Selected Philosophical and Methodological Papers

Selected Philosophical and Methodological Papers

Paul E. Meehl

C. Anthony Anderson and Keith Gunderson, editors

University of Minnesota Press
Minneapolis   Oxford

Acknowledgments and permissions are on p. 545.

Published by the University of Minnesota Press
2037 University Avenue Southeast, Minneapolis, MN 55414.
Printed in the Unisted States of American on acid-free paper.

Library of Congress Cataloging-in-Publication Data

Meehl, Paul E. (Paul Everett), 1920-
    Selected philosophical and methodological papers / Paul E. Meehl ;
edited by C. Anthony Anderson and Keith Gunderson.
       p. cm.
    Includes bibliographical references and index.
    ISBN 0-8166-1855-0 (alk. paper)
    1. Psychology–Philosophy.   2. Psychology–Methodology.
I. Anderson, C. Anthony.   II. Gunderson, Keith.   III. Title
BF38.M42 1991   90-44271
150'.1–dc20   CIP

A CIP catalog record for this book is available from the British Library.

The University of Minnesota is an
equal-opportunity educator and employer

Contents

Foreword

C. Anthony Anderson and Keith Gunderson

The privilege of being able to indulge ourselves in a brief foreword to this distinguished volume stems from the fact that our encouragement might have played a partial causal role in its publication by the University of Minnesota Press at this time. But had it not been for us, others most certainly would in due course have urged the appearance of a collection very much like it. For it contains recognizable "classics" (some collaborative) not all that easily come by and never displayed together, as well as lengthy and deep pieces of philosophical analysis greatly admired by those who are acquainted with them, but slightly hidden from the general view owing to singular appearances in *Festschrift*-type publications. Our own editorial contributions have been exceedingly minimal, and even the task of composing a foreword has been lightened by Meehl's informative preface, which preempted *some* of what we had been poised to say, and by the especially helpful and, we think, accurate assessment of the book by Wesley Salmon who kindly agreed to referee it for the Press. We thank him for articulating with accuracy and elegance what we believe to be the salient virtues of these essays, and for permitting us to quote him at length. Salmon writes:

> This collection of essays is a veritable gold mine. I had previously read a number of them—though by no means all—but rereading them brought back vividly the range and profundity of Meehl's work as well as the sheer delight of his writing style. This collection should be published, and it should be required reading for anyone seriously interested in such areas as philosophy of mind, philosophy of psychology, artificial intelligence, methodology of the social sciences, as well as such specific topics as the foundations of statistics, psychoanalysis, free will, moral responsibility, determinism, punishment, rehabilitation, and ESP.
>
> The world is full of scientists—especially senior scientists—in the physical, biological, and behavioral sciences who are eager to talk and write about the philosophy of their particular branch of science. The vast majority of them

do it very badly. Paul Meehl is an outstanding — perhaps *the* outstanding — exception to that general rule. There are two main reasons. First, he is extraordinarily learned in philosophy, having mastered the thought of a wide variety of important thinkers. Second, he has a superb gift for philosophy, especially philosophy of science. He has benefited from and contributed to the Minnesota Center for Philosophy of Science in important ways over a period of several decades. When he philosophizes, philosophers and psychologists should listen. For example, in essays 2–7, he makes profound contributions to the age-old discussions of freedom of will and its relationship (or lack thereof) to determinism, and the mind-body problem. The great strength of these discussions arises in large part from his philosophically knowledgeable application of scientific details from psychology and neurophysiology to these problems.

The first volume of *Minnesota Studies in Philosophy of Science* was published in 1956, three years after the founding of the Minnesota Center for Philosophy of Science (by Herbert Feigl, Wilfrid Sellars, and Paul E. Meehl). Its subtitle was *The Foundations of Science and the Concepts of Psychology and Psychoanalysis* and included three contributions by Paul E. Meehl: "Construct Validity in Psychological Tests" (co-authored with L. J. Cronbach), "Problems in the Actuarial Characterization of a Person," and "The Concept of Emergence" (co-authored with Wilfrid Sellars). The first two papers are replete with examples of what might be called "applied philosophy of science." In the case of Meehl's writings this usually means philosophy of science applied to issues in theoretical and/or clinical psychology (including psychoanalysis). The third paper, however, is straight ("on-the-rocks") philosophy of mind. It introduces, in the course of effectively criticizing an important argument against emergentism, what seems to us the still very useful distinction between *Physical*$_1$ and *Physical*$_2$ events or entities. Something belongs to the former category if it belongs within a space-time network, whereas something belongs to the latter category if it is "definable in terms of theoretical primitives adequate to describe completely the actual states though not necessarily the potentialities of the universe before the appearance of life." Simple as the distinction may seem, it can be easily overlooked, though it has a crucial relevance with respect to mind-body problems. Arguments which may seem to show that aspects of the mental — sensations, images, "raw feels," or "qualia" — cannot be adequately characterized as *Physical*$_2$ may have little bearing on whether it seems plausible to characterize them as *Physical*$_1$. Meehl and Sellars sketch, without endorsing, an emergentist account of just such mental phenomena which seems to be physicalistic in the first sense but not the second. However, we mention this triad of papers mainly because they indicate some of the range and versatility of Meehl's interests and talent from the time of their appearance to the present. They are also indicative of a certain problem that we faced in helping him to winnow out from his numerous publications the essays for this volume. For if consciously exposing and analyzing the underlying presuppositions or principles of the methods of a discipline constitutes philosophical writing — as it seems to us it does — then a very large proportion of Meehl's writings are philosophical. The first two aforementioned papers did, after all, appear in a Center volume! So their exclusion from this collection was somewhat arbitrary and due to the usual boring constraints concerning length. An earlier selection of his writings entitled *Psychodiagnosis: Selected Papers* is another case in point. It is difficult, if not impossible, to read through many of these without feeling *philosophically* instructed, though the focus of most of them strikes one initially as being on hard-core psychological themes. His paper "Specific Genetic Etiology, Psychodynamics, and Therapeutic Nihilism," for example, includes one section entitled "Philosophical Excursus: Orders of Dispositions" and another "How to Think about Entities and How Not to." His paper "MAXCOV-HITMAX: A Taxonomic Search Method for Loose Genetic Syndromes" begins with a cautionary note concerning the inevitable role of ideologies in science which are, he says, "temporarily resistive to the influence of counterevidence" and then cites Kuhn, Lakatos and Musgrave, and Feyerabend. And so on. Nevertheless, we decided not to include any article already published in that volume and to restrict ourselves in general to those pieces which seemed *most* philosophical or methodological (or a mix of the two), and just plain important. Such a restriction, it should be emphasized, was quite compatible with displaying the scope of Meehl's interests, and the unusual variety of his competencies. We enjoyed the luxury of having a lot to choose from. Although we may have left out some papers that could (and should) have been included, any lingering editorial guilt has been mitigated by an unshakable belief that nothing has been included that should have been left out.

The very choice of subject matters that Meehl's research has focused and refocused on over the years is itself testament to a highly original mind with an unusual blend of intellectual affection for both the theoretical and the almost severely practical: Essays 9–19 comprise a triptych of topics: 1) psychiatry/psychoanalysis; 2) psychology and the law; and 3) ESP (telepathy, psychokinesis). As in the case of freedom and determinism and the mind-body problem, his fascination with the topics has been long-standing. Each topic is addressed by groups of papers appearing over approximately 20-year spans. "The Insanity Defense" (from the second group) is a nice example of Meehl wrestling with a severely practical topic. The article was originally the keynote address at a Minnesota Psychological Association meeting, prompted by concerns of psychologists over what the legislature might do by way of amending the statute covering the defense. Meehl argues for retention of the insanity defense (in Minnesota) but proposes that "the statutory criterion of exculpability . . . be narrowed to psychosis and mental deficiency" and that, ideally, there be a "bifurcated trial with the second trier being a specially qualified and carefully screened panel of lawyer, psychologist, and psychiatrist, plus a layman." He imagines two different cases involving the panel. In the first the defendant is pleading paranoid schizophrenia. Hence, according to Meehl, it is neither dispositive nor even relevant whether he was oriented for time and place, or remembered someone's name or even a phone number. His panel, he presumes, would argue somewhat as follows: "Counsel, the defendant is pleading paranoid schizophrenia as a form of mental illness. Are you unaware that the retention of orientation and ordinary memory is one of the accepted criteria for diagnosis of paranoid schizophrenia? Defendant is not claiming organic brain syndrome or delirious hypermania, so why are you bringing up the irrelevant fact that he was oriented and remembered a phone number?" In the second case, things go the other way. Meehl writes: "if counsel for the defendant tries to bring in the fact that he had an older brother who was a pickpocket, his father was a mean bastard, and his mother was a drunk, none of this bears upon exculpability under the sort of insanity rule that I'm going to propose below." In the wake of developing and arguing for his proposal as well as assessing alleged misuses of the defense, he *also* manages to work in an instructive cameo presentation of the connections between the issues under discussion and more abstract philosophical positions on determinism, compatibilism, etc. Although he is on occasion capable of writing on highly theoretical puzzles the solutions to which may have no obvious practical fallout, he is seldom given to writing about very practical matters (postures regarding the law, clinical procedures, etc.) without bringing to light their philosophical and methodological presuppositions.

The philosophical reader is especially directed to Meehl's essay on the mind-body problem entitled "The Compleat Autocerebroscopist: A Thought-Experiment on Professor Feigl's Mind-Body Identity Thesis."* The autocerebroscope is a fanciful device imagined to be possible in the neurophysiology of the future. The idea was invented by Herbert Feigl (in his "The Mental and the Physical" in *Minnesota Studies in the Philosophy of Science*, Volume II: *Concepts, Theories, and the Mind-Body Problem*, edited by Herbert Feigl, Michael Scriven, and Grover Maxwell; University of Minnesota Press, 1958) but its po-

---

*Editor's note: There is an infelicity in the formal statement of the identity thesis on p. 189 of this volume. To preserve the consequence that there is a unique Φ-event z, it is not sufficient to add the conjunct 'y = z' to the consequent of the first stated "psychophysical correlation-law." One would have to rewrite it as some such thing as

$$(x)(y)[(\psi(x,y) \cdot P(y)) \to (z)((L(z,x) \cdot \Phi(z)) \leftrightarrow y = z)],$$

with a similar formulation of the identity version of the second law. This would also guarantee the consequence claimed on p. 233 of this volume.

C. A. A.

tential in connection with the mind-body problem is only first fully exploited in Meehl's essay.

Meehl constructs thought-experiments to test objections to the Identity Theory, and to explore the conceptual coherence of various alternative views of the mind-body relation. He argues that all objections to the Identity Thesis save one (the "semantical objection") are answerable. And he finds the alternatives coherent and the distinctions between them (e.g., between Interactionism, Parallelism, and Epiphenomenalism) real. Throughout Meehl shows a mastery of psychology, neurophysiology, physics, philosophy, and scientific methodology which is extremely rare (here we echo Salmon's assessment). And he simultaneously displays an equally unusual combination of a sober and sensible respect for the methods of empirical science and a genuine appreciation of the real philosophical problems involved. Here we have an admirable model of the sort of knowledge and methodology requisite for the "compleat" philosopher of mind.

The imagined device, the autocerebroscope, consists of instruments wired directly to the brain of a Utopian neurophysiologist (assume that it's you) which convert current brain activity into one of two symbolic patterns, "R" (for red) or "G" (for green), presented on a visible television screen. The hue of these symbols can be varied independently so as to be either red or green. Of course, if everything is working properly, you will see a red "R" or a green "G." But one day you find yourself experiencing green when the (apparently green-hued) symbol is "R." You are a fully convinced Identity Theorist (as are all good Utopian neurophysiologists). What can have gone wrong? In elaborating this scenario, Meehl makes it extremely plausible that subjective feelings of certainty and the like do not require an outcome incompatible with the Identity Theory. He then argues that the Identity Thesis has empirical content—things could turn out in such a way that the deviant experiences ultimately refute the theory. In making the case for this, Meehl shows that a version of Dualism could turn out to be correct. He describes a way in which the patterning of individually random neuron firings might require (or at least suggest) the postulation of a Cartesian "psychoid." Given the many arguments which have attempted to show that Dualism is conceptually impossible, the contrary view is something that really needs such careful demonstration. (Of course, some will question the real conceivability of Meehl's cases. Let them state their objections with a clarity comparable to Meehl's—and say exactly where the thing becomes incoherent.) Meehl mentions, as a possibility, the idea that quantum indeterminacy might play a real role in brain function and thus in the resolution of the mind-body problem. This has more recently been urged by the mathematician-physicist Roger Penrose (*The Emperor's New Mind* [Oxford: Oxford University Press, 1989]). The matter is, obviously, still highly speculative. Meehl also explores the Inverted Spectrum Problem (in two colors) and considers applicability of such predicates as "Incorrigible," "Indubitable," "Private," and the like, to mental states. Here too the essay is distinguished by its close argumentation and imaginative construction of possibilities. The reader will find therein suggestions reminiscent of more recent work in the philosophy of mind: by Saul Kripke, David Lewis, and Thomas Nagel. There has been some progress (one would like to believe). Donald Davidson and Jaegwon Kim on events are certainly relevant (see, for example, their papers in *Essays in Honor of Carl G. Hempel*, edited by Nicholas Rescher [Dordrecht: Reidel, 1969], and references there given) as is Kripke's sophisticated statement of the "semantical objection" to the Identity Theory ("Naming and Necessity" in *Semantics of Natural Language*, edited by Gilbert Harman and Donald Davidson [Dordrecht and Boston: Reidel, 1972]). (Here again one will find anticipations in Meehl. It is a version of this latter kind of argument that leads him ultimately to conclude that the Identity Theory, taken literally as an identity theory, is "fishy.") But the article as a whole contains a great deal that has not been superseded and that is still highly relevant to the current stage of the debate. This work should be required reading for (advanced) courses in the philosophy of mind. Indeed, the editors confidently maintain that the essay deserves to be considered a "classic."

Another real jewel of a paper is the one jointly authored with Herbert Feigl, entitled "The Determinism-Freedom and Mind-Body Problems." (As a personally necessary aside, one of the editors must insert a record of a scene that occurred in 1968 when an excited Herbert Feigl informed him that *his student*, Paul Meehl, had just been appointed to the rank of Regents Professor—the most prestigious honor the University of Minnesota had [and still has] to bestow upon its faculty. I reminded him that he too had recently received the honor. "But Meehl, think of Meehl," he insisted, ignoring any praise of himself. "He is the youngest of us all. And so accomplished. He was the most brilliant undergraduate we had ever seen. He might have done distinguished graduate work in mathematics, physics, or philosophy. He went with psychology, but he's stayed with us too. Talk with Meehl, you'll learn much from him." And, indeed, that was so. And so, as well, for Feigl, as their collaborations show. But back to their essay.) In it they argue that Popper's worries about the "nightmare" of a deterministic world are not really justified. (Here it might prove interesting to compare their reasons for this with Daniel C. Dennett's interesting discussions ten years later of similar matters in his *Elbow Room—The Varieties of Free Will Worth Wanting*, Cambridge, Massachusetts, and London: MIT Press, 1984.) The main object of such dread is, or should be, the possibility of a "World Formula" and a consequent "World Calendar," which latter would contain a detailed description of all that will ever happen. Such a thing seems to lead to various absurdities: the knowledge of scientific and artistic creations before they are invented or created and the impossibility of avoiding future accidents even with full knowledge of their surrounding conditions. But the possibility of a World Calendar requires the conjunction of three assumptions: 1) a deterministic form for the basic laws of nature, 2) the precise ascertainability of the initial and boundary conditions of all events, and 3) the feasibility of the complex mathematical calculations that would be required for such total predictability. Feigl and Meehl urge that it is 2) and 3) that are false; this leaves the possibility that 1) may be true. Of course, the authors are well aware of the consequences of the currently accepted Quantum Mechanics. And conceivably such an anti-deterministic theory might remain dominant in physics; if so, one would have good (though not conclusive) reason to judge determinism unacceptable. But Feigl and Meehl are only arguing that the impossibilities of prediction mentioned are not in themselves good reason to reject determinism.

This argument, like that (those) in the autocerebroscope piece, is rich in detail and discusses matters currently under intense examination, for example the so-called "Butterfly Effect" of Chaos Theory. Feigl and Meehl bring to bear such diverse considerations as the limitations on the determination of initial conditions imposed by the Theory of Relativity and the possible failure of calculation because of unprovable Goedel formulas. And there is a lucid discussion of what Popper has called "Compton's Problem": if the events in our brains are determined, what sense can we make of the idea of rational acceptance of reasons and arguments? Some have seen here the makings of an argument that determinism itself is irrational. The basic puzzle is very hard to state precisely, but it is plainly very deep. Feigl and Meehl find anticipations (of the fusion of this problem with the mind-body problem) in Plato and Aristotle, in more recent discussions of several Oxford philosophers, and in the work of the American philosophers A. I. Melden and Richard Taylor. (For an even more recent discussion see Robert Nozick, *Philosophical Explanations*, Oxford: Clarendon Press, 1981.) The problem was discussed also by Kant and a popular version of the idea was used by C. S. Lewis in an attempt to refute "Naturalism." The Feigl-Meehl discussion is an extremely detailed and exact statement of a very impressive answer to one version (Popper's) of the puzzle. How, Popper asks, can nonphysical entities such as arguments and reasons have any influence on human behavior if all events in our brains are determined by purely physical causes? (This is, of course, not the only way to focus the puzzle.) Feigl and Meehl argue that, for example, the brain event which corresponds to the acceptance of the conclusion of a syllogism in Barbara (by a logician, say) might be the consequent of a "brain theorem" of future neurological science. (Perhaps an autocerebroscope should have been switched on here! One wonders what might have been found.) It is argued that the logician might have a feeling of compulsion, the brain event might be completely determined, and the causal description of the event might be "complete" in an entirely usual scientific sense. Yet no abstract entities need be mentioned—any more than one need invoke such things as numbers in the complete causal description of a mechanical calculator doing sums. These issues are still hotly debated (now by functionalists and anti-functionalists) but the mentioned counter-argument has rarely (probably never) been stated with such care. If something has gone wrong with this solution of the Compton Problem, one should be able here to locate the faulty premise or fallacious step.

The medley of Meehl's interdisciplinary perspectives, the unusual detail and carefulness in his argumentation, and the originality and boldness of the conclusions, which the last two paper summaries make vivid, are virtues shared by the other essays in this collection. His fascinating attempt at crafting an alternative between chance and determinism in his most recent and very ambitious contribution to the free-will determinism debate (essay 4) will no doubt prove controversial, but the ingenuity and provocativeness of its conjectures seem to us undeniable. Ingenious as well is his strategy for distinguishing telepathic from psychokinetic hypotheses, and his overall suggestions with respect to ESP experimentation in the paired essays 18 and 19.

The intellectual adventures and pleasures of this volume are diverse yet conceptually criss-crossing in remarkable ways. We are honored to be associated with the work and share the sentiments expressed by Wesley Salmon in his closing remarks about it:

> I cannot praise this collection of essays too highly. They are clearly the product of a superb intellect ranging over a broad sweep of areas and issues. And, they are fun to read.

Preface

There are three reasons why a psychologist puts on the philosopher's hat, or sometimes precariously wears both hats simultaneously: (I) Metalinguistic discourse in the ordinary practice of scientific writing; (II) Psychological research and theory in a substantive domain which is intrinsically connected with what are usually considered "philosophical" concepts or questions; and (III) Intrinsic interest in philosophical problems aside from any relevance they have to psychology.

I. In the Course of Doing Science

When discussing psychological theory, and even when interpreting empirical findings in the discussion section of a research article, a considerable portion of the statements made consist of metalinguistic discourse. Theoretical or experimental articles in psychology contain mainly object language proofs in the formalism, description of apparatus, subjects, and procedure, numerical tables concerning measurements and summary statistics, and theoretical text belonging to the substance of the theory. But there are also statements in the metalanguage concerning what something proves or does not prove, whether a technical term is being employed with such and such meaning, reduction of one set of concepts to another, whether a protocol should be received into the corpus, evidentiary weight, probability of inference, the methodological merits of this or that school of inferential statistics, the appropriateness of a significance level, the consistency of such and such claims, the adequacy of certain conceptual definitions, and so on. Many years ago, in *Logical Syntax of Language* (1934/1937), Rudolf Carnap pointed out how frequently scientific discourse not purportedly methodological or philosophical in subject matter contains a sizable amount of what he called the "formal mode of speech." He writes (p. 286),

Accordingly, we distinguish *three kinds of sentences*:

1. *Object-sentences*	2. *Pseudo-object-sentences* = quasi-syntactical sentences *Material mode of speech*	3. *Syntactical sentences* *Formal mode of speech*
Examples: "5 is a prime number''; "Babylon was a big town''; "lions are mammals.''	Examples: "Five is not a thing, but a number''; "Babylon was treated of in yesterday's lecture.'' ("Five is a number-word'' is an example belonging to the autonomous mode of speech.)	Examples: " 'Five' is not a thing-word, but a number-word''; "the word 'Babylon' occurred in yesterday's lecture''; " 'A.~A' is a contradictory sentence.''

See also the striking example (pp. 328–30) from the initial sentences of Einstein's 1905 relativity paper.

Metalinguistic remarks appearing in a purely "scientific" paper are about, or make use of, concepts usually considered to be the province of the philosopher. The "linguistic turn" of philosophy that we connect with the names of Bertrand Russell, the ordinary language philosophers, the logical positivists, and more broadly analytical philosophy in general, usually held that clarification of terms and of the conceptual relations between statements was all that philosophy could consist of. This position is succinctly and dramatically expressed by the early Wittgenstein, *Tractatus*: 4.0031, "All philosophy is critique of language''; 4.112, "The object of philosophy is the clarification of thoughts. Philosophy is not a theory but an activity. A philosophical work consists essentially of elucidations. The result of philosophy is not a number of 'philosophical propositions,' but to make propositions clear''; 4.1121, "psychology is no nearer related to philosophy than is any other natural science.''

One may ask: Why, then, does so much more explicitly metatheoretical discourse take place in the social sciences than in physics, chemistry, or genetics? To answer that, one must first have answered the question, What is it to philosophize? I think it generally agreed that there are two characteristics of discourse that would ordinarily be considered philosophical: First, the extent to which it is metalinguistic, that is, not about facts, formulas, experiments, or laws of nature, but about the relations between concepts, definitional or inferential, about matters of proof, validity, fallacy, inference, meaning, and the like; and second—an aspect that those who made the strong linguistic turn preferred to liquidate or at least not think about—some basic concepts that may or may not be metalinguistic, that are ontological or descriptive or refer to aspects of the physical and mental world, but are of a very high order of generality, the kinds of concepts that used to be called *metaphysical*, in no pejorative sense. Aristotle's categories are the obvious example of the latter; but there is quite a list of object language predicates and object language terms for entities, predicates, and relations that are used in all empirical sciences, and questions raised regarding them do not tip us off about what particular science we are discussing. These interesting terms of high ontological generality are one reason to doubt the adequacy of the Ramsey Sentence as a complete rendering of empirical scientific theories. Examples of these terms are: 'accelerate,' 'adjoin,' 'be composed of,' 'evolve,' 'inhibit,' 'interact with,' 'interval,' 'potentiate,' 'produce,' and 'separate.' See Meehl (1990a) for a more complete list and discussion.

If to philosophize means to engage in metatalk about the relation of concepts and statements to one another, or object language talk of this highly general pervasive metaphysical sort, it should not surprise us that more explicitly methodological discourse takes place in the social sciences than in the more developed sciences of physics, chemistry, astronomy, physiology, and genetics. The more trouble you are in, the more you are pushed to question and clarify the most general ideas and the most general rules of the scientific game. So far as I am aware, there are no theoretical disputes in chemistry which are so deep and intractable that chemists holding two different theoretical positions can hardly have a rational conversation with each other. But it is well known that a solid-gold Skinnerian operant behaviorist can hardly have a civilized conversation with an equally orthodox Freudian. Nor can it be said that this is because the behaviorist has a science and the Freudian does not. A conversation between a typical operant behaviorist and a psychometrician engaged in factor analysis of individual differences traits would be almost, although not quite, as difficult to conduct. One has to engage in a certain amount of method talk willy-nilly, whether one chooses to label it "philosophy" or not.

A philosophically sophisticated psychologist is uncomfortably aware of how much shoddy, home-baked, third-rate philosophy, bulging with mistakes, is committed by psychologists who are proud of avoiding philosophical matters and even contemptuous of philosophy of science as a discipline. Mark Twain, speaking of the concept of a "self-made man," said that, in his experience, it normally illustrates the horrors of unskilled labor. I am not suggesting that all psychological scientists must perforce do a large amount of philosophizing. I am only saying there are some kinds of questions that arise in psychological science that are *inherently* epistemological or logical in character, and that cannot be deprived of these intrinsic features by the psychologist disclaiming an interest in philosophical questions. When the unphilosophical psychologist finds himself unavoidably stuck with such questions, it is my experience that what he produces under these conceptual pressures is likely to be rather shabby.

The proportion of metatheoretical discourse varies from one area of psychology to another and depends upon a number of factors which I will not develop here. When a colleague of mine studies the electrophysiology of the retina, very few occasions arise when he is forced to raise questions of a metatheoretical nature. When an equally "scientific" colleague in the field of differential psychology is faced with the task of adopting a solution to the rotation problem in multiple factor analysis, he has to talk about things like scientific realism and the so-called law of parsimony whether he likes it or not, because, for example, the Varimax solution is a quantitative generalization of Thurstone's simple structure, and the rationale of simple structure is not mathematical, *and cannot be made purely mathematical since it is a methodological preference.* When I was a graduate student, we had hot disputes about whether one could reduce the various Freudian defense mechanisms to learning theoretical concepts. It wasn't hard to Skinnerize or Hullianize the mechanisms of repression or displacement; it was a little more difficult to deal with something like reaction formation; and it was extremely difficult to deal with identification. The metaproblem that arose with the latter was, "In incorporating identification into our model of the mind, what weight should be given to the fact that we cannot at this time reduce it to learning theoretical terms?" Similarly, experimental psychologists, or clinicians like myself with a history of rat experimentation and learning theory concerns, tended to view Freud's *Inhibitions, Symptoms, and Anxiety* (1926/1959) as of major importance in his theoretical development, because of the shift from the hydraulic notion of libido being converted into anxiety (my colleague, David Lykken, likes to say, "anxiety was rancified libido") to the notion that the anxiety signal puts the defense mechanism into gear and *it* then dams up the libido (i.e., inhibits the impulse expression except as a distorted derivative). This latter theory is much easier to interpret with a suitable mix of classical and operant conditioning than is the transformed libido doctrine. Query just how much weight should be given to ease of conceptual reducibility from the Freudian level of analysis to the learning theory level? That is inherently a "philosophical" question, involving the aims of science, the concept of *theoretical reduction*, and optimal strategy at a given stage of scientific growth.

II. "Philosophical" Concepts Intrinsic to a Substantive Domain at the Interface

The branch of scientific psychology that is most likely to require explicit and frequent use of "philosophical" concepts is what has come to be known as cognitive psychology including AI, both the weak and strong form. Empirical research and theorizing about the cognitive processes of perception, reasoning, problem solving, remembering, and formulating experiences, unavoidably have to talk about logical and epistemological matters. Likewise, a philosopher who works in areas such as perception epistemology needs to know something about the substance of scientific psychology. Failure to see this overlap at the interface of the two disciplines makes for bad mistakes. Thus, one may read a philosopher discussing perception and reality and using an example such as a tilted penny appearing elliptical rather than round; in fact a tilted penny appears round to a human observer and can be made to "look elliptical" only by strenuous efforts to undo what the brain automatically does by way of correction for the angle of perspective. It is worth pointing out in this connection that even the currently derided "armchair" or "a priori" epistemology of traditional philosophy was always *empirical*, when the latter term is used in its dictionary sense. Psychologists have an obnoxious tendency to identify the empirical with the experimental, and sometimes with the quantitative, which leads to such absurd statements as "Freud has an interesting theory although it is not empirical." What they mean is that it was based upon listening to patients on the couch rather than setting up experimental manipulations or carrying out statistical analyses. Some may think that Freud was a clumsy, inefficient, or biased "empiricist," but to say that he was not proceeding empirically is careless language. The great philosophers in the Western empirical tradition relied upon ordinary life observations and generalizations that for the most part did not require systematic experimentation in the laboratory or quantitative or statistical treatment. It is a misuse of language to say that Locke, Berkeley, and Hume did not rely on empirical facts in conducting their epistemological investigations. One easy way to see this is via what I call Maxwell's Thunderbolt (to be included with Occam's Razor and Hume's Guillotine as basic principles). While I was still enough of a mixed positivist and Popperian to say that I wanted my epistemology to be a priori and not based on empirical sociology or psychology, Grover Maxwell dealt with that position deftly and permanently, with his question "Well, Paul, tell me what epistemological or methodological principles you can derive from the postulates of Whitehead and Russell's *Principia Mathematica?*" The answer, obviously, is "None."

I am inclined to doubt that cognitive psychology will have very much to offer on the positive side to the philosopher of science engaged in the enterprise of criticism, rational reconstruction, and the formulation of helpful advice or guidelines for the working scientist. My prediction is that the main contribution of cognitive psychology will be negative, e.g., the body of research, already sizable, that testifies to the ubiquity of nonoptimal strategies and irrational mental habits among humans, including scientists (Dawes, 1988; Faust, 1984; Hogarth, 1987; Kahneman, Slovic, & Tversky, 1982; Lord, Ross, & Lepper, 1979; Nisbett & Ross, 1980).

There is a little semantic problem about semiotic here, because discourse that we would normally count as metalinguistic (because it treats relations of evidence, proof, inference, subsumption, etc., between object language concepts and statements) will appear in the object language of the cognitive psychologist. Thus a given string of words could be considered either object language or metalanguage, or both; that is a little messy, but there it is. I suppose there is no harm in this so long as everybody is clear about what is happening and why.

Even animal behavior cannot be safely excluded from the subject matter domains that force us to make some use of the philosopher's kit of tools. For example, in attempting to formalize expectancy theory of learning, MacCorquodale and I wanted to do justice to Tolman's intentions, but at the same time to be as "operational" about his behaviorism as possible in delineating the concept of response, and in saying how one can, without hidden imputation of anthropomorphic intentionality to the rat, give an adequate characterization of the behavior flux. We found that discussants at the Dartmouth conference and critics of drafts of our chapter on Tolman in the Dartmouth conference book (MacCorquodale & Meehl, 1954) had no trouble permitting a portion of the behavior flux to be characterized by a conjunction or disjunction of two topographical properties or two manipulandum events; but they were troubled by a conditional "If . . . , then . . . " The easiest way to diffuse that anxiety was to remind them that the horseshoe of material implication—better called the conditional—is explicitly definable by means of conjunction and negation, or disjunction and negation. Again, in discussing the dependency of operant strength upon reinforcement probability, one wants to be clear in a biological framework about what "teleological" formulations as to the adaptive character of such an adjustment are permissible without anthropomorphizing the rat or dragging in the Great Designer. A final example would be our explaining to the skeptic what we mean by referring to an unconscious motive, so that whether he *believes* it or not, at least he will not find it *conceptually objectionable* on metatheoretical grounds.

III. Intrinsic Philosophical Interests

A psychologist whose subject matter does not interface with philosophy, and whose theorizing is so close to the facts that almost no metalanguage discourse is involved except to point out that a certain mathematical derivation is or isn't valid (a question we hardly think of as "philosophical"), may still enjoy putting on the philosopher's hat because of an intrinsic interest in philosophical questions. In this respect the psychologist interested in philosophy is not different from a geologist interested in chess, a chemist interested in figure skating, or an astronomer interested in politics. I must emphasize to psychological readers that this third way of wearing the philosopher's hat is often present with me. I have always been careful to explain to students in my philosophical psychology class that I avoid the claim that *all* of my philosophical interests have helped me — although I hope they have not hindered me! — in my work as a psychologist. Thus, for example, I don't know any psychologist or, for that matter, any other social, biological, or physical scientist who really worries, *qua* scientist, about Hume's problem of induction, or the related problem of the nature of nomic necessity. All the psychologists I know presuppose — they don't even explicitly premise, they *presuppose* — that there are laws of nature, that these do have some kind of necessity, and that it is important to distinguish causal laws from "mere statistical associations," what the philosopher formulates as the difference between natural laws and accidental universals. When I have my psychologist's hat on and am considering the strengths and weaknesses of a statistical technique such as path analysis for unscrambling the causal order in a complex social network, I don't worry about Hume's problem of induction either. Nevertheless, when I put on the philosopher's hat for this third kind of reason, I find Hume's problem fascinating in its own right.

Thinking Better Under Two Hats

It may be said that the question of what hat you have on is already prejudicial and, perhaps, needless. The linguistic turn doubtless improved the quality of philosophical writing (e.g., I dare say no future philosopher will make the kinds of bloopers that Hegel made in confusing the *is* of predication with the *is* of identity and erecting a whole system upon that undergraduate mistake). But from a post-positivist viewpoint, one might prefer to say there is only one kind of question after all, and that we can ask a meaningful and important question without worrying about what building on the campus we inhabit. Here we find Sir Karl Popper strongly opposed to the position taken by Wittgenstein in the quotes above. Popper writes:

Language analysts believe that there are no genuine philosophical problems, or that the problems of philosophy, if any, are problems of linguistic usage, or of the meanings of words. I, however, believe that there is at least one philosophical problem in which all thinking men are interested. It is the problem of cosmology: *the problem of understanding the world — including ourselves, and our knowledge, as part of the world.* All science is cosmology, I believe, and for me the interest of philosophy as well as of science lies solely in the contributions which they have made to it. For me, at any rate, both philosophy and science would lose all their attraction if they were to give up that pursuit. Admittedly, understanding the functions of language is an important part of it;

but explaining away our problems as merely linguistic "puzzles" is not. (Popper, 1935/59, 15)

The papers reprinted in this collection are samples of all three of the above ways in which a psychologist wears a philosopher's hat. Perhaps a word is appropriate about my general stance as an amateur philosopher. Like most bright people of my generation, I was a logical positivist in my youth, although I was already having doubts about the meaning and value of the verifiability criterion of meaning when the great Vienna positivist Herbert Feigl came to Minnesota in the academic year 1940–41, my senior year at Minnesota. I certainly cannot label myself today as a positivist, logical empiricist, Popperian, Lakatosian, or whatever. My general stance is broadly "analytic philosophy," if that language is not taken to mean a self-imposed injunction against asking interesting questions, whoever's bailiwick they fall into. My thinking as a psychologist—whether I was interpreting experiments on latent learning in the white rat, formulating a theory of schizophrenia that would be testable by appropriate taxometrics, trying to clarify the problem of psychoanalytic evidence in the interview, or trying to understand what we mean when we claim validity for a psychological test—has been greatly helped by the analytic philosophers, many of whom disagree strongly with one another on major issues. I have never, I think, employed philosophy of science as a club, in polemics about substantive psychological issues, a practice common in the heyday of logical empiricism and operationism, as these were abused in some quarters. I think that now the views of Thomas Kuhn are being similarly employed in an illegitimate way. I expect this influence to be far worse than that of the positivists, because it can be employed for obscurantist purposes, which theirs never were.

Nor is my reliance upon concepts and principles of metatheory merely window dressing. Some readers (more likely philosophers, but some of the younger generation of psychologists) may wonder why they find almost no reference to the ordinary language philosophers. There is no point in pussyfooting about that, and in fact I feel a certain obligation to speak out strongly, especially for the benefit of my brethren in the "soft" fields of psychology (clinical, counseling, personality, social, developmental, community psychology). I have not found the writings or lectures of ordinary language philosophers the least bit helpful in my work as a psychologist, and—of less interest, being merely autobiographical—I have found them pretty boring when I put on the philosopher's hat of intrinsic interest in philosophical problems. (The exception is ethics, and perhaps political theory—I am unclear why.) I would be suspicious of myself, given that there is quite a lot of ordinary language philosophy around, except for the fact that I am not identifiable as an adherent of any particular philosopher's metatheory. I have not been, except for a few months as a Popperian, after the English translation of Popper's *Logic of Scientific Discovery* appeared in 1959, and the logical positivism I held as an undergraduate. Relying either on introspection, or the detailed protocols of the early sessions of the Minnesota Center for Philosophy of Science in the 1950s, and most of all upon my publications in psychology, I could easily prove to any fair-minded person that when I am putting on the philosopher's hat as an adjunct to my work as a psychologist, *I treat the philosopher's table as a cafeteria or smorgasbord*—I gladly take anything I can get, whatever its source and however it is labeled, however popular or unpopular it may be within the philosophers' own trade union, if it helps me with what I am doing as a psychologist. Thus I can cite chapter and verse of my writings showing the marked influence of Bergmann, Carnap, Feigl, Hempel, Nagel, Pap, Popper, Reichenbach, and Sellars (older generation of analytical philosophers) as well as Glymour, Grünbaum, Hacking, Kitcher, Kordig, Lakatos, Laudan, Maxwell, and Salmon (younger generation of the same). So I am certain that I do not approach Austin, Hampshire, Malcolm, Moore, Strawson, Toulmin, Wisdom, or the later Wittgenstein with a bias because I am a committed positivist, Popperian, Reichenbachian, or disciple of Lakatos. If the ordinary language philosophers had anything helpful to say to me, I would welcome it; it is simply a fact that they do not. Wittgenstein's *Tractatus* was almost a Bible to the Vienna circle (although they did some eisegesis, beginning with the very first section on atomic sentences!). If I approached the later Wittgenstein with any prejudices, they were positive. Recently, I have been rereading the *Tractatus*, along with Max Black's *Companion*, with pleasure and profit. It seems to me that the early Wittgenstein had some important insights and, perhaps equally important (certainly for anyone with Popperian sympathies), his incorrect "insights" were profound and interesting, so that seeing what makes them incorrect is itself illuminating. It is strange that the ordinary language philosophers have been so little help to me, because I have done theoretical and empirical work in six different areas of psychology which would seem obvious candidates for illumination by the analysis of ordinary language: trait attribution, forensic psychology, psychoanalytic interpretation, the interpretation and validation of psychological tests, the concept of mental illness, and the distinction between dimensions and types in personality and psychopathology. I find it hard to conceive of any branch of science — social, biological, or physical — in which the nature of the problems seems better suited to aid from ordinary language philosophy than these. All I can say is that it just isn't so. *Examples*: In considering the distinction between psychosis and neurosis, which is of both forensic and theoretical importance, one might suppose that the question "What does the ordinary speaker mean if he says somebody is crazy?" would be helpful. Well, perhaps a smidgen, but no more. If one does not move from that level to the crudest clinical refinement by the technically trained psychologist or psychiatrist, the ordinary language gloss is of no value. Similarly, when discussing the concept of general intelligence, one starts by delimiting a broad class of tasks that can be labeled "cognitive," but from that point on the psychometrics (factor analysis and predictive statistics) take over, powerfully controlling all further interpretive discourse. Even the initial delimitation of what is a "cognitive" task does not rely on ordinary language in any strong way. Suppose somebody objects to the original list of subtests in an omnibus intelligence test on the grounds that it merely represents "middle-class school teachers' biases" (an erroneous cliché of the frenzied egalitarians). One simply asks those who think something else is cognitive to devise some feasible tests to get at it, and we throw them into the candidate pot. It turns out that if we put endurance of pain or rapidity of speech or color discrimination or balancing on a narrow board into the pot, the subsequent statistical analysis informs us that, whatever these tasks are getting at, they are not getting at *whatever is tapped* by the ability to solve puzzles, to discern analogies, to understand the meaning of words, to duplicate a complex visual pattern, to remember facts, or to give appropriate commonsensical solutions to everyday occurrences.

There is also a metatheoretical question about the claims of ordinary language philosophy that I have yet to see answered. Why should one presume that ordinary language is adequate to tasks of even moderate conceptual complexity? This has not turned out to be the case with any domain investigated by the sciences (see Maxwell & Feigl, 1961). One defender told me that it ought to be in pretty good shape for matters like human trait description, because all of us, whether psychologists or not, have dealt with quite a few other people and have been practically forced to attribute dispositions to them. I find that no more persuasive than arguing that I should read the Farmer's Almanac instead of consulting a meteorologist, on the grounds that we have all been exposed to quite a bit of good and bad weather. But this is not the place to mount an assault upon ordinary language philosophy. I suppose I should adopt the stance "let a hundred flowers bloom," except that if it turns out that they are mostly weeds when grown in the soft areas of psychology, I have a scholarly interest in stamping them out. I have already refereed some silly (Bertrand Russell's word) papers on schizophrenia which were based on ordinary language, and which would, if published and believed, exert a thoroughly malignant influence on scientific research.

I am not a historian of science, so I do not know how accurate Thomas Kuhn's historical views are, although it is a matter of common knowledge that many historians of science, perhaps the majority, have not been persuaded. Whatever the validity of Kuhn's view about history of physics, I am convinced that the application of his precepts to the "soft areas" of psychology is not only unhelpful, it is positively bad. A glance at some of the current literature in the soft fields, and even more, serving as a referee for manuscripts submitted to psychological journals, will convince anybody who is not a devout Kuhnian that the psychologists who are fondest of quoting Kuhn—also misquoting or misattributing—are those who have a stake in obscurantism. I don't notice my colleagues in the really scientific areas of psychology quoting Kuhn. Kuhn-citing almost always comes from psychoanalysts, social psychologists, personality theorists, etc., and it is practically always linked with a (usually uninformed) variant of what Laudan calls "positivist-bashing." (Of course there are exceptions, e.g., Donald T. Campbell, David Faust, James J. Jenkins.) As a clinician who practices psychotherapy and came into the field because of an interest in Freud, but who also knows something about mathematical statistics and genetics, I am aware that one of the most difficult tasks for clinical psychology is to become more scientific. By this I do not prescribe some narrow, hyper-operationalist philosophy of science (I don't hold one). By "scientific" I mean merely that the initial, basic data and the relation of those data to the theories can command the assent of almost all informed rational minds. I count myself a 40% Freudian (who used to be a 60% Freudian), and I still put some of my patients on the couch and proceed more or less classically. But I do not and never did hold the illusion that psychoanalysis is a science, nor that it is a technology based upon a science. It is now a century since Freud's earliest cases of modifying the cathartic technique into what became classical analysis, and no fair-minded person could say that we now *know* what proportion of his theoretical concepts are substantially correct. This could fairly be described as a scientific scandal. But rather than admitting that it is, and trying to figure out some way to clean it up, the current tendency among some defenders of psychoanalysis is to quote Kuhn and company, which enables them to say that of course one's observations are permeated with theory, so how can you expect a non-Freudian to make the right observations or interpret them properly, and so on and on. I don't even accept Kuhn's thesis that all observations are theory laden; that may hold for nuclear physics and for astrophysics because of their very special character, but certainly does not hold for psychology. I refer the reader to my paper on subjectivity in psychoanalytic inference (essay 11 in this volume).

I cannot resist the impulse to say something in the interest of historical justice in response to the current positivist-bashing. Psychologists grinding an obscurantist ax because they chafe under the burden of proof usually have an acquaintance with logical postivism or logical empiricism largely confined to a superficial reading of its critics. I have read psychologists who refer to Hans Reichenbach as a positivist, whereas anyone who has even glanced at his great 1938 book *Experience and Prediction* knows that he consistently used the word 'positivist' to describe his Viennese adversaries! I have even heard references to Karl Popper as a logical positivist, whereas in his autobiography he raises the question "Who killed logical positivism?" and proudly confesses to have been the murderer. What am I to think of psychologists who are so sloppy in their scholarship as to make attributions of this sort? These obscurantists attribute to the logical positivists or logical empiricists views that, so far as I know, none of them held, or only a few of them held for a short period of time, and they take these views as the core features of the movement. *Example*: I have heard psychologists say that according to the logical empiricists, science is simply and solely a kind of automatic buildup from a small set of incorrigible protocols; that this being so, there is no possibility of being mistaken except by some sort of clerical mistake; that scientists routinely proceed by concocting a formal calculus and then setting alongside it a separate text which is its interpretation; that all allowable terms must be directly linked to ("operationally defined by") observable predicates which it requires no special skill or training to reliably discriminate; that the simple straight rule of induction will invariably generate empirical truths; that all statements in mentalistic language can be completely rendered by the description of behavioral dispositions; and the like.

Now, Herbert Feigl was a core member of the Vienna Circle, and in fact it was Feigl and Kaufmann who suggested formalizing the group and having regular weekly meetings. The very phrase "logical positivism," the English language designation of the Vienna Circle, was invented by Feigl and presented in the first paper on the Vienna Circle's views ever published in the English language (Blumberg & Feigl, 1931), five years before Ayer's (1936) influential *Language, Truth and Logic*. I don't know how many hundreds of hours I have spent in Herbert Feigl's company, first as his student and subsequently as a coinstructor in the philosophy department and during the meetings of the Minnesota Center. I can assert that Feigl did not hold any of the views stated above. To the extent that some things some positivists had said sounded close to any of them, he saw them as mistakes which had, fortunately, been rectified.

In his critique of a recent paper of mine, Donald T. Campbell (1990) kindly refers to my paper with MacCorquodale on hypothetical constructs (essay 8, this volume) and my subsequent article on construct validity with Cronbach (Cronbach & Meehl, 1955) as "liberating," as freeing him and other psychologists of his generation with methodological interests from the constraints of logical positivism. Personally, I never felt much "constrained" even when I was a logical positivist as an undergraduate, especially after Feigl came to Minnesota. Between those two articles, there appeared (partly inspired by discussions of my 1948 paper with MacCorquodale) Feigl's (1950) much neglected paper on existential hypotheses.

Most theories in the soft areas of psychology are not supported by the sort of evidence that would suffice to persuade every open-minded, rational, but critical person that any one of them has high verisimilitude. If any psychologist claims to have such a theory, I would challenge him to show me how he would have been estopped from engaging in his theorizing, or conducting empirical research to test his theory, by the teachings of the logical empiricists as amended, say, from the middle 1930s. I offer that as a serious challenge to the younger generation of psychologists who are positivist-bashers. Cronbach and I were criticized by some hyper-positivistic psychologists for our construct validity position, and they were particularly offended by my strong defense (people say they know which text is

Cronbach's and which is Meehl's) of Pap's *open concepts*. I daresay that some psychologists, unfamiliar with the history of the Vienna Circle, would say that a defense of open concepts is strongly against the core ideas of the logical positivists. This shows they are unfamiliar with Carnap's (1936) classic paper on testability and meaning which was explicitly the takeoff point for Pap's (1953) seminal paper and Waismann's (1945) related paper on open texture. My current research in the taxometric approach to schizophrenia genetics stems from *combining the metatheory of open concepts with the Popperian emphasis upon strong tests* (Meehl, 1989, 1990b, 1990c; Meehl & Golden, 1982). To the extent it represents "a loosened tolerant empiricism," it is in the tradition of the later Carnap, Feigl, Reichenbach, and others. To the extent that it aims to tighten up loose concepts and, when that is not immediately feasible, *to objectify the kind and degree of looseness* via the use of new kinds of taxometric statistics, it can be considered neo-Popperian. I am much indebted to the tradition of the positivists, and to the views of Sir Karl Popper, as the metatheoretical framework within which that taxometric research is being carried out. But I repeat, nothing I have found in Kuhn and Co., or the later Wittgenstein and Co., has given me help in those endeavors. One might have supposed, for instance, that Wittgenstein's "family resemblance" would have been useful to someone struggling with the open concept of an entity like schizophrenia, but it was not. I once tried to see where it would lead me, and came to the conclusion that, if I were a better logician, I would be able to prove that taking Wittgenstein's idea of a family resemblance literally, you could prove that everybody had a family resemblance to everybody else. Some symbolic logician should apply himself to that task. It is not clear, reading Paragraphs 65–67 of the *Investigations* how the family resemblance problem of "games" (or "Hapsburgs") is distinguished from the nonproblem that 'game' is also used to characterize rotting meat. Clearly, the mere multivocality of a word is not what he is calling attention to. Since it's not that, and yet—as he correctly argues—not a common property *or strict logical disjunction of properties*, what is it?

I came to know Herbert Feigl's intellect as intimately as I have known anyone's, over a period of thirty years. Because of the Minnesota Center, I was privileged to exchange views orally with other members of the logical empiricist movement and other spinoff analytical philosophers, so that I have spent time in discussion—frequently in strong disagreement—with Carnap, Hempel, Feyerabend, Pap, Popper, Salmon, and others. On the basis of personal contact plus considerable familiarity with their writings, as well as discussion with psychology students who have studied under them (e.g., Gustave Bergmann at Iowa), I am prepared to make a strong statement about the logical empiricists: Whatever was the matter with them as a group or as individuals, *not a single one of them was stupid*. When a positivist-basher expounds the position in a way that implies they were stupid, I have to conclude that the positivist-basher's position is stupid.

But enough of polemics. On the positive side, what do I tell the students in my philosophical psychology class about the value of philosophy of science for them? I tell them that it probably won't help them to concoct clever theories or design ingenious experiments; that its main function other than being fun is critical; but that it may be *prophylactic* against buying a half-baked (and home-baked) philosophy of science that is roughly a half-century out of date in some respects (e.g., simplistic, intolerant "operationalism" as to scientific terms). I also tell them that, while I disapprove of using metatheory as a cudgel to beat up on the substantive opposition in one's field, it is all right to employ it as a *defensive* instrument because there is so much abuse of philosophy of science by those psychologists who do employ it as a cudgel. Thus, for instance, when I first began publishing my views about schizophrenia, its open concept character was the basis of criticism by psychologists who disliked the whole idea of mental illness and had swallowed the Szasz dogma that there is no such thing. These critics said there couldn't be such a thing as schizophrenia inasmuch as nobody had ever given a "strictly operational definition" of it. It was helpful to refer them to Carnap's "Testability and meaning" (1936–37) and the further development of it by Arthur Pap (1953, 1958, chapter 11) and to Hempel's *Fundamentals of Concept Formation in Empirical Science* (1952). As for metatheory in its own right—not merely as a handmaiden of the psychologist who is confronted with a mixed substantive-methodological problem—I am unabashedly old-fashioned in my belief in Reason, that science differs from superstition in being more rational, and that the only important way that metatheory differs from nonphilosophical "history of science" is in its aim of rational reconstruction, which in turn eventuates not in strict rules of "scientific method" but in guidelines, principles, and helpful advice to the theorizing scientist (Meehl 1984, 1990a, 1990d).

I am deeply indebted to my philosopher colleagues Tony Anderson and Keith Gunderson for their initiative in proposing this collection of writings by an avocational (non-union card) philosopher, and for their competence and diligence in seeing it through. Thanks are also due to Philip Kitcher and Wesley Salmon for accepting the onerous task of reviewers and for their enthusiastic recommendations to go ahead with the project.

Paul E. Meehl
Minneapolis, Minnesota
March 6, 1990

References

Ayer, A. J. 1936. *Language, Truth, and Logic.* New York: Oxford University Press.

Ayer, A. J. 1940. *Foundations of Empirical Knowledge.* New York: Macmillan.

Black, M. 1964. *Companion to Wittgenstein's "Tractatus."* Ithaca, N.Y.: Cornell University Press.

Blumberg, A. E., and Feigl, H. 1931. Logical Positivism. *Journal of Philosophy* 28: 281–96.

Campbell, D. T. 1990. The Meehlian Corroboration-Versimilitude Theory of Science. *Psychological Inquiry 1*: 142–47.

Carnap, R. 1936–37. Testability and Meaning. *Philosophy of Science* 3: 420–71; 4: 2–40. Reprinted with corrigenda and additional bibliography, New Haven, Conn.: Yale University Graduate Philosophy Club, 1950. Reprinted in *Readings in the Philosophy of Science*, eds. H. Feigl and M. Broadbeck. New York: Appleton-Century-Crofts, 1953, 47–92.

Carnap, R. 1937. *The Logical Syntax of Language*. London: K. Paul, Trench, Trubner & Co. (Originally published in German in 1934.)

Cronbach, L. J., and Meehl, P.E. 1955. Construct Validity in Psychological Tests. *Psychological Bulletin 52*: 281–302. Reprinted in P. E. Meehl, *Psychodiagnosis: Selected Papers*. Minneapolis: University of Minnesota Press, 1973, 3–31.

Dawes, R.M. 1988. *Rational Choice in an Uncertain World*. Chicago: Harcourt Brace Jovanovich.

Faust, D. 1984. *The Limits of Scientific Reasoning*. Minneapolis: University of Minnesota Press.

Feigl, H. 1950. Existential Hypotheses: Realistic versus Phenomenalistic Interpretations. *Philosophy of Science* 17: 35–62.

Freud, S. 1959. "Inhibitions, Symptoms and Anxiety." In *Standard Edition of the Complete Psychological Works of Sigmund Freud* (Vol. 20), ed. and trans. J. Strachey. London: Hogarth Press, 87–172. (Original work published 1926.)

Hempel, C. G. 1952. *Fundamentals of Concept Formation in Empirical Science*. Chicago: University of Chicago Press.

Hogarth, R. M. 1987. *Judgment and Choice: The Psychology of Decision*. New York: Wiley.

Kahneman, D., Slovic, P., and Tversky, A. (eds.) 1982. *Judgments under Uncertainty: Heuristics and Biases*. Cambridge, England: Cambridge University Press.

Lord, C. G., Ross, L., and Lepper, M. R. 1979. Biased Assimilation and Attitude Polarization: The Effects of Prior Theories on Subsequently Considered Evidence. *Journal of Personality and Social Psychology* 37: 2098–2109.

MacCorquodale, K., and Meehl, P. E. 1954. "Edward C. Tolman." In *Modern Learning Theory*, eds. W. K. Estes, S. Koch, K. MacCorquodale, P. E. Meehl, C. G. Mueller, W. N. Schoenfeld, and W. S. Verplanck. New York: Appleton-Century-Crofts, 177–266.

Maxwell, G., and Feigl, H. (1961). Why Ordinary Language Needs Reforming. *Journal of Philosophy* 58: 488–98.

Meehl, P. E. 1984. "Foreword." In Faust, *The Limits of Scientific Reasoning*, Minneapolis: University of Minnesota Press.

Meehl, P. E. 1989. Schizotaxia Revisited. *Archives of General Psychiatry* 46: 935–44.

Meehl, P. E. 1990a. Corroboration and Verisimilitude: Against Lakatos's "Sheer Leap of Faith." (Working Paper MCPS-90-01.) Minneapolis: University of Minnesota, Center for Philosophy of Science.

Meehl, P. E. 1990b. "Schizotaxia as an Open Concept." In *Studying Persons and Lives*, eds. A. I. Rabin, R. Zucker, R. Emmons, and S. Frank. New York: Springer, 248–303.

Meehl, P. E. 1990c. Toward an Integrated Theory of Schizotaxia, Schizotypy and Schizophrenia. *Journal of Personality Disorders* 4: 1–99.

Meehl, P. E. 1990d. Appraising and Amending Theories: The Strategy of Lakatosian Defense and Two Principles that Warrant Using It. *Psychological Inquiry*, 1: 108–41.

Meehl, P. E., and Golden, R. 1982. "Taxometric Methods." In *Handbook of Research Methods in Clinical Psychology*, eds. P. Kendall and J. Butcher. New York: Wiley, 127–81.

Nisbett, R. E. and Ross, L. 1980. *Human Inference: Strategies and Shortcomings of Human Judgment*. Englewood Cliffs, N.J.: Prentice-Hall.

Pap, A. 1953. Reduction-Sentences and Open Concepts. *Methodos* 5: 3–30.

Pap, A. 1958. *Semantics and Necessary Truth*. New Haven, Conn.: Yale University Press.

Popper, K. R. 1959. *The Logic of Scientific Discovery*. New York: Basic Books. (Original work published 1935.)

Reichenbach, H. 1938. *Experience and Prediction*. Chicago: University of Chicago Press.

Waismann, F. 1945. Verifiability. *Proceedings of the Aristotelian Society* 19 (Supplement): 119–50.

Wittgenstein, L. 1933. *Tractatus Logico-Philosophicus*. New York: Harcourt, Brace.

Wittgenstein, L. 1953. *Philosophical Investigations* (3rd ed.). New York: Macmillan.

1

Theoretical Risks and Tabular Asterisks: Sir Karl, Sir Ronald, and the Slow Progress of Soft Psychology

I had supposed that the title gave an easy tipoff to my topic, but some puzzled reactions by my Minnesota colleagues show otherwise, which heartens me because it suggests that what I am about to say is not trivial and universally known. The two knights are Sir Karl Raimund Popper (1959, 1962, 1972; Schilpp, 1974) and Sir Ronald Aylmer Fisher (1956, 1966, 1967), whose respective emphases on subjecting scientific theories to grave danger of refutation (that's Sir Karl) and major reliance on tests of statistical significance (that's Sir Ronald) are, at least in current practice, not well integrated—perhaps even incompatible. If you have not been accustomed to thinking about this incoherency, and my remarks lead you to do so (whether or not you end up agreeing with me), this article will have served its scholarly function.

I consider it unnecessary to persuade you that most "theories" in the soft areas of psychology (clinical, counseling, social, personality, community, and school psychology) are scientifically unimpressive and technologically worthless. Documenting that statement would of course require a considerable amount of time, but you can quickly get the flavor by having a look at Braun (1966); Fiske (1974); Gergen (1973); Hogan, DeSoto, and Solano (1977); McGuire (1973); Meehl (1960/1973a, 1959/1973f); Mischel (1977); Schlenker (1974); Smith (1973); and Wiggins (1973). These are merely some highly visible and forceful samples; I make no claim to bibliographic completeness on the large theme of "What's wrong with 'soft' psychology." A beautiful hatchet job, which in my opinion should be required reading for all Ph.D. candidates, is by the so-

This article is based on a lecture delivered at the meeting of the American Psychological Association, Washington, D.C., September 1976, on the occasion of the author's receiving Division 12, Section 3's Distinguished Scientist Award. The research reported here was assisted by Grant MH 24224 from the National Institute of Mental Health and the University of Minnesota Psychiatry Research Fund. Completion of the article was aided by a James McKeen Cattell Fund sabbatical award.

ciologist Andreski (1972). Perhaps the easiest way to convince yourself is by scanning the literature of soft psychology over the last 30 years and noticing what happens to theories. Most of them suffer the fate that General MacArthur ascribed to old generals — They never die, they just slowly fade away. In the developed sciences, theories tend either to become widely accepted and built into the larger edifice of well-tested human knowledge or else they suffer destruction in the face of recalcitrant facts and are abandoned, perhaps regretfully, as a "nice try." But in fields like personology and social psychology, this seems not to happen. There is a period of enthusiasm about a new theory, a period of attempted application to several fact domains, a period of disillusionment as the negative data come in, a growing bafflement about inconsistent and unreplicable empirical results, multiple resort to ad hoc excuses, and then finally people just sort of lose interest in the thing and pursue other endeavors.

Since I do not want to step on toes lest my propaganda falls on deaf ears, I dare not mention what strike me as the most egregious contemporary examples, so let us go back to the late 1930s and early 1940s when I was a student. In those days we were talking about level of aspiration. You could not pick up a psychological journal — even the *Journal of Experimental Psychology* — without finding at least one and sometimes several articles on level of aspiration in schizophrenics, or in juvenile delinquents, or in Phi Beta Kappas, or whatever. It was supposed to be a great powerful theoretical construct that would explain all kinds of things about the human mind from psychopathology to politics. What happened to it? Well, I have looked into some of the recent textbooks of general psychology and have found that either they do not mention it at all — the very phrase is missing from the index — or if they do, it gets cursory treatment in a couple of sentences. There is no doubt something to the notion. We all agree (from common sense) that people differ in what they demand or expect of themselves, and that this probably has something to do, sometimes, with their performance. But it did not get integrated into the total nomological network, nor did it get clearly liquidated as a nothing concept. It did not get killed or resurrected or transformed or solidified; it just kind of dried up and blew away, and we no longer wanted to talk about it or do experimental research on it. A more recent example is the theory of "risky shift," about which Cartwright (1973) wrote, after reviewing 196 papers that appeared in the 1960s:

> As time went by . . . it gradually became clear that the cumulative impact of these findings was quite different from what had been expected by those who produced them. Instead of providing an explanation of why "groups are riskier than individuals," they in fact cast serious doubt on the validity of the proposition itself (225).

It is now evident that the persistent search for an explanation of "the risky shift" was misdirected and that any adequate theory will have to account for a much more complicated set of data than originally anticipated. But it is not clear how theorizing should proceed, since serious questions have been raised as to whether, or in what way, "risk" is involved in the effects to be explained (226).

After 10 years of research, [the] original problem remains unsolved. We still do not know how the risk-taking behavior of "real-life" groups compares with that of individuals (231).

I do not think that there is any dispute about this matter among psychologists familiar with the history of the other sciences. It is simply a sad fact that in soft psychology theories rise and decline, come and go, more as a function of baffled boredom than anything else; and the enterprise shows a disturbing absence of that *cumulative* character that is so impressive in disciplines like astronomy, molecular biology, and genetics.

There are some solid substantive reasons for this that I will list here, lest you think that I am beating up on the profession, unaware of the terrible intrinsic difficulty of our subject matter. Since (in 10 minutes of superficial thought) I easily came up with 20 features that make human psychology hard to scientize, I invite you to pick your own favorites. Differences as to which difficulties are emphasized will not, I am sure, cause any disagreement about the general fact. This is not the place to develop in detail the thesis that the human mind is hard to scientize, let alone to prove it. Each of the 20 difficulties is, I am aware, debatable; and one could find competent psychologists who would either deny a difficulty's reality—at least in the form I state it—or who, although admitting it exists, would maintain that we have, or will be able to develop shortly, methods adequate to overcome or circumvent it. Each of these alleged difficulties in scientizing the human mind is sufficiently controversial to deserve a methodological article by itself. This being so, to substitute a once-over lightly (and hence inevitably dogmatic) defense of each as a real difficulty is, for those who accept it, a work of supererogation, and for the others, it is doomed to failure. I therefore confine myself to listing and explaining the problems, repeating that my purpose in so doing is to prevent the rest of my article from being taken as a kind of malicious and unsympathetic attack on psychologists (of which, after all, I *am* one!) based on an inadequate appreciation of the terrible difficulties under which we work. In a few cases I have explained at some length and replied to objections, these being cases in which a difficulty is not widely recognized in our profession or in which it is generally held to have been disposed of by a familiar (but erroneous) refutation or solution. Regrettably, some psychologists use "philosophical" arguments that are a generation or more out of date.

Since I am listing and summarizing rather than developing or proving, it seems appropriate to present the set of difficulties as follows:

1. Response-Class Problem

This involves the well-known difficulties of slicing up the raw behavioral flux into meaningful intervals identified by causally relevant attributes on the response side, a problem that exists already in the Skinner box (Skinner, 1938, p. 70), worsens in field study by an ethologist, and reaches almost unmanageable proportions in studying human social behavior of the kind to which clinical, social, and personology psychologists must address themselves (see, e.g., MacCorquodale & Meehl, 1954, pp. 218–231, after a quarter century still considered by some the best statement of the problem; Hinde, 1970, pp. 10–13; Meehl, 1954, pp. 40–44 and chap. 6 passim; Skinner, 1938, pp. 33–43).

2. Situation-Taxonomy Problem

As is well known, the importance of an adequate classification and sampling of environments and situations has received less attention than Problem 1, above, despite emphasis by several major contributors such as Roger Barker (1968), Egon Brunswik (1955), and Saul B. Sells (1963). It seems likely that the problems of characterizing the stimulus side, even though often neglected by the profession or dealt with superficially, are about as intractable as the characterization of the response class. It is not even clear whether identification and measurement of the relevant stimulus dimensions (e.g., size) is the same task as concocting a taxonomy of "situations" and "environments," nor whether the answer to this question would quickly generate rules for an adequate statistical ecology applicable to research design. So I am perhaps lumping under this "situation-taxonomy" rubric three distinguishable but related problems. I am inclined to think that most (not all) of the current methodological controversy concerning traits versus situations is logically and mathematically reducible to this and the preceding category, since I think that traits are disposition clusters, and dispositions always involve at least implicit reference to the stimulus side; but this is not the place to push that view.

3. Unit of Measurement

One sometimes hears this conflated with one or both of the preceding, but, of course, it is not the same. There are questions in rating scales and in psychometrics (as well as in certain branches of nondifferential psychology, in which disagreements persist about such fundamental matters as the necessity of a genuine interval or ratio scale for the use of certain kinds of sampling statistical inference.

4. Individual Differences

Perhaps the shortest way to discuss this one is to point out the oddity that what is one psychologist's subject matter is another psychologist's error term (Cronbach, 1957)! More generally, that fact is that organisms differ not only with respect to the strengths of various dispositions, but, more common and more distressing for the researcher, they differ as to *how* their dispositions are shaped and organized. As a result, the individual differences involved in "mental chemistry" are tougher to deal with than, say, the fact that different elements have different atomic numbers or that elements with the same atomic number vary in atomic weights (isotopes).

5. Polygenic Heredity

It is generally conceded that the measurement and causal inference problems that arise in biometrical genetics are, with some exceptions, more difficult than those found in the kind of single factor dominant or recessive gene situation on which the science of genetics was originally founded. Except for Mendelizing mental deficiencies and perhaps some psychiatric disorders that are transmitted in a Mendelizing fashion, most of the attributes studied by soft-field psychologists are influenced by polygenic systems. Usually we must assume that several totally different and unrelated polygenic systems influence a manifest trait like social introversion. Introversion may be based in part on a unitary (although polygenic) variable, as shown by Gottesman (1963) and others. However, as an acquired disposition of the adult-acculturated individual, it presumably results from a confluence of different polygenic contributors such as basic anxiety readiness, mesomorphic toughness, garden-variety social introversion, dominance, need for affiliation, and the like.

6. Divergent Causality

As pointed out 35 years ago by the physical chemist Irving Langmuir (1943; London, 1946; Meehl, 1954, pp. 60–61; Meehl, 1967/1970b, especially footnotes 1–8 on pp. 395–396), there are complex systems whose causal structure and boundary conditions are such that slight differences — including those that are, for practical predictive and explanatory purposes, effectively "random" (whatever their inner deterministic nature may be)—tend to "wash out," "cancel each other," or "balance" over the long run. On the other hand, there are other systems in which such slight perturbations or differences in the exact character of the initial conditions are, so to speak, amplified over the long run. Langmuir christened the former kind of causality as "convergent," as when we say that the average errors in making repeated measurements of a table length tend to cancel out and leave us with a stable and highly trustworthy mean value of the result. On the other hand, an object in unstable equilibrium can lean slightly toward the right instead of the left, as a result of which a deadly avalanche occurs burying a whole village. Although both sorts of systems are found at all levels of Comte's Pyramid of the Sciences, it seems regrettably true that the incidence of important and pervasive types of divergent causality is greater in the sciences of behavior.

7. Idiographic Problem

It is not necessary to "settle" the long-continued methodological controversies regarding idiographic versus nomothetic methods in psychology and history (e.g., whether they are philosophically, metaphysically fundamentally different) to agree with strong proponents of the idiographic method, such as Gordon Allport (Allport, 1937) or my long-time friendly adversary on the prediction issue, Robert R. Holt (1958), that the human personality—unless one approaches it with the postulate of impoverished reality—has in its content, structure, and, conceivably, even in individual differences as to some of its "laws," and very much in its origins, properties and relations that make the study of personality rather more similar to such disciplines as history, archaeology (historical), geology, or the reconstruction of a criminal case from police evidence than the derivation of the molar gas laws from the kinetic theory of heat or the mechanisms of heredity from molecular biology. Some would argue that such explanatory derivations aside, even the mere inductive subsumption of particulars (episodes, molar traits, persons) under descriptive generalizations is a more difficult and problematic affair in these disciplines than in most branches of physical and biological science.

8. Unknown Critical Events

Related to divergent causality and idiographic understanding but distinguishable from them is the fact that critical events in the history of personality development are frequently hard to ascertain. There is reason to believe that in some instances they are literally never ascertained by us or known to the individual under study, even somebody who has spent 500 hours on the analytic couch. They are sometimes observable events that, however, were not in fact observed and recorded, such as the precise tone of voice and facial expression that a patient's father had when he was reacting to an off-color joke that the patient innocently told at the dinner table at age 7. Every thoughtful clinician realizes that the standard life history that one finds in a medical chart is, from the standpoint of thorough causal comprehension, so thin and spotty and selective as to border on the ludicrous. But there is also what I would view as an important causal source of movement in one rather than another direction of divergent causality, namely, inner events, such as fantasies, resolutions, shifts in cognitive structure, that the patient may or may not report and that he or she may later be unable to recall.

9. Nuisance Variables

Other things equal, it is handy for research and theorizing if we can sort the variables into three classes, namely, (a) variables that we manipulate (in the narrow sense of the word *experimental*), (b) variables that we do not manipulate but can hold constant or effectively exclude from influence by one or another means isolating the system under study, and (c) variables that are quasirandom with respect to the phenomena under study, so that they only contribute to measurement error or the standard deviation of a statistic. Unfortunately, there are systems, especially social and biological systems of the kind that clinical psychologists and personologists study, in which there is operative a nonnegligible class of variables that are not random but systematic, that exert a sizable influence, and are themselves also sizably influenced by other variables, either exogenous to the system (F. M. Fisher, 1966) or contained in it, such that we have to worry about the influence of these variables, but we cannot always ascertain the direction of the causal arrow. Sometimes we cannot even get sufficiently trustworthy measurements of these variables so as to "partial out" or "correct" their influence even if we are willing to make conjectures about the direction of causality. There are some circumstances in which we can extrapolate from experimental studies or from well-corroborated theory to make a high-confidence decision about the direction of causal influence, but there are many other circumstances — in soft psychology, the preponderating ones — in which this is not possible. Further, lacking special configurations such as highly atypical cells in a multivariate space or correlation coefficients that impose strong constraints on a causal interpretation, or provisional assumptions as relied on in path analysis (Li, 1975), the system is statistically and causally indeterminate. (Why these constraints are regularly treated as "assumptions" instead of refutable conjectures is itself a deep and fascinating question that I plan to examine some other time.) The well-known difficulties in assessing the influence of socioeconomic status (SES) on children's IQ when unscrambling the hereditary and environmental contributors to intelligence is perhaps the most dramatic one, but other less emotion-laden examples can be found on all sides in the behavioral sciences. (See Meehl, 1970a, 1971/1973b.)

10. Feedback Loops

A special case in engineering is the usual in psychology, that a person's behavior affects the behavior of other persons and hence alters the schedule imposed by the "social Skinner box." The complexities here are so refractory to quantitative decomposition that yoked box setups came to be used even for the (relatively simple) animal case as a factual substitute for piecewise causal-dispositional analysis. In the human social case, they may be devastating.

11. Autocatalytic Processes

The chemist is familiar under the label *autocatalysis* with a rare but important kind of preparation in which one of the end products of the chemical processes is itself capable of catalyzing the process. Numerous common examples spring to mind in psychology, such as anxiety and depression as affects or economic failure as a social impact. Much of neurosis is autocatalytic in the cognitive-affective-volitional system, as are counterneurotic healing processes. When this kind of complicated setup is conjoined with the critical event, idiographic, and divergent causality factors, and also with the individual differences factor (that parameters relating the growth of one state of schedule to a dependent variable, which itself in turn acts autocatalytically, show individual differences), the task of unscrambling such a situation becomes terribly difficult.

12. Random Walk

There is a widespread and understandable tendency to assume that the class of less-probable outcomes, given constancy of other classes of causally efficacious variables, should in principle be explicable by detecting a class of systematic input differences. Thus, for instance, we try to understand the genetic/environmental contributions to schizophrenia by studying discordant monozygotic twins. If I develop a florid clinical schizophrenia and my monozygotic twin remains sane and wins the Pulitzer Prize for poetry, it is a sensible strategy for the psychologist to consider my case *and similar cases* with an eye for "systematic differences" (such as who was born first, who was in what position in the uterus, or who had a severe case of scarlet fever with delirium) as responsible for dramatic difference in final outcomes. When one reflects on the rather meager yield of such assiduous ferreting out of systematic differences by, say Gottesman and Shields (1972) in their excellent book, one experiences bafflement. On the one hand, the concordance rate for monozygotic twins is only a little over 50%, indicating a very large nongenetic component in causality. Yet, on the other hand, we find feeble or null differences when we look at the list of "obvious, plausible" differentiators between the twins who fall ill and the twins who remain well. Of course, one can always say—and would no doubt be partly right in this—that we just have not been clever enough to hit on the right ones; or even if, qualitatively, they are the right ones, we do not have sufficiently construct-valid measures of them to show up in the statistics.

There is, however, an alternative explanation that, when one reflects on it, is plausible (at least to a clinical practitioner like myself) and that has analogues in organic medicine and in other historical sciences like geology or the theory of evolution, to wit, that we are mistaken to look for a "big systematic variable" of the kind that is already in our standard list of influences, such as organic disease, parental preference, or SES of an adoptive home. Rather, we might emphasize that a human being's life history involves as one form of divergent causality, something akin to the stochastic process known as a "random walk" (Bartlett, 1955, pp. 15–20, 47–50, 89–96; Feller, 1957, pp. 73, 311; Kemeny, Snell, & Thompson, 1957, pp. 171–177; Read, 1972, pp. 779–782). At several points that are individually minor but collectively critical determinative, it is an almost "chance" affair whether the patient does A or not A, whether his girl friend says she will or will not go out with him on a certain evening, or whether he happens to hit it off with the ophthalmologist that he consults about some peculiar vision disturbances that are making him anxious about becoming blind, and the like. If one twin becomes psychotic at the end of such a random walk, it is possible that he was suffering from what was only, so to speak, "bad luck"—not a concept that appears in any standard list of biological and social nuisance variables!

Luck is one of the most important contributors to individual differences in human suffering, satisfaction, illness, achievement, and so forth, an embarrassingly "obvious" point that social scientists readily forget (Gunther, 1977; Jencks, 1972, pp. 8–9, 227–228; Popper, 1974, pp. 36–37; Stoddard, 1929; for further discussion of this see Meehl, 1972/1973g, pp. 402–407, Meehl. 1973d, pp. 220–221). Of course, the fact that a process resembles a random walk does not mean that it is not susceptible to quantitative treatment. Witness the extensive formal development of this sort of process in the field of finite mathematics by engineers and others. The point is that its analytical treatment will not look like the familiar kind of search for a systematic class of differentiating variables like

SES as a nuisance variable in relationship to educational outcome and intelligence.

13. Sheer Number of Variables

I suppose that this is the most commonly mentioned of the difficulties of social science, and I assume that my readers would accept it without further elaboration. But it is worth mention that the number of variables is large from several different viewpoints. Thus we deal on one side with a *large number of phenotypic traits*, conceiving a phenotypic trait as a related family of response dispositions that (a) are correlated to some stipulated degree pairwise and that (b) have some kind of logical, semantic, social, or other "meaning" overlap or resemblance that entitles us to class them together. Or, again, we consider a large number of dimensions on the stimulus side and on the response side that are relevant in formulating a law of behavior acquisition, as well as in the subsequent control and activation dispositions thus acquired. From still another viewpoint, the list of historical causal influences is long and heterogeneous, ranging from such diverse factors as a mutated gene or a never-diagnosed subclinical tuberculosis to a mother who mysteriously absented herself the day after a patient first permitted himself the fantasy that a brutal father would go away, and the like. It should be noted that this matter of sheer number of variables would not be so important (except as a contributor to residual "random variation" in various kinds of outcomes) if they were each small contributors and independent, like the sources of error in the scattering of shots at a target in classical theory of errors. But in psychology this is not typically the situation. Rather, the variables, although large in number, are each nuisance variables that carry a significant amount of weight, interact with each other, and contribute to idiographic development via the divergent causality mode.

14. Importance of Cultural Factors

This source of individual differences, both in acquired response clusters (traits) and in the parameters of acquisition and activation functions, especially when taken together with the genetic factors contributing, for instance, to social competence, mental health, intellect, and so on, makes for unusual complications in understanding how somebody got to be the way he is. We are, for instance, so accustomed to referring to nuisance variables like SES in considering the design of experiments that involve SES-related individual differences that we readily forget something every reflective person knows—that the measures of things like SES are general and not tailor-made for what is idiographically more significant in the development of a particular person. So when we speak of "controlling for SES," that is a loose use of language in comparison with "controlling the temperature" in a Skinner box or controlling the efflux of calories in a physics lab by use of a bomb calorimeter. A treatise on the principles of internal medicine (such as Harrison et al., 1966) sometimes refers to cultural factors, including those that are not at all understood—in the way that, say, dietary deficiency might be mediated by extreme poverty in a backward country—and simply says that for some reason this disease is found more frequently among the rich than among the poor. But the *important* causal chains of prime interest to the physician, even in his role as an advisor of preventive medicine, do not typically involve worry about whether somebody is fifth-generation upper class or the third child of parents who became anxious after the birth of the second oldest sibling. However, this kind of consideration might be crucial in reconstructing the life history of such a person.

15. Context-Dependent Stochastologicals

Cronbach and Meehl (1955/1973) and subsequent writers adopted (from the neopositivist philosophers of science) the phrase *nomological network* to designate the system of lawlike relationships conjectured to hold between theoretical entities (states, structures, events, dispositions) and between theoretical entities and their observable indicators. The "network" metaphor is chosen to emphasize the structure of such systems, in which the *nodes* of the network, representing the postulated theoretical entities, are connected by the *strands* of the network, representing the lawful relationships hypothesized to hold between the entities. What makes such a set of theoretical statements a system (rather than a mere conjunction of unrelated assertions, a "heap of hypotheses") is the semantic fact of their shared terms, an overlap in the propositions' inner components, without which, of course, no deductive fertility and no derivation chains to observational statements would be formally possible. The network is empirical (and "scientifically respectable") because a proper subset of the theoretical terms is coordinated in fairly direct ways ("operationally") with terms designating perceptual or instrument-reading predicates. These latter predicates normally possess the admirable properties of *quick decision, minimal theory dependence*, and *high interpersonal consensus*.

Despite the current distaste for these "objectivist" conceptions, I remain an old-fashioned unreconstructed positivist to the limited extent that I think science—both "normal science" and "revolutionary, paradigm-replacing science"—differs from less promising, noncumulative, and personalistic enterprises like politics, psychotherapy, folklore, ethics, metaphysics, aesthetics, and theology *in part* because of its skeptical insistence on reliable (intersubjective, replicable) protocols that describe observations. Skinner is in better shape than Freud partly because Norman Campbell (1920/1957, p. 29) was right in saying that the kinds of judgments for which universal assent can be obtained are (a) judgments of temporal simultaneity, consecutiveness, and "betweenness"; (b) judgments of coincidence and "betweenness" in space; and (c) judgments of number. I cannot view the increasingly fashionable dismissal of these objectivity-oriented views as other than obscurantist in tendency. (See Kordig, 1971, 1973.)

However, the nomological network, even though correlated directly, here and there, with observational data, is not "operational" throughout, since some of the nodes and strands are connected with the observational data base only via other subregions of the network. As Hempel said (1952):

> A scientific theory might therefore be likened to a complex spatial network: Its terms are represented by the knots, while the threads connecting the latter correspond, in part, to the definitions and, in part, to the fundamental and derivative hypotheses included in the theory. The whole system floats, as it were, above the plane of observation and is anchored to it by rules of interpretation. These might be viewed as strings which are not part of the network but link certain points of the latter with specific places in the plane of observation. By virtue of those interpretive connections, the network can function as a scientific theory: From certain observational data, we may ascend, via an interpretive string, to some point in the theoretical network, thence proceed, via definitions and hypotheses, to other points, from which another interpretive string permits a descent to the plane of observation. (36)

Even though the core of these ideas is sound and important, the word *nomological* is in soft psychology at best an extension of meaning and at worst a misleading corruption of the logician's terminology. Originally it designated strict laws as in W. E. Johnson's (1921/1964) earlier use of "nomic necessity" (p. 61). The lawlike relationships we have to work with in soft psychology are rarely (never?) of this strict kind, errors of measurement aside. Instead, they are correlations, tendencies, statistical clusterings, increments of probabilities, and altered stochastic dispositions. The ugly neologism *stochastological* (as analogue to *nomological*) is at least shorter than the usual "probabilistic relation" or "statistical dependence," so I shall adopt it. We are so accustomed to our immersion in a sea of stochastologicals that we may fail to notice what a terrible disadvantage this sort of probabilistic law network puts us under, both as to the clarity of our concepts and, more important, the testability of our theories. (One still hears the tiresome complaint that a theoretical system cannot be simultaneously concept definatory and factually assertive, despite repeated explanations of how this works. See, e.g., Braithwaite, 1960, pp. 76–87; Campbell, 1920/1957, pp. 119–58; Carnap, 1936–1937/1950, 1952/1956, 1966, pp. 225–26, 265–74; Feigl, 1956, pp. 17–19; Hempel, 1952, 1958, pp. 81–87; Lewis, 1970; Maxwell, 1961, 1962; Meehl, 1977, pp. 35–37; Nagel, 1961, pp. 87, 91–93; Pap, 1958, pp. 318–21, 1962, pp. 46–52; Popper, 1974, pp. 14–73; Ramsey, 1931/1960; Sellars, 1948.)

When the observational corroborators of the theory consist wholly of percentages, crude curve fits, correlations, significance tests, and distribution overlaps, it is difficult or impossible to see clearly when a given batch of empirical data refutes a theory or even when two batches of data are (in any interesting sense) "inconsistent." All we can usually say with quasi-certainty is that context-dependent statistics should *not* be numerically identical in different studies of the same problem. (A dramatic recent example of this was the discovery that some of Sir Cyril Burt's correlation coefficients were *too consistent* to have been derived from the different tests and populations that he reported!)

In heading this section "Context-Dependent Stochastologicals," I mean to emphasize the aspect of this problem that seems to me most frustrating to our theoretical interests, namely, that the statistical dependencies we observe are always somewhat, and often strongly, dependent on the institution-cum-population setting in which the measurements were obtained. Lacking a "complete (causal) theory" of what influences what, *and how much*, we simply cannot compute expected numerical changes in stochastic dependencies when moving from one population or setting to another. Sometimes we cannot even rationally predict the direction of such changes. If the difference between two Pearson correlations were safely attributable to random sampling fluctuation alone, we could use the statistician's standard tools to decide whether Jones's study "fails to replicate" Smith's. But the usual situation is not one of simple cross-validation shrinkage (or "boostage")—rather, it involves the validity generalization problem. For this, there are no standard statistical procedures. We may be able, relying on strong theorems in general statistics plus a backlog of previous experience and a smattering of theory, to say some fairly safe things about restriction of range and the like. However, thoughtful theorists realize how little *quantitatively* we can say with sufficient confidence to warrant counting an unexpected shift in a stochastic quantity as a strong "discorroborator." This being so, we cannot fairly count an "in the ball park" predicted value as a strong corroborator. For example, Meehl's Mental Measure correlates .50 with SES in Duluth junior high school students, as predicted from Fisbee's theory of sociability. When Jones tries to replicate the finding on Chicano seniors in Tucson, he gets $r = .34$. Who can say anything theoretically cogent about this difference? Does any sane psychologist believe that one can do much more than shrug?

Although probability concepts (in the theory) and statistical distributions (in the data) sometimes appear in both classical and quantum physics, their usual role differs from that of context-dependent stochastologicals in social science. Without exceeding space limitations or my competence, let me briefly suggest some differences. When probabilities appear in physics and chemistry, they often drop out in the course of the derivation chain, yielding a quasi-nomological at its termination (e.g., derivation of gas laws or Graham's diffusion law from the kinetic theory of heat, in which the postulates are nomological, the "conditions" are probability distributions, and the resulting theorems are again nomological). Second, when the predicted observational result still contains statistical notions, their numerical values are either not context dependent or the context dependencies permit precise experimental manipulation. A statistical scatter function for photons or electrons can be finely tuned by altering a very limited number of experimental variables (e.g., wave-length, slit width, screen distance), and the law of large numbers assures that the expected "probabilistic" values of, say, photon incidence in a specified band will be indiscernibly different from the observed (finite but huge) numbers.

All this is very unlike the stochastologicals of soft psychology, in which strong context dependence prevails, but we do not know (a) the complete list of contextual influences, (b) the function form of context dependency for those influences that we can list, (c) the numerical values of parameters in those function forms that we know or guess, or (d) the values of the context variables if we are so fortunate as to get past Ignorances a–c. Finally, unlike physics, our sample sizes are usually such that the Bernoulli theorem does not guarantee a close fit between theoretical and observed frequencies—perhaps one of the few good uses for significance tests?

16. Open Concepts

As a consequence of the factors listed supra, especially those numbered 4, 7, 9, 15, it is usually not possible in the soft areas of social science to provide rigorous, explicit, or—the holy word when I was in graduate school—operational definitions for theoretical concepts. This difficulty occurs not because psychologists are intellectually lazy or sloppy, although most of us are at times (some routinely and on principle). Rather, it arises from the intrinsic nature of the subject matter, that is, from the organism's real compositional nature and structure and the causal texture of its environment. As has often been pointed out, one can concoct quick and easy "operational definitions" of psychological terms, but they will usually lack theoretical interest and, except for some important special cases (e.g., purely predictive task-tailored psychometrics and *some* kinds of operant behavior control), generalizable technological power (Lazarus, 1971; Loevinger, 1957). It is remarkable evidence of cultural lag in intellectual life that one can still find quite a few psychologists who are hooked on the dire necessity of strictly operational definitions, and who view open concepts as somehow methodologically sinful, although it is now a quarter of a century since the late Arthur Pap published his brilliant article on open concepts (Pap, 1953, see also chap. 11 of Pap, 1958). To do justice, and highlight the cultural lag, I should mention the related article of Waismann that antedated Pap's by 8 years (Wais-mann, 1945) and even Carnap's of 40 years ago (1936–1937/1950). I cannot name a single logician or a philosopher (or historian) of science who today de-fends strict operationism in the sense that some psychologists claim to believe in it. (They don't really—but you have to listen a while to catch the deviations in *substance* when pseudooperationists are not discoursing dogmatically about *method*.)

The problem of open concepts and their relation to empirical falsifiability war-rants a separate article, with which I am currently engaged, but suffice it to say here that the unavoidability of open concepts in social and biological science tempts us to sidestep it by fake operationism on the one side (if we are of the tough-minded, superscientific orientation) or to be contented with fuzzy verbal-isms on the other side (if we are more artsy-craftsy or literary), thinking that it is the best we can get. The important point for methodology of psychology is that just as in statistics one can have a *reasonably precise theory of probable infer-ence*, being "quasi-exact about the inherently inexact," so psychologists should learn to be sophisticated and rigorous in their metathinking about open concepts at the substantive level. I do not mean to suggest in saying this that the logicians' theory of open concepts is in a highly developed state, but it is far more devel-oped than one would think from reading or listening to most psychologists.

I have elsewhere (Meehl, 1977) distinguished three kinds of openness that are involved in varying degrees in various psychological concepts and that may all be present in the same theoretical construct, namely, (a) openness arising from the indefinite extensibility of our provisional list of operational indicators of the con-struct; (b) openness associated with each indicator singly, because of the empir-ical fact that indicators are only probabilistically, rather than nomologically, linked to the inferred theoretical construct; and (c) openness due to the fact that most of our theoretical entities are introduced by an implicit or contextual defi-nition, that is, by their role in the accepted nomological network, rather than by their inner nature. By their "inner nature" I mean nothing spooky or metaphys-ical but merely their ontological structure or composition as the latter will, with the progress of research, be formulatable in terms of the theoretical entities of more basic sciences in Comte's pyramid. In social and biological science, one should keep in mind that *explicit definition* of theoretical entities is seldom achieved in terms of the initial observational variables of those sciences, but it becomes possible instead by theoretical reduction or fusion. Explicit definition is achieved, if ever, in terms of some more basic underlying science (Meehl, 1977; see also Cronbach & Meehl, 1955/1973; Meehl, 1959/1973f, 1973h, pp. 285–88).

A final remark, which also deserves fuller treatment in another place, is that when we deal with open concepts, as in personality psychometrics of traits or taxa, the statistical phenomenon of *psychometric drift* as a result of bootstrap operations, refinement of measures, and theoretical reflection on the big matrix of convergent and discriminative validities (Campbell & Fiske, 1959) also generates, via our reliance on implicit or contextual definitions of theoretical entities, an associated *conceptual drift*, a meaning shift. When we reassign weight to fallible indicators of an entity to the extent that the very meaning of the term designating that entity is specified by its role in the network, such reassignment of weights—especially under drastic revisions of the system such as dropping a previously relied-upon indicator—constitutes a change in the theoretical concept. Difficult interpretative and research strategy problems arise here, because, on the one hand (especially in psychometrics) we encounter the danger that the resulting conceptual drift has pulled us away from what we started out to measure, but we also recognize that in psychology, as in the other sciences, part of the research aim is precisely that of bringing about revisions of concepts on the basis of revisions of the nomological network that implicitly defines them. We want, as Plato said, to carve nature at its joints; and the best test of this achievement is increased order in our material.

17. Intentionality, Purpose, and Meaning

We do not need to settle the philosopher's question of what is the essential condition for the existence of intentionality, or buy Brentano's famous criterion that intentionality is the distinctive mark of the mental, to recognize that human beings think and plan and intend, that if rats do so they do it at a much lower level, that sunflowers probably do not, and that stones certainly do not. The formulation of powerful functional relationships for systems that do not possess the capacity to think, worry, regret, plan, and intend is obviously on the average an easier task. (But see Vico, 1744/1948, for a view so different that an American social scientist of our time can hardly grasp it.)

18. Rule Governance

Related to intentionality but sufficiently important to deserve a special listing is the fact that human behavior is rule governed. People do something not merely ''in accordance with'' a generalization but because they feel bound to obey the generalization stated in the form of a rule. Nobody has succeeded in coming up with a fully satisfactory definition of when a rule is a rule, but a sufficiently good approximation is to say that a rule differs from an empirical generalization in that a rule is not liquidated by being broken, whereas an empirical generalization is thereby liquidated (assuming that the conditions stated in its antecedent clause are granted, and the violation event is admitted into the corpus). Continued controversies in psycholinguistics reflect the importance of this kind of consideration in any discussion of human conduct.

19. Uniquely Human Events and Powers

In addition to being rule governed, there are several other human features that we do not share with chimpanzees, let alone sponges or boulders. I recall the late Richard M. Elliott saying that the main reason that psychology had done so poorly in its "theories" of humor is that man is the only animal that laughs. I think he had a good point here, since we have learned so much about aspects of human functioning, such as digestion and reproduction, by the experimental study of animals. There are a number of other things that human beings do that no infrahuman animal does, so far as we know. Only man speculates about non-practical, theoretical matters; only man worships; only man systematically goes about seeking revenge, years later, for an injury done to him; only man carries on discussions about how to make decisions; and there are some features of cultural transmission that only man engages in, although the evidence now indicates that numerous other species transmit learned forms of behavior to subsequent generations.

20. Ethical Constraints on Research

This one is so obvious as to need no exposition. One can readily conceive quasi-definitive experiments on the IQ-heredity controversy, or whether there are family dynamics sufficient to make just anyone into a manic-depressive, that cannot be performed because to do so would be immoral.

Not to be overly pessimistic, let me mention (without proof) five noble traditions in clinical psychology that I believe have permanent merit and will still be with us 50 or 100 years from now, despite the usual changes. Some of these are currently unpopular among those addicted to one of the contemporary fly-by-night theories, but that does not bother me. These five noble traditions are (a) descriptive clinical psychiatry, (b) psychometric assessment, (c) behavior genetics, (d) behavior modification (I lump under this rubric positive contingency management, aversion therapy, and desensitization), and (e) psychodynamics. This list should convince you that I am not using methodological arguments to grind any substantive ax. I am probably one of the few psychologists alive today who would list all five of these as great, noble, and enduring intellectual traditions. I particularly emphasize the last, psychodynamics, since I am often perceived as a dust bowl empiricist who does not think that anything can be true or useful if it is not based on either laboratory experiments or statistical correlations. There is not a single experiment reported in my 23-volume set of the standard edition of Freud nor is there a *t* test. But I would take Freud's clinical observations over most people's *t* tests any time. I am confident that psychoanalytic concepts will be around after rubber band theory, transactional theory, attachment theory, labeling theory, dissonance theory, attribution theory, and so on, have subsided into a state of innocuous desuetude like risky shift and level of aspiration. At the very least, psychoanalysis is an interesting theory, which is more than I can say about some of the "theories" that are currently fashionable.

These five noble traditions differ greatly in the methods they use and their central concepts, and I am hard put to say what is common among them. Some of them, such as behavior modification, are not conceptually exciting to those of us who are interested in ideas like Freud's, but they more than make up for that by their remarkable technological power. I shall focus the remainder of my remarks on one feature that they have in common with the developed sciences (physical or biological); to wit, they were originally developed with negligible reliance on *statistical significance testing*. Even the psychometric assessment tradition in its early stages paid little attention to significance testing except (sometimes) for finding good items. Binet did not know anything about *t* tests, but he drew graphs of the developmental change of items. I suggest to you that Sir Ronald has befuddled us, mesmerized us, and led us down the primrose path. I believe that the almost universal reliance on merely refuting the null hypothesis as the standard method for corroborating substantive theories in the soft areas is a terrible mistake, is basically unsound, poor scientific strategy, and one of the worst things that ever happened in the history of psychology.

It is easiest to see this from the methodological viewpoint of Sir Karl Popper, but fortunately we have here a rare instance in which Sir Karl's position yields the same result as the Bayesians', and both give the same result as "scientific common sense" practiced by those chemists and biologists who know nothing about philosophy of science or Bayesian statistics and could not care less about either. Briefly and simplistically, the position of Popper and the neo-Popperians is that we do not "induce" scientific theories by some kind of straightforward upward seepage from the clearly observed facts, nor do we "confirm" theories as the Vienna positivists supposed. All we can do is to subject theories—including the wildest and "unsupported" armchair conjectures (for a Popperian, completely kosher)—to grave danger of refutation, in accordance with the formally valid fourth figure of the implicative syllogism: $p \rightarrow q$, $\sim q$, $\therefore \sim p$, Popper's famous *modus tollens*.

A theory is corroborated to the extent that we have subjected it to such risky tests; the more dangerous tests it has survived, the better corroborated it is. If I tell you that Meehl's theory of climate predicts that it will rain sometime next April, and this turns out to be the case, you will not be much impressed with my "predictive success." Nor will you be impressed if I predict more rain in April than in May, even showing three asterisks (for $p < .001$) in my t-test table! If I predict from my theory that it will rain on 7 of the 30 days of April, and it rains on exactly 7, you might perk up your ears a bit, but still you would be inclined to think of this as a "lucky coincidence." But suppose that I specify *which* 7 days in April it will rain and ring the bell; then you will start getting seriously interested in Meehl's meteorological conjectures. Finally, if I tell you that on April 4th it will rain 1.7 inches (.66 cm), and on April 9th, 2.3 inches (.90 cm) and so forth, and get seven of these correct within reasonable tolerance, you will begin to think that Meehl's theory must have a lot going for it. You may believe that Meehl's theory of the weather, like all theories, is, when taken literally, false, since probably all theories are false in the eyes of God, but you will at least say, to use Popper's language, that it is beginning to look as if Meehl's theory has considerable *verisimilitude*, that is, "truth-likeness." (An adequate reconstruction of the verisimilitude concept has yet to be provided by our logician friends, see, e.g., Popper, 1976, but few reflective psychologists will doubt that some such notion of "nearness to the truth" is unavoidable when we evaluate theories. It is crucial to recognize that verisimilitude is an ontological, not an epistemological, concept that must not be conflated with confirmation, probability, evidence, proof, corroboration, belief, support, or plausibility.)

Popperians would speak of low logical or prior probability, of the high content (forbidding much), because it specifies exactly which days it will rain how many inches. A Bayesian (who would reject Popper's philosophy on the grounds that we want our "theoretical prior" to be *high* to get a nice boost out of Bayes's theorem when the facts turn out right) would express Popper's point by saying that we want what Pap (1962, p. 160) calls the *expectedness*, the prior on the observations that is found in the denominator of Bayes's theorem to be low. An unphilosophical chemist or astronomer or molecular biologist would say that this was just good sensible scientific practice, that a theory that makes precise predictions and correctly picks out *narrow intervals* or *point values* out of the range of experimental possibilities is a pretty strong theory. There are revisions (as I think, necessary) of the classic Popperian position urged on us by his heretical ex-students P. K. Feyerabend and the late Imre Lakatos, but psychologists must reach at least the stage of Bayes and Popper before they can profitably go on to the refinements and criticisms of these gentlemen.

The most important caveat I would adjoin to Sir Karl's falsifiability requirement arises from the considerations pressed by Feyerabend (1962, 1965, 1970, 1971), Lakatos (1970, 1974a, 1974b), and others concerning the crucial role of auxiliary theories in subjecting the main substantive theory of interest to danger of *modus tollens*. As is well known (and not disputed by Popper), when we spell out in detail the logical structure of what purports to be an observational test of a theoretical conjecture T, we normally find that we cannot get to an observational statement from T alone. We require further a set of often complex and problematic auxiliaries A, plus the empirical realization of certain conditions describing the experimental particulars, commonly labeled collectively as C. So that the derivation of an observation from a substantive theory T amounts always to the longer formula $(T.A.C) \rightarrow O$, rather than the simplified schema $(T \rightarrow O)$ that most of us learned in undergraduate logic courses. This presents a problem not perhaps for Popper's main thesis (although some critics do say this) but for its application as a criterion of the scientific status of theories (or the scientific approach of a particular theoretician or investigator?). The *modus tollens* now reads: Since $(T.A.C) \rightarrow O$, and we have falsified O observationally, we have the consequence $\sim (T.A.C)$. Unfortunately, this result does not entail the falsity of T, the substantive theory of interest, but only the falsity of the conjunction $(T.A.C)$; that is, we have proved a disjunction of the falsities of the conjuncts. So the failure to get the expected observation O proves that $\sim T \vee \sim A \vee \sim C$, which is not quite what we would like to show.

One need not subscribe to the famous Duhemian thesis regarding falsification of science as a whole (Grünbaum, 1960, 1962, 1969, 1976) or to the Lakatosian exposition (Lakatos, 1970, 1974a, 1974b) about the protective belt of auxiliaries against which the *modus tollens* is directed versus the hard core of the theory against which the *modus tollens* is, prior to a Kuhnian revolution (Kuhn, 1970a, 1970b, 1970c), forbidden to be directed, to see that there is a difficult problem presented to even a neo-Popperian (like myself), because in social science the auxiliaries A and the initial and boundary conditions of the system C are frequently as problematic as the theory T itself. *Example*: Suppose that a personologist or social psychologist wants to investigate the effect of social fear on visual perception. He attempts to mobilize anxiety in a sample of adolescent males, chosen by their scores on the Social Introversion (Si) scale of the Minnesota Multiphasic Personality Inventory (MMPI), by employing a research assistant who is a raving beauty, instructing her to wear Chanel No. 5 and adopt a mixed seductive and castrative manner toward the subjects. An interpretation of a negative empirical result leaves us wondering whether the main substantive theory of interest concerning social fear and visual perception has been falsified, or whether only the auxiliary theories that the Si scale is valid for social introversion and that attractive but hostile female experimenters elicit social fear in introverted young males have been falsified. Or perhaps even the particular conditions were not met; that is, she did not consistently act the way she was instructed to or the MMPI protocols were misscored.

There is nothing qualitatively unique about this problem for the inexact sciences, but it is quantitatively more severe for us than for the chemist or astronomer, for at least two reasons, which I shall set forth without either proving or developing them here. First, independent testing of the auxiliary theories (which often means validation of psychometric instruments or ascertaining efficacy of social stimulus inputs) is harder to carry out. Owing to unavoidable looseness of the nomological network (Cronbach & Meehl, 1955/1973) plus the factors in the list of 20 difficulties supra, the range of research circumstances in which auxiliaries *A* are problematic is greater than in the exact sciences or in some but not all of the biological sciences. Second, a point to which philosophers of science have devoted little attention, in physics or chemistry there is usually a more intimate connection, sometimes one of contributing to derivability, between the substantive theory of interest *T* and components of the auxiliaries *A*. This is sometimes even true in advanced branches of biology. *Example*: There is a complicated, well-developed, and highly corroborated theory of how a cyclotron works, and the subject matter of that auxiliary "theory of the instrument" is for the most part identical to the subject matter of the physical theories concerning nuclear particles, and so on, being investigated by the physicist. Devices for bringing about a state of affairs, for isolating the system under study, and for observing what occurs as a result are all themselves legitimated by theory.

It seems there is a sense in which auxiliary theories used by physical and biological scientists are at least subtly informed by what may be loosely called *the spirit*, the leading ideas, the core, and pervasive concepts of the main substantive theory *T*, although not rigorously derivable from *T*. When this is not so, scientists are likely to consider the (*T.A*) system as "unaesthetic," "incoherent," even ad hoc. These fascinating matters remain to be analyzed and reconstructed by logicians, but most scientists and historians of science are—however informally— well aware of their influence. (See, e.g., Holton, 1973.)

In the social sciences, no such intimate connection, and almost never a relation of theoretical derivability, exists; hence, the auxiliary theory (such as a theory that the Rorschach is valid for detecting subclinical schizoid cognitive slippage or that Chanel-doused beauteous research assistants are anxiety elicitors) must stand on its own feet. Almost nothing we know or conjecture about the substantive theory helps us to any appreciable degree in firming up our reliance on the auxiliary. The situation in which *A* is merely conjoined to *T* in setting up our test of *T* makes it hard for us social scientists to fulfill a Popperian falsifiability requirement—to state before the fact what would count as a strong falsifier.

I shall illustrate this problem further with a simple example whose adequate exposition will appear elsewhere (Meehl & Golden, 1982). Suppose that I wish to test my dominant gene conjecture (Golden & Meehl, 1978; Meehl, 1972, 1972/1973g, 1977) concerning *schizotaxia* as the central nervous system condition for the development by social learning of *schizotypy* (Meehl, 1962/1973c), which in turn is the personality precondition for the development of a *clinical schizophrenia*—although the latter must then occur only in one fourth of the persons carrying the gene, given the roughly 12% concordance for first-degree relatives as regards diagnosable clinical schizophrenia. (See also Böök, 1960; Heston, 1966, 1970; Slater, 1958/1971.) I might rely on some complex neurological or projective or structured test "sign" as having such-and-such estimated construct validity for the schizotypal personality makeup. Such a quantitative estimate might be made relying on a combination of empirical evidence concerning discordant monozygotic twins of known schizophrenics, protocols of persons tested as college freshmen who subsequently decompensate into a recognizable schizophrenia, and the like. Such numerical estimates will all suffer not only from the usual test unreliability and random sampling fluctuations, but they will also have some unknown degree of systematic bias. For instance, it clearly will not do to assume that the taxon *all compensated schizotypes* would average the same scores on a Rorschach or MMPI indicator variable as do the compensated (discordant) monozygotic twins, the latter being a biased selection, since they have the same potentiating genes that their decompensated twins have. However, there must be something else about them—of an environmental sort—that works strongly in their favor and helps keep them discordant, that is, clinically well. One simply has no way of ascertaining the net impact of these two opposed kinds of forces on the psychometric results.

Suppose that we take some combination of earlier findings on preschizophrenics, remitted schizophrenics, compensated discordant monozygotic twins of schizophrenics, and so forth, and we ascertain that while the valid positive rate p_s among these safely presumed schizotypes varies (even if the sample sizes are huge, it will always vary in an amount unexplainable by random sampling fluctuation), it nevertheless shows a "reasonably close" agreement. (Again, we think like physicists or physiologists instead of like social scientists fooling around with t tests.) So we strike some kind of rough average $\bar{p}_s$ of these several valid positive rates, knowing that it is the best we can do at this point with data on different groups of schizotypes, who, despite their differences, must all have somehow been tagged as such. Given that estimated valid positive rate, and given a false positive rate p_n (also systematically biased because of the undiagnosed compensated schizotypes in any "control population"), we record our numerical predictions for the incidence of our psychometric sign among parent pairs of schizophrenic probands (where, on the dominant gene theory, we expect not only a 50% schizotypy incidence but something stronger; to wit, at least one member of each parent pair must be a schizotype). We also compute it for siblings and dizygotic twins and—although here things get a bit feeble—with sufficiently large samples, maybe second-degree relatives. Thus, for instance, the expected sign-positive rate among parents (and sibs, if they all cooperate) is given by the simple expression $p^+ = \frac{1}{2} p_s + \frac{1}{2} p_n$.

Now the substantive dominant gene theory T, when conjoined with the auxiliary theory A concerning psychometric validity, and assuming that we have identified the right relatives and the probands were all schizophrenics [$= C$], generates point predictions and therefore takes a high Popperian risk *when the conjunction* (T.A.C) *is considered as the "theory" under test.* Hence, the verification of those numerical point predictions as to the values of the psychometric incidence in relatives of different degrees of consanguinity provides a strong Popperian test for that conjunctive "theory." One would then normally say that successful negotiation of this hurdle, the failure to be clobbered *modus tollens* by the outcome of the empirical study, provides a moderate to strong corroboration of the conjunctive theory. Hence, $(T.A.C)$ is doing well; that is, it has escaped falsification despite taking a high risk by making several numerical point predictions.

So far, so good, and Popper as well as his critics would have no complaint. However, the classical Popperian requirement on playing the scientific game fairly involves the theoretician's saying, before doing the research, what would count as a strong basis for rejecting the theory. If "the theory" is taken to be the substantive theory T (which it is, if one is not being philosophically disingenuous) rather than the psychometric auxiliary and diagnostic validity conjectures A and C, then one will be committing what amounts in spirit to a Popperian sin against falsificationism as a method. If the empirical research does not pan out as predicted, one does not abandon T; instead he tells us that either T is incorrect, A is incorrect, or the diagnoses were untrustworthy!

I am not persuaded from his writings or from conversations that I have had with him that Sir Karl adequately appreciates the degree to which this theory and auxiliary problem permeate research in the inexact sciences, especially the social sciences in their soft areas. Whether it presents a general problem for the Popperian formulation of scientific method is beyond the scope of this article and my competence. It is perhaps worth saying, however, for the benefit of philosophically oriented readers, that the above described situation—certainly no rarity in our field or in biology—may represent a social fact about the way science works that presents grave difficulties for the Popperian reconstruction. That is, the stipulation beforehand that one will be pleased about substantive theory T when the numerical results come out as forecast, but will not necessarily abandon it when they do not, seems on the face of it to be about as blatant a violation of the Popperian commandment as you could commit. For the investigator, in a way, is doing what Popper says we ought not to do, and what astrologers and Marxists and psychoanalysts allegedly do, playing "heads I win, tails you lose." But it seems in accordance with much scientific practice and, as far as I have sampled, with most persons' scientific common sense or intuitions, to say that if the combination $(T.A.C)$ generates a high-risk numerical point prediction, such a result really does support all three of the components. The reason it does so seems pretty clear, despite its commonsense, nonformalized character: Because of the lack of intimate inner connection in the inexact sciences between the components of these conjunctions, its would strike us as a *very strange coincidence* if the substantive theory T should have low verisimilitude (which would, were T true, also generate mispredictions of the numerical point values) and yet the two (largely unrelated) "wrongs" of T and A are somehow systematically balanced so as to generate the same numerical prediction generated from the conjecture that T and A both have relatively high verisimilitude.

Such a delicate quantitative counterbalancing of theoretical errors is not impossible, but it seems quite implausible, assuming that nature is (as Einstein says) "subtle but not malicious." So I think we are not being unreasonable to congratulate ourselves on arriving at a successful prediction of high-risk point values or other antecedently improbable observational patterns from the conjunction $(T.A.C)$, despite the fact that we seem to be hedging when we say before the fact that we will not consider our substantive theory T falsified by a bad result if it does not pan out. These are problems that need further exploration by statisticians and philosophers of science, especially in light of work on the history of science, and with special attention to the question of whether there are important differences between the inexact and the exact sciences, or even between the biological and social sciences, as to how a Popperian or neo-Popperian methodology should be explained and applied.

But, you may say, what has all this got to do with significance testing? Isn't the social scientist's use of the null hypothesis simply the application of Popperian (or Bayesian) thinking in contexts in which probability plays such a big role? No, it is not. One reason it is not is that the usual use of null hypothesis testing in soft psychology as a means of "corroborating" substantive theories does not subject the theory to grave risk of refutation *modus tollens*, but only to a rather feeble danger. The kinds of theories and the kinds of theoretical risks to which we put them in soft psychology when we use significance testing as our method are *not* like testing Meehl's theory of weather by seeing how well it forecasts the number of inches it will rain on certain days. Instead, they are depressingly close to testing the theory by seeing whether it rains in April at all, or rains several days in April, or rains in April more than in May. It happens mainly because, as I believe is generally recognized by statisticians today and by thoughtful social scientists, the null hypothesis, taken literally, is always false. I shall not attempt to document this here, because among sophisticated persons it is taken for granted. (See Morrison & Henkel, 1970, especially the chapters by Bakan, Hogben, Lykken, Meehl, and Rozeboom.) A little reflection shows us why it has to be the case, since an output variable such as adult IQ, or academic achievement, or effectiveness at communication, or whatever, will always, in the social sciences, be a function of a sizable but finite number of factors. (The smallest contributions may be considered as essentially a random variance term.) In order for two groups (males and females, or whites and blacks, or manic depressives and schizophrenics, or Republicans and Democrats) to be *exactly* equal on such an output variable, we have to imagine that they are exactly equal *or* delicately counterbalanced on all of the contributors in the causal equation, which will never be the case.

Following the general line of reasoning (presented by myself and several others over the last decade), from the fact that the null hypothesis is always false in soft psychology, it follows that the probability of refuting it depends wholly on the sensitivity of the experiment—its logical design, the net (attenuated) construct validity of the measures, and, most important, the sample size, which determines where we are on the statistical power function. Putting it crudely, if you have enough cases and your measures are not totally unreliable, the null hypothesis will always be falsified, *regardless of the truth of the substantive theory*. Of course, it could be falsified in the wrong direction, which means that as the power improves, the probability of a corroborative result approaches one-half. However, if the theory has no verisimilitude—such that we can imagine, so to speak, picking our empirical results randomly out of a directional hat apart from any theory—the probability of refuting by getting a significant difference in the wrong direction also approaches one-half. Obviously, this is quite unlike the situation desired from either a Bayesian, a Popperian, or a commonsense scientific standpoint. As I have pointed out elsewhere (Meehl, 1967/1970b; but see criticism by Oakes, 1975; Keuth, 1973; and rebuttal by Swoyer & Monson, 1975), an improvement in instrumentation or other sources of experimental accuracy tends, in physics or astronomy or chemistry or genetics, to subject the theory to a greater risk of refutation *modus tollens*, whereas improved precision in null hypothesis testing usually decreases this risk. A successful significance test of a substantive theory in soft psychology provides a feeble corroboration of the theory because the procedure has subjected the theory to a feeble risk.

But, you may say, we do not look at just one; we look at a batch of them. Yes, we do; and how do we usually do it? In the typical *Psychological Bulletin* article reviewing research on some theory, we see a table showing with asterisks (hence, my title) whether this or that experimenter found a difference in the expected direction at the .05 (one asterisk), .01 (two asterisks!), or .001 (three asterisks!!) level of significance. Typically, of course, some of them come out favorable and some of them come out unfavorable. What does the reviewer usually do? He goes through what is from the standpoint of the logician an almost meaningless exercise; to wit, he *counts noses*. If, say, Fisbee's theory of the mind has a batting average of 7:3 on 10 significance tests in the table, he concludes that Fisbee's theory seems to be rather well supported, "although further research is needed to explain the discrepancies." This is scientifically a preposterous way to reason. It completely neglects the crucial asymmetry between confirmation, which involves an inference in the formally invalid third figure of the implicative syllogism (this is why inductive inferences are ampliative and dangerous and why we can be objectively wrong even though we proceed correctly), and refutation, which is in the valid fourth figure, and which gives the *modus tollens* its privileged position in inductive inference. Thus the adverse *t* tests, seen properly, do Fisbee's theory far more damage than the favorable ones do it good.

I am not making some nit-picking statistician's correction. I am saying that the whole business is so radically defective as to be scientifically almost pointless. This is not a technical hassle about whether Fisbee should have used the varimax rotation, or how he estimated the communalities, or that perhaps some of the higher order interactions that are marginally significant should have been lumped together as a part of the error term, or that the covariance matrices were not quite homogeneous. I am not a statistician, and I am not making a statistical complaint. I am making a philosophical complaint or, if you prefer, a complaint in the domain of scientific method. I suggest that when a reviewer tries to "make theoretical sense" out of such a table of favorable and adverse significance test results, what the reviewer is actually engaged in, willy-nilly or unwittingly, is meaningless substantive constructions on the properties of the statistical power function, and almost nothing else.

The feckless activity is made worse by the almost universal practice of what I call *stepwise low validation*. By this I mean that we rely on one investigation to "validate" a particular instrument and some other study to validate another instrument, and then we correlate the two instruments and claim to have validated the substantive theory. I do not argue that this is a scientific nothing, but it is about as close to a nothing as you can get without intending to. Consider that I first show that Meehl's Mental Measure has a validity coefficient (against the criterion I shall here for simplicity take to be quasi-infallible or definitive) of, say, .40 — somewhat higher than we usually get in personology and social psychology! Then I show that Glotz's Global Gauge has a validity for its alleged variable of the same amount. Relying on these results, having stated the coefficient and gleefully recorded the asterisks showing that these coefficients are not zero (!), I now try to corroborate the Glotz-Meehl theory of personality by showing that the two instruments, each having been duly "validated," correlate .40, providing, happily, some more asterisks in the table. Now just what kind of a business is this? Let us suppose that each instrument has a reliability of .90 to make it easy. That means that the portion of construct-valid variance for each of the devices is around one fifth of the reliable variance and the same for their overlap when correlated with each other. I do not want to push the discredited (although recently revived) principle of indifference, but without other knowledge, it is easily possible, and one could perhaps say rather likely, that the correlation between the two occurs in a region of each one's components that has literally nothing to do with either of the two criterion variables used in the validity studies relied on. This is, of course, especially dangerous in light of the research that we have on the contribution of methods variance.

I seem to have trouble conveying to my students and colleagues just how dreadful a mess of flabby inferences this kind of thing involves. It is as if we were interested in the effect of sunlight on the mating behavior of birds, but not being able to get directly at either of these two things, we settle for correlating a proxy variable like field-mice density (because the birds tend to destroy the field mice) with, say, incidence of human skin cancer (since you can get that by spending too much time in the sun)! You may think this analogy dreadfully unfair; but I think it is a good one. Of course, the whole idea of simply counting noses is wrong, because a theory that has seven facts for it and three facts against it is *not* in good shape, and it would not be considered so in any developed science.

You may say, "But, Meehl, R. A. Fisher was a genius, and we all know how valuable his stuff has been in agronomy. Why shouldn't it work for soft psychology?" Well, I am not intimidated by Fisher's genius, because my complaint is not in the field of mathematical statistics; and as regards inductive logic and philosophy of science, it is well-known that Sir Ronald permitted himself a great deal of dogmatism. I remember my amazement when the late Rudolf Carnap said to me, the first time I met him, "But, of course, on this subject Fisher is just mistaken; surely you must know that." My statistician friends tell me that it is not clear just how useful the significance test has been in biological science either, but I set that aside as beyond my competence to discuss. The shortest answer to this rebuttal about agronomy, and one that has general importance in thinking about soft psychology, is that we must carefully distinguish *substantive theory* from *statistical hypothesis*. There is a tendency in the social sciences to conflate these in talking about our inferences. (A neglected article by Bolles, 1962, did not cure the psychologists' disease.) The substantive theory is the theory about the causal structure of the world, the entities and processes underlying the phenomena; the statistical hypothesis is a much more restricted and "operational" conjecture about the value of some parameter, such as the mean of a specified statistical population. The main point in agronomy is that the logical distance, the difference in meaning or content, so to say, between the alternative hypothesis and substantive theory T is so small that only a logician would be concerned to distinguish them. *Example*: I want to find out whether I should be putting potash on the ground to help me raise more corn. Now everybody knows from common sense as well as biology that the corn gets its nutrients from the soil, and furthermore that the yield of corn at harvest time is not causally efficacious in determining what I did in the spring, random numbers aside. If I refute the statistical null hypothesis that plots of corn with potash do not differ in yield from plots without potash, I have thereby proved the alternative hypothesis—that there *is* a difference between these two sorts of plots; and the only substantive conclusion to draw, given such a difference, is that the potash made the difference. Such a situation, in which the content of the substantive theory is logically quasi-identical with the alternative hypothesis, which was refuted by our significance test, is completely different from the situation in soft psychology. Fisbee's substantive theory of the mind is not equivalent, or anywhere near equivalent, to the alternative hypothesis. All sorts of competing theories are around, including my grandmother's common sense, to explain the nonnull statistical difference.

So the psychologist can take little reassurance about the use of significance tests from knowing that Fisher's approach has been useful in studying the effect of fertilizer on crop yields.

Although this presents a pretty depressing picture, I daresay that the Skinner disciples among you will be inclined to think,

> well, that's just one more way of showing what we have known all along. The point is to prove that you have achieved experimental control over your subject matter, as Skinner says. If you have, I am not much interested in tabular asterisks; if you haven't, I'm not interested in them either.

But that is easy for Skinnerians because their theory (it is a theory in Sir Karl Popper's sense) is close to a pure dispositional theory and does not usually present us with the kind of evidentiary evaluation problem that we get with entity-postulating theories such as those of Freud, Hull, Albert Ellis, or, to come closer to home, my conjectures about schizophrenia or hedonic deficit (Meehl, 1972, 1974, 1975, 1962/1973c, 1972/1973g). Those of us whose cognitive passions are incompletely satisfied by dispositional theories, whether Skinnerian or psychometric, should ask ourselves what *kind* of inferred entity construction we want and how it could generate the sorts of intellectual "surprises" that Robert Nozick (1974, pp. 18–22) considers typical of invisible hand theories, which have proved so eminently successful in the physical and biological sciences and — somewhat less so — in economics. Some directions of solution (before I go on to the one that I am using in my own research) follow.

We could take the complex form of Bayes's theorem more seriously in concrete application to various substantive theories to take into account, even if crudely in the sense of setting upper and lower bounds to the probabilities involved, the logical asymmetry between confirmation and refutation (see, e.g., Maxwell, 1974). Second, it may be that the Fisherian tradition, with its soothing illusion of quantitative rigor, has inhibited our search for stronger tests, so we have thrown in the sponge and abandoned hope of concocting substantive theories that will generate stronger consequences than merely "the Xs differ from the Ys." Thus, for instance, even when we cannot generate numerical point predictions (the ideal case found in the exact sciences), it may be that we can at least predict the order of numerical values or the rank order of the first-order numerical differences, and the like.

Sometimes in the other sciences it has been possible to concoct a middling weak theory that, while incapable of generating numerical point values, entails a certain *function form*, such as a graph should be an ogive or that it should have three peaks and that these peaks should be increasingly high, and that the distance on the abscissa between the first two peaks should be less than the distance between the second two. In the early history of quantum theory, physicists relied on Wien's law, which related "some (unknown) function" of wavelength to energy multiplied by the fifth power of wavelength. In the cavity radiation experiment, the empirical points were simply plotted at varying temperatures, and it was evident by inspection that they fell on the same curve, even though a formal expression for that curve was beyond the theory's capabilities (Eisberg, 1961, pp. 50–51).

Talking of Wien's law is a good time for me to recommend that psychologists who disagree with my position have a look at any textbook of theoretical chemistry or physics, where one searches in vain for a statistical significance test (and finds few confidence intervals). The power of the physicist does not come from exact assessment of probabilities that a difference exists (which physicists would view as a ludicrous thing to show), or by the verbal precision of "operational definitions" in the embedding text. The physicist's scientific power comes from two other sources, namely, the immense deductive fertility of the formalism and the accuracy of the measuring instruments. The scientific trick lies in conjoining rich mathematics and experimental precision, a sort of "invisible hand wielding fine calipers." The embedding text is sometimes surprisingly loose, free-wheeling, even metaphorical—as viewers of television's *Nova* are aware, seeing Nobel laureates discourse whimsically about the charm, strangeness, and gluons of nuclear particles (see, e.g., Nambu, 1976). One gets the impression that when you have a good science going, with potent mathematics and accurate instruments, you can be relaxed and easygoing about the words. Nothing is as stuffy and pretentious as the verbal "pseudorigor" of the soft branches of social science. In my modern physics text, I am unable to find one single test of statistical significance. What happens instead is that the physicist has a sufficiently powerful invisible hand theory that enables him to generate an expected curve for his experimental results. He plots the observed points, looks at the agreement, and comments that "the results are in reasonably good accord with theory." Moral: *It is always more valuable to show approximate agreement of observations with a theoretically predicted numerical point value, rank order, or function form, than it is to compute a "precise probability" that something merely differs from something else.* Of course, we do not have precise probabilities when we do significance testing because of the falsity of the assumptions generating the table's values and the varying robustness of our tests under departures from these assumptions.

The only possible "solution" to the theory-refutation problem that I have time to discuss in any detail is what I call *consistency tests* (Meehl, Note 3, this essay). Unfortunately, this approach is not easily available for most theoretical problems in soft psychology, although I am not prepared to say that it is confined to the domain in which I have been developing it, namely, taxometrics, that is, the application of psychometric procedures to detection of a taxonic situation and classification of individuals into the taxon or outside of it. From our conjectures about the latent causal situation, we derive formulas for estimating the theoretical quantities of interest, such as the proportion of schizotypes in a given clinical population, the mean values of the schizotypal and nonschizotypal classes, the optimal cut ("hitmax") on each phenotypic indicator variable for classifying individuals, and the proportion of valid and false positives achieved by that cut. But we realize that our conjectures about the latent situation may be false or that the indicators relied on may have too low validity, or that they may be more correlated within the taxa than desired, and so forth. Second, even if the basic formal structure postulated is approximated by the state of nature (e.g., there is a schizoid taxon, the indicators have sizable validity, the intrataxon distributions are quasi-normal or at least unimodal, the correlation of the indicators within the groups is small, and the departures from these various hypotheses are within the tolerance allowed by the method's robustness), it may still be that we have suffered some kind of systematic bias on one of the indicators owing to a nuisance variable such as social class, or that we have had bad luck in the sample, so the method's numerical deliverances on this occasion are untrustworthy.

Whether the abstract causal structure postulated is unsound or the numerical values found in this sample are seriously in error, we need some method of checking the data internally to find out whether these unfortunate possibilities have materialized. We do this by deriving theorems within the formalism specifying how various numerical values (observed or calculated from the observed) should be related to each other, so that when they are not related as the consistency theorem demands, we are alerted to the danger that something is rotten in the state of Denmark (see Meehl, 1973d). Unfortunately, most of the work, both mathematical and empirical, is as yet only available in mimeographed reports from our laboratory (Golden, 1976; Golden & Meehl, Notes 1 and 2; Meehl, Notes 3 and 4, this essay). What survives scrutiny will be found in Meehl and Golden (1982).

One taxometric procedure, which I have christened *maxcov-hitmax* (Meehl, 1973d) relies on the following theorem: If three fallible indicator variables are negligibly correlated within a diagnostic taxon and within the extra-taxon population, then the covariance of any pair of these is maximized in that class interval on the third indicator that contains the hitmax (optimal, fewest misses) cut on the third indicator. That is, $\text{cov}(yz)$ has its largest value for the subset of patients falling in the hitmax interval on x. Starting from this relation we go through a sequence of calculations yielding estimates of the base rate P of the taxon, the frequency distributions of all three of the fallible indicators, the location of all three hitmax cuts, and the inverse probability of taxon membership (via Bayes's theorem) for a patient who has any given combination of the three signs plus or minus.

Our Monte Carlo runs and our single application to a real case in which we know the true answer and pretend not to know it, namely, biological sex diagnosed by three MMPI femininity keys, have been most encouraging and suggest

Table 1. Description of sample sets

Set	Variable	N	P	M_e	M_t	SD_e	SD_t	D'	SD_t/SD_e	r	F^a
1.1	N	1,000	.5	8	12	2	2	2	1	0[b]	0
1.2		800	.5	8	12	2	2	2	1	0[b]	0
1.3		600	.5	8	12	2	2	2	1	0[b]	0
1.4		400	.5	8	12	2	2	2	1	0[b]	0
2.1	P	1,000	.6	8	12	2	2	2	1	0[b]	3
2.2		1,000	.7	8	12	2	2	2	1	0[b]	2
2.3		1,000	.8	8	12	2	2	2	1	0[b]	8
2.4		1,000	.9	8	12	2	2	2	1	0	0
3.1	D'	1,000	.5	9	12	2	2	1.5	1	0[b]	0
3.2		1,000	.5	10	12	2	2	1	1	0[b]	15
3.3		1,000	.5	11	12	2	2	.5	1	0	0
3.4		1,000	.5	12	12	2	2	0	1	0	0
4.1	SD_t/SD_e	1,000	.5	8	12	1.9	2.1	2	1.1	0[b]	0
4.2		1,000	.5	8	12	1.7	2.3	2	1.3	0[b]	0
4.3		1,000	.5	8	12	1.5	2.5	2	1.7	0[b]	0
4.4		1,000	.5	8	12	1	3	2	3	0	0
5.1	r	1,000	.5	8	12	2	2	2	1	.1[b]	0
5.2		1,000	.5	8	12	2	2	2	1	.3[b]	0
5.3		1,000	.5	8	12	2	2	2	1	.5[b]	8
5.4		1,000	.5	8	12	2	2	2	1	.8	0
										r_e/r_t	
6.1	$r_e/r_t = 4$	1,000	.8	8	12	2	2	2	1	.5/.125	0
6.2	N	800	.8	8	12	2	2	2	1	.5/.125	0
6.3		600	.8	8	12	2	2	2	1	.5/.125	0
6.4		400	.8	8	12	2	2	2	1	.5/.125	0

Note. N = sample size; P = base rate of the taxon; M_e = mean of the extra-taxon class on each indicator; M_t = mean of the taxon on each indicator; SD_e = standard deviation of the extra-taxon class on each indicator; SD_t = standard deviation of the taxon on each indicator; D' = $(M_t - M_e)/S$, where $S = SD_e + SD_t)/2$; r = latent correlation between indicator pairs; F = number of failures of consistency tests in 25 samples.

[a]94% correct.
[b]Parameter estimates are always or nearly always accurate.

that the method is powerful and quite robust under departures from the simplifying hypotheses. But applying it to a situation in which we do not know the true answer (such as "What is the proportion of unrecognized schizotypes in a mixed psychiatric population?"), how much faith should we have in our numerical results? The best way I know to go about this, since mere replication of the inferred parameter estimates does not answer the question, is by the use of consistency tests. For example, one of the consistency tests in this kind of two-category taxonic situation is this: If we form the product of the differences between the inferred latent means on y and z (schizotypes minus nonschizotypes) and then multiply this product $\Delta \bar{y} \, \Delta \bar{z}$ by the product of the inferred schizotypal base-rate P and its complement Q, then it can be shown that this theoretically calculated quantity

Table 2. Consistency test result

Actual Situation	Sample		Total
	Trustworthy	Suspicious	
Accurate	336	36	372
Inaccurate	0	228	228
Total	336	264	600

should equal the grand covariance of y and z computed directly from the observations. We call this the "total covariance consistency test."

Of course, such a relation is not required to be literally true, because it is known in advance that (a) the impoverished theory has imperfect verisimilitude and (b) all statistical estimates are subject to both systematic and random error. (We are *not* going to do a significance test!) What we have is a problem of robustness and detection of excessive departures from the postulated latent conditions. Golden and I arbitrarily said that we would consider a particular sample as delivering sufficiently accurate information if the estimates of base rate and hit rate were within .10 of the true values, and estimated latent means and standard deviations within one class interval of the truth. (Actually we did much better than that on the average. For example, with sample sizes greater than 400, equal variances, two sigma differences of latent means, and zero intrataxon correlations, the average error for P was only .01 and for latent means and sigmas, less than one-fourth standard deviation which is one-half the smallest integral class interval.) But if these tolerances strike you as excessively large, I remind you how much more powerful such numerical claims are in soft psychology than the usual flabby "the boys are taller than the girls" or "the schizophrenics are shyer than the manic depressives." We then imposed tolerances on each of the four most promising consistency tests derived within the formalism. For example, if the total covariance consistency test $T_1 = \text{cov}(yz) - PQ (\bar{y}_s - \bar{y}_n) (\bar{z}_s - \bar{z}_n)$ yields a discrepancy greater than $.64 + .74s^2$, a "robustness cut" chosen by a combination of analytical derivation with preliminary Monte Carlo trials, then this particular sample is considered "numerically inconsistent" with Consistency Test T_1. Now if any one of the four consistency tests is, so to speak, rejected by a given sample, this is a red flag warning us that we ought not to have much faith in the parametric estimates of interest.

The important question then is, how sensitive are the consistency tests to sample departures from the parametric truth in excess of the tolerance allowed? How often will we draw a sample in which the inferred parameters are in error by more than the tolerance limit imposed but all four consistency tests are satisfied within *their* tolerance limits, leading us mistakenly to trust our results? Second, how often is at least one of the four consistency tests numerically inconsistent (i.e., outside its tolerance limit) leading us to *mis*trust the sample when in fact all of the sample estimates of the parameters are within their tolerances? The first of these we might call a "false negative" failure on the part of the consistency tests to function jointly; the second is then a false positive.

I restrict my data presentation to Monte Carlo runs in which the samples are generated from a multivariate normal model, although I want to emphasize that our methods are not generally confined to the normal case. Normality was imposed because of Monte Carlo generating problems. In Table 1, the numbers "Set 1.1, 1.2, . . . " in the first column merely name conditions of fixed population properties and sample sizes, and 25 Monte Carlo samples were drawn per set. The column heads indicate the various population properties, such as taxon base-rate P, the two latent taxon means and standard deviations, the mean difference in standard deviation units, the ratio of latent standard deviations, and the within-group correlations. The important result (F) indicates how many of the 25 samples under the given set conditions were failures of the consistency tests. Thus, the four consistency tests were applied to each sample, which was classified as probably trustworthy (or probably not) in accordance with the tolerance rules for consistency tests. Then the sample was classified as to whether it was *in fact* trustworthy, that is, whether the main latent parameters were all estimated within their allowed tolerance.

Despite the high average accuracy of our taxometric method when evaluated as mean percentage errors in estimating each of the latent parameters (base rate, hit rates, means, standard deviations), if a naïve trusting taxometrist relied blindly on the method, hoping to be accurate on all seven parameters on any sample drawn, he would be misled distressingly often were he to lack consistency tests. Among our 600 Monte Carlo samples, all seven latent parameters of the artificial population were estimated to an accuracy within the tolerance levels in 372 samples; that is, on 228 samples at least one parameter was inaccurate. This shows that a trustworthy device for detecting such bad samples is much to be desired. It will not do a taxonomic scientist much good to be "usually quite accurate" if the procedure relied on is nevertheless often (38% of the time) somewhat inaccurate *and the investigator is without a method that warns him when the untoward event has, on a given occasion, occurred.*

In Table 2 the 600 Monte Carlo samples are tallied with respect to each sample's parameter estimation accuracy and whether it passed all four consistency tests. It is encouraging that overall the consistency tests were 94% accurate. Furthermore, the 6% of the samples in which the consistency tests erred were all samples in which they erred conservatively; that is, one or more of the consistency tests was suspiciously outside its tolerance limits, yet none of the latent parameters estimated by the methods was outside *its* tolerance limits. We have not as yet drawn a single Monte Carlo sample (among 600) in which the four consistency tests were conjunctively reassuring but the sample was in fact misleading. This finding suggests that we were unduly stringent, so that if some small amount of leeway were permitted for errors of the other kind, the consistency tests could be somewhat relaxed and, perhaps concurrently, the tolerance limits on the parameter estimates could be somewhat tightened.

There is some interchangeability between original estimators and consistency tests, and the maxcov-hitmax method itself was originally derived by me as a consistency test before I realized that it could better be used as an original search device (see Meehl, Note 3, pp. 28–29; Note 4, pp. 2–6).

Not in reliance on these results, which I present merely as exemplars of a general methodological thesis, I want now to state as strongly as I can a prescription that we should adopt in soft psychology to help get away from the feeble practice of significance testing: *Wherever possible, two or more nonredundant estimates of the same theoretical quantity should be made, because multiple approximations to a theoretical number are always more valuable, provided that methods of setting permissible tolerances exist, than a so-called exact test of significance, or even an exact setting of confidence intervals.* This is a special case of what my philosopher colleague Herbert Feigl referred to as "triangulation in logical space." It is, as you know, standard procedure in the developed sciences. We have, for instance, something like a dozen independent ways of estimating Avogadro's number, and since they all come out "reasonably close" (again, I have never seen a physicist do a t test on such a thing!), we are confident that we know how many molecules there are in a mole of chlorine.

This last point may lead you to ask, "If consistency tests are as important as Meehl makes them out to be, why don't we hear about them in chemistry and physics?" I have a perfect answer to that query. It goes like this: *Consistency tests are so much a part of standard scientific method in the developed disciplines, taken so much for granted by everybody who researches in chemistry or physics or astronomy or molecular biology or genetics, that these scientists do not even bother having a special name for them!* It shows the sad state of soft psychology when a fellow like me has to cook up a special metatheory expression to call attention to something that in respectable science is taken as a matter of course.

Having presented what seems to me some encouraging data, I must nevertheless close with a melancholy reflection. The possibility of deriving consistency tests in the taxonic situation rests on the substantive problems presented by fields like medicine and behavior genetics, and it is not obvious how we would go about doing this in soft areas that are nontaxonic. It may be that the nature of the subject matter in most of personology and social psychology is inherently incapable of permitting theories with sufficient conceptual power (especially mathematical development) to yield the kinds of strong refuters expected by Popperians, Bayesians, and unphilosophical scientists in developed fields like chemistry. This might mean that we could most profitably confine ourselves to low-order inductions, a (to me, depressing) conjecture that is somewhat corroborated by the fact that the two most powerful forms of clinical psychology are atheoretical psychometrics of prediction on the one hand and behavior modification on the other. Neither of these approaches has the kind of conceptual richness that attracts the theory-oriented mind, but I think we ought to acknowledge the possibility that there is never going to be a really impressive theory in personality or social psychology. I dislike to think that, but it might just be true.

Addendum

My colleague Thomas J. Bouchard, Jr., on reading a draft of this article, faulted me for what he saw as a major inconsistency between my neo-Popperian emphasis on falsifiability and my positive assessment of Freud. There is no denying that for such a quantitatively oriented product of the "dust-bowl empiricist" tradition as myself, I do have a soft spot in my heart (Minnesota colleagues would probably say in my head) for psychoanalysis. So, the most honest and straightforward way to deal with Bouchard's complaint might be simply to admit that the evidence on Freud is inadequate and that Bouchard and I are simply betting on different horses. But I cannot resist the impulse to say just a bit more on this vexatious question, because while I am acutely aware of a pronounced (and possibly irrational) difference in the "educated prior" I put on Freud as contrasted with rubber band theory or labeling theory or whatever, I am not persuaded that my position is as grossly incoherent as it admittedly appears. Passing the question whether attempts to study psychoanalytic theory by the methods of experimental or differential psychology have on the whole tended to support rather than refute it (see, e.g., Fisher & Greenberg, 1977; Rapaport, 1959; Sears, 1943; Silverman, 1976), my own view is that the best place to study psychoanalysis is the psychoanalytic session itself, as I have elsewhere argued in a far too condensed way (Meehl, essay 10, this volume).

I believe that some aspects of psychoanalytic theory are not presently researchable because the intermediate technology required—which really means instruments-cum-theory—does not exist. I mean auxiliaries and methods such as a souped-up, highly developed science of psycholinguistics, and the kind of mathematics that is needed to conduct a rigorous but clinically sensitive and psychoanalytically realistic job of theme tracing in the analytic protocol. This may strike some as a kind of cop-out, but I remind you that Lakatos, Kuhn, Feyerabend, and others have convincingly made the point that there are theories in the physical and biological sciences that are untestable when first propounded because the theoretical and technological development necessary for making certain kinds of observations bearing on them have not taken place. It is vulgar positivism (still held by many psychologists) to insist that any respectable empirical theory must be testable, if testable means *definitively testable right now*.

But I do think that there is another class of consequences of psychoanalytic theory, close to the original "clinical connections" alleged by Freud, Ferenczi, Jones, Abraham, and others that does not involve much of what Freud called *the witch metapsychology*, where no complicated statistics are needed, let alone the invention of any *new* formal modes of protocol analysis. Here the problem is mainly that *none of us has bothered to carry out some relatively simple-minded kinds of analyses on a random sample of psychoanalytic protocols collected from essentially naïve patients to whom no interpretations have as yet been offered.* This second category is, in my view, a category of research studies that we could have done, but have not. *Example*: We can easily ascertain whether manifest dream content of a certain kind is statistically associated (in the simple straightforward sense of a patterned fourfold table) with such and such kinds of thematic material in the patient's subsequent associations to the dream. I would not even object to doing significance tests on a batch of such tables, but to explain why would unduly enlarge what is already an addendum.

I cheerfully admit, in this matter, to the presence of a large distance between my subjective personalistic probability (based on my experiences as analysand and practitioner of psychoanalytic therapy) and the present state of the "intersubjective public evidence." That is what I mean by saying that Bouchard and I are betting on different horses. But one must distinguish, as I know from subsequent conversations that he does, between a criticism (a) that what *is* proper evidence *does* presently exist and is *adverse* to a conjecture and (b) an anti-Popperian claim that falsifiability in principle does not matter. If I thought (as does Popper) that Freudian theory was in principle not falsifiable, then I would have to confess to a major inconsistency. But I do think it is falsifiable, although I agree that *some parts* of it cannot *at present* be tested because of the primitive development of the auxiliary theories and the measurement technologies that would be jointly necessary.

A final point on this subject is one that I hesitate to include because it is very difficult to explain in the present state of philosophy of science, and I could be doing my main thesis damage by presenting a cursory and somewhat dogmatic statement of it. Nevertheless, having made the above statements about psychoanalytic theory and having contrasted it favorably with some of the (to me, trivial and flabby) theories in soft psychology, I fear I have an obligation to say it, however ineptly. Once one sees that it is inappropriate to conflate the concepts *rational* and *statistical*, then it is a fuzzy open question, in the present state of the metatheoretician's art, just when a mass of nonquantitative converging evidence can be said to have made a stronger case for a conjecture than the weak kinds of nonconverging quantitative evidence usually represented by the significance testing tradition. I say "when" rather than "whether," because it is blindingly obvious that *sometimes* qualitative evidence of certain sorts is superior in its empirical weight to what a typical social, personality, or clinical psychologist gets in support of a substantive theory by the mere refutation of the null hypothesis. Take, for instance, the evidence in a well-constructed criminal case, such as the evidence that Bruno Hauptmann was the kidnapper of the Lindbergh baby. I do not see how anybody who reads the trial transcript of the Hauptmann case could have a reasonable doubt that he was guilty as charged. Yet I cannot recall any of the mass of data that convicted him as being of a quantitative sort (one cannot fairly except the serial numbers on the gold notes, they being not "measures" but "football numbers").

All of us believe a lot of things that we would not have the vaguest idea how to express as a probability value (*pace* strong Bayesians!) or how to compute as an indirect test of statistical significance. I believe, for instance, that Adolf Hitler was a schizotype; I do not believe that Kaspar Hauser was the son of a prince; I believe that the domestic cat probably was evolved from *Felis lybica* by the ancient Egyptians; I hold that my sainted namesake wrote the letter to the Corinthians but did not write the letter to the Hebrews; I am confident that my wife is faithful to me; and so forth. The point is really a simple one — that there are many areas of both practical and theoretical inference in which nobody knows how to calculate a numerical probability value, and nobody knows how to state the manner or degree in which various lines of evidence converge on a certain conjecture as having high verisimilitude. There are propositions in history (such as, "Julius Caesar crossed the Rubicon") that we all agree are well corroborated by the available documents but without any *t* tests *or the possibility of calculating any*, whereas Fisbee's theory of social behavior is only weakly corroborated by the fact that he got a significant *t* test when he compared the boys and the girls or the older kids and the younger kids on the Hockheimer-Sedlitz Communication Scale. Now I consider my betting on the horse of psychoanalysis to be in the same kind of ball park as my beliefs about Julius Caesar or the evolution of the cat. But, I repeat, this may be a terribly irrational leap of faith on my part. For the purposes of the present article and Bouchard's criticism of it, I hope it is sufficient to say that one could arguably hold that significance testing in soft psychology is a pretentious endeavor that falls under a tolerant neo-Popperian criticism, and could nevertheless enter his personalistic prediction that *when adequate tests become available to us, a sizable portion of psychoanalytic theory will escape refutation.* So I do not think I am actually contradicting myself, but I am personalistically betting on the outcome of a future horse race.

Reference Notes

1. Golden, R., and Meehl, P. E. *Detecting Latent Clinical Taxa, IV: Empirical Study of the Maximum Covariance Method and the Normal Minimum Chi-Square Method, Using Three MMPI Keys to Identify the Sexes* (Tech. Rep. PR-73-2). Minneapolis: University of Minnesota Psychiatry Research Laboratory, 1973. (a)

2. Golden, R., and Meehl, P. E. *Detecting Latent Clinical Taxa, V: A Monte Carlo Study of the Maximum Covariance Method and Associated Consistency Tests* (Tech. Rep. PR-73-3). Minneapolis: University of Minnesota Psychiatry Research Laboratory, 1973. (b)

3. Meehl, P. E. *Detecting Latent Clinical Taxa by Fallible Quantitative Indicators Lacking an Accepted Criterion* (Tech Rep. PR-65-2). Minneapolis: University of Minnesota Psychiatry Research Laboratory, 1965.

4. Meehl, P. E. *Detecting Latent Clinical Taxa, II: A Simplified Procedure, Some Additional Hit-max Cut Locators, a Single-Indicator Method, and Miscellaneous Theorems* (Tech. Rep. PR-68-4). Minneapolis: University of Minnesota Psychiatry Research Laboratory, 1968.

References

Allport, G. W. 1937. *Personality: A Psychological Interpretation*. New York: Holt.

Andreski, S. 1972. *Social Sciences as Sorcery*. London: Deutsch.

Barker, R. G. 1968. *Ecological Psychology*. Stanford, Calif.: Stanford University Press.

Bartlett, M. S. 1955. *An Introduction to Stochastic Processes*. Cambridge: Cambridge University Press.

Bolles, R. C. 1962. The Difference between Statistical Hypotheses and Scientific Hypotheses. *Psychological Reports* 11: 639–45.

Böök, J. A. 1960. "Genetical Aspects of Schizophrenic Psychoses." In *The Etiology of Schizophrenia*, ed. D. D. Jackson. New York: Basic Books.

Braithwaite, R. B. 1960. *Scientific Explanation*. New York: Harper.

Braun, J. R., ed. 1966. *Clinical Psychology in Transition* (rev. ed.). Cleveland, Ohio: World.

Brunswik, E. 1955. Representative Design and Probabilistic Theory. *Psychological Review* 62: 236–42.

Campbell, D. T., and Fiske, D. W. 1959. Convergent and Discriminant Validation by the Multitrait-Multimethod Matrix. *Psychological Bulletin* 56: 81–105.

Campbell, N. R. 1957. *Foundations of Science*. New York: Dover Publications. (Originally published as *Physics, the Elements*, 1920.)

Carnap, R. 1950. *Testability and Meaning*. New Haven, Conn.: Yale University Graduate Philosophy Club. (Originally published, 1936–1937.)

Carnap, R. 1956. "Meaning Postulates." In Carnap, *Meaning and Necessity*. Chicago: University of Chicago Press. (Originally published, 1952.)

Carnap, R. 1966. *Philosophical Foundations of Physics*. New York: Basic Books.

Cartwright, D. 1973. Determinants of Scientific Progress: The Case of the Risky Shift. *American Psychologist* 28: 222–31.

Cronbach, L. J. 1957. The Two Disciplines of Scientific Psychology. *American Psychologist* 12: 671–84.

Cronbach, L. J., and Meehl, P. E. 1973. "Construct Validity in Psychological Tests." In P. E. Meehl, *Psychodiagnosis: Selected Papers*. Minneapolis: University of Minnesota Press. (Originally published, 1955.)

Eisberg, R. M. 1961. *Fundamentals of Modern Physics*. New York: Wiley.

Feigl, H., 1956. "Some Major Issues and Developments in the Philosophy of Science of Logical Empiricism." *Minnesota Studies in the Philosophy of Science*, vol. 1 *The Foundations of Science and the Concepts of Psychology and Psychoanalysis*, eds. H. Feigl and M. Scriven. Minneapolis: University of Minnesota Press.

Feller, W. 1957. *An Introduction to Probability Theory and Its Applications* (2nd ed.). New York: Wiley.

Feyerabend, P. K. 1962. "Explanation, Reduction, and Empiricism." In *Minnesota Studies in the Philosophy of Science*, vol. 3, *Scientific Explanation, Space and Time,* eds. H. Feigl and G. Maxwell. Minneapolis: University of Minnesota Press.

Feyerabend, P. K. 1965. "Problems of Empiricism, Part I." In *Beyond the Edge of Certainty,* ed. R. G. Colodny. Englewood Cliffs, N.J.: Prentice-Hall.

Feyerabend, P. K. 1970. "Against Method: Outline of an Anarchistic Theory of Knowledge." In *Minnesota Studies in the Philosophy of Science*, vol. 4, *Analyses of Theories and Methods of Physics and Psychology*, eds. M. Radner and S. Winokur. Minneapolis: University of Minnesota Press.

Feyerabend, P. K. 1971. "Problems of Empiricism, Part II." In *The Nature and Function of Scientific Theories*, ed. R. G. Colodny. Pittsburgh, Pa.: University of Pittsburgh Press.

Fisher, F. M. 1966. *The Identification Problem in Econometrics*. New York: McGraw-Hill.

Fisher, R. A. 1956. *Statistical Methods and Scientific Inference*. Edinburgh: Oliver and Boyd.

Fisher, R. A. 1966. *The Design of Experiments* (8th ed.). Edinburgh: Oliver and Boyd.

Fisher, R. A. 1967. *Statistical Methods for Research Workers* (13th ed.). Edinburgh: Oliver and Boyd.

Fisher, S., and Greenberg, P. 1977. *The Scientific Credibility of Freud's Theories and Therapy*. New York: Basic Books.

Fiske, D. W. 1974. The Limits of the Conventional Science of Personality. *Journal of Personality* 24: 1–11.

Gergen, K. J. 1973. Social Psychology as History. *Journal of Personality and Social Psychology* 26: 309–20.

Golden, R. 1976. Psychometric Verisimilitude. Ph. D. dissertation, University of Minnesota.

Golden, R. R., and Meehl, P. E. 1978. Testing a Single Dominant Gene Theory without an Accepted Criterion Variable. *Annals of Human Genetics* 41: 507–14.

Gottesman, I. I. 1963. Heritability of Personality: A Demonstration. *Psychological Monographs* 77 (9, Whole No. 572).

Gottesman, I. I., and Shields, J. 1972. *Schizophrenia and Genetics: A Twin Study Vantage Point*. New York: Academic Press.

Grünbaum, A. 1960. The Duhemian Argument. *Philosophy of Science* 11: 75–87.

Grünbaum, A. 1962. Falsifiability of Theories: Total or Partial? *Synthese* 14: 17–34.

Grünbaum, A. 1969. Can We Ascertain the Falsity of a Scientific Hypothesis? *Studium Generale* 22: 1061–93.

Grünbaum, A. 1976. Ad Hoc Auxiliary Hypotheses and Falsificationism. *British Journal for the Philosophy of Science* 27: 329–62.

Gunther, M. 1977. *The Luck Factor*. New York: Macmillan.

Harrison, T. R., et al. (eds.) 1966. *Principles of Internal Medicine*. New York: McGraw-Hill.

Hempel, C. G. 1952. *Fundamentals of Concept Formation in Empirical Science*. Chicago: University of Chicago Press.

Hempel, C. G. 1958. "The Theoretician's Dilemma." In *Minnesota Studies in the Philosophy of Science*, vol. 2, *Concepts, Theories, and the Mind-Body Problem*, eds. H. Feigl, M. Scriven, and G. Maxwell. Minneapolis: University of Minnesota Press.

Heston. L. L. 1966. Psychiatric Disorders in Foster Home Reared Children of Schizophrenic Mothers. *British Journal of Psychiatry* 112: 819–25.

Heston, L. L. 1970. The Genetics of Schizophrenia and Schizoid Disease. *Science* 167: 249–56.

Hinde, R. A. 1970. *Animal Behavior* (2nd ed.). New York: McGraw-Hill.

Hogan, R., DeSoto, C. B., and Solano, C. 1977. Traits, Texts, and Personality Research. *American Psychologist* 32: 255–64.

Holt, R. R. 1958. Clinical and Statistical Prediction: A Reformulation and Some New Data. *Journal of Abnormal and Social Psychology* 56:1–12.

Holton, G. 1973. *Thematic Origins of Scientific Thought: Kepler to Einstein.* Cambridge, Mass.: Harvard University Press.

Jencks, C. 1972. *Inequality.* New York: Basic Books.

Johnson, W. E. 1964. *Logic, Part I.* New York: Dover Publications. (Originally published, 1921.)

Kemeny, J. G., Snell, J. L., and Thompson, G. L. 1957. *Introduction to Finite Mathematics.* Englewood Cliffs, N.J.: Prentice-Hall.

Keuth, H. 1973. On Prior Probabilities of Rejecting Statistical Hypotheses. *Philosophy of Science* 40: 538–46.

Kordig, R. 1971. The Comparability of Scientific Theories. *Philosophy of Science* 38: 467–85.

Kordig, C. R. 1973. Discussion: Observational Invariance. *Philosophy of Science* 40: 558–69.

Kuhn, T. S. 1970a. "Logic of Discovery or Psychology of Research?" In *Criticism and the Growth of Knowledge*, eds. I. Lakatos and A. Musgrave. Cambridge: Cambridge University Press.

Kuhn, T. S., 1970b. "Reflections on My Critics." In *Criticism and the Growth of Knowledge*, eds. I. Lakatos and A. Musgrave. Cambridge: Cambridge University Press.

Kuhn, T. S. 1970c. *The Structure of Scientific Revolutions* (2nd ed.). Chicago: University of Chicago Press.

Lakatos, I. 1970. "Falsification and the Methodology of Scientific Research Programs." In *Criticism and the Growth of Knowledge*, eds. I. Lakatos and A. Musgrave. Cambridge: Cambridge University Press.

Lakatos I. 1974a. "Popper on Demarcation and Induction." In *The Philosophy of Karl Popper* vol. 1, ed. P. A. Schilpp. LaSalle, Ill.: Open Court.

Lakatos, I. 1974b. The Role of Crucial Experiments in Science. *Studies in History and Philosophy of Science* 4: 309–25.

Langmuir, I. 1943. Science, Common Sense and Decency. *Science* 97: 1–7.

Lazarus, A. A. 1971. *Behavior Therapy and Beyond.* New York: McGraw-Hill.

Lewis, D., 1970. How to Define Theoretical Terms. *Journal of Philosophy* 67: 427–46.

Li, C. C. 1975. *Path Analysis.* Pacific Grove, Calif.: Boxwood Press.

Loevinger, J. 1957. Objective Tests As Instruments of Psychological Theory. *Psychological Reports Monograph* 9: 635–94.

London, I. D. 1946. Some Consequences for History and Psychology of Langmuir's Concept of Convergence and Divergence of Phenomena. *Psychological Review* 53: 170–88.

MacCorquodale, K., and Meehl, P. E., 1954. "Edward C. Tolman." In *Modern Learning Theory: A Critical Analysis of Five Examples,* eds. W. K. Estes, S. Koch, K. MacCorquodale, P. E. Meehl, C. G. Mueller, W. N. Schoenfeld and W. S. Verplanck. New York: Appleton-Century-Crofts.

Maxwell, G. 1961. "Meaning Postulates in Scientific Theories." In *Current Issues in the Philosophy of Science*, eds. H. Feigl and G. Maxwell. New York: Holt, Rinehart and Winston.

Maxwell, G. 1962. "The Necessary and the Contingent." In *Minnesota Studies in the Philosophy of Science*, vol. 3, eds. H. Feigl and G. Maxwell. Minneapolis: University of Minnesota Press.

Maxwell, G. 1974. "Corroboration without Demarcation." In *The Philosophy of Karl Popper*, ed. P. A. Schilpp. LaSalle, Ill.: Open Court.

McGuire, W. J. 1973. The Yin and Yang of Progress in Social Psychology: Seven Koans. *Journal of Personality and Social Psychology* 26: 446–56.

Meehl, P. E. 1954. *Clinical versus Statistical Prediction: A Theoretical Analysis and Review of the Evidence.* Minneapolis: University of Minnesota Press.

Meehl, P. E. 1970a. "Nuisance Variables and the Ex Post Facto Design." In *Minnesota Studies in the Philosophy of Science*, vol. 4, *Analyses of Theories and Methods of Physics and Psychology*, eds. M. Radner and S. Winokur. Minneapolis: University of Minnesota Press.

Meehl, P. E. 1970b. "Theory-Testing in Psychology and Physics: A Methodological Paradox." In *The Significance Test Controversy*, eds. D. E. Morrison and R. E. Henkel. Chicago: Aldine. (Originally published, 1967.)

Meehl, P. E. 1972. "A Critical Afterword." In *Schizophrenia and Genetics*, eds. I. I. Gottesman and J. Shields. New York: Academic Press.
Meehl, P. E. 1973a. "The Cognitive Activity of the Clinician." In Meehl, *Psychodiagnosis: Selected Papers*. Minneapolis: University of Minnesota Press. (Originally published, 1960.)
Meehl, P. E. 1973b. "High School Yearbooks: A Reply to Schwarz." In Meehl, *Psychodiagnosis: Selected Papers*. Minneapolis: University of Minnesota Press. Originally published, 1971.)
Meehl, P. E. 1973c. "Schizotaxia, Schizotypy, Schizophrenia." In Meehl, *Psychodiagnosis: Selected Papers*. Minneapolis: University of Minnesota Press. (Originally published, 1962.)
Meehl, P. E. 1973d. "MAXCOV-HITMAX: A Taxonomic Search Method for Loose Genetic Syndromes." In Meehl, *Psychodiagnosis: Selected Papers*. Minneapolis: University of Minnesota Press.
Meehl, P. E. 1973e. Some Methodological Reflections on the Difficulties of Psychoanalytic Research. *Psychological Issues* 8: 104–15. (Originally published, 1970.)
Meehl, P. E. 1973f. "Some Ruminations on the Validation of Clinical Procedures." In Meehl, *Psychodiagnosis: Selected Papers*. Minneapolis: University of Minnesota Press. (Originally published, 1959.)
Meehl, P. E. 1973g. "Specific Genetic Etiology, Psychodynamics, and Therapeutic Nihilism." In Meehl, *Psychodiagnosis: Selected Papers*. Minneapolis: University of Minnesota Press. (Originally published, 1972.)
Meehl, P. E. 1973h. "Why I Do Not Attend Case Conferences." In Meehl, *Psychodiagnosis: Selected Papers*. Minneapolis: University of Minnesota Press.
Meehl, P. E. 1974. Genes and the Unchangeable Core. *Voices: The Art and Science of Psychotherapy* 38: 25–35.
Meehl, P. E. 1975. Hedonic Capacity: Some Conjectures. *Bulletin of the Menninger Clinic* 39: 295–307.
Meehl, P. E. 1977. Specific Etiology and Other Forms of Strong Influence: Some Quantitative Meanings. *Journal of Medicine and Philosophy* 2: 33–53.
Meehl, P. E., and Golden, R. 1982. "Taxometric Methods." In *Handbook of Research Methods in Clinical Psychology*, eds. P. Kendall and J. Butcher. New York: Wiley, 127–81.
Mischel, W. 1977. On the Future of Personality Measurement. *American Psychologist* 32: 246–54.
Morrison, D. E. and Henkel, R. E., eds. 1970. *The Significance Test Controversy*. Chicago: Aldine.
Nagel, F. 1961. *The Structure of Science*. New York: Harcourt, Brace and World.
Nambu, Y. 1976. The Confinement of Quarks. *Scientific American* 235: 48–60.
Nozick, R. 1974. *Anarchy, State and Utopia*. New York: Basic Books.
Oakes, W. F. 1975. On the Alleged Falsity of the Null Hypothesis. *Psychological Record* 25: 265–72.
Pap, A. 1953. Reduction-Sentences and Open Concepts. *Methodos* 5: 3–30.
Pap, A. 1958. *Semantics and Necessary Truth*. New Haven, Conn.: Yale University Press.
Pap, A. 1962. *An Introduction to the Philosophy of Science*. New York: Free Press.
Popper, K. R. 1959. *The Logic of Scientific Discovery*. New York: Basic Books.
Popper, K. R. 1962. *Conjectures and Refutations*. New York: Basic Books.
Popper, K. R. 1972. *Objective Knowledge*. Oxford, England: Oxford University Press.
Popper, K. R. 1974. "Autobiography." In *The Philosophy of Karl Popper,* ed. P. A. Schilpp. LaSalle, Ill.: Open Court.
Popper, K. R. 1976. A Note on Verisimilitude. *British Journal for the Philosophy of Science* 27: 147–95.
Ramsey, F. P. 1960. "Theories." In *F. P. Ramsey's The Foundations of Mathematics and Other Logical Essays*, ed. R. B. Braithwaite. Paterson, N. J.: Littlefield, Adams. (Originally published, 1931.)

Rapaport, D. 1959. "The Structure of Psychoanalytic Theory: A Systematizing Attempt." In *Psychology: A Study of a Science*, vol. 3, *Formulations of the Person and the Social Context*. New York: McGraw-Hill.

Read, R. C. 1972. *A Mathematical Background for Economists and Social Scientists*. Englewood Cliffs, N.J.: Prentice-Hall.

Schilpp, P. A., ed. 1974. *The Philosophy of Karl Popper*. LaSalle, Ill.: Open Court.

Schlenker, B. R. 1974. Social Psychology and Science. *Journal Personality and Social Psychology* 29: 1–15.

Sears, R. R. 1943. *Survey of Objective Studies of Psychoanalytic Concepts*. New York: *Social Science Research Council Bulletin* No. 51.

Sellars, W. 1948. Concepts as Involving Laws and Inconceivable without Them. *Philosophy of Science* 15: 287–315.

Sells, S. B. 1963. An Interactionist Looks at the Environment. *American Psychologist* 18: 696–702.

Silverman, L. H. 1976. Psychoanalytic Theory: "The reports of my death are greatly exaggerated." *American Psychologist* 31: 621–37.

Skinner, B. F. 1938. *The Behavior of Organisms*. New York: Appleton-Century.

Slater, E. 1971. "The Monogenic Theory of Schizophrenia." In *Man, Mind, and Heredity: Selected Papers of Eliot Slater on Psychiatry and Genetics*, eds. J. Shields and I. I. Gottesman. Baltimore, Md.: Johns Hopkins University Press. (Originally published, 1958.)

Smith, M. B. 1973. Criticisms of a Social Science. *Science* 180: 610–12.

Stoddard, L. 1929. *Luck, Your Silent Partner*. New York: Liveright.

Swoyer, C., and Monson, T. C. 1975. Theory Confirmation in Psychology. *Philosophy of Science* 42: 487–502.

Vico, G. 1948. *The New Science of Giambattista Vico* (3rd rev. ed.), trans. T. C. Bergin and M. H. Fisch. Ithaca: Cornell University Press. (Originally published, 1744.)

Waismann, F. 1945. "Verifiability." *Proceedings of the Aristotelian Society* 19: 119–50.

Wiggins, J. 1973. Despair and Optimism in Minneapolis. *Contemporary Psychology* 18: 605–6.

2

Psychological Determinism and Human Rationality: A Psychologist's Reactions to Professor Karl Popper's "Of Clouds and Clocks"

In the Second Arthur Holly Compton Memorial Lecture, engagingly titled "Of Clouds and Clocks," Sir Karl Popper addresses himself to a long-familiar problem about psychological determinism, indicated by the lecture's subtitle, "An Approach to the Problem of Rationality and the Freedom of Man."[1] The lecture treats of several interconnected themes, ontological, historical, and methodological. I want to emphasize that the present paper is in no sense an "attack" on the lecture as a whole, which abounds with the usual Popper stimulation and perspicuity, and from which I have learned much. Some of the interpretation (e.g., the indeterministic features of classical physics) is beyond my competence even to discuss, let alone criticize. What I consider herein, qua philosophically oriented psychologist, is only one specific thesis, to wit, *psychological determinism is incompatible with human rationality*. The core idea here, in spite of the new aspects illuminated by Popper, is an old one, no doubt familiar in one form or other to almost any undergraduate philosophy major. (I recall first hearing it, when a sophomore, forcefully presented and ingeniously defended by Professor Alburey Castell. I did not buy it then, and I find that, some thirty years having passed, I cannot buy it now. But I trust that my reasons are somewhat better today than they were in 1939, as I am now more cognizant of the genuine puzzles and paradoxes involved.)

It is important to be clear about three matters right off: First, the thesis is ontological, not epistemological, and I therefore bypass evidential questions, freely invoking "what Omniscient Jones knows," "what a Utopian physiologist would say," "what is actually going on," "what is true concerning the state of Nature." The thesis is a claim about incoherence in a deterministic ontology; it says that if all human thought and action were completely determined, then it *could*

I am indebted to the Louis W. and Maud Hill Family Foundation and the Carnegie Corporation of New York for support through summer appointments as professor in the Minnesota Center for Philosophy of Science.

not be rational. That kind of question can of course be examined without reference to the evidential issues of how we could find out that determinism was false, or how we could ascertain that we are rational (?!).

Second, I do not attempt a defense of complete psychological determinism, partly because its truth or falsity would not bear on its consistency with rationality, but also because I am not myself a convinced determinist, and consider the substantive issue in doubt on present evidence.

Third, being a psychologist I am naturally suspect and vulnerable to a kind of *ad hominem* complaint that "You of course defend determinism because of trade-union interests, thinking that your scientific and clinical jobs require an implicit faith in the ultimate strict orderliness of all psychological processes." For me, at least, this is not true. I anticipate that no development of the behavior sciences will eliminate their current stochastic features, and I am not aware of any research programs that would have to be abandoned as fruitless if an element of radical indeterminism were postulated. For example, it seems fair to say that the greatest degree of behavioral prediction and control achieved thus far by psychologists is found in the work of Skinner and his disciples.[2] Aside from the fact that these modest triumphs of "behavioral engineering" are quantitatively tighter when the subjects are pigeons pecking keys than when they are humans speaking words — let alone philosophers engaged in criticism — whether or not one sees the laws as deterministic depends upon the level of analysis. The main dependent variable studied is rate of responding, as represented by the slope of a cumulative response record. The conceptual and mathematical relationships between this "operational" variable and the underlying probability-of-responding — the relation between a finite relative frequency and a "propensity" — have never been precisely explicated by the operant behaviorists. Usually they can go along quite well with their work without a rigorous explication of it. But when radical determinism is under discussion, we need more than a mere showing that a response-curve slope is highly manipulable. Whether or not a rat, pigeon, or human emits a certain response during a small interval $\Delta+$, and whether the response has such-and-such narrowly specified topographic, durational, and intensive properties, are *not* under complete experimental control, but remain probabilistic only. Besides, the various kinds of human psychological activity differ in how "clocklike" versus "cloudlike" they are, and Popper could quite properly argue that any showing that there is quasi-clocklike orderliness in a well-conditioned eyeblink reflex is only faintly relevant to the question "How clocklike are political theorizing, mathematical invention, and philosophical criticism?"

With these disclaimers made about what I am not attempting to do, what I shall attempt is to criticize Popper's view that *if* human thought and behavior were completely determined, *then* they could not be rational. If I understand him rightly, he believes that if strict determinism were true, we could not, in any genuine sense, give reasons, be influenced by reasons, engage in critical thought, etc., and that the validity or invalidity of arguments could not influence the course of human happenings. The line of his argument can best be seen from a few representative quotations. Popper writes:

> [Quoting Compton] "If . . . the atoms of our bodies follow physical laws as immutable as the motions of the planets, why try? What difference can it make how great the effort if our actions are already predetermined by mechanical laws . . . ?"
>
> Compton describes here what I shall call '*the nightmare of the physical determinist.*' A deterministic physical clockwork mechanism is, above all, completely self-contained: in the perfect deterministic physical world there is simply no room for any outside intervention. Everything that happens in such a world is physically predetermined, including all our movements and therefore all our actions. Thus all our thoughts, feelings, and efforts can have no practical influence upon what happens in the physical world: they are, if not mere illusions, at best superfluous by-products ('epiphenomena') of physical events. (7–8)

I believe that the only form of the problem of determinism which is worth discussing seriously is exactly that problem which worried Compton: the problem which arises from a physical theory which describes the world as a *physically complete* or a *physically closed* system. By a physically closed system I mean a set or system of physical entities, such as atoms or elementary particles or physical forces or fields of forces, which interact with each other—and *only* with each other—in accordance with definite laws of interaction that do not leave any room for interaction with, or interference by, anything outside that closed set or system of physical entities. It is this 'closure' of the system that creates the deterministic nightmare. (8)

For according to determinism, any theories—such as, say, determinism—are held because of a certain physical structure of the holder (perhaps of his brain). Accordingly we are deceiving ourselves (and are physically so determined as to deceive ourselves) whenever we believe that there are such things as arguments or reasons which make us accept determinism. Or in other words, physical determinism is a theory which, if it is true, is not arguable, since it must explain all our reactions, including what appear to us as beliefs based on arguments, as due to *purely physical conditions.* Purely physical conditions, including our physical environment, make us say or accept whatever we say or accept; and a well-trained physicist who does not know any French, and who has never heard of determinism, would be able to predict what a French determinist would say in a French discussion on determinism; and of course also what his indeterminist opponent would say. But this means that if we believe that we have accepted a theory like determinism because we were swayed by the logical force of certain arguments, then we are deceiving ourselves, according to physical determinism; or more precisely, we are in a physical condition which determines us to deceive ourselves. (11)

For if we accept a theory of evolution (such as Darwin's) then even if we remain sceptical about the theory that life emerged from inorganic matter we can hardly deny that there must have been a time when abstract and non-physical entities, such as reasons and arguments and scientific knowledge, and abstract rules, such as rules for building railways or bulldozers or sputniks or, say, rules of grammar or of counterpoint, did not exist, or at any rate had no effect upon the physical universe. It is difficult to understand how the physical universe could produce abstract entities such as rules, and then could come under the influence of these rules, so that these rules in their turn could exert very palpable effects upon the physical universe.

There is, however, at least one perhaps somewhat evasive but at any rate easy way out of this difficulty. We can simply deny that these abstract entities exist and that they can influence the physical universe. And we can assert that what do exist are our brains, and that these are machines like computers; that the allegedly abstract rules are physical entities, exactly like the concrete physical punch-cards by which we 'program' our computers; and that the existence of anything non-physical is just 'an illusion,' perhaps, and at any rate unimportant, since everything would go on as it does even if there were no such illusions. (12)

For obviously what we want is to understand how such non-physical things as *purposes, deliberations, plans, decisions, theories, intentions, and values*, can play a part in bringing about physical changes in the physical world. (15)

Retaining Compton's own behaviorist terminology, Compton's problem may be described as the problem of the influence of the *universe of abstract meanings* upon human behavior (and thereby upon the physical universe). Here 'universe of meanings' is a shorthand term comprising such diverse things as promises, aims, and various kinds of rules, such as rules of grammar, or of polite behavior, or of logic, or of chess, or of counterpoint; also such things as scientific publications (and other publications); appeals to our sense of justice or generosity; or to our artistic appreciation; and so on, almost *ad infinitum*. (16)

I believe these quotations suffice to give the essential argument, which purports to show that complete psychological determinism, arising on the basis of complete brain-process determinism ("mind is a function of brain"), renders genuine rationality and purposiveness impossible, and "giving of reasons" a spurious idea or an inefficacious irrelevancy. I turn now to my analysis and criticism of that contention.

There is, at least prima facie, a certain oddity about the position of those who wish to reject psychological determinism on the ground that it precludes human rationality, since part of their reason for insisting upon a "something else" which is not the mere workings of the cerebral machinery is the obvious fact that our conduct *is* causally influenced by "the giving of reasons." If I want to control your behavior with regard to a certain decision, it is true that I may proceed by various kinds of irrational appeals (e.g., after the manner of Hitler); but it is also true that I may proceed by giving you what I believe to be good reasons for your behaving in the way that I desire. In fact, if I know you fairly well and believe you to be a highly rational man, I may well operate on the assumption that the most effective way to control your behavior is to present you with good reasons. Thus we have a situation in which the idea of *control*, or the determination of one event (your action) by means of introducing another event (my giving you good reasons), with reliance upon a kind of regularity ("Jones is influenceable by good reasons," roughly), is combined with the idea of *rationality*. Some hold that these two ideas cannot be thus conjoined in discoursing about human conduct, because, they say, "causes" cannot be "reasons." It is this alleged truism, frequently asserted without further justification, that I wish first to examine.

Let us consider a simple arithmetical example as a "pure case," one in which rational inference plays an absolutely crucial role, in which the inference is one of deductive necessity, and in which (precisely because of this deductive necessity) the behavior is determined as completely as we determine the behavior of macro-objects in ordinary physics. Let us suppose I am a practical jokester of philosophic bent. I put a jar down on the table in front of you and allow you to inspect it at leisure. I swear an oath on the Bible (let us suppose you know me to be a pious Christian believer) that I am not a magician, that there is nothing phony about the construction of the jar, and that I am not going to lie to you or engage in any kind of legerdemain. We presuppose that you take these things as true, and that you believe them with as much certainty as we can generally reach about any empirical matter. While you observe me, I now place five pennies one by one in the jar, counting out loud, and put on the lid. Then I hand you two pennies and invite you to place them also in the jar. After you have replaced the cover, I then say the following: "I want you to believe for ten seconds that there are now eight pennies in the jar. No harm will be done to anybody by your believing this, and I don't require that you assert it. So you don't even have to tell a white lie for the short run, if that would bother your conscience. I'm going, however, to attach a psychogalvanometer to your palms, and then I shall point to the figures 'six,' 'seven,' 'eight,' 'nine' on the blackboard one by one, and the instrument will reveal which numeral corresponds to your actual momentary belief about the contents of the jar. You understand I am only asking you to believe the proposition (that $N = 8$) for ten seconds, so you don't have to worry about developing bad arithmetical habits, or becoming psychotic through chronic reality distortions. Now, if you are able to believe for ten seconds that there are now eight pennies in the jar, I will give ten thousand dollars to your favorite charity. Surely you can have no moral objections or psychological fears about this procedure.''

Now it is perfectly obvious that under these circumstances the experimental subject would very much like to entertain the proposed belief for ten seconds, but if he is a sane man, acquainted with the rules of arithmetic, it would be literally impossible for him to do so. I do not mean he would have a hard time ''willing to do so,'' or that he would be ''rationally reluctant to do so.'' In terms of the utilities involved, it would in fact be rational of him to make up his mind (in the pragmatic metalanguage) to believe this false sentence for ten seconds, but the fact is that it would be impossible. You could afford to wager as much money on the outcome of this experiment as you can on the outcome of a neurologist's tapping the patellar tendon to elicit the knee jerk, or on the color and size of a negative afterimage. Yet it is equally obvious that this behavior control, which is as deterministic as anyone could desire, invloves a rational process, namely, the process of mental addition obeying the rules of arithmetic, as a crucial feature. By placing five pennies in the box and having the subject place two pennies in the box, I *determine* his belief that it now contains seven pennies, and I render it *impossible* for him to believe that there are eight. There is, I submit, little or no more ''play'' in this system than there is in the elicitation of a reflex from a spinal animal or the putting of a sugar lump into solution. If the conditions stipulated are fulfilled, I would lay as large a wager on the outcome of any one of these experiments as on any other.

There are, it seems, two opposite dangers to beware of in discussing causes and reasons in relation to human behavior. The first danger, which is not likely to be made by anyone who is philosophically sophisticated, is to conflate causes and reasons; but there is an opposite danger, one which we sometimes find in philosophically sophisticated persons, to conclude that since causes and reasons are not the same sort of entity, there cannot be any intimate connection between them, so that ''explaining someone's behavior'' must either be a *causal*-analysis enterprise or a *reason*-providing enterprise, but no single instance of behavior-explaining can be both. This radical separation of discourse about causes from discourse about reasons is in my view mistaken when the domain of explananda is human conduct, even though I admit (nay, insist) that the words 'cause' and 'reason' designate utterly different sorts of being. I grant the premise, that the terms 'cause' and 'reason' refer to nonoverlapping classes of designata. But I deny that from this premise we can validly infer the usual conclusion, to wit, that to provide a causal account of a person's behavior is inconsistent with giving an account in terms of his reasons. If this is paradoxical, I can only argue that it is not contradictory, and hope that its paradoxical flavor will be dissipated by sufficient immersion in my examples.

The view that I wish to develop is that while causes and reasons are utterly different sorts of things, and while in an important sense we can say that causes are "in the world" whereas reasons are not "in the world," nevertheless the *giving* of reasons, the *holding* of reasons, the *stating* of reasons, the *tokening* of reasons, the *belief* in reasons, are all psychological events, and as such are very much "in the world," and part of the chain of causality. I wish to maintain further that such psychological events have a *content*, the character of which cannot be fully set forth without employing the categories of logic. Hence, in formulating the causal laws of behavior, at least at the molar level, regarding the influencing of behavior by the tokening of reasons, the question whether or not a certain proposition or belief or sentence is a *good reason* is psychologically relevant. This is a question which can be put without conflating causes and reasons, because while a reason is not an event "in the world," the giving of a reason (or the believing of a reason, or the accepting of a reason) *is* a psychological event and *is* "in the world."

Let us take an example of simple purposive behavior to examine in this light. I mail a letter to a hotel in New York City for the purpose of arranging a room reservation because I am planning to attend a convention there. My plan to attend the convention is a good reason for sending a letter. There is a quasi-lawlike statement relating the sending of letters and the establishment in New York of a room reservation in one's name, which, while it is not a fundamental nomological, can either be made into a nomological by a suitable *ceteris paribus* clause or formulated as a statistical generalization of high p. We then have a kind of "causal law" (belonging in the domain of sociology), which relates one event, the mailing of a letter, to a subsequent event by alleging a causal connection between the two. Now this statistical generalization (or derived nomological, presupposing the *ceteris paribus* fulfilled) is known to me. And taken together with my intention, it provides a good reason for mailing the letter.[3] In causal terms "having-the-intention-cum-believing-the-law" is a composite inner (mental) event or state that acts as an efficient cause of my letter-mailing behavior.

To say, "A reason caused my behavior" is perhaps a harmless ellipsis, but strictly speaking, it involves a confusion of the two realms which we must be careful to avoid. What we should rather say, so as to steer safely clear of this confusion, is, "The tokening of a reason was the psychological cause of my behavior." Or, lest even this formulation be taken wrongly, we could say, "The tokening of a sentence S which expresses a proposition p, where p is a good reason for action A, was the psychological cause of my emitting action A." So, even in this simple example we have at least four linkages or "connections" to consider and distinguish: First, mailing letters is a cause of room reservations expressible as a hypothetical 'If one mails a letter, he gets a room'; second, this causal relation is, *in the realm of inference*, a good reason for mailing a letter, granted the premise that one wants a room reservation; third, my tokening of this good reason functions as a psychological cause of my performing an act whose description occurs in the antecedent statement of the hypothetical (a relation in pragmatics which, in general, is a characteristic of purposive behavior); fourth, an external observer would in turn have a good reason for expecting me to mail this letter, and that good reason would be *his* understanding of the psychological causal law which says that, *ceteris paribus*, if a rational person wills the consequent of a causal law which the person believes, he tends also to will the antecedent. (The *ceteris paribus* clause must, of course, include such qualifiers as 'absent countervailing means-end structures' and the like.) In this analysis I have not, I trust, anywhere conflated causes with reasons. Yet I have explicitly recognized that a critical element in what makes certain kinds of mental events causally efficacious is that they are tokenings of sentences which, in the realm of logic, constitute valid reasons.

Consider next the case of a simple desk calculator. In order for it to compute sums accurately, its internal structure must have some kind of isomorphism with decimal arithmetic. Thus, the machine is constructed so that after a wheel has turned through ten positions, this physical fact causally produces a one-position displacement in the next adjacent wheel, i.e., the wheel which "corresponds" to the next integer to the left. The machine behaves rationally, in that it makes legitimate or valid transitions in the arithmetical language game. If it were not constructed in the way it is, or in some alternative way preserving the necessary machine-arithmetic correspondence, it would not be able to do this. We telephone the company and ask for a repairman to be sent out when the machine begins to make counter-arithmetical transitions, i.e., it "makes mistakes" and "gives the wrong answers." (Even a philosophy professor normally finds these locutions quite natural under such circumstances.) Such a desk calculator is clearly a "clock" rather than a "cloud," but as it gets old and worn out and becomes a little more cloudlike, it also becomes more irrational, i.e., slippage in the gears leads it to make arithmetical mistakes. We can carry the analogy further, still remaining at the level of a mere desk calculator rather than the big modern computers. What the machine will do with the numbers we punch in depends upon our giving it instructions, which is (formally) comparable to the "intention" or "mental set" adopted by a human being as he listens to us giving reasons. It is no objection to this analogy that the machine does not have conscious intentions, because it is imperative to distinguish the components of sentience and sapience,[4] and what we are concerned with in the present section is whether determinism is in any way incompatible with that aspect of *sapience* which we call 'rationality.' (Even in the human being there is, of course, plenty of evidence to say that sapience can occur, and sometimes in very complicated forms, in the absence of reportable phenomenal events. The well-known examples of unconscious literary composition or scientific problem-solving, not to mention the quite complicated content of means-end connections involved in psychoanalytic mechanisms, suffice to show this.)

With the kind permission of Professors Schilpp and Freeman, I would like to quote here a passage from the forthcoming contribution by Professor Feigl and myself to the Schilpp volume on Sir Karl Popper's philosophy.[5]

Returning to the question of the sense in which a physicalistic account in brain-language is "complete" *even though it does not say all that could be said*, we suggest the following as a first approximation to an account which, while maintaining the distinction between logical categories and the categories of physics or physiology, nevertheless insists that a physicalistic micro-account is nomologically complete. We have a calculus, such as arithmetic or the rules of the categorical syllogism. We have a class of brain-events which are identified by appropriate physical properties—these, of course, may be highly "configural" in character—at, say, an intermediate level of molarity (i.e., the events involve less than the whole brain or some molar feature of the whole acting and thinking person, but are at a "higher" level in the hierarchy of physical subsystems than, say, the discharge of a single neuron, or the alteration of microstructure at a synapse). Considered in their functioning as inner tokenings—that is, however peripherally or behavioristically they were originally acquired by social conditioning, considering them as now playing the role of Sellars's *mental word*[6]—there is a physically-identifiable brain-event b_M which "corresponds" (in the mental word sense) to the subject-term in the first premise of a syllogism in Barbara. There is a second tokening event b_P which is a token of the type that designates the predicate-term of the conclusion; a brain-event b_S which corresponds to a tokening of the type that designates the subject-term of the conclusion of the syllogism; and finally a brain-event b_C corresponding to the copula. (These expository remarks are offered with pedagogic intent only. We do not underestimate the terrible complexity of adequately explaining the words 'correspond' and 'designate' in the immediately preceding text.)

A physically-omniscient neurophysiologist [= Omniscient Jones estopped from meta-talk about logic] can, we assume, identify these four brain-events b_M, b_P, b_S, b_C on the basis of their respective conjunctions of physical properties, which presumably are some combination of *locus* (where in the brain? which cell assemblies?) and *quantitative properties of function* (peak level of activation of an assembly, decay rate, pulse-frequency of driving the next assembly in a causal chain, mean number of activated elements participating). For present purposes we may neglect any problem of extensional vagueness, which is not relevant to the present line of argument, although it is of considerable interest in its own right.

Our physically-omniscient neurophysiologist is in possession of a finite set of statements which are the nomologicals (or quasi-nomologicals) of neurophysiology, which we shall designate collectively by L_{phys} [= neurophysiological laws]. He is also in possession of a very large, unwieldy, but finite set of statements about structure, including (a) macrostructure, (b) structure of intermediate levels, e.g., architectonics and cell-type areas such as studied microscopically in a brain-histology course, and (c) micro-structural statements including micro-structural statements about functional connections. We take it for granted that "learned functional connections" *must* be embodied in micro-structure (although its exact nature is still a matter for research) since there is otherwise no explanation of the continuity of memory when organisms, human or animal, are put into such deep anesthesia that all nerve cell discharge is totally suspended for considerable time periods, or when normal functional activity is dramatically interrupted by such a cerebral storm as a grand mal seizure induced in electroshock treatment. Thus the class of structural statements S_t includes two major sub-classes of statements, one being about the inherited "wiring diagram" of a human brain, and the other being the acquired functional synaptic connections resulting from the learning process.

Our omniscient neurophysiologist can derive, from the conjunction (L_{phys}. S_t), a "brain-theorem" T_b, which, to an approximation adequate for present purposes, may be put this way: Brain-state theorem T_b: "Whenever the composite brain events ($b_M b_C b_P$) and ($b_S b_C b_M$) are temporally contiguous, a brain-event ($b_S b_C b_P$) follows immediately." This brain-theorem is formulated solely in terms of the states b_i which are physicalistically identifiable, and without reference to any such meta-concept as class, syllogism, inference, or the like. The derivation of T_b is one of strict deducibility in the object-language of neurophysiology. That is, neurophysiology tells us that a brain initially wired in such-and-such a way, and then subsequently "programmed" by social learning to have such-and-such functional connections (dispositions), will necessarily [nomological necessity] undergo the event ($b_S b_C b_P$) whenever it has just previously undergone the events ($b_M b_C b_P$) and ($b_S b_C b_M$) in close temporal contiguity.

But while for the neurophysiologist this brain-theorem is a theorem about certain physical events *and nothing more*, a logician would surely discern an interesting formal feature revealed in the descriptive notation — the subscripts — of the *b*'s. It would hardly require the intellectual powers of a Carnap or Goedel to notice, *qua* logician, that these brain-events constitute a physical model of a sub-calculus of logic, i.e., that these physical entities [b_M, b_P, b_S, b_C] "satisfy" the formal structure of the syllogism in Barbara, if we interpret

b_M = tokening of middle term b_S = tokening of subject term
b_P = tokening of predicate term b_C = tokening of copula

The "brain-theorem" T_b can be *derived nomologically* from the structural statements S_t together with the microphysiological law-set L_{phys}, given *explicit definitions* of the events $[b_M, b_P, b_S, b_C]$. These explicit definitions are not the model-interpretations, nor are they "psycholinguistic" characterizations. We can identify a case of b_P by its physical micro-properties, *without knowing* that it is a tokening-event, i.e., without knowing that it plays a certain role in the linguistic system which the individual who owns this brain has socially acquired. But brain-theorem T_b has itself a *formal structure*, which is "shown forth" in one way, namely, by the syntactical configuration of the b-subscripts [M,P,S,C]. In this notation, "which subscript goes with what" is determinable, so long as the events b_i are physically identifiable. There is nothing physically arbitrary in this, and there is nothing in it that requires the physically-omniscient neurophysiologist to be thinking about syllogisms, or even, for that matter, to know that there is any such thing as a syllogism. Although again, it goes without saying that he himself must reason logically in order to derive the brain-theorem. But he does not have to meta-talk about rules, or about his own rule-obedience, in order to token rule-conformably in his scientific object-language, and this suffices to derive T_b.

One near-literal metaphor which we find helpful in conveying the essence of the "syllogistic brain-theorem" situation, as we see it, is that the sequence of brain-events $(b_i b_j b_k)$ $(b_j b_k b_l)$ . . . *embodies* the syllogistic rules. Their defined physical structure plus the physical laws of brain-function causally necessitate that they exemplify syllogistic transitions, a fact revealed when the notation designating them is considered in its formal aspects. In the usual terminology of thinking processes and logic, the brain-theorem T_b says, in effect, that the existence of a formal relation of deducibility (truth of logic) provides, in a brain for which the theorem obtains, the necessary and sufficient causal condition for a factual transition of *inference* (a mental process). This assertion may appear to "mix the languages," to "commit the sin of psychologism," to "conflate causes with reasons"; but we maintain that none of these blunders is involved. It is a *physical* fact that a certain *formal* relation is physically embodied. If the formal features of the initial physical state were otherwise, the ensuing physical result would have been otherwise. Hence the physical embodiment of the formal relation—a *fact*, which is "in the world" as concretely as the height, in metres, of Mount Everest—is literally a condition for the inference to occur.

I need hardly say that the idea that strict rationality in a deductive-inference situation is not only compatible with determinism but at the common-sense level requires it—"If I am 100% rational, I will be unable to deny conclusions strictly implied by premises''—is hardly a new insight on my part, and I have not felt it useful to canvass the philosophical or psychological literature for citations. Since the first draft of this paper was written, two explicit statements on this point have been brought to my attention, one by Ruth Macklin, in an illuminating paper entitled "Doing and Happening," where we read:

> The problem of trying to make this distinction [between things a person does and things that happen to him] hold for all cases becomes even more complex when we consider mental acts such as believing, thinking, and wanting. Although choosing, deciding, and forming intentions appear to be mental acts in the sense that they seem to be clear cases of something a person does, what about believing? Does a person choose to believe the things he believes? Or to think the thoughts he thinks? Does he have control over his beliefs in the psychological sense that he can, in fact, avoid believing that p in cases where evidence in favor of the truth of p is overwhelming? If he cannot control his beliefs in such cases, are we to say that believing that p is not something which that person does, but rather something that happens to him? This result is obtained by using an analogue of the physiological control criterion which may be somewhat infelicitously termed "the mental control criterion." It does seem counter-intuitive to claim that believing is not something that someone does; yet it is not clear that either the mental control criterion or another appeal to linguistic usage will answer the question satisfactorily. We do sometimes say, "I cannot help believing that," or "Try as I might, I cannot believe that," indicating that the ability to choose or control our beliefs is open to question. This problem can be met, in part, by making the further distinction between deliberate and non-deliberate doings, and between believings that are reflective and those that are not. Hence, application of the mental control criterion would result in the position that some types of believing are not things that one does, but rather things that happen to one. Perhaps, then, the criterion should be rejected. But on what grounds? Presumably, on the grounds that it conflicts with our intuition that believing is always something persons do. Of course, there is still another alternative, namely, that the distinction between what a person does and what happens to him is inapplicable to mental acts such as believing. On this view, it is inappropriate to claim that believing is *either* something that one does or something that happens to him.[7]

The other quotation, as succinct and explicit a statement of my position as one could easily find anywhere, goes back to 1905, in Max Weber's critique of Eduard Meyer's methodological views.

> The error in the assumption that any freedom of the will—however it is understood—is identical with the "irrationality" of action, or that the latter is conditioned by the former, is quite obvious. The characteristic of "incalcula-

bility," equally great but not greater than that of "blind forces of nature," is the privilege of—the insane. On the other hand, we associate the highest measure of an empirical "feeling of freedom" with those actions which we are conscious of performing rationally—i.e., *in the absence of physical and psychic "coercion," emotional "affects" and "accidental" disturbances of the clarity of judgment*, in which we pursue a clearly perceived end by "means" which are the most adequate in accordance with the extent of our knowledge, i.e., in accordance with empirical *rules*. If history had only to deal with such rational actions which are "free" in this sense, its task would be immeasurably lightened: the goal, the "motive," the "maxims" of the actor would be unambiguously derivable from the means applied and all the irrationalities which constitute the "personal" element in *conduct* would be excluded. Since all strictly teleologically (purposefully) occurring actions involve applications of empirical rules, which tell what the appropriate "means" to ends are, history would be nothing but the applications of those rules. The impossibility of purely pragmatic history is determined by the fact that the action of men is *not* interpretable in such purely rational terms, that not only irrational "prejudices," errors in thinking and factual errors but also "temperament," "moods" and "affects" disturb his freedom—in brief, that his action too—to very different degrees—partakes of the empirical "meaninglessness" of "natural change." Action *shares* this kind of "irrationality" with every natural event, and when the historian in the interpretation of historical interconnections speaks of the "irrationality" of human action as a disturbing factor, he is comparing historical-empirical action not with the phenomena of nature but with the ideal of a purely rational, i.e., absolutely purposeful, action which is also absolutely oriented towards the adequate means.[8]

I have no doubt made my task somewhat easier, as Sir Karl might object, by confining myself to that restricted form of rationality involved in thinking syllogistically. But while the choice of such an example simplifies the problem, I cannot think that the use of such an example is tendentious or prejudicial. And this is the more so since Sir Karl, whose position is under examination here, is such a firm and articulate opponent of the idea that there exists such a thing as "inductive logic." Without making overmuch of the Reichenbachian dichotomy between the context of discovery and the context of justification (a dichotomy which is not clearcut, but still useful for many purposes) I would suggest that those portions of what is ordinarily considered subsumable under "inductive inference" that involve the testing of hypotheses and generalizations can be given a syllogistic form (e.g., *modus tollens*), so that the preceding syllogistic example can function as a paradigm case for dealing with Sir Karl's position in this respect; and that what is not so formulated can *either* (a) be viewed as satisfying or not satisfying some overarching methodological prescription in the pragmatic metalanguage (and hence examinable in an essentially syllogistic way, i.e., we inquire whether a given bit of concrete pragmatics of inference is or is not in accord with the methodological prescription), or (b) really properly relegated to "context of discovery" in the strong sense of the phrase. Since Sir Karl himself explicitly repudiates the problem of the psychology of discovery as not belonging to the logic of the matter, the question how (historically, psychogenetically, sociologically) a particular scientist comes to hit upon a theory or an experimental arrangement is not relevant to our present issue. The possibility of novelty, of genuine "creation" by the scientist or artist, does involve this context-of-discovery question, and Sir Karl adduces it as a further objection to determinism; but that is outside the scope of this paper.[9]

One's philosophical (and perhaps, more importantly, one's "personal, human, existential") discomfort about determinism in relation to the possibility and limits of human rationality is, I suggest, often exacerbated by two mental habits in our thinking about the psychological causation of beliefs and related cognitive processes (e.g., perceiving, inferring, recalling). The first is our habit of associating the idea of psychological causation primarily with the nonrational or irrational class of causes, such as unquestioned beliefs carried over from childhood, political manipulation of mass opinion through propaganda, personal idiosyncratic prejudices having a variety of origins, unconscious determinations of the Freudian type, and the like. One has the impression, in talking with either philosophers or "plain men," that when asked to contemplate the possibility that their own behavior may be completely (or even largely) determined by antecedent causal conditions, they tend to think immediately of such factors as the fried eggs they had for breakfast, or the prejudice they learned from their Norwegian grandmother against the Danes, or the subtle influence of TV advertising upon consumer choice, rather than such psychological facts as the fact that they have been presented with certain evidence in the form of statements from reliable sources, or have been subjected to criticism in the course of discussion with a colleague, or have made certain observations in the laboratory. Thus it seems that our tendency to polarize "human reason" over against "psychological causality" infects our thinking by influencing the very examples that occur to us in this connection, so that we tend to think of psychological causality solely in terms of the kinds of causes which normally are used to explain a piece of human irrationality. No doubt the influence of Freud and Marx, at least among educated persons, is important here, inasmuch as they both stressed the "hidden, nonrational" forces that play a greater role in the molding of man's opinions than had been formerly supposed.

The second habit is our tendency to connect such "psychological determiners" as motives, affects, training, group pressures, psychoanalytic identifications, and the like almost entirely with a person's *particular substantive (object-language) opinion*, forgetting to take into account the fact that these same classes of psychological determiners also exert a powerful causal influence upon his *meta*-talk and *meta*-thought. That is, we readily recognize the possibility that I am a zealous pacifist or jingoist because I have a strong unconscious father-identification and my father was a pacifist or jingoist, as the case may be. But we neglect the possibility (thankfully, one realized in at least an appreciable minority of human beings!) that I am committed to certain overarching procedural or methodological principles, such as rationality, critical discussion, and the examination of contrary evidence, as a result of my psychological history. These overarching methodological habits are, of course, subject to learning by reward or father-identification or peer-group conformity pressures, and it is a mistake to assume that only our specific-issue opinions are "psychologically caused." In common life, we have occasion to characterize persons according to their meta-talk dispositions. We may say of a certain individual, "Well, he's usually a very rational fellow on most subjects, and he tries hard to be fair-minded and to see the other fellow's viewpoint; but you'd better not get him on the race question, because there he goes haywire." What do we mean by a remark of this kind? We mean that this person is one who has developed very strong pervasive "meta-habits" of the kind we call 'rational,' so that we expect that these overarching considerations, e.g., his self-concept of being a rational person, and his sincere desire to find out the truth about matters to which he addresses himself, his compulsion to derive implications from hypotheses and compare them with facts, will *in general* be controlling with respect to his processes of thinking about particular substantive matters; but that this overarching monitor or control system, which causes him to think rationally in general, is not sufficiently strong to countervail the influence of a very strong emotional commitment on this particular substantive issue of the race question. (Each of us has on occasion in his smaller way to make Henry Clay's famous decision on whether we would rather be right than be President!)

It may be objected that in these remarks I have fallen into the confusion I earlier renounced, to wit, mixing the category of "causes" with the category of "reasons." If so, it has been through some subtle philosophical mistake, because in writing the foregoing I had this distinction constantly in mind. But I have permitted myself such locutions as "thinking rationally," or "countervailing influence against rationality," and it is obligatory upon me to explicate the cause-reason relationship indicated by such language.

What, then, is the situation here, as regards the relation of causes to reasons, when we inquire concerning a particular individual's thinking about a certain subject whether it was mainly influenced by "rational" or "irrational" factors? For ease of exposition and to avoid nonrelevant issues in psycholinguistics (but, I hope, without loss of generality), I confine myself to thinking processes sufficiently "symbolic-linguistic" in nature to make appropriate the notion that the individual tokens a sentence. I do not mean thereby to prejudge the question whether all forms of intentionality involve sentence-tokening; but that sort of intentionality which is (debatably) present when I simply image a state of affairs, or when I have an unworded "expectation" that is rudely disappointed (as in Russell's well-known example of a nonlinguistic belief, that of experiencing surprise upon finding another step on the stairs when I thought I had come to the bottom even though I was not consciously "thinking about it" at all) is too dubiously "rational" to be of use for our analysis. I have no stake in asserting that such non-worded, inchoate expectations *cannot* (on some suitable reconstruction) be considered rational; and in fact I tend to believe some of them should be called so. But since the detailed reconstruction is not available, and since some readers would disagree with me, I avoid these marginal cases. The issue is the compatibility of rationality and determinism, and it seems unlikely that the alleged incompatibility would show up in the case of dubiously intentional (mental) acts of a nonsymbolic, nonlinguistic sort, but for some strange reason be lacking in the clear-cut linguistic case. And since the linguistic case is the one which has been subjected to more adequate philosophical analysis, it is the only one I shall consider here.[10]

Consider an example in which I begin without any personal involvement or emotional prejudice one way or the other. I am an educated man but a non-mathematician, and I have no particular philosophical leanings about the idea of infinity. In a semipopular volume on mathematics, I come across the question whether there is a largest prime. I think to myself, "That's an interesting question; it never occurred to me; I shouldn't be surprised one way or the other; and I couldn't care less." I read through Euclid's short and easy proof, which I find convincing. From that moment onward, I firmly believe that there is no largest prime. This would seem to be a rather clear-cut case of practically 100 percent rationality. Now in what sense, if any, can we speak of the "causes of my belief" in the infinity of primes being "rational causes," without conflating the distinct categories of *cause* and *reason*?

It seems to me that there is no great mystery here, that the correct analysis is quite straightforward, and not even paradoxical. In reading through the proof, I token consecutively the sentences which, according to the syntactical rules of the language I speak, constitute (in the realm of logic) a formally valid proof of the infinity of primes. These sentences express propositions which, in the realm of logic, constitute "valid grounds for believing the conclusion." That is, the propositions which these sentences express are *good reasons*. What makes them good (deductive) reasons is, of course, that the conclusion can be reached by a finite number of steps, each step being taken in accordance with the transformation rules of the language. The tokenings (= my *thinking the sentences*) are not, strictly speaking, reasons. The tokenings are psychological causes, that is to say, they are events which go on in my mind (or, if physicalism is true, we can also say "in my brain").[11] What makes them effective causes is the fact that my brain is wired (or, more accurately, we would have to say wired plus programmed) to make language transitions in accordance with certain syntactical transformation rules. When I token a sentence S_1 and a sentence S_2, tokenings of sentences related such that the sentence S_3 logically follows from S_1 and S_2 in accordance with the tranformation rules of the language in which I have learned to "think," I am strongly disposed (to the extent that I am a rational man) to token S_3. What is the mystery about this? Except for vast differences in complexity, how does this differ from the fact that my desk calculator has a mechanical construction such that the movements of its gears "obey the laws of arithmetic"? Elliptically, it is therefore unobjectionable, provided there is no danger of confusion, to say that I am "caused to believe in the infinity of primes by valid reasons." But this locution should probably be avoided in the interests of clarity. The reasons are not causes, but the tokenings of the sentences which express the reasons are causes. If my terminal tokening of Euclid's conclusion is in fact psychologically produced not by admiration of Euclid (for some students the letters Q.E.D. could stand for "quod Euclid dixit"), or by the fried eggs I had for breakfast, but by the fact that my brain has been programmed to token sentences in accordance with transformation rules, then my belief in the infinity of primes is "rationally determined."

I have in this analysis made free use of the notion of an inner "tokening" as if it were an obvious and clear idea, which it admittedly is not. Unfortunately this is one of those concepts in whose consideration philosophy unavoidably overlaps with one of the empirical sciences, namely, psycholinguistics; and psycholinguistics is a science presently in a primitive state of development so that it cannot provide clear-cut, well-established laws (or, hence, adequate implicit definitions of its theoretical entities) for the use of the philosopher interested in semantics. It seems clear that the mental word need not possess a complex internal structure capable of correspondence, or "isomorphism" with the external nonlinguistic event that it designates. For example, a single noise, not capable of division into parts or components which have a separate "meaning," may, to an Eskimo, be equivalent to an English language statement, "There is today a great deal of snow, of a slushy variety." No psycholinguist or philosopher can, in the present state of knowledge, specify in detail what are the necessary and sufficient physical and psychological conditions for an Eskimo to token this word internally. Fortunately, it is not necessary for the philosopher to rely heavily upon technical psycholinguistics in discussing Popper's thesis. All that we need suppose is that there occurs a certain kind of physical event in the brain, whatever its "internal" nature, that has the required relation to an external event such that it is entitled to be called a tokening of a sentence, when that sentence expresses a proposition designating the external event. In the case of an English speaker, the resources of his language are such that he must say "There is a great deal of snow, of a slushy type." Whereas for an Eskimo speaker it may be sufficient to say "glop," which means the same thing to him as the more complicated expression means to an English speaker. The point for our purposes is that *whatever* physical event in the brain has come (by social learning) to possess this kind of statistical correspondence to slushy snow, perceptions normally produced by slushy snow, expectations about correlates of slushy snow, etc., constitutes the physical tokening of the proposition. The occurrence of slushy snow is physically describable. The occurrence of a particular token event is also physically describable. (I set aside ontological dualism for the time being; but since determinism and not materialism is in issue, I do not believe that prejudices our present discussion. Would not Popper's objection hold against a deterministic dualistic interactionism, if it holds against a deterministic identity thesis?) Examining the role of a given kind of tokening event in the total tokening system of an individual belonging to a particular culture, we can (in principle) determine the external event to which it "refers" (insofar as it refers precisely, which it almost never does). Having determined that, we understand the "meaning" of the sentence which the individual tokens. And if he tokens that sentence when the external event does not occur, then we say that he "tokens falsely."

Of course we know that the formulation of semantic rules on the basis of studying a natural language ("English as she is spoke") will always involve a certain element of arbitrariness, because we may or may not choose to embody certain statistically deviant locutions in the rules. This will depend upon their statistical rarity, in large part, although not wholly. (Cf. the dictionary-maker's problem of deciding between "second usage" and "erroneous usage.") Thus Carnap[12] says that after observing the verbal behavior of people who speak a particular language B and noticing that 98 percent of the time they use the word 'mond' to mean the moon, but 2 percent of the time use 'mond' to refer to a kind of lantern, we are free to formulate the semantics of language B either to include this special and rare usage or not. That is, the formulation of a pure semantics, like any idealization or rational reconstruction, is something done with *attention to* (and *on the basis of*) the empirical statistics of descriptive semantics and pragmatics, but cannot usefully aim to *exactly correspond* to the latter. (If it did, as a desideratum, it would not be rule-construction, since a rule is, by definition, something capable of being violated.)

In the present state of knowledge of how the human brain mediates behavior and experience (on *either* a dualistic or "identity" view of the mind-body problem) it is pointless to speculate philosophically about possibilities as regards detail. Nor can one anticipate with any confidence just where on the cloud-clock continuum various kinds of psychological processes will be located when psychophysiology has reached a relatively advanced state. When the contemporary psychologist deals with rational behavior, such as that of a logician performing the task of classifying a simple syllogism as formally invalid, he proceeds in the same way as the philosopher or the layman does, namely, at what is usually called the "molar" level of analysis.[13] That is to say, in forecasting Professor Popper's verbal response to a syllogism which commits an Illicit Distribution of the Major, we do not—in part because we *cannot,* at the present state of knowledge of brain function—mediate this prediction in the language of neurophysiology. Instead we rely upon dispositional properties (setting aside for the moment whether these are probabilistic or nomological) of the "whole organism," the man Popper, whom we know to be sane, sober, attentive to his task, and who has a history of having been educated in formal logic. The fact that our predictions of his verbal behavior are mediated on this molar basis gives rise to an interesting problem in the methodology of those sciences that deal with the behavior of human beings, namely, to what extent must the behavior scientist employ the concepts of the logician?

It is important to make some distinctions here which are sometimes overlooked. A logical category, such as "valid syllogism," can be involved in the psychologist's task in three different ways. First, the psychologist wants to proceed rationally in his own scientific thinking, i.e., it is necessary that he himself as a knowing organism *exemplify* or *be obedient to* the laws of logic. That is to say, in his own (object-language) discourse he must avoid committing fallacies. Second, we recognize that a considerable amount of scientific writing and discussion involves, in addition to object-linguistic assertions describing observations or propounding theories, processes of rational criticism. Here the psychologist moves periodically into the metalanguage as he engages in such processes as evaluating experimental evidence, examining the theoretical derivations offered by himself and others, carrying on rational inquiry about the internal consistency of a system of theoretical propositions, and the like. So far as I can discern, in these two respects the behavioral scientist's "use" of logic does not differ in any essential way from that of the botanist or the astronomer. All scientists must think logically, whether in the object language (substantive derivations and classifications) or in the metalanguage (criticism, evaluation, and research strategy). But it seems that insofar as the psychologist treats of human cognitive processes at the molar rather than at the neurophysiological level, he is forced to employ the concepts of logic in a third way, a way that is unique to social science as a subject matter. The reason for this peculiarity of psychology, sociology, economics, etc., as Professor Popper would be the first to emphasize, is, put most simply and directly, that plants and stars do not think, but human beings do.

This undisputed fact (did even John B. Watson *really* doubt it?) about the special nature of the psychologist's subject matter gives rise to the paradox that *concepts customarily regarded as metalinguistic unavoidably appear in the psychologist's object-linguistic discourse whenever he is attempting to mediate predictions about rational human behavior*. It might be supposed that more adequate behavioristic formulation of rational behavior could, in principle, dispense with the employment of such metalinguistic concepts. Quite apart from the fact that this hope refers to a Utopian state of behaviorism, whereas we all admit that the psychologist, like the layman or the philosopher, can successfully mediate high-probability predictions given the present *non*-Utopian state of the psychology of cognition and psycholinguistics, I must further point out that it is far from obvious that even in a Utopian state of these molar disciplines it would be theoretically possible to dispense with the logician's metalanguage in giving a psychological description or causal analysis of rational human behavior. Since the possibility of their permanent indispensability at the molar level of analysis is the alternative most favorable to Professor Popper's position, let us scrutinize the consequences of this alternative in more detail.

Consider again the simplified, idealized example of a logician being confronted with a syllogistic argument containing an Illicit Major. We set aside the empirical problems involved in ascertaining those aspects of the individual's emotional and motivational state which are relevant to his momentary disposition to think rationally. That is, we assume that the "test conditions" for activating his disposition to classify an argument as Illicit Major are known to be momentarily fulfilled. The usual gambit for an arch-behaviorist who aims at eliminating any vestige of "mentalistic concepts" from his descriptive or theoretical language is to invoke the individual's learning history and to infer from it that the logician has a very strong "habit" of responding with the phrase "Illicit Major" when he is presented with a certain stimulus, say, the formally invalid syllogism appearing in three lines on a clearly printed page. Leaving aside the current controversies in psycholinguistics (which call into serious question the theoretical adequacy of any "stimulus-response" model of verbal processes) let us proceed on the (probably false) assumption that such an analysis could be given and satisfactorily corroborated. That is, let us assume that the molar behaviorist can make good on his claim of accounting for the logician's current disposition to token the metalinguistic expression "Illicit Major" as a response to the printed tokens of such a formally invalid syllogism. The question now arises, how is the stimulus class to be characterized in molar language? As is well known, there are terrible difficulties involved in the whole problem of pattern recognition, such that no one has as yet provided an adequate theoretical model of the necessary structures which, if we were in possession of it, would enable us to construct and program a computer to duplicate even fairly simple visual pattern-recognition functions of the human brain.[14] We shall set this whole class of difficulties aside also, and assume as an oversimplified situation that the typeface, size, spacing, etc., are physically identical with those which have been presented to the logician in his previous experiential history.

But even these idealizations and oversimplifications do not, it seems to me, get rid of the behaviorist's fundamental problem. We know that it is possible to present the logician with *any* syllogism having the requisite formal structure of an Illicit Major, and confidently predict that his response will be a tokening of

'Illicit Major,' or some equivalent thereof. (Let us set aside the problem of what are "equivalent responses" and confine our attention solely to the problem of identifying the stimulus class.) Now the fact that the presented visual stimulus, a syllogism on the printed page, need not be physically identical in terms of mounds of ink with any stimulus previously presented to the logician is not in itself a serious objection to the behaviorist's analysis, it being admitted on all sides that some underlying concept of stimulus equivalence or stimulus generalization will be required by any adequate molar theory (since from the sheer standpoint of their physics no two stimulus inputs, at least among those occurring in ordinary life, are strictly identical). That is, what Skinner in *The Behavior of Organisms* calls "the generic nature of the concepts of stimulus and response" is taken for granted by psychological theorists of many different persuasions. The scientific problem here is not (at the molar level) to derive or explain the basic phenomenon of stimulus equivalence or stimulus generalization, which is rather taken as a rock-bottom fact, a basic postulate in any molar behavior theory, and presumably finds its own explanation in turn at another level of causal analysis, i.e., at the neurophysiological level. The problem at the molar level, once having included some suitable theoretical postulate regarding stimulus equivalence or stimulus-generalization gradients, is that of *formulating*, in the descriptive language which we employ to characterize the stimulus side, what the *common property of the stimulus inputs which belong to a stimulus-equivalent class must be*. Or, speaking not in terms of strict stimulus equivalence but rather in terms of the stimulus-generalization gradient, the problem is one of formulating the relevant features of the physical dimensions which constitute the input variables with respect to which the generalization gradient is to be plotted as a hyper-surface in a stimulus hyperspace. To avoid the mathematical complexities involved here, we shall simplify further by speaking of stimulus equivalence rather than stimulus-generalization gradients, i.e., we shall dichotomize the syllogism inputs into illicit and licit distributions. We shall also neglect the fact that even for a logician there might be certain formal presentations which would be more "seductive" in leading him to misclassify the syllogism as valid when it is actually fallacious.[15] Our problem then becomes, how do we characterize the stimulus input in a molar-psychological formulation of the stimulus side, of a verbal habit whose response side consists of the tokening 'Illicit Major'?

Now it is a truism, routinely pointed out to students in an elementary logic course, that the fallacious character of such a syllogism is revealed by its form alone, so that one can identify an Illicit Major even if the terms (other than the logical constants) are terms whose meaning is not known to the classifier. For that matter they could be neologisms which have no meaning, in anybody's natural or artificial language. So that when we present to the logician a syllogism which says, "No glops are klunks; all klunks are fabs; ergo, no glops are fabs," we will be perfectly confident that he can respond with the tokening of 'Illicit

Major' in spite of the fact that the terms 'glop,' 'klunk,' and 'fab' are novel to him. And we have this confidence because we know that, for a logician, the defining property of an Illicit Major is its possession of a certain syntactical form, i.e., all syllogisms of this form are stimulus-equivalent to him as determiners of the verbal response 'Illicit Major.' The possession of this syntactical form is both a necessary and a sufficient condition for the logician to token the fallacy's name.

It might be argued by the staunch behaviorist that he can describe the syllogism-input stimulus class without making use of the logician's concept *Illicit Major*. Now no one wants to maintain that the behaviorist must employ the logician's *terminology*, i.e., he need not employ the actual expression 'Illicit Major' to mediate his prediction. But does this get around the behaviorist's difficulty? I do not think it does. After all, the metalinguistic expression 'Illicit Major' is introduced by the logician through explicit definition and, therefore, is in principle eliminable from *his* discourse as well. But the point is that when the behaviorist attempts to really deliver the goods on his claim to be able to *characterize* the stimulus side of the logician's disposition, he will find himself unavoidably driven to set forth the formal (syntactical) characteristics of the adequate stimulus class; and these characteristics will (if the logician is really a logical logician!) be identical with the defining syntactical property which the logician expresses by the shorthand phrase 'Illicit Major.'

It would therefore seem more honest for the behaviorist to admit from the start that he employs the syntactical category referred to by the metalinguistic expression 'Illicit Major,' and that being the case, he might just as well include the logician's phrase in his scientific vocabulary and be prepared to utilize it in object-language derivations.

Should this distress him? I think not. Consider an analogous infrahuman example. An animal psychologist is studying form discrimination in the monkey, say in a Skinner-box situation, where the discriminative stimulus is the presentation of a visual pattern on an illuminated screen and the response alternatives are to depress one of two levers. During the training phase of the experiment, the monkey is reinforced if he presses the right-hand lever in the presence of an isosceles triangle composed of three straight lines, and he is also reinforced for pressing the left-hand lever if the visual stimulus is a single circle of approximately the same size as the triangle. After this discriminative control is thoroughly established, the experimenter then presents the monkey with a visual pattern consisting of three small circles in a triangular arrangement and lacking symmetry of placement such that the circle which constitutes the top vertex is displaced leftward from the midline between the other two. So the novel visual stimulus on test trials consists not of an isosceles triangle formed out of three visible straight-line segments, as in training trials, but rather of the three vertices only, arranged so that they define a scalene triangle, and the vertices are circles which, although of smaller size, are, as circles, members of the same geometrical class as the original training stimulus for pressing the *left*-hand lever. It is likely that if these circles were made very large and close to collinear, the monkey would respond to them as approximately stimulus-equivalent to the original circle; if they are made very small, almost points, he may or may not respond; and with a considerable departure from collinearity he will (one hopes) respond to them as triangular, in spite of the fact that the physical lines connecting the vertices of this triangle are missing.

Suppose the psychologist, by trying various combinations after such original training, finds that the probability or strength of the response disposition to the right versus left lever depends in a complicated way upon (a) the absolute size of the original negative circle, (b) the absolute sizes of the test circles used as vertices, (c) the ratio between these circular areas, (d) the degree of departure from collinearity of the three points in the test trial, (e) the distances between the vertices in relation to the angles of the test triangle, and so forth. Let us imagine that (whether on theoretical grounds or by a blind, curve-fitting process) the investigator succeeds in constructing a complicated configural function which relates the response strengths of the two lever-pressing operants to these geometrical features. That is, he writes response-strength equations or probability equations of the type $P_R = F(L_1, L_2, R_1, R_2, \theta)$ and $P_L = G(L_1, L_2, R_1, R_2, \theta)$. Obviously, in explaining what these variables are, our psychologist employs concepts of analytic geometry and trigonometry, i.e., he has to explain that the variable θ which appears in these response-strength functions refers, say, to the smaller of the two angles between the lines connecting the vertices of the circles on the test trial, and so forth. Thus he employs, in his descriptive discourse characterizing the stimulus side, an interpreted formalism, i.e., physical geometry.

Now suppose either a hard-nosed behaviorist or an anti-behaviorist philosopher with intent to gore the behaviorist's ox were to object to this procedure by saying, "But, my dear fellow, you said that you were a behaviorist; that is to say, you alleged that stimuli and responses, which are mere physical energy inputs and effector events, would constitute your subject matter. Now I find you forced to employ a set of nonbehavioral concepts — namely, those of geometry. Furthermore, you do not employ them merely in the sense that you use your knowledge of geometry in designing the apparatus or what not. No, you employ them in a *susbstantive* way — that is to say, you use concepts from a nonbehavioral formal discipline as an essential part of the language with which you characterize the monkey's stimulus input. This seems to me to be contradictory to your expressed behaviorist aim.''

I cannot imagine anyone voicing this complaint, and if anyone did, I cannot imagine any behaviorist taking the objection seriously. *Of course* he must at times employ mathematical formalism in other ways than as transformation rules in making theoretical derivations. Physical objects exemplify formal properties, and these properties are behaviorally relevant. It is just not possible to characterize certain stimulus inputs if one is precluded from employing the language of geometry. One way of viewing this is that we generally take the physical language, whether the ordinary physical-thing language or the theoretical language of physical science, as *including* certain portions of the languages of formal disciplines. That is, we do not forbid the physicist to write a Riemann integral, or the descriptive statistician to write down the expression for the gamma function, on the grounds that physics and descriptive statistics are supposed to deal with physical things which are ''in the world,'' arguing that hence these sciences may not employ abstract or formal categories such as those found in mathematics or in an uninterpreted calculus. We are less accustomed to think of the formal features of a printed syllogism as a kind of ''geometrical configuration,'' although Carnap made the point explicitly in his great work of 1934:

> Pure syntax is thus wholly analytic, and is nothing more than *combinatorial analysis*, or, in other words, the *geometry* of finite, discrete, serial structures of a particular kind. *Descriptive syntax* is related to pure syntax as physical geometry to pure mathematical geometry; it is concerned with the syntactical properties and relations of empirically given expressions (for example, with the sentences of a particular book).[16]

> It is just as possible to construct sentences about the forms of linguistic expressions, and therefore about sentences, as it is to construct sentences about the geometrical forms of geometrical structures. In the first place, there are the analytic sentences of pure syntax, which can be applied to the forms and relations of form of linguistic expressions (analogous to the analytic sentences of arithmetical geometry, which can be applied to the relations of form of the abstract geometrical structures); and in the second place, the synthetic physical sentences of descriptive syntax, which are concerned with the forms of the linguistic expressions as physical structures (analogous to the synthetic empirical sentences of physical geometry, see §25). *Thus syntax is exactly formulable in the same way as geometry is.*[17]

> The sentences of syntax are in part sentences of arithmetic, and in part sentences of physics, and they are only called syntactical because they are concerned with linguistic constructions, or, more specifically, with their formal structure. Syntax, pure and descriptive, is nothing more than the mathematics and physics of language.[18]

The point is made repeatedly and with beautiful clarity in several papers by Wilfrid Sellars, although I shall content myself with only two brief quotations from his early (and insufficiently noticed) ''Pure Pragmatics and Epistemology.'' Discussing the necessity of a pure pragmatics that avoids the philosopher's sin of psychologism, Sellars writes:

Today, then, the analytic philosopher establishes his right to attack psychologism with respect to a given concept if he is able to show that it is capable of treatment as a concept the nature and function of which is constituted by its role in rules definitive of a broader or narrower set of calculi. The issue was joined first over the concepts of formal logic and pure mathematics, and it can be said with confidence that the attack on factualistic and, in particular, psychological accounts of these concepts rest on solid ground. Logic and mathematics are not empirical sciences nor do they constitute branches of any empirical science. They are not inductive studies of symbol formation and transformation behavior. (And if, at a later stage in our argument, we shall find *formal* science dealing with language *facts*, it will not be because logic is discovered by a more subtle analysis to belong to empirical science after all, but rather because of a less naive analysis of the relation of language to fact.) This first battle was won because of the development of pure syntax. The concepts of formal logic and pure mathematics were clarified through being identified with concepts which occur in the formation and transformation rules definitive of calculi. These rules constitute a logic of implication and deducibility. In this stage of the battle against psychologism, an apparently clear-cut distinction arose between *symbol-behavior* and *formal system*, a distinction sometimes summed up as that between *inference as fact* and *deducibility as norm*.[19]

And later in the same article he says:

On the other hand, if we are asked, "Isn't it absurd to say that syntactical properties do not apply to symbol behavior?", we should find it extremely difficult not to agree. How, indeed, can we characterize an *inference*, for example, as valid, unless it makes sense to attribute syntactical properties to symbol-behavior in the world of fact? If we say that syntactical properties belong in the first instance to expressions in a calculus or language which is a model or norm for symbol behavior, can we then go on to say that in the second instance they belong to language as *behavioral fact*? But to say this would be to put metalinguistic predicates into the object-language. Is there, then, no way out of our dilemma? Must we hold either that syntactical predicates are object-language predicates, or that syntactical predicates are not applicable to language as behavioral fact? Perhaps we can find a way out by drawing a distinction between language *as behavior* (that is, as the subject-matter of empirical psychology), and language behavior *to the extent that it conforms, and as conforming, to the criteria of language as norm*; or, in the terminology we shall adopt, between language behavior *qua* behavioral fact, and language-behavior *qua tokens* of language as type.[20]

A difficult question which arises in connection with microanalyses of systems that perform logical and mathematical operations is the following: Suppose we deal with such a system, one which is clocklike rather than cloudlike, and we present a detailed causal analysis of the workings of the mechanism, including of course those *structural* and *configural* characteristics of the machine by virtue of which it "mirrors" or "embodies" logical and mathematical rules. If we do this microanalytic job adequately, it seems that we have performed the task of causal analysis, and yet we seem to have *left something out of our account*, namely, that which the mechanism is "achieving" or "doing." This puzzle arises in the philosophical analysis of conduct at least as far back as Plato (in the *Phaedo*) and continues to bother us today.

It seems not to be a mere matter of omitting adequate description of how the parts are arranged. It is obvious that one cannot be said to "describe" an ordinary desk calculator if he merely *lists* the parts, as such-and-so gears, levers, cams, cogwheels, and the like, even if he also gives a description of how a gear "works" (i.e., how it acts upon another gear in terms of the laws of mechanics) but omits to specify how the gears are physically arranged in the calculator. So, "calculating purpose" aside, it is clear that no one can claim to have provided a complete physical description of the machine if he leaves out an account of the arrangement of its parts, "how it is all put together." Let us suppose such a complete physical description to have been given. But let us suppose that the knower who carries out this "internal" analysis in terms of the principles of mechanics is a Martian visitor who uses a binary or duodecimal number system. (Or, even if he used ours, he might be unacquainted with the particular sign vehicles [= numerals] which we employ to designate the natural numbers.) That is to say, he has his own mathematical equipment (which is necessary for him to be able to solve the equations of mechanics involved in describing the inner workings of the machine); but he is not in possession of the rules of translation between his number system and ours, and therefore he might (conceivably) be forced to treat the Arabic numerals which are stamped on the keys, and which pop up in the register dials, as uninterpreted forms. If the calculator is structurally intact and functioning "properly," the rules of decimal arithmetic are perfectly embodied in the machine's structure, so that the operations of arithmetic are in perfect isomorphism with certain corresponding changes of state of the machine. The machine is—in the technical sense of the logician—a (physical) *model* of the interpreted calculus *arithmetic*. Thus, for example, punching the key marked '1' in the extreme right-hand column and then punching the key marked ' + ' is a physical operation sequence corresponding to the abstract specification "taking the successor of an integer." It is evident that the Martian *could*, in principle, possess a mathematics adequate for a science of mechanics that would provide a "complete causal analysis" of the functioning of the machine, and *not* thereby (necessarily) understand the correspondence between the machine's structure (and structure-determined functional properties) on the one hand, and the Earthlings' numerical system on the other.

There is a sense in which, when the Martian has given his structural and functional analysis of the workings of the mechanism, he *has* "said everything that can be said," in the sense that nothing is "left out" of the causal analysis. But there is another sense, which is equally important, in which the Martian has *not* "said everything that can be said" about the properties of the machine, because he has not said that the machine "does arithmetic," or, less teleologically, that the machine's wheel movements constitute a model of a decimal arithmetic (= the wheel movements and positions satisfy the postulates of arithmetic). It is partly a matter of semantic convention how we choose to employ the locution 'saying everything that can be said.' But it is not purely conventional that one can distinguish between the following two kinds of *text* (I speak of 'text' because I want to emphasize that the following distinction is not a distinction of "mere descriptive pragmatics"):

1. A text is stated which consists of a conjunction of sentences exhaustively descriptive of the physical structure-dependent properties of the machine, and which suffice to entail all true statements about the machine's dispositions.

2. A conjunction of sentences (1) is stated, *together with all theorems which flow as consequences of the conjunction (1) given certain definitions.*

Now what *is* conventional or stipulative about the locution 'saying everything that can be said' is, of course, the possibility of stipulating that an individual who asserts the postulates also implicitly asserts the theorems. If anyone wishes to adopt this locution for certain purposes of logical analysis, I shall not complain of it. The fact remains that a text may contain the postulates without the theorems, or it may contain both the postulates and the theorems. And it is a familiar truth that while one in some sense "implicitly holds" the consequences of his postulates, in the sense that if he is consistent and rational he *ought* to believe the theorems that follow from them, the limitations of the finite intellect are such that we often do not hold all of the theorems which flow from our postulates because, for example, nobody has as yet succeeded in showing whether a certain well-formed formula is a theorem, or a counter-theorem, or even whether it is decidable. E.g., we do not know whether Fermat's Last Theorem is true or false; and we know that no one has as yet presented a valid proof of it, or a proof of its undecidability; so that it is somewhat misleading to say that we "believe it" or "hold it" or "know it to be true," supposing that Omniscient Jones knows it to be true, i.e., to be a consequence of the postulates of arithmetic. It is not, I think, an excessive reliance upon the usages of vulgar speech to ask that metalanguage stipulations avoid needlessly paradoxical consequences, such as that I am bound to hold that my late grandmother believed the number of her noses to be $-e^{\pi i}$.

Now it might be said that whereas the Martian would lack (better, *could* lack) our semantics for interpreting the numerical sign vehicles that pop up in the dials of the desk calculator, and if he were a particularly rigid or stupid Martian he might not develop insight into the translatability of the physical properties of the machine into a number system which was in turn transformable into his own, he could, nevertheless, ''predict everything about the machine's behavior,'' because we have just assumed that he gives a complete mechanical-causal analysis of its micro-structural (and, as a consequence, micro-function) properties. And it seems evident that one who understands everything that happens in the causal order about any mechanism ought to be able to forecast—since we are assuming that the machine is completely clocklike and has no cloudlike ''slippage'' in its gears—all its dispositions. However, I believe there is an important sense in which even this is not quite true, unless stated very carefully and with all the necessary qualifications. The ''results'' of performing certain ''operations'' with the machine, definable in terms of what sorts of physical sign patterns pop up in the ''answer'' (cumulative bank) register are, after all, among the dispositional properties of the machine. And some of the strict uniformities (and statistical generalizations) in these ''results'' cannot, oddly enough, be predicted by a knower who has not made the cognitive identification of certain functional consequences of the machine's micro-structural features with the abstract concepts of arithmetic.

Consider the following example: A set of instructions is provided for carrying out division operations, and for recording their results, such that one obtains a sequence of ''outcomes'' (semantically uninterpreted by the Martian) that in fact constitute successive answers to the question ''Is this integer prime?'' We also have the Martian concurrently performing the task of keeping track of the proportion of such outcomes that have cumulated up to the nth integer, although of course he doesn't know that is what he is doing. Finally, we assume that the Martian knows logarithms (or at least that we can instruct him in the sheer mechanics of entering a logarithm table). Then it can be asked whether the proportion of outcomes of the ''prime type'' accumulated up to any point in this sequence of operations exceeds the reciprocal of the natural logarithm (i.e., the Martian is, so to speak, ''empirically'' examining Gauss's law of the density of distribution of primes). We now ask the Martian to predict, from his complete causal understanding of the machinery, how far along in the sequence he will have to go before he can be certain that the cumulated proportion of outcomes of the ''prime'' type will at some point have *exceeded* the Gauss approximation, instead of falling on the low side as it will at first. Now this number, Skewe's number, is

$$10^{10^{10^{10^{34}}}}$$

which is believed to be larger than the cardinal number of all of the atoms in the universe. So of course the Martian will never reach this value, before which—we don't know how much before—the prime proportion ''flips over'' so that Gauss's asymptotic formula errs on the high side of the actual value. We Earthlings, who *have* made the coordination—or for that matter an Earthling who *knows nothing about the machinery but only knows that the calculator "does arithmetic"*—can correctly state a lower bound for the number of such consecutive operations necessary to achieve this proportion of outcomes; whereas the Martian, or anyone else who has not made the coordination between the machine's structural properties and the axioms of arithmetic, could not make such a prediction. It seems obvious that this constitutes in some sense a genuine "cognitive edge," and that it is therefore false, or at least very misleading, to say that one who had described the internal mechanical structure, but has not made the explicit identification of the machine's states and operations with arithmetical concepts, would have "said everything that can be said." He would have said something which, given the appropriate explicit definitions and interpretations, *suffices to derive everything* that can be said, given the further assumption that he is an omniscient mathematician who is able to derive all the theorems that validly flow from the arithmetical postulates embodied in the structure of the machine. But if you don't say something that can be said, it is misleading to characterize your description as having said everything that can be said, even if what you have said is capable of entailing everything which can be said.

Nevertheless, recognizing this fact does not force us to postulate a "something more" going on *causally* in the machine, i.e., we do not infer from this that there is some sort of an additional arithmetic spook at work which sees to it that the calculator "obeys the postulates of arithmetic." Whether or not any such additional causal entity needs to be invoked depends upon whether our analysis of the situation amounts to a projection or a reduction, in Reichenbach's sense.[21] A desk calculator, an electronic computer, or—if physicalism be true—a human brain is a reductive complex of its elements. Nevertheless we have to insist that even in the case of a reductive complex, there is an important sense in which one may not have said everything that can be said about the complex, even though he may have said everything about the elements, and have included *certain ways of stating* everything about their relations, such that everything about the reductive complex follows of necessity from the statements which he *has* formulated. Thus if I recognize that a wall is a reductive complex of the bricks, and then I give the bricks numbers 1, 2, 3, and so forth, and state that Brick #1 is adjacent to Brick #2 and Brick #3 is located immediately above the first two and symmetrical with respect to them, and so forth, the vast conjunction of all true statements of this kind entails a "molar" statement about the wall. (They are not equivalent, since, as Reichenbach points out, the molar statement about the wall, while entailed by this conjunction of statements about the bricks, does not entail this conjunction; because the same molar statement about the wall is also a consequence of alternative conjunctions about the bricks.) What I have said about Bricks #1, #2, #3, and so forth may entail the "molar" statement that the wall is 50 feet high; but if I do not make this latter statement, it is misleading to say, at least for certain purposes and in certain contexts, that I have "said everything that can be said." And it is at least theoretically possible for an individual to have a "complete understanding" of each of the statements about the elements and, depending upon the complexities of the structure, not to be (psychologically) able to derive a molar consequence that validly flows from these statements.

This is not an appropriate place, even if I had the technical competence, to enter upon a detailed consideration of the formal or structural relationships that must obtain between a physical system and a specified molar means-end process in order for the system to be capable of performing the specified process. And I certainly do not mean to suggest that Professor Popper is unfamiliar with the problems in this area. I rather imagine he knows more about them than I do. Nevertheless, I must point out that his paper reads as *if* he believed a proposition which I am confident that he does not believe, to wit, "If a predicate 'P' designating a property P does not appear in a language adequate to describe a sequence of events related by causality, those events being considered at a certain level of analysis, it follows that the property P cannot, without inconsistency, be predicated of the system as a whole, or at another level of analysis." I do not myself know of any compelling reason for holding such a meta-proposition; and it is pretty clear that adopting it would generate some difficult (and, as I think, needless) puzzles. Example: Suppose we are talking political science, it would be a major lacuna in any characterization of Dwight Eisenhower to omit the statement that Eisenhower was a Republican. But even the most consistent identity theorist would consider it a category mistake to predicate of one of Mr. Eisenhower's cerebral neurons that the neuron was Republican. Must we say that since none of Eisenhower's neurons was Republican, therefore Eisenhower could not be such? Or, at the molar level, since none of Eisenhower's letter-forming actones[22] (e.g., engraphing the mark 'a') may be meaningfully characterized as Republican, hence he wrote no Republican-oriented manuscripts? If the activities of the living human brain were—as I do not assert—completely "clocklike"; or if they were largely clocklike but with a certain irreducible element of "cloudiness"; or if they were extremely "cloudy," with only a small "clocklike" element present; in any case, no description of the cerebral processes at the micro-level, formulated in neurophysiological language, will include the predicate 'Republican.' It does not seem to me that this point about the appropriateness of certain predicates being confined to what one may loosely call "the whole person and his molar acts" has any relation to the question where the human nervous system is located on the cloud-to-clock continuum.

To stay away from the technical complexities of modern computer theory, consider an ordinary Hollerith punch-card machine. We have a batch of cards in a military personnel unit which are encoded in a certain way, i.e., the row and column positions have been, by some physical procedure, set into correspondence with properties, whether simple physical ones or extremely complicated social ones, of the miltary personnel whom the cards "represent." Professor Popper need not fear that I am surreptitiously avoiding the problem by shifting it backward to the encoding process. On the one hand, certain aspects of the encoding process do not involve "intentional mental acts" on the part of any encoder; but of course some do, and the ones that do will present a problem of microanalysis in relation to molar analysis of the same kind we are here considering. I am not, I trust, arguing circularly that there is no difference between the human brain and a Hollerith machine, a view I would vigorously repudiate. I am only saying that a Hollerith machine encodes information by a correspondence rule relating one set of properties, sometimes very complex ones, to another set, namely, a hole or non-hole at a specified locus on the card. That a human operator rationally intends the encoding process for his conscious purposes is true but irrelevant for my purpose at this point. Suppose that at induction a soldier fills in a response-box set opposite to a named occupation on a checklist. We cannot presume that in filling in the box the soldier *has* to call up thoughts or images of his occupational activity, although of course he *might* do so. The more usual situation would be that a man who in civilian life has acquired the skills involved in making bread, and who has a pre-induction history of being paid to do this, will also be an individual who has acquired the verbal disposition to token 'baker' in response to the question 'What is your occupation?' Notice that there is no necessary overlap in the physical subsystems of the soldier's brain involved in these vocational activities and in his self-descriptive tokenings, nor does the self-descriptive tokening of 'baker' necessarily involve any concurrent or antecedent tokenings designating the activities of a baker. These dispositions are correlated in the English-speaking population by virtue of what R. B. Cattell calls "an environmental mould," that is to say, a cluster of topographically dissimilar dispositions which go together in a given culture or subculture by virtue of the fact that any human organism that learns the one will also have learned the other.[23] The correlation is similar to that which exists between a person's motoric skills in making an incision into living flesh and his disposition to respond verbally to the question "What is a Billroth II?" There is negligible overlap between these dispositions, either on their stimulus side or on their response side; and there is nothing about either one of them which suggests any appreciable overlap in the functioning of the cerebral machinery. The fact remains that they would be very highly correlated, because anyone who possesses certain incision-making skills at a given level of proficiency is certain to be a surgeon, and surgeons in the course of their training also learn to state verbally what a Billroth II is.

To return to our inductee-baker, he fills in a square box on an occupational checklist which the machine further encodes by punching a hole in a certain position on the card representing this soldier. Ditto for his height, weight, and eye color. (These can be coded mechanically, if desired.) Now suppose we want, for some strange reason, to select from a regiment all the enlisted men who are over six feet tall but weigh less than 180 pounds, who have blue eyes, and who were bakers in civilian life. The machine's board is wired accordingly, and the cards are run through the sorter ending up with a stack of cards in which are punched the serial numbers of all soldiers having this particular combination of properties. The functioning of this machine is very far toward the clocklike rather than the cloudlike end of Professor Popper's continuum. With a little care we can render it as clocklike as desired. Now suppose concerning any particular card which emerges from such a sorting process, we say, "Give me a detailed causal account of how this particular card happened to drop out during the sorting." This question can be answered in physical language describing the structures and processes of the machine without any reference to the vocational activities of the bakers, or to concepts of height, weight, and eye color. Nothing is left out of this causal account. If we start with the initial conditions on how the machine is wired, and how a batch of cards representing the entire regiment is punched, nothing *need* be said which cannot be completely expressed in terms of such concepts as brushes, electrical contacts, punched holes, the geometry of the coordinate positions at which holes are punched, and the like.

Now this causal account of the card-sorting operation, which *leaves nothing out* (in one perfectly legitimate sense of the phrase 'leaves nothing out'), does not preclude a sentence of the following kind being literally true: "The sorter is picking out the cards of blue-eyed bakers over six feet tall and weighing less than 180 pounds." This is a perfectly good account of what the sorter is "doing." This sentence employs concepts which did not appear at the lower level of analysis of the machine's inner workings. Furthermore, it employs concepts which are *not translatable into the minimum vocabulary adequate to give an account of the machine's mechanical and electrical workings*. Is there any puzzle here? If so, it is resolved by recognizing the role of the previous encoding process, in which certain complex properties possessed by the soldier were set into a certain correspondence with loci punched on the cards. And corresponding to the fact that the cards can be repeatedly sorted is the logical particle 'and' joining the predicates 'blue-eyed,' 'baker,' 'weight less than 180 pounds,' and 'height over six feet.'

In order for me to be capable of making rational inferences or having intentions, it is necessary that my brain have a certain kind of structure. There are alternative physical arrangements that are equally capable of providing this necessary structure, the human brain being one of them. As long as the brain is capable of some kind of consistent encoding procedure, it can "represent" external facts, such as someone's being a baker, by nervous connections which, *when examined at their own level of analysis*, do not partake, however faintly, of "bakerhood." And even if the sequence of activation of individual nerve-cell dispositions were completely clocklike, this would not show, or even tend to show, that our beliefs, intentions, or volitions find no place in the world or that they have no causal efficacy.

It may be illuminating at this point to reexamine a famous puzzle about intentionality propounded by Sir Arthur Eddington.[24] Suppose a man from Mars arrives on the earth mysteriously possessed of such a Utopian knowledge of Earthling neurophysiology that he is able, by a combination of behavioral and microtechniques (such as single-unit stimulation and the like), to give a complete causal account, *in neurophysiological terms*, of all the activities and dispositions of any given members of *Homo sapiens*. In particular, he observes (and was able to predict) that on November 11, 1918, great numbers of people in many cities of the world stand about in the public square waving their arms and shouting. Now, says Eddington, there is apparently "nothing left out" of this causal account; and yet the Martian would not know the most important thing there is to know about this social occurrence—namely, that these people are celebrating the armistice. This is true, if the Martian confines his attention to the momentary activities, but it is false if he allows himself to consider dispositions as well. There is surely no reason for saying, given Eddington's own assumption of a Utopian state of Martian neurophysiology, that the Martian is forbidden to include the dispositions of nerve cells in his description of the state of affairs. If these micro-dispositions are included, I contend that Eddington is incorrect in saying that the Martian would not understand the "meaning" of the celebration. The reason is very simple: *Given a complete micro-account of the neural dispositions, one possesses all of the information necessary to construct a descriptive semantics.* He would, for example, know *that* (and he will also know *why*) persons waving their arms and shouting in the public square would be disposed to reply, if asked why they are carrying on in this crazy way, "The war is over." And, of course, his complete catalogue of neuronal dispositions would locate the word "war" in the descriptive semantic space, i.e., he would know what the word 'war' *means* to English-speaking human beings. Since we know that one can learn a language by recording the molar dispositions of its speakers (as, for example, an explorer or missionary *must* be able to do when he is the first visitor to a tribe of aborigines), a fortiori one would know the language if he knows all the micro-dispositions. Because, of course, the micro-dispositions entail the molar dispositions, but not conversely; and not all molar dispositions are realized in any finite behavior sample. Now it is perfectly true that the Martian is not *forced* to carry out any such descriptive-semantic research. He may, if he is only interested in neurophysiology, confine his explanations, predictions, and concepts to the micro-level. Whether such a confining to the micro-level "leaves something out" (in the causal sense) depends upon how far back in the causal chain it is desired to analyze the celebration. The immediate causal ancestor of a man's standing in Times Square and shouting would be, say, his looking at a newspaper headline "War is over." But the remoter causal ancestor is a complex of behavioral events at Compiègne, which the Martian would describe by a phrase in his language that is approximately synonymous with the English expression 'agreement to a cessation of hostilities.'

Can anything philosophically important about the mind-body problem, or the cloud-clock problem, be inferred from the fact that *if* physicalism is assumed true, the Martian *need not* pursue the causal chain that far backward but, on the other hand, that he *can* do so; or from the fact that he can predict "armistice behavior" successfully without tracing the causal chain back, confining himself to the momentary brain-cell dispositions; or from the fact that he could even infer the "meaning" of the celebration? I think not. These considerations do help to illuminate matters somewhat. Thus, for example, we are thereby reminded of the distinction between a statistical regularity of descriptive semantics (inferable by the Martian from nerve-cell dispositions) and the *non*psychological concept of a *semantic rule*, which is not a behavioral regularity but a prescription that the Martian formulates in his own Martian metalanguage.[25] A Utopian knowledge of the nerve-cell dispositions would be a Utopian knowledge of descriptive semantics, and a Utopian knowledge of descriptive semantics, together with a Utopian knowledge of the tokening dispositions of the celebrators, would obviously inform the Martian—*assuming he himself has the level of abstraction equipment which Eddington must presuppose in order for him to carry out the hypothesized microanalysis*—what the "content" of the celebration is all "about." All of which aids in dissipating the paradoxical flavor of the situation, but cannot help us to decide whether (a) physicalism and (b) determinism are true doctrines about mind.

Professor Popper is disturbed by the notion that a "clockwork" view of the human mind implies that the behavior scientist would be able to "write" the symphonies of Beethoven through his knowledge of Beethoven's physical states, even though the scientist himself were completely ignorant of musical theory.[26] Why does this distress him? He says "all this is absurd." But is it really absurd? I will go him one better (partly to test the limits of my own convictions in the matter!). Consider the following example. Suppose a Utopian neurophysiologist studies the brain of a mathematician who is currently working on Fermat's Last Theorem. We will assume that this neurophysiologist knows the kind and amount of applied mathematics he needs to carry on ordinary calculations upon physiological measures, but that he is completely ignorant of pure mathematics, including number theory. Thus we assume that he has never even heard the phrase 'Fermat's Last Theorem,' let alone understands what it designates. Let us further suppose (with Professor Popper) that the cerebral mechanism has certain clocklike features but others that are cloudlike. In particular, let us suppose that there occur occasions on which the strengths of the neuronal activity in two systems of cell assemblies "competing" for command of the output channel are so close that a difference in only a few critically located "trigger" neurons firing or not will show up as a molar output difference. It is irrelevant for our present purposes whether at another level of analysis—say, by the physical chemist—this cloud-like feature arises from the quasi-random character of distributions of initial conditions of intra-neuron particles whose individual chemical and physical transitions are, nevertheless, completely clocklike; or whether it arises from a fundamentally indeterministic feature of nerve-cell action quantum-theoretical in nature, as has been postulated by some physicists and neurophysiologists.[27] In either case, the point is that a randomizing component is built into the functioning of our mathematician's cerebral system, super-imposed upon the clocklike features that are involved in his being thoroughly trained in mathematical manipulation (so that he always treats an exponent differently from a base, and the like). Suppose our Utopian neurophysiologist, ignorant of number theory, is able to show *at the micro-level* that there exists a set of alternative tokening dispositions, each of which is itself a chain of subdispositions to perform particular mathematical operations. That is, our neurophysiologist sees that the mathematician is "capable of" (= has non-zero probability of emitting) several alternative work-product sequences on a given day. Within each of these alternative chains, there are points at which the cerebral machinery functions clocklike, and there are other points at which it functions cloudlike. (And even if it functioned clocklike at all points in the chain, the cloudlike selection of the *initial member* of a chain is unpredictable by the neurophysiologist.) So he doesn't know *which* of the chains will actually take place, but he can list all the physically possible alternatives. And if his psychophysiology is truly Utopian he can associate probabilities with each of these alternatives. (It is perhaps better to assume that the Utopian neurophysiologist is a considerably evolved species as respects his brain, studying a mathematician of *Homo sapiens*. Otherwise there may be information-theoretical difficulties involved in Brain$_1$ carrying out the requisite microanalysis of Brain$_2$.[28] These can presumably be avoided by setting no time limit on the neurophysiologist's derivation, so that he may continue work for months or years after the mathematician has quit. Or we may assume breakthroughs in computer engineering permitting superhuman computer brains. Or we may substitute "quasi-Omniscient Jones," who represses number theory, for the physiologist.)

Now, his microanalysis of each chain will obviously enable him to characterize the motor output—that is, the effector movements of the muscles of the mathematician's hand; and, consequently, from skeletal structure and biomechanics he knows what each virtual sequence of sign designs will be, i.e., *he knows what mathematical expressions the mathematician would write down*, if he carried out a given ("possible") cerebral sequence. Viewed thus, as the mere graphical residues of a molar class of finger movements (Neurath's "mounds of ink"), the potential work product might be devoid of meaning to our physiologist, yet its potential occurrence would be derivable by him from the Utopian microanalysis.

So our Utopian neurophysiologist is able to list a set of mutually exclusive and exhaustive "behavior outcomes," namely, all the mathematician's potential work products for the day, although he does not know which one will actually take place but has only the probabilities associated with each. Finally, let us suppose that one of these "possible work products" is a valid proof of Fermat's Last Theorem. But, regrettably, it is a sequence having (for this particular mathematician) an extremely low probability; and it is not the sequence which in fact eventuates on the given day. ("The potential proof remains unactualized.") Having worked on the problem for several weeks, our unlucky mathematician becomes discouraged, and thereafter pursues other interests.

Now this mathematician was in some sense "capable of" a proof of Fermat's Last Theorem (assuming for the moment that a valid proof of this theorem does exist) but he in fact never discovers it. However, the neurophysiologist has now before him a list of alternative potential work products, only one of which ever came into being, and that actualized one is not a valid proof. The psychophysiologist takes the whole stack of hypothetical work products (each of which is directly derivable as a consequence of the effector movements terminating a chain of CNS events) to the Department of Mathematics. I remind you that the neurophysiologist doesn't know anything about number theory. He doesn't "understand what the mathematician is working on." Yet, the low-probability valid proof, which was never actually carried out by the mathematician, would be recognized as a valid proof by the Department of Mathematics. Thus the neurophysiologist in some sense could "discover" a valid proof of Fermat's Last Theorem without understanding mathematics, by studying the brain of a mathematician who, while in some sense potentially capable of developing such a proof, never in fact does so. I readily agree that this sounds counterintuitive. But I do not see anything contradictory about it. And I think the reader will agree with me that it is interesting.

I have argued above that statements about human behavior or experience which attribute causal efficacy to reasons have a meaning which should be acceptable both to a philosopher-logician and to a determinist psychologist, but that such statements are elliptical so that unless carefully unpacked they are likely to be misleading. Thus I have said that, strictly speaking, a valid argument, considered as a certain formal structure (an abstract universal) is not an event "in the world," at least in any ordinary sense; and therefore it cannot function as a causal agent with respect to an event, e.g., a human locomotion, manipulation, or phonation. The ontology of universals, the reality of abstract entities, and the more technical aspects of the traditional nominalism-realism debate are not—it is hoped—relevant, because a serious discussion of them is, regrettably, beyond my competence. My colleague Professor Maxwell thinks I am wrong, or at least terminologically ill-advised, to say that logical relations (such as deducibility) are not "in the world." As he—rather compellingly—puts it, "*Everything* has got to be 'in the world'; where else *could* it be?'' Professor Popper even writes recently of a "third world," whose denizens are abstract ideas.[29] I confess I do not understand Sir Karl here; but perhaps Professor Maxwell's demand is met by my agreement with Carnap and Sellars on linguistic structures; see footnotes 16–20 and associated text *supra*. In any event, by saying that there are Platonic universals but they are not in the world, I have made my position more difficult, and Professor Popper's easier, to maintain. I have argued that when a bit of rational behavior is being fitted into the causal framework, the question whether certain logical categories (such as the category Illicit Distribution) are required in formulating the behavioral laws or quasi-laws depends upon the level at which the behavior analysis is being conducted. If we are attempting to formulate psychological laws either in mentalistic language or in molar behaviorese we will find such formal categories indispensable, because we will be unable to characterize a stimulus class which functions as a discriminative stimulus for such verbal responses as 'Illicit Major' on the part of a logician-subject *unless that stimulus class is characterized by reference to its syntactical structure*. Whether the mentalistic or molar-behavioristic psychologist actually employs the logician's *terminology* or not is irrelevant, inasmuch as he will be driven, in his account of the subject's behavior or experience, to introduce a specification of the syntactical features of the stimulus input, which specification will in fact *be* the logician's definition of 'Illicit Major.' But I have also maintained that the same is not necessarily the case, given a complete Utopian micro-description, although the complete Utopian micro-description will *entail* (within the nomological network) the same syntactical statements at the molar level which would have to be invoked by the molar behaviorist in predicting or explaining rational behavior. This is because the whole organism and its molar activities are reductive complexes of the micro-structures and micro-events, and hence the statements about the whole person follow from the statements about his component parts and part processes, analogously to the way in which statements about a wall follow from conjunctions of statements about the bricks. But we have also seen that there is an important sense in which, unless one *asserts* these molar statements which are consequences of the statements about the elements, he has not literally "said everything that can be said" about such a reductive complex.

The anti-determinist or, perhaps more strongly, the ontological dualist may object to this analysis with the following: "You say that your refurbished behaviorism, including as it does a physical$_2$ microanalysis, and a recognition of the molar-indispensability of certain logical categories such as *valid form*, does justice to the logician's legitimate claims, while still maintaining physicalism and determinism in the domain of mental life. In this you attempt to please both parties; you want to have your cake and eat it too. I do not know whether the hard-nosed behaviorist will buy this, but I, as a firm believer in the genuine efficacy of reasons, cannot buy it. Because, while you tell me that the micro-account *entails* those statements at the molar level which are characterizations of stimulus inputs as logical forms, the fact remains that you also maintain the dispensability of concepts like *valid reason* in a complete causal analysis. Because while you admit that one who fails to assert some of the consequences of those statements which he does assert has failed (in a sense) 'to say everything that can be said,' nevertheless it remains true that you hold it possible to present a complete causal account of human actions without reasons entering the causal chain as *reasons*. That is, you maintain that it would in principle be possible, within a Utopian neurophysiology, to detail the processes in a person's brain confining oneself to physiological descriptions at the level of 'neuron-language,' such that the resulting molar output, e.g., punching somebody in the nose, could be predicted and completely understood causally at this level of analysis; and it is obvious that no reference to the good reasons he may have had for punching somebody in the nose would occur in such a micro-causal analysis. This is what I mean by insisting that you are depriving rules and reasons and validity of all genuine efficacy in human affairs. If you can give a complete causal account of what a person does and why he does it without at any point mentioning the reasons *for which* he does it, then it seems to me that you have, in effect, eliminated the reasons from any significant role. You throw a sop to me and my friends the indeterminists, emergentists, Cartesians, etc., by telling us that certain conjunctions of micro-statements entail molar-level statements which—given suitable metalanguage definitions of logical notions like 'implies' and 'negates'—in turn entail statements about a person's *reasons*, in our full sense of 'reasons.' But you also insist that one *need not do this* in giving the complete micro-causal account. You, so to speak, 'permit' us to mention reasons; but you insist that you yourself are not *compelled* to mention them. But, surely, if they need not be mentioned, they are dispensable. And this we cannot admit.''

Since I myself admit—nay, I insist, as against a certain kind of behaviorist—that reasons are psychologically efficacious, i.e., that the hearing of reasons and the thinking of reasons and the tokening of valid arguments play a role, and for rational men may play the crucial or determinative role, in the guiding of their actions and utterances, it is the more obligatory upon me to answer this objection. It seems to me that the core issue here can, without prejudice, be formulated thus: Has one "dispensed with" the causal efficacy of a configural property of a physical state or system as playing a role in a causal explanation *whenever he avoids explicitly characterizing that configural property*, confining himself to description at a lower level of analysis ("lower" in the sense of a reductive complex), provided that (a) what he *does* assert in his lower level description can be shown to entail nomologically the configural statements and (b) if asked, he concedes—as he must in consistency—that these configural consequences are entailed by his lower level statements? Is there not a considerable element of conventional or stipulative usage involved here, about which it is pointless and fruitless to argue? One who describes a physical system omitting dispositional statements about it which flow as necessary consequences of the statements he has made, might be said, on one convention, to have "left something out," because he did not say everything that could, and (strictly speaking) everything that *must*, if the question is raised, be said. But so long as he is not inconsistent, so long as he is quite willing to *admit* the necessary consequences of what he has said, and those consequences of course *include* the entailed configural properties of the system, the locution "He thinks these configural properties are irrelevant to an adequate account" is surely misleading. In what sense can I be said to think that any feature of a physical system is "irrelevant," if I concede that this feature is a necessary consequence of features to which I have attributed relevance, and further, that if the system *lacked* these (entailed) configural features, its "output" characteristics (e.g., tokening an implied conclusion when one has tokened the premises) would be different from what they in fact are?

In assessing the conventional element in whether we would think it convenient and clarifying to say that such a scientist "leaves something out" or "considers something causally inefficacious," one consideration might be whether the physical system includes a subsystem which functions as a kind of controller, guider, evaluator, or selector, with respect to another subsystem, such that, among the intermediate or molar-level theorems that flow from the axioms of which the system is a model, there is a statement which says, roughly speaking, that the monitor or selector system will "accept" or "reject" a certain product or message from the monitored or controlled subsystem, depending upon whether that product or message possesses or fails to possess such-and-such formal properties. Thus, for example, when we program an electronic computer to perform certain computational checks upon its own work and to report to us the presence of inconsistencies; or when we program it to inform us that our own program is itself defectively written—in such cases it seems very natural, and not just a computer engineer's whimsy, to use the connective 'because' in sentences like the following: "The computer rejects these data *because* they include entries in a correlation matrix which exceed unity." It is true that in this kind of case it is also possible to describe and explain the operation of the monitoring or evaluating subsystem in micro-terms. But it remains true that we can identify two such functional subsystems, and we can correctly (and literally) say that the monitoring subsystem *classifies* the states and outputs of the monitored subsystem with regard to their possession or nonpossession of certain formal properties. It seems to me that one can arrange a continuously graded series of physical systems, each of which is a physical embodiment of certain formal rules (i.e., each of which is, in the logician's sense of the word, a "model" or provides an "admissible interpretation" of a formal calculus) from one extreme at which it would be a very marked departure from ordinary usage to employ the connective 'because' followed by a characterization in terms of validity or logical structure, to another

extreme at which a failure to include this intermediate or molar-level characterization would be looked upon as some sort of prejudice or inadvertence. Take,
for instance, the case of a beam balance, which we do not ordinarily think of as
performing logical or mathematical operations. We place three one-gram weights
in one pan, and we place two one-gram weights in the other pan, and we observe
as a causal consequence of these physical operations that the beam becomes and
remains nonhorizontal. It would not ordinarily occur to anyone to describe this
state of affairs by saying, "The balance tips *because of a truth of arithmetic*,
namely that 3 > 2." But there is a perfectly legitimate sense in which such a
statement would be literally correct. If there is a Platonic sense in which the
truths of arithmetic are not "in the world," there is another sense in which they
are, namely, that since these theorems are analytic, all physical objects do in fact
exemplify them. (Cf. Wittgenstein, "It used to be said that God could create everything, except what was contrary to the laws of logic. The truth is, we could
not say of an 'unlogical' world how it would look. To present in language anything which 'contradicts logic' is as impossible as in geometry to present by its
coordinates a figure which contradicts the laws of space; or to give the coordinates of a point which does not exist. We could present spatially an atomic fact
which contradicted the laws of physics, but not one which contradicted the laws
of geometry."[30]) If we move along this continuum of "rule representation" from
the beam balance (which "exemplifies," "instantiates," "physically embodies" the axioms of arithmetic, as well as the formalism expressing the laws of
mechanics — the former necessarily, the latter contingently) to the ordinary desk
calculator, it still seems somewhat inappropriate, but much less so, to characterize its operations by using the connective 'because' followed by an arithmetical
truth. I note that even here we are more likely to do so in an extreme or "special"
instance such as an inadvertent division by zero, where we say, "The machine
keeps running and doesn't pop up with an answer, because you divided by zero."
(We here correlate the mechanical fact that it would "run forever" if the gears
didn't wear out with the arithmetical notion that

$$\frac{N}{X} \to \infty \text{ as x} \to 0,$$

or roughly put, that if division by zero were allowed the answer would be "infinity.") The fact that the gear wheels in the calculator are toothed in isomorphism with the decimal system, and that they are arranged from left to right in
isomorphism with the way in which we place numerals in the decimal system to
represent the powers of 10, facilitates our intuitive appreciation of a more explicit
embodiment of the "rules of arithmetic" in the machine's structure than we
readily feel in the beam balance case. Just how natural it seems to employ the
locution 'because' followed by an arithmetical truth seems, in the case of a desk
calculator, to depend partly upon the complexity of the operation involved, a psy-

chological aspect which does not reflect any fundamental physical or logical difference. For example, suppose I am given a printed instruction the rationale of which I do not understand, as follows: I first set a number into the upper (cumulator) register; then I proceed to subtract the consecutive odd numbers, 1, 3, 5, . . . until I get all zeros in the register; then I record the number which appears in the lower (counting) register. If I now clear the machine and operate upon this recorded result with itself through the multiplication key, the machine presents an "answer" in the upper (cumulator) register, and that answer is the number that I started out with. Suppose I am baffled by this, and I ask the question "What is the explanation of this remarkable mechanical phenomenon?" I would probably be satisfied, unless I were specifically interested qua mechanician in the internal workings of a desk calculator, by someone's saying, "Oh, that happens because it is a theorem of arithmetic that the sum of the first k odd numbers is equal to the square of k." It seems to me that whether one views this use of 'because' as literal or figurative is a matter of adopting a semantic convention, rather than a psychological, ontological, or epistemological issue about which there can be a genuine cognitive disagreement. If, for example, one were to require, in stipulating what constitutes a legitimate use of the word 'because' followed by a theorem of some formal science (logic, set theory, arithmetic, differential equations) that the physical system should in some suitable sense be *tokening the theorem* (rather than merely exemplifying it), then he would say that the use of 'because' in the present instance would be incorrect usage (or, at best, metaphorical). But there seems to be no compelling reason for adopting such a stringent stipulation regarding the word 'because.' We employ logic and mathematics to describe the world, whether in its inanimate or animate features. A configural feature of a physical system, whether animate or inanimate, is literally characteristic of it. A formal theorem, whether of logic or mathematics or set theory or whatever, that is exemplified by the system's states and lawful transitions is, I submit, literally attributable to factual (contingent) structure-cum-events of the physical order. Unless some strong counter-consideration were advanced, such as the danger of confusion or of anthropomorphic projection (e.g., of feeling states of experienced motives) into an inanimate system, it is hard to see why such locutions should be conventionally forbidden.

If it is now objected that 'because' cannot be stipulated as allowable usage without doing great violence to both ordinary language and technical conventions, on the ground that the rule exemplified is not in the causal chain, I am at a loss how to reply beyond repeating what I have already said, to wit, that while the *rule* is not in the physical order, an *embodiment* (model, satisfier) of the rule *is* in the physical order. I would say further that the legitimate element of "necessity" which most logicians today would be willing to concede (in spite of Hume) is clearly present in this type of situation. That is to say, if we reconstruct a post-Humean notion of causal necessity as a combination of (a) logical necessity, (b) analysis of reductive complexes, and (c) the distinction between fundamental nomologicals and derivative nomologicals, then we properly assert that the calculator gives the answers which are *arithmetically* necessary, and that it does so "necessarily," given the presupposition that the laws of physics hold and that the machine is not broken, worn out, or the like.

When we move to the modern electronic computer, an additional element enters which makes it still more natural to refer to logical and mathematical theorems in explaining the machine's behavior, namely, that the machine contains a physically identifiable subsystem which stores "instructions" of a nature less generic than the ever-binding laws of logic and arithmetic. And as these instructions become more and more complicated, as when we instruct a computer to examine a certain result with respect to some property (such as whether it is odd or even, or whether it is greater than a certain value) and, depending upon the result of this examination, to operate upon this result in one or another way, then we feel quite at home with such explanations phrased in terms of rules of logic and arithmetic and the word 'because.'

There is, however, still something lacking in the computer which we might wish to require before we employ the word 'because' followed by a reference to a logical rule, namely, a physical subsystem which corresponds to a psychological *motive*. If we can distinguish motives from nonmotivated intentional states, one can say that a computer has intentional states, i.e., applies rules, but does not have motives, i.e., it does not desire things. I myself can discern no division point (other than the phenomenal or consciousness criterion) on the complexity-of-goal-seeking dimension which is other than arbitrary. When Samuels's checker-playing computer[31] (which *learned* to defeat him, the programmer!) examines a set of possible eight-move sequences, and selects the initial move of that sequence which optimizes certain features of the resulting position, I would insist that this is an unquestionably intentional, goal-directed, criterion-applying process, *except* for the "sentience" component. The same can be said for the Logic Theorist computer program, which cooked up a shorter and more elegant proof of the *Principia Mathematica* Theorem *2.85, done in three steps rather than Russell and Whitehead's nine, relying on fewer axioms, and rendering a certain lemma superfluous.[32] (This kind of thing weakens Professor Popper's argument from "novelty" or "creativity," I think—even though the example deals with the propositional calculus where neither Church's Theorem nor Gödel's troubles us.)

Here again one has a problem of stipulation. I myself would include, as a necessary ingredient of "desire," the subjective phenomenal, experiential component, which I presume to be lacking in an electronic computer (regardless of the logical complexity of its "intentional" features). As to "goal," I am quite neutral. As to "selection," I say the computer *selects*. At this point the sapience aspect of the mind-body problem borders on the sentience aspect, which is not the subject matter of this paper. It is, I think, arguable that adopting a convention requiring a raw-feel experiential aspect as a necessary component of the construct *motive* would be very inconvenient. It might preclude the animal psychologist or ethologist from attributing motives to animals at certain levels, where the phylogenetic continuity in many goal-directed aspects of behavior does not seem to be interrupted, but where it becomes increasingly dubious whether any such subjective or raw-feel component is present. But more important, while one may entertain (as I do) grave doubts about the validity of considerable portions of the Freudian picture of the mind, I am prepared to argue that one of its core characteristics, the same basic idea of the controlling influence of motive-like variables or states which are not reportable by the subject as having an inner-phenomenological aspect, seems rather well corroborated. It would be very inconvenient, both theoretically and in clinical practice, if we were forbidden to refer to an individual's motives except in those cases in which he is able to give an introspective report of them. I suspect that most psychologists would, like myself, put greater emphasis here upon theoretical generality than upon vulgar speech. Hence the preference to use 'motive' after the manner of Freud or Tolman, the conscious/unconscious distinction being made not by noun choice but by an adjective (conscious motives are contrasted with unconscious motives). But of course if someone wants a noun (e.g., 'desire') that always means *conscious motive*, well and good. These semantic preferences are stipulative, and it is silly to hassle over them. What is *not* stipulative is the empirical finding that much of human behavior is controlled by internal state variables or events that (a) have most of the usual causal properties of reportable motives but yet (b) are not reportable as having a subjective-experience aspect. It is not easy to improve on Freud and Tolman[33] in spelling this out.

If a human brain, like an electronic computer, has a structure which makes it susceptible of storing instructions concerning the allowability of certain kinds of transitions, it would seem appropriate to say that a person accepts a particular argument "*because* it is valid" and rejects another one "*because* it is invalid." That one could carry out a complete causal analysis without referring to these logical meta-categories (because he might do it instead at the micro-level) does not invalidate the literal truth of this statement, although it is commonly thought to do so. One way of seeing this is to put the question "Would the argument be accepted by the individual if it were not formally valid?" The answer, of course, is that if the argument were not formally valid, then it follows (from the fact that the microlaws entail the macro-laws and the macro-state is a reductive complex of *the micro-states that—literally—compose it*) that the cerebral mechanism would reject the argument. Hence, if the critic says, "According to your view the validity of the input argument *makes no difference in what happens*," we would have to reply that the critic is simply mistaken in saying this. Because it can be shown from the microanalysis that if the input argument were invalid, the macrobehavior, i.e., the logician's tokening response, would be to say, "This argument is an Illicit Major." Any configural property of an input which "makes a difference," in the sense that if it were lacking, the individual would say "No," but if it is present the individual will say "Yes," surely must be said to "make a difference" in the most stringent use of that expression.

While the complexities of the reconstruction vary widely, and while the presence of a state or event which constitutes a "guiding motive" (*properly* so-called) makes a great difference, the fundamental point I am making seems to be exemplified both in inanimate and animate contexts; and, within animate systems, is exemplified both in the "psychological" and the "purely physiological" domains. In physics there are problems such that the state to which a system moves can be derived by alternative methods which are not contradictory but which do represent analyses at different levels of description. Thus, we may invoke highly general principles of a quasi-teleological sort (such as conservation principles or least-action principles), but we may sometimes achieve the same result (less easily and elegantly) without invoking these principles, by proceeding at the micro-level of causal analysis. Or, again, a certain theoretical concept may be one which has a summary function, or which characterizes a complex configuration by reference to certain summarizing quantities, so that the attribution of a certain value of the summarizing quantity follows necessarily from what would be a huge conjunction (or disjunction of conjunctions) of statements about the components. In such situations, there is a noncontroversial sense in which one who omits mention of the summarizing quantity may be said to have "left something out of his description," because he did not say everything that might correctly be said. Putting it more strongly, he omitted saying something that is necessarily true on the basis of those things he has in fact said. But I think we should not say that he has given a *defective* causal account because of this omission, inasmuch as the omitted statement concerning the summarizing quantity is virtually present (in the sense of logical entailment) given the nomologicals, and/or explicit definitions, in the statements he has made. Example: I place a block of ice in the center of a room which is being kept warm by a roaring fire in the fireplace. An omniscient physicist provides me with the monstrous conjunction of micro-statements regarding the collisions of individual air molecules with the molecules at the icecake's surface and a blow-by-blow quantum-mechanical account of the manner in which the intra-molecular forces holding each particular molecule in its position in the ice crystal are counteracted, so that this molecule becomes free of the crystal, i.e., becomes part of the fluid. At no point does he employ the terms 'crystal,' 'melt,' 'fluid,' and even his references to the internal geometry of the ice crystal are clumsily formulated by a complicated conjunction that avoids reference to planes, lattices, and the like. Now the true statements involving all of these macro-and intermediate-level concepts are, given the explicit and contextual definitions of these terms in physical theory, to be found among the sentences that follow nomologically from this vast conjunction of sentences characterizing the micro-states and micro-events which he does utter. I do not believe that anyone could object to such an account, other than on aesthetic grounds or because of its cumbersomeness. That is, one could not object by saying that the causal account has been rendered somehow incomplete by the failure of the physicist to include mention of all the sentences, and therefore the words that would normally occur in such sentences, at a more molar level of causal understanding. No one would object to this account by saying, ''That's all very well, but it won't do as a complete causal explanation of what took place, because you have described the situation as if the difference in temperature between the cake of ice and its surroundings was irrelevant, i.e., that such a temperature differential had no efficacy, that the fact that the ice was colder than the fire-heated air *made no difference*.'' To say that this micro-account is defective because it suggests that the temperature difference between the ice and the surrounding air ''had no effect,'' ''was irrelevant,'' ''made no difference,'' or that it was some kind of a ''supernumerary,'' ''mere parallel,'' or ''epiphenomenon,'' would be misleading. The complete characterization of the situation concerning the surrounding air, and the causal explanation of that situation by reference to the chemical changes taking place in the fireplace, obviously do ''make a difference,'' in the literal sense that if those circumstances had been other than they in fact were, the micro-events described in the huge conjunction of statements about the freeing of the individual molecules of water from their crystalline state would not have been true. The conjunction of a vast set of sentences about the molecular motions of the air together with the conjunction of statements about the molecules in the ice, entail a statement that the summarizing quantity known as ''temperature'' will be higher in the one than in the other.

Consider a nonpsychological case in the animate domain. A biochemist describes the processes which go on in a man's blood chemistry over a period of years at the biochemical level. A physical chemist explains the micro-details of how these various values of blood concentrations bring about a deposition of lipids in the intima of the coronary artery. A physicist gives us a detailed micro-account (in terms of Euler's equations, etc.) of the hydrodynamic situation at this site, resulting from the narrowing of the arterial lumen. A physiologist provides an explanation of what happens in the individual cells of the cardiac muscle itself as a consequence of the reduced oxygen supply and deficient rate of removal of metabolic products, including a micro-characterization of processes which a cytologist, *if asked*, would recognize as constituting ''death of the individual cell.'' Now one might legitimately complain of this account (especially if he were in the life-insurance business, or a close friend of the family's, or the attending physician) that it fails to state something that was literally true, something that should appropriately be said at another level of analysis, namely, that the patient suffered a myocardial infarction as a result of a coronary occlusion. But it would be misleading for this objector to say that the team (physical chemist + biochemist + physicist + physiologist + cytologist) had "left something out of the account," if by that is meant that there was some further event, entity, or process at work influencing the chain of causality and that this something had been omitted from the description. It would be very wrong of the critic to say, "You have described this as if it made no difference in causing the man's death that he had a coronary occlusion which produced a myocardial infarction." Nothing of the sort. The conjunction of lower level statements made by our five-man basic science team, when taken together with the explicit definitions of the science of pathology, is an assertion that the patient suffered a coronary occlusion leading to a myocardial infarction.

Again, suppose we consider two flywheels having the same mass but different physical dimensions, whereby one has a much larger radius of gyration than the other. We inquire about the torque necessary to accelerate these flywheels to a specified rate of revolution, but we do this by considering the transmission of the applied force through the material particle by particle, and by literally summing these billions of components, rather than performing the usual integration analytically from the geometry of the two flywheels. Of course it turns out that in spite of their equal masses, a greater torque is required to achieve a stated angular acceleration in the case of the flywheel whose mass can be considered as concentrated at a greater distance from the center. But we do not explicitly mention this in our causal explanation. Would anyone object to our causal account, saying it was "incomplete" because it "treated the radius of gyration as something lacking in relevance or effect"?

Whether or not one would "normally" or "naturally" employ locutions of an intentional or quasi-purposive type in vulgar speech is, of course, largely lacking in scientific or philosophical interest. So long as we understand the causal and logical categories and their relationships to one another in the various contexts, whether we opt for one or another label is uninterestingly stipulative. My intuitions about what the usage of vulgar speech would be in a given setting are, like everyone else's, armchair speculations based on anecdotal impressions and lacking in such scientific support as might be obtained through a properly designed sampling procedure with the best available methods of psycholinguistic investigation. What sentences the alleged "plain man" would be willing (or reluctant) to token in regard to the behavior and "mental processes" of a digital computer which beats him at a game of checkers is one of the dullest topics imaginable, and cuts no philosophical or scientific ice so far as I am concerned. My own references in this paper to what (in my armchair opinion) we would "ordinarily" or "naturally" say are intended pedagogically and psychotherapeutically, and nothing really hinges upon these educated guesses of mine. I am not interested in armchair psycholinguistics, whether Oxbridge or Minneapolis style; and I should not dream of deciding a scientific or philosophical question on the basis of what

I guessed would be the verbal behavior of a (hypothetical) uninformed layman were he asked to think about difficult and obscure matters which he does not in fact think about, and lacks adequate conceptual equipment to think about.

It is, nevertheless, instructive from the standpoint of curing one's own intuitive resistances to pinpoint their source, considering a variety of examples with an eye to analyzing carefully those in which one experiences considerable ambivalence with respect to the use of quasi-mentalistic or quasi-purposive labels as applied to an inanimate system. Speaking for myself (and I invite the reader to consider whether this may be true of him also), it is my impression that when the element of sentience either is excludable in high probability or is irrelevant (because it is not supposed to be causally efficacious, or because it is clearly present in *both* systems under comparison), the human/subhuman or even animate/inanimate dichotomy sometimes receives less subjective weight in our readiness to employ purposive or intentional locutions than does the question whether the process under study has in it some features of "matching" or "comparison" of the actual with the ideal. So that when an inanimate physical system has a structure which enables it to function as a kind of "judge" or "comparator," which "applies criteria," we readily employ mentalistic verbs such as 'sort,' 'classify,' or 'test'; whereas we are reluctant to employ such language, *even with respect to an organic system*, if this element of judging, of comparing, of determining whether something satisfies a condition is utterly lacking.

It is true that in such cases we are aware of the fact that a human mind constructed the inanimate mechanism for a certain purpose, and it is sometimes argued that *this* understood origin and (human) purpose is what justifies the use of such mentalistic language in speaking of a calculating machine. There is no doubt considerable truth to this, and I have no wish to play it down. However, I wish to maintain that such an empirically based comprehension of the human designer's purpose in building the inorganic machine is, while typically present, not a necessary condition for properly applying some (not all) of these "criteria"-flavored words. For example, there are machines the function of which, *part by part*, a layman with a rudimentary understanding of mechanics and mathematics could be brought to understand, but the overarching industrial or scientific purpose to which they were put might baffle him. He might not have anything like an adequate comprehension of the desired "end product" envisaged by the engineer who built the machine to satisfy certain human motives, but he might nevertheless be capable of *characterizing the properties* of the end product satisfactorily. Or, to take a science-fiction example, suppose we find, on geological excavation in the pre-Cambrian rock strata, several complicated apparatuses on which no written instructions are provided in a language we understand, but there is a small plate showing a picture of what appears to be a large bird fastened in the machine. We get ourselves an adult male ostrich and find that he "fits into the machine" with a little adjusting here and there, and when we start the thing running it turns out that what it does is to pluck prime-numbered feathers in a line running down the ostrich's back. This would be pretty spooky, and we might have a very difficult time understanding what a pre-Cambrian somebody was up to, but after experimenting with several ostriches on several of these "extinct machines," we would be entitled to say that, odd though it is, there is good evidence that the "purpose" or "function" of the machine was to pluck out the prime-numbered feathers from ostriches. Point: One does not need to understand the overarching "why," the *ultimate* "end in view," of the maker of the machine in order to infer something about the characteristic end product, as *proximate* "end in view," which results from the machine's operation. In fact, we do not always presume a designer (or plan or prevision) when asking quasi-teleological questions; witness the atheist zoologist or anatomist who undertakes research to answer the question "What is this organ *for?*" — a question which is, given careful formulation, surely sensible aside from one's views on natural theology. The most incisive and illuminating discussion of this problem that I know of is by Nagel.[34]

At the risk of boring the reader, let me consider one last example, to highlight the problem of causal analysis in relation to abstract universals, when the latter are allowed to go unmentioned in a (purportedly complete) causal account. We have a simple industrial testing machine, a plate with an elliptical-shaped hole in it, the hole being made slightly larger than any of a batch of elliptical-shaped tiles which the machine is to "test." The machine has "arms" that place each tile in position above the hole, and then proceed to rotate the tile slightly in both directions from its initial position, the rotation being smooth (or at least by steps of very small angles) so that an optimal placement will not be inadvertently "missed." The relationship between the distribution of sizes of the ellipses and the amount of "play" in the hole is such that an elliptical tile whose major and minor axes are in any ratio between 6:8 and 7:8 will be capable of falling through the hole and dropping into a collecting box below. Otherwise the machine throws the tile aside. Now suppose someone provides a detailed account of exactly what happens in the sequence of operations involved in testing 100 consecutive tiles on this machine. He describes the form of the testing slot by stating the coordinates of a very large number of points on its edge (located, say, 1 millimeter apart). Thus he does not write any mathematical function in the familiar algebraic form, although he does in effect write a function for it in the sense of providing a finite set of ordered pairs of numbers. After having thus "tested" 100 tiles, ending up with 97 of them in the box (these having passed through the test slot successfully) and 3 "rejects," and having given a detailed account of the sequence of events as each tile was being tested, our nonmathematical mechanic offers this as a complete causal account of what happened. But now a critic advances the following: "You are assuming, in your alleged complete causal account, that the elliptical shape is of no relevance, that the relation of the major to minor axes in the tiles makes no difference." He makes this objection on the ground that we have not made any reference to the word 'ellipse,' or said anything about major and minor axes. Would this criticism be valid? We would admit that critic is now pointing out something which is literally and physically true about the sequence of events, namely, that *whether or not a particular tile ends up in the box or as a reject depends upon whether it meets or fails to meet a certain geometrical specification.* This specification, that of 'being an ellipse' (with a certain range of tolerance permitted in the ratio of the axes), has been ''left out'' of our account. So we have not said everything that could be said. But would one infer from this that mechanism or physical determinism must be false as an ontology of testing machines, or that a reified platonic universal (some sort of ideal elliptical tile laid up in heaven) must get into the act somewhere to see to it that things go properly?

An ellipse is an abstraction, a universal belonging to the domain of a formal science, which certain material objects may ''model'' (in the usual sense that a model is a set of entities that satisfies a calculus). What we have presented, in our allegedly complete physicalistic description of the slot, when we specified the coordinates of the points running along the edge 1 millimeter apart, is a set of statements which collectively entail that a tile which passes through is of elliptical shape, with axes in the range 6:8 to 7:8.

Keeping in mind my exclusion of the two considerations beyond the scope of this paper (the subjective-experiential aspect of the mental and the motivational or purposive), let us imagine a critic who adopts Popper's view about the causal efficacy of universals to advance the following: Your account leaves out any reference to the abstract universal *ellipticity*; you describe what goes on as if ellipticity was irrelevant, as if it made no difference to what happens. But the truth of the matter is the ellipticity is the core of the whole process of sorting by this machine; it is precisely the fact and amount of ellipticity of a particular tile that makes the difference between the two grossly different outcomes of a test—to be 'accepted' or to be 'rejected' by the machine. Evaluating ellipticity is what the machine does, and you have left that out entirely. How can your account be complete, when it treats the abstract universal *ellipticity* as an irrelevancy, as something one can mention or not as he pleases, since it makes no difference to what happens?

In order to decide how much truth there is in this objection, we must first explicate what it means to say that the fact of ellipticity is treated by the microanalyst as ''making no difference to what happens.'' The most straightforward explication of the phrase 'such-and-such a factor *makes no difference*' would seem to be that the outcome, given the factor's presence, is indistinguishable in all respects from the outcome that would have eventuated assuming the factor to have been absent. So we unpack the criticism ''You say that ellipticity makes no difference'' as being an assertion by the critic to the following effect: ''The non-mathematical mechanician, by putting forth (as allegedly complete) a causal analysis which makes no mention of ellipticity, thereby implies that if the shape of the testing matrix had been other than elliptical, the results would have been the same as they in fact were. Or, in terms of an individual tile (axes 7.5:8) which was accepted, if that tile had been circular, or had axes in the ratio 5:8, it would nevertheless have been accepted.'' But of course this is false, and is not being asserted by the mechanician. Not only does the mechanician avoid asserting this false counterfactual; he does not assert anything which implies it. On the contrary, what he says *does* imply a counterfactual contradictory to the one imputed, namely, ''If the shape of the sorting machine slot had been other than elliptical, the outcome would have been different, i.e., the tiles which dropped through and the tiles which were cast aside ('rejected') would have been different from the tiles that were in fact passed and cast aside.'' It is one thing to point out, quite rightly, that the mechanical account of the machine's operations fails to mention something which is true, and which follows necessarily from what was mentioned. In this sense the critic is correct in saying ''Something has been left out of the account.'' But this something which has been left out is not a something which involves any new ontological commitments about the furniture of the world, nor is it something which gets us into trouble with the thesis of mechanical determinism. What *would* involve some sort of additional ontological commitments, and would presumably mean that the causal account of the micromechanical determinist was defective (i.e., literally left something out, failed to mention a causally significant property), would be an asserted or implied counterfactual, ''The elliptical form as a universal instantiated by this particular machine is irrelevant to what the machine does.'' But that counterfactual is neither asserted nor implied; on the contrary, its contradictory is implied by the mechanical account, even though that account does not use the word ''ellipse'' or any short synonym thereof. What the account does contain is the large conjunction of sentences giving coordinates of points on the edge, and these coordinates satisfy the equation of an ellipse. Putting aside the necessary refinements of tolerance, physical discontinuity, etc., the mechanician's clumsy conjunction of statements entails (given the definition of an ellipse) that ''ellipticity makes a difference in what happens.'' What more does the critic want?

It is difficult to summarize the argument presented in the preceding pages. There are five related lines of thought. First, I warn against the temptation to identify ''determining factors'' in human belief with ''non-rational'' (e.g., Freudian, Marxian) factors, emphasizing that we have all learned logic as well as other things and that ''to think logically'' is part of our cerebral computer's programming. Second, I hold that *logical* categories are unavoidable for the psychologist who wishes to deal with human behavior. Third, I argue that the Platonic universals of logic (e.g., Rule of Detachment, *modus tollens*, *dictum de omni et nullo*) are physically modeled by certain subsystems of the human brain, so that—absent countervailing *non*rational forces of Freudian or Marxian type—it tends (statistically) to ''think rationally.'' Fourth, I hold that when a physical system models a calculus, a knower K_c who understand the calculus and knows how to derive theorems within it will have a genuine cognitive edge over a less well-informed knower K_m who knows *everything* K_c knows about the machine's parts + arrangement + laws of mechanics, but who lacks K_c's expertise with the calculus. This genuine cognitive edge is literally *physical* in its content, inasmuch as K_c can actually make correct predictions about the future movements of the machine which K_m cannot make. Fifth, I argue that even if a complete physicalistic micro-causal account might be given of human, rational decision-making — an account that contains no explicit reference to *reasons* — the truth of such a complete micro-causal account would be compatible with a "molar" account truly asserting that *reasons decisively influenced the choice*.

As I stated at the beginning, none of these arguments is intended to show that complete psychological determinism obtains, a thesis which I consider open on present evidence, and unnecessary for the current conducting of psychological research.

Notes

1. K. R. Popper, "Of Clouds and Clocks: An Approach to the Problem of Rationality and the Freedom of Man," the Arthur Holly Compton Memorial Lecture presented at Washington University, April 21, 1965 (St. Louis: Washington University, 1966). All quotations of Popper's language are from this source.

2. In recognizing the unblinkable fact that Skinner's epoch-making book *The Behavior of Organisms* (New York: Appleton-Century-Crofts, 1938) gave rise to a technology of behavior control which has, to an unprejudiced mind, no real competitors, I do not commit myself as regards its long-term *theoretical* adequacy. As would be true for most of my philosophical readers, I have grave reservations about Skinner's account of language, in his *Verbal Behavior* (New York: Appleton-Century-Crofts, 1957), vigorously attacked by N. Chomsky, "Review of *Verbal Behavior*, by B. F. Skinner," *Language*, 35 (1959), 26–58. But see K. MacCorquodale, "On Chomsky's Review of Skinner's *Verbal Behavior*," *Journal of the Experimental Analysis of Behavior*, 13 (1970), 83–99. I also believe the Skinnerian group underestimates the importance of genetic factors — and resulting real taxonomic entities — in behavior disorder, and hence they underrate the importance of formal diagnosis, although there is nothing about the theoretical position that requires this attitude. Finally, as a psychotherapist I have reservations about the adequacy with which Freud's constructs are translated into behaviorese by J. G. Holland and B. F. Skinner in *The Analysis of Behavior* (New York: McGraw-Hill, 1961), a programmed text which I recommend to readers approaching this subject matter for the first time. Another good introductory presentation can be found in B. F. Skinner, *Science and Human Behavior* (Cambridge, Mass.: Harvard University Press, 1951). See also, but requiring varying amounts of technical preparation, B. F. Skinner, *Cumulative Record* (New York: Appleton-Century-Crofts, 1961); T. Verhave, ed., *The Experimental Analysis of Behavior: Selected Readings* (New York: Appleton-Century-Crofts, 1966); T. Ayllon and N. Azrin, *The Token Economy: A Motivational System for Therapy and Rehabilitation* (New York: Appleton-Century-Crofts, 1968); L. Krasner and L. P. Ullmann, eds., *Research in Behavior Modification* (New York: Holt, Rinehart and Winston, 1965); L. P. Ullmann and L. Krasner, eds., *Case Studies in Behavior Modification* (New York: Holt, Rinehart and Winston, 1965); R. Ulrich, T. Stachnik, and J. Mabry, eds., *Control of Human Behavior* (Glenview, Ill.: Scott, Foresman, 1966); B. F. Skinner, *The Technology of Teaching* (New York: Appleton-Century-Crofts, 1968); C. B. Ferster and B. F. Skinner, *Schedules of Reinforcement* (New

York: Appleton-Century-Crofts, 1957); W. K. Honig, ed., *Operant Behavior: Areas of Research and Application* (New York: Appleton-Century-Crofts, 1966); and A. C. Catania, ed., *Contemporary Research in Operant Behavior* (Glenview, Ill.: Scott, Foresman, 1968).

3. See C. G. Hempel, "The Concept of Rationality and the Logic of Explanation by Reasons," pp. 463–86 in his *Aspects of Scientific Explanation* (New York: Free Press, 1965); G. H. von Wright, "The Logic of Practical Discourse," pp. 141–67 in R. Klibansky, ed., *Contemporary Philosophy* (Florence: Nuova Italia, 1968); A. Pap, *An Introduction to the Philosophy of Science* (New York: Free Press, 1962), pp. 263–67; a very stimulating analysis and criticism of "the view that meaningful human actions are not amenable to causal, scientific explanation" is May Brodbeck's "Meaning and Action," *Philosophy of Science*, 30 (1963), 309–24. Because her mode of resolution is incommensurable with mine, and repudiates the mind-body identity thesis presupposed in Professor Popper's formulation of "Compton's problem"—see her "Mental and Physical: Identity versus Sameness," in P. K. Feyerabend and G. Maxwell, eds., *Mind, Matter, and Method* (Minneapolis: University of Minnesota Press, 1966), pp. 40–58—I have not found it feasible under space limitations to integrate Professor Brodbeck's discussion into my paper.

4. Essays 3 and 7, this volume; H. Feigl, *The "Mental" and the "Physical": The Essay and a Postscript* (Minneapolis: University of Minnesota Press, 1967).

5. Essay 3, this volume.

6. W. Sellars, "Empiricism and the Philosophy of Mind," in H. Feigl and M. Scriven, eds., *Minnesota Studies in the Philosophy of Science*, vol. I (Minneapolis: University of Minnesota Press, 1956), p. 328. Also in *Science, Perception, and Reality* (New York: Humanities, 1963); W. Sellars, "Thought and Action," in K. Lehrer, ed., *Freedom and Determinism* (New York: Random House, 1966); R. Chisholm and W. Sellars, "Intentionality and the Mental," in H. Feigl, M. Scriven, and G. Maxwell, eds., *Minnesota Studies in the Philosophy of Science*, vol. II (Minneapolis: University of Minnesota Press, 1958), Appendix, pp. 507–39.

7. Ruth Macklin, "Doing and Happening," *Review of Metaphysics*, 22 (1968), 246–61, quoted from 257–58. See also the same author's "Action, Causality, and Teleology," *British Journal for the Philosophy of Science*, 19 (1969), 301–16.

8. M. Weber, "A Critique of Eduard Meyer's Methodological Views" (1905), in Max Weber, *Methodology of the Social Sciences*, ed. E. A. Shils and H. A. Finch (New York: Free Press, 1949). I am indebted to my Law School colleague Professor Carl Auerbach for calling this reference to my attention.

9. See, however, essay 3, this volume.

10. For a fascinating—although, in the end, somehow unsatisfying—analysis of the concept *rational* as applied to imaginary dance-language of bees, see J. Bennett, *Rationality* (London: Routledge and Kegan Paul, 1964).

11. See essay 7, this volume, pp. 188, 231-233.

12. R. Carnap, *Foundations of Logic and Mathematics*, vol. 1, no. 3 of *International Encyclopedia of Unified Science*, ed. O. Neurath (Chicago: University of Chicago Press, 1939), pp. 6–7.

13. E. C. Tolman, *Purposive Behavior in Animals and Men* (New York: Appleton-Century-Crofts, 1932), pp. 3–23 and *passim*; E. C. Tolman, *Collected Papers in Psychology* (Berkeley: University of California Press, 1951); C. L. Hull, *Principles of Behavior* (New York: Appleton-Century-Crofts, 1943), pp. 19–21; B. F. Skinner, *The Behavior of Organisms* (New York: Appleton-Century-Crofts, 1938), pp. 3–6, 33–43; R. A. Littman and E. Rosen, "Molar and Molecular," *Psychological Review*, 57 (1950), 58–65; H. A. Murray, *Explorations in Personality* (New York: Wiley, 1938), pp. 55–58, 96–97; K. MacCorquodale and P. E. Meehl, "Edward C. Tolman," in W. K. Estes *et al.*, *Modern Learning Theory* (New York: Appleton-Century-Crofts, 1954), especially pp. 218–31; and the operant behaviorists generally, cited in footnote 2 *supra*.

14. K. Sayre, *Recognition: A Study in Artificial Intelligence* (Notre Dame, Ind.: University of Notre Dame Press, 1965).

15. R. S. Woodworth and S. B. Sells, "An Atmosphere Effect in Formal Syllogistic Reasoning," *Journal of Experimental Psychology*, 18 (1935), 451–60; for a summary of this and related studies, see generally R. S. Woodworth, *Experimental Psychology* (New York: Holt, 1938), pp. 810–17.

16. R. Carnap, *Logical Syntax of Language*, trans. Amethe Smeaton (New York: Humanities, 1937), p. 7.

17. *Ibid.*, pp. 282–83.

18. *Ibid.*, p. 284.

19. W. Sellars, "Pure Pragmatics and Epistemology," *Philosophy of Science*, 14 (1947), 181–82.

20. *Ibid.*, pp. 184–85. No philosopher or psychologist concerned with the "rules-and-facts" problems of semiotic can afford to leave Sellars's contributions unread or unstudied. See especially his "A Semantical Solution of the Mind-Body Problem," *Methodos*, 5 (1953), 45–85, and "Intentionality and the Mental [correspondence with Professor Roderick Chisholm]," in Feigl, Scriven, and Maxwell, eds., *Minnesota Studies in the Philosophy of Science*, vol. II, Appendix, pp. 507–39. See also "Epistemology and the New Way of Words," *Journal of Philosophy*, 44 (1947), 645–60; "Realism and the New Way of Words," *Philosophy and Phenomenological Research*, 8 (1948), 601–34; "Mind, Meaning, and Behavior," *Philosophical Studies*, 3 (1952), 83–94; "Some Reflections on Language Games," *Philosophy of Science*, 21 (1954), 204–28; "Empiricism and the Philosophy of Mind," in Feigl and Scriven, eds., *Minnesota Studies in the Philosophy of Science*, vol. I; and "Empiricism and Abstract Entities," in P. A. Schilpp, ed., *The Philosophy of Rudolf Carnap* (LaSalle, Ill.: Open Court, 1964).

21. H. Reichenbach, *Experience and Prediction* (Chicago: University of Chicago Press, 1938), pp. 110–14.

22. H. A. Murray, *Explorations in Personality* (New York: Wiley, 1938), pp. 55–59, 96–101.

23. R. B. Cattell, *Description and Measurement of Personality* (Yonkers-on-Hudson: World, 1946), pp. 64–66, 74, 496; *Personality* (New York: McGraw-Hill, 1950), pp. 33–36.

24. A. S. Eddington, *Science and the Unseen World* (New York: Macmillan, 1929). The book is inaccessible to me at this writing so that while the basic puzzle is due to Eddington, the formulation of conditions is mine and may not accord precisely with his original setup.

25. See Sellars, publications cited in footnote 20 *supra*.

26. Popper, "Of Clouds and Clocks," p. 11.

27. E.g., N. Bohr, *Atomic Theory and the Description of Nature* (New York: Macmillan, 1934); J. C. Eccles, "Hypotheses Relating to the Brain-Mind Problem," *Nature*, 68 (1951), 53–57; J. C. Eccles, *The Neurophysiological Basis of Mind* (Oxford: Oxford University Press, 1953), pp. 271–86; A. S. Eddington, *The Philosophy of Physical Science* (Cambridge: Cambridge University Press, 1939), pp. 179–84; *The Nature of the Physical World* (New York: Macmillan, 1929), pp. 310–15; *New Pathways in Science* (New York: Macmillan, 1935), pp. 86–91; P. Jordan, *Science and the Course of History* (New Haven, Conn.: Yale University Press, 1955), pp. 108–13; I. D. London, "Quantum Biology and Psychology," *Journal of General Psychology*, 46 (1952), 123–49; P. E. Meehl, "Determinism and Related Problems," chapter VIII, especially pp. 190–91, and footnotes 30, 31, pp. 213–15, and Appendix E, "Indeterminacy and Teleological Constraints," pp. 328–38, in P. E. Meehl *et. al.*, *What, Then, Is Man?* (St. Louis: Concordia, 1958; while I no longer hold the theological position presupposed in that discussion, the treatment of determinism and speculative brain processes still appears to me as essentially defensible); Meehl, essay 7, this volume, pp. 199-201; M. H. Pirenne and F. H. C. Marriott, "The Quantum Theory of Light and the Psychophysiology of Vision," in S. Koch, ed., *Psychology, a Study of a Science*, vol. 1: *Sensory, Perceptual and Physiological Formulations* (New York: McGraw-Hill, 1959), pp. 288–361; F. Ratliff, "Some Interrelations among Physics, Physiology, and Psychology in the Study of Vision," especially pp. 442–45, in S. Koch, ed., *Psychology, a Study of a Science*, vol. 4: *Biologically Oriented Fields* (New

York: McGraw-Hill, 1962). For criticism of the notion that quantum-indeterminacy at the single-unit micro-level could be relevant to psychological determinism at the level of molar behavior or experience, see E. Schroedinger, *Science and Humanism* (Cambridge: Cambridge University Press, 1951), pp. 58–64; A. Grünbaum, "Causality and the Science of Human Behavior," in H. Feigl and M. Brodbeck, eds., *Readings in the Philosophy of Science* (New York: Appleton-Century-Crofts, 1953); Lizzie S. Stebbing, "Causality and Human Freedom," in her *Philosophy and the Physicists* (London: Methuen, 1937), pp. 141–242; and section X, pp. 13–14, of Professor Popper's lecture.

28. J. R. Platt, *The Step to Man* (New York: Wiley, 1966), pp. 147–49. The point has been made by several writers.

29. K. R. Popper, "Epistemology without a Knowing Subject," in B. Van Rootselaar and J. F. Staal, eds., *Logic, Methodology and Philosophy of Science*, vol. III (Amsterdam: North-Holland, 1968), pp. 333–73.

30. L. Wittgenstein, *Tractatus Logico-Philosophicus* (London: K. Paul, Trench, Trubner, 1922), Propositions 3.031–3.0321; see also K. R. Popper, "Why Are the Calculi of Logic and Arithmetic Applicable to Reality?" in his *Conjectures and Refutations* (New York and London: Basic Books, 1962), pp. 201–14.

31. A. Samuels, "Some Studies in Machine Learning Using the Game of Checkers," *IBM Journal of Research and Development*, 3 (1959), 210–29.

32. A. Newell, J. C. Shaw, and H. A. Simon, "Empirical Explorations with the Logic Theory Machine," *Proceedings of the Western Joint Computer Conference*, 11 (1957), 218–30; "Report on a General Problem Solving Program," *Proceedings of the International Conference on Information Processing* (Paris: UNESCO, 1959), pp. 256–64. See generally E. Hunt, "Computer Simulation: Artificial Intelligence Studies and Their Relevance to Psychology," in P. R. Farnsworth, M. R. Rosenzweig, J. T. Polefka, eds., *Annual Review of Psychology*, 19 (1968), 135–68. A. Newell, J. C. Shaw, and H. A. Simon, "Note: Improvement in the Proof of a Theorem in the Elementary Propositional Calculus," C.I.P. Working Paper no. 8, January 13, 1958.

33. S. Freud, "The Unconscious," in J. Strachey, ed., *Standard Edition of the Complete Psychological Works of Sigmund Freud*, vol. 14 (London: Macmillan, 1957), pp. 159–216; Tolman, *Purposive Behavior in Animals and Men*.

34. E. Nagel, *The Structure of Science* (New York: Harcourt, Brace and World, 1961), chapter 12. See also C. G. Hempel, "The Logic of Functional Analysis," in L. Gross, ed., *Symposium on Sociological Theory* (New York: Harper, 1959); reprinted with alterations in C. G. Hempel, *Aspects of Scientific Explanation* (New York: Free Press, 1965), pp. 297–330.

3

The Determinism-Freedom and Body-Mind Problems

with Herbert Feigl

Our cherished friend, Sir Karl, has very penetratingly and challengingly dealt in several essays[1] with two of the most difficult and controversial issues of modern philosophy and science. In accordance with Popper's own designations we shall speak of "Compton's problem" and "Descartes's problem." Compton's problem is how to account for free choice and genuine (artistic or scientific) creativity; Descartes's problem concerns the relation of the mental to the physical. These problems are closely related, and both are viewed by Popper in the light of modern physics, biology, psychology and the theory of language. Although we do not pretend to know of any definitive solutions of either problem, and although we tend to agree with several important points made by Popper, we propose to submit to him a number of critical reflections. What we hope to show is that the "plastic" (or "cloudlike") control stressed by Popper does not necessarily require a basic indeterminism; and that the role of meanings and reasons in the representative and argumentative functions of language does not necessarily imply a dualism of mind and body.

I

Popper's "nightmare of determinism" — very much like the dread of the "block universe" of William James — seems to us to rest on identifying determinism with strict predictability. We can hardly believe that Popper regards these terms as synonymous. If so, this could only be due to an unrelinquished remnant of positivistic thinking in the keenest and most outstanding contemporary critic of positivism. It seems quite unlikely that Popper, for once, and quite contrary to his general enlightened attitude, has fallen victim to a verificationist prejudice. This would indeed be inconsistent with his pronouncements in other places on the *metaphysical*, i.e., untestable nature of the doctrine of determinism. In any case, we think that complete predetermination becomes a "nightmare" only if one as-

97

sumes that some sort of Laplacean World Formula could ever be produced by scientists. Such a World Formula would then—inserting the total set of specific numerical values for the initial and boundary conditions—furnish a World Calendar. In such a calendar one could look up one's own future, the future of mankind and of our planet in general, etc., in perfect detail; and if the basic laws are temporally symmetrical (as they are at least in classical physics), one could also reconstruct any phase of the historical, prehistorical, or cosmological past. It is the attainability of a World Formula thus understood which leads to absurdly paradoxical and abhorrently unpalatable consequences. Fatalism would then seem the only possible attitude. Any avoidance reaction to predictions of unpleasant or disastrous events would itself have to be derivable from the World Formula, and the well-known phenomenon of a self-annulling prediction would be logically impossible—as long as we assume the World Formula to be correct. Precise and detailed predictions of future works of art, of scientific theories, of the rise or decline of civilizations, etc., would all be attainable in terms of an accurate physicalistic description of every and all spatiotemporal events—indeed including the "putting of ink marks on paper"—be it a future composer's symphonic score, or the manuscript of a great mathematician or theoretical physicist of the year 2500! If such precise predictions were possible, then we might have full knowledge of scientific theories, or achievements of works of art, long before they were—respectively—invented or created. This is surely as logically incoherent an idea as is that of H. G. Wells's time machine! Furthermore, if the World Formula permitted the prediction of a fatal automobile accident which someone is to suffer at a definite place and a precise date—in the future, then he could not succeed in conveniently staying at home, and thus avoid the disaster. By a curious and intricate concatenation of circumstances he would nevertheless be "destined" to die in precisely the predicted circumstances, and in the specified space-time region. If the World Calendar contained a prediction of even some highly desired event, one could not—merely for the sake of disproving the World Formula—change the course of events such that the predicted one would not take place.

Considerations such as these have often been adduced as a reductio ad absurdum of determinism. But it should be clear that it is rather the attainability of the World Formula which the foregoing arguments refute. Now, as is agreed on all hands, the idea of the World Formula is to be understood as a logical conjunction of *three* propositions: (1) the doctrine of the deterministic form of all basic natural laws, (2) the precise, complete (and simultaneous) ascertainability of all initial and boundary conditions, (3) the mathematical feasibility of the hopelessly complex computations necessary for precise and complete predictions (or retrodictions). Now, as no one knows better than Popper (though this is really a matter of the most elementary propositional logic), if a conjunction of several independent propositions entails a false or absurd conclusion, not every one of the conjuncts is (necessarily) false. In the empirical sciences there are experimental or statistical methods to pinpoint the "culprit" (or culprits) among the conjoined premises. In our problem this is obviously impossible. Nevertheless, there are excellent reasons for regarding propositions (2) and (3) as false at any rate, thus leaving the hypothesis of determinism at least open for further consideration.

We should make it quite clear immediately that neither in the above remarks nor in what follows are we pleading for the doctrine of determinism. We consider it quite possible that the indeterminism of present quantum mechanics (or something akin to it) may never be overcome. On the other hand, it is conceivable that a future theory regarding a further substratum of micro-microevents might have deterministic form and be nonemergentist. The question as to what form—deterministic or statistical—the "rock bottom" laws of the universe have, is indeed never conclusively decidable; and this for the simple reason that there is not and could not be a criterion by which to recognize the "rock bottom" of nature. As David Bohm has suggested, it is logically conceivable that our universe may be "infinitely deep"—layer upon layer without end. Hence, the only sensible question to ask is whether at a given stage of scientific (experimental and theoretical) investigation the (on that level) basic laws are strictly causal (deterministic) or statistical (probabilistic). Hence, while we agree with Popper that neither the doctrine of determinism nor that of indeterminism is conclusively decidable,[2] we think that empirical evidence, that is reasons, can be adduced that justify a tentative endorsement of one or the other doctrine. Surely, if the triumphant successes of classical mechanics, and of the nineteenth-century field theories had continued to furnish adequate explanations in every domain of the empirical sciences, determinism would have remained a highly plausible frame hypothesis.

Since it is imperative for our conception of determinism to separate it quite radically from all references to prediction and predictability, perhaps an explicit formulation of "strict lawfulness" is needed. We suggest the following definition: Any event in the world (as described in the four-dimensional representation) instantiates a nomological proposition—i.e., either a basic or a derived law. Thus understood, the frame hypothesis of determinism is not hopelessly untestable. Indeed, it was the unexpected development of quantum physics in our century that for the first time cast *serious* doubt upon the determinism doctrine. But before we turn to the implications of indeterminism for "Compton's problem," let us show that the two other conjuncts in the World Formula doctrine are much more vulnerable than the idea of determinism. As Popper himself has shown,[3] even under the presupposition of the determinism of classical physics, there is a fundamental (we should think set-theoretical) impossibility in ascertaining and recording the initial and boundary conditions of a closed system. As long as the observing-measuring instrument and/or observer is part of the system under scrutiny, not all the system can be "mapped" on to part of itself. This would indeed seem a *logical* impossibility as regards proposition (2), i.e., of the full ascertainability of the total set of conditions. To this might be added the basic physical impossibility of knowing about incoming ''inputs'' before they have arrived. According to the extremely well-corroborated principles of the special theory of relativity, any ''messages,'' ''information'' (really any sort of propagation of causal influences) cannot occur at a velocity greater than the speed of electromagnetic waves. Hence—strictly speaking—there can be only ex post facto explanations of events—but no rigorous and completely reliable predictions of them. Only the events in Minkowski's ''passive light cone of the past'' can be adduced for predictions. Any events ''outside the cone'' can become known only after a certain time has elapsed. While Bergson (who never quite understood Einstein's theory) did not base his early pronouncement of free will (in the sense of prior unpredictability of action) on relativistic principles, he was, nevertheless, correct in claiming that most actions could be causally explained only after they had occurred. Hence, we agree with Popper that even on the basis of the theories of classical physics (including the special and general theories of relativity) complete and precise prediction is logically and physically impossible.

We disagree with Popper, however, if he views these impossibilities of prediction as arguments against determinism. (They are, we insist, decisive arguments only against the feasibility of the World Formula.) We view the doctrine of determinism as meaningful, coherent, though, of course, only very inconclusively testable. Perhaps this merely reveals that—Popper's critique to the contrary notwithstanding—we are not as radically anti-inductivistic as he is. The very fact that one could *reason* from the successes of classical physics to the (then) plausible assumption of determinism; and that the laws of classical physics are deterministic in their mathematical formulation—all this indicates that one can understand the meaning of determinism even if this doctrine is operationally and practically inconsequential. We do understand the counterfactual proposition: ''If the totality of initial and boundary conditions could be precisely ascertained; and if the laws are deterministic; and if the immensely complex computations could be accomplished, then every event in the universe could be exactly predicted (or retrodicted).'' This is the conjunction of our three propositions all over again. The idea of determinism by itself need not be wrong. It could—as it has for a long time—still serve as the guiding maxim of scientific research. It is merely ''sour grapes'' policy of scientists or philosophers of science, if they maintain that ''statistical causality'' is just as good as fully deterministic lawfulness. Einstein's well known opposition to regarding quantum mechanics as complete, emphatically expressed his conviction that nature ''at rockbottom''(?) is strictly deterministic. Having succeeded twice (viz., in his special and general theory of relativity) in a ''geometrization'' of physics, he hoped to succeed once more—in his attempts toward a unified field theory—to design a new fundamental account, and thus to eliminate the idea of ''absolute chance'' conclusively from all future science. To his great disappointment he failed in this ambitious endeavor.

On a much lower level of sophistication this "faith" in determinism is clearly exemplified by the traditional view of the games of chance. Which way spinning coins, or dice, or roulette balls, will come to rest is considered a matter of *relative chance*. The thought here is that the—no matter how complex and delicate—initial and boundary conditions strictly determine the outcome. And if we only knew their precise total constellation, we could predict the outcomes with full certainty and precision. The very concept of relative chance then presupposes determinism. Chance in this sense is relative in a twofold way: (1) Relative to our knowledge (or ignorance) the event in question is not precisely predictable. (2) The many factors or conditions relevant for the outcome have a high degree of causal independence from each other. This is the way we customarily view "accidents" or "coincidences," be it a cosmic collision of stars, or an automobile accident. Essentially this rests on the causally contingent relations of events that occur at a distance from one another and are (roughly) simultaneous. In the well-known four-dimensional representations this is indicated by the crossing of world-lines. In the games of chance (and as we shall see in a moment, also in the kinetics of molecules), there is the further very important aspect of the most "delicate" dependence of outcomes upon extremely small variations in the initial conditions. Whether, for example, a coin will come up heads or tails; or whether a ball on the Galton board will turn left or right after impinging on a given nail, will often depend—according to classical mechanics—on minimal differences in original positions, speeds, friction encountered, etc. Surely, here is one more extremely powerful argument for the impossibility of precise and certain predictions even under the presupposition of strict determinism.

Ascertaining by measurement of the initial conditions would have to be *completely* exact, for even infinitesimally small differences in the causal antecedents may result (by various amplification processes) in enormous differences in the ensuing effects. In other words, continuous variations in the initial conditions can bring about discontinuous changes in highly relevant features of the causal results. The ball coming down from a nail on the Galton board may finally reach one electric relay that brings about the ringing of a bell; or it may trigger off another relay, and thereby cause the explosion of a bomb. And if the initial conditions were such that the ball were coming down exactly vertically upon the nail, it should—after a few dampened bouncings—come to rest, in unstable equilibrium right on top of the nail. This latter—unheard of—event would, however, be excluded by the random (heat) motion of the molecules, both in the surface of the ball and in that of the nail. Since all measurements—even from the classical-deterministic point of view—are achieved by using macroinstruments, and since molecular motion (at least at temperatures above absolute zero) is unavoidable, there is even in the classical theory an ineluctable inaccuracy (i.e., an element of chance) in the results of even the most refined measurements.

There is no need, we are sure, for any elaborate argument regarding the overwhelming complexity of the calculations that would be required for precise predictions for any but the most simple (and idealized) systems and their "development." As all the world knows, this is the *raison d'être* of the statistical approach—be it in the games of chance, in matters of insurance, or in the kinetic theories of molecular motions. The sort of system of equations that would be required for detailed and precise predictions would obviously involve difficulties far surpassing those of the astronomical *n*-body problem. It is, moreover, quite conceivable that the pure mathematics of such calculations might run up against insoluble mathematical problems—in the sense of the undecidability discovered by Kurt Gödel.

However, all these considerations, we repeat, do not establish conclusive argument against determinism as such. To illustrate in terms of Popper's own example, the "behavior" of soap bubbles can be explained, as Ludwig Boltzmann might well have claimed, within a deterministic point of view. To be sure, precise predictions (e.g., of the moment of the bubble's bursting) are impossible—for the reasons already mentioned. Yet, according to Boltzmann's convictions, the kinetics of the air molecules inside and outside the bubble, as well as of the molecules constituting the thin "skin" of the bubble, might be construed in the light of Newtonian determinism. Boltzmann might have said that we have very good reasons for assuming such an "underlying" determinism, in spite of the hopelessness of detailed and exact predictability. Classical determinism (involving, of course, only concepts of *relative* chance) thus would provide a perfectly intelligible basis for the "plastic control" that Popper emphasizes. As he admits, "clouds" may well be "clocks" in this sense, after all. Very much, however, depends on what one means here by "in this sense." As Popper rightly sees, there is a continuum of degrees that lies between extreme cases of "clouds" and extreme cases of "clocks."

Analogous considerations apply to the differences of organisms and machines. Admittedly, there are tremendous differences between a simple mechanical machine (such as a system of levers and pulleys, or of cog wheels) and even the simplest organism, such as a protozoan. Perhaps even a difference in kind must be admitted between noncybernetic mechanisms and mechanisms involving self-regulation. We must not prejudge the issue by any simplistic "man a machine" conceptions. We are inclined to think that in any case machines made of hardware (vacuum tubes, transistors, wires, transmission gears) no matter how ingeniously constructed, will, at best, simulate (or perhaps even "outdo") only certain segments of human activities. Very likely only a structure composed of the proteins of the nervous system can function in the "creative" manner of the highest human achievements. An anecdote about a conversation between a brilliant avant-garde engineer and a great musician poignantly illustrates the issue. The engineer said: "Now we can build machines that compose works of music."

The musician replied: "Then you should also build some machines that will appreciate that sort of music." The point is well taken. Electronic "music" of the "aleatory" type is one of the atrocities of our age of technology. We agree wholeheartedly with Popper that human creativity cannot be explained on the basis of a "clock" (simple machine) theory of cerebral functioning.[4] We also agree that the combination of a machine with a built-in randomizer will not suffice either. But it has become increasingly clear that systems with "organismic" structures, i.e., involving Gestalt and cybernetic features, may well exemplify the typically "teleological" aspects of a great variety of physiological processes. This, together with whatever "randomizing" factors may be at play, could go a long way toward a deterministic explanation of the delicately attuned, but never fully predictable biological and psychological functions and occurrences.

As we understand Popper's views (especially in *Of Clouds and Clocks*), he rejects determinism to make room for an (unfortunately none too explicitly formulated) *emergentism*. Here again it seems imperative to us to distinguish between emergence in the sense of unpredictability, and emergence as involving a basic indeterminism. As has often been pointed out,[5] the impossibility of prediction in the cases of emergent novelty does not necessarily imply a denial of determinism. The familiar examples of the impossibility of predicting the properties of complexes (e.g., chemical compounds; organisms; social groups) on the basis of the properties of their constituent parts or components (e.g., chemical elements, cells, individual persons), do not establish an argument against the possibility of deterministic theories that would explain the properties of the "organic wholes." The arguments for "genuine emergence," along with the arguments for ("irreducible") holism appear plausible only as long as they are couched in *epistemic* terms. That is to say, if the properties of the parts or components have been explored only in "splendid isolation," there would hardly be any clue as to what sort of wholes (compounds, organisms, etc.) they might form when brought into interactions with each other. This is strikingly true even on the most elementary level of modern microphysics. A study of the behavior of "free" electrons (as in the cathode rays) would never suggest their "configurational behavior" in the context of even the simplest atoms. Pauli's exclusion principle (which is an independent postulate of quantum mechanics) may be considered a fundamental composition law; just as in classical mechanics the law of vectorial addition (i.e., the well-known parallelogram of forces) is a basic empirical law, logically independent of the other Newtonian laws of motion and of gravitation.

Just how far we have to explore more and more complex situations, constellations, and configurations in order to "glean" (pardon the "inductivism"!) the total set of laws sufficient for purely computational (i.e., mathematical, including geometrical) inference of regularities of complexes (wholes) cannot be decided in an a priori manner. By and large, the extant evidence encourages the view that chemistry is in principle reducible to atomic and quantum physics; and that biology (especially since the recent advances in the knowledge of the molecular structure of the nucleic acids) is equally—in principle (!)—reducible to modern physics. (This is not to deny that there are still grave unsolved problems in connection with the specifics of evolution, and other biological problems.)

The doctrine of "genuine emergence" is incompatible with the sort of reductionism just sketched only if new sorts of regularity were to crop up indefinitely at levels of higher complexity, and if these new regularities were absolutely underivable from the laws of some level of lower complexity. As we see it, there is no reason for such pessimism about the possibility of unitary scientific explanation. Quite to the contrary, there are important instances of the prediction of novel features on the basis of theories that were formulated *before* the resultant features of "compounded wholes" had been empirically known: Consider Mendeleev's predictions of new chemical elements, their properties, and the properties of their compounds; or the prediction of (artificial) fission and fusion of atomic nuclei; predictions of the phenotypical characteristics of organisms on the basis of the theory of genes, etc.

Even if such striking feats of prediction had not been achieved, the very possibility of *theories* from which the properties of "wholes" can be derived can certainly not be denied on a priori grounds; and, as just indicated, that possibility is becoming increasingly plausible in the light of empirical evidence. This is at least one type of argument for the compatibility of (epistemic) emergence with (theoretical or "ontological") determinism. And even disregarding high-level theories, the conditions and consequences of "emergence" could be stated in the form of empirical laws. Once the resultants of compounding processes have been observed, laws formulating antecedents as causally implying their consequents would be subject to corroboration. Of course, these laws may have deterministic form (as in most cases of chemical compounding) or they may be statistical (as in genetics). If they are ineluctably statistical, then a certain measure of indeterminacy would be characteristic of emergence. If they are deterministic, then one could always (retrospectively) formulate the regularities in terms of dispositional properties of the components. (For example, sodium and chlorine are "apt" to combine into ordinary salt.)

In general, the logical situation in regard to emergence seems to be as follows: Only if the concepts of the theories (or laws) which are to be reduced (i.e., derived, explained) are explicitly definable in terms of the concepts of the reducing theory, can the reduction (derivation) be accomplished. But, since this is merely a necessary and not a sufficient condition, emergence in the sense of nonderivability may yet obtain, even if the definability condition is fulfilled. Hence, we regard the problem of emergence as an empirical question.

It is generally agreed that, e.g., laws of electromagnetism are not derivable from the laws of classical mechanics. Thus one could say that the phenomena of electromagnetism are "emergent" with respect to mechanical phenomena. It is even tempting to say that a sort of "interaction" between the electromagnetic forces and the (mechanical) masses takes place — as in the cases of "ponderomotoric" electric forces or in the phenomena of light pressure. But it is highly questionable whether an analogous interaction may be assumed between mental states (once they have emerged — be it in the course of phylogenetic evolution or in the course of ontogenetic development) and the respective nervous systems. The resistance to this sort of doctrine among natural scientists and physicalistically oriented philosophers is not merely due to its "spookiness." The idea that "immaterial" mental factors somehow interact with, or intervene in, the physiological processes is not necessarily untestable, let alone meaningless. Of course, one would want to know more precisely what is meant by "immaterial" or "nonphysical." But once that is at least in outline specified, the remaining question is whether a hypothesis of this kind is needed. If some sort of nonphysical agent (let us call it "psychoid") is required to account for free choice and creativity, how are we to square this with all that is known about the factors that are relevant for the formation of the character, personality, and intelligence of human beings? Hereditary constitution as based on the genetic makeup, together with all the influences of maturation, education (positive and/or negative reinforcements in the physical and social environments), emulation of "father figures" (or oedipal reactions against them), etc., seems to offer a sufficient basis — and one that may well be, in principle, susceptible of a physicalistic account.

The repudiation of dualistic-interactionistic explanations can be understood, if not justified, in the light of all the accumulated scientific evidence that speaks for a view of causality that is "closed" in the physical world, i.e., not open to "miraculous" interventions by nonphysical causes. The retreat of animism and vitalism is surely due to the ever growing scope of physical explanations. Driesch, the well-known vitalist, some forty years ago postulated entelechies which, though not in space, were assumed to "act into space." And anyone who assumes that the indeterminism of modern physics allows for "loopholes" or a "leeway" for the intervention of nonphysical forces proposes in our century a doctrine homologous to the one proposed by Descartes in the seventeenth century. Descartes had to postulate a "breach" in the mechanical laws in the case of mental-physical interaction. Similarly, if there is to be anything testable in the twentieth-century idea that quantum indeterminism allows for (at least slight) influences of immaterial mental states upon the ongoing atomic processes in human brains, some sort of "breach" in, or deviation from, the statistical regularities would have to be assumed. Perhaps this sort of "violation" could be made more palatable by assuming that the local frequencies of quantum transitions (or the like) would be in keeping with the physical theory, but that a sort of "patterning" in the firing of neurons takes place which is not derivable from physical theory alone, and would thus require the intervention of a "psychoid." Hence, both Descartes and Compton alike make assumptions, which—if testable—deviate from what the physics of their respective times (seventeenth and twentieth centuries) would imply.

Naturally, all the remarks just made are merely the results of logical analyses. It does not seem likely that an experimental test will be forthcoming in the foreseeable future. Physicalistically oriented thinkers will insist that Compton merely repeated Descartes's mistaken reasoning on the more sophisticated level of twentieth-century science. Thinkers opposed to physicalism find this type of interactionism not so terribly "strange" after all. What we intended to point out is merely that some "tampering" with physical laws is unavoidable—even if the laws are partly (or largely) statistical, as they are in quantum mechanics.

Before turning to the role of meaning, rules, and norms in human behavior—and thus to "Descartes's problems," a few more remarks on free will are in order. Let us candidly admit that we, too, can feel the sting of this perennial puzzle. Surely, if we human beings are solely the products of "nature and nurture," i.e., of our inherited constitutions and all the influences that have impinged upon us ever since the fertilization of the ovum from which we developed—how are we to understand the sentence asserting "in the given life situation we *could have acted differently* from the way we actually did." G.E. Moore's well-known answer "we could have acted differently, had we wanted to" merely shifts the vexing question to the freedom of "wanting." Some misguided thinkers even went so far as to question the very idea of moral responsibility by pointing out that we did not make or choose our character or personality. The current revolt against the Hume-Mill-Schlick-Hobart "dissolution" of the free will versus determinism issue indicates that perhaps we latter-day "compatibilists" should add a few further clarifying observations to the old issue. Surely it must be admitted that, for example, Schlick, despite the great clarity of his thought on the issue, did, in part, misdiagnose its roots. Schlick was very likely wrong in thinking that the trouble stems from confusing descriptive (natural) law with prescriptive (judicial) law. We are not aware of any important philosopher who committed this error. But the "compatibilist" school of thought seems to us to have provided some very important and very illuminating considerations. There is first, the obvious distinction between voluntary and compelled action. Both can be understood on the basis of deterministic assumptions. Even purely behaviorally there are (almost in the sense of physics) "degrees of freedom" with respect to the environmental context of our voluntary action. The ball on the inclined plane is "bound to" roll down. But the rabbit on the hillside might well go up or sideways. And a human being on that same hillside may sing a song, write a letter or poem, do gynmastic exercises, or eat his lunch, etc. While this is only a beginning in the explication of "freedom of choice," it is an indispensable first step. It could be formulated in terms of the comparative predominance of the internal (intradermal) factors over the external (extradermal) ones in the causal determination of behavior. However, to define "free choice" merely negatively by the absence of compulsion, coercion, or constraint, though stating necessary conditions, is not by itself sufficient. Positively, there is the undeniable fact that in voluntary action, we are the doers of our deeds. Our character and personality, and our desires, express themselves in our deliberations, decisions, and actions. And although the causal account cannot as yet be given in all of its detail, it should be clear that we are essential links in the causal chains of such voluntary actions. Any choice we make after surveying and contemplating the possible avenues of actions reflects our character, our momentary attitudes, sentiments, and moods. Of course, any precise and fully reliable predictions are precarious, if not impossible. Nevertheless, even the very incomplete and inexact knowledge we have acquired of our relatives, friends, and close acquaintances, often enables us to foretell, with a high success frequency, their reactions to various life situations. We know what will please, amuse, or annoy them; we know their preferences — be it in the choice of foods or drinks, or in voting for political candidates. We know that employees practically always cash their salary checks (sooner or later — usually sooner).

The ascription of responsibility for an action necessarily involves (in addition to any moral-normative considerations) causal imputation. In common language this manifests itself even in locutions that have nothing to do with moral judgments. We say, e.g., "the earthquake is responsible for the devastation," "the landslide is responsible for the change in the river's course," etc. The work of a great artist or scientist is *his*, for the simple reason that *he* produced it — never mind in that context what "produced him"! If the music of Beethoven in his late quartets (Op. 127 to Op. 135) "reflects" something of his personality of that period, does this not mean that there is a causal relation between the composer and his work? To be sure, one must not be so naïve as to expect any simple and predictable relation here. Mozart produced some of his most serene and happy-sounding music in periods of great stress — if not distress. Nevertheless, there is no reason for abandoning the scientific approach which — no matter how qualified by probabilistic considerations — is after all *causal* analysis. And causal analysis, in modern interpretation, amounts to nothing else but the search for relevant variables and their lawful functional relationships. Surely coincidences of all sorts may have to be taken into account. Beethoven is reported to have been stimulated occasionally by hearing a popular tune whistled by someone in the streets of Vienna. Is this *fundamentally* different from the changes brought about in planetary motions by an "accidental" approach of a comet?

Summing up, we submit that what we know, cherish, and designate as "free choice" is not only compatible with determinism, but actually presupposes a large measure of it for the processes constituting human actions. As Popper rightly stresses, nothing is gained by the assumption of absolute chance — i.e., of completely uncaused action. What, then, could indeterminism do for genuine freedom? All it could do, we recapitulate, is to give us one more (and we admit, of course, fully decisive) argument against the attainability of the World Formula. It seems to us that the "nightmare" of the World Formula is indeed—on all counts—a chimera, a fantasy gone wild. It is in this sense on a par with theological doctrines of predestination. Divine omniscience poses exactly the same problem, and some brilliant theologians (like Jonathan Edwards) have seen quite clearly that this is perfectly compatible with human free will and moral responsibility.

Now let us face the free will perplexity once more in its moist poignant form: If strict determinism were true then there are no genuine alternatives for human action. "I could have done otherwise" can mean only that if I had been different (e.g., wiser or better) I would have acted differently. But precisely because human nature is "flexible," i.e., capable of learning from the lessons of experience, it can change from one occasion to the next. This is certainly a most important feature in which human beings (but also many species of animals) differ from *simple* automata whose internal structure is rigidly fixed, and thus not responsive to the "lessons of experience." The sentiment of regret, while phenomenologically directed upon the past act ("I wish I had not done it"), finds its pragmatic significance in the resolution to "reform" ("Next time I'll behave differently"). Moral responsibility presupposes responsiveness to the sanctions of society. The severely insane are therefore not held responsible. Does "making an effort" make a difference? It certainly does, at least sometimes. Why not view the human conscience (somewhat as Freud suggested in his "anatomy of the personality") as a subsystem of the person (physicalistically: the organism)? As such the superego is indeed involved in highly subtle interactions with other subsystems (the ego and the id). Hence if, for example, a certain type of education results in the formation of a powerful superego, this may well manifest itself in the type of conduct a person displays.

We repudiate the idea that such free will as we possess is an illusion, arising from the ignorance of the causal conditions of our actions. There are situations in which we know the relevant antecedents quite well, and nevertheless do what we do "of our own free will." For example, we know that we are very fond of our great friend Sir Karl; hence we quite voluntarily try to write in a manner that will not offend him. Only a detailed, complete foreknowledge such as the chimerical World Formula could provide would deprive us of our feeling of free choice.

If all of the foregoing considerations do not remove the sting of the free will versus determinism problem, then perhaps only a word of practical wisdom can help. It is morbid to contemplate universal causation while engaged in making decisions in the context of practical urgencies. Fortunately, it is rather difficult, if not psychologically impossible, simultaneously to combine the attitude of the spectator and causal analyst with that of the goal-pursuing agent. (To the complementarity philosophers a word of warning: this has nothing whatever to do—except for a very remote analogy—with the complementarity formulated in the Copenhagen interpretation of quantum mechanics!)

We conclude that the testimony of introspection, as well as the objective observation of behavior at "choice points" quite clearly reveals the efficacy of deliberation and effort. Even if deliberation, preference, choice, and action were completely determined by causal antecedents, it is still *free* choice (as contrasted with decisions imposed on us by any form of compulsion—from the normal cases of coercion to the peculiar cases of hypnosis or "brainwashing"). If "classically" oriented scientists—from Laplace to Einstein—after careful consideration of all relevant reasons came to accept and defend a deterministic point of view, their convictions are "rational" only to the extent that they responded to the available evidence, and with their mastery of a variety of theoretical schemes, in a manner that might well be ultimately explainable in causal terms. This seems basically not different from the trial and error-elimination process involved in all cases of learning. In fact, it seems to us that (to use Sir Karl's way of formulating the matter) the refutation or the corroboration of theories had better be intelligible in causal-psychological terms, if it is not to consist of "snap judgments."

Although we grant, of course, that in many contexts the words "cause" and "reason" are used (and should be used) in categorially different ways, we submit that there are contexts in which they are practically synonymous. And even where they are not—there are subtle relations between them. This is one of the main points to be discussed in the following section.

II

Turning now to Popper's views regarding Descartes's problem, i.e., the "body-mind" problem, it will be well to point out the primary issues in the cluster of questions that are traditionally and controversially discussed under that heading. We think it useful to distinguish three major parts of that cluster: Sentience, Sapience, and Selfhood. Of these it is *sapience* which is in the foreground, both for Descartes and for Popper. The problems of sapience concern the intellectual capacities and activities of human beings—in relation to the processes occurring in their nervous systems, particularly in the cortices of their brains. Everything that is relevant for perceiving, knowing, reasoning, problem solving, and the like is here comprised under "sapience." "Sentience," by contrast, designates the qualities of immediate experience, and the problem here also is to give a consistent, coherent, and scientifically acceptable account of its relation to the neurophysiological process. "Selfhood," in turn designates the "identity" of the human person—among other persons—and as a continuant throughout a span of time. Here, too, there are questions as to the relationships between both the introspective and the common-life descriptions of a person, and the (ultimately

physical) scientific account of the organism as the "embodiment of a mind."
Popper, most understandably and justifiably, focuses on the problem of sapience.
We can best set the stage for our critical examination of his position (that human
sapience is incompatible with determinism) by gathering together the chief passages in *Of Clouds and Clocks* which most explicitly assert and argue this incompatibility. Popper writes:[6]

> [Quoting Compton] If . . . the atoms of our bodies follow physical laws as
> immutable as the motions of the planets, why try? What difference can it
> make how great the effort if our actions are already predetermined by mechan-
> ical laws . . . ?
>
> Compton describes here what I shall call *"the nightmare of the physical
> determinist."* A deterministic physical clockwork mechanism is, above all,
> completely self-contained: in the perfect deterministic physical world there is
> simply no room for any outside intervention. Everything that happens in such
> a world is physically predetermined, including all our movements and there-
> fore all our actions. Thus all our thoughts, feelings, and efforts can have no
> practical influence upon what happens in the physical world: they are, if not
> mere illusions, at best superfluous by-products ('epiphenomena') of physical
> events. [p. 8]
>
> I believe that the only form of the problem of determinism which is worth
> discussing seriously is exactly that problem which worried Compton: the
> problem which arises from a physical theory which describes the world as a
> *physically complete* or a *physically closed* system [29]. By a physically closed
> system I mean a set or system of physical entities, such as atoms or elemen-
> tary particles or physical forces or fields of forces, which interact with each
> other—and *only* with each other—in accordance with definite laws of inter-
> action that do not leave any room for interaction with, or interference by, any-
> thing outside that closed set or system of physical entities. It is this 'closure'
> of the system that creates the deterministic nightmare [30]. [p. 8]
>
> For according to deteminism, any theories—such as, say, determinism—
> are held because of a certain physical structure of the holder (perhaps of his
> brain). Accordingly we are deceiving ourselves (and are physically so deter-
> mined as to deceive ourselves) whenever we believe that there are such things
> as arguments or reasons which make us accept determinism. Or in other
> words, physical determinism is a theory which, if it is true, is not arguable,
> since it must explain all our reactions, including what appear to us as beliefs
> based on arguments, as due to *purely physical conditions*. Purely physical
> conditions, including our physical environment, make us say or accept what-
> ever we say or accept; and a well-trained physicist who does not know any
> French, and who has never heard of determinism, would be able to predict
> what a French determinist would say in a French discussion on determinism;

and, of course, also what his indeterminist opponent would say. But this means that if we believe that we have accepted a theory like determinism because we were swayed by the logical force of certain arguments, then we are deceiving ourselves, according to physical determinism; or more precisely, we are in a physical condition which determines us to deceive ourselves. [p. 11]

For if we accept a theory of evolution (such as Darwin's) then even if we remain sceptical about the theory that life emerged from inorganic matter we can hardly deny that there must have been a time when abstract and non-physical entities, such as reasons and arguments and scientific knowledge, and abstract rules, such as rules for building railways or bulldozers or sputniks or, say, rules of grammar or of counterpoint, did not exist, or at any rate had no effect upon the physical universe. It is difficult to understand how the physical universe could produce abstract entities such as rules, and then could come under the influence of these rules, so that these rules in their turn could exert very palpable effects upon the physical universe.

There is, however, at least one perhaps somewhat evasive but at any rate easy way out of this difficulty. We can simply deny that these abstract entities exist and that they can influence the physical universe. And we can assert that what do exist are our brains, and that these are machines like computers; that the allegedly abstract rules are physical entities, exactly like the concrete physical punch-cards by which we 'program' our computers; and that the existence of anything non-physical is just 'an illusion', perhaps, and at any rate unimportant, since everything would go on as it does even if there were no such illusions. [p. 12]

For obviously what we want is to understand how such non-physical things as *purposes, deliberations, plans, decisions, theories, intentions*, and *values*, can play a part in bringing about physical changes in the physical world. [p. 15]

Retaining Compton's own behaviorist terminology, Compton's problem may be described as the problem of the influence of the *universe of abstract meanings* upon human behavior (and thereby upon the physical universe). Here "universe of meanings" is a shorthand term comprising such diverse things as promises, aims, and various kinds of rules, such as rules of grammar, or of polite behavior, or of logic, or of chess, or of counterpoint; also such things as scientific publications (and other publications); appeals to our sense of justice or generosity; or to our artistic appreciation; and so on, almost *ad infinitum*. [p. 16]

These passages mention several distinguishable components of human mental life (e.g., our feelings, our desires, our reasonings) some of which are more clearly sapient (= cognitive) than others. Thus, for example, a person's "desire for water" would ordinarily be viewed by the psychologist as a fairly complex state of the organism, including such component aspects as water depletion in the peripheral body tissues, afferent nerve impulses arising from local dryness of the throat and mouth, chemical conditions of the extracellular fluid surrounding and bathing nerve cells in the thirst-specific and drinking control centers of the hypothalamus, a heightened "arousal" of the generalized sort associated with any strong biological drive, selective perceptual sensitization to water-related exteroceptive cues, differential activation of acquired instrumental habits (including verbal ones!) that have been strengthened by water reinforcement in the past, and so on. It seems safe to assume, on present evidence (both scientific and commonsense) that those states of the organism that we ordinarily subsume under such generic state-terms as "desire," "feeling," "motive," and the like are partly sapient, partly sentient, and partly neither. For example, unconscious wishes are, by definition, not sentient, and they are (quasi-) sapient only by a complicated—and still disputed—extension of familiar meanings.[7]

It is not our intention to consider separately each of the distinguishable kinds of mental events to which Sir Karl alludes in these passages. We do not believe this is necessary, even if our limited space permitted it. We suggest that the core philosophical objection is best represented by the "pure case" of human sapience, to wit, *rational inference* by a calm, nonhungry, nonthirsty, sexually satisfied, unfrightened, nonangry scholar, whose regnant motive is that upon which Aristotle relies in the first sentence of the *Metaphysics*.[8] We are confident that if ratiocination can be reconciled with psychological determinism, none of the other less "pure" cases, such as involve means-end selections based upon the combination of "knowledge" and "desire," will present insuperable difficulties. On the other hand, a satisfactory deterministic analysis of motivational ("goal-oriented") behavior, such as the mechanism for selecting instrumental responses tending to find sexual gratification or avoid social anxiety, might leave us with persistent doubts about the compatibility of determinism with rationality. One could put it succinctly thus: If ratiocination is compatible with determinism, then, so are purposiveness, goal-directedness, motivated choice, contemplation of alternatives, means-end appropriateness, the "influence of our desires on events," and so forth. Whereas, if determinism is *in*compatible with ratiocination, Popper's case is proved, whatever might be shown about any or all of these. We therefore submit that the issue will not be prejudiced by our concentrating on the single question, "Is the doctrine of psychological determinism compatible with the existence of human rationality?"

A common ground with Professor Popper can perhaps be found in the following noncontroversial observation: "It is frequently the case that we influence other persons, and find ourselves influenced by them, through the giving of *reasons*." We employ the weak verb "influence," where many determinist psychologists would prefer to say "determine" or "control," since these stronger words beg the (empirical) question of precisely how rigidly "clocklike" human behavior is. We do not here enter into the substantive issue, which is qualitatively no different in psychology from that presented by the other biological and social sciences (or, for that matter, as Professor Popper himself emphasizes, the physical sciences) of whether certain systems are or are not plausibly viewed, on the basis of all available theory and evidence, as ontologically deterministic apart from the question of our "instrumental" ability to predict and control them. As pointed out earlier in this chapter, it is sometimes a rational extrapolation for the scientist to postulate that a system obeys strict laws, i.e., that all the events of a domain are instantiations of nomologicals, even though the limitations of his measuring technology are such that the determination of the initial and boundary conditions of the system make it unfeasible to predict other than statistically. For example, staying away from the human case for the moment, the animal psychologist observes a steady trend toward increased order and regularity in learning curves as he increases his control of the organism's previous history and, especially, his control of the current stimulating field. The smoothness and high-confidence predictability of cumulative response curves obtained in the "Skinner box" is the main reason for its increased use in the study of learning, emotion, psychopharmacology, etc., in preference to the previously popular maze. The lawfulness of the rat's behavior in the Skinner box is sufficiently great (better, for example, than most "physiological" research data) so that a psychologist is sometimes in the position of being able to instruct his research assistant, "See what's the matter with the apparatus," because the curve purportedly produced by a particular rat is one which he can confidently say is *psychologically impossible*, given the animal's previous training and present stimulating conditions. To quote our colleague, Professor Kenneth MacCorquodale, "These data are impossible; God is a better engineer than Foringer (manufacturer of Skinner-boxes and associated programming and recording apparatus)." It is a matter of degree, not of kind, when the experimental psychologist—or, for that matter, the clinical psychologist, relying upon Freud's investigations—makes the usual scientific extrapolation and assumes until further notice that this fact of increased control (or even well-knit retrospective understanding) suggests that, in the limit, the system would be predictable or, putting it ontologically, that "in itself" the system is deterministic. Again, we do not propose to argue the empirical merits of the substantive questions here (especially the vexed issue, "how do persons differ from rats?")[9]

It is worth nothing that there are *non*experimental occasions on which an extremely high degree of predictability, as high as we can normally obtain in an ordinary undergraduate physics laboratory experiment, is present even in the case of complex human behavior involving rational processes. If I take certain rather elementary steps to ascertain that a colleague is in a "normal" state of mind, i.e., that he is not hypnotized or psychotic or drugged or the like, I can predict his answer to certain questions (putting it another way, I can therefore, by asking these questions, control his verbal output) with essentially 100 percent certainty. Thus, we know that, if we present to Professor Popper a certain sort of invalid syllogistic argument and ask him to "comment on this *qua* logician," he will reply, "Illicit distribution of the major," or some synonymous expresson. The predictability of this kind of "rational" human behavior is considerably higher than that which obtains in other areas of human behavior (e.g., falling in love, disliking a political figure), and it is also considerably higher than that which obtains in, say, organic medicine, or even in certain domains of the physical sciences (e.g., meteorology).

Furthermore, what appears from the behavioristic standpoint as a practically perfect predictability or controllability of verbal behavior can also be observed introspectively by a nonbehaviorist philosopher of, say, dualist persuasion; and the subjective experience of an individual in this type of situation is consonant with the behaviorist's impression of it, i.e., *one feels subjectively that he is completely powerless to think otherwise*. Of course, he is capable of *speaking* otherwise, and will do so if certain other motivating conditions are provided. For example, one might (as a nefarious Svengali-type psychologist) inform Professor Popper that somebody was going to put a logician's question to him in an effort to "prove the thesis of psychological determinism," and as a result of such instruction Professor Popper might be motivated to show that his behavior is *not* thus neatly predictable, and as an "act of counterwill" refuse to classify the obviously fallacious syllogism as an Illicit distribution of the Major, calling it instead an Undistributed Middle, or saying that it was all right. Here the predictability of what he *would* say is rather low, but (knowing his position on determinism) the predictability that he *would not* say what we would ordinarily expect him to say as a logician might be very high indeed. But these questions involve his overt speech output. In either case, from the subjective standpoint, he would find himself incapable—we do not say "unwilling," we mean literally *incapable*—of cognizing a fallacious syllogism as being valid. If we, as behavior-engineers, told him, "Sir Karl, we are now going to determine your thought for the next few seconds, provided you are willing to listen to what we say next. Consider the following argument . . . ," he might refuse to listen to us, or decline to read an argument on a sheet of paper (i.e., we might lack adequate control of his orienting and attending behaviors). But *if* he met these conditions, i.e, if he listened to us and thought about what we were telling him, we would have attained substantially perfect control of *what* he would think about what we said. It is worthwhile emphasizing this subjective aspect, because there is a tendency, when philosophers and psychologists quarrel about this matter, to identify *determinism* with *behaviorism*. And while unquestionably these positions show certain historical connections (and temperamental affinities?) they are related by no logical necessity, as Professor Popper has been careful to remind us.

One source of philosophical (and, even more, of one's personal, "existential") rejection of the idea of psychological determinism is our tendency to associate it with those theorists and ideologists who have laid emphasis upon the *irrational* determiners of human thought and action. If you ask the typical cultivated, educated nonpsychologist for his immediate associations to the idea of psychological determinism, he will usually mention Freud, and with fair probability will add Marx, Pavlov, and—depending upon how much he has kept up with the controversy or how recent his formal education—Skinner. Now whereas Freud was a complete psychological determinist and therefore held that the "rational, reality-testing functions of the ego" were determined as much as anything else, he seemed to feel no tension, let alone logical contradiction, between his own very high valuation of rationality in the scientist's thinking, and the notion that such thinking, as much as the scientist's knee-jerk reflex or digestion, was completely determined. The main thrust of Freud's contribution was the *extent* to which irrational forces control "the surface," and the *extent* to which we are often deceived in giving a purportedly rational account of our conduct. Thus one of the Freudian Mechanisms—contributed not by Freud himself but by Ernest Jones—has the title "Rationalization," the process of giving reasons (perhaps even objectively valid reasons) for actions or beliefs that were, in fact, psychologically produced by internal forces of a very different, nonrational character. It was, of course, no *qualitatively* new discovery on Freud's part that people deceive themselves about their own beliefs and conduct; but the working out of some of the details of the machinery by which this self-deception is carried out, the *quantitative* emphasis upon its being more frequent and more powerful than had generally been supposed, and the elaboration of the *content* of the unconscious processes (e.g., what kinds of impulses are being defended against) have had an impact upon our culture which can hardly be exaggerated. The same is true of Marx who, although he never denied that rational calculation occurred (e.g., when the capitalist asks himself how he can maximize his profits), nevertheless saw a great deal of both individual mental life and cultural development as primarily reflecting economic forces which did not always appear on the surface. Thus we have the stereotype of the kind of vulgar Marxism which would "explain" Darwinism as nothing but the biologist's rationalization of Victorian competitive capitalism, or would "explain" the rise and decline of cubism in terms of the pig-iron production of French industry.

Now, without entering into the empirical question whether Freud somewhat exaggerated this (admittedly) pervasive influence of the irrational, what we wish to emphasize here is the following: Whether one describes the mind in psychoanalytic terminology, or in the terminology of an experimental psychology of perception and learning, the most deterministic psychologist does not deny the existence of specific cognitive dispositions—of "habits" or "ego-structures"—that are rational in nature. Thus, for example, in Freudian theory we distinguish between the so-called "primary" and "secondary" processes, between the "pleasure principle" and the "reality principle" of mental functioning, between a relatively strong ego—that means, in large part, a realistic or rational one—and a weak ego, as is found in a young child or a regressed psychotic. One should avoid the very common temptation to think immediately, when psychological determinism is under discussion, of such determiners as one's unconscious hatred for his father or the subtle influence of a blood chemistry attributable partly to the fried eggs one had for breakfast. Popper himself succumbs to this temptation, in discussing the theoretical predictability of Mozart's or Beethoven's composing, in terms of whether they "had eaten lamb, say, instead of chicken, or drunk tea instead of coffee" (*CC*, p. 11). Sometimes unconscious conflicts or fried eggs are strong enough to impair the ego's rational functions; sometimes, fortunately for the conduct of ordinary affairs as well as the advancement of science, the fried eggs simply produce the necessary biological energy to keep the machine working, but do not, in any psychologically or philosophically important way, determine the *direction* or *content* of the ego's cognitive processes. One should not, in contemplating the social and existential implications of psychological determinism, think only of the fact that a man had a permissive mother or an authoritarian father or a vitamin deficiency, to the neglect of such equally important factors as that he inherited a high conceptual intelligence, that he read many books during his teens, that he was exposed to an excellent undergraduate course in logic, and the like.

In this connection it is important to keep in mind the distinction between object language habits and metalanguage habits. Not only do we learn by a complicated mixture of (a) direct reinforcement ("reward") for thinking straight (or, alas, crooked, as the case may be), and (b) by identification with significant figures in our environment who present models of straight or crooked thinking, and (c) by formal precept in school and university, to obey logical rules; we *also* learn a set of powerful metahabits, *such as talking to oneself about the rationality of one's own arguments* (which in the case of philosophically disposed persons may maintain the ascendancy in behavior control over many and strong competitive forces). It must be confessed that tendencies of this sort are not as widespread in humankind as one might desire, and it is a presently unsolved question to what extent this sad fact is a matter of poor education or limitations in basic intelligence and temperament. But even the uncultivated layman of low education does possess a rudimentary set of such metahabits, which can be successfully appealed to, if the counterforces are not too great, to control his behavior along rational lines.

Finally, we all acquire certain *self-concepts* in the process of acculturation. For some persons, the self-concept "I am a reasonable fellow, I do not go around committing gross fallacies" is as fundamental and important a part of their personality organization as those kinds of self-concepts more familiar in the literature of psychotherapy, such as "I am an unlovable person" or "I am strong, I do not need to depend upon anybody," or "Nobody can tell me what to do!" or "I am a beautiful woman, all men are attracted to me," and so forth. Here again, while the social and clinical psychologists have attempted, with arguable success, to fill in many details about the mental *machinery* and the family constellation that contribute to mental *content*, it is noteworthy that the basic situation in such matters has always been understood (in its essentials) by thoughtful men. Everyone knows that in discussing controversial matters, say of politics or economics or sexual morality or foreign policy, we often find ourselves trying to judge whether we can successfully appeal to a person's "need to be rational" when that second-order need, involving the possibility of a threat to his self-concept, is, on a particular substantive issue, placed in opposition to what we (from the outside) view as nonrational or irrational commitments. So we may say of a person, "He's a straight thinking, sensible, fair-minded fellow, and you can almost always learn something from him, and teach him something in a discussion; but I must warn you that he admires his father very much, and his father is a classical representative of the old Southern Bourbon type. So on the race question, you have to handle him with kid gloves; there is one issue where he can sometimes become rather illogical when pressed."

It may be objected that, when the psychologist employs locutions such as "self-concept of being a rational person," he is surreptitiously plugging a nondeterministic concept (i.e., that of *rationality*) into a behavioristic-mechanistic-deterministic theoretical framework in which such meta-categories have no place. One of us (Meehl, 1968) has examined this question at length elsewhere, and the reader may be referred to that[10] for elaboration of the position we adopt on this question. Over against the dualistic, antireductionist philosopher, we hold that there is no contradiction involved in saying, "Jones's thinking is logical [on such and such an occasion]" and saying, "Jones's thinking [including its logicality] is strictly determined by his present neurophysiological state, together with the momentary stimulus inputs; and his current neurophysiological state is in turn completely determined by his antecedents, i.e., genetic equipment interacting with his life experiences."

On the other hand, we must say (against certain kinds of neobehaviorists) that the psychologist's scientific task — whether its explanatory, predictive, or controlling aspects are emphasized — cannot be carried out *at a molar level of analysis*, unless the psychologist employs certain of the logician's concepts and rubrics in his, the psychologist's, object language. This is not the place to develop that argument in detail, for which development the reader is referred to the article cited above by Meehl. Briefly, the position is that, in order to explain, predict, and control, let us say, the verbal behavior of a logic professor when presented with a formal fallacy such as Illicit Distribution, the psychologist must be able to *characterize the stimulus side*, i.e., the perceptual input to which the logician responds with such an utterance as "Illicit Major." And the point is that the psychologist's use of such concepts as "stimulus equivalence" or "verbal generalizations" must not be employed by him to hide a very important fact: When the psychologist is forced to make explicit the *configural* properties of a stimulus input that will render it "stimulus-equivalent" to the subject logician, so that, for example, the logician can properly classify a syllogism whose terms—except for the logical constants—are terms of which he does not know the meaning, and to which he has never been previously exposed; the only way to characterize this stimulus input is in terms of its *formal structure*. An adequate characterization of that stimulus class, regardless of what terminology the psychologist might employ in describing it, will, of course, turn out upon careful analysis to correspond to the characterization found in a logic text. It is of no substantive interest whether the behaviorist psychologist actually employs the logician's sign vehicle "Illicit Major," since it must be admitted that whatever (nonphilosophical) sign vehicle the psychologist employs, his *definition* of it will involve specifying the very same formal features which the logician specifies in defining the term "Illicit Major." For this reason we hold that when Skinner[11] speaks of logic being "embraced by our [the radical behaviorist's] analysis," although he is literally correct if he means that reasonable behavior, and the tokening of metalinguistic terms belonging to logic, have a causal history in the learning process; he is incorrect if he means that this behaviorist "embracing" involves the liquidation, or a showing of irrelevancy, of the logician's *categories* in a psychological analysis of "reasonable verbal behavior." *The molar behaviorist psychologist who concerns himself with language and with rational, cognitive, ego-functions must reconcile himself to the fact that he cannot dispense with the logician's formal categories.*

We mean by this something much stronger than what would be meant if we said it about a physicist or a botanist. Every scientist has to come to terms with the logician in two ways, namely, (a) He must exemplify logical processes in his object-linguistic discourse, i.e., he must think rationally about his subject matter; and (b) Since a great deal of scientific discussion and scholarly writing is not simply reports of observations, or formulation of theory, but is critical discussion of theories (their relationship to one another and to observations, the validity of one's own and other people's inferences, and the like), the scientist must also make use of the logician's categories in his metalinguistic discourse, i.e., in the process of scientific criticism. In respects (a)-(b) psychology is not essentially different from the other sciences. However, there are no other sciences in Comte's pyramid of the sciences below the level of psychology (we are assuming economics, sociology, anthropology, and political science all appear "above" psychology in this well-known pyramid) which are forced to employ the categories of the logician or philosopher in their object language.

It is not clear why this necessity should be distressing to a biological or social scientist, but for some reason it often seems to be. Whether it should distress the philosopher depends upon whether there is some kind of paradox or contradiction involved in *meta*linguistic terms, such as "valid," or "Illicit Distribution," appearing in the *object* language discourse of an empirical science. But, if this represents a problem for the philosopher, it represents a technical problem in logical theory, so we content ourselves with merely calling attention to the oddity. (Our colleague Professor Keith Gunderson suggests that, since this unavoidable reference by the molar behaviorist to formal categories is so evident, any logician's theory about object language/metalanguage relationships that precludes it is, *ipso facto*, suspect.)

A final question concerning any reduction-determinist view of the psychology of beliefs, arguments, inquiry, criticism, and the like is the question, "Would a complete causal account, *formulated in terms of the microlevel* (e.g., electrical and chemical events at neural synapses) be incompatible with our intuitive conviction that our beliefs and actions are influenced by reasons?" It is our contention, as opposed to Sir Karl's, that there is no such incompatibility, although at first impression it does appear that there must be. Suppose one takes the expression "a valid reason" as designating a kind of abstract Platonic universal which *in some sense* "exists," and would exist even if there were no thinking brains (a position we are not here espousing, but will adopt as a premise *arguendo*, since it is the one most unfavorable to the determinist analysis of human thought and action); then we hold that "the existence of a valid reason" (in some such abstract, metaphysical, Platonic sense) is a question belonging to the critical domain of logic, broadly conceived. But the *thinking* of such a reason by a living, concrete human person, the *stating* of a reason, the *hearing* of a reason, the *mentioning* of a reason, *the tokening of a sentence which expresses a proposition which is a good reason for another proposition*—there are all events very much "in the world" and "belonging to the causal order." And we maintain that one does not have to conflate reasons with causes, or to commit the fallacy of psychologism in logic (or the naturalistic fallacy in ethics), to be justified in saying that, although the validity of an argument, or the soundness and cogency of a reason, is an abstract Platonic truth about universals, nevertheless the thinking of a reason is an event, is a something which happens in space-time, in a living brain (just as the uttering of a valid reason happens in a human larynx), and instantiates nomologicals.

Admittedly there is something initially strange about the notion that a man's beliefs or actions are influenced by reasons, i.e., as we say a man is to this extent and in this matter "reasonable," and nevertheless hypothesizing—as a promissory note, until further notice, as an orienting "faith" of the scientific investigator—that the brain processes involved could, in principle, be formulated by Omniscient Jones *at a level of causal analysis which would dispense with the logician's categories*. But, although this does seem to us a bit odd, and to some readers will doubtless be highly paradoxical, we are not persuaded by Professor Popper's paper, or by any arguments that have been thus far brought to our attention, that there is anything contradictory in it. What must be understood, if we are right in our view of the matter, is that when one gives a complete causal account of a physical process at a certain level of analysis, *he does not thereby claim*, in making a metaclaim to "causal completeness," *that he has asserted everything true that could properly be asserted about the system*. In other words, it is the difference between telling the truth and telling the *whole* truth.

It is important to notice here that, whereas Professor Popper's distinction between "Compton's problem" (puzzles about determinism) and "Descartes's problem" (puzzles about the mind-body relationship) is a valid and useful one, at this stage of our discussion they are seen to be intimately related; and if the reader will turn back to the series of quotations from Popper at the beginning of this section, he will notice that Professor Popper himself has at times conflated them, we think perhaps unintentionally but unavoidably. Although the (Compton) question "How can I be rational and purposive if determined?" can be seen as presenting a philosophical problem even within a framework of radical (ontological) mind-body dualism, its bite is greatly sharpened if, instead, the determining (and determined) events are all set in a purely physicalistic ontology. Roughly put, it is bad enough if my "mind" is determined; but it is worse if my "mind" is nothing but a complex configuration of events or states, a sequence of occurrents that deterministically befall continuants that are themselves "nonmental" in nature. This fusion of the Compton problem and the Descartes problem has, of course, a venerable history, being already formulated clearly and powerfully by Plato (in the *Phaedo*, 98c-99b) and Aristotle (in the *Metaphysics*, Book 9, Chap. 6, 1048b—18-30). It has received considerable attention from several contemporary Oxford philosophers, and from the Americans A. I. Melden and Richard Taylor, to mention only notable examples. It is perhaps foolhardy for us in this limited space to attempt a resolution of such an ancient and recondite question, to which so many able thinkers have addressed themselves (and, on the current scene, emerged with answers very different from ours). But we are satisfied that no one has formulated the determinist-monist analysis of rationality (or purposive action) *quite* in the manner we propose, and that our kind of "levels" picture of the situation, whether ultimately refutable or not, will at least constitute a contribution to the ongoing philosophical discussion of this venerable controversy.

Consider first a nonpsychological example. If I give a detailed, blow-by-blow mechanical account of a sequence of operations carried on by an ordinary desk calculator, I can properly say, in conclusion, that "causally speaking, nothing has been 'left out' of this account." But it is evident that such a detailed account in terms of the laws of mechanics (as applied to the structure-dependent properties of the machine in respect to its inner workings) does not *have* to contain such (true) statements as, "The machine is dividing 3,746 by 125." Yet that is, quite literally, what the machine is doing. It does not occur to us, in such simple, in-animate system cases, to postulate the existence of some kind of an "arithmeti-cal" *deus ex machina* as a necessary addition to the causal system first described. Nevertheless, one can shift the level of description upward to a more "molar" level, as an instructor in a statistics laboratory would do in talking to a student about how to operate the machine. At that (more "molar"-behaviorist) level of analysis, the instructor formulates quasi-causal laws (they are tight nomologi-cals, as long as the machine is not broken or worn out) in which such concepts as addition, division, multiplication, and the like occur in the formulation.

We think that there is a temptation, when philosophers consider the implica-tions of psychological determinism for the possibility of human rationality and genuine criticism, to move from the (correct) statement, "At level L_c of causal analysis, not everything which might truly be said has been said" to the false (as we think) statement, "Therefore, at level L_c of analysis, the causal account is radically incomplete." If certain definitions are given at one level of analysis, and then certain reductions are carried out (given acceptance of a suitable theo-retical network), it will then be clear that the things which were left unsaid follow necessarily from those things which were said, when the latter are taken together with the explicit definitions. So that, whether or not it is literally correct to say of a microphysiological account of a complicated human thought process that the account "leaves something out," depends upon a clarification of what is meant. If the speaker means to say that something has been left unsaid which could truly be said, he is right; but if he means that the causal account will not be complete unless some additional *theoretical entity* is introduced into the causal chain, then—assuming that the reductionist thesis is empirically correct—he is wrong.

In speaking of "reduction" and "definition" in the preceding paragraph, we are perhaps inviting a major misunderstanding which we shall now endeavor to forestall. Our position is not, we trust, a surreptitious reduction of the *logical* to the *physical*, as if to say that conceptual relations (e.g., class-inclusion, formal deducibility, contradiction) could be defined in terms of "nonlogical" notions (e.g., mass, rigidity, proximity, protoplasm, synaptic resistance). We take it that everyone—whether philosopher, physicist, psychologist, computer engineer, and whether determinist or not, "physicalist" or not—would agree with Sir Karl that any such reduction is impossible in principle. Logical and arithmetical relation-ships are *sui generis*, not definable in terms of physical or biological categories or dimensions, and we wish to make it crystal clear that we accept this truth un-qualifiedly and without equivocation.

In what sense, then, can we properly speak of "explicit definition" in the pre-ceding line of argument? Reflect again upon the desk calculator problem. Reply-ing to an imagined critic (one who has Cartesian, antibehaviorist, antiphysicalist, or emergentist views about this machine), and who complains that our detailed microaccount of the machine's transitions "leaves out the main point, namely, that the calculator is adding the numbers 4 and 3 to get the (valid) answer 7," we say the following: "It is a true statement that you offer as supplementary to our mechanical account; the machine is, quite literally, 'adding numbers,' and, furthermore, it is 'getting the correct answer.' And it is true that our mechanical description did not anywhere include this arithmetical assertion. You are therefore entirely right in saying that our account does not 'say everything that can properly be said.' What we deny is that we have 'left something out' in the causal sense; specifically, we deny that there occurs any event, state, or process involving any *theoretical entity* [= entity playing an explanatory role in the nomological net, possessing causal efficacy] over and above the physical entities included in our 'nonarithmetical' account." We wish to maintain that the following statements are jointly compatible:

1. Our causal account A_c of "how the calculator works," as a physical mechanism, is complete.
2. The words "sum," "addition," "integer," etc., do not occur in A_c. (Names *of* integers may, of course, occur in the account A_c; mathematics is part of the object language of mechanics, of course. We do not talk metamathematics in describing the machine's physical operations; we do not even *mention* arithmetical theorems. We do, however, *rely upon* such theorems; and, of course, we use numerical *concepts* [e.g., "the second gear underwent three forward tooth-displacements"].)
3. "Number" is not a theoretical (causal) entity contained in, or acting upon, the machine.
4. The machine (literally) *adds numbers*.

We invite the reader to try developing a genuine contradiction from these four statements. We think there is none. What there is, is a kind of oddity — the kind of oddity that wears off, however, with sufficient familiarity. Not that we would for a moment countenance invoking oddity as a negative criterion, especially in these deep matters.

On the positive side, perhaps the shortest formulation (aimed at therapeutic erosion of the oddity-response) would be something like the following: Abstract "entities," such as formal (numerical, logical, set-theoretical) relations considered as Platonic universals, are not "in" the machine, in the sense that its *parts* are *in* it. Nor are they "in" the *event*-sequence, as, say, a wheel displacement is. But the physical entities (whether continuants or occurrents) which *are*, literally, *in* the machine, do (in some respects) exemplify those abstract universals. The cardinal number 3 is not, obviously, in the machine. But sets of structures and events of cardinality 3 are there.

In discussing with colleagues our approach to this aspect of Popper's problem, we were once met with the objection that our analysis really consisted of saying that the desk calculator (or a "logic machine," or the human brain) is a physical model satisfying the laws of arithmetic, which *all* physical entities necessarily satisfy; from which, the critic argued, it would follow that no calculators (or brains) can err. This complaint rests upon a confusion among physical levels. We must be clear about *which* physical entities and processes are taken as elements and relations of the physical model corresponding to the elements and relations of the calculus. It is, of course, true that the physical set formed by conjunction of a set of three iron atoms and a set of two iron atoms is a set having cardinality 5, even though the gear in which these five atoms lie is part of a worn-out calculator (which "makes arithmetical mistakes"). But the cardinal number of interest is not that of the constituent atoms, it is the number of tooth-displacements. Or, treating the machine "molar-behavioristically," the cardinal number of interest is either (a) The number of punch-and-cumulate operations or (b) The cardinal number designated in English, by the numeral [= "3"] on a key punched and cumulated once. And it is obvious that *these* (= "molar") physical events do not necessarily satisfy the laws of arithmetic. *If* the wheels are not worn out, prone to slippage, etc., then three punchings and cumulations of key labeled "1" will result in a state of three-tooth-displacement; this state will persist until two further unit-additions occur. It being a theorem of arithmetic that $3 + 2 = 5$, we know that 3 physical displacements "plus" 2 physical displacements leads to a terminal state of 5 net displacements. It is (trivially) analytic to say that "If the machine satisfies the axioms, it satisfies the theorems." But the point is that, whereas its constituent atoms satisfy the axioms, the "molar"-level parts and processes may fail to be a model of arithmetic, when the physical operations occur in time and the numbers are used to characterize resulting positions rather than historical facts. The statements S_1: "Gear G has undergone three forward displacement events during interval $(t_1 - t_0)$" and S_2: "Gear G has undergone two forward displacement events during interval $(t_2 - t_1)$" jointly entails S_3: "Gear G has undergone five forward displacement events during interval $(t_2 - t_0)$." This truth of arithmetic, that $S_1.S_2 \rightarrow S_3$, cannot fail to be satisfied by the machine, worn-out or not. But the conjunction $S_1. S_2$ does *not* entail S_4: "At t_2, Gear G is in a state displaced five steps from its state at t_0." Gear G may have "slipped" backward at some time during the interval. And similar considerations apply a fortiori when a causal interaction between different gears is supposed to model arithmetical operations.

Unavoidably, any causal reconstruction of rational mental processes in terms of brain events will suffer, at the present state of our knowledge, either from extreme generality — amounting to little more than a restatement in pseudo-brain-language of such general formal concepts as "model" — or, if it becomes more specific than this and attempts to deliver the goods, so to speak, *scientifically*, it will be on the fringe of current empirical knowledge and readily objected to by the critic as not only unproved but excessively speculative. We do not take it as our task, in examining Professor Popper's objections, to present a brain model. And since his objection is essentially philosophical (rather than directed at what is wrong with any specific substantive theory of learning, perception, or thinking in the present state of the behavior sciences) we are confident he will not complain in either of these two ways, so long as we make quite clear which enterprise we are engaged in, i.e., a highly generalized statement of the conditions for the brain to think rationally although determined, or, on the other hand, a specific physicalistic *example* which exhibits the philosophical point we wish to make but lays no claim at all to scientific correctness.

Returning to the question of the sense in which a physicalistic account in brain language is "complete" *even though it does not say all that could truly be said*, we suggest the following as a first approximation to an account which, while maintaining the distinction between logical categories and the categories of physics or physiology, nevertheless insists that a physicalistic microaccount is nomologically complete. We have a calculus, such as arithmetic or the rules of the categorical syllogism. We have a class of brain events which are identified by appropriate physical properties—these, of course, may be highly "configural" in character—at, say, an intermediate level of molarity (i.e., the events involve less than the whole brain or some molar feature of the whole acting and thinking person, but are at a "higher" level in the hierarchy of physical subsystems than, say, the discharge of a single neuron, or the alteration of microstructure at a synapse). Considered in their functioning as inner tokening—that is, however peripherally or behavioralistically they were originally acquired by social conditioning, considering them as now playing the role of Sellars's *mental word*[12] — there is a physically identifiable brain event b_M which "corresponds" (in the mental word sense) to the subject term in the first premise of a syllogism in Barbara. There is a second tokening event b_P which is a token of the type that designates the predicate term of the conclusion; a brain event b_S which corresponds to a tokening of the type that designates the subject term of the conclusion of the syllogism; and finally a brain event b_C corresponding to the copula. (These expository remarks are offered with pedagogic intent only. We do not underestimate the enormous complexity of adequately explaining the words "correspond" and "designate" in the immediately preceding text.)

A physically-omniscient neurophysiologist [= Omniscient Jones estopped from metatalk about logic] can, we assume, identify these four brain events b_M, b_P, b_S, b_C on the basis of their respective conjunction of physical properties, which presumably are some combination of *locus* (where in the brain? which cell assemblies?) and *quantitative properties of function* (peak level of activation of an assembly, decay rate, pulse frequency of driving the next assembly in a causal chain, mean number of activated elements participating). For present purposes we may neglect any problem of extensional vagueness, which is not relevant to the present line of argument, although it is of considerable interest in its own right.

Our physically-omniscient neurophysiologist is in possession of a finite set of statements which are the nomologicals (or quasi-nomologicals) of neurophysiology, which we shall designate collectively by L_{phys} [= neurophysiological laws]. He is also in possession of a very large, unwieldy, but finite set of statements about structure, including (a) macrostructure, (b) structure of intermediate levels, e.g., architectonics and cell-type areas such as studied microscopically in a brain-histology course, and (c) microstructural statements including microstructural statements about functional connections. We take it for granted that "learned functional connections" *must* be embodied in microstructure (although its exact nature is still a matter for research) since there is otherwise no explanation of the continuity of memory when organisms, human or animal, are put into such deep anesthesia that all nerve cell discharge is totally suspended for considerable time periods, or when normal functional activity is dramatically interrupted by such a cerebral storm as a *grand mal* seizure induced in electroshock treatment. Thus the class of structural statements S_t includes two major subclasses of statements, one being about the inherited "wiring diagram" of a human brain, and the other being the acquired functional synaptic connections resulting from the learning process.

Our omniscient neurophysiologist can derive, from the conjunction $(L_{phys} \cdot S_t)$, a "brain theorem" T_b, which, to an approximation adequate for present purposes, may be put this way: Brain-state theorem T_b: "Whenever the composite brain events $(b_M b_C b_P)$ and $(b_S b_C b_M)$ are temporally contiguous, a brain event $(b_S b_C b_P)$ follows immediately." This brain theorem is formulated solely in terms of the states b_i which are physicalistically identifiable, and without reference to any such metaconcept as class, syllogism, inference, or the like. The derivation of T_b is one of strict deducibility in the object language of neurophysiology. That is, neurophysiology tells us that a brain initially wired in such and such a way, and then subsequently "programmed" by social learning to have such and such functional connections (dispositions), will necessarily [nomological necessity] undergo the event $(b_S b_C b_P)$ whenever it has just previously undergone the events $(b_M b_C b_P)$ and $(b_S b_C b_M)$ in close temporal contiguity.

But, whereas for the neurophysiologist this brain theorem is a theorem about certain physical events *and nothing more*, a logician would surely discern an interesting formal feature revealed in the descriptive notation — the subscripts — of the b's. It would hardly require the intellectual powers of a Carnap or Gödel to notice, *qua* logician, that these brain events constitute a physical model of a subcalculus of logic, i.e., that these physical entities $[b_M, b_P, b_S, b_C]$ "satisfy" the formal structure of the syllogism in Barbara, if we interpret

b_M = tokening of middle term b_S = tokening of subject term
b_P = tokening of predicate term b_C = tokening of copula.

The "brain theorem" T_b can be *derived nomologically* from the structural statements S_t together with the microphysiological law-set L_{phys} given *explicit definitions* of the events $[b_M, b_P, b_S, b_C]$. These explicit definitions are not the model-interpretations, nor are they "psycholinguistic" characterizations. We can identify a case of b_P by its physical microproperties, *without knowing* that it is a tokening event, i.e., without knowing that it plays a certain role in the linguistic system which the individual who owns this brain has socially acquired. But brain theorem T_b has itself a *formal structure*, which is "shown forth" in one way, namely, by the syntactical configuration of the b-subscripts [M,P,S,C]. In this notation, "which subscript goes with what" is determinable, so long as the events b_i are physically identifiable. There is nothing physically arbitrary in this, and there is nothing in it that requires the physically-omniscient neurophysiologist to be thinking about syllogisms, or even, for that matter, to know that there is any such thing as a syllogism. Although again, it goes without saying that he himself must reason logically in order to derive the brain theorem. But he does not have to metatalk about rules, or about his own rule-obedience, in order to token rule-conformably in his scientific object language, and this suffices to derive T_b.

One near-literal metaphor which we find helpful in conveying the essence of the "syllogistic brain theorem" situation, as we see it, is that the sequence of brain events $(b_ib_jb_k)$ $(b_jb_kb_l)$ . . . *embodies* the syllogistic rules. Their defined physical structure plus the physical laws of brain function causally necessitate that they exemplify syllogistic transitions, a fact revealed when the notation designating them is considered in its formal aspects. In the usual terminology of thinking processes and logic, the brain theorem T_b says, in effect, that the existence of a formal relation of *deducibility* (truth of logic) provides, in a brain for which the theorem obtains, the necessary and sufficient causal condition for a factual transition of *inference* (a mental process). This assertion may appear to "mix the languages," to "commit the sin of psychologism," to "conflate causes with reasons"; but we maintain that none of these blunders is involved. It is a *physical* fact that a certain *formal* relation is physically embodied. If the formal features of the initial physical state were otherwise, the ensuing physical result would have been otherwise. Hence the physical embodiment of the formal relation—a *fact*, which is "in the world" as concretely as the height, in meters, of Mount Everest—is literally a condition for the inference to occur.

Comes now the emergentist or Cartesian dualist advancing an objection as follows: "Even granting, which I do not, that there are any such strictly deterministic brain nomologicals as L_{phys}, and assuming *arguendo* that your concept of a physically-omniscient neurophysiologist (who is ignorant of metastatements in logic) could actually carry out the derivation of T_b from $(L_{phys} \cdot S_t)$, I must interpose a philosophical objection which is surely available to us upon present knowledge, and does not rely upon speculations, whether optimistic or pessimistic, about the future development of brain science. My philosophical objection is a very simple one, and it is this. While you, in your imaginary reconstruction of the derivation possibility for the physically-omniscient neurophysiologist, can carefully avoid any reference to the syllogism, or to the formal validity of the inference which is 'embodied' in these brain events, *you yourself* do have in mind that this is the brain of a thinking human being, and you do intend me to understand that these brain events are his valid thinkings. Yet you say that you give an exhaustive account of what happens, and that you can explain, i.e., derive nomologically, given the structural statements S_t, all that went on. Now if it is true that you can derive everything that goes on within the object language of the physically-omniscient neurophysiologist, then the fact that this brain event sequence is [known to you and me but not to him] a process of valid inference, that the individual whose brain we are studying is *correctly thinking a syllogism in.Barbara*, turns out to be an irrelevant fact, a supernumerary, something that doesn't make any difference at all. Whereas I want to hold that this is the most important fact about these happenings. How can you say that you have given a complete account of what is taking place in this person, that you have 'explained everything' about the happenings under consideration, when you have not any-where said the most important thing there is to say, namely, *that he is making a valid inference*? If the physically-omniscient neurophysiologist can derive the brain theorem T_b without even knowing that inference is going on in this person's brain (I should, of course, prefer to say 'mind,' but I will make concessions to your strange materialist verbal habits), then the validity of the inference makes no difference. Whereas, of course, I know perfectly well, brain physiology aside, that whether a certain inference is permissible makes all the difference in the world, and you yourself have said the same thing earlier in the present discourse. I simply do not understand how you can say that the account is causally complete when it leaves out the most important fact, which is a *logical* fact, namely, that a valid inference is being made when the person passes from tokening 'M is P' and 'S is M' to tokening 'S is P.' ''

Now the first thing to see about this Cartesian or emergentist objection is that it contains an important element of truth, which it is both dishonest and unnec-essary for the determinist-materialist to deny. The objector points out that, in the microphysiological account of the brain events which is assumed to be offered by the physically-omniscient neurophysiologist, something that is literally true has not been said, to wit, *that a valid syllogism is being tokened*. Having freely ad-mitted this, our next question is, does it follow from the fact that something which could be truly literally said has not been said, that the causal account is incomplete? This is the crucial issue, and we want to urge that the proper answer to this question is in the negative. But, of course, in order to examine this ques-tion, one has to arrive at some suitable convention for the use of the metalinguistic expressions "everything that can be said" and "a complete causal account of the events."

Let us first point out that there are many obvious and noncontroversial cases, lying quite outside the realm of the mind-body problem (or the determinism problem, or the intentionality problem) where it is clear that a complete causal account of a series of events can be given without explicitly saying everything that would, if said, be literally true. Examples are so numerous as to be almost pointless, so we will mention only one. Suppose that I give a causal account of the displacement of the piston in a cylinder by an expanding gas, and this account is given at the microlevel—in the extreme case, by the long, but finite, set of sentences describing the components of momenta, the positions, the impacts on the wall of the container, etc., of the individual gas molecules. Nothing is left out of this account from the standpoint of physical understanding. I do not, however, mention that the number of molecules in this batch of gas is prime. Let it not be objected that this is a silly instance. That the number of these molecules is prime is just as much a physical fact as is the set of numbers characterizing the components of their respective momenta. It is not, however, a fact we find it necessary to *mention* in giving a complete causal account of how the gas displaces the piston. This example suffices at least to show, what is really a rather trivial and unexciting truth, that one can say everything that is causally relevant in accounting (at all levels of causal analysis) for a certain phenomenon, without saying everything that is literally true about it.

But we will readily concede to the Cartesian critic that this example is, while sufficient to prove the just stated general thesis, not a fair analogy to the brain theorem problem. Because what he is objecting to in our brain theorem case is not only that we have left out something that is literally true (that the brain is thinking about a syllogism in Barbara), but that the *outcome* of the thinking is critically influenced by the *logical fact* that the inference is valid. And while it is literally true that the number of molecules in the gas is prime, this is not a fact which makes any difference to the outcome.

This last locution, the phrase "makes any difference to the outcome," contains, we think, the core of the objection, and also provides us with the essence of our answer to it. What do we mean when we say that something's being the case, or not the case, "makes any difference"? Depending upon one's views concerning causality, a number of things might be meant; but we assume that at least a minimum condition for its being appropriate to say that "such and such makes no difference" is that if such and such *had not* obtained, the outcome *would have been* the same as the outcome in fact was when such and such *did* obtain. Whatever else one might mean about something "making no difference," he surely must mean at least this counterfactual. Now is it literally correct to say, as the critic does here, that the causal account provided by the physically-omniscient neurophysiologist shows that the validity of the inference, as a formal truth, makes no difference? That is, does it follow, from the metafact that the physical microaccount provided by the neurophysiologist does not contain any reference to the formal structure (revealed by the subscripts on the b's), that *if this formal structure were not present, the terminating brain event $(b_S b_C b_P)$ would occur nevertheless*? Clearly not. The brain theorem is stated in terms of b's with distinguishable subscripts, and these subscripts are formally related, *within the theorem* T_b, in a certain way. Thus, we do not have a brain theorem stating the following: "Whenever brain events $(b_S b_C b_M)$ and $(b_P b_C b_M,)$ occur in close temporal contiguity, they are immediately followed by brain event $(b_S b_C b_P)$." In fact, if the brain under study is that of an always-rational man, we will instead have a countertheorem here, which states that this particular contiguity will never be immediately followed by the third event, i.e., this being the brain of a perfectly rational man, he never commits the fallacy of Undistributed Middle. Now the point is that the physically-omniscient neurophysiologist *does not have to mention* this formal feature about the b-subscripts in order for his account to be causally complete, because the statements he *does* mention jointly entail, as a matter of nomological necessity, that the brain events will be related in such and such a way, i.e., that they will in fact be models of the syllogism in Barbara, a consequence which is revealed by the syntactical configuration of the subscripts. And it is literally false to say that the same "conclusion" $(b_S b_C b_P)$ would be tokened in this brain if the subscripts designating the physical events preceding this conclusion-tokening had been different from what they in fact were. In a way, the point is really quite trivial, being essentially no more than to say that if any set of properties makes a causal difference, then any other set which can be explicitly defined in terms of the first set also "makes a difference," for if those higher-level properties were not in fact what they are on a particular occasion, then, since they are defined explicitly in terms of the lower-level properties, it follows that the lower-level properties could not have been what they in fact are; and therefore the outcome would have been physically different.

It still seems admittedly a little strange that one does not have to mention the validity of the syllogism thus exemplified or embodied by the brain processes in giving a complete physical-causal account. We believe that this strangeness arises mainly from the fact that the causal account offered by the physically-omniscient neurophysiologist *begins* with certain microstructural premises contained in the collection of sentences S_t and that *these sentences collectively constitute the physical description of the microstates which embody the dispositions to compute rationally in this brain*, dispositions that have been socially learned when the individual acquired the habits of "thinking straight." That is the historical account of why these microstructural facts are what they are. But we may start our explanation of the brain theorem T_b at a given moment in time, forgetting about the learning history; then we represent only the *results* of social learning (to think straight) by statements about microstructures at the synapse, considered neuron by neuron. This way of describing the matter of course yields a paradoxical effect, because it now appears that the all-important "fact of rationality" has been left out of the picture. But the point is that the all-important fact of rationality has not really been left out of the picture, *it has instead been stated* (admittedly opaquely) *by referring to the microstructures which embody the "rational dispositions."* There is, of course, a familiar sense in which one may be considered to have expressed everything in a theoretical system when he expresses the postulates, in that he is considered to "assert" implicitly all of the theorems that follow therefrom. From this point of view, our physically-omniscient neurophysiologist therefore "asserts" the brain theorem T_b, and he therefore "asserts" the syntactical relationships holding among the b_i-subscripts in the terms that are contained in the brain theorem. And he therefore "asserts," although not expressly (since he speaks no metalanguage), the crucial fact that this brain is a rationally reasoning brain.

Whether a purportedly complete causal account deserves criticism because of its failure to assert explicitly one or more of the necessary consequences of what it *does* assert, depends upon several considerations such as human social interest, level of analysis as defined by the pragmatic context of one's investigation, and the like. Therefore to leave out a statement that follows from the conjunction of other statements, to the effect that the number of molecules in a contained gas is prime, would not ordinarily strike us as a very serious omission, although it would be a valid comment that "a true statement was left unsaid." But even if we remain at the level of inorganic processes, where purpose and knowledge are not attributable to the system under study, it is easy to think of instances in which something is left unsaid that one would normally think of as a very serious omission, yet that something is not something that one *must* say in giving a complete causal account of what took place. Example: I drop an ice cube in a cup of boiling tea, and physically-Omniscient Jones gives a detailed microaccount of the ensuing process of its dissolution. That is, he considers the tea, molecule by molecule, and considers the face of the ice, molecule by molecule, describing each molecular collision, the interplay between the mechanical forces of impact and the intermolecular forces tending to maintain the solid state of the ice crystal, etc. We end up with all of the water molecules that were in the ice being dispersed among the water molecules in the tea, and our story is closed. Here is a situation where, unlike the silly case of the prime numbered gas molecules, we are strongly impelled to say, at the close of the account, "Well, that's all very fine, but you know you never said once that the main thing going on here was that hot tea was losing heat to cold ice and cold ice was taking up heat from hot tea, and the result of this whole process is that an ice cube in a cup of hot tea has dissolved and disappeared. You didn't say that. You left that out. *And what you left out is the most important thing that went on.*" Our point is that the question of "importance" refers to a number of considerations, which collectively may or may not lead us to be critical of an account which omits to mention something that is literally true and that in fact follows deductively — given certain already available nomologicals and explicit definitions — from the statements that were made in the account.

In the case of the human brain thinking syllogistically, it is obvious that there are at least two kinds of things that could be said that are not said in stating and deriving the "brain theorem" T_b, and which make us critical of the account. The first is the role of "purpose" (motivation, intention, goal-orientation) in the thought processes, which we might express either with reference to the reinforcement history of this individual (as a consequence of which his brain cells have acquired the syllogistic dispositions that they have); or, alternatively, by reference to the state of distress (surprise, disconfirmed expectancy, shame or guilt, or whatever) that the individual is disposed to experience if he finds himself committing a formal fallacy. This motivational feature is one that has not until recently engaged the attention of computer-simulation investigators, and it will unquestionably come in for a great deal of systematic attention in the near future. See, for example, Simon.[13] It was, of course, not our intention to pretend that such goal-oriented factors are absent in the above account, but we presume that Sir Karl will agree that, in spite of their intimate relations to human thought, *intentionality* and *intention* are different concepts; that one thinks rationally and that one desires to think rationally are two different facts, although they are intimately related.

Second, we also omitted reference to those metatalk dispositions of the sort that we imagined our physically-omniscient neurophysiologist to lack. We restricted his omniscience to physical events, and kept him out of the metalanguage of logic for our purpose in discussing the physical derivability of the "brain theorem." But it does not appear to us that any new issue of principle concerning determinism and rationality is raised by the introduction of the metalanguage. Whether there are any insuperable set-theoretical or Gödel-related difficulties in computer-hardware analogs to the human mind is not the province of this paper and is beyond our scholarly competence. Fortunately for us, Sir Karl has not made such considerations the focus of his attention (except insofar as there is a set-theoretical problem involved in the world-calendar idea, dealt with in Section I above).

Of course, in the real world no such "brain theorem" as T_b will be validly deducible from realized conditions S_t together with the cerebral nomologicals L_{phys}, inasmuch as all actual human thinkers (even philosophers!) do at times commit formal fallacies. It does not appear to us that this qualification is germane to the analysis we are proposing, however; it merely indicates that the human brain is, as we readily agree with Sir Karl, not a complete "clock" but a mechanism having some "cloudy" properties. For expository purposes we have considered the idealized case, that is, the brain of a thinker who never reasons fallaciously. The necessary modifications are easy and obvious ones which do not, as we think, affect the point of our line of argument. There are two ways to modify the above brain theorem example which would render it more realistic, one of which accepts a determinist picture of the world and the other a quasi-determinist picture with "random" components included as part of the system. On a completely determinist view, the conjunction $S_t L_{phys}$ is explained in such a way that the various causal *sources* of fallacious reasoning, e.g., of failure to conclude validly in Barbara, are ruled out as initial conditions by restrictively characterizing S_t in sufficient microdetail. (Another way of doing this, still preserving the determinist position, is to consider three classes of determiners, one of which is the structural determiners, the second of which is again L_{phys}, but the third of which is "momentary state-variables" such as emotion or the presence of some kind of unconscious Freudian dynamism, or unusual stimulus input or the like.) Alternatively, however, we may choose to do justice to what we, like Popper, suppose to be a certain cloudlike feature in the cerebral quasi-clock (even as causally understood by Omniscient Jones) in which case we must replace the brain theorem T_b in its nomological form by a brain theorem T'_b in stochastic form. In this case, the relationship between the stochastic brain theorem T'_b and the formal structure of the syllogism in Barbara (as shown forth in the subscripts on notation designating the brain states about which the theorem speaks) would be analogous to the familiar distinction between the statistical data that constitute an anthropologist's or a psycholinguist's "descriptive semantics" of a language, and the idealized semantical rules (*prescriptive* sense of "rule") which the dictionary writer, semantician, or logician sets down on the basis of this descriptive survey. Obviously, the overwhelming preponderance of successor states to the "premise-tokening" brain states will, in an intelligent nonpsychotic brain, be such as to reveal the same formal structure as in our idealized example. So that a perspicacious logician would have no more difficulty discerning the formal structure in the stochastically formulated theorem than he would in the nomological form, since he would immediately notice the high probability outcome $(b_S b_C b_P)$ and then discern that its subscripts are Barbara-related to the subscripts on the antecedent cerebral events. But, of course, while identifying the usual (valid, "rational") sequence would take care of the needs of the logician who is attempting to understand whether, and how, this particular brain "thinks correctly," the molar psychologist has an equally great interest—whether Freudian or less clinical in bent—in understanding causally why the brain theorem is merely stochastic, and in identifying the major classes of interfering factors which operate to produce departures from "validity" on certain occasions.

Conclusion

We must leave to the reader to judge, in the light of Sir Karl's rejoinder,[14] whether our criticisms of his argument are sound or not. In either case, we anticipate that his reply, like the papers to which we have reacted herein, will be stimulating and illuminating. We have not taken the reader's time nor the volume's limited space to emphasize our numerous points of agreement with Sir Karl (as, e.g., the untenability of those muddled and malignant varieties of societal determinism he so brilliantly refutes in *The Poverty of Historicism* and *The Open Society and Its Enemies*). Nor have we bestowed superfluous encomiums upon this great man. We have been engaged in an attempt to control his, and the reader's, cognitive processes — but by the method Sir Karl has so well defended in all of his writings, the method of rational criticism. We are confident that his own position will grow in clarity and depth by reaction to these criticisms of ours, as we have been moved (quasi-determined) to think afresh about the determinist position as a result of his objections.

It is perhaps unnecessary to add some final disclaimers about what we have *not* been doing. We have not been trying to make the positive case for radical determinism, which neither of us can presently hold for physics, and which is a methodological prescription as well as a promissory note, for molar psychology — the latter unlikely, for reasons Sir Karl persuasively adduces, ever to be fully paid. We have not been engaged in making a positive case for materialist monism (the "identity thesis" as a solution of the ontological mind-body problem), regarding which we both entertain doubts, mainly because of semantic difficulties with sentience (raw feels) but also, in part, owing to the puzzling data on telepathy and precognition. We have not attempted to reduce the categories of logic or semantics to those of physics or biology, knowing as we do that all such efforts necessarily involve philosophical mistakes of the most fundamental kind. Finally, we have not been so foolish as to offer a specific brain model, or to propound a molar theory of cognition, which is one of the most primitive and least understood domains of scientific psychology. Our purposes have been much more modest and limited in aim, namely, to criticize the philosophical arguments by which Sir Karl has tried to show — thus far unsuccessfully, as we think — that a doctrine of determinism or quasi-determinism (= physiological determinism qualified by cerebral randomizing systems) is *incompatible* with the admitted facts of (a) practical unpredictability, (b) creative novelty, and (c) rationality (insofar as it exists) in human affairs. If our critique contributes constructively to the development of Sir Karl's thought and to further clarification of the profound and difficult issues involved, we shall be satisfied.

Notes

1. K. R. Popper, *Of Clouds and Clocks: An Approach to the Problem of Rationality and the Freedom of Man* (St. Louis, Missouri: Washington University, 1966). Also: "Indeterminism in Quantum Physics and in Classical Physics, I and I," *The British Journal for the Philosophy of Science*, 1, No. 2 (1950), 117–33, and No. 3, 173–95. *Conjectures and Refutations: The Growth of Scientific Knowledge* (London: Routledge & Kegan Paul, 1963; New York: Basic Books, 1963), esp., "On the Status of Science and of Metaphysics," pp. 184–200; "Language and the Body-Mind Problem," pp. 293–98; "A Note on the Body-Mind Problem," pp. 299–303.

2. They are not decidable for the simple reason that their formulation requires universal as well as existential quantifiers. (But many scientific propositions have this form.)

3. K. R. Popper, "Indeterminism in Quantum Physics and in Classical Physics," Part I. *The British Journal for the Philosophy of Science*, 1, No. 2 (August, 1950), 117–33; *Ibid.*, Part II, 1, No. 3 (November, 1950), 173–95.

4. Although it is worth mentioning that the very clocklike electronic computer, programmed to discover proofs in the elementary propositional calculus by heuristic means (i.e., without the use of a systematic algorithm or decision procedure) succeeded in finding a proof for Theorem *2.85 of *Principia Mathematica* which required three steps and relied upon five earlier theorems, whereas Russell and Whitehead's proof required nine steps and relied upon seven additional theorems, including a lemma whose only use in *PM* is to help prove Theorem *2.85 (and which in turn required 11 steps, yielding a total of 20 steps needed by these human logicians). This strikes us as a rather impressive display of rational creativity by the clocklike computer, and those with expertise in the field assure us that they have hardly begun to tap the machine's resources. Prophecy by two nonexperts: A next major advance might well be metaprogramming for a wide class of mathematical structures, with a randomizer, so that the machine will *invent theories*. It will still have its built-in plus programmed limitations—there will be "theories which it cannot think." But then, as Kant would emphasize, the same is true of us. See A. Newell and H. A. Simon, "The Logic Theory Machine: a Complex Information Processing System," *Transactions on Information Theory* (Institute of Radio Engineers, September, 1956), Vol. IT-2, No. 3, pp. 61–79; A. Newell, J. C. Shaw, and H. A. Simon, "Empirical Explorations of the Logic Theory Machine," *Proceedings of the Western Joint Computer Conference* (Institute of Radio Engineers, February, 1957), pp. 218–30; A. Newell and J. C. Shaw, "Programming the Logic Theory Machine," *ibid.*, pp. 230–40; A. Newell, J. C. Shaw, and H. A. Simon, "Elements of a Theory of Human Problem Solving," *Psychological Review*, 65 (1958), 151–66; L. T. Allen Newell, J. C. Shaw, and H. A. Simon, "Note: Improvement of a Proof of a Theorem in the Elementary Propositional Calculus" (unpublished Carnegie Institute Proceedings Working Paper No. 8, Carnegie-Mellon University, January 13, 1958).

5. K. F. Schaffner, "Approaches to Reduction," *Philosophy of Science*, 34, No. 2 (1967), 137–47. John Kekes, "Physicalism, the Identity Theory and the Doctrine of Emergence," *Philosophy of Science*, 33, No. 4 (1966), 360–75. C. G. Hempel, *Aspects of Scientific Explanation* (New York: The Free Press; London: Collier-Macmillan, 1965), pp. 259–64. J. J. C. Smart, *Philosophy and Scientific Realism* (New York: Humanities Press, 1963). Ernest Nagel, *The Structure of Science* (New York: Harcourt, Brace & World, 1961), pp. 367–80, 433-35. Gustav Bergmann, *Philosophy of Science* (Madison: University of Wisconsin Press, 1957), pp. 140–71.

6. K. R. Popper, *Of Clouds and Clocks: An Approach to the Problem of Rationality and the Freedom of Man* (St. Louis: Washington University, 1966). Hereinafter cited as *CC*.

7. For a remarkably sophisticated treatment of this issue, cf. S. Freud, *The Unconscious* (1915, Standard Edition, XIV, pp. 161–215, [London: Horgarth Press, 1957]). The *locus classicus* for a molar-behavioristic defense of "cognitions" as inferred theoretical entities in infrahuman animals

(and, hence, not known to have a subjective, phenomenal aspect), is, of course, Edward Chace Tolman's great *Purposive Behavior in Animals and Men* (New York: Century Company, 1932).

8. "All men by nature desire to know."

9. The interested reader is referred to such sources as W. Honig, ed., *Operant Behavior: Areas of Research and Application* (New York: Appleton-Century-Crofts, 1966); L. P. Ullmann and L. Krasner, eds., *Case Studies in Behavior Modification* (New York: Holt, Rinehart & Winston, 1965); L. Krasner and L. P. Ullmann, eds., *Research in Behavior Modification* (New York: Holt, Rinehart & Winston, 1965); R. Ulrich, T. Stachnik, and J. Mabry, eds., *Control of Human Behavior* (Glenview, Ill.: Scott, Foresman, 1966).

10. Essay 2, this volume.

11. B. F. Skinner, "The Operational Analysis of Psychological Terms," *Psychological Review*. 52 (1945), 270–77.

12. W. Sellars, "Empiricism and the Philosophy of Mind," *Minnesota Studies in the Philosophy of Science*, Vol. I, *The Foundations of Science*, p. 328. Also in *Science, Perception, and Reality* (New York: The Humanities Press, 1963). W. Sellars, "Thought and Action," in *Freedom & Determinism*, ed. by K. Lehrer (New York: Random House, 1966). W. Sellars, "Intentionality and the Mental," *Minnesota Studies in the Philosophy of Science*, Vol. II (Appendix).

13. Herbert A. Simon, "Motivational and Emotional Controls of Cognition," *Psychological Review*, 74 (1967), 29–39.

14. K. R. Popper, "Replies to My Critics," in P. A. Schilpp (ed.), *The Philosophy of Karl Popper* (La Salle, IL: Open Court, 1974), pp. 962–1197.

4

Psychological Determinism or Chance: Configural Cerebral Autoselection as a Tertium Quid

I begin by responding to two thoughts that I daresay are in the reader's mind, as they were in mine when I debated with myself about accepting the invitation to write on this topic. Is it possible to say anything really new about this ancient problem in the present state of philosophical, neurological, and psychological knowledge? I myself often think that since Jonathan Edwards's great work (1754/1969) and the important papers of Hobart (1934), the University of California Associates (1938), and C. D. Broad (1934), very little incisive and illuminating has been done, and hardly anything radically *new*. One might except from this generalization the recent formulations of free action via the concept of a rational second-order value-coherency that is compatible with determinism (see Dworkin, 1970a; Frankfurt, 1971; Neely, 1974; Slote, 1980; Watson, 1975). In connection with rationality and determinism I urge a reading of my paper against Popper (essay 2, this volume) which, I fear, Sir Karl has chosen to deal with in a rather cavalier manner, as he did Professor Feigl's and my contribution to the Schilpp volume (essay 3, this volume; Popper, 1974, pp. 1072–78, and see comments on this by Mackie, 1978, pp. 365, 371). I think I may have something

---

This topic is the last one I discussed with Grover Maxwell, and the argument has benefited greatly from his (as always) fair, open-minded, but searching, "no-nonsense" criticisms. I should perhaps record that the amended form (read at a Philosophy Department Colloquium, April 10, 1981) failed to convince him that I had concocted a *via media* between determinism and chance in human choice. I am indebted to Tony Anderson for his forceful "10 little roulette wheels" objection at the colloquium. The basic idea of relying on Bernstein's Theorem and command neurons was propounded by me during early meetings (1953–54) of the Minnesota Center for the Philosophy of Science, and I no longer recall what sharpenings of the issue came from Herbert Feigl, Wilfrid Sellars, and Michael Scriven. Previous publications on selected aspects appear in Meehl, 1958, pp. 213–15, 328–38, essay 7 this volume, pp. 199–201, essay 19, pp. 537–41. While I no longer subscribe to the Lutheran theology in the first of these, the rest of the metaphysical analysis therein still seems to me quite acceptable.

I did not have the opportunity to read the indeterminism volume of Sir Karl Popper's *Postscript* (1983) before writing this essay.

refreshingly new to say about the concept of "determining a person to be genuinely free," without an abuse of language; and my speculative neurophysiology does rely on (a) the notion of command neurons, and (b) the Bernstein case in mathematical statistics, neither of which is generally familiar to philosophers.

Second, as to the question "Who cares anyway?", one does not know how many philosophers today are compatibilists vs. incompatibilists on the matter of determinism and moral responsibility. But one knows that there are at least some people on the fence who remain troubled by incompatibilist arguments despite Edwards, Hobart, the California Associates, and perhaps the majority of contemporary language analysts. I myself believe that C. D. Broad makes a very strong case—almost dispositive—against compatibilism. Even at the practical "real-life" level, I know of lawyers and judges—including the highly influential and sophisticated David Bazelon—who accept the incompatibilist view. They think that if criminal conduct were strictly determined by the influence of genes and conditioning on the momentary state of the brain, no ordinary-language analysis of words like "can" and "choose" would permit the attribution of blameworthiness (and, hence, punishment as just deserts) to an offender. I don't want to defend this incompatibilist view, about which I hold no firm opinion, but merely wish to indicate that in nonphilosophical circles the old-fashioned traditional stomach ache about freedom and responsibility is still a live one. Readers may wish to consult the collections by Berofsky (1966), Dworkin (1970b), Hook (1958), and Lehrer (1966), which I think show that despite varied emphasis and ingenious arguments, the *basic moves* available in the game are extremely limited. So far as I know, the approach taken in the present essay is a genuinely novel one.

My essay is not directed at ordinary-language analysis or refutation of the compatibilist position. But since I am going to use some speculative neurophysiology, I have an obligation to answer the kind of objection that says, "Don't talk to me about nerve cells, or about whether they 'can' or 'cannot' do something. Such talk is a category mistake if we are dealing with total actions performed by the whole human person." Now I am not so naïve as to think that one can properly refer to one of Mr. Reagan's neurons as being Republican. Nor do I hold the view that the *semantics* of intentional words can be completely rendered in neurologese. However, that one cannot reduce the semantics of 'intending to mail a letter' to statements about single nerve cells is one thing; that my neuronal firing patterns have no *causal* importance in understanding my letter-mailing is quite another thing. The possibility and usefulness of a purely molar (Littman and Rosen, 1950) description at the level of action (or phenomenology) does not make the micromachinery irrelevant when concepts like "possible" are under discussion. True, I can know what I mean by saying Mr. Reagan is a Republican without knowing anything about brain cells; I can know how to find out whether he is; I can be sophisticated about the avoidance of category mistakes when relating his Republicanism to his brain cells; but none of these things — about which I take it there would be no argument — permits us to declare independence of *all* statements about his Republicanism from all possible conjunctions of statements about his brain cells. Thus, if asked to predict whether he will be a Republican a year hence, it might be relevant to know whether his brain cells are undergoing senile changes.

There is a view that when we talk about human choices, decisions, intentions, and actions we are, by virtue of having chosen that level of description, emancipated from consequences of a theory of how the head works. This view strikes me as rather like that of some molar behaviorists who, in discussions of the alleged phenomena of latent learning, where one theoretical model for explaining the molar behavior is the possibility of the rat forming stimulus-stimulus connections not mediated by peripheral muscular events, argued that they had *absolutely zero* interest in whether the auditory and visual perception brain areas are internuncially connected, even by a huge bundle of axons. I vividly remember Michael Scriven pointing out to me, when I took this "Iowa-1950" position *arguendo*, that one can no more declare a relevant fact nonrelevant to a theoretical claim than one can decide by fiat that a logically *ir*relevant fact should be counted as part the evidence! Of course if a behaviorism is purely dispositional, as Skinner's approaches being, then each of the two sets of facts stands on its own feet; neither is privileged. If there *seems* to be an incompatibility between correctly deducible consequences of generalizations about how the brain is built and generalizations from Skinner box data at the molar level, the only thing one can do is wait around to see which set of generalizations turns out to be incorrect.

This approach will not wash for behaviorism less purely dispositional than Skinner's. Thus, it will not work for Hull's or Tolman's (or, needless to say, for nonbehaviorist entities like Freud's). Both the indefinitely extensible class of brain-facts and that of molar behavior facts are incompletely known, and the latter do not entail the molar theories, they merely tend to corroborate them. So if well-corroborated brain-wiring-facts were to render S-S learning antecedently probable, a weakly corroborated molar theory that precludes such learning is suspect. The "facts," as first-order generalizations of observations, may (almost, sometimes) speak for themselves; but since the domain of experimental contexts is still rather scantily mapped, "the facts" cannot speak so strongly for one molar theory as to exclude a competitor.

I think, in this connection, of a grandfather clock. A molar behaviorist (or ordinary-language analyst) might tell me that he neither needs nor desires to enter into discussion of the clock's innards. But if he complains and expresses mystification about the fact that the grandfather clock tends to run slow in summer and fast in the winter, he shouldn't put his fingers in his ears when I tell him that that's because the brass pendulum follows the physicist's law of linear expansion with increase in temperature, and the period of the pendulum follows Galileo's law of varying as the square root of the length; and therefore, of causal necessity, a grandfather clock being built the way it is built, it is going to run slow when warm and fast when cool.

I don't mean to prove anything substantive by these analogies, but only to motivate the discussion and prepare you to read some speculative neurophysiology, in answer to what begins as a seemingly straightforward question at the level of molar behavior and conciousness. At the risk of displaying my philosophical ignorance, I venture to say that the alleged exhaustive dichotomy "determinism/ chance" is "frame-analytic" (see essay 7, this volume, p. 246, fn 1). The exhaustiveness of the dichotomy is surely neither a truth of logic nor obtainable from one by substituting synonyms (I usually refer to this broader analyticity, that requires semantics, as "Webster-analyticity"). Therefore it must, if it is analytic, be what I call frame-analytic. I leave it to the logicians to tell me exactly what that is, but it's obvious that there has to be some such thing if we're to understand physics and mathematics. Now I don't know any way to show that an alleged exhaustive dichotomy is *not* frame-analytic when we deal with a loose, nonformalized, and very incomplete "conceptual frame" like psychophysiology. When a dichotomizer claims it is frame-analytic, in my experience he usually pushes that by saying, in effect, "Well, tell me what else it could be? If your behavior on a given choice occasion is not strictly determined, then you are saying that it's not a causal function of anything; and that *means* it's a matter of chance, doesn't it?" But my speculative psychophysiology aims to present a fairly simple and consistent alternative. If coherent, this alternative, being clearly *not* chance and clearly *not* determinism, shows that the frame-analyticity is an illusion.

I'm going to permit myself free use of the concept of a nomological and assume we all agree—however the future logicians manage to fix it up for us—that some rather basic distinction must be made between nomologicals and accidental universals. The research scientist (say, in a field like psychopharmacology) can't even set up an experiment and discuss its meaning if he can't have a nomological underlying his understanding of counterfactuals. He needs counterfactuals to talk about a "control group," to apply his results to advising individual patients in the future, to advocate public-health measures, and so on. I am also fairly happy with the notion of causal necessity, because given the fundamental nomologicals, all of the nomologicals that are derivable from them are "necessary" in as strong a sense of necessity as any of us wants or needs, namely, deductive necessity. And the relations between particulars that instantiate those nomologicals are then necessary as well. It goes without saying that a hard-core Humean (are there any? not among scientists I know) who consistently rejects even the faintest whiff of "causal necessity" will find the rest of the essay of no interest, since he should have no moral or political stomach ache about free choice, or any epistemological worry about the possibility of rational belief, to begin with.

If I am a strict psychophysiological determinist, what does this mean for the ordinary-language analysis, whether by Jonathan Edwards or one of the moderns, of the statement, "Jones stole the money, but he could have done otherwise"? Suppose someone pushes incompatibilism by saying (a) he couldn't have done otherwise and (b) invoking Kant's dictum that 'ought' implies 'can.' I suppose the commonest compatibilist reply is to say that whether he's determined or not (i.e., whether or not his behavior instantiates nomologicals), what we *mean* by "can" or "could have" in a molar statement about conduct is something like: "He could have had he chosen to." Here I could examine that gloss on "could have," where we distinguish an act that is impossible because of the mechanical limitations of human musculature, or an act that is impossible because the individual has never learned a certain motor skill, from any of the senses of "possible" that refer to motivations. We say that in ordinary language 'to be unable to do otherwise' means that it would be counternomological in these first two ways (strength or skill) but not in the third (motivational state). Ringing the changes on this one has consumed trainloads of wood pulp, but I cannot perceive most of it as illuminating, or even as geniunely engaging Broad's rigorous, deep-level thesis.

This gloss on the word 'possible' (= can or could) in "He could have done otherwise" does not help me one bit if I am stuck with the incompatibilist dilemma by Kant's principle. Suppose I am a thorough-going psychophysiological determinist like Freud or Skinner. One of the strongest meanings of the word 'impossible' (the strongest one I know of other than violating the laws of logic) and the meaning used in common life, in theoretical science, in medicine, and in the law courts—with the same meaning—is that the counterfactual particular contemplated would be counternomological. We say, "That can't happen," because we believe for it to happen would violate the laws of physics or chemistry or biology. That's not quite as bad as violating the laws of logic, but it's pretty bad! It's plenty bad enough to use the word 'impossible' whether in the laboratory, the parlor, or the courtroom. And if for the individual who stole the money to have done otherwise, to have resisted temptation, to have avoided stealing, it would have been necessary for his muscles to do, at the molar level of action, something that his brain cells *could not* transmit the physically necessary impulses for them to do, given the state of his brain at that time; then for him to resist stealing was impossible in a full-bodied, potent, nonmetaphorical meaning of that term. He is like the grandfather clock who loses time at the molar level because of the way his innards are put together and of the hot weather. My objection to the ordinary-language dissolution of this problem from Jonathan Edwards (or, for that matter, Calvin, Luther, and Augustine) to the moderns is simple: If the gloss on "he could have done otherwise" means he could have done otherwise had he willed to, or had he chosen to, or had he wanted to badly enough (inasmuch as he had the necessary conceptual knowledge, motor skills, and muscular strength), then the conclusion of these two lines of reasoning is that "under certain circumstances people can do things that are impossible." Since I find it hard to attach meaning to that sentence, I am, if I'm a consistent physiological determinist, pushed to reject an ordinary-language compatibilist gloss on "could have done otherwise." The gloss is more confusing than clarifying. The discussion of this "possible/impossible" problem in the criminal responsibility context by Wilson is the best that has come to my attention (Wilson, 1979, Part V) although I cannot quite accept all of it.

So much for the motivation, and now for my speculative psychophysiology. I first introduce the concept of a "command neuron," known in some earlier writings as "pontifical neuron" or "trigger neuron." This is not a new discovery, the earliest replicable finding of a command neuron being now some thirty years old (Wiersma, 1952). For information about the command-neuron concept and summaries of experimental evidence corroborating my statements in text following, the reader may consult Grillner and Shik (1975), Hubel and Wiesel (1962), Perkel and Bullock (1969), Rosenbaum (1977), Rosenbaum and Radford (1977), Schiller and Koener (1971), Wilson (1970), and see summary of concept's status by Kupfermann and Weiss (1978). There are conceptual controversies among neurophysiologists about defining properties at the furry edges of this concept, but they are not relevant here. The basic idea of a command neuron is that it is a single nerve cell which by spiking, either in a series of impulses or in some instances by one single impulse, controls (given a certain background of other neuronal action) a sizable number of later neurons in the chain to bring about the performance of a complex act, whether motoric or perceptual. Thus, for instance, there is one single command neuron in a certain species of crayfish which, when it spikes (a single pulse!), commands the integrated firing of some 300 neurons that jointly accomplish a complicated defensive reflex in one half of the animal. Command neurons were originally discovered in invertebrates but subsequently found in vertebrates, including cat and monkey. Since they involve microelectrode stimulation methods, it is not easy to study them directly in humans, and there isn't consensus among neurophysiologists about whether there are command neurons in the human, although many believe there are. There are molar behavior data that some take to corroborate the existence of command neurons in the human, and I am going to conjecture that we have them, like our primate relative the monkey. Since my paper is conceptual, aimed at showing the abstract possibility of a state affairs that is neither deterministic nor chance, I may be allowed to play with this empirical hypothesis, it being a plausible extrapolation not contradicted by present scientific evidence. To give you some idea of how far some neuroscientists are willing to push it, one of the leading neurophysiologists in the world, Dr. Theodore Bullock, when teasingly asked at a symposium, "Surely you don't think that I have a 'Ted Bullock-perceiving' command neuron in my visual system?'', replied that he thought that was quite possible, maybe even likely!

For expository purposes I am going to postulate that a certain action has 10 components (never mind whether some are simultaneous and others serially integrated); and that in an acculturated, morally educated, and prudential human being, an act like stealing money out of the till when your employer isn't looking involves 10 such components; and that each of these components is subject to inhibition by one command neuron. I am going to set aside Freudian parapraxes, whereby an abortive act is performed as a result of mental conflict. I'm going to postulate that the remainder of the cerebral system, whose complicated neural networks (both wired genetically and acquired by learning) are the cerebral subsystems for money-lust, fear of jail, recalling your Sunday school lessons, and whatever else enters into the picture, is strictly deterministic, although I think nothing crucial to my discussion hinges upon that simplification. Given a momentary cerebral state produced by perception of the money, hearing the employer slam the door as he leaves for the afternoon, and the like, and the recent memory of one's wife saying this morning she would like a mink coat if we could afford it, and so forth; then if there *were* no such inhibitor-command neurons, the rest of the system would run off in a certain predictable way in accordance with the nomologicals, leading to either stealing the money or resisting temptation, as the case may be. Note that I am *not* locating the brain's "prudential (or moral) engrams" in these command neurons. The prudential and ethical memory banks are located elsewhere; and it is only when they are activated in a suitable deterministic way that the command neurons even enter into the system. I will say more about that later.

Second, I'm going to conjecture the existence of genuine quantum indeterminacy of some, although not all, brain events. The presynaptic cells that synapse on the command neurons may be the locus of that quantum indeterminacy; or it may be that at the individual synaptic knobs which stimulate a command neuron there is a sort of "local outcome" uncertainty in the synaptic space events.

Now imagine a series of temptations of, say, 10 occasions over the course of the year when the individual is tempted to steal out of the till. Let us impose some indeterministic restrictions (that sounds funny but it's what I mean) on the events involved. Considering an individual command neuron on 10 successive occasions, assume it fires or not at random, although a run this short wouldn't suffice to *show* that it satisfies Mises's criterion of randomness. It has probability each time $p = \frac{1}{2}$ of spiking, and that probability does not depend on any place selection. Further, the Utopian biophysicist, after studying the local circumstances at the terminal button, tells us that the distances, energies, and times involved are of such an order of magnitude as to be possibly quantum uncertain, so he would not be surprised to find they are statistically indeterminate. The question whether quantum indeterminacy at the synapse plays a significant role in molar behavior remains unanswered, although Hecht's half-century-old conjecture (Hecht, 1934) that it could do so at the retinal receptor element seems generally accepted. For discussion pro and con of its "behavioral" relevance see Eccles (1951), Eccles (1953, pp. 271–86), Eddington (1929, pp. 310–15), Eddington (1935, pp. 86–91), Eddington (1939, pp. 179–84), Jordan (1955, pp. 108–13), London (1952), Pirenne and Marriott (1959), and Ratliff (1962). For criticism of the notion that quantum-indeterminacy at the single-unit micro-level could be relevant to psychological determinism at the level of molar behavior and experience see Grünbaum (1953), Popper (1966, pp. 13–14), Schroedinger (1951, pp. 58–64), and Stebbing (1937, pp. 141–242). Unfortunately, the terms 'quantum' and even 'quantum hypothesis' have been used by neurophysiologists to denote certain conjectures concerning the amounts and step-functional effects of transmitter substance released at the synaptic interface, which would seem only remotely related, if at all, to the indeterminacy question. Since the present essay concerns conceptual analysis (as bearing on certain metaphysical arguments), I permit myself the assumption *arguendo* that genuine Heisenbergian quantum indeterminacy obtains for some—we need not say all, or even most—synaptic events. That is, of course, an empirical question, not settled on present evidence.

We find further that there is pairwise independence between the local events, that is, the depolarizing inputs from the precommand cells. On those occasions *when the command neurons are in the system at all* the molar outcome is unpredictable and the sequence of response attributes "steal/not steal" satisfies Mises's criterion. So everything appears to be chance—until we reflect on the astounding fact that the 10 command neurons always act in concert. That is, there are no Freudian parapraxes or abortive actions, so that while we never know what will happen at a particular locus, and we cannot tell from what happens at locus A on command neuron I what will happen on locus B of command neuron X, we do know that if command neuron I spikes, so does command neuron X, and so do all eight of the others. So what we have is a radical indeterminacy (not due to ignorance—I'm talking about an ontological indeterminancy of the kind physicists believe in) at the level of the local synaptic events, as well as a complete indeterminacy at the molar level of action, provided that the actions studied are those in which the command neurons have been in the system at all. So that everything would look like a big random mess of quantum uncertain events, except for the astonishing fact that the command neurons always act configurally. That is, in concert they manifest a kind of joint intentionality with respect to their "necessary cooperation in the integrated outcome," so that the 10 part actions are either all performed (when I steal) or all inhibited (when I resist the temptation).

Such a system is clearly not determined, at either the micro or molar level; but it seems equally clear that it is not "pure chance." With 10 command neurons operating, each of which has a random firing probability of ½ on any one occasion, when all spike or all fail to spike, we are already past the traditional statistician's .01 significance level ($p < 10^{-3}$); and for such patterning to happen on 10 occasions over the course of a year has a probability that is minuscule.

On our antecedent knowledge that the spike-probability for each neuron, given a concurrent brain state sufficient to throw the command neurons "into the system," is and remains at $p = \frac{1}{2}$, an occurrence of 10 firing in concert shows that something nonrandom—something patterned, orderly, "configural"—is taking place. Even a single such coherent occasion might legitimate such an inference of nonrandomness at a statistical significance level customary in the life sciences, the probability of coordinated firing on the chance model being 2^{-10}. In this extreme case, we need not know anything about the effector events controlled (in this case inhibitorily) by the neuron to make a "nonchance" inference. A *fortiori*, we need not know how the achievement response class (MacCorquodale and Meehl, 1954, pp. 218–31)—the instrumental molar act—corresponding to that disjunction of effector movements is socially, legally, or ethically categorized. A totally nonethical cognizer from Saturn would be able to recognize the statistical evidence for a nonrandom, configural, "patterned" process. However, it is also true in this simple, clear case that having made the identification of the 10-spike event as highly unlikely on a chance basis, one can then go on, if he *has* the available action semantics, to characterize the molar outcome that is closely correlated with the (neurally necessitated) effector activities. The conjoint event is in itself "nonchance," but is also "nonchance *such that* . . . [achievement-characterized R-class] . . . . "

A more interesting case: There are 10 command neurons, 6 of which activate certain components (whether simultaneous or sequential) of a complex molar action, and 4 of which inhibit effector-patterns that would interfere—perhaps the 4 components of an "alternative action" at the molar level. On a particular occasion, the Utopian neurophysiologist observes a 6:4 split as to spiking, a split very close to the chance expected value. Neither expected value nor mode is appreciably larger than this one. So there would be no basis to infer anything "systematic" (nonchance) if we consider only the firing pattern of the command neurons on this occasion. However, if we supplement our microphysiological knowledge with information about the effectors thus controlled, and can also characterize the effector pattern in terms of an achievement class (e.g., stealing, speaking French, apologizing) we can discern the configurality at the command neuron level, *but only by reference to the molar action outcome, intentionally characterized*. So this is an interesting case philosophically. The Utopian physiologist takes note that if any of those that fired, or refrained from firing, on the particular occasion of a 6:4 split under study, had performed the other way, a "nonsense" action, like a fumbling or an asphasic outburst or a parapraxis, would have occurred. The reasoning here is very like the geneticist's in recognizing a "nonsense coding" that takes place when even a single base in the codon triplet (say, thymine) is replaced by adenine, out of a string of 200 or 300 triplets, each designating an amino acid, coded to control the synthesis of a particular polypeptide chain. A nonsense code makes a nonsense protein; which means, in turn, one that doesn't "do its job" in the metabolism of the cell.

It is worth noting that the kind of conceptual equipment the Utopian physiologist must possess to discern this, if he comes from Alpha Centauri, varies with the action-domain under scrutiny. It is possible to recognize some effector sequences as instrumental nonsense acts without employing ethical or social categories. For instance, a rat does something with some of his muscles that leads to the lever not being pressed, although the rest of the musculature does what it usually does, effector sequences that would get the lever down except for this one aberrant subsequence. In other cases, the "nonsense" would be discernible only by reference to higher level social concepts, such as the economic, legal, or moral significance of the instrumental action.

Consider an introspective account where one says, "I chose freely, after reflecting on the pros and cons, being influenced one way by my desire for the money and, opposing this, by moral and prudential reasons against stealing it." The corresponding brain state should presumably involve a causal dependency of the command neurons' functioning, or their being in the system at all, on activation of prudential and ethical memory banks. Let us suppose there is a "scanning" cerebral subsystem that plays a critical role in putting and keeping the command neurons "in the system." It is not Utopian (merely improving existing single-unit stimulation and recording techniques) to ascertain what happens if artificial means are employed to suppress activity in the ethical and prudential memory banks, or to interfere with the scanning subsystem's operations. Suppose we find that on the subset of occasions when such artificial interference prevents the counterconsiderations from even being available—cerebral tokenings of the argument sentences cannot neurophysiologically occur—the money motive always wins out, because the command neurons do not show their "normal" activity of inhibiting on half the occasions. I suggest that this is a plausible account of what, at the molar behavior and phenomenological level, we mean when we say that radical, existential freedom of choice in nontrivial situations involves the weighing of alternatives, the evaluating of reasons, the computing of utilities, the counterbalancing of motives, and the like. It would be incorrect to make the too-easy inference, found in Hobart and Jonathan Edwards, that *if* these counterconsiderations play a significant "influencing" role, *therefore* they must determine the outcome. It is true that these considerations (I prefer to say, "The cerebral events that are tokenings of sentences expressing the considerations") must play a significant influencing role if we have a kind of indeterminism that is affirmatively meaningful as a form of personal freedom, a real choosing. What they determine is that the outcome is indeterminate. That is shown by showing that preventing their usual activity, while leaving the rest of the cerebral system to run off as it normally would, yields a molar choice stealing probability no longer ½ but $p = 1$. On such occasions, the behavior is consistently "controlled by the strongest motive," the money drive, no countermotive being available.

After Hobart's powerful "If my action is not determined by my character, it is not *my* actions, and *I* am not responsible, capable of blame or regret," I think the next strongest (but, as I hope to show, rebuttable) objection to radical free will, as I used to hear it from Professor Feigl and other positivist colleagues, goes like this: "Look, the action is either determined, or it is a matter of chance. You *either* behave as you do because of a combination of internal and external causes (including your acquired cognitive and motivational dispositions, considered as causal), *or* you respond at random. You can't have it any other way, because there *is* no other way." When this plausible molar dichotomy is reduced to conjectural brain models, it still seems seductive to most philosophers and psychologists. When I talk about command neurons and indeterminacy they reply with, "Well, you still are trying to have it both ways. If the local micro-event is truly quantum indeterminate—that is, it's a chance happening—then no matter how you wire things up and no matter how many such local synaptic outcomes you consider, you still get a big random mess; you are trying to have your cake and eat it too, by alleging that the microevents are, both epistemologically and ontologically, indeterminate. Yet somehow you want to claim the macro-event is not merely a big random cascade effect, like the final distribution of marbles at the bottom of a Galton Board. That's inconsistent of you. If the component events are random, then the whole thing is random, however cleverly you fiddle with ways of describing that make it appear otherwise."

Now this, plausible as it sounds, is mistaken. It is presented as analytic—as a *conceptual* dichotomy, not requiring empirical data. As a conceptual dichotomy, it must rely on formal or semantic implications of the concepts "random" and "independent." There are three purely formal (mathematical) truths that all contradict such a dichotomist thesis, although in different ways at different levels of analysis:

1. Given $p(E_1/C_1) = $ ½ and $p(E_2/C_2) = $ ½ (even if $C_1 \leftrightarrow C_2$) then any correlation $[-1 \leq \phi(E_1E_2) \leq +1]$ may be assigned without contradiction.

2. Pairwise independence of events does not entail total configural independence within the system (Bernstein's Theorem, Cramér, 1946, p. 162; Feller, 1957, p. 117).

3. Numerical values of pairwise dependencies among *non*independent events do not suffice to deduce the values of higher-order dependencies by adding probability increments: There can be interaction effects, as recognized in standard analysis of variance formulas, the extreme, "pure configural" case being where significant interaction terms exist despite absence of an overall main effect.

The first of these principles assures us that the 10 command neurons may regularly fire (or not-fire) "in concert," despite each one's firing being indeterminate at $p = $ ½, this p-value remaining constant over an indefinitely extended

Fig. 1

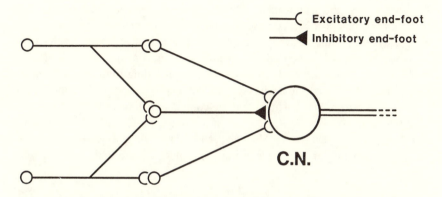

time-sequence of occasions. This suffices to refute the determinism/chance di-chotomist. The other two principles are helpful when we examine various *pre-synaptic deterministic* cases. Consider the situation in Figure 1. Here the command neuron ("C.N.") is deterministically controlled by input from two presynaptic neurons. The wiring is such that if either presynaptic cell fires alone, the command neuron fires; if neither fires, C.N. doesn't; and if *both* fire, C.N. does not fire, because of the cross-inhibition represented by the shaded triangular end-knobs. Figure 2 shows another way to get the result. (Empirical examples

Fig. 2

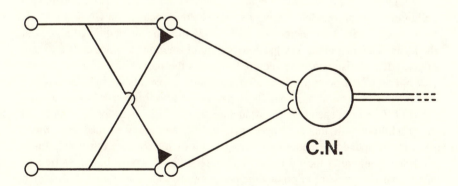

like this have been reported.) Assume that, given the extra-command neuron cerebral state necessary and sufficient to put the command neurons into the system, the input neurons each have indeterminate firing probability $p = \frac{1}{2}$ and their fire-probabilities are independent. This implies that the command neuron fires half the time. Suppose the same values obtain for the other nine command neurons. Then each of the presynaptic events is indeterminate at $p = \frac{1}{2}$; each pair of presynaptic events is independent, whether they are on the same or different command neurons; each trial is independent of preceding trials; but a *tetrad* of presynaptic events associated with only *two* command neurons is not configurally independent, given our constraint that the command neurons fire "in concert."

While formally possible, Case I may strike you as far-fetched. Case II (Figure 3) is less "rigged"-appearing. Here also, the command neurons fire deterministically as a function of their (indeterministic) inputs, iff 2–3 loci (+). The local

Fig. 3

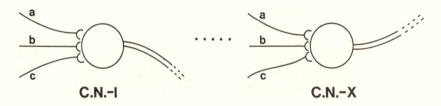

C.N.-I   **C.N.-X**

events on each C.N. are pairwise and three-wise independent ($p = \frac{1}{2}$). Table 1 shows the eight event-patterns, and the resulting "fire"/"not-fire" outcome on each. From the $(2+)$ input firing condition we compute that the firing probability conditional on a (+) at any locus is .75; and the inverse probability (that a locus is (+), conditional on command neuron firing) is also .75. The conditional probability of locus a_{II} on CN-II being (+), given that locus a_I on CN-I is (+), is then $(.75)^2 = .5625$, an increment of only .625 over the unconditional $p = \frac{1}{2}$ at the locus. This increment is what conventional Fisherian statistics calls a "main effect." If a statistician were required to guess the probability of a local event (say b_{II}) on CN-II being (+), conditional upon (+) events $a_I{}^+ b_I{}^+$ on CN-I together with (−) event $a_{II}{}^-$ on CN-II, he would reason thus: "There's a main effect of .625 from each (+) event, and a reasonable guess is approximate main effect additivity—if this stuff acts anything like agronomy or medicine. Since pairwise independence obtains between loci on each C.N., there is no reason to think that conjoining the (−) event $a_{II}{}^-$ alters the $b_{II}{}^-$ probability. So (recognizing that I'm guessing) I predict the $p(b_{II}{}^+/a_I{}^+ b_I{}^- a_{II}{}^-)$ at around .625, which I get by simply adding the two main effect increments." But this value is way off

Table 1

INPUT STATE			C.N. fires?
a	b	c	
+	+	+	+
+	+	−	+
+	−	+	+
+	−	−	−
−	+	+	+
−	+	−	−
−	−	+	−
−	−	−	−

$$p_I(F) = .50$$

$$p_I(F/a^+) = .75$$

$$p_I(F/b^+) = .75$$

$$p_{II}(F) = .50$$

$$p_{II}(a^+/F) = .75$$

$$p_{II}(b^+/a^+) = .50$$

$$p_I(a_{II}^+/a_I^+) = (.75)^2 = .5625$$

Increment $\Delta p = .0625$ "Main Effect"

But owing to "in concert" constraint on C.N.s, $p(b_{II}^+/a_I^+ \ b_I^+ \ a_{II}^-) = 1$

the mark, because the condition $(a_I{}^+ b_I{}^+)$ fires CN-I for sure, so if CN-I and CN-II always fire in concert, this requires two $(+)$ loci on CN-II; but locus a_{II} is negative, hence both remaining loci b_{II}, c_{II} must be $(+)$.

Case III (Figure 4) is one I concocted 30 years ago during an argument with

Fig. 4

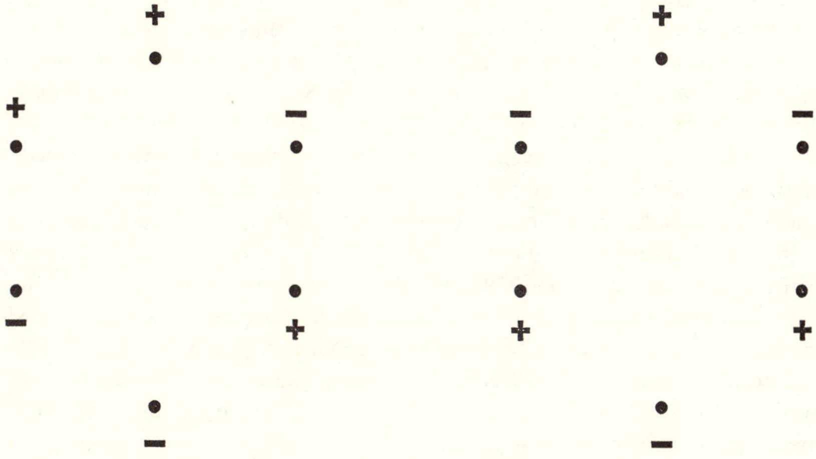

Pattern A   Pattern B

Professors Feigl and Sellars in the early days of the Minnesota Center for Philosophy of Science. Previous published treatments appear in Meehl (1958, pp. 213–25, 328–38), Meehl (essay 7, this volume, pp. 199–201), and Meehl (essay 19, pp. 537–41 this volume and *passim*). There are six loci, each has a (+) probability $p = \frac{1}{2}$, and the controllee neuron fires iff two or more *adjacent* loci are (+), very like the way in which neurons do respond. So Pattern A spikes the command neuron and Pattern B does not. Suppose exactly half the loci are (+) on each occasion. Then we cannot have pairwise independence between one command neuron's inputs (as in Cases I and II). But we can have pairwise independence between local inputs on *different* command neurons (unlike Case II). Note that by adjusting the *p*-values we can set the controllee neuron's spike-probability anywhere in the closed interval [0, 1], despite *all* the local outcomes being strictly indeterminate at $p = \frac{1}{2}$, Mises's criterion holding over the long run for each.

Suppose it happens that my fellow clerk (Figure 5), over the series of occasions when he perceives that I am tempted, sometimes tries to influence my conduct by purely moral appeals, and sometimes relies on prudential ones. For easy arithmetic, suppose the relative frequency of these two approaches is one half, although you will see in a moment that nothing qualitative hinges upon an even split. Assume that I am (deterministically) disposed to respond only to prudential arguments, being completely cold to moral ones. So the deterministic cerebral state throws the command neurons into the system only on the occasions of a prudential argument. On the other half of the occasions, faced with the totally inefficacious moral appeal, I deterministically follow the stealing motive. Among the remaining half of the occasions, acting under the influence of the efficacious prudential arguments, the command neurons are in the system and (indeterministically) inhibit stealing half the time. So that over the long run I succumb to the stealing temptation 75% of the time. Among those succumbing occasions, the Utopian neurophysiologist knows that two out of three of them were determined, and the remaining third were free. In 25% of the total series of occasions, I refrain from stealing, all of those taking place under the influence of the prudential arguments. I submit that it is then literally correct to characterize my dispositions as we ordinarily would: We may properly say that Meehl is often tempted to steal; that he is uninfluenceable by moral considerations when so tempted; that he is, however, influenceable by prudential arguments; that when so influenced he successfully resists temptation half the time; and on those occasions when he is acting under the prudential appeal influence — choosing sometimes to steal and sometimes to refrain — either way, his choice is radically free.

To the preceding conjectural brain models (presupposing the general philosophical points made at the beginning about counternomological impossibility and ordinary language analysis), a critic advances the following: "This is all

Fig. 5

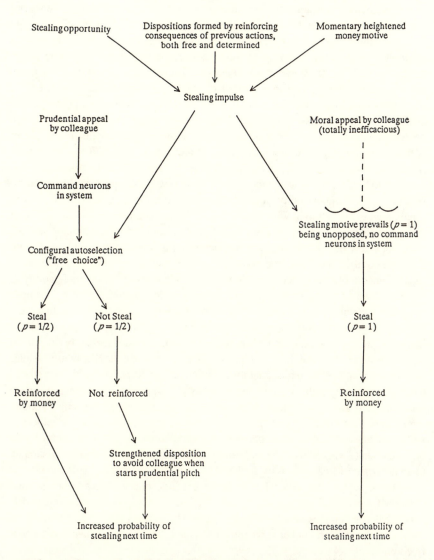

very interesting, and especially illuminating as to the dichotomist position, which I am prepared to grant you've shown to be false by constructing an internally consistent and plausible alternative to either determinism or pure chance. But I am unpersuaded that it will reassure the freewillite, or, *a fortiori*, the incompatibilist. Their original objection to determinism was that I 'cannot' refrain from stealing because for me to refrain would involve counternomological events in my brain, and counternomological events are *impossible*, in the strong strict literal meaning of that term. Your analysis disposes of the ordinary language gloss on 'could have done otherwise' and related expressions. As you say, it is difficult to attach any meaning to the sentence, 'Jones could have done otherwise, although the brain events involved in his actual doings and decidings, being necessarily determined in accordance with the nomologicals, were the only ones physiologically possible.' So I agree with your criticism that when the ordinary-language gloss on 'He could have done otherwise' combines with a proper analysis of *possibility* in terms of nomologicals, the conclusory statement is that 'Sometimes people can do things that are impossible,' and I don't countenance that statement, which, like you, I consider absurd. The incompatibilist who wants us to hold a thief nonaccountable or nonblameworthy appeals in the determinist frame to the impossibility of his having done otherwise, because he is, so to speak, merely the victim of what his neurons were (deterministically) doing. Now on your analysis he cannot say he was the victim of the deterministic action of his neurons, but surely he can still say he is the victim of his command neurons, which are firing randomly. That is, we are holding him accountable for something that is the molar outcome of a sequence of random cerebral micro-events. The thief can say to us, 'Look, we were originally troubled by your considering me a free moral agent — hence an accountable and blameworthy individual — for doing something that ordinary language says I could have refrained from doing. We rejected that ordinary-language claim on the grounds that, according to determinism, for my brain cells to have have fired otherwise than they did would have been nomologically impossible. You have substituted the notion that for my brain cells to have fired otherwise would have been nomologically possible, but that they fired the way they did was a chance affair. It's as if the molar action I finally perform — despite my performing it following reflection on the arguments of my fellow clerk, whether prudential or ethical — still, at that last critical stage, depends upon the outcome of the spinning of 10 little organic roulette wheels in my head. I fail to see why that should give any reassurance to an advocate of free will. Why should it leave me any less exculpable than if, instead of being little roulette wheels, they were little preset clocks? For the final choice — I repeat, following upon my deliberations, considering the arguments delicately balanced on the existential knife edge — to be a matter of chance doesn't seem preferable over the original case where we had the deterministic stomach ache about freedom.' "

Now this is a powerful objection, and it remains pretty impressive even when we correct the objector by pointing out that he is not quite entitled to say that what happened in the command neurons is literally a matter of "chance." In our conjectural brain model, while *individually* the command cells act as if by chance, and a subsequence of the molar sequence of temptation occasions satisfies Mises's criterion, yet the 'total cerebral event' involved in the choosing is seen *not* to be a matter of chance, because of the clearly ''nonchance'' patterned coherence of the several (local) outcomes. This is especially clear when what the nonchance pattern of that configural outcome at 10 loci *has to be* (teleolonomically) is inferred by considering significant social or moral properties of the final effector event defined as a molar achievement class.

Before meeting the objection head on, we may inquire what is the meaning of 'chance' that we think the consistent incompatibilist freewillite, given his original objections to determinism, ought to find equally objectionable here? The overinterpretation of 'chance' in this setting—and we don't know whether the critic is overinterpreting unless we press him to expand it further, but the passage above sounds suspiciously as though he is—is the connotation we dislike in such verbal correlatives as 'capricious,' 'meaningless,' 'blind,' 'unreasoning,' 'unmotivated,' 'without regard for such things as reasons or anticipated consequences,' and, perhaps the best word here, *'unintentional.'* Now to think properly about this we must parse the concept labeled 'chance' or 'random,' and ask which of the different (and, in most ordinary contexts, closely correlated) meanings apply.

The first ''chancey'' condition in the model is local unpredictability at the individual synapse, which we are postulating as present for quantum physics reasons. So the individual elements of the cerebral event are, by that definition, a matter of chance. Second, for the subset of all stealing temptation occasions in which the remainder of the cerebral system is in such a state as to put the command neurons effectively into the system at all (regardless of what they finally do jointly), there is sequential randomness; that is, the series of molar outcomes in the subset that are nondeterministic satisfies Mises's criterion, so the system is chance in that second respect also. But consider the strong, total system requirement that the 10 local events that jointly ''decide'' the final outcome (the firing or nonfiring of the 10 command neurons) should be *totally random*, i.e., satisfying the mathematician's condition of total independence. That requirement we have seen does not obtain in the present case; and the possibility of that total event being ''nonchance'' despite local indeterminacy and the Mises's criterion for the subsequence, arises from Bernstein's Theorem. Finally, a meaning of ''chance'' not expressed above, would be a ''mentalistic'' molar characterization of the events immediately preceding the final act of stealing or inhibiting, namely, that *reasons, motives, values, the weighing of considerations* and so on would play no genuine (efficacious, significant) role in the internal process terminated by the final action. Part of what is objectionable about the language ''10 little roulette wheels in my head'' is that such a locution makes it appear that the reasons offered by the fellow clerk, and one's reflection on them in the light of his prudential memory-bank activations, only seem subjectively to be relevant in what finally comes out but in actuality are not so. This is related to a point made by

C. A. Campbell in his distinction between the "inner" and "outer" aspect of a free choosing (1951 in Berofsky, 1966, pp. 131–33).

I fear that the basic question involved in the objection, and the possibility of answering it, is that perennial problem of philosophy about persons, "What is the 'I'?" Here a preliminary terminological observation, from which I don't intend to get much mileage but simply to alert the reader and myself to a tempting semantic danger: The language of the objector, "I am a victim of my command neurons, which are acting like 10 little roulette wheels," makes it sound rather as if the 'I' in that sentence is an entity wholly distinct from the command neurons. And on most (I'm going to argue below, on *all*) plausible solutions to the mind/body problem, this is misleading. That is, it is not as if there are command neurons and then, in addition, there is a psychophysical 'I' separate from them, whereby they do something first and then, as a consequence of that doing as an efficient cause, a something else befalls the 'I' of the sentence. The command neurons are part of the 'I,' insofar as it is a continuant (albeit a composite one); and ditto for the rest of the cerebral system that provides input to the command neurons and that responds to their commands. The 'I' is my total psychophysical system, the activities of which (when we move to a molecular level of analysis from the molar level of behavior and experience) *consist of* the firing of the neurons, command and otherwise, deterministic and indeterministic. Therefore one must speak with care to avoid falling into a subtle form of category mistake we would make if we said one of Mr. Reagan's neurons is Republican. I don't mean to adduce this warning as more than a warning. It is not, just as it stands, a cure for the stomach ache of our critic. If the determinist had a stomach ache that persisted after reading Hobart (or Bradley's letter to James [Perry, 1935, pp. 238–40]) where the 'I,' once in being and however composed at another level of analysis, is now acting, choosing, etc., the mere fact that this 'I' is a physical composite, and the command neurons are part of that composite, doesn't answer the objection, if the *properties of the elements* of that composite (under the deterministic scheme) make it impossible to choose otherwise than one did. I will say more on this below.

One might hope, as I did in a colloquium reading of this essay, to avoid getting into the morass of the mind/body problem; but it seems that cannot be managed. I do think it possible to show that the several still live options to the solution of the mind/body problem do not differ importantly with respect to my "solution" of the determinism/chance problem, the possible exception being what I shall call 'Strong Dualism,' to be explained in a moment. I suggest that we can give an explication of 'the Ego' that permits asking the questions that need to be asked about the above criticism, and to answer them, at both the molar and micro level, in a way that answers the critic as well. My classification of solutions to the mind/body problem differs somewhat from the usual, and I would try to put it in the usual way if I thought it made any difference, which I don't believe it does.

Even if it does, I believe readers will find they can make their own reclassification and restate the rest of the business accordingly.

By the *identity theory* I mean the strong interpretation of Feigl, Smart, Armstrong and Co. that mental events are literally and numerically identical with physical$_2$ (Meehl and Sellars, essay 6, this volume) brain events. I take this as an empirical thesis, and a meaningful claim, despite the familiar semantic objection concerning how I can know the meaning of a quality word like 'red' before knowing what, how, or even *that* red-perceiving events occur in my brain (essay 7, this volume). Suppose the identity thesis is denied, while the existence of mental events is granted as against a miniscule number of probably inconsistent behaviorists (I am not myself sure there are any quite like this). Then I would prefer, as I gather most philosophers do, a theory I shall label *Event Dualism*, in which the mental entity is a ''short-lived-continuant.'' That is, it comes into being and (quickly — the specious present) passes away. There is no truly mental entity considered to exist continuously between these happenings. I call it 'Event Dualism' to distinguish it from the Strong Dualism of a Descartes, but one then has the problem of how short-lived an ''ephemeral continuant'' can be before we don't count it as a continuant anymore. Thus, for instance, are nuclear particles with half lives of 10^{-20} microseconds ''continuants''? Or, for that matter, when an electron ceases to be at energy level K and appears at level L in an atom (without traversing space between them!), is there any basis for saying it's ''the same electron,'' rather than that an electron ceased to be at one level and, simultaneously, another one was created at another? However, I don't see that anything hinges upon that semantic convention of how short-lived a continuant can be and what kind of genidentity (or intercausal connections between its appearances) must obtain for it to be a continuant rather than an event or state. If most of the physicist's short-lived decay particles live long enough to be called continuants, the specious present of mental events — whether atomized or Gestalted — is surely long enough for Event Dualism. We do not want to call it a 'brain state,' because that language makes it appear as if we are still pushing some form of identity thesis.

The two kinds of Event Dualism are epiphenomenalism and interactionism. In epiphenomenalism the mental event is a causal descendant of the neurophysiological (= brain) event, but it is not itself a causal ancestor of anything, either of a subsequent mental event or of acting back (''interacting'') causally upon the stream of brain events. In the other form of Event Dualism, interactionism, we postulate a two-way causal influence, in which the transitory continuant or ''mental event'' acts upon the subsequent brain events in the brain-event stream whose earlier members gave rise to it. Physical analogies exist, such as self-induction (and the resulting dispositional concept of reactance). The theoretical distinguishability of epiphenomenalism and interactionism, contrary to the views of some philosophers who deny that, even in principle, there could be a way to tell them apart, is developed in essay 7 of this volume, pp. 192-93, 201.

Finally, we have Strong (Cartesian) Dualism, or what one might call *Substance Dualism*, in which we postulate a long-lived continuant (normally one thinks of it persisting during the life of the individual to whose body it is causally connected)—a psychoid, diathete (Kapp, 1940, 1951), soul, mind, or spirit. While not space filling, and not possessing such physical properties as charge, spin, or mass, being a thinking substance rather than an extended substance, the psychoid is nevertheless space located, by a semantic convention that (like Aquinas's angel) *it is where it acts*, it is wherever the physical$_2$ neural events are that are causal ancestors of its states and upon which it acts causally in certain ways (essay 7, this volume, pp. 198ff). This psychoid is a continuant that in itself undergoes states and dispositional changes, long- and short-term, and its states or events are causally efficacious, acting as efficient causes with regard to the sequence of brain states. A side benefit of our quantum uncertain neuron model is the possibility of this kind of old-fashioned ontological dualism, even if we insist that all the conservation laws of the physical$_2$ realm must obtain in the brain, since there is nothing about the conservation laws that prevents nonrandom "throwing" of a local quantum uncertain event. So that the psychoid, so to speak, "throws the switches," "selects the configuration of local outcomes" in the command neuron model.

In formulating a dualist theory I consider 'The Ego' as being the total integrated causally connected psychophysical subsystem that engages in the thinking and deciding process when I am tempted to steal, reflect upon the considerations pro and con, and decide to steal or not, as the case may be. Nothing philosophically important hinges upon precisely how widely we delimit that subsystem. We call it a '*sub*system' because we consider it obvious that if, say, a small region of my parietal lobe were activated briefly owing to slight pressure on my foot from a crinkled shoe as I listen to my fellow clerk make his pitch against stealing, this would not play a critical role in whether I decide to steal or not. There might be special circumstances under which it would; but under such special circumstances, that portion of the total cerebral system would be included in the subsystem that we are calling The Ego. We know that if a certain average overall ambient input for various modalities (including body surface pressures, etc.) is prevented by special experimental means, as in stimulus-deprivation research, changes take place in the ego, including, for some people at least, its very capacity to track, think logically, and know "who it is." Our clerk is not, however, in a stimulus-deprivation experiment, and what we do with that class of special conditions is what we ordinarily do in psychology, law, medicine, or genetics. We presuppose a certain *causal field* (Mackie, 1974) in whose (unusual) absence questions about causality could not be put in their usual form, but whose other "normal range" variable properties do not make any difference as to the outcome.

I think that unless one is a Strong Dualist he cannot coherently object to a microanalysis of The Ego and its actions in which The Ego has parts and part-functions. I mean here both physically located parts and mental events, although on the commonest view of Strong Dualism the psychoid, while it is "part" of The Ego, does not itself have parts, one of Socrates's arguments for the immortality of the soul. If you are not a Strong Dualist, The Ego is neurons and their dispositions and actions, which actions are efficient causes of short-term mental events, which in turn either act back on the neurons (interactionism) or are nomological danglers (epiphenomenalism). The only alternative to this, if one is not a Strong Dualist but doesn't want to say that The Ego is "made up of parts" (like brain cells), is the conclusion of the Buddhist King Milinda dialogue that there *is* no ego.

Just what is it that the thoroughgoing reflective freewillite wants to say literally about The Ego? He wants to say that The Ego—this psychophysical system that I have just briefly sketched—is influenced by motives (e.g., avarice, wish to keep his job, aim to be an honorable man, desire to please his wife with a mink coat); that it perceives as meaningful inputs the fellow clerk's arguments; that it remembers previous experiences; that it reflects, considers, deliberates, and after being pulled one way and another by the conflicting motives it chooses (*freely*— but "in the light of the preceding reflections"). If the muscle system works, the person acts. We note that all of these requirements except "chooses *freely*" are also satisfied by the determinist model. The question is, what help, if any, is provided by the quantum uncertain command neurons in preserving the other desired features found in determinism (and which the freewillite wants, or *ought to want* for the kinds of reasons Hobart adduces) but yet provides the possibility of choosing both "freely," *and* "in the light of the preceding deliberations and memories"?

Let me introduce a Utopian neurophysiology device which is, however, merely a technological improvement over things we already have, which I will call Dr. Schwitzgebel's Super-Machine. The original Schwitzgebel Machine (Schwitzgebel, 1967; Meehl, essay 14, this volume, p. 437 note 11) was for monitoring paroled criminals but our super one combines telemetric monitoring of single unit [= neuron] brain events with telemetric single-unit stimulation by implanted micro-electrodes. Dr. Schwitzgebel is at the console of his Super-Machine on the second floor of the retail store in which I am undergoing my stealing temptation and listening to the prudential arguments of my fellow clerk. Dr. Schwitzgebel receives moment-to-moment readings on states of those several cerebral subsystems that are the physical$_2$ components of The Ego. How might he detect, for instance, that the fellow clerk's prudential arguments are "influential"? First, the machine readings enable him to trace the firing sequence, and from general knowledge of how the brain is put together he knows what the main functional connections are from one Brodmann area to another. He combines this with whatever idiographic research was necessary on me as a particular subject to ascertain any microstructural peculiarities of my individual brain. Dr. Schwitzgebel knows, both from his TV screen image of the molar behavior and what the cerebroscopic machine tells him about my moment-to-moment brain states, that when my fellow clerk starts making his prudential arguments, my attentional scanner sends impulses to my prudential memory-bank neurons, thus stimulating them to fire to other neurons (in a different subdivision of the scanner mechanism, that is, the "pick-up" rather than the "eliciting" part of the scanner). These scanner neurons feed into neural subsystems which are presynaptic to the command neurons, *providing part of their input*. That normal sequence of events is already well known to him from previous research.

We have, corresponding to all this, the subject's molar ability to report (at the time or later) that "I considered the reasons that my fellow clerk was presenting." We also find an increase in the delay time and other molar indications (e.g., tremor of the hand, frowning, drumming on desk, subtle striped-muscle action-potential conflict indicators) showing that a state of conflict, distress, indecision has been induced. This conflictual state is different from the state induced if the clerk makes no arguments. In the case we were imagining, it differs greatly from the state induced when he makes ethical arguments, since I am an amoral person in this respect and respond only to prudential ones. Finally, over a *series of occasions* (over the years of my employment before the cops finally catch me), if we identify the molar subset of occasions in which I am not appealed to by my fellow clerk, or am appealed to by the inefficacious ethical reasons, the molar probability of thievery is $p = 1$; whereas on those occasions when the clerk argues prudentially (and in those cases we find the scanner activates the prudential memory banks which feed in a certain pattern to the command neurons) the probability of stealing is $p = \frac{1}{2}$. Behold, further, that the cases of successful temptation resistings *are that one-half of cases in which the command neurons fire to inhibit the stealing components*, even though, on the other half of the occasions (when the command neurons fail to fire) they are receiving the same kind of input from the precursors, including those precursor neurons that are being controlled by input from the activated prudential memory banks.

Dr. Schwitzgebel can intervene with his Super-Machine by pressing the red button which suppresses what would otherwise be the "normal reaction" of the prudential memory banks to the scanner's arousal of them. It turns out that in those cases the prudential arguments of the fellow clerk have the same consistent inefficacy as the moral arguments, and I regularly succumb to temptation under those artificial circumstances. Finally, the experimenters can get an interesting introspection from me (I don't know about Dr. Schwitzgebel's presence upstairs, and maybe I don't even know about my brain being microwired), for I say, "You know, that last time it was kind of funny, it was different from the way it usually is, in that Joe started making this pitch about I didn't want to go to the clink, and I heard his words, and I even understood their meaning as I usually do—but for some reason it was impossible really to keep my mind on it. I mean it was as if I just couldn't make myself think about those arguments the way I usually do. Very strange." To which the answer is, literally, "That's right, it *was impossible* for you fully to think those arguments, because Dr. Schwitzgebel was suppressing your prudential memory banks by pushing the red button."

Under these circumstances, when Dr. Schwitzgebel avoids pressing the button, we are entitled to say that The Ego chooses, as per the above freewillite list of desiderata for a genuinely free Ego. All of the conditions are met, including the one that is not met under the determinist scheme. The Ego chooses freely, the outcome of its choice situation can be either to steal or not steal, without either result being counternomological. What is the role of the command neurons in this kind of analysis? They permit this last condition to be fulfilled, which determinism does not. Even on the determinist thesis, it is possible literally to say "I [= Ego = the whole psychophysical subsystem] reflected, weighed and chose." Under this analysis we can add to the preceding sentence (which, even under determinism, is taken literally) the term 'freely.' The sentence without the adverb 'freely' is literally true, given determinism. It becomes false if the adverb 'freely' is added, because to have done otherwise than I did would have been counternomological and, hence, literally impossible for me at the time, in that state, with my past, etc. With the indeterminate command neurons in the system, everything else is as before. It is possible to say that I reflected, weighed and chose, and now we can add 'freely' because to have chosen otherwise than I did is not counternomological, that is, it was literally *possible to have done otherwise*.

Now this literal statement is not falsified, or even attenuated, by our going on to say, "The entity called 'Ego' in the above sentence is itself a composite. It is made up of neurons, and its actions consist of its various states and the patterned firing of those neurons in an organized fashion that is not random *as a system* but is not deterministic either."

I think it important to ask whether we can, if pressed (but under "fairly" stated conditions), formulate this at a purely molar level, turning the indeterminate command neuron conjecture into simply an interesting empirical speculation. If I am a freewillite, I want my decision to be *influenced by*, but *not strictly determined by*, motives and reasons. In what follows I shall avoid the usual metaphors of "I am a victim of," "My acts spring from me," or "I have to exercise my powers of . . . " and shall formulate things as literally as the subject matter permits. To avoid these metaphors and also to steer clear of microphysiology, it is necessary to make use of *ceteris paribus* clauses in certain places, and to presuppose that the molar behavior is "orderly" (by which I do not mean that it is strictly deterministic but that there are orderly relations between the molar conditions and the probabilities of certain molar outcomes). To begin with, the free-willite takes it as obvious that he is influenced by the mink-coat motive, that the current activated money drive was heightened by his wife's morning remark. That I will take as obvious and part of the causal field in stating the counterfactuals to follow. The question we want to answer in molar terms is what does it mean to say that I'm influenced by the prudential appeals of my fellow clerk? The most straightforward explication of the phrase 'influenced by . . . ' in causal contexts (which I have no trouble assimilating to "motives" or "reasons" contexts, despite a widespread opinion to the contrary) is that used in interpreting results of scientific investigations utilizing control groups, as in a drug study, namely, a suitably formulated counterfactual. In the present case some of the counterfactuals hold literally *casewise*, that is, assuming the external situation of employer's absence and the internal situation of mink-coat motive. (Molar behaviorism and phenomenology can refer to inner motives without saying anything about microstates other than in psychological language.) Other counterfactuals apply to subcollectives only and not to nomologically formulated casewise outcomes, that is, they have to state changes in the odds. Consider the following counterfactuals that may hold casewise:

a. Fellow clerk makes no appeal; I steal; had he made a moral appeal, I would have stolen ("anyway").
b. Fellow clerk makes prudential appeal, I refrain from stealing; had he not done this, *I would have stolen.*
c. Fellow clerk makes prudential appeal, I steal; had he made a moral appeal, I would have stolen ("anyway").

These, it seems to me, are straightforward (given the *ceteris paribus* clause), and they apply casewise as well as to the whole collection of cases meeting the stated conditions. This should satisfy one who is not a frequency theorist but a propensity theorist and who views the single occasion as involving *a propensity that is not realized*, quite apart from what the relative frequency might be in the long run. Frequency theorists will have to do this by some kind of Reichenbachian posit, the application of a frequency number to decision-making about the individual case.

There are some other equally important counterfactuals that apply only to the odds changes on the subcollectives, or on the propensity for the individual case once identified by the statement of its conditions, as:

d. Fellow clerk makes moral appeal, I steal; the subcollective probability of stealing here is $p = 1$. Had he made a prudential appeal instead of a moral appeal, it is possible that I would have stolen; it is also possible that I would have resisted stealing. Neither steal nor nonsteal is counternomological on the prudential appeal conditions, but within that subcollective $p = \frac{1}{2}$ instead of the $p = 1$ which the realized protasis sets.

We can take the shaping of habits further along this line so as to recognize what everyone knows about character formation under the influence of rewards and punishments. Being an amoral individual, I experience negligible guilt on those occasions when I steal, but perhaps I experience a good deal of selfish regret on those occasions when I resist. The result of such a reinforcement schedule may be that I avoid my fellow clerk as soon as he says enough to reveal that his objections will be prudential, but I remain relatively willing to listen to him when the appeal is moral. These second-order dispositions to listen or avoid listening are themselves deterministic, once established in me; but note that the very learning process that strengthens those differential dispositions to hear arguments of one kind versus those of another are the outcome of the consequences (having the stolen money or regretting that I don't have it) following (deterministically!) upon genuinely free acts of choice on a proper subset of occasions. So we make allowance for the laws of reinforcement, the attribution of stable traits, and the shaping of traits over time by one's life experiences, none of which is contradictory to the thesis of there being a subset of choosings that are radically, metaphysically free.

I must emphasize again that the subset which is indeterministic is still properly characterized as being "nonchance," and the genuinely free choosings are made in consideration of the (sometimes effective) prudential arguments. If the prudential arguments were not made, I would always succumb to the temptation — as I do when the inefficacious ethical arguments are made. Consequently, our ordinary view, that the arguments are irrelevant if they are without influence, is preserved by the model. But this "influence" takes the *statistical* form of altering a probability via introducing the command neurons, which does not require us to admit, following Edwards and Co., that the prudential arguments strictly determine what I do.

Consider a nonpsychological example, the Schroedinger cat experiment, not with the usual emphasis given it (the paradoxical mixed state of a molar cat who we know is actually either alive or dead) but simply with regard to the *determinacy* of his demise or survival. The single photon aimed precisely at the dividing line of a half-silvered mirror will pass through or will be reflected to a photocell, which outcome electrocutes the cat as a quantum indeterminate event. If the apparatus is misadjusted, say a millimeter to the left, it is determined that the cat lives. An opposite bias a millimeter to the right of the midline determines that the cat dies. How do we describe what the research assistant does if he detects such a misalignment and adjusts it properly? We say that he has determined to bring about a quantum uncertain event. What he has determined by his adjustment is that the outcome will be quantum uncertain, not that a certain outcome occurs. We have to speak carefully of what he does. If it was initially misadjusted for certain survival, we could arguably (but with a certain danger of misunderstanding) say that he had "killed the cat" by centering it properly, if the outcome of the quantum uncertain event is reflection of the photon. If he moved it from a millimeter left to a millimeter right of the midline, we would be entitled to say he had deterministically killed the cat. An adjustment in the opposite direction would clearly entitle us to say he had saved the cat's life. Suppose he moves it from the clear death position to the indeterminate position. What we say then depends upon the outcome of the uncertain event, because if the cat lives, we are surely entitled to say that he saved him, whereas if the cat dies despite the read-justment, we have to say something more complicated like, "Well, he gave the poor beast a fighting chance."

Let's apply this to a case where I argue with my fellow clerk, as I perceive he is tempted to steal the money. Whether I offer him prudential or moral arguments, what am I doing on this model? This is the kind of case where the dichotomist says that there would be no point in arguing with him if I didn't think that I was determining his conduct, an objection I here vigorously dispute. It may be that he is cerebrally determined to steal unless I, by my objections, throw his brain into such a state that the command neurons enter the causal system. But it may also be that my arguments are compelling, that my words lead to some cerebral scanning of his moral or prudential engrams or memory banks, which scanning determines him to resist stealing on this occasion. The point is that I do not need to know *which* of these circumstances obtains to make it rational for me to argue with him. Because if he is determined to steal when the command neurons aren't in the system, and my arguments put him on the existential knife-edge by throwing the command neurons into the system, then he's like Schroedinger's cat in that now he has a fighting chance to resist. If my arguments, instead of making him have an even chance, determine him to resist, that's all right too. In my state of ignorance of the microdetails of his cerebral system, I can't lose. A decision theorist would say here that arguing with the clerk dominates nonarguing, whatever the (unknown) state of nature. Notice that this model combines the notion of genuine (radical metaphysical knife-edge) "free choice" with the obvious fact, known to all sane persons centuries before Freud and Skinner, that people learn and develop habits, including the habits of reflection (or not) and the ability (or inability) to resist temptation. Any freewillite who does not deal with this obvious truth of human conduct is, of course, in serious implausibility trouble. There is a total sequence of molar choices of a clerk who, by repeatedly succumbing to temptation, becomes a habitual thief or who, by repeatedly resisting, becomes a reflexly honest character. That total sequence obviously does not satisfy Mises's randomness criterion over time, and it should not do so. Any theory of the mind that ignores the empirical laws of reinforcement or psychodynamics we must reject. But at the micro-levels, the Utopian neurophysiologist knows that there is a proper subset of occasions which, unfortunately for free will with regard to stealing, become scarcer as we go through the fellow's life. On these occasions, the *rest of the cerebral system* is determined by the history of previous choices and their consequences and the current stimulation (and, for all I know, by sun spots or barometric pressure) to throw the command neurons into the system. On that subset of occasions, the man is radically free to choose. Knowledge of the molar circumstances and the micro-level, including the bio-physicist's most detailed knowledge of the synapse, will not enable us to predict how he will choose before he does. That subset of molar occasions does satisfy Mises's criterion. We also know that on those occasions, whose *occurrence* may be determined and predictable, but whose outcome when they occur is radically unpredictable (not just epistemologically but ontologically so), the *system* is not behaving like "pure chance" because the configural effect shows that something orderly and, if I may so speak, "intentional" or "teleological" is taking place.

It is interesting to conjecture what the introspections might be that correspond to these funny brain events. What the freewillite objects to when the positivist determinist tells him that his only alternative to determinism is "pure chance" is that the subjective experience of moral or prudential choice under conflict and with reflection *seems* very "unchancey," whether or not an external observer could predict what *I* finally decide. I think my model shows that there is a soundness to this instinct. Consider the uninteresting case of a person being asked whether he wants chocolate or strawberry ice cream for dessert. He doesn't care much about dessert at all, and the only reason he gives an answer is to get rid of the waitress. He doesn't much like ice cream to begin with, he doesn't want any dessert, and even to the extent he slightly enjoys them on occasion, he has absolutely zero stable preference as between the two flavors. Now this system might be molar indeterminate, but without involving a micro-indeterminacy of command neurons. They would probably not even be in the system. The *molar* indeterminacy here might be the same sort as the molar indeterminacy of a steel ball rolling down the Galton board, which we usually assume (*pace* Popper!) is nevertheless strictly determined by the laws of mechanics, friction, biased dropping, slight variations of the pin position, and so forth. The Utopian microphysiologist might know that when a person has genuinely no preference (as in some of Thurstone's research on the intransitivity of unreliable food preferences, where no latent hedonic scale can appear if they're too close together, and no utility function derived) there is a microdetermined wavelike oscillation between chocolate and strawberry, with a certain period; and then there is a decision tension while the waitress waits; and a tension threshold for speaking one's decision. So the Utopian microphysiologist knows from the initial state that it will take 4.7 seconds for the decision tension to reach the critical score at which the man will speak, and he also can predict that at that instant the sine wave for ice cream flavors will be such that strawberry is momentarily in the ascendancy. So what is molar uncertain is microdeterminate. When you ask this chooser to introspect, he says, "What the hell. I couldn't care less either way, I just said something because I had to say something. I don't like ice cream." And if we press him further on his introspections about how he did decide, he says, "I don't know, I just picked one. Who cares?" This introspective report is, of course, totally unlike the introspective report following an intense moral or prudential conflict over a life-significant contemplated action like stealing, or leaving the Communist Party, or proposing to Drusilla, or whatever.

It is conceivable that the intensity of the conflict, the introspection "It took an awful lot of willpower to resist that temptation, believe me!" might involve some kind of quantitative difference in the number of command neurons that have to fire, which requires a more complicated set-up than the one I have imagined. The point is that our phenomenology of significant conflict, the consideration of reasons, the weighing of the utilities, etc., is very unlike the capricious, whimsical, "random" choice of ice cream flavors by someone who genuinely doesn't care. I am arguing that there must be a corresponding difference at the microlevel.

I now have to address a question which has doubtless occurred to the reader: "How could such a thing possibly be?" I might turn it around and ask, "Why do we find such an idea—despite the plausibility of both command neurons and quantum uncertainty existing in the brain, and the simple mathematical point of Bernstein's Case—so spooky and unlikely?" I am not up on the recent literature of reductionism in philosophy of science, so perhaps it is rash for me to consider this; but I am going to do it anyway, because I think it's fairly clear what the source of our uneasiness is about such a spooky business. It's the notion of 10 anatomically separated command neurons acting in concert when each is on a quantum uncertain knife-edge to spike or not to spike; we find that kind of "co-ordinated action at a distance," so the speak, something that we don't believe could happen in a brain. I am of the "we," I don't believe it either.

Why couldn't it happen? The best I come up with is that we Western materialists (we are almost all that at heart and in mind, whatever our official philosophy) find it incredible that there could be configural effects, patterns defined by a teleological specification of "outcome," unless that configurality is itself deducible as a theorem from a conjunction of statements about (a) properties of the parts and (b) their physical arrangement, as in the grandfather clock example. Discussion of this would involve the current state of arguments about emergence, concerning which I am insufficiently informed; but it seems that there are some kinds of "emergent" properties that do not distress us from the standpoint of our scientized metaphysics, and others that do. We are not, for instance, distressed when a computer can solve differential equations or carry out complicated iterative procedures to improve its approximation of a communality in factor analysis, although a single transistor in the computer's innards cannot do these things. It seems that certain kinds of configurality, at certain levels in the pyramid of the sciences, trouble us more than others.

I give two examples from physics, neither of which bothers the physicists, as far as I'm aware. Niels Bohr took some flack about his old quantum theory from people who said that it was simply a transcription of the Balmer formula. There is a smidgeon of truth in this criticism, so such people were pleased when de Broglie's later idea of an electron as a bunch of waves permitted derivation of the impossibility of electrons being between two Bohr energy states, because the waves would get in each other's way. There you have a configural principle about possible energy levels for an electron to exist in, that was (on the old Bohr model) *derived*, and in that sense "reduced" or "explained" by the properties of the parts. Not quite like a grandfather clock, but still . . . .

Compare this with the Pauli Exclusion Principle which, as I understand it, is *not* derivable as a theorem from more elementary principles, yet which is clearly configural in nature, simply forbidding two elementary particles belonging to the same system to share all four quantum numbers. If I knew more physics, I would be tempted to ask why nobody tried to derive it as a theorem. My hunch is that you would have to start talking about some kind of waves or globs or particles, say, Paulons, that would be sent from one electron to another, and before you were through you would have to reduplicate the Pauli Principle about these "informers," having gained nothing except more particles to worry about. In any case, what interests me here is that the physicist is not bothered by having a rock-bottom principle that is configural, even though he was pleased about the electron wave-cancellation business. It seems to be part of our reductionist conjecture about the universe that, despite the numerous remarkable emergent properties of living systems, we find it intellectually offensive if a configural property has to be simply postulated, and is not (at least potentially) a theorem flowing from statements about the parts and their arrangement. That's not very good, but it is the best I can do at present. It adds insult to injury, for most of us, if the very *statement* of that configural property has a teleological, intentional or purposive component, as in the present case.

Finally, it occurs to me as worth pursuing some other time the question whether such a configural cerebral autoselection might give aid and comfort to the metaphysical dualist? Suppose the integrated action of 10 command neurons were left for a very long scientific time period on the shelf as a rock-bottom, underived configural principle. We might just get used to saying, "Well, that's the way brains are! When brains get complicated enough, they start showing this funny kind of internal autocerebral configural selection of local events with respect to molar outcomes." One thinks of the arguments that if computers became sufficiently complicated, even though made out of hardware rather than amino acids and colloidal dispersions and so on, a certain kind of complexity itself would make consciousness emerge. We have all had fantasies (Prof. Gunderson published one in 1963) about the kind of conversation with a super computer concerning whether it had a subjective side that would lead us, however reluctantly, to conclude that it did. Somebody who remains offended by action at a distance, and fascinated by the intentional molar-outcome-oriented coherence of spiking/

nonspiking by command neurons, might ask whether this provides at least a little basis for the idea of a psychoid, entelechy, or Kapp's "diathete" (1940, 1951, 1955). A dualist might conceive a mental entity coordinated uniquely with a certain brain and, at times, getting into the act as the neurophysiologist Eccles has conjectured in his writings (particularly in the recent work with Popper). I, of course, disagree with Eccles and Popper in their view that quantum indeterminacy couldn't have anything to do with free will and choice. I suspect they have both been convinced by the dichotomist argument that the only alternative to determinism at the micro-level is randomness there and at all "higher" levels.

Finally, since I, after all, do belong mainly to a Psychology Department, and wouldn't want any scandalous rumors to reach my brethren over there, let me report that while I think this is an interesting kind of model, whose very possibility refutes the strong dichotomist position, showing that there are conceivable circumstances under which we would distinguish a *free choice* both from a "chance whim" on the one side and a strictly determined result on the other, I don't myself expect Utopian neurophysiology to find such a state of affairs. If I had to lay my own bets, I would be with Freud and Skinner as a psychological determinist.

References

Berofsky, B., ed. 1966. *Free Will and Determinism*. New York: Harper & Row.

Bohr, N. 1934. *Atomic Theory and the Description of Nature*. New York: Macmillan.

Broad, C. D. 1971. Determinism, Indeterminism, and Libertarianism (1934). Reprinted in *Broad's Critical Essays in Moral Philosophy*, ed. David Cheney. London: Allen & Unwin.

Campbell, C. A. 1951. Is "Freewill" a Pseudo-Problem? *Mind*, 60: 446–65. Reprinted in *Free Will and Determinism*, ed. B. Berofsky. New York: Harper & Row, 1966.

Cramér, H. 1946. *Mathematical Methods of Statistics*. Princeton: Princeton University Press.

Dworkin, G. 1970a. Acting Freely. *NOÛS* 4: 367–83.

Dworkin, G., ed. 1970b. *Determinism, Free Will, and Moral Responsibility*. Englewood Cliffs, N.J.: Prentice-Hall.

Eccles, J. C. 1953. *The Neurophysiological Basis of Mind*. Oxford: Oxford University Press, 271–86.

Eccles, J. C. 1951. Hypotheses Relating to the Brain-Mind Problem. *Nature* 68: 53–57.

Eddington, A. S. 1929. *The Nature of the Physical World*. New York: Macmillan. pp. 310–15.

Eddington, A. S. 1935. *New Pathways in Science*. New York: Macmillan. pp. 86–91.

Eddington, A. S. 1939. *The Philosophy of Physical Science*. Cambridge: Cambridge University Press. pp. 179–84.

Edwards, J. 1969. *Freedom of the Will*, eds. A. Kaufman and W. K. Frankena. New York: Bobbs-Merrill. (Originally published, 1754.)

Feller, W. 1957. *An Introduction to Probability Theory and Its Applications* (2nd ed.). New York: Wiley.

Frankfurt, H. 1971. Freedom of the Will and the Concept of a Person. *Journal of Philosophy* 68: 5–20.

Grillner, S., and Shik, M. L. "Command Neurons in the Cat." Paper presented at the International Conference on Control of Locomotion, Valley Forge, Pa., September 29–October 2, 1975.

Grünbaum, A. 1953. "Causality and the Science of Human Behavior." In *Readings in the Philosophy of Science*, eds. H. Feigl and M. Brodbeck. New York: Appleton-Century-Crofts.

Gunderson, K. 1963. Interview with a Robot. *Analysis* 23: 136–42.

Hecht, S. 1934. "The Nature of the Photoreceptor Process." In *Handbook of General Experimental Psychology*, ed. C. Murchison. Worcester, Mass.: Clark University Press.

Hobart, R. E. 1934. Free Will as Involving Determinism and Inconceivable without It. *Mind* 43: 1–27.

Hook, S., ed. 1958. *Determinism and Freedom in the Age of Modern Science*. New York: Collier.

Hubel, D. H., and Wiesel, T. 1962. Receptive Fields, Binocular Interaction, and Functional Architecture in the Cat's Visual Cortex. *Journal of Physiology, London* 160: 106–54.

Jordan, P. 1955. *Science and the Course of History*. New Haven, Conn.: Yale University Press, pp. 108–13.

Kapp, R. O. 1955. *Facts and Faith: The Dual Nature of Reality*. New York: Oxford University Press.

Kapp, R. O. 1951. *Mind, Life, and Body*. London: Constable.

Kapp, R. O. 1940. *Science vs. Materialism*. London: Methuen.

Kupfermann, I. and Weiss, K. R. 1978. The Command Neuron Concept. *The Behavioral and Brain Sciences* 1: 3–39.

Lehrer, R., ed. 1966. *Freedom and Determinism*. New York: Random House.

Littman, R. A., and Rosen, E. 1950. Molar and Molecular. *Psychological Review* 57: 58–65.

London, I. D. 1952. Quantum Biology and Psychology. *Journal of General Psychology* 46: 123–49.

MacCorquodale, K. and Meehl, P. E. 1954 "Edward C. Tolman." In *Modern Learning Theory*, eds. W. K. Estes, S. Koch, K. MacCorquodale, P. E. Meehl, C. G. Mueller, W. N. Schoenfeld, and W. S. Verplanck. New York: Appleton-Century-Crofts.

Mackie, J. L. 1965. Causes and Condtions. *American Philosophical Quarterly* 2: 1–20.

Mackie, J. L. 1974. *The Cement of the Universe: A Study of Causation*. Oxford: Oxford University Press.

Mackie, J. L. 1978. Failures in Criticism: Popper and His Commentators. *British Journal for the Philosophy of Science* 29: 363–75.

Meehl, P. E., Klann, R., Schmieding, A., Breimeier, K., and Schroeder-Slomann, S. 1958. *What, Then, is Man?* St. Louis: Concordia Publishing House.

Neely, W. 1974. Freedom and Desire. *Philosophical Review* 83: 32–54.

Perkel, D. H., and Bullock, T. H. 1969. "Neural coding." In *Neurosciences Research Symposium Summaries*, eds. F. O. Schmitt, T. Melnechuk, G. C. Quarton, and G. Adelman. Cambridge, Mass.: M.I.T. Press, pp. 405–527.

Perry, R. B. 1935. *The Thought and Character of William James II: Philosophy and Psychology*. Boston: Little, Brown & Co.

Pirenne, M. H., and Marriott, F. H. C. 1959. "The Quantum Theory of Light and the Psychophysiology of Vision." In *Psychology: A Study of a Science*, vol. 1, *Sensory, Perceptual and Physiological Formulations*, ed. S. Koch. New York: McGraw-Hill. pp. 288-361.

Popper, K. R. 1966. *Of Clouds and Clocks: An Approach to the Problem of Rationality and the Freedom of Man*. St. Louis: Washington University. Reprinted as Chapter 6 in K. R. Popper, *Objective Knowledge*. Oxford: Clarendon Press, 1972.

Popper, K. R. 1974. "Replies to My Critics." In *The Philosophy of Karl Popper*, ed. P. A. Schilpp. LaSalle, Ill.: Open Court.

Ratliff, F. 1962. "Some Interrelations among Physics, Physiology, and Psychology in the Study of Vision." In *Psychology: A Study of a Science*, vol. 4, *Biologically Oriented Fields*, ed. S. Koch. New York: McGraw-Hill (especially pp. 442–45).

Rosenbaum, D. A. 1977. Selective Adaptation of 'Command Neurons' in the Human Motor System. *Neuropsychologia* 15: 81–90.

Rosenbaum, D. A., and Radford, M. 1977. Sensory Feedback Does Not Cause Selective Adaptation of Human 'Command Neurons.' *Perceptual and Motor Skills* 41: 497–551.

Schiller, P. H., and Koerner, F. 1971. Discharge Characteristics of Single Units in Superior Colliculus of the Alert Rhesus Monkey. *Journal of Neurophysiology* 34: 920–36.

Schroedinger, E. 1951. *Science and Humanism.* Cambridge: Cambridge University Press, pp. 58–64. For criticism of the notion that quantum-indeterminancy at the single-unit micro-level could be relevant to psychological determinism at the level of molar behavior or experience.

Schwitzgebel, R. K. 1967. Electronic Innovation in the Behavioral Sciences: A Call to Responsibility. *American Psychologist* 22: 364–70.

Slote, M. A. 1980. Understanding Free Will. *Journal of Philosophy* 77: 135–51.

Stebbing, L. S. 1937. *Philosophy and the Physicists.* London: Methuen.

University of California Associates. 1938. "The Freedom of the Will." In *Knowledge and Society.* New York: Appleton-Century Co. Reprinted in *Readings in Philosophical Analysis*, eds. H. Feigl and W. Sellars. New York: Appleton-Century-Crofts, 1949.

Watson, G. 1975. Free Agency. *Journal of Philosophy* 72: 205–20.

Wiersma, C. 1952. Neurons of Arthropods. *Cold Spring Harbor Symposium in Quantitative Biology* 17: 155–63.

Wilson, D. M. 1970. "Neural Operations in Arthropod Ganglia." Chapter 38 in *The Neurosciences: Second Study Program*, ed. F. O. Schmitt. New York: Rockefeller University Press, pp. 397–409.

Wilson, E. 1979. *The Mental as Physical.* London: Routledge and Kegan Paul.

5

A Most Peculiar Paradox

The "empirical identity" view of the denotata of neurophysiological and phenomenal terms has been challenged as follows: Assume complete determinism in the physical (brain-state) series, and a parallelism between it and the phenomenal (mind-state) series. Suppose the parallelism is interrupted so that the subject experiences a phenomenal state different from that which has been invariably correlated with the present brain-state. No "interaction" occurs, so that all the physical laws hold as usual; yet the subject "would surely know" that he was having the one experience rather than the other. Thus, if an external observer informed him as to the current state of his brain, he would be "aware" that the usual correspondence had broken down. Such a hypothetical failure of isomorphism, even if in fact it never occurs, does not involve a contradiction. This possibility renders any "identity" of the neural and phenomenal unacceptable.

I wish to show that this argument involves certain rather paradoxical consequences. For simplicity, suppose there are only two brain-states, G and R. The (hitherto exceptionless) phenomenal accompaniments of these states are mind-states g ("experiencing green") and r ("experiencing red"). Causally dependent upon the brain-states G and R are subsequent brain-states G' ("naming green") and R' ("naming red"), and dependent upon these are peripheral-motor events G" ("uttering word 'green' ") and R"("uttering word 'red' "). The identity view asserts that if an exceptionless regularity holds coordinating g and r to G and R, the role of the former in the whole law system is indistinguishable from that of the latter, so that empirical identity can be asserted, on the usual grounds. The critic claims that even if the physical sequence continues to be wholly lawful, a subject would "know" that he was seeing r rather than the usual g.

But just what, and how, would such a subject "know"? The physical sequence runs off as usual, Green light →Retinal state for green→G→G'→G". But corresponding to G occurs phenomenal r instead of the usual g. If no physical laws are violated, what are the consequences? (1) The subject will utter "green"

169

although he "knows" he is seeing red. (2) If asked, "You said 'green,' did you mean to say 'red'?" he will answer "No, I mean 'green,' " since *replying* is a physical event and the physical series continues as usual. (3) He will hear himself say "green" and will not contradict himself by a subsequent remark, since to do this would mean that the usual physical consequences of a state, say H_G (brain-state produced by stimulus of own utterance), have been affected by the substitution of r for g, contrary to the hypothesis. (4) If asked in a subsequent epistemological discussion, "Do your utterances about color agree with your phenomenal field?" he will say "Yes, of course," as otherwise the physical sequence etc. (5) If asked by a philosopher, "Is there something you have discovered about epistemology or the mind-body problem, which for some reason you are unable to communicate to us by words or gestures?" he would reply, "No, there is not."

All this is not merely the familiar behaviorist thesis about the "other one," for these points apply where *oneself* is the "knowing subject." What do *I* "know," having experienced r instead of g? If I read the same books, insist that I hold the identity view, argue the same views on epistemology, publish the same opinions, what kind of "knowledge" is this? Could I, for example, "remember" this miracle? I could not say or write anything to suggest it to myself; all obtainable records of my reports would lead me to wonder whether I had not "really seen" g as usual (although I could not wonder aloud, nor with subvocal speech!). This is certainly a peculiar sort of knowing.

6

The Concept of Emergence

with Wilfrid Sellars

Somewhat over a quarter of a century ago, Professor Stephen Pepper published a paper on "Emergence" (1) which was (and still is) symptomatic of a certain way of thinking on this topic. The paper had the virtues of brevity and clarity, and, which is more important, it went to the heart of the matter. The fact that the crucial step in its argument is a simple *non sequitur* by no means detracts from its diagnostic value as a document in the controversy over emergence.

Before we examine Professor Pepper's argument, two introductory remarks are in order.

1. Our aim is not to defend an emergentist picture of the world, but rather to criticize an argument which, if successful, would make this picture indefensible. As we see it, the question whether the world is to be conceived along emergentist lines is a scientific question which cannot be settled on a priori grounds.

2. The question "Does the world contain emergents?" requires to be answered in terms of a scientific account of observable phenomena, and although with reference to a given scientific picture of the world the question is a *logical* one which concerns the formal structure of this picture, taken absolutely, the question shares the inductive character, and hence corrigibility in principle, of the scientific enterprise. Indeed, since science presents us today not with one integrated interpretation of the totality of observable phenomena, but rather with a large number of partially integrated theories of more limited scope, the question inevitably takes on a *speculative* character, and becomes an attempt to anticipate the logical structure of a theoretical framework which is still in gestation. This speculative dimension must, of course, be distinguished from the previously noted corrigibility (in principle) of any answer to the question "Are there emergents?"

I

Professor Pepper writes,

> Emergence signifies a kind of change. There seem to be three important kinds of change considered possible in modern metaphysical discussion. First, there is chance occurrence, the assertion of a cosmic irregularity, an occurrence about which no law could be stated. Second, there is what we may call a "shift," a change in which one characteristic replaces another, the sort of change traditionally described as invariable succession and when more refined described as a functional relation. Thirdly, there is emergence, which is a cumulative change, a change in which certain characteristics supervene upon other characteristics, these characteristics being adequate to explain the occurrence on their level. The important points here are first, that in discussing emergence we are not discussing the possibility of cosmic chance. The emergent evolutionists admit a thoroughgoing regularity in nature. And secondly, we are not discussing the legitimacy of shifts. These also are admitted. The issue is whether in addition to shifts there are emergent changes.
>
> The theory of emergence involves three propositions: (1) that there are levels of existence defined in terms of degrees of integration; (2) that there are marks which distinguish these levels from one another over and above the degrees of integration; (3) that is impossible to deduce the marks of a higher level from those of a lower level, and perhaps also (though this is not clear) impossible to deduce marks of a lower level from those of a higher. The first proposition, that there are degrees of integration in nature, is not controversial. The specific issue arises from the second and third propositions. The second states that there is cumulative change, the third that such change is not predictable.
>
> What I wish to show is that each of these propositions is subject to a dilemma: (1) either the alleged emergent change is not cumulative or it is epiphenomenal; (2) either the alleged emergent change is predictable like any physical change, or it is epiphenomenal. I assume that a theory of wholesale epiphenomenalism is metaphysically unsatisfactory. I feel the more justified in making this assumption because I have been led to understand that the theory of emergent evolution has been largely developed as a corrective of mechanistic theories with their attendant psycho-physical dualisms and epiphenomenalisms. (241)

The distinctions drawn in the first of these paragraphs provides the basic framework of Pepper's argument. Pointing out, quite correctly, that indeterminism is neither essential to, nor characteristic of, theories of emergent evolution, Pepper draws a distinction between two possible types of regularity: (a) "shifts" — that is to say regularities of the kind "traditionally described as invariable succession''; (b) regularities ''in which certain characteristics supervene upon other characteristics.'' Notice, however, that to his description of the second kind of regularity he adds the phrase ''these [latter] characteristics being adequate to explain the occurrences on their level.'' By adding this phrase, Pepper implies that there could be no such thing as a regularity in which certain characteristics supervene upon other characteristics but in which the lower level characteristics were not adequate to explain the occurrences on their level. In other words, he implies that ''supervening'' or emergent characteristics are, merely by virtue of being such, unnecessary to the explanation of occurrences at the lower level—that is to say, of occurrences insofar as they exemplify nonemergent characteristics. And, indeed, he implies that this is such a well-known and generally accepted fact that its use requires no justification in this day and age. We are not surprised, then, to find him claiming, without further ado, in the fifth paragraph, that ''a theory of emergent qualities is palpably a theory of epiphenomena'' (p. 242).

Now the claim that emergent qualities are (''palpably'') epiphenomenal can scarcely be just the claim that emergent qualities have necessary-and-sufficient conditions. ''Epiphenomenal'' carries, and is intended by Pepper to carry, the connotation ''making no difference.'' Obviously ''having a necessary-and-sufficient condition'' is not identical in sense with ''making no difference.'' Yet the idea that emergent qualities must be epiphenomenal is clearly tied up with the idea that a certain context specified in terms of lower level characteristics is the necessary-and-sufficient condition for the appearance of the emergent quality. A glance at the conventional diagram will show what is going on.

$$H$$
$$\uparrow$$
$$(A) \qquad \Phi_0 \longrightarrow \Phi_1 \longrightarrow \Phi_2$$

This diagram is designed to be a representation of the following propositions: (1) Φ_0 is a sufficient condition of Φ_1; (2) Φ_1 is a sufficient condition of Φ_2; (3) Φ_1 is also the necessary and sufficient condition of H. But while this is all that the diagram is *intended* to represent, it strongly suggests that H is, in the proper sense of the term, an epiphenomenon. That this suggestion is unwarranted, that the information summed up in the diagram leaves open the question as to whether H is an epiphenomenon, will be established at a later stage in our argument. For the moment we shall limit ourselves to some reflection on the phrase ''making no difference.''

It is obvious that if H is to ''make a difference'' there must be a difference between situations in which it is present and situations in which it is not. That there is one such difference is clear; H-situations differ from non-H-situations in that the former are also Φ_1 situations and the latter not. But this difference, far from being a difference that would keep H from being epiphenomenal, is at least part of what is meant by calling H an epiphenomenon. And, indeed, if there were no other difference between H-situations and non-H-situations, H *would* be epiphenomenal. But what other difference could there be? Clearly it is a mistake to look for this new difference in the form of another characteristic that is present when H is present and absent when H is absent. There remains only the possibility that H-situations are governed by different laws than non-H-situations. And this not in the trivial sense that H-situations conform to the law "H if and only if Φ_1," whereas non-H-situations do not (save vacuously), but in the important sense that the lower level characteristics themselves exhibit a different lawfulness in H-situations. In other words, for emergent qualities to make a difference which removes them from the category of the epiphenomenal, in any significant sense of this term, there must be "emergent laws." We hasten to add that the last few remarks are informal in character, and are intended to be hints and signposts of what is coming, rather than definitive clarifications.

II

Pepper's "first dilemma," designed to prove that "either the alleged emergent change is not cumulative or it is epiphenomenal," begins with a distinction between those theories of emergence according to which what emerges are *qualities* and those according to which what emerges are *laws*. He points out that in Alexander's system it is new qualities which emerge; but he expresses the conviction that "most emergent evolutionists have theories of emergent laws" (p. 242). As we have already noted, he claims that "a theory of emergent qualities is palpably a theory of epiphenomena." On the other hand "it is not so obvious that a theory of emergent laws must also be such — or else cease to be a theory of emergence" (p. 242). But though he finds the latter claim "not so obvious," it is, as he sees it, equally true, and it is to the task of showing it to be true that he now turns.

Before we take up his argument, some remarks on his classification of theories of emergence are in order. Once again we find fewer alternatives presented than are abstractly possible. Postponing (with Pepper) the question as to what could be meant by "emergent law," the dichotomy "emergent quality" — "emergent law" yields a trichotomy of emergentist theories: (a) theories of emergent qualities without emergent laws; (b) theories of emergent qualities with emergent laws; (c) theories of emergent laws without emergent qualities. Now we have already suggested that of these three only the first is "palpably" committed to epiphenomenalism (unless, that is, a theory of emergent qualities is "epiphenomenalistic'' merely by virtue of that fact that it recognizes that emergent qualities have necessary-and-sufficient conditions). We now notice that to make this first alternative consistent with determinism (which is not in question in this paper) we must either refuse to call the regularities between emergent qualities and the contexts in which they emerge ''laws,'' or, calling them ''laws,'' we must deny that they are ''emergent.'' Pepper, in effect, by drawing his distinction between ''shifts'' and ''superveniencies'' takes the former alternative. In these terms, the regularities in diagram (A) between Φ_0 and Φ_1, and between Φ_1 and Φ_2 would be shifts, whereas that between Φ_1 and H would be a regularity of supervenience. And in these terms, the three alternatives above become (a') theories of emergent qualities without emergent shifts; (b') theories of emergent qualities with emergent shifts; (c') theories of emergent shifts without emergent qualities. But from the standpoint of one whose concern is with the question ''Does emergence involve epiphenomenalism?'' and who is convinced that emergent qualities must as such be epiphenomenal, this trichotomy reduces to this dichotomy: theories without emergent shifts—theories with emergent shifts. And from this standpoint, and in these terms, the issue would be ''Do emergent shifts involve epiphenomenalism?''

But this is not how Pepper sets up his problem. In his first formulation, as we have seen, he makes use of the general notion of *law*, and sees his purpose as that of showing that ''a theory of emergent laws . . . must be [a theory of epiphenomena] or else cease to be a theory of emergence.'' Then, after drawing a distinction between *laws* and the *regularities* they describe, he reformulates his task as that of showing that ''all natural regularities are shifts.'' At first sight this is puzzling indeed, for as the term ''shift'' was introduced, it amounts to the task of showing that no natural regularities are regularities in which ''certain characteristics supervene upon other characteristics.'' And since the understood context is ''under pain of epiphenomenalism,'' this amounts, in turn, to the task of showing that supervening *characteristics* must be epiphenomena. But at first sight this is only verbally different from the task of showing that emergent qualities are epiphenomena—and this for Pepper, is no task, since the *demonstrandum* is ''palpably'' true.

Now the key to the resolution of this difficulty is the philosophical virtuosity of the term ''characteristic.'' Often used in the sense of *property*, frequently used to cover both *properties* and *relations*, it is here being used in so broad a sense that even *regularities* become characteristics. Pepper, indeed, is thinking of an emergent law as a *supervening regularity*—as, so to speak, a regularity which rides piggy-back on a lower level regularity. It is little wonder that, approaching it with this mental set, he finds the notion of an emergent law absurd. As he sees it, the emergentist who speaks of emergent laws is able to swallow this absurdity because he mistakes a ''whole hierarchy of different laws''—each of which, according to Pepper, describes ''the same natural regularities''—for a ''ladder of cosmic regularities.'' Pepper does not develop this point. However, in terms of contemporary controversy, the initial mistake of the emergentist, according to Pepper, is to be so fascinated by the difference between one framework of concepts and laws (e.g., biology) and the proximate lower level framework of concepts and laws (e.g., organic chemistry) that he finds it difficult to believe that the one could be reducible to the other. What is not clear is whether Pepper believes that the denial (in principle) of reducibility involves the absurdities he finds in the notion of emergent laws.

III

Be this as it may, the fact remains that Pepper does find the emergentist view absurd, and offers an argument to prove it. He seeks, as we have seen, to show that ''all natural regularities are shifts.'' Now this thesis is equivalent to ''there are no emergent (supervening) regularities'' only if ''shifts'' is being used in such a way that it connotes absence of supervenience. Given this connotation, Pepper's formulation of his task is equivalent to our formulation at the end of the preceding section, namely, ''Do emergent shifts involve epiphenomenalism?'' Indeed, in the terminology of that section, it becomes ''Is the notion of an emergent shift absurd?'' Here is his argument:

> Let us suppose a shift at level B is described as a function of four variables q, r, s, and t. Let us then suppose that r and s constitute an integration giving rise to level C at which level a new cosmic regularity emerges that can be described as a function of four variables r, s, a, and b. r and s must necessarily be variables in this emergent law even though they are variables of level B, because they constitute part of the conditions under which the emergent law is possible. Theoretically, to be sure, the emergent law may be thought of either as a function of new variables or as a new function of C-level variables. But actually only the former is possible. For if the new law were not f_1, (q,r,s,t), but were f_2 (q,r,s,t), then, of course, it would *never* be f_1 (q,r,s,t), unless the event were a chance occurrence in which case no regularity could be described anyway. The point is, either f_1 adequately describes the interrelationships of (q,r,s,t) or f_2 does; or if neither adequately describes the interrelationships there is some f_3 that does, but there cannot be two adequate descriptions of the same interrelationships among the same variables.
>
> An emergent law must, therefore, involve the emergence of new variables. But these new variables either have some functional relationship with the rest of the lower level variables or they haven't. If they haven't, they are sheer epiphenomena, and the view resolves itself into a theory of qualitative emergence. If they have, they have to be included among the total set of variables

described by the lower level functional relation; they have to drop down and take their places among the lower level variables as elements in a lower level shift.

Such being the case, our dilemma is established so far as concerns cumulative change—either there is no such thing or it is epiphenomenal . . . (pp. 242–43)

Before embarking upon a more general discussion, we shall examine the argument in Pepper's form. It can be restated as follows:

1. If a function f_1 (q,r,s,t) "adequately describes the interrelationships" among four variables q, r, s and t, then no other function f_2, nonequivalent to f_1, of these variables can do so. "There cannot be two adequate descriptions of the same interrelationships among the same variables."

2. If f_2 "adequately describes the interrelationships" among these variables *after* the 'integration' (and putative emergence) then, since sheer difference of time has no material consequence, f_2 must also be the adequate description of these interrelationships before the integration. Consequently f_1 could only be the adequate description of these interrelationships before the integration if it were equivalent to f_2, which, *ex hypothesi*, it is not.

3. Hence, if f_2 "adequately describes the interrelationships" after the integration, f_1 cannot adequately describe the relationships which obtain before the integration. "The point is, either f_1 adequately describes the interrelationships of (q,r,s,t) or f_2 does; or if neither adequately describes the interrelationships, there is some f_3 which does . . . "

But surely this is too strong—a veritable *ignoratio elenchi*. What the emergentist says is that there is a region in the fourspace $qrst$ within which f_1 (q,r,s,t) = 0 holds. This region is the "lower level of integration"—e.g., physicochemical processes which are not occurring in protoplasm. On the other hand, there is another region—the "emergent" region—in which f_2 (q,r,s,t) = 0 holds, $f_1 \neq f_2$. And a claim of *this* kind is mathematically unexceptionable, since it amounts to no more than the claim that a function may graduate the empirical data in restricted regions but break down when extrapolated. Such a "breakdown" does not mean, however, that the fit attained in either the subregion fitted by f_1 or that fitted by f_2 is a "chance occurrence." The fit may be excellent, and the demarcation of the regions precise (or, if gradual, thoroughly lawful) so that the "chance occurrence" interpretation is as definitely excludable as it ever can be by inductive methods. It should be noted that phenomena in describing which scientists speak of "laws of composition" belong to this category.

But while the notion of different regions in the fourspace $qrst$ exhibiting different functional relationships is mathematically unexceptionable, is it emergence? Here the first thing to note is that the notion, as such, involves no "supervenience." For (a) no emergent variables have been introduced; f_1 and f_2

being functions of the same four variables; and (b) it is not being claimed that there are 'piggy-back' regularities. When a situation exhibits a constellation of values of q, r, s, and t falling within region$_1$ of the fourspace, it is not exhibiting a constellation falling within region$_2$ and vice versa. When a situation conforms to f_2, it is not conforming to f_1, and vice versa. Thus, to the extent that 'emergence' connotes the simultaneous presence in a single situation of two or more levels, the notion we have been analyzing is not, *as such*, a matter of emergence. This, however, is not to say that there is no philosophical use of "emergence"—a use, that is, to connote something of philosophical interest—according to which cases of this kind are cases of emergence. Thus, the mere fact that the highly complex organic compounds which are found in protoplasm made their appearance late in the history of the universe would *not* be a fact of emergence in any philosophically interesting sense. But if we add to this the notion that protoplasm exhibits a constellation of physicochemical variables which belongs in a region of the n-space defined by those variables that conform to a different function than do the regions to which belong constellations exhibited by less complex physicochemical situations, then the use of the term "emergence" seems not inappropriate. And, indeed, many philosophers who have made use of the concept of *levels of integration* or *levels of causality* seem to have had something like the above in mind.

But it is reasonably clear that most emergentist philosophers have had something more in mind. They have spoken of the emergence of *properties*. And while there is a usage of "property" (in the sense of *dispositional property*) in which to mention a property of an object is to mention a functional correlation exhibited by that object—so that to say, for example, that protoplasm has an emergent property would be just another way of saying what was said above in terms of different functions holding for different regions in the n-space of physicochemical variables—not all the 'properties' that have been said to 'emerge' can be given this interpretation. Thus, the qualia of feeling and sensation have been said to emerge. It must be confessed, however, that emergentists have tended to lump into one category of "emergent properties" items which require radically different treatment, e.g., *sense qualities, life, purpose, value, thought.*

IV

We are now in a position to make a more penetrating analysis of Pepper's claim that theories of emergent qualities are committed to epiphenomenalism. If determinism is assumed, so that these qualities are themselves lawfully related to the lower level variables, then it must be granted that descriptive laws predicting the course of the latter can, in principle, always be formulated in terms of them alone. For suppose the emergents to be a and b, depending for their appearance upon, say, appropriate values of q, r, s and t, so that, for example,

$$a = g(q,r)$$
$$b = h(s,t)$$

then the function which adequately describes the interrelationships of the inclusive set of variables (q,r,s,t,a,b), call it $E(q,r,s,t,a,b)$, can be written without a and b, for it can be written as $E[q,r,s,t,g(q,r),h(s,t)]$ or $f_3(q,r,s,t)$.

Now Pepper at this point develops an argument which can be represented as follows:

1. Unless $f_3(q,r,s,t)$ is equivalent to $f_1(q,r,s,t)$, they cannot both hold (and, of course, Pepper is quite right *if* both f_3 and f_1 are intended to cover the entire four-space determined by these variables).

2. But for f_3 to be equivalent to f_1, is for a and b to be epiphenomenal. (Again Pepper is quite right on the same condition we have pointed out in our comment on 1.)

3. Thus, if f_3 holds, and a and b are *not* epiphenomenal, then f_1 cannot hold. In other words, if f_3 holds and a and b are not epiphenomenal, then f_3 must hold both 'before' and 'after' the appearance of a and b.

4. But $f_3(q,r,s,t)$ is just another way of writing $E(q,r,s,t,a,b)$. Therefore, both 'before' and 'after' integration the phenomena in question are adequately described by the function $E(q,r,s,t,a,b)$.

5. Thus, the supposed emergents a and b "have to be included among the total set of variables described by the lower level functional relation; they have to drop down and take their place among the lower level variables as elements in a lower level shift" (pp. 242–43).

However, once we drop, as we have seen we must, the assumption that f_3 and f_1 are intended by the emergentist to hold for the same regions in qrst-space (f_3 presumably holds for all regions, f_1 only for the "lower level of integration"), the argument falls apart. For while the emergentist must indeed admit that if f_3 and f_1 are equivalent, then a and b make no difference, it is open to him to say that the difference made by a and b is just the fact that $f_1(q, r, s, t)$, which holds in regions of qrst-space which are unaccompanied by a and b, is not equivalent to the function which holds of these variables for regions in which they are accompanied by a and/or b.

V

A survey of the literature makes it clear that 'sense quality,' 'sensa,' 'raw feels,' '(sensory) consciousness' — the terms are almost as numerous as the authors — are among the more confidently backed candidates for the role of emergent. And it may be helpful to conclude our examination of emergence on the more concrete note of a discussion of certain logical aspects of this particular claim. In doing so, however, we shall avoid, as far as possible, those labyrinthine issues concerning the sense, if any, in which sense qualities, supposing them to be emergent, can appropriately be said to be 'in' the brain. It should, however, be pointed out that this problem concerns the structure of a (future) *scientific* account of sensory consciousness, and it must be carefully distinguished from the problem of analyzing ordinary language to determine the relation of talk about seeing colors, feeling pain, having an itch, etc., to talk about the body and bodily behavior. Science has the task of *creating* a way of talking about the sensory activities of the central nervous system, not that of analyzing antecedent ordinary language about sense experience. After all, we were talking about seeing colors and itching long before there was such a notion as that of the C.N.S., and long before it was realized that the brain had anything to do with these matters. Our present concern is with a possible logical feature (namely emergence) of the coming scientific account of what goes on "in Jones" when common sense correctly says that Jones is seeing green or has a toothache, etc.

Now, to suppose that "raw feels," as we shall call them, will be found to be emergent—though not epiphenomenal—in this future scientific account, is to suppose that raw feels (or, better, raw feel dimensions) are the a's and b's in the *generalized* function

$$E(q,r,s,t,a,b) = f_3(q,r,s,t)$$

where

$$a = g(q,r)$$
$$b = h(s,t)$$

That is, raw feels depend upon the variables q,r,s,t which also characterize pre-emergent situations. But raw feels do not occur in the presence of matter generally; only matter as it is in the living brain. The function $f_1(q,r,s,t)$ which fits the behavior of matter everywhere else, breaks down when applied to brains. This, as we have seen, is the sense in which raw feels "make a difference."

But how will the scientist be led to introduce raw feels into his picture of the world? Will he, indeed should he, not be content with noting that one region of qrst-space conforms to f_1 whereas another region (roughly brains) conforms to f_2? Or, to put it differently, constructing the function $E[q,r,s,t,g(q,r),h(s,t)]$ which combines these into one function holding for the entire space, what would lead him, as scientist, to speak of the part-functions g and h as correlating values of the lower level variables q, r, s, and t with values of raw-feel variables? Now one answer would be that, after all, we experience raw feels, and it is the business of science to fit them into its world picture. And even in the present primitive state of psychophysiology we can confirm certain crude functional dependencies both of the (psychophysical) kind g and h, and of the (physicopsychical) kind $f_3(q,r,s,t,g,h)$.

But the controversy over Behaviorism has made us sensitive about the scientific standing of 'sensations,' 'images,' and 'raw feels' generally. Thus, it is often thought that the only concept of 'seeing green' that belongs in a scientifically constructed psychology is one that is defined in terms of molar behavior. And it is obvious that at best such concepts would designate *correlates* of raw feels, and not the latter themselves. But how could we legitimately introduce raw feels or other emergent qualities into the "psychology of the other one"? Here we have to distinguish between "descriptive" and "theoretical" aims. While it is true that prior to the examination of living brains, the function f_1 was quite adequate, and though afterwards we saw that f_2 was required for the case of brains, this does not force us to introduce the new variables a and b. For, as we have seen, a and b are eliminable from the descriptive laws. Nevertheless, the introduction of these new variables might be 'forced' upon us by theoretical necessities (insofar as we are ever forced to make theoretical sense by the postulation of hypothetical entities). For example, a brain consists of matter of special kinds in certain arrangements. Complex hydrocarbon molecules, potassium ions, free iron, and electromagnetic fields exhibit certain "exceptionless" regularities (outside of brains) which correspond to Pepper's f_1. Many arrangements turn out to be such that we can deduce their properties, including the ways in which the components will behave *in situ*, from the f_1 functions. But for living brains this turns out not to be the case. The flow of electrons at the synaptic interface "breaks the laws." But it is not lawless, since the more general function f_3 takes care of it. However, we were able to *derive* f_1 from other laws, those of the microtheory, involving only variables q,r,s,t. When we have succeeded in working up a theory which will enable us to derive f_3, the theoretical primitives include other terms than those which were sufficient for an explanation of pre-emergent phenomena. These other terms—α_1, α_2, α_3, etc.—are the items to which the variables a and b pertain; and while we can write a and b as functions (g and h) of q, r, s, and t, it should not be supposed that the α's have thereby been shown to be analyzable into the entities for which q, r, s, and t in turn suffice as descriptive functors. If this seems odd, one should remember that whenever a theory is "correct" it means that we have succeeded (among other things) in formulating a lawful relation between a value, x, appertaining to the theoretical entity and a value, y, taken on by the observed. Hence, in the present case we can write an equation explicitly relating these *values*,

$$x = f(y)$$

But the fact that we can write this equation obviously does not mean that the entity to which the value x appertains is being equated with the situation to which the value y appertains, any more than the discovery of a functional relation between a person's height and weight would require us to suppose that somehow a person's height is the same thing as his weight.

Now an argument offered by Pepper in the closing section of his paper hinges partly on a failure to make this last distinction.

It is a natural ideal of science to derive all laws from a certain limited number of primitive laws or principles—not necessarily from one single law—and so to convert science into a mathematics. If it could be assumed that there are no chance occurrences such a system of laws should be obtainable, though it might look very different from the traditional mechanics. The assumption of science appears to be that such a system is obtainable. I do not know what else the dissatisfaction of science with inconsistencies could mean.

Now, there seems to be no intention on the part of emergent evolutionists to deny that such a system is possible or to assert that there are chance occurrences. If that is so, they seem to be faced with the following dilemma: either the emergent laws they are arguing for are ineffectual and epiphenomenal, or they are effectual and capable of being absorbed into the physical system. But apparently they want their laws to be both effectual and at the same time no part of the physical system . . . (pp. 243–44)

First a terminological point. Among the various meanings of the word *physical* let us distinguish the following for present purposes:

Physical$_1$: an event or entity is *physical*$_1$ if it belongs in the space-time network.

Physical$_2$: an event or entity is *physical*$_2$ if it is definable in terms of theoretical primitives adequate to describe completely the actual states though not necessarily the potentialities of the universe before the appearance of life.

Now, an emergentist account (of the kind we have been constructing) of raw feels denies that the latter are *physical*$_2$. But this in no way involves the denial that they are *physical*$_1$. And indeed this emergentist account definitely gives them a *physical*$_1$ status. And if the equations

$$a = g(q,r)$$
$$b = h(s,t)$$

permit the elimination of a and b from the descriptive function relating the *physical*$_2$ variables q,r,s, and t, this fact, as we have just seen, by no means involves that the emergent entities with which the variables a and b are associated must also be *physical*$_2$.

Whether or not there are any emergents in the sense we have sought to clarify is an empirical question. Our only aim has been to show that Pepper's "formal" demonstration of the impossibility of non-epiphenomenal emergents is invalid.

Reference

Pepper, Stephen C. 1926. Emergence. *Journal of Philosophy* 23:241–45.

7

The Compleat Autocerebroscopist: A Thought-Experiment on Professor Feigl's Mind-Body Identity Thesis

Professor Feigl's mind-body identity thesis, which may be characterized as a daring hypothesis of "empirical metaphysics," asserts that human raw-feel events are literally and numerically identical with certain physical$_2$ brain-events. By physical$_2$ events he means, adopting the terminology of Meehl and Sellars (essay 6, this volume), events which can be exhaustively described in a language sufficient to describe everything that exists and happens in a universe devoid of organic life. Given the set of descriptive terms (predicates and functors) which would be capable of describing without residue all continuants and occurrents in an inorganic world (say, perhaps, our world in the pre-Cambrian period), we need not supplement this conceptual equipment to describe everything that exists and happens when a human being experiences a red sensation ("has a red raw feel," is the locus of a red-qualitied phenomenal event).

It is not my purpose here to attack or defend this identity thesis, concerning which I have, in fact, no settled opinion. Rather, I hope to clarify its meaning by examining some implications and alternatives presented when we apply it to a plausible thought-experiment involving Professor Feigl's "autocerebroscope" (Feigel, 1958, p. 456).

I. The Thought-Experiment

The autocerebroscope is an imaginary device, differing only in arrangement and technological development from instruments already used by psychologists and neurophysiologists, which would enable a subject to receive continuous and nearly instantaneous information regarding the momentary physical$_2$ state of his own brain while he is experiencing raw feels. For simplicity of exposition as well as avoidance of irrelevant substantive problems (e.g., vagueness in the applicability of certain phenomenal predicates), I shall consider the case of two clearly distinguished color qualities, *red* and *green*. The subject is a nonaphasic, nonpsychotic, cooperative, English-speaking neurophysiologist thoroughly pretested for possession of normal color vision. To avoid the terrible difficulties of methodological behaviorism and to highlight his epistemological dilemma, it will be convenient to speak of this subject in the first person; and I invite readers to read what follows taking themselves as the "I" so spoken of.

The apparatus consists of instruments leading directly off my cerebral cortex which convert the pattern of my current brain activity into either of two symbolic patterns, R (for "red") and G (for "green"), presented on a television screen directly in front of me. The apparatus is wired and adjusted so that symbol R appears whenever the physical$_2$ state of my visual-perceptual cortical area is that known (by Utopian neurophysiology) (a) to be produced by retinal inputs of red light waves in persons with normal color vision, and (b) to ordinarily produce a tokening of "red" in cooperative English-speaking subjects. This brain-state we designate by the lower-case italic letter r; also by "Φ_r."

The same conditions hold, *mutatis mutandis*, for the television symbol G in relation to the green brain-state ($= g$). It is important to be clear that the apparatus's symbol presentation depends solely upon the *visual*-cortical state, and is not wired so as to be directly influenced by other events. If, while the visual cortex is in state r, the cerebral tokening mechanism should happen (for whatever reason) to token "green," or the light waves entering the eye should be in the physical$_2$-green spectral region, these events are without causal influence upon the television symbol presentation.

However, the television system of the apparatus is also (and independently) arranged so as to vary the hue of whatever symbol is being presented, and the symbol (regardless of whether it is R or G in type) is sometimes colored red and sometimes green, this coloration persisting from, say, 5 to 20 seconds before it changes, and the variable interval lengths being randomly determined.

Under these conditions it is psychologically possible for me as subject to attend simultaneously to two rather simple aspects of my momentary visual experience, i.e., the *shape* and the *hue* of the presented symbol. By this arrangement we avoid the old stomach ache about when introspection is "really" short-term retrospection, and at least minimize the touchy problem of how many things a subject can attend to simultaneously.

What instructions are given to me as subject in this Utopian experiment? We first agree that I am to use the words "red" and "green" to designate *experienced color qualities*. For simplicity and speed of reporting, the single hue-quality word "red" (or "green") will be conventionally taken as elliptical for "I am now experiencing a visual raw feel of red (or green) hue quality," respectively. As a neurophysiologist I am, of course, aware of the fact that I, and other normal English-speakers, have historically acquired our shared color language by a rather complicated process of social learning. Since the thing-predicate "red" is employed ambiguously in vulgar speech, referring indiscriminately to (a) surface physico-chemical properties of external objects, (b) the distribution of light waves such objects are disposed to reflect in "standard" illumination conditions, and (c) the raw-feel quality normally produced in persons exposed to such stimulation, a terminological stipulation is required for more exacting experimental purposes. In common life, the ambiguity is not often a source of malcommunication because either the three conditions are simultaneously realized or the context makes the speaker's intention clear. In special cases, as when a person asserts "That's red" in a red-illuminated darkroom, it may be necessary to question him as to his intention, and decide for the truth or falsity of his claim accordingly. In the present context, I as subject am instructed to employ the color predicate "red" in its phenomenal usage, i.e., as a predicate descriptive of the experienced raw-feel hue-quality.

If all goes as expected, I find myself tokening "red" as descriptive of my experienced color whenever the television symbol has the shape R, and tokening "green" when it presents the symbol G. In speaking the phenomenal language, it seems clearly appropriate to token "red" (labeling the experienced hue) and "R" (labeling the experienced sign-shape) quasi-simultaneously. If necessary, I can be instructed to report the experienced hue orally and the experienced sign-shape by depressing one of two keys. In speaking the physical thing-language, with the intention of denoting the external physical$_2$ properties of the distal stimulus, I find myself willing (on the *basis* of my raw feel but with *reference* to the objective television screen) to allege that the screen is displaying a red-colored letter R, or a green-colored letter G, as the case may be. The received laws of psychophysiology seem to be instantiated, and I am so far content with the status of my mental health as well as the soundness of Utopian neurophysiology. Both my brain and the autocerebroscope appear to be functioning satisfactorily.

But now a frightening aberration unexpectedly occurs. One day, after an otherwise "normal" run has gone on for several minutes, I find that I am experiencing green when the (apparently green-hued) symbol is R-shaped. I announce this disparity to my research assistant, who takes a long look himself and embarrassedly informs me that the R symbol looks appropriately red to *him*. Perhaps, he suggests timidly, I am mis-speaking myself? I take stock carefully, and remain very sure that I am at the moment experiencing a green-hued phenomenal event. I find no difficulty articulating the *word* "red," and by shutting my eyes I find that I am (being an excellent color visualizer) able voluntarily to call up a pretty good red-hued image. But upon opening my eyes, I continue to "feel certain" that the raw-feel predicate "green" is the correct description of what I see when looking at the screen. I am not in the state of a severe compulsive patient who feels involuntarily impelled to utter the "wrong word," nor of the aphasic who hears himself speak a word he knows isn't what he helplessly wants to say. The word "green" seems perfectly appropriate to me, given the instructions to describe my momentary raw-feel experience. The concurrent "inappropriateness" feeling arises not from doubt or vagueness about the phenomenal quality, but solely from my scientific knowledge about the causal network in which I and my experiences are presumably embedded. The autocerebroscope informs me that my visual cortex is in the r-state, which it *should* be because the television screen is (according to my assistant) emitting red light. I can, of course, dispense with the assistant's report and substitute other multiple observers, plus additional physical apparatus, to confirm that my objective retinal input is physically red light.

Suppose now that I carry out detailed and thorough checking and testing of the entire apparatus, as well as gathering the testimony of multiple observers. And suppose that all of the obtainable evidence continues to indicate, via numerous tightly knit nomological relationships and overdetermined particulars, that there do occur unpredictable but repeated occasions in which my visual cortex is in physical$_2$ state r, that state being causally determined by objective inputs of physical$_2$-red light from the physical$_2$-red-colored screen, and yet I am, on those occasions, momentarily certain that I am experiencing phenomenal green. Over an extended series of trials, this happens in about 10% of my phenomenal reports. A critical question here is, of course, what precisely this "momentary certainty" amounts to (e.g., is it more than the fact of psychological indubitability?). We shall set this question aside for now, because we can approach it more fruitfully after examining some further ramifications of the autocerebroscopic thought-experiment in its causal-scientific aspect. Proceeding still at a "common-sense" level (Utopian-science common sense, that is), how do I meta-talk about my situation as aberrant autocerebroscopic subject? I want to token "I experience green" in obedience to the instructions, and I do not need to infer this raw-feel proposition from any other propositions. If my colleagues ask me *why* I persist in saying "I experience green," I can only remind them of their instructions, which require me to describe my phenomenal events, rather than to make causal claims about the apparatus or the physical$_2$ state of my visual cortex. If asked whether I consider "I experience green" to be incorrigible, I reply that all empirical propositions are corrigible—perhaps adding that if I keep my sanity I may end up being forced to correct "I experience green" in particular! However, I confess that I can't cook up a genuine *doubt* that I am now experiencing green. This means that while I sincerely admit corrigibility, I am at the moment unable "seriously to entertain the notion" that the future evidence will, in fact, turn out that way. I know in general what such evidence would consist of, and I firmly believe that it *would* be rational of me, in the face of such evidence, to conclude that my presently tokened "I experience green" was false. I hope that I am a rational enough man so that I *would* at such time find it psychologically possible to abandon the proposition. And if I were not to turn out in the event to be that rational, still I am prepared *now* to say that such a development would prove me to be less rational than I had supposed. Nevertheless, I am not now psychologically able to make myself seriously doubt that I am experiencing green, and hence I don't seriously entertain the notion that the situation will arise. In short, I remain confident that, if we keep looking, we will succeed in locating the "bug" in the autocerebroscope which, I hypothesize, is the true explanation of these crazy events.

Is there any dishonesty, unreasonableness, or inconsistency in this combination of assertions and expections? If I am a Utopian identity theorist, I consider it $physical_2$-impossible to "experience a green raw feel" while my brain is in state r. To assert such a thing would be like saying "This soup, while very hot, consists of motionless molecules." Such a statement is frame-analytically[1] false within the nomological network of physics; one who holds the kinetic theory of heat might go so far as to call such a statement meaningless.

Suppose that exhaustive tests of all conceivable kinds fail to reveal any defect in the autocerebroscope's structure, function, or brain-attachments. At some point I become convinced that there are times when my visual cortex is in state r but I am simultaneously tokening "I see green," and that this (inner) tokening "seems clearly descriptive of my raw feel." What are the possibilities open to me for making *causal* sense of such a bizarre state of affairs?

We begin with the received doctrine of Utopian neurophysiology, which accepts the identity thesis and which further identifies a particular brain region (or, better, system of related cell-assemblies) as the $physical_2$ locus of events whose occurrence *constitutes* a visual raw-feel event. (I believe that Professor Feigl is clearly committed, although he is not very happy about it, to saying that a raw-feel event is literally, in a $physical_2$ sense, *in the head*—since otherwise he contradicts Leibniz's Principle. See Section IV below.) Presumably, Utopian psychophysiology asserts—or, better, for one who accepts its nomological network, "implicitly defines"—a one-many relationship between raw-feel predicates and $physical_2$ brain-state functors. A set of structural assertions about neurons (numbers, positions, and synaptic connections of a very complex kind) identifies the cerebral system which is the *locus* of visual raw-feel events; thus, visual raw-feel events cannot occur in the transverse gyrus of Heschl (auditory projection area), but they can occur in the calcarine cortex (or Brodmann's area 18?). We designate by "V" the cortical region or functional subsystem which is the locus of visual raw-feel events. Given an appropriately structured cerebral subsystem, its momentary state is exhaustively characterized by a set of $physical_2$ functors. These might be simple (e.g., strength of electromagnetic and electrostatic fields), or, more likely, complex (e.g., second time-derivative of a proportion of instantaneously activated synaptic knobs on cells of type X in cell-assemblies of structure S). The received neurophysiological network asserts that a necessary and sufficient condition for experiencing a red raw feel (or, the theoretical *definition*, within this causal framework, of brain-state r) is that a cerebral system of type S must be in a state described by a complex conjunction of physical$_2$ functor inequalities:

P: One-place predicate designating the phenomenal quality,

L: Two-place predicate locating a brain-event in the brain of a person,

Ψ: Two-place predicate designating the internal *Erlebnis*-relation, " . . . experiences phenomenal event . . . ,"

Φ: One-place predicate designating the complex physical$_2$ property which a brain-event has when its physical$_2$ functors satisfy certain inequalities (the relation of raw feel to brain-state being, presumably, one-many),

x: Variable ranging over persons,

y: Variable ranging over phenomenal events,

z: Variable ranging over physical$_2$ brain-events.

Reference to time is omitted, taken as quasi-simultaneous.

Then the empirical "psychophysical correlation-laws" are:

$$(x,y) \; Ψ \; (x,y) \cdot P(y) \rightarrow (E!z) \; L \; (z,x) \cdot Φ(z)$$
$$(x,z) \; L \; (z,x) \cdot Φ(z) \rightarrow (E!y) \; Ψ \; (x,y) \cdot P(y).$$

The Feigl theory consists of conjoining to each of these correlation-laws the identity-assertion

$$(y = z).$$

But we have so far not done justice to the advanced development of Utopian neurophysiology. Although our thought-experiment began by wiring and attaching the autocerebroscope only to provide information about events occurring in the cerebral locus of visual raw-feel events, Utopian knowledge of brain function includes much besides this. For the "normally functioning brain," we also possess scientific understanding of the causal relations obtaining in other cerebral systems, including the tokening mechanism. This means that certain problems of methodological behaviorism, and certain philosophical difficulties arising from reliance upon vulgar speech, have been "solved"—insofar as empirical knowledge ever solves problems. The differences between raw-feel utterances which are "correct," "false because of lying," "false because of mis-speaking," "false because of being hypnotized," "false because of aphasia," "false because of slovenly language training," "false because of having previously mis-read an English-German dictionary," etc., are formulable by reference to *where* in the intracerebral causal chain the tokening process and its controls have gone awry. Presumably Utopian neurophysiology will have isolated a cerebral system T (= the tokening system) which is the physical$_2$ locus of events t_r, t_g, etc., these events being the inner tokenings of raw-feel predicates "red," "green," etc. These tokening events are the immediate causal descendants of raw-feel events in the visual system V; and they are the immediate causal ancestors of events in intermediate instrumental systems which arouse, trigger, and monitor subsequent motor-control systems that give rise to families of overt acts of the reporting kind (vocalizing "red" or pressing a red-colored lever). Detailed experimental and clinical analysis will have made clear which system does which, and it will be precisely known how, for example, a red-qualitied visual raw feel gives rise to vocalizations of "red," "rot," or "rouge" in a trilingual subject, depending upon the instructions given him or his perception of the momentary social context. Obviously none of the three cell-assembly systems on the motoric side which control *utterances* of "red," "rot," or "rouge" would be considered as the primary tokening mechanism, especially for purposes of philosophical discussion. We need not here decide upon the precise conditions necessary for identifying the primary tokening system T, since for our purposes it will suffice to place certain conditions upon it. It must at least undergo states which are physical$_2$-distinguishable, and these distinguishable states must be correlated (in a normal person) on the one side with the raw-feel events, and on the other with "appropriate" states in the first-order motoric system. That is, T is the locus of events t_r and t_g which are the causal descendants of raw-feel states r and g respectively; and the states t_r and t_g are the causal ancestors of events m_r and m_g respectively, these latter being events in the "English-set motor-control system" which—*certeris paribus*—give rise to differentiated chains continuing through the motor area to effector-organ events (vocalizations of "red" or "green"). In this scheme, the tokening mechanism T is the physical$_2$ locus of tokening *propositions* (= "making judgments"), whereas the events m are tokenings of sentences. For present purposes, a subject *tokens "red"* when the primary tokening system T is the locus of physical$_2$-event t_r regardless of whether he utters, or "tends to utter" (by covert laryngeal twitches) the English word "red" or the French word "rouge," or even if the process is for some reason stopped short of affecting any part of the instrumental reporting mechanism.[2] What we require, in short, is that system T must be the locus of physical$_2$-differentiable events t_r and t_g with input and output conditions appropriately correlated. It will not suffice, for example, to find a system which is activated whenever a visual raw-feel event *recurs*, and whose correlated report is one of mere "familiarity" (e.g., "I have experienced this color before"). When the hue of a raw feel is our subject matter, the primary tokening mechanism must be the locus of distinguishable symbolic events that are hue-correlated.

The nomologicals of Utopian neurophysiology not only assert causal dependencies between raw-feel events in V and tokenings in T (e.g., $r \Rrightarrow t_r$, $g \Rrightarrow t_g$) but they also permit these nomologicals to be derived as theorems. That is, the structural statements about how the brain is organized genetically, when combined with more fundamental laws of neurochemistry and physics, suffice to explain neurophysiological laws of such intermediate molarity as

($g \ggg\!\!\rightarrow t_g$). Gross (and merely stochastic) regularities at the level of molar behavior (e.g., "Normal people almost always report 'red' as an afterimage of
green stimulus inputs") are shown to be physical$_2$-deducible from a combination
of neurophysiological laws of intermediate level with detailed narration of social
learning histories. These intermediate-level laws are themselves deducible from
structural laws about how the human brain is wired, together with microlaws expressed in terms of microanatomy, biochemistry, and physics. The stochastic
character of the more molar laws is itself explained within the system, and provides a causal account of the vagueness intrinsic to most ordinary phenomenal
predicates.

If Utopian neurophysiology embodies Feigl's identity thesis, it does so on the
basis of much more evidence than that available to Feigl in the mid-1960s. Why
has Utopian neurophysiology augmented its psychophysical correlation-law with
the conjoined identity statement? Why has it not preferred a psychophysical interactionist nomological of form $g \ggg\!\!\rightarrow \Psi_g \ggg\!\!\rightarrow t_g$, which speaks of a raw-
feel event Ψ_g that is not physical$_2$ but only physical$_1$ (belonging in the space-time
network)?

I submit that the reason for this scientific decision would not be different from
any other option in which the scientist dispenses with a supernumerary event or
entity in concocting and corroborating his causal picture of the world. He does
not feel under any obligation to "rule out" alleged events Ψ_g, but only to show
that they are causally dispensable. His situation is like that of the geneticist, who
began with Mendelian "factors" (evidenced on the molar side by certain phenotypic breeding statistics) and ultimately *identifies* them with genes (i.e., with
chemical packets found in specific chromosomal loci). We do not ask the geneticist to "prove that there aren't factors 'associated with' genes," once he has
shown that the causal role played by factors in explaining the phenotypic statistics is indistinguishable from the causal role assigned to genes in physiological
genetics.

I am not here attempting to beg the crucial philosophical question, whether it
can even *make sense* to identify a simple phenomenal predicate's intension with
the meaning of a complex physical$_2$ expression. Our Utopian neurophysiologist
may be guilty of a philosophical mistake, through not seeing that the mind-body
problem involves semantic (or epistemological?) issues which are unique. This
question we shall examine below. My point here is that *if* it is philosophically
admissible to assert the identity thesis, *if* it can be considered meaningful at all,
then the empirical grounds for embodying it in the network will be of the usual
scientific kind. The scientific aim is to concoct a nomological network in which
all events find their place; if the causal antecedents and consequences of Ψ_g are
indistinguishable from those of g, we have merely two notations for one and the
same scientific concept. The abstract possibility that Ψ_g should be retained to
designate a kind of event distinct from g which *might conceivably exist* "along-

side it,'' but lacking any causal efficacy, would not impress any scientist. He would properly point out that when *Lactobacillus bulgaricus* was shown to be the causative agent behind the curdling of milk, the lowliest *Hausfrau* ceased to speak of brownies; that geneticists do not hypothesize factors ''parallel with'' or ''mediating the action of'' genes; and that caloric has been dropped from physical vocabulary since the kinetic theory of heat. There ''could still be'' such things as brownies, factors, and caloric; received science may be in error, and one cannot refute an existential proposition. But when the previously assigned causal role of a hypothesized entity is found to be either unnecessary or identical with a more fully known entity, the separate existence of the old one is no longer seriously maintained.

The ''possibility'' of a parallel event lacking causal efficacy has a special interest in the raw-feel case, which it may be profitable to examine here. It is sometimes argued that psychophysical interactionism, psychophysical parallelism, and epiphenomenalism are meaningless pseudotheories because they could not in principle be distinguished. In the diagram we represent causal connection by the arrow $\ggg\!\!\!\rightarrow$, distinguishable mental events by Ψ_i, distinguishable physical$_2$ events by Φ_i, and time relationships by the correlated subscripts i. The issue of simultaneity versus precedence in causation is set aside for present purposes.

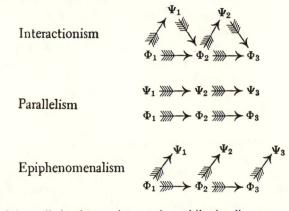

Critics of these distinctions point out that while the diagrams make it appear that we deal with three theories, they achieve this (misleading) effect by arbitrarily dropping selected arrows which represent perfectly good nomologicals. If Φ_1 is a necessary and sufficient condition for Φ_2 and also for Ψ_1, then the conjunction $\Phi_1 \cdot \Psi_1$ is necessary and sufficient for Φ_2; and which nomologicals we elect to draw in as ''causal arrows'' is surely arbitrary. Hence the three theories have indistinguishable content.

In spite of a fairly widespread acceptance of this analysis, I believe it to be mistaken, or at least in need of further justification by invoking an ancillary principle which I see no good reason to adopt. The usual practice in science, when inquiring as to the existence and direction of causal arrows, is to carry out the analysis at all levels. When an experimental separation of confluent factors is technologically (or even physically) precluded, we do not abandon our attempt to unscramble the skein of causality by distinguishing merely correlated from causal relations. The commonest method of doing this is microanalysis, which in advanced sciences is extremely powerful, and often suffices to satisfy any reasonable theoretical interest. In the biological and social sciences, where much of our evidence (especially in "field" and "clinical" studies) consists of correlations within the material as we find it, the only reasonable basis for choice may lie in moving our causal analysis to a lower level of explanation.

In the psychophysical problem, it should not be assumed that the physical$_2$ events designated by the Φ's are incapable of further analysis. If we characterize Φ_1 and Φ_2 by conjunctions of physical$_2$ expressions designating their respective microdetails, so that Φ_1 is written out as a complex conjunction of physical$_2$ functors (limiting case: elementary physical particles, electromagnetic fields), we ask whether the intermediate-level law ($\Phi_1 \gg\!\!\!\rightarrow \Phi_2$) is derivable from the fundamental nomologicals (the structure-dependent features of Φ_1 being now packed into the microconjunction). If ($\Phi_1 \gg\!\!\!\rightarrow \Phi_2$) is microderivable, then our causal account of Φ_2 is complete without the "mental correlate" Ψ_1 being required. The nomological relation between Ψ_1 and Φ_2 is a universal correlation but not a relation of causal dependence. If we retain Ψ_1 in our network, it will have to be for an extrascientific reason, such as a philosophical argument refuting the identity thesis analytically.

Having thus distinguished interactionism from the other two, can we tell *them* apart? Suppose that the phenomenal events themselves have sufficient richness to permit characterizing each of them by, so to speak, crude "phenomenal quasi-functors" (e.g., the color solid, the smell prism). Then we can try to formulate various intraphenomenal causal laws involving these dimensions and their combinatorial laws, and we can ask whether these combinatorial laws are in turn theorems derivable from a more basic set of Φ-Ψ laws. If they are, the usual scientific practice would be to decide for epiphenomenalism, on the ground that parallelism leaves the intraphenomenal combination-laws unexplained. Another approach would, of course, be experimental separation. The Utopian neurophysiologist can induce Φ_2 directly by imposing an artificial intracerebral stimulus, interrupting the immediately preceding events, whereby Φ_2 occurs without Φ_1—or Ψ_1!—having preceded it. If the phenomenal event Ψ_2 then occurs, we conclude that its "regular" phenomenal antecedent Ψ_1 is not part of the causal ancestry. The normal causal role of Φ_1 is unchallenged because the artificial stimulation is physical$_2$-identical with that "normally" imposed by Φ_1.

The ancillary principle alluded to above, which would be needed to defend the indistinguishability of the three psychophysical theories, is that whenever an event is time-place correlated with another, it must be taken to be causative unless shown *not* to be. I see no reason for adopting such a principle in dealing with the mind-body problem, since we do not adopt it anywhere else.

As Utopian neurophysiologist, I have adopted the identity thesis because everything I know about raw-feel events enables me to plug them into the nomological network at the place I have plugged in physical$_2$ brain-states. For ordinary purposes, I continue to use the phenomenal predicates "red" and "green," just as the heating engineer talks to a householder in terms of "winter" and "B.T.U.'s" rather than in the theoretical language of meteorology or kinetic theory. The epistemological peculiarities of raw-feel propositions may be of no interest to me, but if they are, I find it easy to explain them. By "explain," I do not of course mean that all logical and epistemological *concepts* are reducible to physical$_2$ *concepts* (compare Sellars, 1953). I mean only that, given these philosophical concepts, the fact that they apply in certain unique ways to raw-feel propositions is causally understandable. Why do I have privileged access to my raw feels? Because my tokening mechanism T which tokens propositions descriptive of my raw feels is in my head, wired directly to the locus of my raw-feel events; and this is not true of your tokening mechanism in relation to my raw-feel events (compare Skinner, 1945; Reichenbach, 1938, pp. 225–58). Why are some raw-feel properties not further analyzable, their predicates not further "definable" in raw-feel language (the "ineffable quale")? Because the physical$_2$ components of certain raw-feel events have not been separately linked to distinguishable reactions of my tokening mechanism, and some of them *cannot* be so linked. Why are my raw-feel predications associated (usually!) with such subjective certainty? Because this special class of tokenings has a history of thousands of reinforcements, with near-zero failures. Why does it seem that raw feels are immediately given, not requiring inference? Because that's how I learned to token raw-feel propositions, by a direct $g \rightarrow t_g$ transition, unmediated by other tokening events linking propositions to other propositions.

Within this causal network, my problem with the aberrant raw feels is pretty clearly defined. *Something has gone wrong between my raw-feel events* (locus in visual-cortical system V) *and my primary tokening events* (locus in tokening mechanism T). We have established by repeated experimentation that the causal sequence is running off as usual up to (and including) events in V. That is, the objectively red television screen is emitting red light which produces the normal photochemical effect in the cones of my retina, which produces the normal pattern of nerve impulses through my second cranial nerve and is relayed normally in my lateral geniculate bodies and back through my optic radiations to my visual cortex. Similarly on the instrumental (output) side, my primary tokening t_g is activating the motoric systems for the utterance "green" and my laryngeal muscles are working satisfactorily. The motivational-affective systems whose activity constitutes a "feeling of appropriateness" between my primary tokening event t_g and my overt utterance are also functioning normally, and I do not feel that I am "unable to express what I experience." In short, each system is functioning normally, in obedience to the received nomologicals, except the linkage system between V and T. The "privileged access" nomological $(r \Longrightarrow t_r)$ seems to have broken down.

But we are not stuck with this as a rock-bottom fact. It is a complex fact, a fact with "parts" (the event has literal, physical$_2$ *parts* which constitute it). Since we know that the erstwhile law $(r \Longrightarrow t_r)$ is a *theorem*, derivable from the conjunction of *micro*structural and *micro*functional propositions descriptive of a "normal human brain," and of the events r and t_r occurring within such a brain, it follows that my brain must not be a normal brain, assuming that the fundamental nomologicals (physics) are valid.

What sort of abnormality might this be? For our thought-experimental purposes, one kind will do as well as another. If none of my other functions are impaired (e.g., affectivity, verbal reasoning, auditory discrimination, rote memory, motor coordination) it is presumably not a general biochemical defect of single-neuron function, which should produce detectable aberrations in other systems as well. If my verbal learning history has been normal, the enduring microstructural residues of color-tokening activity should be the same as other people's—if the initial microstructure was normal. The best guess is, therefore, that my "visual-associative" system's wiring diagram was initially aberrated microstructurally, so that the imposition of a standard color-learning history upon it has yielded an acquired microstructure such that the control linkage between V and T is stochastic rather than nomological.

To carry the analysis further we must raise the question whether Utopian neurophysiology is strictly deterministic. The stochastic character of nervous activity (e.g., Lorente de No's "optional transmission" at the synapse, or the spontaneous discharge of unstimulated neurons) may be attributable to intracellular events which are intrinsically deterministic but, from the standpoint of the neurophysiologist, essentially random. In addition, it is possible that genuine quantum indeterminacy operates, considering the distances and energies involved at the synaptic interface between a single terminal knob and the cell membrane of the postsynaptic neuron (see Bohr, 1934, pp. 116–19; Eccles, 1951; Eccles, 1953, pp. 271–86; Eddington, 1939, pp. 179–84; Jordan, 1955, pp. 108–13; London, 1952; Meehl, 1958, pp. 190–91, 214–15, 328–37). Whether one or both of these factors are responsible, the stochastic character of spontaneous discharge and synaptic transmission may be taken as an empirical fact. Approximation of intersystem stochastic control to nomologicality can be achieved by sufficient overdetermination through involvement of large numbers of elements. Thus it is known that many, perhaps most, synaptically induced discharges are produced by presynaptic activity in excess of that needed to get the cell over threshold. It must not be forgotten, however, that a very great deal of behavior is only stochastically predictable, presumably reflecting the fact that even strong linkages may allow for low but nonzero probabilities of control failure.

The normal brain is so wired that the long-term consequence of social learning is a microstructure yielding complete control between V and T. (Query whether this is literally true. Only, I suspect, if we assume that all mislabeling of pure hues is ''Freudian,'' which is at least debatable.) This must mean that in spite of spontaneous discharge and optional transmission, the number of neurons involved in a simple hue-tokening is so large, given their arrangement, that it yields a quasi-nomological. (We must still prefix ''quasi,'' since if $p > 0$ for failure to transmit at each synapse, $p > 0$ for system failure. But this magnitude may be such that neurophysiology pays it no more heed than physicists pay to Eddington's ice cube heating up the warm water.) So we conclude that anyone *might*, theoretically, token ''green'' when experiencing red, without having anything structurally wrong with his brain. It follows that I *might* be the victim not of a miswired brain but of the binomial theorem. This latter, however, involves such an infinitesimal probability that we determine to accept it only as a last resort.

The obvious next step in investigating my aberrated tokening is to examine the microstructure of my tokening mechanism. My single-cell biophysics (e.g., spike amplitude, speed of transmission, afterpotentials) being established as normal, we already know that the terminal impulses arriving from V are of the appropriate kind. If necessary, this can be checked directly by microleads from these termini, by study of the microfields and transmitter substances there produced, etc. A plausible guess is that the number and spatial distribution of synaptic knobs, either those arriving from V or those linking the neurons into cell-assemblies within T itself, are inadequate to ''overdetermine'' the tokening events t_r and t_g. By convergence and divergence, a subset of ''trigger'' neurons in the input subsystem of T, when discharged by presynaptic activity at the termini of V-fugal fibers, normally suffices to determine t_r or t_g in T as a larger system of cell-assemblies. But if this overdetermination is insufficient, the probability becomes nonnegligible that the pattern of optional transmissions and spontaneous firing of the subset of ''trigger'' elements will result in the ''wrong'' tokening. In my case this probability has reached, let us suppose, the easily detectable value $p = .10$.

Being a zealous scientist, and considering the low risks attendant upon Utopian neurosurgery, I suggest that a biopsy be performed to corroborate the hypothesis of aberrant synaptic-knob distribution. Previous research has shown what this distribution is in a random sample of normal persons; and theoretical calculations have shown that the density and placement of knobs is such that $p < 10^{-3}$ for the average individual's tokening mechanism to discharge in pattern t_g when receiving input from a modal r-state. It is now noted with interest that, in the researched sample of presumed "normals," individuals lying beyond the 2σ point (some 2–3% of the population) would develop p values as high as 10^{-2}, suggesting that a small but nonnegligible minority of the population are tokening hue predicates erroneously 1% of the time. Since 1% is still quite rare, and since the phenomenon itself is of no clinical interest and each single occurrence likely to go unnoticed or explained away (e.g., "Freudian slip," "I'm tired"), we are not surprised to find that only the autocerebroscopic experiment, performed luckily on an unusually deviant subject, has even called it to anyone's attention.

The biopsy being performed, statistical study of the sections reveals a peculiar "thinning" and "clumping" of synaptic knobs, differing from their normal distribution. Theoretical calculation shows that my T mechanism should be expected to mistoken as between a pure red and a pure green on approximately 12% of occasions under the special condition of continuous, randomly alternated retinal inputs provided by the experiment. This value differs well within combined errors of instrumentation and sampling from the observed 10% in experimental runs on me to date.

Scientifically speaking, everything is again satisfactory. The data are in excellent accord with theory and the particularistic hypothesis about me. If I retain my belief in the identity thesis, I will say: "Because of a structural defect in my tokening mechanism, I token 'green' around 10% of the times when I am experiencing a red raw feel, and conversely. These mistokenings of course 'seem right' at the time, because what T tokens is propositions, not English sentences; and to 'seem wrong' a mistokening must occur farther along the intracerebral causal chain, as when I can't find the right *word*. In my case, the *word*-tokening 'green' is the normal one for a primary tokening event t_g in T, so no tendency to feel or report a disparity occurs. It is therefore literally correct to say what many philosophers have considered nonsense, namely, sometimes my raw feels *seem to be green when they are in fact red*."

It is important in contemplating this paradoxical statement to keep in mind that until some sort of tokening-of-a-universal occurs, we cannot properly raise questions of "being right," "being sure," or "knowing." It is extraordinarily tempting to forget this, especially in dealing with raw-feel judgments. Thus, in philosophical conversation, I may imagine myself to be experiencing green, and the impulse is to say exasperatedly, "But surely I couldn't be wrong about *that*!" The trouble is that this imagery of green leads me to think that *if* I were to call *that* imaged green "green," I could not conceivably be mistaken. And if my image is green, this is certainly true, being tautologous when set forth propositionally; i.e., if I am experiencing green, it cannot be a mistake to call it "green." The trick is in the imagery, whereby I subtly introduce the hypothesis that I *am correctly labeling my experience*. Nor does this tempting error, I think, have any special relation to the identity thesis. A complete metaphysical dualist, for whom phenomenal green is a state of a nonspatial psychoid causally connected to a brain, must also realize this is a mistake and be wary of it. There simply is no necessary connection between "Jones tokens 'green' at t" and "Jones experiences green at t," regardless of one's Jonesian ontology.

II. Empirical Character of the Identity Thesis

The outcome of our autocerebroscopic studies, while scientifically satisfactory, suggests a disturbing philosophical thought. Professor Feigl insists that his identity thesis, while somewhat speculative and touching on some rather metaphysical questions about the nature of things, is nevertheless a form of *empirical* metaphysics. This means that the identity thesis might, in principle, be discorroborated by scientific evidence. It occurs to us that we imagined the autocerebroscopic thought-experiment to have come out in a particular way, a way compatible with the identity thesis. Was this too easy? What sort of empirical result could have led to our rational abandonment of it? It seems only fair, if we are dreaming up Utopian neurophysiology, to test the allegedly empirical character of the identity thesis by imagining an adverse outcome of the autocerebroscopic research. If we can't do so, something is wrong with viewing the identity thesis as an empirical claim.

To cook up an adverse empirical outcome, let us again proceed in the ordinary scientific way, by postulating a theory contradictory to the received one and deriving its consequences. Suppose there exist psychoids ("minds," "souls," "diathetes") which are substantive entities, not composed of physical$_2$ parts of substances, not space-occupying, and of such nature that most of the predicates and functors appropriate to physical$_2$ occurrents and continuants are inappropriate to them. Thus we can ask about the mass, spin, diameter, charge, etc., of physical$_2$ particles; we study the velocity, amplitude, and wave length of physical$_2$ waves; at the level of ordinary physical things, we treat of their color, shape, volume, temperature, texture, and the like. But if one were to ask about the specific gravity of an angel, we would know he had failed to grasp the idea, as when Haeckel defined God as a "gaseous vertebrate." It will be convenient, however, to adopt the convention that psychoids can be spoken of as being at a place in physical$_2$ space, even though they cannot *occupy* a region in the ordinary sense. This convention is perhaps dispensable, although somewhat inconveniently; but it introduces no confusion if we stipulate (as Aquinas did for angels) that "a psychoid is located where it acts" (i.e., where it exerts causal efficacy upon physical$_2$ entities). It goes without saying that psychoids must share *causality* with physical$_2$ entities (i.e., they must be physical$_1$) for us to be able to know about them. A disembodied and causally disconnected psychoid would be unknowable by us humans in the present life, as Professor Feigl has clearly shown (Feigl, 1958; see also essay 5, this volume). The form of ontological dualism we shall consider makes the further hypothesis that each psychoid is "connected to" an individual human brain, meaning by this that it has a bidirectional causal relation to the physical$_2$ states of one and only one brain. Finally we hypothesize that no physical$_2$ events affect the psychoid except those occurring in the brain to which it is specially connected, nor does it exert any causal influence upon other physical$_2$ events. Thus, for simplicity, we assume that clairvoyance and psychokinesis (as distinguished from telepathy) either do not exist, or are special types of brain-mediated transactions.

The psychoid is conceived to *undergo states*, which change over time and whose occurrences are the causal ancestors and descendants of specific physical$_2$ events in the brain to which each psychoid is coordinated. The existence of a psychoid and its being causally linked to a particular human brain are taken as fundamental facts of the physical$_1$ order, like the fact that there are electrons.

Suppose now that among the transitory "states" into which psychoids get are states of visual experience. When a human brain undergoes state r in its visual cortex system V, the coordinated psychoid ψ_i is causally influenced so as to experience phenomenal state ρ. This state of affairs may be designated by $\rho\,(\psi_i)$ and the psychophysical correlation-law can only be written properly with use of the psychoid notation. The psychoidal event $\rho(\psi_i)$ is linked by a psychophysical nomological to the physical$_2$ tokening event t_r, and we shall assume that this tokening event occurs upon the confluence of physical$_2$ inputs from V and the concurrent physical$_1$ action upon T by ψ. Diagrammatically,

Utopian neurophysiology would presumably have considered this theoretical possibility even prior to discovery of the aberrant autocerebroscopic findings, and would have accepted or rejected it depending upon the microderivability of the $(r \ggg\!\!\rightarrow t_g)$ quasi-nomological as a physical$_2$ theorem. The theoretically expected departures from strict nomologicality would, of course, be conceptualized as due to the rare confluence of indeterminate microevents having low, but non-zero, joint probability. Prior to the aberrant autocerebroscopic findings, Utopian neurophysiology might have been erroneously (but, on the extant data, quite properly) betting on the identity thesis.

What are the logically available possibilities?

1. $r \ggg\!\!\rightarrow t_r$ holds. This, a theoretical consequence of received Utopian neurophysiology, is now refuted by the autocerebroscopic experiment. The putative (raw feel $\ggg\!\!\rightarrow$ tokening) "law" was microderivable as a physical$_2$ theo-

rem, so the micropostulates must be modified *or supplemented by postulates concerning additional theoretical entities*.

2. $r \ggg_p \nrightarrow t_r$ holds. The (raw feel → tokening) law is stochastic, and its low-probability deviations have now been brought to our attention. Under this case, two subcases are distinguishable: (a.) The incidence and micropatterning of deviations are "random," and microderivable from the physical$_2$ microlaws by applying probability theory to the empirical distribution of initial microconditions. (b.) The incidence and micropatterning of deviations are "systematic," and cannot be derived as in (a).

This exhausts the possibilities. Clearly both (1) and (2a) are compatible with the identity theory. The former yields a strict deterministic identity theory, the latter an indeterministic one. Neither requires postulation of additional theoretical entities mediating the empirical (raw feel → tokening) relation. The first involves strict nomologicals linking the physical$_2$ raw-feel event to the tokening event; the other involves probability linkage only, and the numerical probabilities are derivable from the microconditions.

It is in case (2a) that the psychoids can reveal themselves by exerting causal influence. Suppose it is shown that when a subset of microevents (e.g., synaptic events at individual end-feet) are locally indeterminate, i.e., the physical$_2$ microlaws make k local outcomes quantum-uncertain, the joint probability of a certain outcome pattern is p_1, another such p_2, and so on. Suppose further that the sum of all p's associated with a tokening t_g as intermediately molar outcome is $p(t_g)$. Finally, suppose that $p(t_g)$ is significantly smaller than its observed value over a sufficiently long series. Then we have discorroborated the "random" hypothesis and may be impelled to concoct a theory embodying a "systematic selection" process determining the locally random microevents. One such theory could be the existence of psychoids, which "select" locally indeterminate outcomes *teleologically* (i.e., the psychoid "throws" a subset of indeterminate events so as to yield a patterned tokening event t_g).

It might be thought that this contradicts our hypothesis of physical$_2$ indeterminacy—that the system is either "random" or "lawful" but we can't have it both ways. This objection, while superficially plausible, is not sound. There is no contradiction between asserting that the individual microevents are "locally random," and that their *Gestalt* is systematic with respect to the molar outcome. A simple example will suffice to demonstrate this, as follows:

Consider a circular arrangement of elements, each of which "fires" on exactly half of the "occasions." Adjacent elements are wired so as to send stimulating termini to common elements in the next system, these latter elements requiring simultaneous stimulation by two inputs in order to be discharged. Hence the next system will be activated only if adjacent elements in the control system fire concurrently, but not if only nonadjacent ones do. Thus firing pattern A will be effective, whereas firing pattern B will not:

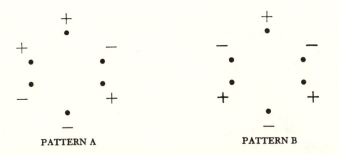

PATTERN A   PATTERN B

It is evident that we can impose "random" requirements upon each individual element, such that it fires exactly half the time and that its firing probability on any occasion is invariant with respect to its preceding firing series, and still be free to select *patterns* which will yield anywhere from zero to 100% activation of the controlee system. A statistical test will tell us whether there is evidence of a "pattern-selection bias," which if found would be evidence for the operation of a "systematic" selector agent, e.g., a psychoid. (For extended discussion see Meehl et al., 1958, Appendix E.) It is assumed, of course, that the received physical$_2$ nomologicals provide no explanation for the tendency. Whether the (V → Ψ) correlation is stochastic or nomological depends upon the level of causal analysis. At the molar level, our autocerebroscopic data discorroborate any (V ⟫⟶ Ψ) nomological, because they show that a red-type cortical state r is sometimes coexistent with phenomenal green. However, since the Φ-Ψ relation is many-one when Φ is microcharacterized, it is logically possible for the aberrated Ψ-occasions to be either nomological or stochastic functions of the V-states when these are subdivided on the basis of their microproperties.

I do not wish to defend such a psychoid theory, which is admittedly rather impoverished in content (although, I think, not empty or frivolous). On the evidence stated, it would seem imparsimonious to postulate such enduring continuants as psychoids. We might better conceive of some sort of "Ψ-field," an occurrent characterized by suitable phenomenal quasi-functors, and acting back upon the physical$_2$ system. Examples like self-induction in physics are helpful in dispelling the anxiety sometimes aroused by the "emergent" features of such psychophysical theories. Of course self-induction is emergence only epistemologically, not ontologically, since Omniscient Jones knows that the field about a coil—its existence and all its quantitative features—is derivable from statements about the fields associated with the elementary particles of which current-in-coil is composed. A scientist who had already carried theoretical analysis of electric current to a "deep" enough microlevel would have been able to *predict* the self-induction effect. So we have here emergence in the context of discovery, but not emergence in the "ontological" sense required by the physical$_1$-physical$_2$ distinction. This clarification may itself be helpful in getting clearer about the physical$_1$-physical$_2$ distinction. How could we know whether to call a theoretical entity like a "Ψ-field" physical$_1$ or physical$_2$?

The Meehl-Sellars definition of physical$_2$ has the oddity of making a *world-historical* reference in stating the nature of a theoretical construct. "An event or entity is *physical$_2$* if it is definable in terms of theoretical primitives adequate to describe completely the actual states though not necessarily the potentialities of the universe before the appearance of life" (essay 6 this volume, p. 182). Suppose Utopian neurophysiology, even after discovery of the aberrant autocerebroscopic effects, is able to provide an adequate causal account of everything that happens by speaking of nothing but elementary particles, electromagnetic and electrostatic fields, etc. The relation of raw feels to "life" might be explicable in terms of certain structural peculiarities of complex carbon molecules, such that the configural relations among elementary physical$_2$ functors needed to render any raw-feel quasi-functor nonzero cannot arise without a kind and order of complexity to which only the carbon atom lends itself chemically. The raw-feel quasi-functor is then a number characterizing certain mathematical features of the physical$_2$ functor *relations*, which is why it is permissible to speak of "identity." That is, the raw-feel event r is physically *constituted* or *composed* of the elementary particles with their associated fields and forces. A raw feel is an occurrent, whose physical$_2$ nature is a certain configuration of elementary physical$_2$ continuants; and the "richness" of this configuration presupposes a structural and causal complexity not physical$_2$-possible except with carbon compounds. If it should be technically possible to synthesize organisms built around silicon, such androids (Scriven, 1953) would be confidently said to "have experiences," and of course their verbal and other expressive-reportive behavior would be consistent with this. The notion that they might "merely be talking *as if* they 'had experiences' " would not be a theoretically admissible notion, since we constructed them and "a raw feel" would be *constitutively* defined by reference to the configuration of fundamental physical$_2$ functors. Similarly, such classical puzzles as the experiences of dogs or earthworms would be soluble, simply by substituting in the expressions for phenomenal quasi-functors the physical$_2$ functors determined experimentally by studying the brain functions of these creatures.

How could there be any such entity as a physical$_1$ raw-feel event or state which was not physical$_2$ by the Meehl-Sellars criterion? It would have to be an entity not constituted of physical$_1$ entities, an entity not composed of physical$_2$ "phases" or "parts" or "substates," and which literally *comes into being* for the first time when physical$_2$ entities enter into a certain configuration. The occurrence of this requisite physical$_2$ configuration is necessary and sufficient for the existence of the new entity, but the latter is not itself the configuration. It seems that we would have here a truly fundamental nomological, a rock-bottom feature of the world. This brute fact would qualify as one of the "insoluble mysteries of the universe," and DuBois-Reymond would have been vindicated in calling it one of the seven such. I do not know whether there are any comparable cases in current physical$_2$ science; but it is safe to say — as a matter of logic! — that at *any* given stage of knowledge, even the fictitious "final, Utopian, complete" stage, there will necessarily be some primitive theoretical propositions. One or more of these may be purely dispositional, designating properties whose actualization is contingent within a world-family and "novel" at time *t* in an actual world. Such a property would be a true emergent in one acceptable sense of that tricky word. Professor Paul Feyerabend has suggested to me the physical$_2$ possibility of a two-particle universe, say a pair of electrons, placed at a distance such that their gravitational attractive force exactly equals their electrostatic repellent force. Stable thus, no electromagnetic field exists; but this universe has the potential to develop one if somehow (e.g., by the finger of God) a relative motion were to occur between them.

These considerations show that a non-physical$_2$ Ψ-field might be similar to what we ordinarily call "mental," or it might not. Suppose all efforts to analyze it failed, and we found it impossible to develop a theory of its fine structure, to break it conceptually into parts or components, to specify any sort of spatial regions or intensity gradients — in short, to say anything about it except its causal role in the physical$_1$ brain-system. Now this would be a very exciting scientific position, because our analysis of case 2a showed a kind of "teleology" in the selective influence exerted by Ψ over the locally indeterminate physical$_2$ outcomes in the tokening mechanism. Crudely put, we could say that "Whatever the nature of Ψ may be, as a causal agent it 'acts purposefully,' it throws the physical$_2$-indeterminate subset of microevents in system T 'so that' the molar outcome is the meaningful tokening t_r, rather than the physical$_2$-probable disjunction of micro-outcomes which would lead to a meaningless pseudo-token (e.g., a neologism), or a jamming of the mechanism, or tokening something inappropriate to the modality (e.g., 'C sharp' when the current physical input is from the visual cortex). All efforts to microanalyze Ψ having thus far failed, all we are able to say about it is that it is a nonextended, homogeneous, unitary, non-space-filling whoozis, which mediates tokenings by teleological selection of subsets of physical$_2$ micro-events." I suggest that it would be quite appropriate to say that such a combination of negative and positive properties and powers is rather like the "mental" of traditional dualism. If I am right in this, it means that a radical ontological dualism must be regarded as having empirical — even "scientific" — meaning, contrary to what was alleged by the Vienna positivists and some of their philosophic descendants.

A philosophically relevant result of this analysis of the scientifically available outcomes of our thought-experiment is that the admissibility of "I seem to be experiencing green but I am really not because my cortex is in state r" hinges upon prior acceptance of a specified nomological network. If case 1 obtains, no one would ever be impelled to *say* such a thing, but it would be admissible because a person *could* (physical$_2$ possibility) have a structurally defective tokening mechanism. If case 2a obtains, the paradoxical remark might be made, and correctly. If case 2b obtains the remark would be proper or not depending upon whether the net allows for "slippage" between Ψ and T, between r and Ψ, or both. The micronomologicals between r and Ψ (i.e., laws relating phenomenal quasi-functors characterizing Ψ to their determining physical$_2$ functors in r) might be such that "slippage" between the molar r-state and phenomenal qualities is theoretically derivable, whereas the psychophysical correlations relating Ψ and r jointly to the molar tokening events are strict (nomologicals). If that were so, an observer would know (scientifically) that any impulse to token the paradoxical sentence should be resisted, because the object-language "I am experiencing green" will always be correct. (We assume here an autocerebroscopically confirmed *ceteris paribus* regarding other potentially interfering cerebral systems, such as Freudian slips.) Per contra, if the total evidence corroborates a network in which the $(r \Rrightarrow\!\!\rightarrow \Psi)$ law is tight and the joint $(\Psi \cdot r \Rrightarrow\!\!\rightarrow_p \rightarrow t_r)$ law loose, the paradoxical statement is not only admissible, but mandatory. Intermediate cases (both anchorings of Ψ stochastic) would lead to varying probabilities, the paradoxical statement being sometimes right and sometimes wrong.

III. Some Alleged Metapredicates of Raw-Feel Statements

In the light of this thought-experiment, let us examine some of the metapredicates traditionally attributed to raw-feel statements, together with some of the familiar grounds for attributing them. I shall distinguish (without prejudging their independence) claims that raw-feel statements are (not perhaps always, but sometimes) *noninferential, incorrigible, inerrant, indubitable, private*, and *ineffable*.

1. *Noninferentiality*: Lord Russell, precisely reversing the line of methodological behaviorism, distinguished the physical from the mental by the epistemic criterion that the former is inferred and the latter is not. Both Russell and the (neo) behaviorists are right, inasmuch as the mental events of other people are inferred by me but noninferred by them; and my mental events are inferred by other people but noninferred by me. This is true only if "mental" is taken as synonymous with "phenomenal," a convention which is so inconvenient for clinical psychology that it has been abandoned there. But in the present context, where the mind-body problem is stated in terms of its *raw-feel component* rather than its *intentionality component*, Freud's theories are irrelevant. Our "mental" is—roughly—Freud's "conscious." The intentionality component of the mind-body problem has been solved, in its essentials, by Sellars (1953). While expressions such as "immediately given," "known by acquaintance," "hard data," "true by ostensive definition," and the like have been powerfully criticized as misleading, equivocal, and downright false, still it is generally

agreed that all these expressions aim at *something* which is uniquely true of raw-feel statements. Just what that something is remains a matter of controversy, and I have here chosen "noninferential" as the least misleading, least disputed, and most central or "core" component of the explicandum.

It is important that "noninferential" does not mean *noninferable*. If raw-feel events are in the physical$_1$ network, then raw-feel statements are inferable from non-raw-feel statements. I presuppose throughout that phenomenal events, whether physical$_2$ or not, are physical$_1$. If phenomenal events were not even stochastically *correlated* with human speech, writing, or other signals, nor with stimulus events, nor with internal bodily (brain) events, there would be no "mind-body" problem, no identity theory, and no conversation about such matters among philosophers. It is doubtful whether one could even be said to "know about" his own phenomenal events in such a world (see essay 5, this volume). If Jones tokens "I see red," Smith may infer probabilistically that Jones sees red; Smith's evidence for "Jones sees red" is the statement "Jones tokens 'I see red,' " a statement whose *content* is behavioral (and linguistic), not phenomenal (and nonlinguistic). Smith may alternatively infer "Jones sees red" from other statements, such as "The apparatus is transmitting 7000 Å light waves to Jones's retina," "Jones is fixating a neutral gray wall after having looked for a minute at a green circle," "The neurosurgeon is electrically stimulating Jones's brain (etc.)," "Jones's GSR changes in response to stimulus word 'red.' " These inferences are probabilistic, but they are (probabilistically) valid inferences. Since these other evidential statements are also available to Jones, it follows that he *could* infer his own phenomenal statement, as Smith does. So we see that the autocerebroscopic situation is not epistemologically unique, but merely tightens the net by providing more "direct" readings from the brain.

We have now put the necessary hedges around the claim that raw-feel statements are noninferential. It does not mean that they *cannot* be inferred; it does not mean that they are never *in fact* inferred; it only means that they are *sometimes made without being inferred*, and typically so by the knower whose raw feels are their subject matter. The familiar sign that a raw-feel statement belongs to the class of noninferred raw-feel statements is, of course, the statements' use of egocentric particulars. Jones *may* properly say "Jones sees red," and in philosophical or autocerebroscopic contexts he might actually adopt the third-person locution; but normally Jones says "I see red" to designate that state of affairs which Smith would designate by "Jones sees red."

Although other statements *might* be adduced as evidence for "I see red," and although I may now or later admit evidence against "I see red," it is nevertheless true that knowers sometimes token "I see red" without having antecedently tokened any statements from which "I see red" could be inferred. This fact of descriptive pragmatics is perhaps the minimum content of a claim that raw-feel statements are noninferential; but what is philosophically relevant is our generally accepted belief that such noninferential tokenings are sometimes legitimate moves, so that a knower who tokens "I see red" without antecedently tokening any statements from which it can be inferred is not necessarily tokening illegitimately or irresponsibly. How can such a thing be?

It has sometimes been said that the "evidence" which justifies a raw-feel statement (under the usual noninferential conditions) is "the experience itself." I do not wish to condemn such talk as utterly without merit, since I believe that it intends something true and fundamental. But if we adopt the generally accepted convention that "evidence for . . . " means "providing a basis for inferring . . ." and remind ourselves that inferability is a relation between statements or propositions, it follows that we cannot properly speak of an experience (something nonpropositional) as being "evidence for" a statement (something propositional). It seems then that noninferential raw-feel tokenings are, strictly speaking, tokenings of statements "in the absence of evidence." On the other hand, we do not ordinarily countenance the tokening of raw-feel statements by a knower who is not concurrently experiencing the raw feel designated by the statement tokened. If Jones makes a practice of tokening "I see red" on occasions when he is not in fact seeing red (a fact which we infer from other evidence, which may include his own subsequent admission that he lied, or mis-spoke, or "just felt like saying it") we consider him irresponsible, because he tends to token illegitimately.

I do not have anything illuminating to add to what others (e.g., Sellars 1954) have said by way of expounding what is involved here. A knower is considered to token egocentric raw-feel statements legitimately when his tokening behavior is rule-regulated, whether or not he antecedently tokens the rule itself (which he normally does not). There is a degenerate, uninformative semantic rule, " 'Red' means *red*," to which an English-speaking knower's tokenings may or may not conform. It may be viewed, within pure pragmatics, as a language-entry rule, conformity to which legitimates an egocentric raw-feel tokening. We may employ special words like "legitimate" (applied to particular tokenings) and "responsible" (applied to a knower who tokens legitimately) as distinct from the word "rational," since the latter refers to intertokening (intralinguistic) relations, e.g., inferability, conformance to language-*transition* rules, which we have seen is not at issue for the typical egocentric raw-feel statement. A tokening "I see red" by a knower who is not concurrently the locus of a red-qualitied raw-feel event is false; the act of so tokening is illegitimate (i.e., semantic-rule-violative); knowers who tend to token illegitimately are sense-defective, psychotic, or irresponsible. We need terms other than "irrational" in this context, because we reserve the latter for a disposition to violate language-transition rules, i.e., to token against, or without, (propositional) *evidence*.

Speaking epistemologically, the legitimacy of tokening egocentric raw-feel statements without antecedently tokening any statements as evidence (and in most cases, without being able to do so upon demand) depends upon the token-ing's conformity to the semantic rule. There is in this notion of a legitimate ego-centric tokening a small but inescapable element of "psychologism," that amount and kind of reference to the nonlinguistic which is not a philosophic sin because it falls under the heading of pure pragmatics — the *coex* relationship of Sellars (1947, 1949). Speaking psychologically, the English-speaker's over-whelmingly strong impulse to token "red" when experiencing a red-qualitied raw feel has its causal account in intimate wiring plus verbal reinforcement his-tory. We are all trained against tokening non-raw-feel statements without ante-cedently tokening statements from which they can be inferred, or at least without being able to offer such on demand. "Just because," or "I say what I mean," or "I need no evidence" are childish or neurotic responses to "Why do you say that?" for non-raw-feel statements, and are finally beaten out of all but the most irrational. But we are permitted to token raw-feel statements without evidence, so long as we do it in a rule-regulated way (i.e., in what the reinforcing verbal community takes, on all of *its* evidence, to be conformable to the language-entry rule " 'Q' means *Q*").

2. *Incorrigibility*: It has been shown above that noninferentiality does not mean noninferability, that while egocentric raw-feel statements are commonly and legitimately tokened without inference, their allocentric equivalents are reg-ularly inferred and even the egocentric ones can sometimes be. Since raw-feel statements can be inferred, it follows directly that their contraries can be discor-roborated. Hence a raw-feel statement "Jones sees green" can be argued against by evidence supporting "Jones sees red," given the grammar of these phenom-enal color predicates. And while this is clearest in the case of allocentric raw-feel statements, it is true of egocentric ones also. Since evidence supporting "Jones sees red" is evidence against "Jones sees green," and such evidence is also, at times, available to Jones himself, it follows that Jones can have evidence tending to discorroborate his egocentric raw-feel statements. It is puzzling why so many philosophers have doubted this, when it follows rigorously from two universally accepted theses: (a) Raw-feel events have knowable causes and effects (either would do!); (b) Some raw-feel statements are incompatible with others.

Incorrigibility of a raw-feel statement would require that, while counterevi-dence can unquestionably be brought to bear upon it, the amount and character of such counterevidence could never be sufficient to warrant abandoning it. While this doctrine seems widely held, I have never seen any cogent proof of it. I per-sonally find the autocerebroscopic thought-experiment very helpful in this re-spect. My dilemma as Utopian neurophysiologist is to decide whether any suffi-ciently massive and interlocking evidence could corroborate "I am seeing red" more than all of my evidence corroborates the claim that I always token in obe-dience to the language-entry rule " 'Green' means *green*." It cuts no ice at all to "feel sure," since "Meehl feels sure that he always tokens in conformity with the language-entry rules'' clearly does not entail that he does in fact so token. The kind of evidence hypothesized in our thought-experiment provides an adequate explanation of my aberrated ''green'' tokenings, as well as of my strong feeling of subjective certainty. Given that other evidence can be *relevant* to the truth of a raw-feel statement, it is hard to see any reason for insisting that it could not conceivably be countervailing against the unevidenced raw-feel statement, unless we accept the metaproposition "All egocentric raw-feel statements are true,'' a proposition which is surely not analytic. And, if it is itself empirical, it cannot be made untouchable by all amounts of discorroboration.

3. *Inerrancy*: Without making the strong claim of incorrigibility (no egocentric raw-feel statement could, *in principle*, be opposed by evidence sufficient to require its abandonment), it might be hoped that nevertheless no such statements are *in fact* false. A specious plausibility is lent to this view by the widespread habit of putting ''et cetera'' after a list of interfering factors which are at present known to produce illegitimate tokenings. Thus a philosopher writes, ''An English-speaking plain man, not lying or afflicted with aphasia, etc., cannot err in tokening 'I see red.' '' Great danger lies in the innocent-looking ''etc.,'' which has to do duty for all the unlisted sources of mistokening. The statement that one *cannot* token an egocentric raw-feel statement incorrectly without misunderstanding English, being aphasic, having a Freudian slip, being drugged, obeying a posthypnotic suggestion, *and so forth* is analytic only if ''and so forth'' is short for ''any other causal source of mistokening.'' Can the list be written out, substituting an extensional specification for ''etc.,'' rather than the intensional ''causal source of mistokening''? Obviously no such extensional list could be compiled, lacking an admittedly complete causal theory of experiencing-and-tokening. Is anyone prepared to say on present evidence that we already *know* all possible sources of mistokening? *Could* anyone claim this while the mind-body problem remains *sub judice*? If anyone did so claim, would his claim be incorrigible with respect to the autocerebroscopic experiment? What this argument for inerrancy really comes down to when explicated is a tautology plus a bow to psychic determinism, namely: ''An egocentric raw-feel statement cannot be erroneously tokened unless some disturbing factor leads to the knower's violating the language-entry rule,'' i.e., an egocentric raw-feel tokening is legitimate unless something causes it to be made illegitimately. This triviality cannot sustain a philosophical claim of inerrancy. Since we already have indisputable evidence that mistokenings do in fact occur, why would we venture on the unsupported empirical claim that the presently known list is exhaustive?

Neither common-sense examples nor philosophical arguments suffice to destroy in some people the conviction that ''I just *couldn't* be wrong in 'attentively (etc.)' characterizing the hue-quality of my momentary raw-feel.'' By way of softening up such a reader, I recommend study of a fascinating experiment by Howells (1944) in which he showed that repeated association between a color (red or green) and a tone (low or high, respectively) produced in his subjects a growing disposition to mislabel the colors when presented unsaturated along with the "inappropriate" tone. The experimenter infers (as I do, tentatively) that the subjects came to actually *experience* the wrong color; other psychologists opt for the alternative hypothesis that they came to *token* erroneously. It seems rather implausible that VIIIth-nerve inputs to Heschl's gyrus could acquire such control over the visual-experiencing cortex; but it also seems hard to believe that they began to say "red" when seeing green. The point is that Howells's results are compatible with either interpretation; and reading them should, I think, at least attenuate one's intuitive faith in the "obvious infallibility" of raw-feel statements.[3]

4. *Indubitability*: By this word I mean the psychological inability to doubt our egocentric raw-feel statements at the time we token them. Does this inability, if it in fact obtains, have any philosophic relevance? I think it has none, unless we presuppose that "Jones is psychologically incapable of genuinely doubting *p* at time *t*" entails, nomologically or analytically, "*p* is true." I take it that no one will wish to maintain that a knower's psychological lack of power to doubt a proposition implies the latter's truth, the implication being either a law of nature or a truth of logic. I do not myself believe that psychological indubitability is even incompatible with the knower's sincere assertion that *p* is corrigible. Readers will have to judge this for themselves, with respect to "sincerity of assertion." But the metalinguistic statement "I know that there could be strong countervailing evidence against *p*" is surely compatible with "As of this moment, I find myself unable to entertain seriously the notion that *p* is in fact false." In the autocerebroscopic situation, our Utopian neurophysiologist continued to collect discorroborative evidence against his own raw-feel statements, because he rationally recognized that he *ought*, if such counterevidence were forthcoming, to correct these raw-feel statements. But during the course of this evidence-collecting, he "felt certain" that a bug would be found in the apparatus, because the raw-feel statements were currently indubitable by him. This would be "inconsistent" cognitive activity for one who held that a knower's inability to doubt entails the truth—analytically, in logic or epistemology—of the indubitable statement. But our neurophysiologist holds no such indefensible view.

5. *Privacy* ("privileged access"): It is agreed that no other person is the locus of my raw-feel events. This simple truth can be formulated either epistemically or physiologically, as follows: a. A raw-feel event *x* which belongs to the class C_1 of events constituting the experiential history of a knower K_1 does not belong to the class C_2 of a different knower K_2. b. The tokening mechanism whose tokenings characterize the raw-feel events of organism K_1 is wired "directly" to K_1's visual cortex, whereas the tokening mechanism of K_2 is not directly wired to the visual cortex of K_1.

It seems that (a), stated in philosophic language, is an analytic truth (but see below), whereas (b), stated in physiological language (except for "tokening"), is synthetic. Query whether the contradictory of the second half of (b), while counterfactual for all historical organism-pairs, is counternomological? Given Utopian neurophysiology, we can at least conceive a procedure whereby the tokening mechanism of K_2 might be wired to the visual cortex of K_1 in such a way that the "causal intimacy" of K_2's tokening events would be as "close" to the events occurring in K_1's visual cortex as are the tokening events of K_1. Or, without such direct anatomical wiring, Utopian neurophysiology could presumably impose a pattern upon K_2's tokening mechanism which was physical$_2$-indistinguishable (within tolerance limits set narrower than those yielding "no difference" reports or discriminations for the single specimen) from the pattern imposed by K_1's visual cortex upon K_1's tokening mechanism. While I don't wish to liquidate any valid philosophical problem by shifting the grounds to biology, it is worth emphasizing that from the standpoint of physical$_2$ causality, the "privacy" of my raw-feel events consists of the rather unexciting fact that "I" (= the person whose body is the locus of the tokening mechanism which tokens the egocentric raw-feel statement in question) am causally related to "my" (= visual-cortical states located within that body) raw-feel events in a close-knit, causally direct way; whereas "you" (= the person whose body is the locus of the tokening mechanism which tokens the allocentric equivalent of the egocentric raw-feel statement in question) are causally related to "my" raw-feel events by a causal chain having more links and therefore, normally, having greater possibility of "slippage" (i.e., of intervening nuisance variables which may prevent complete correspondence). From the physical$_2$ point of view, there is nothing mysterious or special about the fact that Jones knows he has a stomach ache under circumstances when Smith does not know that Jones has a stomach ache. Jones's knowing (= tokening) system is linked fairly directly to Jones's stomach; Smith's knowing system is normally linked to Jones's stomach only via Jones's knowing system, thus: Jones's stomach → Jones's tokening system → Jones's reporting system → Smith's receptor system → Smith's tokening system. It being a physical$_2$ fact that each of these causal connections is only stochastic, every link involves a further attrition of probabilities: hence the correlation between events in Smith's tokening system and events in Jones's stomach will be lower than that between events in Jones's tokening system and events in Jones's stomach.

Such an analysis of the causal basis of the epistemic situations suggests that, in principle, there *could* be special physical$_2$ arrangements in which the linkage between Smith's tokening system and Jones's stomach would be more dependable than that between Jones's tokening system and the latter's own stomach. And we already know of such clinical examples, e.g., the recently operated patient who "feels sensations in his leg" when the surgeon knows that the leg has been amputated. Such examples serve to remind us that the "privacy" which is philosophically interesting involves central (brain) events rather than peripheral conditions. The autocerebroscopic experiment pushes this "privacy" as far back as it can be taken from the physical$_2$ standpoint, and this extreme is the *only* stage of causal analysis that is of intrinsic philosophical interest for the mind-body theorizer. Here we have the situation in which two quasi-nomological links are set in (apparent) opposition. The subject's tokening system is considered to be very intimately linked to his visual raw-feel states; and the autocerebroscope is also very intimately linked with them. If the Utopian microanalysis supports Feigl's identity theory, either in form (1) or (2a) above, we must conclude that the usual "privacy" (= privileged access) of raw-feel events merely reflects the usual organic condition of intimate wiring, and the usual lack of an equally tight independent access; but that special physical$_2$ conditions *can* be set up in which the causal linkage between artificial apparatus and raw-feel events is more trustworthy than that provided by nature's cerebral anatomy. The progress of science will merely have carried the "stomach-to-brain" kind of analysis inward, so to speak; and educated Utopians will recognize that scientific instruments are (while fallible) less fallible than the tokening mechanism with its socially learned linkage to events in other cerebral subsystems. Less educated Utopians will absorb this understanding by downward seepage through the Sunday supplement section, and the Utopian "plain man" will feel nothing absurd about such locutions as "Jones thinks he is experiencing a pain, but he's really not."

Given the frame of Utopian identity theory, analytic thesis (a) can also be *stated* physicalistically, but it is no longer clearly analytic. We say, "A raw-feel event occurring in the visual cortex of organism K_1 cannot occur in the visual cortex of organism K_2." (I mean this literally, of course; there is nothing analytic, or even plausible, about a denial that raw-feel events having the *same properties* can occur in two different brains. The statement is about identity of particulars.) This would be frame-analytic given a biological law "A visual cortex V cannot belong to two organisms K_1 and K_2 at the same time," which is contingently true but not clearly nomological, since Utopian neurophysiology may provide surgical techniques whereby two organisms can share their visual cortices. Admittedly such a Siamese-twin brain-fusion would necessitate adoption of a convention as to what "two organisms" will be taken to mean. But it would seem to be a reasonable, nonarbitrary stipulation that if two bodies were so joined as to possess a common visual cortex but shared nothing else (e.g., each has a separate tokening mechanism wired equivalently to the common visual cortex; each has its own motivational cortical subsystems; each retains its own stock of memory-storage and "self-concept" subsystems), Utopian physiology would properly speak of "two organisms having a shared visual cortex." The raw-feel *knowings* of these joined individuals being conventionally taken as their distinct propositional (= tokening) events, Utopian epistemology would allow the locution "Knowers K_1 and K_2 share visual raw-feel events," so that (a) not only is seen to be nonanalytic but is empirically false. It is worth noting that this Utopian situation is not utterly unlike our present situation, when we say that "Raw feel *x* belongs to knower K,'' even though knower K may be identifiable over a twenty-year period only by the fact of genidentity (i.e., most of the matter constituting K's brain has been replaced during the 20-year time interval). It is not easy to say precisely why a particular 20-years-past raw-feel event belongs to ''K's set'' of raw-feel events *except* that it belongs to the set historically associated with a body genidentical with K's present body. This line of thought may be worth pursuing on another occasion, because it suggests the possibility that the inaccessibility of another's mind amounts fundamentally to the same problem as the reliability of memory in relation to the solipsism of the present moment; so that he who ''resolves'' the latter—by whatever means—will thereby have also resolved the former.

How would the privacy problem shape up if Utopian neurophysiology were led by the evidence to adopt an ontological dualism of the kind hinted at in Section II? Surprisingly enough, this does not seem to make any important difference. It having been shown experimentally that (nonphysical$_2$) raw-feel events are causal descendants of physical$_2$ brain-events in the visual cortex and that a raw-feel event produced by a state of cortex V_i cannot influence tokening events in tokening system T_j unless T_j is simultaneously ''physical$_2$-close'' (and perhaps neurologically wired) to V_i, we adopt the location-convention that a (non-physical$_2$) raw-feel event ''occurs at (or, even, *in*)'' the brain B which contains properly juxtaposed and wired subsystems V_i and T_i and in which the nomological subnet

is being instantiated. The physical$_2$ conditions necessary and sufficient for such instantiation would be known, and it would be a technological problem to realize them by surgical methods of brain-fusion. Suppose that somehow, without hopelessly disrupting the general cerebral arrangements needed for preserving minimal ''personhood,'' we could juxtapose each of the two tokening systems T_1 and T_2 to each of two visual systems V_1 and V_2, so that the surgeon's electrical stimulation of *either* V_1 or V_2 would produce raw-feel events which influence events in *both* T_1 and T_2. Our experimental analysis continues to support the notion that only a single raw-feel event (or short-lived continuant) is produced by such stimulation. Our dualistic network looks like this:

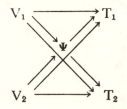

When we stimulate V_1, both subjects token "I see red." Similarly they both token "I see red" when we stimulate V_2. There seems to be no reason, behavioristically, introspectively, or neurophysiologically, for attributing either of these
raw-feel events to one of the subjects rather than the other, unless we adopt a
convention that the person whose *visual* cortex is causative of (an otherwise
shared) raw-feel event is the person who "has" it. Given a Utopian psychophysiology *in dualist form*, such a convention would, I think, be rejected as arbitrary,
counterintuitive, and systemically inconvenient. Even adopting such a convention, however, we can modify the situation by reverting to a shared cortex—a
third person's, or a chimpanzee's, or even a synthetic one!—and dealing with a
setup diagramed thus:

Here everything is symmetrical. The "red" physical$_2$ state Φ_S occurring in
(shared) visual cortex V_S produces one raw-feel event Ψ_S (= phenomenal red)
which in turn combines with the physical$_2$ neurophysiological links to elicit appropriate tokenings in both T_1 and T_2. Surely we do not want to say, "This raw-
feel event occurs, but belongs to no person's experiential history." Unless the
now deceased chimpanzee is a candidate, the raw-feel event must be assigned to
one of our subjects; and there is not the slightest reason for choosing between
them. Note that physicalism and methodological behaviorism are not involved
here. The ontology is explicitly dualistic; and if you were either subject, you
would indignantly oppose a philosopher's asserting that—because of the oddity
of the context—your momentary raw feel "does not really belong to you, but
belongs to the other fellow (or the deceased chimpanzee)."

The most fascinating feature of these fantastic thought-experiments, and the
feature having most philosophic relevance, is that they force us to re-examine the
analyticity of epistemic-pragmatic statements about "I," by bringing out our implicit assumptions concerning the nature and identity of *persons*. Unless a person
is a "simple"—an entity without "parts," "regions," "components," "subsystems"—there must be some criteria by which part-events are assigned to their
appropriate persons. In phenomenal or dualistic language, we currently take it as
analytic that "a particular raw-feel event cannot belong to the class C_i of raw-feel
events constituting the *Erlebnis*-history of person I and also to the class C_j constituting the *Erlebnis*-history of a nonidentical person J." But the analyticity of
this is not a simple dictionary-analyticity like "No woman x is the wife of any
bachelor y." If analytic, it is frame-analytic, involving the nomological network

which embodies our received metaphysic of "persons." If a "person" is *defined* by specifying a class of raw-feel events, how is the class to be specified except by reference to the genidentity of a body whose cortical states are the immediate causal ancestors of the raw-feels being classified? And if we do it this way, the statement about persons' raw-feel sets being disjoint hinges upon the supposition that two bodies' cortical states must necessarily be disjoint. This in turn depends upon the alleged impossibility of two brains sharing parts of cortices — namely, the "parts" whose states are the immediate causal ancestors of raw-feel events. I cannot see any clear reason why such a state of affairs is impossible.

One must, of course, beware of the temptation to imagine an inner observer-of-raw-feels, a manikin who is located elsewhere than the visual cortex and who "inspects" the raw feels occurring in the visual cortex. The locus of the phenomenal red quality is the raw-feel event Ψ, and the only "manikin" is the tokening mechanism, which *tokens* but does not *experience*. If someone insists that by "I" he means "whatever subsystem is the raw-feel locus," then there are not two "I"-persons when the brains are conjoined so as to share a visual cortex, but one "I." We have then to remind such a subject that he must avoid token-reflexive discourse about his visual raw feels, because the "I" who *tokens* is not the "I" whose raw feel is being tokened about. Alternatively, if the subject insists that token-reflexive statements be allowed because, he holds, the "I" referred to is not genidentical with that psychophysical system whose tokening mechanism is being used but rather with that psychophysical system which contains the visual cortex genidentical with the experiencing one, then he is committed to saying "I am a (dead) chimpanzee's brain."

The upshot of these considerations seems to be roughly this: If "privacy" means "privileged access," it is a matter of degree as regards the closeness (tightness) of causal connection between a tokening mechanism and a visual raw-feel event. Under ordinary circumstances (lacking autocerebroscopes, supersurgery, and the like) the causal chain connecting a person's raw-feel events to his tokening events is more trustworthy than the chain connecting his raw-feel events to another's tokening events. But this is no absolute principle, for the same reason that a person might sometimes be well advised to accept the autocerebroscopic verdict on his own raw-feel events in preference to the deliverances of his own "direct-line" tokening mechanism.

If "privacy" is taken to mean "absolute noninspectability," in the sense that the nonoverlap of two persons' raw-feel-classes is analytic, I have tried to show that it is at least not dictionary-analytic but, at most, frame-analytic within an (arguable) nomological network about "persons." And I have *suggested* that this network of constraints about what is possible of persons may really not be nomological but only contingently universal, and perhaps purely technological.

How stands it with the old puzzle about whether my raw-feel qualities are qualitatively the same as yours? If the identity thesis is correct, the problem is solved experimentally, by investigating the physical$_2$ functor conditions present in your brain when you token "red" and in my brain when I token "red." (I hold, as against Professor Feigl, that *if* his identity thesis is correct, he cannot formulate the inverted-spectrum problem in his Utopian theoretical language. It would make no more sense than it would to ask, "Granting the kinetic theory of heat, is the 'hotness' of this bucket of hot soup the same as the 'hotness' of that one, given that their molecules have the same mean kinetic energy?")

What if Utopian psychophysiology is dualistic, along the lines sketched above? We know that English-speaking subjects normally satisfy the causal law network

$$\text{Red surface} \ggg\!\!\to \text{Red light} \ggg\!\!\to \ldots \ggg\!\!\to \Phi_r \ggg\!\!\to t_r$$

with Ψ_r above Φ_r

in which the *form* of the tokening event t_r is learned but the other connections are nomologically necessitated by the (innate) wiring diagram plus the mysterious fundamental nomologicals which entail the raw-feel event Ψ_r whenever the physical$_2$ "red" cortical state Φ_r occurs in a normally constructed visual cortex. The question is whether the raw-feel event Φ could play this causal role in two brains but be of red quality in one and green quality in another. Concentrating for the moment on the "input" side, a Utopian scientist would probably argue that some such overarching principle as "same cause, same effect" should apply here as elsewhere in scientific thinking. The intersubjective nomological network being well corroborated, we "believe in it" until further notice. It tells us that there are two events Φ_i and Φ_j which occur in the brains of persons I and J, and they have certain common physical$_2$ functor properties which are causative of two events Ψ_i and Ψ_j that also share all known causal properties. If there is a property that is nonefficacious, in the sense that it is only a causal descendant but not a causal ancestor (i.e., a nomological "dangler"), our Utopian scientist would probably feel it imparsimonious to hypothesize that this nonefficacious property was different in the two individuals. He might say, "I find no reason why it *should* differ, being consequent upon similar causal conditions, so I shall assume that it *doesn't.*" I must confess that this argument strikes me as convincing, but I don't know what to say if someone challenges the "same cause, same effect" principle.

Perhaps the Utopian thought-experiment can help us gain further insight into this idea of the "phenomenal red quality" as a noncausal property of the raw-feel event Ψ_r. If the phenomenal red quality is noncausal, what can the privileged-access dualist be taken to mean by raising his question? If I am a dualist arguing for absolute, analytic privileged access, how do I frame the question in Utopian physiologese? I say, "While scientific findings may show that my raw feel Ψ_r has causal properties identical with your raw feel Ψ_r, I cannot infer—even in probability—that the *non*causal property *red quality* is present in yours, whereas I know that it is present in mine." Since we have agreed that merely experiencing a raw feel cannot be identified with "knowing that it has a certain quality," I as a dualist must at least be claiming that I can token "red" in obedience to the language-entry rule " 'Red' means *red*." (I do not raise here the incorrigibility or infallibility question, settled above in the negative. All that I claim for the sake of argument is that I "know" in the limited sense of high-confidence probability.) Is my tokening "red" in any way determined by the presence of the red quality in Ψ_r? Not if this quality is taken to be noncausal. If this is true, then my tokening in obedience to the language-entry rule is solely due to the *correlation* between the (causally inefficacious) red quality and the (causally efficacious) physical$_2$ event Φ_r conjoined with the *other* (causally efficacious) properties of Ψ_r. I do not, on such a view, token correctly *because* of the red quality, but because of other factors. *If* I tend to token in obedience to the language-entry rule, it is only because of the nomological dangler which relates the noncausal red quality of Ψ_r to its antecedents. *Consequently I have no stronger ground for trusting my own raw-feel tokenings than for trusting those of others.* In both cases, I must rely upon the "same cause, same effect" principle to infer the noncausal red quality from its *input* conditions. If the phenomenal quality is conceived of as noncausal, as a dangler, I can't know—except by trusting the dangler—that you experience red qualities; but I can't know that I do either!

One way of saying this is that, although a semantic rule and a causal nexus are two very different things, yet in the case of noninferential egocentric raw-feel statements, "legitimated" solely by their obedience to the language-entry rule, *a semantic tie requires a causal tie*. One need not, of course, *assert* the causal tie to "justify" such tokenings as they occur. But if he repudiates the claim that there *is* a causal tie, he cannot maintain in metalinguistic discourse about "privacy" that he trusts the semantic tie and therefore "knows" that he correctly characterizes his own raw-feel events.

There is something at least pragmatically strange—I do not say literally inconsistent—about Professor Feigl's view that phenomenal qualities are not intersubjective, not part of science, not in the public domain. Let us set aside the question as to whether an intersubjective test exists for the inverted-spectrum hypothesis, and consider the broader issue whether the world of science, the causal order, the physical$_1$ network, finds raw-feel qualities theoretically dispensable. Why does Professor Feigl pose the mind-body problem in the first place? What is the "puzzle" which identity theory intends to solve? If you ask him whether there are phenomenal qualities, he says, "Of course there are—this is why we *have* a mind-body problem." I take this to mean that Professor Feigl would not philosophize about the mind-body problem (nor would he be able to understand the discourse of another who did so) except for his own acquaintance with raw-feel qualities. I conclude from this that raw-feel qualities make a difference (i.e., they influence the verbal behavior of Professor Feigl *qua* philosopher). Hence they are causally efficacious, the world would be different in both physical$_1$ *and* *physical*$_2$ ways without them, and they must find a place in the nomological network. Must they not then be "part of science," like everything else that is causally efficacious?

It would seem so. Yet we must do justice to the claims of a rigorous and consistent epiphenomenalism, such as that defended by Lachs (1963). I am unable to detect any flaw in Lachs's incisive analysis, and feel compelled to retreat to a weaker thesis, namely, "If raw-feel qualities are dispensable from the theoretical entities of physical$_1$ science, as Professor Feigl maintains, then he must also hold that *his* concern with the mind-body problem does not originate from his own acquaintance with raw feels. Hence, he must hold that he would philosophize about the mind-body problem *exactly as he does* (compare essay 5, this volume) if, counterfactually, he experienced no raw feels of any kind whatever." I do not tax Professor Lachs with this consequence, which, I take it, would not disturb him; but I know (personal communication) that Professor Feigl finds it unacceptable. It distresses him — as it does me — to be in the very counterintuitive position of saying, "When I raise the mind-body problem, I am talking about my raw feels and their qualities; the very *meaning* of the mind-body problem involves the existence of these raw-feel qualities; a being which thinks (computes, ratiocinates, engages in rule-regulated language transitions) but lacks raw feels could not *understand* the mind-body problem. Nevertheless my raw-feel events have no causal influence upon my tokening behavior." The fascinating question whether, and how, a genuine semantic tie, " 'Red' means *red*," could exist for a knower, lacking any causal (raw feel $\ggg\!\!\rightarrow$ tokening) tie, I shall not attempt to treat here.[4]

We therefore decide that the phenomenal red quality should be taken as causally efficacious. Hence the tokening event t_r is partially controllable by phenomenal qualities of Ψ_r. (I should perhaps remind the reader, in case "phenomenal qualities of a mental event" seems redundant, that Utopian psychophysiology will have introduced the dualistic entity Ψ_r as a theoretical construct required to make sense of the entire body of evidence, so that Ψ_r might — presumably would — have properties in addition to phenomenal ones.) In short, *whether Ψ_r is* *phenomenally red or phenomenally green makes a causal (output) difference.*

I have passed over for expository simplicity the fact that the form of t_r, a conventional sign, is learned, as is its connection with the $\Phi_r - \Psi_r$ complex. This psychological fact gives rise to the distressing possibility of systematic difference between the "content" of two persons' language-entry habits. Granted that "phenomenal red" and "phenomenal green" are causally differentiable, two persons could have learned to *token* pseudoappropriately if the ($\Phi \rightarrow \Psi$) links were consistently reversed between red and green. Can Utopian science find this out, given that the phenomenal hue is causally efficacious?

I think that it can. "Mr. Normal" has learned to token "red" according to the chain

$$\text{Red surface} \ggg\!\!\to \text{Red light} \ggg\!\!\to \ldots \to \Phi_r \ggg\!\!\to t_r \quad \Psi_r$$

and he therefore obeys the language-entry rule " 'Red' means *red*" consistently. "Mr. Funny" has something wrong with his idiographic ($\Phi \to \Psi$) "nomologicals" such that he experiences (consistently) phenomenal green when his visual cortex is in the red-state Φ_r. He will, however, *appear* to be normal, since he tokens in accordance with the causal system

$$\text{Red surface} \ggg\!\!\to \text{Red light} \to \ldots \ggg\!\!\to \Phi_r \ggg\!\!\to t_r \, . \quad \Psi_g$$

If the language-entry rule were " 'Red' means *red-surfaced object*" Mr. Funny would be tokening obediently. And since this is the pragmatic context of verbal learning (see Skinner, 1945), he appears all right to the rest of us. When, as a sophisticated adult pursuing philosophy, he intends to shift to the phenomenal language, in which " 'Red' means *red phenomenal quality*" is the language-entry rule, he fails—but he doesn't know it (i.e., he unwittingly tokens disobediently to the rule) and neither do we. This is the inverted-spectrum problem in two colors.

According to the proponents of absolutely privileged access, this fact can never be brought to light, even by Utopian science. Let us see.

We have agreed that the phenomenal qualities must be allowed causal efficacy. That is, Mr. Funny's appropriate tokenings of "red" are causally dependent upon the copresence in his brain of physical$_2$ state Φ_r and the (consistently aberrated) phenomenal event Ψ_g. While this connection has been learned, *once learned, it makes a causal difference*. Suppose we perform the Utopian neurosurgery necessary to bring Mr. Funny's visual cortex into intimate causal connection with Mr. Normal's tokening mechanism, meanwhile disconnecting or functionally suppressing Mr. Normal's visual cortex. Now Mr. Normal's tokening mechanism is controllable by physical$_2$ inputs of type Φ_r and by physical$_1$ influences of type Ψ_r so as to token "red" when these are copresent. What will happen when the novel input ($\Phi_r \cdot \Psi_g$) "from Mr. Funny's visual cortex" is imposed? Without detail of Utopian microtheory, we can't say. But *something* odd should occur, since Ψ_g is causally differentiable from the usual Ψ_r, and—taken alone—should tend to produce the tokening "green" in Mr. Normal. Better yet, suppose we know from previous research that a somewhat "weakened" or "jammed" physical$_2$ input will not prevent a clear, strong raw-feel event from exerting nonchance discriminative control over a well-learned tokening process. Then we can interfere with the physical$_2$ chain between V and T while allowing the physical$_2$ event Φ_r (and, therefore, the raw-feel event Ψ_g) to occur in full strength and clearness. We might find our subject reporting, "It's a peculiar experience—nothing quite like I'm familiar with—but it *is* a color, and it's green—yet I also feel an impulse to say 'red'—but 'green' is stronger." By ingenious surgical cross-wirings, and well-timed suppressions or chain-interruptions, we could study the tokening consequences of various combinations of physical$_2$ inputs and raw-feel influences upon each subject's several brain-subsystems. The results might very well be so consistent that we would feel confident in saying, "When Mr. Funny normally tokens 'red,' his visual cortex is in the same physical$_2$ state that red light produces in Mr. Normal and the rest of us. But his raw feels are of phenomenal green quality under these circumstances. The rest of us have learned to token 'green' when our tokening mechanisms are under the intimate influence of a green-qualitied raw feel, so when *his* raw feels are allowed to control our tokening mechanisms, we token accordingly." But why are they Mr. Funny's raw feels? It's delightfully arbitrary to say *whose* they are. I would say that they are shared, given the Utopian supersurgery cross-wiring.

Of course I do not believe any such circumstance could arise, since I have metaphysical faith in the "same cause, same effect" principle. Another way of saying this, less offensive to modern ears, is that I decide resolutely to pursue the scientific aim of concocting a nomological net which will include everything that happens (Popper, 1959, 1962). If ontological dualism is true, we have the aim to fit our psychoids into the net (i.e., "Everything is physical$_1$, whether it is physical$_2$ or not"). The Utopian physiologist would insist that there can't be two utterly different hue qualities arising from the same brain-condition Φ_r, even though they are in different brains. And he would persist doggedly in searching for the as-yet-undiscovered physical$_2$ functor which makes Mr. Funny have the "wrong hue quality" when his visual cortex is in state Φ_r.

It may be argued against the brain-joining experiment that we *still* do not have any basis for inferring to the "private" raw-feel qualities, because it could be that "everything changes" owing to the special character of such Utopian cerebral rearrangements. This is of course logically possible. My only answer would be to point out that this possibility is always present when we invoke nomologicals to infer to states of affairs only "indirectly known." There is, so far as I can see, nothing peculiar in *this* respect about the mind-body problem. If I infer the chemical constitution of the stars from spectrographic evidence, and cross-check this inference by employing other avenues of inference, it still *could be* that "everything is different" out there—provided it is "different" in a sufficiently systematic way. The "privileged-access" absolutist cannot rely upon the truism "Our postulated nomologicals may not hold, in reality," unless he is willing to concede that the "privacy" of our raw-feel qualities has the same source as does the general fallibility of human knowledge. The philosophically distressing form of the "privacy" problem is not that which merely concedes the possibility of error; it is that which denies the possibility of a human knower's even getting evidence which is relevant to the question about another knower's raw-feel qualities. Since "getting relevant evidence about event Y" is a matter of latching on to other events X and Z to which Y is causally linked, absolute "privacy" means acausality. I have argued that anyone who admits that raw feels are caused has no positive reason for hypothesizing that they differ qualitatively when produced by similar brain-antecedents. And I have further argued that one who admits that raw feels are causally efficacious—in the required sense that the raw-feel quality is causally relevant as a critical determiner of our own raw-feel tokenings, making it possible for each of us to token obediently to even a purely "private" language-entry rule—must allow as logically possible a thought-experiment in which one knower can token responsively to a raw feel which also "belongs to" the experiential history of another knower. If Smith's tokening mechanism is controllable by the phenomenal qualities, making it possible for him to token consistently "red" when a raw-feel event in his brain is of red quality and "green" when it is green, then if we can locate a raw-feel event belonging to Jones's experiential history so as to give it causal control over Smith's tokenings, *what* he tokens will be evidential as to the raw-feel qualities of Jones.

It is worth noting that the inverted spectrum is usually taken by philosophers as an "obviously possible" contingency, whereas the psychological situation is actually far more complicated; and it is very doubtful whether such a concept can be made structurally consistent. Color experience involves more than hue, and hue is not independent of the other phenomenal dimensions of visual experience. When we combine the findings of phenomenologists, classical introspectionists, Gestalt psychologists, and contemporary "eclectic" students of perception, we have to deal with an extraordinarily rich, complex, interknit set of relationships, both "internal" and "external," and we cannot treat of a simple hue dimension that is unrelated to anything else. It would probably be impossible to construct a formal model representing the visual-experience domain with hue order reversed such that the verbal reports and other discrimination behavior exactly matched that of normal-seeing persons in all respects. The same objection holds for C. I. Lewis's stronger hypothesis about interchanging sensory modalities, such that my red hue is your C sharp tone. In this "switched modality" case, things are worse than with intramodality inversions, because here even the dimensionality may not correspond. I think all psychologists would agree that no such switched modalities are possible, given the internal correlations — the phenomenal *struc-ture* — of the several modalities as we know them. This of course does not refute a hypothesis which merely says " . . . some *other* qualities with isomorphic structure . . . ," understanding that the "other qualities" cannot be any of those we know (i.e., there must be a radically new modality). With this understanding, the idea becomes rather less interesting; and its abstract possibility is still not obvious. I am not sure just what it means to say, "There *might* be a phenomenal modality different from vision, hearing, taste, touch, kinesthesis, etc. — utterly unlike any sensory qualities we know — whose structure was precisely the same as that of the visual modality." This modality must be related to inputs as vision is; it must be related to the subject's experience of his own movements in objective space as vision is (a very tricky requirement, perhaps impossible to meet); it must possess the appropriate number of phenomenal dimensions; and these must be related to one another (internally) and to light stimulation of the retina (externally) in exactly the way hue, saturation, "grain," brightness, size, distance, interposition, direction, etc., are. I am not prepared to say that there could not be such a modality; I merely wish to enter a psychologist's caveat against the too-easy assumption that it could be worked out. And the familiar form of the idea, in which a phenomenal dimension is simply reversed or two modalities are interchanged, is almost certainly impossible.

6. *Ineffability*: It is commonly said that "the quality of a raw feel cannot be communicated." As it stands, this is ambiguous. One interpretation is, "By to-kening a raw-feel predicate, knower K_1 does not inform K_2 as to the quality of K_1's denoted raw feel." Whether this is correct or not depends upon the privacy issue, since if K_1 and K_2 are *in fact* tokening in obedience to the same language-entry rule, each tokening "red" when he experiences the red hue, then K_1 *does* communicate to K_2 by telling him, "Now I am experiencing the red hue." Of course K_1 may at times token erroneously, and on such occasions K_2 will receive misinformation. This kind of mistokening, in which K_1 fails to conform to his own language-entry rules (i.e., he tokens color words inconsistently), is not unique to the raw-feel problem but is also possible when K_1 tokens erroneously in the physical thing-language or in the theoretical language. We do not say that communication is impossible merely because particular communications may (and do) mislead. "Ineffable" means "unspeak*able*," which is a good deal stronger than "sometimes unspoken" or "sometimes mis-spoken." If Smith and Jones have each learned to token "red" whenever their visual cortices are in state Φ_r, or their psychoids are in state Ψ_r, then they normally communicate by so tokening. I am not here appealing to the usages of vulgar speech, i.e., what we "ordinarily take as communication," an appeal which is forestalled by the very posing of the inverted-spectrum problem. What I mean here is that if Smith and Jones do in fact obey the same language-entry rule, then Jones's token "I see

red" communicates *fully* to Smith, and conveys to Smith no less about Jones's raw feel than Smith conveys to himself by his own raw-feel tokenings.

Another unpacking of "ineffability" is "The meaning of raw-feel words can only be conveyed by providing the appropriate raw-feel experience." This is not true for complex raw-feel events, unless we assume the ineffability of simple ones. It is possible for me to explain to you the meaning of "visual image of a centaur" in language permitting you to recognize such a visual image (or even to create one); and this is true for the same reason that "centaur" in physical thing-language is verbally explicable without recourse to ostensive procedures. But I believe we can agree that it is true, in some sense, that certain "elementary" or "simple" raw-feel predicates cannot be thus verbally explained. I could probably convey the meaning of "orange" to a person whose visual history had been rigged so as to exclude any experiences in the (broadly specified) orange region, by telling him "Orange is a color between red and yellow, it's kind of a red-yellow mixture." But I could not do the same for yellow itself (which led some psychologists to reject a trichromatic theory of color on the ground that "yellow is a 'simple,' " although yellow can be matched on the color wheel by a suitable mixture of red and green). While there can be disagreement about many marginal cases, let us here grant for argument's sake that there exist *some* phenomenal predicates which designate raw-feel qualities of this "simple, unanalyzable, rock-bottom" kind. We would find it impossible to formulate in language a definition of the predicate in terms of more elementary concepts, concepts which taken separately are not synonymous (or even near-synonymous) with the predicate in question. A centaur is not simple—it has parts or components, it is "made out of" elements, "centaurhood" is a complex quality. Hence we can translate sentences about centaurs (and, derivatively, about centaur-images) into sentences about hooves, horses, men, etc. But if, say, *red* is a simple quality, we cannot thus reduce the predicate "red" to non-hue-characterizing expressions, enabling learner to token appropriately in the future.

But even this is not quite true, taken literally as just stated. It would be possible to teach someone to token "red" appropriately, at least under many circumstances, by stating a special kind of semantic rule. We might, for instance, say " 'Red' designates the color of apples"; or " 'Red' designates the color you experience when light waves of wave length λ stimulate your eye." The availability of these verbal meaning-specifications is not philosophically important in the present context, because they will "work" only if the learner then proceeds to *put himself* into the described circumstances (i.e., to look at some apples or have a physicist stimulate his retina with wave length λ). So that our definition of "red" is, in effect, a prescription to him for learning obedience to the language-entry rule. Instead of training him ourselves—the usual way we enable children to acquire color words—we instruct him how to train himself. If we don't permit him to go through this intermediate process of self-tutelage, our definition of "red" will not enable him to token appropriately.

The ineffability of phenomenal simples can be trivialized by saying, "If a person has not been given the opportunity to learn a language, then, of course, he will be unable to speak it." As we discussed above in regard to the noninferential character of egocentric raw-feel statements, such statements are often *inferable* from other statements even though typically they are not, in fact, inferred. When tokened noninferentially, they have no "grounds" or "evidence" or "reasons" or "justification." The tokening occurs "on the basis of" a nonlinguistic occurrence, i.e., the raw-feel event itself. The relation is (a) causal and (b) semantic, but the semantic rule is degenerate and uninformative. We learn to token in obedience to it by training, in the same way a dog learns to sit up or roll over. The required linkage is not intraverbal, as in rational inference or propositionally mediated knowledge; the required linkage is between language and the nonlinguistic. And just as we have to be *trained* to perform intralinguistic transitions, so we have to be *trained* to perform language-entry transitions. From one point of view, since there is nothing philosophically earthshaking about the fact that a person cannot "give the right answer" to $(317 \times 48 = ?)$ if he has never learned the multiplication table, why is it considered so very special that a person cannot "correctly name a raw-feel color quality" unless he has learned the color language?

IV. Is "Acquaintance" with a Raw-Feel Quality Cognitive?

This is perhaps an appropriate place to examine briefly what a person "knows" by virtue of having experienced a raw feel. Suppose that knowers K_1 and K_2 share knowledge of the Utopian scientific network, including, of course, the psychophysiology of vision and the psycholinguistics of color language. However, K_2 is congenitally blind and although he has recently undergone a corneal transplant, it is very shortly postsurgery and he has not as yet experienced any visual raw feels. Does K_1 know anything that K_2 does not know?

I have put this question to a number of "plain men" as well as to some not so plain. The natural tendency is to say that K_1 knows something that K_2 does not know, to wit, "*what red looks like*." Without taking vulgar speech or the theories it embodies as criteria of truth, I must confess that my own instincts in this matter are very like those of the plain man. It is pointed out by Professor Feigl that mere "living-through," "having," "experiencing" is not cognitive. While one might cavil at the persuasive definition of "knowing" presupposed by this exclusion, let us accept it for argument's sake. We may still question the conclusion that K_1 differs from K_2 only as to "*mere* experiencing." The raw-feel experiences of K_1 have been systematically correlated with color-word tokenings by himself and others during the course of his language-learning history, and he has been thoroughly trained to token "red" in accordance with the language-entry rule " 'Red' means *red*." He has not *merely* experienced the red and green hue qualities; rather he has coexperienced the red hue quality with "red"-tokenings and the green hue quality with "green"-tokenings. One reformulation of the plain man's notion that K_1 "knows how red looks, which K_2 does not" might be that *K_1 knows how to apply a language-entry rule which K_2 does not*. It is true that K_2 knows that there *is* a language-entry rule " 'Red' means *red*." He can token the rule itself. He can discuss the pragmatics of the rule (e.g., how people acquire the habit of obeying it, why he himself cannot as yet token in obedience to it, what the physical$_2$ functor values of the visual cortex are for brain-states Φ_r and Φ_g). He can describe precisely what needs to be done by him, or to him, so that he will be rendered capable of tokening in obedience to the rule in the future. Nevertheless he cannot token in obedience to it at present. Is the ability to obey a semantic rule "cognitive"?

There are two related approaches to this question which seem to me to justify at least a tentatively affirmative answer. The first approach asks how it happens that a knower can know a semantic rule and yet be incapable of tokening in obedience to it. We can understand that people lie, make jokes, or mis-speak on a Freudian or other basis. But our knower K_2 *cannot* token color terms consistently with the semantic rules he "knows" (i.e., rules that he can token, and can fit into Utopian pragmatics). It is all very well to explain this oddity by causal analysis; it may even be somewhat illuminating to trivialize it as we did above by the statement "No one can speak a language he hasn't learned." But these psychological accounts, while perfectly correct as causal explanations, do not remove the oddity in its philosophic aspect. The more strictly philosophical question is: Granted that we can easily explain K_2's status as a psychological consequence of his impoverished visual history, what, precisely, *is* that status with respect to the semantic rules " 'Red' means *red*" and " 'Green' means *green*"? The obvious answer, of course, is that ability to token a semantic rule, and the sincere motivation to emit other tokenings in obedience to it, does not suffice for doing the latter *unless one understands what the rule means*. Putting this affirmatively, we may say: "A person who understands the meaning of a rule can obey it if he wishes (provided, of course, that the action — in this case, tokening — is physically performable by him)." Therefore, if K_2 wishes to obey the rule but cannot, it must be that he does not understand it. I, like the plain man, am inclined to say that he does not fully understand it. To understand the semantic rule " 'Rouge' means *red*" one must understand the meaning of "red." When blind K_2 tokens " 'Red' means *red*" or " 'Rouge' means *red*" he cannot fully intend all that K_1 intends by this utterance. He cannot, because "red" designates a hue quality and, as our plain man says, a blind person "does not know what red looks like." I am not able to push this argument any further, and I shall simply have to ask

Professor Feigl whether he wants to say that a person who has never linked the words "red" and "green" to the hue qualities *red* and *green* can fully understand the semantic rules " 'Red' means *red*" and " 'Green' means *green*." Surely there is something intended by the seeing who enunciate this rule that is not intended by the blind who enunciate it?

It may be objected that our truism, "A person who understands the meaning of a rule can obey it if he wishes," was insufficiently qualified by the stipulation that the required action be physically performable by him. This way of putting it, focusing entirely upon the *action* (output) side, leaves open the question of his lacking sufficient information, and the latter is equally necessary for rule-obedience. If I am to obey the rule, "The king may not be put into check," it is insufficient that I am physically able to move the chessman; I must also know the position. Any rule which specifies an action appropriate to a condition will normally require for its consistent obedience that the action be physically performable and that the condition be knowable at the time of action-choice. And a semantic rule is such a rule—it makes specified tokenings licit conditional upon the occurrence of certain raw-feel events. The truism must be formulated more carefully so as to take this into proper account. A hard-nosed consistent identity theorist (tougher than Professor Feigl—say one like Professor P. K. Feyerabend) might argue thus: In order for K_2 to token in obedience to the rule " 'Red' means *red*," he has to possess the information that he is experiencing a red-hued raw feel. We know (Utopian identity theory) that a red-hued raw feel is (*sic!*) a physical$_2$ state Φ_r in the visual cortex. Hence the semantic rule is " 'Red' means Φ_r," and in order to be rule-obedient, one must token "red" if one's brain is in the Φ_r-state. Now the Φ_r-state is explicitly definable in terms of certain physical$_2$ functor inequalities, the satisfaction of which is ascertainable via the cerebroscope. Further, by means of the autocerebroscope (or an autocerebrophone, since K_2 has not yet learned visual form discrimination, so he couldn't read the television screen's symbols), K_2 can ascertain whether his brain is currently in state Φ_r or Φ_g, and he can do this upon the *first* postoperative occasion that red or green light enters his eyes. We have agreed that K_2 knows all the Utopian psychophysiology and the psycholinguistics that K_1 knows, so he will of course be able to understand the workings of the autocerebrophone and will token "red" (if, say, the instrument's high-pitched tone indicates his brain is in state Φ_r) and "green" (low-pitched tone indicating brain-state Φ_g) appropriately. It is therefore incorrect to say that K_2 "must not understand" the semantic rule, on the ground that he can't token in obedience to it. He can—provided he is given the necessary information.

Now this is an interesting move, and its use by an identity theorist testifies to his theoretical consistency. If the identity theory is taken literally—if a red-hued raw-feel event *is* literally, numerically identical with a physical$_2$ brain-event— then the autocerebrophone (or -scope, or -tact, or whatever) is a perfectly good

epistemic avenue to that which is denoted variously in phenomenal, behavioristic, and neurophysiological languages. I rather suspect that this move is some
kind of touchstone for an identity theorist's wholeheartedness; and I take note of
the biographical fact that (in conversations) Professor Feigl finds the move somewhat distressing, as contrasted with Professor Feyerabend who sees it as *the* most
straightforward approach and employs it aggressively and unapologetically.

Granted that K_2 could, by using the autocerebrophone, enable himself to obey
the semantic rules even upon the first postoperative occasions of his experiencing
red and green raw feels, what does this prove? Let us recapitulate the argument.
We began with the principle that a person can, if he desires, obey a rule whose
action-side is physically performable. We argued that just-operated knower K_2
cannot token in obedience to the semantic rule " 'Red' means *red*," even though
he desires to, and even though he is able to perform the tokening act itself (i.e.,
he has long since learned how to *pronounce* "red" in the course of studying Utopian science). Therefore, we argued, he must not understand it. To this argument
was offered the objection that the possibility of rule-obedience involves knowing
the conditions which are to be compared to the rule's conditions, and that if K_2
were permitted to know the conditions (by using the autocerebrophone) then he
would be able to token appropriately. Hence it has *not* been demonstrated that K_2
"does not understand the meaning of the rule."

This brings me to the second approach to "Does K_1 know something which
K_2 doesn't?" The reason we—most of us, I mean—are not happy with the au-
tocerebrophonic basis of K_2's rule-obedient tokening is that it is an alternative
avenue, one which K_1 can dispense with because he has "more direct access." I
do not expect this to disturb a good materialist like Professor Feyerabend, who of
course views the situation as symmetrical in two indicator instruments: the tokening mechanism (biologically wired and learning-calibrated) and the autocerebrophone (scientifically built and calibrated), with the latter presumably being
more reliable! Perhaps our dissatisfaction points the way to an argument not rebuttable by invoking the autocerebrophone?

Try this one: "If, given a shared system of propositions T and identical momentary physical inputs S_1 and S_2, a knower K_1 can predict a future external
event E which K_2 cannot predict, then K_1 understands T more fully than K_2 understands it." Here T refers to the entire system of propositions known to Utopian science and shared by our two subjects, including the semantic rules. (It
does not, however, include all particulars concerning the present experiment.)
Inputs S_1 and S_2 are red light stimuli which we shine into the eyes of K_1 and K_2
(thereby giving the latter a red-hued raw feel for the first time). As we present
this visual stimulus, we also give the following instructions to each subject: "I
am going to shine this same light into the eyes of 10 normal-visioned English-
speaking subjects with the request to 'name the color.' What will they say?"

These instructions augment T somewhat, but equally for both subjects. The momentary stimulus inputs (while not identical) are "relevantly identical" in that they are clearly red (or can be made so by repeatedly stimulating K_2 before presenting the instructions). Yet we know that K_1 will be able to predict the verbal behavior of other subjects, whereas K_2 will not. Since both knowers have the same system T, the same instructions, the same momentary input, but differ in their predictive ability, we conclude that K_1 understands something about T that K_2 does not. (I say "understands something," rather than "knows," because they can both token T's propositions, can both derive portions of T from other portions, can both engage in meta-talk about object-language parts of T, etc.) Of course the reason that poor K_2 cannot predict the verbal behavior of others is that merely being informed in our instructions that they will be stimulated by "this same light" does not entail that he will be informed what color the light is; hence he cannot move within the T-network to reach the semantic rule " 'Red' means *red*" or its pragmatic counterpart "English speakers token 'red' when they experience *red*." He knows these rules, but he—unlike K_1—cannot apply them to solving his cognitive problem. And there is, I submit, a very simple reason for his inability to apply them: *he doesn't fully understand them.* If he fully understood " 'Red' means *red*," he would know that the light entering his own eye was inducing red-qualitied raw feels in him; hence he would infer that "this same light" would have that effect upon others; and hence, finally, that they would token "red" in obedience to the rule.

Unless there is some flaw in this example and argument, it provides a refutation of the view that "knowing how to obey a language-entry rule is not cognitive." Because surely everyone will admit that he who can, by virtue of some extra "know-how," predict an external event which another lacking that "know-how" cannot predict has a genuine *cognitive edge* over the latter. Admittedly there is a considerable element of arbitrariness in where the line is drawn between "knowing that" and "knowing how," so that, whereas "knowing how" to solve physical problems by using calculus would be universally considered equally a "knowing that" and unquestionably cognitive, knowing how to obey linguistic rules is less clearly so. Our example suggests a fairly broad stipulation here, since we have seen that knowing *how* to obey a semantic rule can lead (via linguistic transitions) to a definite surplus of knowing *that*, i.e., rational prediction of a future external event. Knowing a language is conventionally considered cognitive; and we have good reason to follow conventional usage here. Not that anything philosophically critical hangs upon how tolerant a convention we adopt for labeling those marginal "knowings that" which are mainly "knowings how" as "cognitive." If a very narrow convention were adopted, it would still be true that possessing habits of semantic-rule-obedience gives one a cognitive edge, even if the habits themselves are classified as noncognitive. Suppose someone then maintains that raw-feel qualities can be deleted from the scientific world-picture, since that picture deals only with the cognitive, and the having of a raw feel is not cognitive. To this we reply the following:

1. A knower who has never experienced the raw-feel quality designated by a phenomenal predicate Q cannot mediate predictions (in the domain of descriptive pragmatics) which can be mediated by a knower who has experienced this raw-feel quality but who is in all other respects equivalently trained and informed.

2. This is because the inexperienced knower cannot employ the semantic rule " 'Q' means Q" and the pragmatic rule "L-speakers token 'Q' when experiencing Q" to make the necessary derivations.

3. His inability to employ these semantic and pragmatic rules in derivation chains arises not from ignorance of these rules, since he "knows" both of them.

4. Rather he is unable to employ them because he does not fully understand them.

5. Specifically, he does not fully understand " 'Q' means Q" because he is unacquainted with the raw-feel quality Q which "Q" designates.

6. But if there is (exists, occurs) anything designated by "Q"—which must be so, if the inexperienced knower's predictive disadvantage is to be explained—then that something is left out of any world-account which does not include mention of Q.

7. A world-account which does not include "Q" when there is a cognitive edge favoring knowers who understand the meaning of "Q" is cognitively defective.

The basic point of all this, it seems to me, is really quite simple. What makes it seem difficult is our (understandable) phobia about "the given," "knowledge by acquaintance," "incorrigible protocols," and "the ineffable quale." If we shuck off these things (without adopting an untenable dispositionalism or logical behaviorism as our account of raw feels) the matter can be formulated as follows: Part of my knowledge consists of knowing when the people who speak "my" language use its various words. If I don't know this, if I cannot recognize a particular circumstance as being one for which the language has a certain expression, then there is clearly something about the language and its users that I do not know. But *what* is it about the language that I don't know? I know all of the language-transition rules; I even know—in a sense—the language-entry rules. But in another and critically important sense I do not fully "know" the language-entry rules, because there occur some situations legitimating a language entry in which others are able to make the prescribed entry but I am not. The common-sense explanation of this disability is that I cannot make the entry because I don't fully understand the meaning of some of the words involved. I am skeptical as to whether philosophese can improve fundamentally on this account of the matter.

Some have felt that this line of thought is adverse to the identity theory, but I am unable to see why. The identity theorist may agree that a knower who has experienced red-hued raw feels "knows" something, as shown by his ability to predict events under circumstances such that the prediction can only be mediated by the knower's habit of obedience to the language-entry rule " 'Red' means *red*." What bearing does this have upon the identity theory? We have adopted a tolerant conception of "the cognitive," and we therefore say that, while *mere experiencing* of a red-hued raw feel is not cognitive, such experiencing together with an appropriate tokening "red" (by another, or by oneself if thereupon reinforced by another) is a "cognitive" event in the derivative sense that it generates a "cognitive" disposition, to wit, the ability to token in conformity with the semantic rule; and he who knows how to obey the semantic rule "knows" something. Let it be further admitted that if K_1 can perform a rule-regulated language-entry under physical input conditions such that K_2 cannot, K_1 knows more than K_2 knows—in the present case K_1 knows "what quality the word 'red' designates." Does this prove, or have any tendency to prove, that "red" does not designate the physical$_2$ cortical state Φ_r? I am not yet raising the question whether (and, if so, how) a hue-quality term can designate a physical$_2$ cortical state (i.e., whether the "meaning" of "red" can *conceivably* be identified with any complex of physical$_2$ functor inequalities). I am only considering the anti-identity argument which arises from the K_1-K_2 cognitive edge. Can anything be inferred about ontological identity from the admission that a knower who is historically acquainted "by direct experience" with raw-feel quality Q can, by virtue of that acquaintance, recognize a new instance of it and token appropriately, whereas a knower who lacks such acquaintance "by direct experience" cannot do so?

How does identity theory handle this? In the reconstructed theoretical language of identity theory, the semantic rule " 'Red' means *red*" can, of course, still occur; but there is also a more informative semantic rule which provides an explicit definition of "red" in terms of physical$_2$ functor inequalities, i.e., the rule " 'Red' means the brain-state functor condition Φ_r." This semantic rule has been adopted (conventionally but nonarbitrarily) on the basis of a well-corroborated object-linguistic generalization that a red-hued raw-feel event *is* (in fact) a cortical state, characterizable in terms of functor inequalities represented by the explicitly defined symbol Φ_r. Within this revised language, we define *in usu*:

1. "Knower K experiences a raw feel y of red-hued quality at t" means that K's visual cortex is in physical$_2$ state Φ_r at t.

2. "Knower K is directly acquainted with the meaning of 'red' " means that he has experienced a raw feel of red-hued quality concurrently with a tokening of "red." (I neglect here the psychological refinements which would be necessary for completeness, e.g., we would have to distinguish between such "opportunities to become acquainted" and effectively "becoming acquainted.")

Then we have, in descriptive pragmatics, an empirical law which asserts, roughly,

3. A knower cannot token (extra-chance) in conformity with the semantic rule " 'Red' means Φ_r," unless either (a) He is directly acquainted with the meaning

of "red," as in (2); in which case he tokens correctly by a language-entry only. Or (b) He is provided with other information as to the state of his brain or its physical$_2$ inputs; in which case he tokens correctly by a combination of *other* language-entries and language-transitions (i.e., he makes rational inferences).

We note in passing that each of these molar-level laws is in turn microderivable within the identity theory.

The appropriate tokening of "I see red" can occur so long as the knower's tokening mechanism is somehow brought under the causal control of his visual-cortical events. The causal chain from Φ_r to t_r, the "direct access" link, is available if he has learned the raw-feel language, but otherwise not. "Knowledge by acquaintance" consists, causally analyzed, in having established this intrabrain direct-access linkage.

Dualists often object to the identity theory on the ground that a person can know the meaning of "red" without knowing anything about brain-states. There is, at least to me, a troubling force to this objection if it goes to the intension of "(phenomenal) red," a point to which we shall return later. However, insofar as the objection lays its emphasis—as it commonly does—upon the pragmatic fact that a knower can consistently token in obedience to " 'Red' means *red*" without knowing anything about brain-states, I believe it has no force against the reconstructed identity theory. In order for this pragmatic fact to speak against the identity theory, we must show that the identity theory itself entails something to the contrary. But this is surely impossible to show in physical$_2$ terms. We would have to prove, within the identity frame, that in order for an organism's tokening mechanism to be differentially responsive (by tokening "red" versus "green") to the physical$_2$ states Φ_r versus Φ_g in the visual cortex, that same organism's tokening mechanism must also respond to the several physical$_2$ *component aspects* of Φ_r and Φ_g by tokening theoretical physical$_2$-language statements descriptive of these components. There is, of course, nothing about the laws of learning or the microphysiology of the brain which would even remotely suggest such a consequence. Insofar as the identity theory is, after all, a scientific theory—its substantive content being assertions in the physical$_2$ object-language—a refutation based upon the laws of tokening behavior must proceed within the theory's network and show therefrom that an entailed correlation among tokening dispositions is empirically false. The theory identifies red-hued raw-feel events with Φ_r-states in the visual cortex. A Φ_r-state consists of a conjunction of component conditions, such as, say, "The second time-derivative of the proportion of simultaneously activated termini of the synaptic scales on cells of type M in cell-assemblies of form F lying within Brodmann's area 17 has a value $l_1 \leq d^2p/dt^2 \leq l_2$." Nothing within the theory need entail the consequence that a subject whose tokening system has been brought (through learned microconnections) under stochastic control of such a part-condition has also been trained to token so much as the word "derivative," let alone the whole collection of scientific statements involved in Φ_r. The tokening system is itself a complex entity, and its connections (wired-in plus conditioned) with the visual cortex are also complex. Tokening "red" is an event of immensely complex physical$_2$ composition, the components of which are not themselves tokenings. Nor are the microcomponents of the state Φ_r themselves raw feels. (Does anyone imagine, even if he is an identity theorist, that a single neuron "experiences the red quality" when that neuron undergoes a single discharge as part of its sustained firing contribution to the Φ_r-pattern?) There is just no reason to expect, on the identity theory's own grounds, that everyone who is able to token correctly in accordance with " 'Red' means *red*" should be able to token the theoretical statements contained in the explicit definition of state Φ_r. Given the causal laws and structural statements of the theory, we have no more reason to expect tokenings characterizing the microcomponent events or state-values than we have for expecting in the kinetic theory of heat that our thermometers should provide readings in terms of the mean free path or average velocity of the molecules in a bucket of hot soup. Therefore the fact of descriptive pragmatics that persons can "know what red is" (i.e., can know when they are themselves experiencing red-hued raw feels) without "knowing what a Φ-state is" (i.e., without knowing that their momentary brain-states fulfill certain functor conditions) provides no grounds for rejecting the identity theory *as being an inadequate causal account of raw-feel tokening behavior*.

V. The Identity Theory and Leibniz's Principle

This causal analysis has its more strictly philosophical counterpart in the well-known qualification upon Leibniz's Principle, to wit, that it does not bind in intentional contexts. Actually our attempted refutation of the identity theory proceeds by ignoring this qualification, which in other philosophical disputes is routinely applied. The dualist is here arguing, in effect, that "K knows that he is experiencing a red raw feel," when conjoined with the identity theory's equivalence, "Experiencing a red-hued raw feel *is* having a Φ_r-state in one's visual cortex," entails "K knows that he is having a Φ_r-state in his visual cortex," a conclusion which is factually false (for all contemporary knowers, and for most knowers in Utopia). But the inference proceeds through substitution of the (red-hued raw feel = Φ_r-state) identity into the first statement "K knows . . . " a substitution via Leibniz's Principle in a forbidden intentional context.

Arguments against the identity theory which rely on Leibniz's Principle fall naturally into two classes, depending upon whether the allegedly unshared property is physical or mental. The commonest objection of the first class invokes one of the classic distinctions between the physical and the mental, to wit, that the former is "in space" and the latter is not. (Whether "in space" means space-

filling or spatially *located* I shall not consider, although this refinement may be important in deciding upon a suitable convention for categorizing theories as monistic or dualistic.) Critics of the identity theory point out that physical$_2$ brain-events are literally, anatomically, spatially *located in the head*; if Professor Feigl means what he says, and a red-hued raw feel is identical with a Φ_r-state, then since the Φ_r-state is in the head, he is committed to asserting that the red-hued raw feel is in the head. And the critic considers this a *reductio ad absurdum* on the ground that a raw feel is "obviously" *not* located in the head.

As stated above, I believe Professor Feigl is so committed by his theory, although I know him to feel a bit queasy about asserting "My phenomenal events are in my head." I shall attempt to show that this is an unobjectionable locution, and one which we *must* adopt if we take the identity theory seriously and literally.

Consider the phenomenal event which occurs in the ordinary negative after-image experiment. Following upon fixation of a red circle in a booklet, I now fixate the gray wall 20 feet away and I "see there" a large, unsaturated, blue-green circle. While it is true that I do not *believe* it is "out there" (i.e., I do not assert that the causal ancestor of my current visual experience is a circular object on the wall), the "out there" character of the phenomenal event is strong, involuntary, and quite unmistakable.

Let us designate the color quality of this afterimage by the predicate "P," its apparent size by "Q," and its spatial ("out there") quality by "R." It does not matter whether "R" is 1-place or 2-place, since even if "my body" needs to be put in the second place, this "spatial" relation must, of course, be understood phenomenally, i.e., the red patch is *phenomenally external* to my *phenomenal body*. We use the 2-place predicate "L" as before, to mean " . . . is located (literally, spatially, anatomically) in the head of . . . "

Then when *a* is experiencing the afterimage we write, in our original notation for the psychophysical correlation-law and conjoining the identity statement:

$$(E!y)\ \Psi\ (a,y) \cdot P(y) \cdot Q(y) \cdot R(y) \cdot (E!z)L(a,z)\Phi(z) \cdot (y = z).$$

Which requires us to assert, substituting,

$$(E!y)L(a,y),$$

i.e., "The phenomenal event y is located in *a*'s head," which leaves us asserting the conjunction

$$(E!y)L(a,y) \cdot R(y),$$

i.e., "There is a phenomenal event located in *a*'s head and this event has the phenomenal property of seeming external to *a*'s head." This entailed conjunction is deemed contradictory by the critic, and is therefore taken to refute the identity conjunct $(y = z)$.

But L(a,y) · R(y) is not self-contradictory, because the predicate L characterizes the physical$_2$ location of the phenomenal event, whereas the predicate R characterizes one of the phenomenal event's internal phenomenal properties. It is a phenomenal property of the afterimage to "appear out there," that is, the "externality" is *a quality of the experience*. In simpler notation, if v is a visual raw feel and b a brain-event, the identity theorist says

1. v is "out there (phenomenally)."
2. b is "in the head (anatomically)."
3. v and b are identical.

Spelling these out a bit more,

1'. The visual phenomenal event v possesses as one of its phenomenal properties an "out-there" quality.

2'. The brain-state b occurs in the head.

3'. The phenomenal event is the brain-state.

Hence we are required to say, "There occurs in the head a phenomenal event one of whose phenomenal properties is the 'out-there' quality." This kind of talk seems a bit odd, but what is there actually contradictory about it? R is a phenomenal predicate characterizing an experienced quality *of* the phenomenal event; whereas L is *not* a phenomenal predication and does *not* characterize the event as possessing or lacking experienced locus as a visual quality, but instead tells us where the phenomenal event is in physical$_2$ space. The critic relies on an allegedly clear truth, that

$$(x,y)[L(x,y) \supset \sim R(x,y)],$$

i.e., nothing can be "inside" and "outside" a person at the same time. But L means "physically inside" and R means "having the phenomenal quality 'outside,' " so nothing as to the predicability of R is inferable from the identity theory's universal predication of L. It goes without saying that the reconstructed theoretical language of Utopian identity theory will identity the phenomenal "out-there" property with certain physical$_2$ functor conditions in the brain-state, different from those identified with phenomenal hue, size, etc.

VI. Summary as to Nonsemantic Objections

Beginning with the autocerebroscopic thought-experiment, we have examined some of the commoner objections to the identity theory and, I believe, found them answerable. I have tried to show in what sense the theory can be genuinely empirical, by suggesting how Utopian neurophysiology might provide experimental results either corroborative or discorroborative of identity or dualism. In the light of the autocerebroscopic thought-experiment, I have briefly examined (with no claim to exhaustive treatment) several of the more familiar claims regarding raw-feel statements, especially those which are thought to militate against the identity theory. Most, if not all, of these claims would fail as refutations even if true, because they are claims about *knowledge* and therefore do not permit substitution via Leibniz's Principle. But I also tried to show that none of these claims is clearly correct, and that some are clearly incorrect. Raw-feel statements are, if I am right,

1. Noninferential normally, but not always, even when tokened egocentrically;
2. Corrigible;
3. Sometimes errant;
4. Indubitable, normally; but not always;
5. Private, contingently, but not nomologically or analytically;
6. Ineffable, when simple; but not in the sense of "incommunicable."

Finally I have discussed the question whether knowledge of raw feels by direct acquaintance is cognitive (I conclude that it is), and whether the occurrence of such knowledge without knowing the physical$_2$ nature of one's brain-events is ground for rejecting the identity thesis (I conclude that it is not).

The net result of these ruminations is, I think, to leave the identity theory in pretty good shape as an internally consistent hypothesis of "empirical metaphysics." The positive grounds for adopting it have not been discussed, and are too well known to require discussion. It must, I believe, be admitted that the evidence in its support, even within the limitations of current science and common sense, is fairly strong. Further, the purely *conceptual* difficulties we meet in trying to formulate even a sketch of ontological dualism (e.g., in getting clear "where Smith's non-physical$_2$ raw feels are" for purposes of their causally influencing events in Jones's brain) should discourage a scientifically oriented theorizer from working along dualistic lines, at least until the more manageable monism runs into serious scientific difficulties.

VII. The Strongest Objection to Identity Theory: Semantic

I have left to the last the only objection (other than certain parapsychological phenomena) which I find continues to bother me somewhat. It involves the problem of intension—of "what sense-quality words *mean*"—in a way which is, I fear, rather too technical to be usefully discussed by a psychologist lacking the philosopher's union card. I shall therefore treat it only briefly in this place.

As a first approximation to formulating the difficulty, let the dualist advance the following: Your theory says that a red-hued raw feel is literally, numerically identical with a cortical Φ_r-state. According to this view, that which I experience as a red quality is—not "depends upon," "arises from," "correlates with," "corresponds to," "is produced by," but *is*—a complex of electromagnetic and electrostatic fields, alterations in potassium ion concentrations, disarrangements of membrane molecules, and the like. You have explained satisfactorily how it is that I can know *when* my brain is in this state, and how I can token "I am experiencing a red-hued raw feel" in obedience to the semantic rule " 'Red' means Φ_r," without knowing the physical$_2$ nature of the state Φ_r. You have resolved a paradox in pragmatics by combining a microcausal analysis of my learned tokening dispositions with a philosophical reminder that Leibniz's Principle does not bind in an intentional context. It is, as I now see, a mistake to attack you in the domain of pragmatics. But the problem has also a reflection in semantics. Surely you will concede that "red" and "green" designate raw-feel *qualities*. And these qualities do not appear anywhere in your theoretical reconstruction. When I examine the component expressions in the explicit definition of "Φ_r" I find physical$_2$ predicates and functors, but where are the red and green raw-feel qualities mentioned? They have gotten lost in the shuffle. I can't help feeling that, whatever you *have* done, you have *not* dealt with the problem we started to worry about, which was the nature of raw feels. Whatever else may be true of raw feels — and you have made it very doubtful whether anything else is uniquely true of them — at least it is true that they have qualities. And this, the sole distinguishing feature of raw feels, has been liquidated in the course of your analysis. I maintain that "red" designates a quality; that the *meaning* of "red" is this quality; and that there occur raw feels *of* this quality, i.e., "red-hued raw feel" denotes as well as designates. These qualities are in the world (if anything is!). But they find no place in your world-account. Therefore I must reject your account.

Professor Feigl himself has apparently some difficulties with the identity theory on this score. It might be said that his view is not entirely consistent, insofar as he takes the inverted-spectrum problem seriously. If the identity theory is correct, there can be no such *philosophical* problem, because Utopian science will presumably find out that your and my tokenings of "red" are correlated with the same kind of state Φ_r and that will settle the matter. If the identity theorist persists in philosophic doubt after that point in science is reached, or if he *adds* some sort of argument from "analogy," or appeals to "induction" or "determinism" or "parsimony" or "same cause, same effect," we know that he does *not* believe that a red-hued raw feel is literally identical with a Φ_r-state, since if it is, then there *is* no "other something" which requires analogy, etc., to infer.

Similarly, one may question Professor Feigl's emphasis upon the intersubjective and causal features of scientific knowledge insofar as this knowledge is contrasted with our "knowledge" of raw feels. If the identity theory is understood literally, raw feels are as much in the nomological network as anything else, and therefore they are part of the "public, intersubjective" world-picture. As I have argued above, it is also necessary for them to be causally efficacious. If a red-hued raw feel *is* a Φ_r-state, and what distinguishes it from a green-hued raw feel is a difference in the physical$_2$ conditions, then the qualities *red* and *green* are represented by physical$_2$ expressions which are not nomologically different from those of nonpsychological science.

Within the frame of identity theory, can it be properly said that the occurrence of phenomenal qualities is "a contingent fact"? If we mean by this that the world could have been otherwise in its fundamental nomologicals, of course. Also if we mean that a different world of our world-family might have produced no living brains, and hence realized no Φ-states of raw-feel complexity. But what the identity theorist may *not* say is that the world could have been "just as it is, except for the absence of raw feels." It is not contingent (granting identity theory) that for every Φ$_r$-state there is a red-hued raw feel. This truth is analytic for an identity theorist. That the world could have contained no Φ$_r$-states is logically (and even nomologically) possible, but any world which *does* contain Φ$_r$-states contains red-hued raw feels. To return again to the kinetic theory analogy, a physicist who believes in kinetic theory can say:

1. Kinetic theory is empirical. It might be false; and, if true, it might have been false.

2. Even if kinetic theory is true, it might have been false that there ever existed such an entity as hot soup.

It is a contingent fact that the world has molecules in it. Given that there are molecules, it is a contingent fact that certain aggregates of molecules exist and have a certain mean kinetic energy. But what a physicist who believes in kinetic theory *cannot* say is:

3. It is a contingent fact that soup is hot when its molecules are moving rapidly.

The physicist who adopts kinetic theory has—until further notice—committed himself to a theory which demands obedience to the semantic rule " 'Hot' means *containing fast-moving molecules*." If subsequent evidence leads him to abandon the theory, he will again revise the semantic rules. But while he continues to hold the theory, statements like "The molecules of this hot soup are motionless" are analytically false. Similarly, for an identity theorist such statements as "Jones is experiencing no visual raw feel and his visual cortex is in state Φ$_r$," are analytically false. While disagreement exists among logicians as to which statements of a scientific theory are implicitly definitional of its constructs and which—if any—remain contingent even after adoption of the theory, I believe it is clear that what we may call *constitutive* statements always belong to the former class. Theoretical reductions in which complex physical$_2$ events are allegedly analyzed into their "parts" or "components," thereby permitting an explicit definition of the complex in terms of other theoretical primitives in the revised language, are constitutive in this sense. So that while one may adopt kinetic theory and (according to some) still view "Hot soup raises the mercury column of a thermomenter placed in it" as contingent, as not frame-analytic, one may not adopt kinetic theory and yet view "Hot soup contains fast-moving molecules" as contingent. (I need hardly say that I am here using the phrase "hot soup" as a predicate of the physical thing-language and not as a predicate of a phenomenal sense quality.) The reduction of raw-feel statements to physical$_2$ statements is obviously constitutive within identity theory.

If the experienced properties of a raw feel were taken to *be* the raw feel instead of *properties of it*, the identity thesis could be refuted easily by any knower who was directly acquainted with them. The refutation relies upon what Wilfrid Sellars calls the "difference in grain" between raw feels and physical$_2$ brain-states.[5] Suppose I am experiencing a circular red raw feel, large, clear, saturated, "focusing all my attention" upon its center. Granted that rapid fluctuations in attention can occur, that sensory satiation will take place, that the hue and "clearness" at the circle's edge may differ from those at its center; nevertheless, the most careful and sophisticated introspection will fail to refute the following statement: "There is a finite subregion ΔR of the raw-feel red patch Ψ_r, and a finite time interval Δt, such that during Δt *no* property of ΔR changes."

The properties of a phenomenal event being the properties it "appears to have," we state the above in phenomenal object-language and avoid any unnecessary reference to knowing. This is important because the desired refutation utilizes Leibniz's Principle. We say of the physical$_2$ state Φ_r (by substituting Φ_r for Ψ_r as allowed by the theory): "There is a finite region ΔR of the brain-state Φ_r and a finite time interval Δt, such that during Δt no property of ΔR changes." But this, as even pre-Utopian neurophysiology shows us, is factually false. The region ΔR and the interval Δt are not infinitesimals, they are finite values taken small enough to satisfy the raw-feel statement of constancy. Thus, during, say, 500 milliseconds, the 5° region at the center of my phenomenal circle does not change in any property, whereas no region of the physical$_2$ brain-event can be taken small enough such that *none* of its properties changes during a 500-millisecond period.

This "grain" objection cannot, of course, be answered by saying that a property of the brain-state, such as an average value of a certain complex physical$_2$ functor, remains constant during Δt, analogizing to the relation between macrotemperature and molecular motion (compare Feyerabend, 1963, p. 53). The phenomenal assertion is stronger than this rebuttal can meet, because it says " . . . no property changes . . . " not " . . . some property remains constant . . . "

This "grain" argument seems to me to provide a clear refutation of the identity theory, provided we identify "the raw-feel event" or "the phenomenal entity" with the experienced circular red patch. But we need not do this, and the identity theorist will, of course, not do it. He will instead speak of the entity as *having the properties* red, circular, saturated, etc. He thinks of the denotatum as a *tertium quid*, whose existence becomes "known" to science either via the internal linkage to a tokening mechanism ("knowledge by acquaintance") or via the external linkage to the cerebroscope (hetero- or auto-, it doesn't matter). From Professor Feigl's standpoint, the identity of a raw-feel event as known "from the inside'' with a raw-feel event as known ''from the outside'' is of the same sort as the identity between the morning star and the evening star. He relies upon the principle that identity of denotata does not imply identity of designata.

Many find this analogy unsatisfying, myself among them. Let me try to say why it bothers me. Since the morning star example involves an individual, it will be preferable to use another of Professor Feigl's own examples, to wit, the diverse indicators of an electric current. Passage of an electric current is associated with several indicators of its occurrence, two among them being a heating effect and an electromagnetic field effect. A temperature rise in the conductor or its vicinity is an ''avenue of knowledge'' to the *tertium quid*: electric current, as is the deflection of a compass needle near the wire. Professor Feigl wishes to say that the phenomenal quality *red* (known ''by acquaintance,'' ''directly,'' ''from inside'') and the cerebroscopically indicated neurophysiological facts (known ''by description,'' ''indirectly,'' ''from outside'') are related to the one brain-event in the same way that thermoelectric and electromagnetic indicators are related to the one electric current.

In critically examining this analogy, I first take note of the fact that a temperature rise and a compass deflection are events (or states) distinct from the denotatum of ''electric current.'' The entity *designated* and *denoted* by ''electric current'' is a movement of electrons through the conductor. This entity is nomologically linked to two other sorts of events, but theory does not identify them with it any more than with each other. We say that *when* and *because* the electrons move through the conductor, the latter's molecules increase their average velocity (which we detect by means of a thermometer) and an electromagnetic field surrounds the conductor (which we detect by means of a compass). There are *three* designata, and *three* denotata, thus:

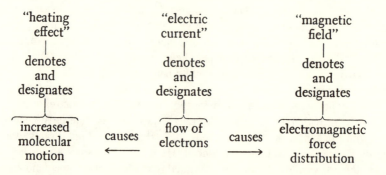

I note also that we do not consider our theory complete unless it provides a theoretical (derivable) answer to the question why the passage of electrons can be detected by thermometers and compass needles, i.e., why the indicators work.

Now if Professor Feigl took the view that the only ''inside indicator'' was the tokening event itself, his analogy would be strictly accurate. We would have the following:

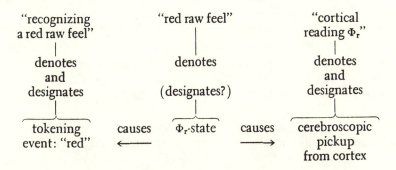

("Red raw feel" only *denotes* the Φ_r-state as tokened egocentrically, although it also *designates* the Φ_r-state as tokened by a sophisticated Utopian believer in the identity theory.) The above diagram represents Professor Feyerabend's view of the identity theory, since he rejects the claim that phenomenal quality words designate anything other than the vaguely understood Φ-states to which they are linked by language-entry habits.

However, the above diagram does not represent Professor Feigl's view of the matter, since he admits—nay, insists—that phenomenal predicates *do* designate something, and that their "meaning" is known to us by acquaintance. That is, the *red quality* is itself an indicator, the tokening "red" being still further along in the indicator chain. If a person fails to token "red" on certain occasions when he experiences a red raw feel, there nevertheless occurs an instance of the red quality, according to Professor Feigl's view. How is this interpretation to be diagramed? Following the analogy, we have:

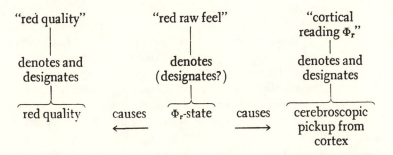

But surely this won't do. We have a something called "red quality" being *produced by* the Φ_r-state. Such an interpretation is objectionable on at least two counts. First, qualities are *of* existents, they do not exist on their own. Second, if there is a red quality which is "produced by" the Φ_r-state, the physical$_2$ reduction sought by the identity theory is endangered. "Red" as a phenomenal predicate is not to be found among the physical$_2$ functors and predicates of physical theory. If there is a property designated and denoted by the quality-word "red" which does not "belong to" (or is not "part of") the physical$_2$ Φ_r-state, then the identity theory is not—literally—an *identity* theory; it is only a weaker claim that all mental events are physical$_1$, i.e., nomologically linked to physical$_2$ occurrents and dispositions. This claim is, of course, quite compatible with dualism (interactionistic or epiphenomenalistic, assuming that the latter can be made consistent).

But if there is no numerically distinct entity (even, so to say, a "short-lived continuant") to which the Φ_r-state gives rise, then the quality-word "red" must denote *a property of the Φ_r-state itself*. The causal and semantic situation would then be represented thus:

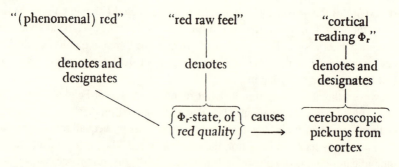

In this interpretation, "red-hued" is a property of the physical$_2$ brain-state Φ_r. But since, as Professor Feigl holds, "red" as a phenomenal predicate is absent from the list of fundamental predicates and functors of theoretical physics— speaking object-linguistically, among the elementary properties and dimensions of the world there is no such thing as a red quality—how is it theoretically possible for *red* to be a property of the physical$_2$ brain-state Φ_r? So far as I can see, the only way this would be possible is if "red-hued" designates a *configural property* of the complex physical$_2$ state Φ_r. That is, "red-hued" designates a complex conjunction of physical$_2$ functor inequalities, analogously to the way in which "hot" (physical thing-language, not phenomenal language!) designates a summary statement about molecular motion, or "charged" designates a configural statement about the distribution of elementary particles on the plates of a condenser.

Such an analysis, forced upon us by our determination to maintain a genuine *identity* thesis, brings us back again to the counterintuitive difference in "grain" between the intension ("by acquaintance") of "red hue" and the intension ("by description") of "Φ_r" formulated in terms of physical$_2$ functors. But in the course of returning full circle to that objection on the basis of meanings, we have, I fear, precluded Professor Feigl from one kind of defense. Initially, he was able to answer the "grain" objection by distinguishing *property* from *entity* and *designatum* from *denotatum*. This rebuttal is no longer available to him because now the "grain" objection is reiterated at the level of *properties* rather than at the level of occurrents or continuants themselves. Can anyone who knows the red quality "by acquaintance" really allow, on the basis of any theoretical reconstruction, that this quality is a configural property of physical$_2$ components?

I must confess that I do not know how to put this question in a less "intuitive" form, which leaves me in an unsatisfactory philosophical position vis-à-vis a radical materialist like Professor Feyerabend (who, when I put it to him, looks me right in the eye and answers "Yes"). I am impelled to pursue the argument in terms of "understanding the equivalence," but I do not know how to do this with any philosophic rigor. It strikes me as very odd that I could fully understand the intension of the phenomenal predicate "red-hued," this predicate designating a configural physical$_2$ property, and could also fully understand the intension of the physical$_2$ predicate "Φ_r"; and yet not "understand why" they designate the same *property*. This seems to me radically different from the situation where I can understand two designating expressions without knowing that only one denotatum satisfies them. In the morning star–evening star example, it is easy to see why I can understand the meaning of each expression and yet be uninformed as to the factual identity. We deal there with the difference between propositional functions and the (otherwise unknown) individuals whose names or definite descriptions can be filled into the variable positions; whereas in the present case we are dealing not with values of the variables but with the intension of the predicates. Not to understand that "author of *Waverley*" denotes the same entity as "author of *Rob Roy*" is compatible with understanding both expressions, because understanding the identity involves knowledge of *facts*. Similarly, understanding the meanings of "specific etiology of paresis" and "specific etiology of tabes" is compatible with ignorance that their denotata are identical, again because factual information is involved. But the identity theory—if held consistently—identifies the *property* designated by "red" with the complex physical$_2$ *property* designated by Φ_r."[6] I do not see how one can fully understand the intension of two property expressions which designate the same property—one expression being shorthand for the other, which is complex—without understanding their equivalence.

And, be it noted, this lack of understanding can be expected to continue even *after* a claim of identity has been made within the revised theoretical language. Consider a Utopian neurophysiologist who is not blind and who has learned to speak the ordinary color language, but who has *not studied either psycholinguistics or psychophysics* (i.e., he knows all about the fundamental nomologicals—the laws of physics—but he does not know those structure-dependent quasi-nomologicals that are provided by the contingent facts of his verbal culture and the characteristics of organic transducers). He does not, therefore, know *all* of Utopian science, because that corpus includes such disciplines as descriptive pragmatics and the psychophysiology of vision. He does, however, know cortical anatomy and neurophysiology. We provide him with the following information about experimental particulars:

1. *Stimulus*: A bright, saturated red light is made to fall upon his retina.

2. *Proposition*: "A light stimulus, possibly but not necessarily of this kind, was applied to Subject X, a physically normal individual."

3. *Proposition*: "The cerebroscopic reading off X's visual cortex under that stimulation was Φ_r."

Query: "Was X stimulated with the same light you were?"

What will be our Utopian's epistemic situation given these inputs? Having learned the habit of obedience to the language-entry rule (i.e., knowing the meaning of "red" by acquaintance) he can correctly token "I experience *red*" and, via nomologically legitimated language-transitions, can thereby also token correctly, "If X was stimulated by this same light, X experienced *red*." He also knows that X's visual cortex was in state Φ_r as a result of whatever light stimulation he received. There is nothing about this physical$_2$ description of X's brain-state that he does not "fully understand." Why then can he not tell us whether the state "Φ_r" matches "experienced *red*"?

The situation here is different from that of our congenitally blind Utopian, who could not solve his cognitive problem because he did not *know the language*. It is also different from that of a non-Utopian, who does not know all about the fundamental nomologicals (or, at least, does not fully understand the microphysiology represented by the physical$_2$ description Φ_r). Our present subject "knows all there is to know" about the state Φ_r which occurred in the brain of X. He "knows all there is to know" about the phenomenal quality *red*, including how to designate it (by "red"). If "red" is a shorthand expression for the physical$_2$ configural property Φ_r, he should be able to say that the states are the same. But, of course, he cannot.

Nor will it do for the identity theorist to complain that we have unfairly rigged the thought-experiment by withholding crucial information, when we disallowed him knowledge of psycholinguistics and the visual-system transducers. It is not relevant to the *nature* of state Φ_r that it is induced by the "usual" (retina → . . . → lateral geniculate → . . .) causal chain. Nor is it relevant to the rule " 'Red' means *red*" that people historically learn it in a certain way. Our subject knows the rule, and he knows that X knows the rule. He knows what "red" *means*; and *he knows that it means the same to X as to himself.* And he knows the configural state of X's brain. If *red* is, literally, nothing but a configural property of the Φ_r-state, it is very strange indeed that he cannot match "red" with "Φ_r" so as to postdict X's stimulus input.

And what about after we inform him? Even *after* he knows that phenomenal red consists of (*sic!*) the physical$_2$ configuration Φ_r, will this seem in any way "appropriate" or "comprehensible" to him? It is always dangerous to anticipate science, especially in the negative. But I cannot conceive that any theoretical reconstruction involving the fundamental physical$_2$ functors would enable me to "see how" the red phenomenal quality *consisted* of such and such a configuration of fields, ions, disrupted neuron membranes, and the like. And I do not believe that Professor Feigl envisages any such possibility either.

I have not been able to formulate the psychophysical correlation-law and, as a separate claim, the identity thesis, by means of a notation essentially different from that of Section I; nor has Professor Feigl suggested any such (personal communication). It would seem not only natural but unavoidable, in meeting Professor Feigl's own conditions on the epistemological status of the identity thesis, that our notation should represent the entities to be identified — the raw-feel event and the brain-state — by bound *variables*; whereas the raw-feel qualities predicated of the former, and the physical$_2$ functor conditions characterizing the latter, should occur in the role of descriptive constants. I think that the notation brings out more clearly than words what is intuitively unsatisfying about the morning-star kind of analogy. It also shows why Professor Feigl's invocation of the designatum-denotatum distinction, while important in forestalling certain alleged refutations relying upon unnecessary puzzles in pragmatics, does not quite succeed in clearing matters up. Consider a critic who attempts to refute the identity thesis by saying, "A psychophysical correlation-law presupposes that there are *two 'somethings'* being correlated; you admit that there is such a law, and that it is empirical. How then can you turn about and assert that there is only *one 'something'* without contradicting these very statements which constitute your main scientific ground for adopting the identity thesis in the first place?" Contemplation of the logical form of our correlation-law provides the answer to this objection. We have

$$(x,y)\Psi(x,y) \cdot P(y) \to (E!z)L(z,x) \cdot \Phi(z)$$
$$(x,z)L(z,x) \cdot \Phi(z) \to (E!y)\Psi(x,y) \cdot P(y)$$

which shows that a raw-feel event y is characterized by phenomenal hue quality P and related (Ψ) to a person x; a brain-state z is characterized by the complex physical$_2$ functor condition Φ and related (L) to the body of that same person. The correlation-law asserts that the necessary and sufficient condition for a person to be the experiential locus of a raw-feel event having property P is that his brain should be in state Φ. Obviously there is nothing about this formally which estops us from a subsequent assertion that the event and the state are identical. The critic cannot complain of a "shift" here from speaking about two entities to speaking about only one, unless he is prepared to maintain that there is something impermissible logically about saying "One individual wrote *Waverley*," and "One individual wrote *Rob Roy*," following these with "And these ('two') individuals are the same ('one')." The psychophysical correlation-law merely informs us that whenever there is an entity satisfying one pair of propositional functions (P,Ψ), there is a unique entity which satisfies another pair of propositional functions (L,Φ); it leaves open the question as to whether one or two numerically distinct entities are involved. So Professor Feigl is correct in answering *this* criticism in terms of the usual distinction between designatum and denotatum.

But the notation also shows clearly why such an attack is misconceived, being aimed at the *variables* instead of at the descriptive constants. If Sellars is right in seeing an insuperable objection to the identity thesis *even on present knowledge* to be the difference in "grain" between phenomenal events and physical$_2$ brain-states, then the proper focus for attack is not the conjoined identity claim "(y = z)" itself, but (via Leibniz's Principle) its *consequence*, to wit, that

$$(f) \ (fy \equiv fz)$$

from which we conclude that, given the correlation-laws,

$$(y) \ (Py \supset Pz)$$

i.e., the physical$_2$ brain-state must possess the red hue quality. And since the predicate "P" designating the red hue quality is not to be found among the component physical$_2$ functor conditions $\phi_1, \phi_2, \ldots, \phi_m$ which jointly constitute the explicit definition in our theoretical language of the brain-state property Φ, we must conclude that "P" designates the configural physical$_2$ property Φ itself. Quite apart from the possibility that property P is causally inefficacious (epiphenomenalism), or that "P" does not designate the same quality in Professor Feigl's language and in mine, we have his insistence that "P" does designate something that exists, that there are phenomenal qualities "in the world." Nor does it help him to argue—if indeed he can successfully—that they are not includable within the intersubjective world-network of physical$_1$ science. Be that as it may, he is concerned about the mind-body problem *qua* philosopher (if not "of science," then "as empirical metaphysician") because he holds that phenomenal predicates have a referent, that they denote something, namely, the raw-feel qualities themselves. He stoutly maintains that he has raw feels and is acquainted with their qualities; he cheerfully admits that others have them too. So we are initially agreed that the phenomenal predicate "P" does refer to an existent quality. Granted that there is such a quality, the identity thesis entails via Leibniz's Principle that it be literally attributable to the brain-state. Hence in the reconstructed theoretical language of identity theory, we should adopt the semantic rule

$$\text{"P" means } \Phi$$

which I, like Sellars, find it quite impossible to make myself genuinely intend.

Can the "grain" objection be restated in terms of properties? Yes, it can, and in a tight, simple form which is unavoidable except by denying its premises. If "Sim (. . .)" is a second-type one-place predicate designating the property *simple* (a property of first-type properties) we assert:

$$Sim(P)$$
$$\sim Sim(\Phi)$$
$$\therefore P \neq \Phi$$

by Leibniz's Principle applied to properties. The only trouble with this direct hammerblow is that "Sim(P)" itself is not provable, although it has a strong intuitive obviousness to most (but, alas, not all) thinkers. And while its intuitive claim upon me (and, interestingly, upon Professor Feigl) is compelling, I am hardly prepared to insist that English or epistemologese has a clear language-entry rule about *simplicity* which is violated by a denier of the premise "Sim(P)."

Another approach to rigorous formulation of the "grain" argument, also involving predicates of higher type, relies upon the alleged nontransitivity of the "equal," "nondiffering," "indiscriminable," or "indistinguishable" relation among phenomenal qualities. Some have argued that "indistinguishability" is transitive for physical$_2$ properties but is nontransitive for phenomenal properties. The highly technical issues involved in that allegation are beyond the scope of this paper, and I shall content myself with making two critical observations. First, the commonly assumed nontransitivity of phenomenal "equality" rests upon experimental facts interpreted via an arbitrary definition of the difference threshold (e.g., the old 75 percent criterion, which is wholly without logical, psychometric, physical, or physiological justification). Second, the autocerebro-scopic thought-experiment and its attendant theoretical speculations should have made it clear to the reader that it is *not* absurd, meaningless, or self-contradictory to say that two raw feels "seem equal but are not," the reason being that "seem-ing," when carefully analyzed, invariably turns out to be a matter of *tokenings or other intervening or output events*. I must emphasize that no dispositional or log-ical-behaviorist analysis of mind is presupposed in saying this; it must be obvious that I reject all such analyses. Nor is the identity thesis or any variant of "mate-rialism" presupposed. I am simply insisting that "seeming equal" is a state, pro-cess, event (whether physical$_2$ or not) which, while a causal descendant of the raw-feel event and correlated with the latter's properties, is certainly not to be identified with the raw-feel event or its properties. "These two phenomenal [*sic*!] greens seem equal to me," which expresses a *judgment about* experience that is numerically distinct from the experience, does *not* entail phenomenal equality. Taking these two considerations jointly into account, I do not believe we are compelled by the available psychological evidence to assert that "equality" is nontransitive for phenomenal properties.

I warned the reader at the start of this concluding section that I was not competent to present a rigorous philosophical objection on purely semantic grounds, and I am acutely conscious of not having done so. It remains my conviction that there is something fishy about the identity thesis when interpreted literally, i.e., as a genuine *identity* thesis. Professor Feigl must, I think, make his mind up as to whether or not there are any raw-feel qualities, i.e., whether phenomenal predicates denote anything. I do not believe that he has solved the basic problem by emphasizing the designatum-denotatum distinction, because this only takes care of the relation between the tokening of phenomenal predicates and the neurophysiological readings off the visual cortex. He — unlike Professor Feyerabend — maintains that the reference of phenomenal predicates is to raw-feel *qualities*. This insistence creates a dilemma for him: if these qualities are other than complex physical$_2$ functor conditions, then the "identity thesis" is misleadingly named; for there is something in the world — and a causally efficacious something at that — which is not reducible to the theoretical entities of physics. Alternatively, if these qualities are *not* other than physical$_2$ functor conditions, they must be configural combinations of the latter. It does not seem to me that they can possibly *be* that, but I leave it to a competent philosopher to prove what to me is only intuitively obvious as a matter of "grain."

If the identity of raw-feel red with a physical$_2$ configural property can be shown impossible upon rigorous *semantic* grounds, the identity theory is demolished; and the outcome of an autocerebroscopic experiment is thereby rendered partly irrelevant and partly predictable. Per contra, if the equivalence of "phenomenal red" and "brain-state Φ_r," is free of semantic difficulty, then I think it must be admitted that the identity theory is in a very strong and easily defensible position. In particular, I have tried to show in this essay that some of the commonly advanced nonsemantic refutations of it are without merit.

Notes

1. Throughout this essay I use the expression "frame-analytic" to mean, roughly, true by "theoretical definition"; which latter phrase in turn means, roughly, stipulation of meaning (explicit or implicit) in terms of other theoretical constructs which are themselves "defined implicitly" by the accepted nomological network. While such frame-analytic truths therefore rest in one sense upon conventions, these conventions are far from "arbitrary," but are adopted on the basis of our theoretical knowledge — our current best available notion of "how the world is." The deeper issues raised here (e.g., status of so-called conventions in empirical science, clarity and defensibility of the traditional analytic-synthetic distinction) are beyond the scope of this essay and of my competence. Frame-analyticity is closely related to truth by P-rules, by meaning-postulates or A-rules, and the like. See, for example, Carnap (1950, 1952), Maxwell (1961), Sellars (1948, 1953), Feyerabend (1962). I do presuppose in employing the phrase "frame-analytic" that whatever may be the final resolution of this cluster of technical philosophical problems, some important distinction will be pre-

served between the kinds of analyticity involved in "bachelor = unmarried male" and "temperature = mean kinetic energy of molecules."

2. This formulation does not, I would think, prejudice the philosophical issues, and is simpler to talk about for present purposes. If no such mediating judgmental tokening occurs, then for the "propositional," primary tokening event t we would presumably have to substitute some sort of conjunction of (1) an "English-set" superordinate event, elicited by one's perception of the audience as being English-speaking, and (2) the first link in an English-verbalizing event-sequence, which link is activated (instead of French or German) *because of* the superordinate "English-set" regnancy. These are presently unsettled issues in psycholinguistics.

3. I am indebted to Dr. Milton Trapold for calling this experiment to my attention.

4. I am indebted to Professor Sellars for bringing home to me, when I was defending epiphenomenalism, the full force of this objection.

5. I am not sure that I correctly understand Sellars's use of the term "grain," but I learned the term, and this objection to the identity theory, in discussions with him. Roughly put, "grain" refers to an admittedly vague cluster of properties involving continuity, qualitative homogeneity, unity or lack of discrete parts, spatiotemporal smoothness or flow, and the like, which many raw feels possess in ways that their corresponding physical$_2$ brain-states do not. Thus a small phenomenal red patch is typically experienced as a continuous, homogeneous expanse of red hue. The identity theory makes the phrase "phenomenal red patch," in the revised theoretical language, refer both to this entity and to that "gappy," heterogeneous, discontinuous conglomerate of spatially discrete events that are described in a physical$_2$ account of the brain-state Φ_r. The issue raised is similar to Eddington's problem about "which table is the real table" — the solid object of ordinary experience or the inferred entity of physical theory, mostly empty space sparsely occupied by gyrating electrons? Whereas Eddington's problem is fairly easily dissolved by proper linguistic analysis (both tables are real, being the same table, and the macrodispositions being causally analyzed in terms of the microstructure), its analogue in the identity theory is more refractory. The objection is termed "semantic" because it is, fundamentally, based upon an alleged radical difference in (*intensional*) *meanings* (= designata) of phenomenal and physical$_2$ predicates, taken together with Leibniz's Principle.

6. Professor Feigl does not, of course, assert this identification of properties; quite to the contrary, he wishes to deny it. But I hope that my discussion up to this point has shown that a genuine, consistent identity theory cannot escape such an identification of the property *phenomenal red* with the property Φ_r.

References

Bohr, N. 1934. *Atomic Theory and the Description of Nature*. New York: Macmillan.

Carnap, R. 1950., Empiricism, Semantics, and Ontology. *Revue Internationale de Philosophie* 11:20–40.

Carnap, R. 1952. Meaning Postulates. *Philosophical Studies* 3:65–73.

Eccles, J. C. 1951. Hypotheses Relating to the Brain-Mind Problem. *Nature* 168:53–57.

Eccles, J. C. 1953. *The Neurophysiological Basis of Mind*. Oxford: Oxford University Press.

Eddington, A. S. 1939. *The Philosophy of Physical Science*. Cambridge: Cambridge University Press.

Feigl, H. 1958. "The 'Mental' and the 'Physical'." In *Minnesota Studies in the Philosophy of Science*, vol. II, *Concepts, Theories, and the Mind-Body Problem*, eds. H. Feigl, M. Scriven and G. Maxwell. Minneapolis: University of Minnesota Press, pp. 370–497.

Feyerabend, P. K. 1962. "Explanation, Reduction, and Empiricism." In *Minnesota Studies in the Philosophy of Science*, vol. III, *Scientific Explanation, Space, and Time*, eds. H. Feigl and G. Maxwell. Minneapolis: University of Minnesota Press, pp. 28–97.

Feyerabend, P. K. 1963. Materialism and the Mind-Body Problem. *Review of Metaphysics*. 17:49–66.

Howells, T. H. 1944. The Experimental Development of Color-Tone Synesthesia. *Journal of Experimental Psychology* 34:87–103.

Jordan, P. 1955. *Science and the Course of History*. New Haven, Conn.: Yale University Press.

Lachs, J. 1963. The Impotent Mind. *Review of Metaphysics* 17:187–99.

London, I. D. 1952. Quantum Biology and Psychology. *Journal of General Psychology* 46:123–49.

Maxwell, G. 1961. "Meaning Postulates in Scientific Theories." In *Current Issues in the Philosophy of Science*, eds. H. Feigl and G. Maxwell. New York: Holt, Rinehart and Winston, pp. 169–83.

Meehl, P. E., Klann, H. R., Schmieding, A. F., Breimeier, K. H., and Sloman, S. S. 1958. *What, Then, Is Man?* St. Louis: Concordia Publishing House.

Popper, K. R. 1962. *Conjectures and Refutations*. New York: Basic Books.

Popper, K. R. 1959. *The Logic of Scientific Discovery*. New York: Basic Books.

Reichenbach, H. 1938. *Experience and Prediction*. Chicago: University of Chicago Press.

Scriven, M. 1953. The Mechanical Concept of Mind. *Mind* 62:230–40.

Sellars, W. 1948. Concepts as Involving Laws and Inconceivable without Them. *Philosophy of Science* 15: 287–315.

Sellars, W. 1953. Is There a Synthetic A Priori? *Philosophy of Science 20:121–38*.

Sellars, W. 1947. Pure Pragmatics and Epistemology. *Philosophy of Science* 14:181–202.

Sellars, W. 1948. Realism and the New Way of Words. *Philosophy and Phenomenological Research* 8:601–34. Reprinted in *Reading in Philosophical Analysis*, eds. H. Feigl and W. Sellars, pp. 424–56. New York: Appleton-Century Crofts, 1949.

Sellars, W. 1953. A Semantical Solution of the Mind-Body Problem. *Methodos* 5:45–84.

Sellars, W. 1954. Some Reflections on Language Games. *Philosophy of Science* 21:204–28.

Skinner, B. F. 1945. The Operational Analysis of Psychological Terms. *Psychological Review* 52:270–77.

8

On a Distinction between Hypothetical Constructs and Intervening Variables

with Kenneth MacCorquodale

As the thinking of behavior theorists has become more sophisticated and self-conscious, there has been considerable discussion of the value and logical status of so-called 'intervening variables.' Hull speaks of "symbolic constructs, intervening variables, or hypothetical entities" (1943, p. 22) and deals with them in his theoretical discussion as being roughly equivalent notions. At least, his exposition does not distinguish among them explicitly. In his presidential address on behavior at a choice point, Tolman (1938, p. 13) inserts one of Hull's serial conditioning diagrams between the independent variables (maintenance schedule, goal object, etc.) and the dependent variable ('behavior ratio') to illustrate his concept of the intervening variable. This would seem to imply that Tolman views his 'intervening variables' as of the same character as Hull's. In view of this, it is somewhat surprising to discover that Skinner (1938, pp. 436, 437) apparently feels that his formulations have a close affinity to those of Tolman, but are basically dissimilar to those of Hull. In advocating a theoretical structure which is 'descriptive' and 'positivistic,' he suggests that the model chosen by Hull (Newtonian mechanics) is not the most suitable model for purposes of behavior theory; and in general is critical of the whole postulate-deductive approach.

Simultaneously with these trends, one can still observe among 'tough-minded' psychologists the use of words such as 'unobservable' and 'hypothetical' in an essentially derogatory manner, and an almost compulsive fear of passing beyond the direct colligation of observable data. 'Fictions' and 'hypothetical entities' are sometimes introduced into a discussion of theory with a degree of trepidation and apology quite unlike the freedom with which physicists talk about atoms, mesons, fields, and the like. There also seems to be a tendency to treat all hypothetical constructs as on the same footing merely because they are hypothetical; so that we find people arguing that if neutrons are admissible in physics, it must be admissible for us to talk about, e.g., the damming up of libido and its reversion to earlier channels.

The view which theoretical psychologists take toward intervening variables and hypothetical constructs will, of course, profoundly influence the direction of theoretical thought. Furthermore, what *kinds* of hypothetical constructs we become accustomed to thinking about will have a considerable impact upon theory creation. The present essay aims to present what seems to us a major problem in the conceptualization of intervening variables, without claiming to offer a wholly satisfactory solution. Chiefly, it is our aim here to make a distinction between two subclasses of intervening variables, or we prefer to say, between 'intervening variables' and 'hypothetical constructs' which we feel is fundamental but is currently being neglected.

We shall begin with a common-sense distinction and proceed later to formulations of this distinction which we hope will be more rigorous. Naïvely, it would seem that there is a difference in logical status between constructs which involve the hypothesization of an *entity, process*, or *event* which is not itself observed, and constructs which do not involve such hypothesization. For example, Skinner's 'reflex reserve' is definable in terms of the total available responses without further conditioning, whereas Hull's 'afferent neural interaction' involves the notion of processes within the nervous system which presumably occur within the objective physical system and which, under suitable conditions, we might observe directly. To take examples from another science in which we psychologists may have less stake in the distinction, one might contrast the notion of 'resistance' in electricity to the notion of 'electron.' The resistance of a piece of wire is what Carnap has called a *dispositional concept*, and is defined by a special type of implication relation. When we say that the resistance of a wire is such-and-such, we mean that ''so-and-so volts will give a current of so-and-so amperes.'' (For a more precise formulation of this see Carnap, 1936, p. 440.) Resistance, in other words, is 'operational' in a very direct and primitive sense. The electron, on the other hand, is supposedly an *entity* of some sort. Statements about the electron are, to be sure, supported by means of observational sentences. Nevertheless, it is no longer maintained even by positivists that this set of supporting sentences exhaust the entire *meaning* of the sentences about the electron. Reichenbach, for example, distinguishes *abstracta* from *illata* (from Lat. *infero*). The latter are 'inferred things,' such as molecules, other people's minds, and so on. They are believed in on the basis of our impressions, but the sentences involving them, even those asserting their existence, are not reducible to sentences about impressions. This is the epistemological form, at rock bottom level, of the distinction we wish to make here.

The introduction of the word 'entity' in our discussion has served merely to indicate the distinction, but in any crucial case there could be dispute as to whether a stated hypothesis involved the positing of an entity. For instance, is Hull's 'habit strength' an entity or not? Is 'drive' an entity? Is 'superego'?

Previous analyses of this difference may enable us to give a somewhat more precise formulation. These two kinds of concepts are variously distinguished by writers on philosophy of science. Feigl (personal communication) refers to *analytic* versus *existential* hypotheses. Benjamin (1937) distinguishes between *abstractive* and *hypothetical* methods. In the abstractive or analytic method we merely neglect certain features of experience and group phenomena by a restricted set of properties into classes; relations between such classes can then be discovered empirically, and nothing has been added to the observed in the process. The hypothetical method, on the other hand, relates experiences "by inventing a fictitious substance or process or idea, in terms of which the experiences can be expressed. A hypothesis, in brief, correlates observations by adding something to them, while abstraction achieves the same end by subtracting something" (p. 184).

This quotation suggests to us at least three ways of stating the distinction we have in mind. First, it may be pointed out that in the statement of a hypothetical construction, as distinguished from an abstractive one, there occur words (other than the construct name itself) which are not explicitly defined by (or reduced to) the empirical relations. Once having set up sentences (postulates) containing these hypothetical words, we can arrive by deduction at empirical sentences which can themselves be tested. But the words themselves are not defined directly by or reducible to these empirical facts. This is not true of abstractive concepts, such as resistance or solubility or, say, 'drive' as used by Skinner. (We may neglect wholly noncommittal words such as *state*, which specify nothing except that the conditions are internal.)

A second apparent difference between abstractive and hypothetical concepts is in their logical relation to the facts, i.e., the observation-sentences and empirical laws which are the basis for believing them. In the case of sentences containing only abstractive concepts, the truth of the empirical laws constitutes *both the necessary and sufficient conditions* for the truth of the abstractive sentences. For sentences involving hypothetical concepts, this is well known to be false. The empirical laws are necessary for the truth of the hypothetical sentences, since the latter imply them; but they are not sufficient. All scientific hypothesizing is in the invalid 'third figure' of the implicative syllogism. We neglect here the impossibility, emphasized by Reichenbach and others, of equating even an abstractive sentence or empirical 'law' to a *finite* number of particular observation sentences; this is of importance to philosophers of science but for help in the understanding of theories is of no particular consequence. We shall be assuming the trustworthiness of induction throughout and hence will treat 'direct' observational laws as universal sentences or as sentential functions. One can deduce empirical laws from sentences involving hypothetical constructs, but not conversely. Thus, beginning with the hypothesis that gases are made up of small particles which obey the laws of mechanics, plus certain approximating assumptions about the relation of their sizes to their distances, their perfect elasticity, and their lack of mutual attraction, one can apply mathematical rules and eventually, by direct substitution and equation, lead without arbitrariness to the empirical equation $PV = K$. However, one cannot rigorously reverse the process. That is, one cannot commence with the empirical gas law $PV = K$ and arrive at the full kinetic theory. The mathematics is reversible, granted that certain arbitrary breakups of constants, etc., are permitted; but beginning with the empirical law itself there is no basis for these arbitrary breakups. Furthermore, aside from the equations themselves, there are coordinated with these equations certain existence propositions and assertions about the properties of the entities hypothesized. We state that there exist certain small particles, that they collide with the walls of the container, that the root mean square of their velocities is proportional to the temperature, etc. These assertions cannot, of course, be deduced from the empirical law relating pressure and volume.

This suggests a third distinction between concepts of the two kinds. In the case of abstractive concepts, the quantitative form of the concept, e.g., a measure of its 'amount,' can be derived directly from the empirical laws simply by grouping of terms. In the case of hypothetical concepts, mere grouping of terms is not sufficient. We are less assured of this distinction than of the other two, but we have not been able to think of any exceptions. It seems to us also that, in the case of Hull, this is the point which makes our distinction between hypothetical constructs and intervening variables most obvious. Let us therefore consider Hull's equations as an example.

In *Principles of Behavior*, the influence of certain independent variables, such as number of reinforcements, delay in reward, stimulus-response asynchronism, etc., upon response strength is experimentally investigated. In the study of the influence of each of these, the other independent variables are held constant. The experimental findings lead to the formulation of the separate laws of dependence as a set of growth and decay functions. We shall neglect for the moment the complication of drive and of all other variables which intervene between the construct $_sH_r$ and the empirical measure of response. That is to say, we shall deal only with the variables introduced in Hull's Postulate 4. The mathematical statement of Postulate 4 is

$$_sH_r = M(1 - e^{-kw})e^{-jt}e^{-ut'}(1 - e^{-iN}).$$

(1943, p. 178)

This equation asserts that habit strength is a certain joint function of four variables which refer to direct empirical quantities — number of reinforcements, delay in reinforcement, amount of reinforcement, and asynchronism between the discriminative stimuli and the response. It is important to see that in this case Hull does not distinguish the four experimentally separated laws combined in the equation by separate concept-names; the only intervening variable introduced is habit strength, which is written as an explicit function of four empirical variables w, t, t', *and* N. It would be quite possible to introduce an intervening variable referring to, say, the last bracket only; it might be called 'cumulative reinforcement' and it would be a function of only one empirical variable, N. This would be the most reasonable breakdown of habit strength inasmuch as the other three growth functions (two negative) serve merely to modify the asymptote M (1943, p. 181). That is to say, given a certain (maintained) rule for the amount of reinforcement given and two time-specifications concerning the constant relation of the response to two other operations, we have determined a parameter m for a dynamic curve describing the course of acquisition of habit strength. The quantity $(1 - e^{-iN})$ (which we are here calling 'cumulative reinforcement') is then an intervening variable which is multiplied by the parameter m in order to determine the value of habit strength after N reinforcements have occurred.

Suppose now that a critic asks us whether our 'cumulative reinforcement' really *exists*. This amounts to asking whether we have formulated a 'correct statement' concerning the relation of this intervening variable to the anchoring (empirical) variables. For since the statement of 'existence' for the intervening variable is so far confined to the equations above, the 'existence' of cumulative reinforcement reduces strictly to the second question. And this second question, as to whether the statement about the intervening variable's relation to the facts is correct, is in turn equivalent to the question, "Are the empirical variables related in such-and-such a way?" In other words, to confirm the equation for habit strength, it is merely necessary to state that (as Hull assumes in his earlier chapters) with drive, etc., constant, some empirical measure of response strength R is a linear function of habit strength. Then we can write directly,

$$R = C(_sH_r) = C \cdot F(w)G(t)H(t')J(N) = Q(w, t, t', N).$$

To confirm or disconfirm this equation is a direct empirical matter. It is possible to multiply out the bracketed quantities in various combinations, so as to make the arbitrary groupings disappear; what will mathematically persist through all such regroupings will be the rather complicated joint function Q of the four empirical variables w, t, t', and N. By various arbitrary groupings and combinations we could define 15 alternative and equivalent sets of intervening variables. Thus, we might multiply out three of the four brackets in the basic equation but for some reason choose to put $e^{-ut'}$ separately into the denominator. This would give us

$$R = \frac{F(w,t,N)}{e^{ut'}}$$

as the particular form for our empirical relation. $F(w, t, N)$ could then be given an appropriate 'intervening variable' name, and the stimulus-response asynchronism t' would then define an intervening variable $e^{ut'}$.

It may be objected that 'habit strength' presumably refers to some state of the organism which *is* set up by reinforcing N times under specified conditions; whereas $e^{ut'}$ cannot refer to any such state. This seems plausible; but the point is that to establish it as a state, it would be necessary to coordinate to the groupings within equations certain existence propositions, i.e., propositions that do *more* than define a term by saying "Let the quantity $G(x, y, z)$, where x, y, z are empirical variables, be designated by the phrase so-and-so." This setting up of existence propositions could presumably be done even for a quantity such as $e^{ut'}$, by referring to such hypothetical processes as, say, diminishing traces in the neural reverberation circuits activated by a certain discriminative stimulus.

In the above example we have considered the fractionation of the intervening variable $_sH_r$ into others. This reasoning can also be extended in the upward direction, i.e., in the direction of fusion rather than fractionation. Let us treat 'habit strength' as Hull would treat our 'cumulative reinforcement,' by not giving it a name at all. It is still possible to set up equations to fit the Perin-Williams data (Hull, 1943, pp. 229, 255) without referring to habit strength, writing merely

$$n = F(N,h),$$

where N and h are again both purely empirical variables.

We do not mean to imply that the divisions made by Hull (or Tolman) are of no value. It is convenient to have some term to refer to the result of a certain maintenance schedule, instead of having to say "that part of the general multivariable equation of response strength which contains '*hours since eating to satiety*' as an independent variable." We merely wish to emphasize that in the case of Hull's intervening variables, it is both necessary and sufficient for the truth of his 'theory' about the intervening variables that the empirical facts should be as his equations specify. The latter are merely names attached to certain convenient groupings of terms in his empirically fitted equations. It is always possible to coordinate to these quantities, which as written mathematically contain parameters and experimental variables only, certain existence propositions which would automatically make the construct 'hypothetical' rather than 'abstractive.' This giving of what Reichenbach calls 'surplus meaning' automatically destroys the equivalence between the empirical laws and the theoretical construct. When habit strength *means* the product of the four functions of w, t, t' and N, then if the response strength is related to these empirical variables in the way described, habit strength 'exists' in the trivial sense that the law holds. Our confidence in the 'correctness' of the intervening variable formulation is precisely as great as our confidence in the laws. When, however, habit strength means not merely this product of empirical functions but something more of a neural or other physiological nature, then the theory could be false even if the empirical relations hold.

It seems to us that Tolman himself (1938, p. 13), in using one of Hull's serial conditioning diagrams as a set of intervening variables, departs from his original definition. He has first described the situation in which the 'behavior ratio' is a complex function f_1 of the independent experimental variables. He goes on to say,

A theory, as I shall conceive it, is a set of intervening variables. These to-be-inserted intervening variables are 'constructs' which we, the theorists, evolve as a useful way of breaking down into more manageable form the original complete f_1 function (1938, p. 9).

His reason for introducing intervening variables does not seem to us very cogent as he states it. He says that empirically establishing the form of f_1 to cover the effects on behavior of all the permutations and combinations of the independent variables would be a 'humanly endless task.' If this means that all of the verifying instances of a continuous mathematical function cannot be empirically achieved it is true; but that is equally true for a function of one variable only. In order to utilize the proposed relationship between Tolman's function f_3 (1938, p. 10) which describes the relation of the behavior to the intervening variables, it is still necessary to establish empirically that the relationship holds—which amounts essentially to trying several of the infinitely many permutations and combinations (as in the Perin-Williams study) until we are inductively satisfied by ordinary scientific standards.

However cogent the arguments for intervening variables may be, it seems clear from Tolman's description that they are what we are calling *abstractive* rather than *hypothetical*. His notion of them involves nothing which is not in the empirical laws that support them. (We may speak of 'laws' here in the plural in spite of there being just the single function f_1, just as Boyle's and Charles's laws are distinguished in addition to the more general gas law $PV/T = R$.) For Tolman, the merit of an intervening variable is of a purely 'summarizing' character. One can determine the function f_1 by parts, so to speak (1938, p. 17), so that the effect of a given maintenance schedule upon one part of f_1 may be referred to conveniently as *drive*. For a given drive, we can expect such-and-such behavior ratios in a diversity of situations defined by various combinations of the other independent variables.

It has been observed earlier that in introducing one of Hull's well-known serial conditioning diagrams as an example of intervening variables outside Tolman's own system, we see a departure from the definition Tolman gives. The Hull diagrams contain symbols such as r_g (fractional anticipatory goal response) and s_g (the proprioceptive impulses produced by the movements constituting r_g). These symbols refer to hypothetical processes within the organism, having an allegedly real although undetermined neuromuscular locus. These events are in principle directly observable. In fact, here the case for speaking of an objective reality is even stronger than Reichenbach's examples of electrons, molecules, etc.; since even the criterion of *technical* verifiability, admitted by all positivists to be too strong a restriction, would not exclude these hypotheses as empirically meaning-less. Even without penetrating the organism's skin we have some direct observa-tional evidence of r_g in the work of Miller (1935). Whether r_g occurs and actually plays the role described is not relevant here; the point is that the diagrams and verbal explanations of Hull involve the supposition that it does. He assumes the existence of certain processes which are not logically implied by the empirical laws in the sense of strict equivalence. Even if, by using the notion of fractional anticipatory goal response, Hull deduced all of the empirical laws relating inde-pendent and dependent variables, alternative hypotheses could be offered. Be-cause of the 'surplus meaning' contained in concepts like r_g and s_g, these con-cepts are not really 'anchored' to the facts in the sense implied by Tolman's definition of intervening variables or by Hull's diagram on page 22 of the *Prin-ciples*. Hull states in reference to this diagram,

> When an intervening variable is thus securely anchored to observables on both sides it can be safely employed in scientific theory (1943, p. 22).

We presume that Hull means in this statement that the anchoring in question is not only a sufficient but a necessary condition for scientific admissibility. We feel that the criterion is too strong, assuming that the structure of modern physical science is to be allowed. This sort of anchoring makes the intervening variable strictly reducible to the empirical laws, which is, to be sure, what Tolman's orig-inal definition implied. But it excludes such extremely fruitful hypotheses as Hull's own fractional anticipatory goal responses, for which the strict reducibility does not exist.

It occurs to us also in this connection that Hull seems to have moved in the direction of Skinner and Tolman in his treatment of intervening variables. The use of the postulate-theorem approach is maintained more as a form in the *Prin-ciples* than as an actual instrument of discovery. In this respect, the *Principles* is much less like Hull's Newtonian model than was the *Mathematico-deductive the-ory of rote learning*. The justification of 'postulates' in the usual sense is their ability to mediate deductions of empirical laws which are then verified. In the *Principles*, the 'postulates' are verified directly, by the experimental device of holding all variables constant except the one for which we want to find a law. This is quite unlike the derivation of the gas law in physics. The only sense in which any postulates are 'assumed' is in the assumption, referred to by Hull on page 181 of the *Principles*, that the separately verified parts of Postulate 4 will in fact operate according to his equation 16 when combined. This is certainly a 'postulate' only in a very attenuated sense, since it amounts essentially to an em-pirical extrapolation which can be verified directly, as Hull suggests.

At this point any distinction between the type of theory advocated by Hull and that advocated by Skinner or Tolman would seem to disappear, except for the relatively noncontributory 'neural' references contained in the verbal statement of Hull's postulates. Insofar as this neural reference is taken seriously, however, we are still dealing with concepts of a hypothetical rather than abstractive character. There are various places in Hull's *Principles* where the verbal accompaniment of a concept, which in its mathematical form is an intervening variable in the strict (Tolman) sense, makes it a hypothetical construct. Thus, the operational definition of a *pav* of inhibition (1943, p. 281) would seem merely to mean that when we know from the independent variables that the combined habit strength and drive, together with a discriminative stimulus located so many j.n.d.'s from the original, would yield a reaction potential of so many wats, it requires an equal number of pavs of inhibition to yield an effective reaction potential of zero. However, in the accompanying verbal discussion (1943, p. 281) Hull refers to the removal of the inhibitory substance by the bloodstream passing through effector organs as determining the quantitative law of spontaneous loss of inhibition as a function of time. 'Afferent neural interaction' is another example of a concept which is mathematically represented as a relation of intervening variables in Tolman's sense, but to which are coordinated verbal statements that convey the surplus meaning and make it a hypothesis.

The question might be raised, whether this is not always the difference—that the mathematical assertions are definitive of intervening variables but the verbal additions lend the hypothetical character to such concepts. We do not believe this is the essential difference. There are mathematical expressions whose meaning is not defined in the absence of verbal existential accompaniment, because the quantities involved refer to nonobservational (i.e., hypothetical) processes or entities. There are other mathematical expressions for which this is not true, since their component symbols have direct observational reference. In the case of our 'cumulative reinforcement' term $(1 - e^{-iN})$, no coordinated existential proposition is required. We simply say, "Response probability is such-and-such a multivariate function of such-and-such experimental variables. Within this function can be isolated a simple growth function of one variable, whose value as a function of N is referred to as *cumulative reinforcement*." This may be taken as an adequate reference for $(1 - e^{-iN})$. On the other hand, in the derivation of the law $PV = K$ there occur statements such as "When the gas is maintained at the same temperature, $\overline{mv^2/2}$ does not change." Neither m nor v is an empirical variable. This statement does not tell us anything *until* we are informed that v refers to the velocity which each molecule of the gas could be assumed to have in order that their mean kinetic energy should be what it is. In other words, in the derivation of the gas laws from kinetic theory there occur mathematical assertions whose meaning is unclear without the accompanying existence assertions, and *which cannot be utilized to take the subsequent mathematical steps in the chain of inferences unless these assertions are included.* Thus, to get from a purely mathematical statement that a molecule on impact conserves all of its momentum, to a mathematical statement whose terms refer to the empirical concept of 'pressure on the walls,' it is necessary to know (from the accompanying verbal description) that in the equations of derivation, m refers to the mass of a hypothetical particle that strikes the wall, v to its velocity, and so on. This example shows that some mathematical formulations are themselves incomplete in the sense that they cannot mediate the desired deductions unless certain existential propositions are stated alongside, so as to render certain necessary substitutions and equations legitimate. Therefore it is not merely the matter of mathematical form that distinguishes a 'pure' intervening variable from a hypothesis.

In the second place, it seems to us that the use of verbal statements without mathematical formulations does not guarantee that we are dealing with a hypothetical construct rather than an intervening variable. Consider Skinner's definition of emotion as a 'state of the organism' which alters the proportionality between reserve and strength. This is not defined as a direct proportionality, and in fact Skinner nowhere deals with its quantitative form. No mathematical statement is given by him; yet we would contend that the use of the word 'state' does not in any way make the notion of emotion existential, any more than drive is existential in Skinner's usage. The 'state' of emotion is not to be described in any way except by specifying (a) The class of stimuli which are able to produce it and (b) The effects upon response strength. Hence, emotion for Skinner is a true intervening variable, in Tolman's original sense. We conclude from these examples that whether a given concept is abstractive or hypothetical is not merely a matter of whether it is an equation with or without accompanying verbal exposition.

On the basis of these considerations, we are inclined to propose a linguistic convention for psychological theorists which we feel will help to clarify discussion of these matters. We suggest that the phrase 'intervening variable' be restricted to the original use implied by Tolman's definition. Such a variable will then be simply a quantity obtained by a specified manipulation of the values of empirical variables; it will involve no hypothesis as to the existence of nonobserved entities or the occurrence of unobserved processes; it will contain, in its complete statement for all purposes of theory and prediction, no words which are not definable either explicitly or by reduction sentences in terms of the empirical variables; and the validity of empirical laws involving only observables will constitute both the necessary and sufficient conditions for the validity of the laws involving these intervening variables. Legitimate instances of such 'pure' intervening variables are Skinner's *reserve*, Tolman's *demand*, Hull's *habit strength*, and Lewin's *valence*. These constructs are the behavioral analogue of Carnap's 'dispositional concepts' such as solubility, resistance, inflammability, etc. It must be emphasized that the setting up of a definition or reduction for an intervening variable is not a wholly arbitrary and conventional matter. As Carnap has pointed out, it often happens that we give alternative sets of reduction sentences for the same dispositional concept; in these cases there is empirical content in our statement even though it has a form that suggests arbitrariness. The reason for this is that these separate reductions for a given dispositional concept imply that the empirical events are themselves related in a certain way. The notion of amount of electric current can be introduced by several different observations, such as deposition of silver, deflection of a needle, hydrogen separated out of water, and so on. Such a set of reductions has empirical content because the empirical statements together with the reductions must not lead to contradictions. It is a contingent fact, not derivable from definitions alone, that the deposition of silver will give the same answer for 'amount of current' as will the deflection of a needle. A similar problem exists in Hull, when he sets up 'momentary effective reaction potential' as the last intervening variable in his chain. In the case of striated muscle reactions, it is stated that latency, resistance to extinction, and probability of occurrence of a response are all functions of reaction potential. Neglecting behavior oscillation, which does not occur in the formulation for the second two because they involve many repetitions of the situation, this means that the empirical variables must be perfectly correlated (nonlinearly, of course). The only possible source of variation which could attenuate a perfect correlation between probability of occurrence and resistance to extinction would be actual errors of experimental measurement, since there are no sources of uncontrolled variation left within the organism. If we consider average latency instead of momentary latency (which is a function of *momentary* effective reaction potential and hence varies with behavioral oscillation), latency and resistance to extinction should also be perfectly correlated. It remains to be seen whether the fact will support Hull in giving simultaneously several reductions for the notion of reaction potential.

As a second linguistic convention, we propose that the term 'hypothetical construct' be used to designate theoretical concepts which do *not* meet the requirements for intervening variables in the strict sense. That is to say, these constructs involve terms which are not wholly reducible to empirical terms; they refer to processes or entities that are not directly observed (although they need not be in principle unobservable); the mathematical expression of them cannot be formed simply by a suitable grouping of terms in a direct empirical equation; and the truth of the empirical laws involved is a necessary but not a sufficient condition for the truth of these conceptions. Examples of such constructs are Guthrie's M.P.S.'s, Hull's r_g's, S_d's, and *afferent neural interaction*, Allport's *biophysical traits*, Murray's *regnancies*, the notion of 'anxiety' as used by Mowrer, Miller, and Dollard and others of the Yale-derived group, and most theoretical constructs in psychoanalytic theory. Skinner and Toman seem to be almost wholly free of hypothetical constructs, although when Skinner invokes such notions as the 'strain on the reserve' (1938, p. 289) it is difficult to be sure.

We do not wish to seem to legislate usage, so that if the broader use of 'intervening variable' has become stuck in psychological discourse, we would propose alternatively a distinction between intervening variables of the 'abstractive' and of the 'hypothetical' kind. Since our personal preference is for restricting the phrase *intervening variables* to the pure type described by Tolman, we shall follow this convention in the remainder of the present paper.

The validity of intervening variables as we define them cannot be called into question except by an actual denial of the empirical facts. If, for example, Hull's proposed 'grand investigation' of the Perin-Williams type should be carried out and the complex hyperspatial surface fitted adequately over a wide range of values (1943, p. 181), it would be meaningless to reject the concept of 'habit strength' and still admit the empirical findings. For this reason, the only consideration which can be raised with respect to a given proposed intervening variable, when an initial defining or reduction equation is being written for it, is the question of convenience.

In the case of hypothetical constructs, this is not so clear. Science is pursued for many reasons, not the least of which is *n Cognizance*. Since hypothetical constructs assert the existence of entities and the occurrence of events not reducible to the observable, it would seem to some of us that it is the business of a hypothetical construct to be 'true.' It is possible to advance scientific knowledge by taking a completely 'as if' attitude toward such matters, but there are always those whose theoretical-cognitive need dictates that existential propositions should correspond to what is in fact the case. Contemporary philosophy of science, even as represented by those who have traditionally been most cautious about discussing 'truth' and most highly motivated to reduce it to the experiential, gives psychologists no right to be dogmatic about the 'as if' interpretation of theoretical knowledge (see especially Carnap, 1946, p. 598, Kaufmann, 1944, p. 35, Russell, 1940, Introduction and Chapter XXI, and Reichenbach, 1938, *passim*). We would find it rather difficult to defend the ingenious conditioning hypotheses developed in Hull's series of brilliant papers (1929–) in the *Psychological Review* on the ground that they merely provide a "convenient shorthand summarization of the facts" or are of value in the 'practical manipulation' of the rat's behavior. We suspect that Professor Hull himself was motivated to write these articles because he considered that the hypothetical events represented in his diagrams may have actually *occurred* and that the occurrence of these events represents the underlying truth about the learning phenomena he dealt with. In terms of practical application, much (if not most) of theoretical psychology is of little value. If we exclude the interesting anecdotes of Guthrie, contemporary learning theory is not of much use to school teachers. As a *theoretical* enterprise, it may fairly be demanded of a theory of learning that those elements which are 'hypothetical' in the present sense have some probability of being in correspondence with the actual events underlying the behavior phenomena, i.e., that the assertions about hypothetical constructs be true.[1]

Another consideration may be introduced here from the standpoint of future developments in scientific integration. Even those of us who advocate the pursuit of behavioral knowledge on its own level and for its own sake must recognize that some day the 'pyramid of the sciences' will presumably catch up with us. For Skinner, this is of no consequence, since his consistent use of intervening variables in the strict sense genuinely frees him from neurophysiology and in fact makes it possible for him to impose certain conditions upon neurophysiological explanations (1938, pp. 429–31). Since he hypothesizes nothing about the character of the inner events, no finding about the inner events could prove disturbing to him. At most, he would be able to say that a given discovery of internal processes must not be complete because it cannot come to terms with his (empirical) laws. But for those theorists who do not confine themselves to intervening variables in the strict sense, neurology will some day become relevant. For this reason it is perhaps legitimate, even now, to require of a hypothetical construct that it should not be manifestly unreal in the sense that it assumes inner events that cannot conceivably occur. The 'as if' kinds of argument sometimes heard from more sophisticated exponents of psychoanalytic views often seem to ignore this consideration. A concept like *libido* or *censor* or *super-ego* may be introduced initially as though it is to be an intervening variable; or even less, it is treated as a merely conventional designation for a class of observable properties or occurrences. But somewhere in the course of theoretical discussion, we find that these words are being used as hypothetical constructs instead. We find that the libido has acquired certain hydraulic properties, or as in Freud's former view, that the 'energy' of libido has been converted into 'anxiety.' What began as a name for an intervening variable is finally a name for a 'something' which has a host of causal properties. These properties are not made explicit initially, but it is clear that the concept is to be used in an explanatory way which requires that the properties exist. Thus, libido may be introduced by an innocuous definition in terms of the 'set of sexual needs' or a 'general term for basic strivings.' But subsequently we find that certain puzzling phenomena are *deduced* ('explained') by means of the various properties of libido, e.g., that it flows, is dammed up, is converted into something else, tends to regress to earlier channels, adheres to things, makes its 'energy' available to the ego, and so on. It is naïve to object to such formulations simply on the grounds that they refer to unobservables, or are 'hypothetical,' or are not 'statistical.' None of these objections is a crucial one for any scientific construct, and if such criteria were applied a large and useful amount of modern science would have to be abandoned. The fundamental difficulty with such theories is two-fold. First, as has been implied by our remarks, there is the failure explicitly to announce the postualtes concerning existential properties, so that these are introduced more or less surreptitiously and *ad hoc* as occasion demands. Second, by this device there is subtly achieved a transition from admissible intervening variables to inadmissible hypothetical constructs. These hypothetical constructs, unlike intervening variables, are inadmissible because they require the existence of entities and the occurrence of processes which cannot be seriously believed because of other knowledge.

In the case of libido, for instance, we may use such a term legitimately as a generic name for a class of empirical events or properties, or as an intervening variable. But the allied sciences of anatomy and physiology impose restrictions upon our use of it as a hypothetical construct. Even admitting the immature state of neurophysiology in terms of its relation to complex behavior, it must be clear that the central nervous system does not in fact contain pipes or tubes with fluid in them, and there are no known properties of nervous tissue to which the hydraulic properties of libido could correspond. Hence, this part of a theory about 'inner events' is likely to remain metaphorical. For a genuine intervening variable, there is no metaphor because all is merely short-hand summarization. For hypothetical constructs, there is a surplus meaning that is existential. We would argue that dynamic explanations utilizing hypothetical constructs ought not to be of such a character that they *have* to remain only metaphors.

Of course, this judgment in itself involves a 'best guess' about the future. A hypothetical construct which seems inherently metaphorical may involve a set of properties to which hitherto undiscovered characteristics of the nervous system correspond. So long as the propositions about the construct are not stated in the *terms* of the next lower discipline, it is always a possibility that the purely formal or relational content of the construct will find an isomorphism in such characteristics. For scientific theories this is enough, since here, as in physics, the associated mechanical imagery of the theorist is irrelevant. The tentative rejection of libido would then be based upon the belief that no neural process is likely to have the *combination* of formal properties required. Strictly speaking, this is always problematic when the basic science is incomplete.[2]

Summary

1. At present the phrases 'intervening variable' and 'hypothetical construct' are often used interchangeably, and theoretical discourse often fails to distinguish what we believe are two rather different notions. We suggest that a failure to separate these leads to fundamental confusions. The distinction is between constructs which merely abstract the empirical relationships (Tolman's original intervening variables) and those constructs which are 'hypothetical' (i.e., involve the supposition of entities or processes not among the observed).

2. Concepts of the first sort seem to be identifiable by three characteristics. First, the statement of such a concept does not contain any words which are not reducible to the empirical laws. Second, the validity of the empirical laws is both necessary and sufficient for the 'correctness' of the statements about the concept.

Third, the quantitative expression of the concept can be obtained without mediate inference by suitable groupings of terms in the quantitative empirical laws.

3. Concepts of the second sort do not fulfill any of these three conditions. Their formulation involves words not wholly reducible to the words in the empirical laws; the validity of the empirical laws is not a sufficient condition for the truth of the concept, inasmuch as it contains surplus meaning; and the quantitative form of the concept is not obtainable simply by grouping empirical terms and functions.

4. We propose a linguistic convention in the interest of clarity: that the phrase *intervening variable* be restricted to concepts of the first kind, in harmony with Tolman's original definition; and that the phrase *hypothetical construct* be used for those of the second kind.

5. It is suggested that the only rule for proper intervening variables is that of convenience, since they have no factual content surplus to the empirical functions they serve to summarize.

6. In the case of hypothetical constructs, they have a cognitive, factual reference in addition to the empirical data which constitute their support. Hence, they ought to be held to a more stringent requirement insofar as our interests are theoretical. Their actual existence should be compatible with general knowledge and particularly with whatever relevant knowledge exists at the next lower level in the explanatory hierarchy.

Notes

1. It is perhaps unnecessary to add that in adopting this position we do not mean to defend any form of metaphysical realist thesis. The ultimate 'reality' of the world in general is not the issue here; the point is merely that the reality of hypothetical constructs like the atom, from the standpoint of their logical relation to grounds, is not essentially different from that attributed to stones, chairs, other people, and the like. When we say that hypothetical constructs involve the notion of 'objective existence' of actual processes and entities within the organism, we mean the same sort of objective existence, defined by the same ordinary criteria, that is meant when we talk about the objective existence of Singapore. The present discussion operates within the common framework of empirical science and common sense and is intended to be metaphysically neutral.

2. We are indebted to Dr. Herbert Feigl for a clarification of this point.

References

Benjamin, A. C. 1937. *An Introduction to the Philosophy of Science*. New York: Macmillan.

Carnap, R. 1936. Testability and Meaning, Parts I–III. *Philosophy of Science* 3:419–71.

Carnap, R. 1937. Testability and Meaning, Part IV. *Philosophy of Science* 4:1–40.

Carnap, R. 1946. Remarks on Induction and Truth. *Philosophy and Phenomenological Research* 6:590–602.

Hull, C. L. 1943. *Principles of Behavior*. New York: Appleton-Century.

Kaufmann, F. 1944. *Methodology in the Social Sciences*. London: Oxford University Press.

Miller, N. E. 1935. A Reply to "Sign-Gestalt or Conditioned Reflex." *Psychological Review* 42:280–92.

Reichenbach, H. 1938. *Experience and Prediction*. Chicago: University of Chicago Press.
Russell, B. 1940. *Inquiry into Meaning and Truth*. New York: Norton.
Skinner, B. F. 1938. *Behavior of Organisms*. New York: Appleton-Century.
Tolman, E. C. 1938. The Determiners of Behavior at a Choice Point. *Psychological Review* 45:1–41

9

Psychopathology and Purpose

When I received an invitation from Dr. Paul H. Hoch to address the American Psychopathological Association, I was, of course, pleased and honored; but I was also conflicted, because the topic that came to my mind was so smacking of heresy for most psychologists and psychiatrists that I wondered whether it would even be taken seriously. Furthermore, I have spent many hours arguing over the question with the (then) treasurer of the association, Dr. Bernard C. Glueck; and as a former analysand of his, I could hardly avoid the thought that my choice of topic might be partly determined by some residual negative transference. In proposing a critical re-examination of received doctrine, it is difficult to draw the line between being challenging and being cantankerous. I hope I shall succeed in being one without being the other.

The concept of "purpose," while it has an essential role in psychopathology, is currently overemphasized; this overemphasis gives rise to needless theoretic puzzles and, more important, rationalizes psychotherapeutic strategy and tactics which are sometimes useless and even countertherapeutic.

Freud's discovery that the concept of purpose could be powerfully applied in contexts where it had previously been thought irrelevant is justly regarded as a major intellectual achievement, and stands in no need of proof or eulogy. But, like other great ideas in the history of thought, it has been overgeneralized—humankind being incapable of grasping an important truth without making it into the *whole* truth (which, of course, it never is).

Bypassing philosophic questions and pseudoteleologic laws in physical science (e.g., "least action" principles), we can identify two broad classes of purposive concepts in biologic and social science. First, there is what the logicians call "motive talk," in which we explain a person's actions by referring to his drives, goals, motives, intentions, etc. Such explanations are usually signaled by connective phrases such as "in order to," "so that," "lest," "because he wanted," and the like. The demonstration that these connectives are often appropriate even when the content of the dependent clause is nonreportable is perhaps most clearly and cogently made in Freud's 1915 paper "The Unconscious."

A second kind of purposive statement, which I shall dub with the neologism "biopragmatic," occurs in discourse about the biologic function of organs, substances, or processes. Even the most hardheaded anatomy professor is not offended by the question: What is this organ *for?* In experimental psychology, the perceptual constancies have a striking biopragmatic aspect. The apparent size of objects is a close correlate of their actual size. If our nervous systems were wired so that the geometric dependency of retinal image size upon object distance was determinative of experienced size, we would have a tough time getting around in the physical environment.

The laws of operant learning provide another example. A hungry rat in a Skinner box may be reinforced by delivery of a food pellet every time it presses the lever; or reinforcement may be given following only *some* of the lever pressings (i.e., on an "intermittent schedule"). The response strength turns out to be very delicately geared to the reinforcement schedule, so that slight alterations in the objective payoff-probability control the rate of responding. Continuous reinforcement maintains higher average rates than does intermittent. However, if *all* reinforcement is now withheld, extinction proceeds faster, and with far fewer total responses, following a history of continuous reinforcement. Biopragmatically, it is "sensible" for organisms to adjust their work output to objective payoff; however, if payoff probability *has been* = 1 and suddenly falls to zero, the chances are that something funny is going on in the external world, and until things get back to normal it is biologically expedient to quit trying—and quickly.

Are such biopragmatic statements part of the corpus of behavioral science? My answer is no, because they do not actually appear in any theoretic derivation. They are *true*, but they belong to another science, namely, genetics (including evolution), which has the task of explaining how organisms with such biopragmatic properties came into being.

Now this distinction is not one of mere philosophic precision, because it makes a difference whether you treat biopragmatic statements as laws of behavior (which they are *not*) or more like editorial comments imported from a nonpsychologic subject matter (which is what they are). In general, the inclusion of biopragmatic assertions in behavioral science gives rise to more problems than it solves. A rat can be trained to put out 200 responses per pellet, a ratio which leaves him ahead of the game calorically. But if this schedule is suddenly imposed on a rat who has been performing at 20:1, he will extinguish, and can actually be starved to death in an environment where food is objectively available. A biopragmatic principle such as, "Organisms adapt to their environment," leads to paradoxes which a rat clinician might be tempted to resolve by *ad hoc* hypotheses (e.g., death instinct). Whereas by confining our conceptual system to the substantive learning principles of reinforcement and discriminative control, we can *derive* the necessity of proceeding to large ratios by gradual steps. The important truth illustrated by this laboratory example is that the biologic "adaptiveness" or "utility" of behavioral laws is only *stochastic*, and cannot be validly applied to make derivations about individual specimens and circumstances. Let me emphasize that we are not discussing rats who are somehow aberrant — any normal rat can be starved to death with food available by appropriate choice of the reinforcement schedule's parameters.

Another point of this example is that the organism is a repository not only of *motives* and *emotions*, but also of *habits*. There is a vast experimental literature dealing with the acquisition, shaping, control, activation, and extinction of habits, and psychopathologists who consider this body of facts irrelevant to their concerns are profoundly mistaken, because there are behavioral phenomena which cannot be understood, especially in their quantitative aspects, except in terms of learning principles.

Let us turn now to clinical material. Since Freud, we are accustomed to ask, "*Why* is the patient doing this?", anticipating an answer formulable in motive talk. My thesis is that this is sometimes a mistake. It is worth noting that Freud expressed a somewhat similar conclusion in *Beyond the Pleasure Principle*. The "repetition compulsion" strikes most of us as a rather poor explanatory construct because it represents an abandonment of that insistence upon finding motivational explanations which made Freud's early discoveries so illuminating. The "death instinct" is Freud's metaphysical effort to subsume what he reluctantly recognized as nonpurposive clinical phenomena under a principle which, although counterintuitive and no longer biopragmatic, still preserves an odd kind of teleologic character.

In understanding a trait or symptom, the question "What is the patient getting, or avoiding (or 'trying' to get or avoid)?" may be inappropriate for a variety of reasons, of which time permits me to mention only three. First we have the distinction between classic (Pavlovian) conditioning and instrumental learning by reward (Thorndike's "Law of Effect"), corresponding to Skinner's distinction of respondents and operants. Salivating when you hear the dinner bell is a respondent. It does not manipulate the environment, it does not bring about the presence of food, and it belongs to that class of responses, occurring in smooth muscle and gland, controlled by the autonomic system. By contrast, saying to the waitress, "I'll have a hamburger," is an operant (like lever pressing), which acts upon the external environment to bring about the presence of food, occurs in striped muscle, and is controlled by the skeletal nervous system. Respondents are "conditioned" in the original Pavlovian sense, and the question "What does the dog 'get out of' salivating?" is not behaviorally meaningful (although it obviously has a good biopragmatic answer). Operants, on the other hand, are learned and maintained by reward, and it *does* make behavioral sense to ask what the organism gets out of them.

The operant-respondent distinction is crucial for understanding the relation between psychosomatic phenomena and conversion symptoms. The former are respondent and are therefore not "purposive." The latter are operant and are "purposive." The question "What is Mr. X getting out of his stomach ulcer?" is not only scientifically unsound but partakes of a certain element of injustice. I don't think it is always correct to say that the patient is getting *anything* out of his ulcer, although of course even an ulcer (like a conversion symptom) may provide secondary gains. But there is no good evidence that conditioned respondents can be strengthened, or their strength maintained, by reward; so that the secondary gains of a psychosomatic symptom are pragmatically of less importance because they do not, theoretically, contribute to symptom maintenance.

Even in the operant case, one can be misled into asking pseudoquestions by overteleologizing the reward concept. The late, great psychologist E. C. Tolman once argued in print against the Law of Effect on the curious ground that it could not explain a man's persistence in smoking Luckies when Old Golds would satisfy the smoking drive equally well! This is a beautiful example of what can happen when a bit of biopragmatics is allowed to metastasize, and the fact that such an able mind as Tolman's could fall into the trap testifies to our pervasive and ineradicable tendency to think teleologically. The Law of Effect (or, the principle of operant reinforcement) does not refer to hypothetic occurrences (what *would* happen *if* something else happened) but states that organisms tend to emit the responses that have been reinforced. There isn't any basis for expecting the fellow to shift from Luckies to Old Golds, nor is there anything paradoxical about his persistence. His learning history is that he has been asking for Luckies, getting Luckies, and smoking Luckies. This is the behavior that has been emitted, and it is this behavior that has been reinforced. He hasn't been asking for Camels or Old Golds, and, consequently, that behavior has not been reinforced. The Law of Effect tells us that he will do what he has been rewarded for doing; what he *could* get rewarded for doing, as seen from the vantage point of the outside observer, is behaviorally irrelevant.

A similar error occurs in the thinking of many clinicians when trying to understand neurotic behavior. A patient ought, we think, to be doing so-and-so because this would lead to need gratification. Why doesn't he? In contemporary psychodynamics, the first place we look is for something which is "in the way," i.e., we look for some kind of counterforce or impedance which prevents the individual from emitting the healthy response and getting the healthy gratification. Now often there are such roadblocks, especially in the early phases of treatment. But even if there aren't, the clinician who thinks biopragmatically will search until he *finds* them—which, given the complexity of behavior and a moderate ingenuity, he can almost always do. Whether or not the patient will *buy* his interpretation, and whether, if he does buy it, it has a therapeutic consequence, is another question.

But, as we have seen, responses may fail to occur for other reasons; and one of the commonest causes of response failure is the quantitative inadequacy of reinforcement. Once we abandon the assumption that maladaptive behavior always reflects the influence of interfering forces and therefore should, so to speak, "clear up by itself" when these adverse influences are lifted by the therapeutic process, we can recognize that, in addition to incompatible habits and disruptive affects, there are also failures to have acquired or maintained instrumental responses at sufficient strength. The therapeutic task then becomes partly one of building up such healthy responses. Of course, to attempt this while the counterforces are still present makes no more theoretic sense in terms of the experimental psychology of learning than it does in terms of, say, classic analytic theory. I am not suggesting that we throw overboard what we know about the role of defense in maintaining maladaptive behavior, returning to some kind of Couéism or other suggestive-suppressive therapy. I am concerned with a kind of problem which I am sure every psychotherapist present has met repeatedly, namely, the patient who has worked through a great deal of material, freed himself from many neurotic defenses, learned to tolerate less distorted derivatives, but who persists in not doing the obvious things that he himself says would now be in order, and who sometimes even raises spontaneously the mysterious question of why he doesn't get around now to doing them. This clinical problem is *not* effectively approached by searching for some yet uncovered counterforces or by postulating excessive amounts of *thanatos*, and the like. Instead, we recognize that the individual's interfering habit systems have been considerably reduced by psychotherapy, but that he lacks sufficiently strong instrumental response chains of the gratification-seeking type to get the behavior out and to keep it going under the reinforcement schedule of adult life. The stochastic nature of socially mediated reinforcement schedules here becomes particularly important. Very little of our interpersonal behavior is on a total reinforcement schedule. When we tell a joke, people are not always amused; when we go to a party, we are sometimes bored; when we accept a patient for therapy, the patient does not always improve; and so forth. When an individual has been impeded by neurotic counterforces from acquiring a stable and well-differentiated system of instrumental responses, removal of the impeding factors constitutes a necessary but not a sufficient condition for development of healthy behavior. Uncovering psychotherapy is primarily aimed at reducing defense, which means in learning-theoretic terms that it tries to extinguish *avoidant* operants and the conditioned anxiety respondents which underlie them. Neither of these changes has any intrinsic tendency to strengthen operants of the *adient* class. Relying upon the uncovered impulses to do this is often like expecting the rat to switch without stepwise retraining gradually to a new schedule, merely on the grounds that he is hungry. Moral: *Drive is not enough.*

Weak operants are in danger of extinction because a respectable payoff probability may easily fail to materialize in a short run of trials. Suppose, for example, that you are treating a patient whose neurosis has greatly restricted his heterosexual history. As the treatment frees him up a bit, he starts tentatively exploring. If his long-run odds of a "success"-experience are, say, 20%, there is one chance in nine that he will have a run of ten consecutive failures — which might lead the healthiest male to get a little discouraged. The patient is not being sabotaged by his *thanatos*, or his will to defeat the therapist, or by his unconscious guilt; he is merely a victim of the binomial theorem.

Recognizing that habits and reinforcement schedules are just as important in understanding learned behavior as drives or affects suggests the modification of psychotherapeutic procedures along lines of response strengthening and shaping through positive reinforcement. Specifically, we ought not assume that whenever the anxiety signal is sufficiently extinguished and the defensive system has been sufficiently worked through by interpretative methods, the drive system of the organism will somehow automatically do the rest. There is no theoretic reason why we should expect this to happen; and it is quite apparent that many psychotherapists today are acutely conscious of the clinical fact that it frequently does not happen. Since our clinical experience is in such excellent accord with theoretic expectations, it would seem appropriate to modify and adapt our procedures so that they will be more in harmony with the principles which have been discovered by the experimental study of the learning process.

The technical suggestions which arise upon adopting this view would require detailed discussion, and rather than give a misleading picture by characterizing them generically, or even by listing them *in extenso*, let me take only two specific tactical examples. The first of these involves the amount and kind of positive reinforcement administered by the therapist himself. Because of the notorious fact that ordinary unsophisticated reassuring tactics of the type used by the patient's friends and family are ineffective, there is a widespread professional opinion that explicit positive rewards ought not be administered by the therapist. The complications which can arise from an unsuitable use of tactics such as encouragement are too well known to need discussion. But we should surely distinguish between the unskilled and blanket reassuring procedures employed by the patient's peer group (without *first* reducing the neurotic counterforces), and the skillful application of verbal rewards at suitable stages of therapy. Therapists show here a kind of double standard. When they talk about an approved therapeutic tool, such as interpretation, they wish its efficacy to be judged in terms of its skillful and optimal use. But when asked to consider interview tactics such as "priming" or reassurance or encouragement or explicit approval for doing something healthy, they tend to denigrate them as "mere symptomatic treatment," assimilating all such to the unskilled operations of nonprofessional helpers. An experimental psychologist would expect that the proper dosage of reward for behavior in the healthy direction, even if objectively *unsuccessful* on a given environmental trial, should help to build up the desired response strength and keep the behavior coming out sufficiently so that the patient has a fighting chance of getting a few pellets.

A more controversial tactic is task setting. While Freud discussed task setting in connection with phobias, he did not develop his own technique along these lines; furthermore, the task setting experiments of certain other workers (such as Ferenczi) brought the whole concept into disrepute. On learning principles, one would expect task setting to be an extremely powerful ancillary procedure at certain stages in therapy; and under some circumstances, with some patients, it might even be a necessary condition for getting a patient over the hump. Here also, the contraindications and numerous dangers (e.g., with respect to the therapeutic relationship) are admitted. However, the existence of dangers and complications ought not rule out therapeutic experimentation, especially since our current methods can hardly be considered so powerful as to be beyond improvement.

A third situation in which the motive question is inappropriate resembles Freud's repetition compulsion, and is admittedly more speculative than the cases of respondent conditioning or low operant strength. On present evidence, we cannot exclude the possibility that at least some "negative" psychic conditions are simply the result of a thoroughly overlearned, massively conditioned CNS state. The patient is not seeking or avoiding—he is just repeating, and that's the end of the story. Whether this type of central "state repetition" occurs, and whether it obeys the laws of respondent conditioning and extinction, are factual questions of great clinical importance. If the baffling and discouraging behavior of some of our patients is thus mediated (especially if the "statistical physiology" of the situation leads to maintenance of a steady state, or to a kind of automatic self-reconditioning by sheer repetition and without primary reinforcement), the implications for therapeutic tactics are quite different from those derivable from either an impulse-defense or a hedonic-control model.

In summary, I have tried to suggest some of the theoretic and experimental reasons which lead me, as a clinician and erstwhile rat psychologist, to believe that contemporary psychodynamics systematically overgeneralizes the concept of purpose and neglects other variables whose control over behavior is well established. It is my further conviction that when this error is rectified, the full conceptual power of Freud's emphasis on motives will be manifested because it will no longer be attenuated by misapplication, and that our ability to help patients will thereby be materially increased.

10

Some Methodological Reflections on the Difficulties of Psychoanalytic Research

Whatever the verisimilitude[1] of Freud's theories, it will surely be a matter of comment by future historians of science that a system of ideas which has exerted such a powerful and pervasive influence upon both professional practitioners and contemporary culture should, two-thirds of a century after the promulgation of its fundamental concepts, still remain a matter of controversy. That fact in itself should lead us to suspect that there is something methodologically peculiar about the relation of psychoanalytic concepts to their evidential base.

Let me begin by saying that I reject what has come to be called "operationism" as a logical reconstruction of scientific theories. Practically all empiricist philosophers (e.g., Carnap, Feigl, Feyerabend, Hempel, Popper, Sellars), thinkers who cannot by any stretch of the imagination be considered muddleheaded, obscurantist, or antiscientific in their sympathies, have for many years recognized that strict operationism (in anything like the form originally propounded by Bridgman) is philosophically indefensible.[2] In saying this, they do not, however, prejudge those issues of scientific research *strategy* that arise between a quasi-operationist like Skinner and a psychoanalytic theorist. And it is commendable that Skinner and his followers (unlike some psychologists) have been careful to avoid invoking "philosophy of science" in their advocacy of either substantive views or research strategy.

Associated with my rejection of operationism is the recognition that biological

AUTHOR'S NOTE: Revised and expanded version of a paper read at a joint session of the Division of Experimental Psychology and the Society for Projective Techniques, seventy-fourth annual convention of the American Psychological Association at New York City, September 6, 1966.

This work was largely done during my summer appointments as professor in the Minnesota Center for Philosophy of Science, under support from the Carnegie Corporation of New York. I should also like to express my indebtedness to colleagues Herbert Feigl, Carl P. Malmquist, and Grover Maxwell for the stimulation, criticism, and clarification provided, as always, at Center discussions.

272

and social sciences are forced to make use of what have come to be known[3] as "open concepts," the "openness" of these concepts having two or three distinguishable aspects which space does not permit me to develop here. One important consequence of this openness is that we must reject Freud's monolithic claim about the necessity to accept or reject psychoanalysis as a whole. This is simply false as a matter of formal logic, even in explicitly formalized and clearly interpreted theoretical systems, and such a systematic "holism" is a fortiori untenable when we are dealing with what is admittedly a loose, incomplete, and unformalized conceptual system like psychoanalysis. It is well known that proper subsets of postulates in physics, chemistry, astronomy, and genetics are continually being changed without "changing everything else" willy-nilly, and it is absurd to suppose psychoanalytic theory, unlike these advanced sciences, is a corpus of propositions so tightly interknit that they have to be taken "as a whole."

I would also reject any requirement that there should be a *present mapping* of psychoanalytic concepts against constructs at another level of analysis, such as neurophysiology or learning theory. All that one can legitimately require is that psychoanalytic concepts ought not to be *incompatible* with well-corroborated theories of the learning process or nervous system function. But the situation in these two fields is itself so controversial that this negative requirement imposes only a very weak limitation upon psychoanalytic theorizing.

I would also combat the tendency (found in some psychonomes) to treat the terms "experimental" and "empirical" as synonymous. An enterprise can be empirical (in the sense of taking publicly observable data as its epistemic base) *without* being experimental (in the sense of laboratory manipulation of the variables). Such respectable sciences as astronomy, geography, ecology, paleontology, and human genetics are obvious examples. We should not conflate different dimensions such as the following: experimental-naturalistic; quantitative-qualitative; objective-subjective; documentary-behavioral. It is obvious, for example, that one can carry out objective and quantitative analysis upon a nonexperimental document (e.g., diary, personal correspondence, jury protocol).

I should make clear that while I am not an "orthodox Popperian," I find myself more in sympathy with the logic and methodology of science expounded by Sir Karl Popper[4] than with that of any other single contemporary thinker. While I share with my Minnesota colleagues Feigl and Maxwell reservations about Sir Karl's complete rejection of what he calls "inductivism," I agree with Popper in emphasizing the extent to which theoretical concepts (often implicit) pervade even the so-called "observation language" of science and of common life; and I incline to accept refutability (falsifiability) as the best criterion to demarcate science from other kinds of cognitive enterprises such as metaphysics.

There is a certain tension between these views. What I have said about operationism, open concepts, and the scientific status of nonexperimental investigation makes life easier for the psychoanalytic theorist; but the Popperian emphasis upon falsifiability tends in the opposite direction.

As a personal note, I may say that, as is true of most psychologists seriously interested in psychoanalysis, I have found my own experience on the couch, and my clinical experience listening to the free associations of patients, far more persuasive than any published research purporting to test psychoanalytic theory. I do not assert that this is a good or a bad thing, but I want to have it down in the record. In the ''context of discovery''[5] this very characteristic attitude is worth keeping in mind.

The inventor of psychoanalysis took the same view, and it might be good research strategy to concentrate attention upon the verbal behavior of the analytic session itself. If there is any strong empirical evidence in support of Freud's ideas, this is perhaps the best place to look, since this is where he hit upon them in the first place! We have today the advantage which he regrets not having, that recording an analysand's verbal behavior is a simple and inexpensive process. Skinner points out that what makes the science of behavior difficult is *not*— contrary to the usual view in psychoanalytic writing—problems of *observation*, because (compared with the phenomena of most other sciences) behavior is relatively macroscopic and slow. The difficult problems arise in slicing the pie, that is, in classifying intervals of the behavior flux and in subjecting them to powerful conceptual analysis and appropriate statistical treatment. Whatever one may think of Popper's view that theory subtly infects even so-called observation statements in physics, this is pretty obviously true in psychology because of the trivial fact that an interval of the behavior flux can be sliced up or categorized in different ways. Even in the animal case the problems of response class and stimulus equivalence arise, although less acutely. A patient in an analytic session says, ''I suppose you are thinking that this is really about my father, but you're mistaken, because it's not.'' We can readily conceive of a variety of rubrics under which this chunk of verbal behavior could be plausibly subsumed. We might classify it syntactically, as a complex-compound sentence, or as a negative sentence; or as resistance, since it rejects a possible interpretation; or as negative transference, because it is an attribution of error to the analyst; or, in case the analyst hasn't been having any such associations as he listens, we can classify it as an instance of projection; or as an instance of ''father theme''; or we might classify it as self-referential, because its subject matter is the patient's thoughts rather than the thoughts or actions of some third party; and so on and on. The problem here is not mainly one of ''reliability'' in categorizing, although goodness knows that's a tough one too. Thorough training to achieve perfect interjudge scoring agreement *per rubric* would still leave us with the problem I am raising.

There are two opposite mistakes which may be made in methodological discussion on the evidential value of verbal output in a psychoanalytic hour. One mistake is to demand that there should be a straightforwardly computable numerical probability attached to each substantive idiographic hypothesis, of the sort which we can usually compute with regard to the option of rejecting a statistical hypothesis. This mistake arises from identifying "rationality in inductive inference" with "statistical hypothesis testing." One need merely make this identification explicit to realize that it is a methodological mistake. It would, for instance, condemn as "nonrational" all assessment of substantive scientific theories, or the process of inference in courts of law, or evaluation of theories in such disciplines as history or paleontology. No logician has succeeded in constructing any such automatic numerical "evidence-quantifying" rules, and many logicians and statisticians are doubtful whether such a thing could be done, even in principle. It is obvious, for instance, that a jury can be put in possession of a pattern of evidence which makes it highly rational to infer beyond a reasonable doubt that the defendant is guilty; but no one (with the exception of Poisson in a famous ill-fated effort) has tried to *quantify* this evidential support in terms of the probability calculus. Whether a distinction can be made between quantifying the corroboration of nomethetic theories[6] and quantifying the probability of particularistic (= idiographic) hypotheses is difficult to say, although we should pursue that line of thought tenaciously. Ideally, I suggest, a Bayes Rule calculation on the idiographic constructions of psychoanalysis should be possible.

The opposite error is the failure to realize that Freud's "jigsaw-puzzle" analogy does not really fit the psychoanalytic hour, because it is simply not true (as he admits elsewhere) that all of the pieces fit together, or that the criteria of "fitting" are sufficiently tight to make it analogous even to a clear-cut criminal trial. Two points, opposite in emphasis but compatible: Anyone who has experienced analysis, practiced it, or listened to taped sessions, if he is halfway fair-minded, will agree that (1) there are sessions where the material "fits together" so beautifully that one is sure almost any skeptic would be convinced, and (2) there are sessions where the "fit" is very loose and underdetermined (fewer equations than unknowns, so to speak), this latter kind of session (unfortunately) predominating.

The number of theoretical variables available, and the fact that the theory itself makes provision for their countervailing one another and reversing qualities (e.g., the dream work's sometime expression of content by opposites), lead to the ever-present possibility that the ingenuity of the human mind will permit the therapist to impose a construction which, while it has a certain ad hoc plausibility, nevertheless has low verisimilitude. What we would like to have is a predictive criterion, but the trouble is that the theory does not claim to make, in most cases, highly specific content predictions. Thus, as Freud himself pointed out, while we can sometimes make a plausible case for the occurrence of certain latent dream thoughts which were transformed through the dream work into the manifest content of a dream, the same set of dream thoughts *could* have been responsible for a manifest content completely different. Similarly, in paleontology, the fossil data may be rationally taken to lend support to the theory of evolution, but there is nothing in the theory of evolution that enables us to predict that such an organism as the rhinoceros will have been evolved, or that we should find fossil trilobites. Or, again, the facts may strongly support the hypothesis that the accused had a motive and the opportunity, so he murdered the deceased; but these assumptions would be equally compatible with his having murdered him at a different time and place, and by the use of a knife rather than a revolver. I do not myself have any good solution to this difficulty. The best I can come up with is that, lacking a rigorous mathematical model for the dream work, and lacking any adequate way of estimating the strengths of the various initial conditions that constitute parameters in the system, we should at least be able to apply crude counting statistics, such as theme frequencies, to the verbal output that occurs during the later portions of the hour when these are predicted (by psychoanalytically skilled persons) from the output at the beginning of the hour. I look in this direction because of my clinical impression that one's ability to forecast the *general theme* of the associative material from the manifest content of the dream plus the initial associations to it, while far from perfect, is nevertheless often good enough to constitute the kind of clinical evidence that carries the heaviest weight with those who open-mindedly but skeptically embark upon psychoanalytic work. Let me give a concrete example of this (one on which I myself would be willing to lay odds of $90 to $10, and on more than a mere "significant difference" but on an almost complete predictability within the limits of the reliability of thematic classification). If a male patient dreams about fire and water, or dreams about one and quickly associates to the other (and here the protocol scoring would be a straightforward, objective, almost purely clerical job approaching perfect interscorer reliability), the dominant theme in the remainder of the session will involve *ambition* as a motive and *shame* (or triumph) as an affect. In 25 years as a psychotherapist I have not found so much as a single exception to this generalization. This kind of temporal covariation was the essential evidential base with which Freud started, and I suggest that if sufficient protocols were available for study, it is the kind of thing which can be subjected to simple statistical test. Since there is no obvious phenotypic overlap in the content, a successful prediction along these lines would strongly corroborate one component of psychoanalytic theory, namely that involving the urethral cluster. Now I believe that there are many such clustering which could in principle be subjected to statistical test, and my expectation is that, if performed, they would provide a rather dramatic support for many of Freud's first-level inferences, and a pretty clear refutation of others.

Whether or not one is a convinced "Bayesian" is largely irrelevant here, provided we can set *some* safe empirical bounds on the priors, which we can presumably do for the "expectedness" (of our test-observation) in the denominator of Bayes's Formula, relying on statistics from a large batch of unselected interviews. Even expectedness values $\simeq$ ½ can become a basis for fairly strong corroborators if there are several all "going the right direction." And if we *are* real, feisty, honest-to-goodness "Bayesian personalists" about probability, it might be plausibly argued that a fair basis for assigning the priors would be guesstimates by academic psychologists largely ignorant of Freud. This basis of prior-probability assignments permits us to go outside the analytic session into those diverse contexts (for which explicit statistics are lacking) of daily life, history, biography, mythology, news media, personal documents, etc. — data sources which collectively played a major role in convincing the nontherapist intelligentsia that Freud "must have something." Example: No philosophically educated Freudian would have trouble guessing which of these four philosophers wrote a little-known treatise on *wind*: Kant? Locke? Hume? Santayana? A Freudian would call to mind Kant's definition of a moral act as one done *solely* from a sense of duty (rather than, say, a spontaneous loving impulse or a desire to give pleasure); the pedantic punctuality of his daily walk, by which the Königsberg housewives allegedly set their clocks; his remarkable statement that "there can be nothing more dreadful than that the actions of a man should be subject to the will of another"; and his stubborn refusal over many years to speak with a sister following a minor quarrel. But I doubt that a panel of (otherwise knowledgeable) psychologists, ignorant of Freudian theory, would tend to correctly identify Kant as having a scholarly interest in wind—even if we helped them out by adding the fact of Kant's excessive concern with constipation in his later years. The same is no doubt true of my rash prediction (upon first descending the stairs inside the Washington monument) that the wall plaques would show more financial contributions by fire departments than by police departments. (They do.) Point: The very "absurdity" or "farfetched" character of many psychoanalytic *connections* can be turned to research advantage, because the prior probabilities of such-and-such correlations among observables are so very differently estimated by one thinking outside the Freudian frame.

As must be apparent from even these brief and (unavoidably) dogmatic remarks, I locate the methodological difficulties of testing psychoanalytic theory differently from many—perhaps most?—who have discussed it, whether as protagonists or critics. For example, I do not waste time defending[7] the introduction of unobservable theoretical entities, knowing as I do that the behaviorist dogma "Science deals only with observables" is historically incorrect and philosophically ludicrous. The *proper* form of the "behavioristic" objection is, as always in sophisticated circles, to the *kind* of theoretical entity being invoked (read: its role in the postulated nomological network, including linkages to data statements). Methodological insight quickly shifts our attention away from such philosophical issues to examination "of the merits," as the lawyers would say. Let me emphasize that I do not rely tendentiously upon philosophy-of-science considerations as a *defense* of psychoanalytic theory either. To rebut a dumb objection is merely to rebut a dumb objection; it does not make a scientific case. Those of us who are betting on a respectable verisimilitude in the Freudian corpus must beware of taking substantive comfort in this indirect way, as some "Chomskyites" are currently taking comfort from (easy) refutations of unsound philosophical positions employed by certain of their S-R-reinforcement opponents. We must try to be honest with ourselves even though we are (as always in science) "betting on a horse race." It simply won't do to get relaxed about the dubious methodological status of, say, a postulated "bargain between ego and superego" as explaining why Smith cuts himself shaving before visiting his mistress, on the ground that the superego is a theoretical construct, and that's peachy, since physicists can't see the neutrino either!

Having mentioned the neutrino, I am led to a comment on falsifiability in the inexact sciences. You will recall that when Pauli cooked up the neutrino idea in 1931 — solely to preserve the conservation laws ad hoc! — the theory itself showed that the neutrino hypothesis was probably not falsifiable, because the imagined new particle had zero charge and zero rest-mass. It was not until 1956, 25 years later, that a very expensive, never-replicated experiment by Reines and Cowan successfully detected the neutrino (more) "directly." The auxiliary assumptions involved (e.g., would the cross section of cadmium nucleus be large enough?) were themselves *so* problematic that a negative experimental result could just as plausibly have counted against *them* as against the theory of interest. While Popper's stress on falsifiability (and the correlative idea that theories become well corroborated by passing stringent tests) is much needed by the psychologist, partly as an antidote to the current overreliance on mere null-hypothesis refutation as corroborating complex theories,[8] it has become increasingly clear that a too-strict-and-quick application of *modus tollens* would prevent even "good" theories (i.e., theories having high verisimilitude) from getting a foothold. "All theories are lies, but some are white lies, some gray, and some black." The most we can expect of psychodynamic theories in the foreseeable future is that some of them are gray lies. My own predilection is therefore for a neo-Popperian position, such as is represented by Feyerabend, Lakatos, and Maxwell.[9] But what precisely this methodological position means for the strategy of testing psychoanalytic theory is difficult to discern in the present state of the philosophers' controversy. My own tentative predilection is for stronger theories,[10] such strong theories being subjected to more tolerant empirical tests than Popper or Platt seems to recommend. Discussion of this very complicated issue would take us too far afield, but suffice it to say that I now view the position presented in my 1967 paper as overly stringent, although its main point is still, I think, a valid one.

Perhaps the psychologist should first learn Popper's main lesson, including why Popper considers such doctrines as psychoanalysis and Marxism to be nonscientific theories like astrology (because all three are pseudo-"confirmable" but not refutable), and then proceed to soften the Popperian rules a bit. Whether these suggested "softenings" really conflict with a sophisticated falsification-ism, or whether Popper himself would consider them objectionable, we need not discuss here.[11] Specifically, I advocate two "cushionings" of the Popperian fal-sifiability emphasis:

1. A theory is admissible not only if we know how to test it, but if we know *what else we would need to know* in order to test it.
2. A theory need not be abandoned following an adverse result, if there are fairly strong results corroborating it, since this combination of circum-stances suggests that either (a) the auxiliary hypotheses and *ceteris paribus* clause of the adverse test were not satisfied, or (b) the theory is false as it stands but possesses respectable verisimilitude (i.e., is a gray lie), or both.

I think that these are sensible methodological recommendations that can be rationally defended within a "neo-Popperian" frame, and they do not appear to me to hinge upon resolution of the very technical issues now in controversy among logicians and historians of science. But I hasten to add that such "soft-ening" of the pure, hard-line *modus tollens* rule must not be accompanied by a theoretical commitment such that we persist indefinitely in what Popper stigma-tizes as "Parmenidean apologies," clinging to the cherished doctrine in spite of all adverse evidence.[12] *When* Parmenidean apologies are desirable, *which kinds* and *how long* to persist in them ("theoretical tenacity") are difficult questions.[13]

One big trouble with the application of neo-Popperian strategies to a theory such as Freud's is that the best case for either Parmenidean apologies or continu-ing use of a "gray-lie" theory in the face of strong and accepted falsifiers is the concurrent existence of strong corroborators, and this usually (not always) re-quires that the theory have made successful *point* predictions (i.e., predictions of antecedently improbable numerical values). The successful prediction of a mere directional difference is not of this kind, having too high a prior expectedness in Bayes's Formula absent the theory of interest. (If I am right, this atheoretical ex-pectedness in the social and biological sciences approaches ½ as the power of our significance test increases, Meehl 1967.) Yet an attempt to formulate psychoan-alytic theory so as to generate such high-risk numerical point predictions is hardly feasible at present. For one thing, the auxiliary hypotheses which are nor-mally treated as (relatively) unproblematic in designing a test experiment are un-available pending the development of powerful, well-corroborated *non*-psy-chodynamic theory (e.g., psycholinguistics). I must say that this state of affairs renders the prospects for cooking up strong tests rather gloomy.

From the standpoint of the experimental psychologist, for whom the experi-ment (in a fairly tough, restrictive usage of that term) is the ideal method of cor-roborating or discorroborating theories, the obvious drawbacks of the psychoan-alytic hour as a data source are two, one on the "input" (= control) side and the other on the "output" (= observation) side. On the input side, unless the analyst's enforcement of the Fundamental Rule relies entirely upon the psychological pressure of a silence—a technical maneuver which is sometimes the method of choice but other times, I think, clearly not—we have the problem of the timing and content of the analyst's interventions as being themselves "biased" by his theoretical predilections. (It would be interesting to play around with the psychoanalytic analogue to a yoked-box situation in operant behavior research.) On the output side, the problem of "objectifying" the classification of the patient's verbal behavior is so complex that when you begin to think hard about it, the most natural response is to throw up your hands in despair. Tentatively I suggest two contrasting methods of such objectification, to wit: First, we rely upon some standard source such as *Roget's Thesaurus* or the Palermo-Jenkins tables or a (to-be-constructed) gigantic atlas of couch outputs emitted under "standard" conditions of Fundamental Rule + analyst silence, for determining whether certain words or phrases are thematically or formally linked to others. Such a "scoring system" bypasses the skilled clinical judge and hence avoids theoretical infection of the data basis. I need hardly point out its grave defect—so grave that a negative result would not be a strong falsifier—which is that the mainly idiographic theme indicators (those which make psychoanalytic therapy fun!) would be lost.

Alternatively, we permit the judgment of a skilled clinician to play a part in classifying the responses, but we systematically prevent his having access to other portions of the material (e.g., to the manifest content of the dream with which the patient commenced a session) so that he will not be "contaminated" by this material. Point: As much as any area of research in clinical psychology, the study of the psychoanalytic interview brings home the importance of solving, by ingenious methods, the perennial problem of "How do we get the advantages of having a skilled observer, who knows what to listen for and how to classify it, without having the methodological disadvantage that anyone who is skilled (in this sense) has been theoretically brainwashed in the course of his training?" In my view, this is *the* methodological problem in psychoanalytic research.

This brings me to my final point, which is in the nature of a warning prophecy more than a reaction to anything presently happening in psychoanalytic research. The philosophical and historical criticisms against classical positivism and naïve operationism have (quite properly) included emphasis upon the role of theory in determining what, when, and how we observe. But most of the discussion of these matters has drawn its historical examples from astronomy, physics, and chemistry. In these examples, as I read the record, what the experimenter *relied* on in "making observations" was (relatively) nonproblematic and independently corroborated portions of the theoretical network for, say, constructing apparatus. The theory of interest was not "relied on" in that sense, although of course in another sense it was "relied on" in deciding what to do and what to look for. It seems to me important to distinguish these two sorts of reliance on theory, and if they are conflated under the broad statement "Theory determines what we observe," I think confusion results. Furthermore, it is misleading (for several reasons) to equate a mass spectrometer or a piece of litmus paper with a psychotherapist as an "instrument of observation." I seem to discern in some quarters of psychology a growing obscurantist tendency — partly anti-empirical but also even at times antirational — which relies upon the valuable and insightful writings of Kuhn and Polanyi[14] for what I can only characterize as nefarious purposes. It would be unfortunate indeed if efforts to objectify psychoanalytic evidence and inference were abandoned or watered down because of a comfortable reliance on such generalizations as "Scientists have commitments," "We often must stick to a theory for want of a better," "You have to know what you are looking for in order to observe fruitfully," "There is no such thing as a pure observational datum, utterly uninfluenced by one's frame of reference." These are all true and important statements, although the last one needs careful explication and limitation. I do not think general comments of this nature are very helpful in deciding how much an analyst subtly shapes the analysand's discourse by the timing of his interventions ("uncontrolled input"), or whether he classifies a bit of speech as "anal" in a theoretically dogmatic manner ("observer bias in recording output"). If the exciting developments in contemporary philosophy of science are tendentiously employed for obscurantist purposes, to avoid answering perfectly sensible and legitimate criticisms, it would be most unfortunate. The good old positivist questions "What do you mean," "How do you know" are still very much in order, and cannot be ruled out of order by historical findings about where Einstein got his ideas! "Millikan relied upon a lot of physical theory, treated as unproblematic, when he 'observed' the charge on the electron" is a correct statement of the case. But such a statement is not, most emphatically *not*, on all fours with "Blauberman[15] is a qualified psychoanalyst, therefore we can rely upon his use of psychoanalytic theory when he classifies a patient's discourse as phallic-intrusive." What one *observes* in the psychoanalytic session is words, postures, gestures, intonation; everything else is inferred. I think the "lowest level" inferences should be the main object of study for the time being — we should be objectifying and quantifying "low-level theoretical" statements like "Patient is currently anxious, and the thematic content is hostile toward his therapist," rather than highly theoretical statements like "He has superego lacunae" or "His dammed-up libido is flowing back to anal channels." In the process of such objectifying-and-quantifying research, I can think of no better methodological prescription than the one with which Aristotle sets the standards of conceptual rigor as he begins his considerations of ethics, "It is the mark of an educated man to look for precision in each class of things just so far as the nature of the subject admits." No more — but no less, either.

Notes

1. K. R. Popper, *The Logic of Scientific Discovery* (New York: Basic Books, 1959); *Conjectures and Refutations* (New York: Basic Books, 1962).

2. But see F. Wilson, "Is Operationism Unjust to Temperature?" *Synthese*, 18 (1968): 394–422; "Definition and Discovery: I, II," *British Journal for the Philosophy of Science*, 18 (1967): 287–303, and 19 (1967): 43–56.

3. Following the late, great philosopher Arthur Pap, "Reduction Sentences and Open Concepts," *Methodos*, 5 (1953): 3–30; *Semantics and Necessary Truth* (New Haven, Conn.: Yale University Press, 1958). See also L. J. Cronbach and P. E. Meehl, "Construct Validity in Psychological Tests," *Psychological Bulletin*, 52 (1955): 281–302.

4. Popper, *The Logic of Scientific Discovery* and *Conjectures and Refutations*; and see M. Bunge, ed., *The Critical Approach: Essays in Honor of Karl R. Popper* (New York: Free Press, 1964).

5. H. Reichenbach, *Experience and Prediction* (Chicago: University of Chicago Press, 1938), but see I. Lakatos, "Criticism and the Methodology of Scientific Research Programmes," *Proceedings of the Aristotelian Society*, 69 (1968): 149–86.

6. An algorithm for which, says Lakatos, p. 324, is precluded by Church's theorem. I. Lakatos, "Changes in the Problem of Inductive Logic," in I. Lakatos, ed., *The Problem of Inductive Logic* (Amsterdam: North-Holland, 1968), pp. 315–417.

7. Else Frenkel-Brunswik, "Psychoanalysis and the Unity of Science," *Proceedings of the American Academy of Arts and Sciences*, 80 (1954): 271–350.

8. See W. Rozeboom, "The Fallacy of the Null-Hypothesis Significance Test," *Psychological Bulletin*, 67 (1960): 416–28; D. Bakan, "The Test of Significance in Psychological Research," *Psychological Bulletin*, 66 (1966): 423–37; P. E. Meehl "Theory-Testing in Psychology and Physics: A Methodological Paradox," *Philosophy of Science*, 34 (1967): 103–15; D. T. Lykken, "Statistical Significance in Psychological Research," *Psychological Bulletin*, 70 (1968): 151–59.

9. P. K. Feyerabend, "Attempt at a Realistic Interpretation of Experience," *Proceedings of the Aristotelian Society*, 58 (1958): 143–70; "On the Interpretation of Scientific Theories," *Proceedings of the Twelfth Congress of Philosophy* (Venice and Padua), 5 (1958), 151–59; "Explanation, Reduction, and Empiricism," in H. Feigl and G. Maxwell, eds., *Minnesota Studies in the Philosophy of Science*, vol. III, *Scientific Explanation, Space, and Time* (Minneapolis: University of Minnesota Press, 1962), pp. 28–97; "Problems of Microphysics," in R. G. Colodny, ed., *Frontiers of Science and Philosophy* (Pittsburgh: University of Pittsburgh Press, 1962), pp. 189–283; "How to Be a Good Empiricist—A Plea for Tolerance in Matters Epistemological," in B. Baumrin, ed., *Philosophy of Science: The Delaware Seminar*, vol. 2 (New York: Wiley, 1963), pp. 3–39; "Realism and Instrumentalism: Comments on the Logic of Factual Support," in Bunge, ed., *The Critical Approach: Essays in Honor of Karl R. Popper*, pp. 280–308; "Problems of Empiricism," in R. G. Colodny, ed., *Beyond the Edge of Certainty* (Englewood Cliffs, N.J.: Prentice-Hall, 1965), pp. 145–260; "Reply to Criticism," in R. S. Cohen and M. W. Wartofsky, eds., *Boston Studies in the Philosophy of Science*, vol. II (New York: Humanities, 1965), pp. 223–61; "Review [of Nagel's *Structure of Science*]," *British Journal for the Philosophy of Science*, 17 (1966): 237–49; "On the Improvement of the Sciences and the Arts, and the Possible Identity of the Two," in R. S. Cohen and M. W. Wartofsky, eds., *Boston Studies in the Philosophy of Science*, vol. III (Dordrecht: Reidel, 1968), pp. 387–415; "Problems of Empiricism, II," in R. G. Colodny, ed., *The Nature and Functions of Scientific Theories* (Pittsburgh: University of Pittsburgh Press, 1971); "Pro-Parmenides: A Defense of Parmenidean Apologies" (forthcoming); I. Lakatos, "Criticism and the Methodology of Scientific Research Programmes," *Proceedings of the Aristotelian Society*, 69 (1968): 149–86; "Changes in the Problem of Inductive Logic," in Lakatos, ed., *The Problem of Inductive Logic*, pp. 315–417; "Falsification and the Methodology of Scientific Research Programmes," in I. Lakatos and A. Musgrave, eds., *Criti-*

cism and the Growth of Knowledge (Cambridge: Cambridge University Press, 1970); G. Maxwell, "Corroboration without Demarcation," in P. A. Schilpp, ed., *The Philosophy of Karl Popper* (LaSalle, Ill.: Open Court, 1974).

10. J. R. Platt, "Strong Inference," *Science,* 146 (1964): 347-53; but see E. M. Hafner and S. Presswood, "Strong Inference and Weak Interactions," *Science*, 149 (1964): 503-10.

11. But see the distinction between $Popper_0$, $Popper_1$, and $Popper_2$ in Lakatos, "Criticism and the Methodology of Scientific Research Programmes."

12. K. R. Popper, "Rationality and the Search for Invariants," address to International Colloquium on Philosophy of Science, July 11, 1965.

13. To get the feel of them I recommend reading of P. K. Feyerabend, "Pro-Parmenides: A Defense of Parmenidean Apologies"; also "Realism and Instrumentalism: Comments on the Logic of Factual Support."

14. T. S. Kuhn, *The Structure of Scientific Revolutions* (Chicago: University of Chicago Press, 1962); and M. Polanyi, *Personal Knowledge* (London: Routledge and Kegan Paul, 1958).

15. Lillian Ross, "The Ordeal of Doctor Blauberman," *New Yorker*, 37 (May 13, 1961): 39-48; reprinted in Lillian Ross, *Vertical and Horizontal* (New York: Simon and Schuster, 1963).

11

Subjectivity in Psychoanalytic Inference: The Nagging Persistence of Wilhelm Fliess's Achensee Question

An alternative subtitle to this essay, which my non-Freudian Minnesota colleagues urged upon me, would have been, "Whose mind does the mind-reader read?" To motivate discussion of a topic not deemed important by some today, consider the story of the last "Congress" between Freud and Fliess, the rupture of their relationship at Achensee in the summer of 1900—the last time the two men ever met, although an attenuated correspondence continued for a couple of years more. Setting aside the doubtless complex psychodynamics, and the prior indications (from both content and density of correspondence) that the relationship was deteriorating, I focus on the intellectual content of the final collision. Fliess had attacked Freud by saying that Freud was a "thought reader" who read his own thoughts into the minds of his patients. Freud correctly perceived that this choice of content for the attack was deadly, that it went for the jugular. Freud's letter to Fliess after the meeting (Freud 1954) indicates that Fliess had written, apparently to soften the blow of the criticism, something about "magic," which Freud again refused to accept and referred to as "superfluous plaster to lay to your doubts about thought reading" (p. 330). A year later Freud is still focusing on the thought-reading accusation, and writes, "In this you came to the limit of your penetration, you take sides against me and tell me that 'the thought-reader merely reads his own thoughts into other people,' *which deprives my work of all its value* [italics added]. If I am such a one, throw my everyday-life [the parapraxis book] unread into the wastepaper basket" (p. 334). In a subsequent letter Freud quotes himself as having exclaimed at Achensee, "But you're undermining the whole value of my work" (p. 336). He says that an interpretation of Fliess's behavior made the latter uncomfortable, so that he was

Expansion of a paper read at the Confirmation Conference; an earlier version was prepared for and presented in the Lindemann Lecture Series celebrating the 25th anniversary of the founding of the Institute for Advanced Psychological Studies at Adelphi University (March 11, 1977).

"ready to conclude that the 'thought-reader' perceives nothing in others but merely projects his own thoughts into them . . . *and you must regard the whole technique as just as worthless as the others do*" (p. 337, italics added).

Not to belabor the point, it seems that when Fliess wanted to hurt, he knew precisely what was the tender spot, and so did Freud. So that in addressing myself to this vexed topic of the subjectivity of psychoanalytic inference, I am at least in good company in thinking it important. Surely it is strange that four-fifths of a century after the publication of the *Interpretation of Dreams* it is possible for intelligent and clinically experienced psychologists to reiterate Fliess's Achensee question, and it is not easy to answer it.

One has the impression that the epistemology of psychoanalytic inference is less emphasized today than it was in Freud's writings, or in the discussions as recorded in the minutes of the Vienna Psychoanalytic Society. Despite the scarcity of psychoanalytic tapes and protocols (relative to, say, Rogersian and rational-emotive modes), and the lack of any verbatim recordings from the early days, it seems safe to say that the kinds of inferences to unconscious *content* and *life history episodes* that so fascinated Freud, and played the dominant role in his technique, are much less emphasized today. We cannot ignore the fact that Freud considered the dream book his best book. Why is there less emphasis upon discerning the hidden meaning, whether in the restrictive sense of "interpretation" or the more complicated sense of a "construction," than there used to be? I suppose one reason is the tendency among analysts to say, "Well, we don't worry as much about it, because we know the answer." The trouble with that is that there are *two* groups in American psychology who think we now "know the answer," and their answers are very different, consisting of the Freudian answers and the non-Freudian answers. Nor are the non-Freudian answers found only among experimentalists or behaviorists or dust-bowl psychometrists. They are found widely among practitioners and psychotherapy teachers.

One source of the lessened attention to psychoanalytic evidence is the long-term shift—especially complicated because of Freud's never having written the promised treatise on technique—from the original Breuer-Freud abreaction-cartharsis under hypnosis, to the pressure technique focusing upon specific symptoms, to the more passive free association (but still emphasizing the content of the impulse defended against or the memory repressed), to resistance interpretation and, finally, the heavy focus on interpretation of the transference resistance. So that today a large part of analytic intervention is directed at handling the momentary transference, aiming to verbalize the patient's current transference phenomenology with interpretations that are hardly distinguishable from a Rogersian reflection during Rogers's "classical nondirective" period. Such sessions sound and read uninteresting to me. My first analyst was Vienna trained in the late twenties and my second was a product of the Columbia Psychoanalytic

Clinic under Rado's aegis, and both spent quite a bit of effort on a variety of interpretations and constructions, the Radovian very actively.

Perhaps the seminal papers of Wilhelm Reich on character analysis — despite Reich's own objection to analysts simply "floating in the patient's productions" and "permitting the development of a chaotic situation" or as Fenichel somewhere puts it, "communicating intermittently and unselectively various thoughts that occur as they listen" — nevertheless had the long-term effect, because they focused on resistance and specifically on the characterological resistances as interferences with obedience to the Fundamental Rule, of narrowing interpretive interventions almost wholly to varying forms of the question, "How are you feeling toward me right now?"

The playing down of the importance of old-fashioned interpreting and constructing I see, perhaps wrongly, as related to an oddity in the views expressed by some well-known institute-trained analysts who, though in good standing with the American Psychoanalytic Society, adopt strange positions. Take Dr. Judd Marmor, whose views are expressed in the preface to the huge tome he edited, *Modern Psychoanalysis: New Directions and Perspectives* (Marmor 1968). Before touching gingerly on the topic of nonmedical analysts and considering ambivalently the nature and purpose of the training analysis, he has told us that modern psychoanalysis builds upon the great work of that genius Freud, whose followers we are, and who discovered for the first time a powerful and truly scientific way of investigating the human mind. But we are also told that of course today the classical psychoanalytic technique is not used much because it doesn't work, and that the constructs in Freud's psychoanalytic theory need not be taken very seriously. It is clear that Dr. Marmor is jealous of the designation "psychoanalyst" and "psychoanalysis," but I find it hard to see why. An imaginary analogy: Suppose I tell you that I am a microscopist, that I stand in the succession of that great genius, the founder of true scientific microscopy, Jan van Leeuwenhoek, upon whose discoveries, made by means of the microscope, we contemporary microscopists build our work. Nobody practices microscopy, or is entitled to label himself "a microscopist," who has not attended one of our van Leeuwenhoekian night schools. Of course we no longer use the microscope, since it doesn't work as an instrument; and the little animals that van Leeuwenhoek reported seeing by the use of this device do not exist. What would we think of such a position? It seems to me incoherent. One can argue that if our practice consists almost entirely of handling the moment-to-moment transference phenomenology that occurs during interviews, then the study of Freud's writings is largely a waste of time in preparation for practice of psychoanalytic therapy, and should be classed along with requirements that one study brain physiology or correlational statistics, as tribal educational hurdles for the coveted Ph.D. or M.D. degree that must be met, pointlessly, by would-be psychotherapists! One recalls Carl Rogers's famous view, pushed by him toward the end of World War II, that it takes only a few weeks of intensive training in client-centered therapy to become skillful at it and that most of what therapists study in medical school or graduate school is a waste of time.

I have taken somewhat too long on these preliminary remarks, but I wished to sketch the historical and current sociological context in which Fliess's question is, I think wrongly, often set aside. I must also mention four matters I am *not* considering here, although all of them have great interest and importance. First, I am not concerned to discuss the therapeutic efficacy of classical analysis or psychoanalytically oriented therapy, on which my views are complicated, especially since in recent years I have been doing quite a bit of modified RET (Rational Emotive Therapy), and only recently returned to mixing RET with a modified psychoanalytic approach. Rational emotive therapy and behavior modification are probably the treatments of choice for 80 or 90 percent of the clientele. This view is not incompatible with a view I hold equally strongly, that if you are interested in learning about your mind, there is no procedure anywhere in the running with psychoanalysis. Second, I am not going to address myself to the validation of metapsychological concepts, even though I think that a view like Marmor's is in need of clarification. Third, I'm not going to talk about the *output* aspect of analytic interpretation, i.e., the timing and wording of interventions, but only about the *input* (cognitive) side, i.e., the way one construes the material, whatever he decides to do with it, including the usual decision to wait. Finally, I shall set aside entirely the experimental and statistical studies, not because I think them unimportant but because I am not very familiar with them except through summaries such as the recent paper by Lloyd H. Silverman in the *American Psychologist* (1976). I believe a person would not become convinced of the truth or falsity of the first-level theoretical corpus of psychoanalysis solely on the basis of the experimental and statistical studies, and that most psychologists who are convinced that there is a good deal in psychoanalytic theory have become convinced mainly by their own experience with it as patient and therapist.

It goes without saying, for anyone familiar with current philosophy of science, that there is a complicated two-way relationship between facts and theories. On the one hand, we can say that clinical experience with psychoanalytic material provides some sort of prior probability when we come to evaluate the experimental and correlational evidence, both when it's positive and when it's adverse; and, on the other hand, whatever general principles can come from the study of either human beings or animals, even of the somewhat attenuated, distantly related kind reported in Robert R. Sears's (1943) classic survey on objective studies of psychoanalytic concepts, can in turn give support to inferences made during the psychoanalytic session itself. My own view, despite my Minnesota training, is that if you want to find out what there is to psychoanalysis, the psychoanalytic hour is still the best place to look. It would be strange — although not logically contradictory — to say that we have in that hour a set of important discoveries that a certain man and a few of his coworkers hit upon while listening to what patients said about their dreams and symptoms and so on, under special instruction for how to talk (and even a prescribed physical posture while talking); but that setting is not a good one for investigating the matters allegedly brought to light! So: The rest of my remarks will deal wholly with the subjectivity in inferences reached from the verbal and expressive behavior the patient displays during the psychoanalytic hour.

I realize that I have not given a clear statement of the problem, and it's not easy. The patient speaks; I listen with "evenly hovering attention" (and background reliance upon my own unconscious). From time to time I experience a cognitive closure that, its content worded, characterizes an inferred latent psychological state or event in the patient's mind. For example, it occurs to me that the patient is momentarily afraid of offending me, or that the dream he reported at the beginning of the session expresses a homoerotic wish, or that the Tyrolean hat in the manifest content is connected with his uncle who wore one, and the like. The essence of psychoanalytic listening is listening for that which is not manifest (Reik 1948), for an inferred (and theoretical) entity in the other's mind that has then imputed to it a causal status. Fliess's Achensee question is: "What credentials does this kind of alleged knowledge bring? When you listen to a person talk, you can cook up all sorts of plausible explanations for why he says what he says. I accuse you, therefore, of simply putting your own thoughts into the mind of the helpless patient."

The epistemological scandal is that we do not have a clear and compelling answer to this complaint eighty years after Fliess voiced it, and a century after Josef Breuer discovered his "chimney sweeping" hypnocathartic technique on Anna O. We may motivate the topic as one of great theoretical interest, which I confess is my main one, as it was Freud's. From the clinical standpoint, however, we "mind-healers" do have the long-debated question as to whether, and how, processes labeled "insight," "uncovering," and "self-understanding" work therapeutically. Non-Freudian therapists like Joseph Wolpe, Albert Ellis, and Carl Rogers have argued plausibly that psychoanalytic efficacy (marginal as it is) is an incidental byproduct of something other than what the analyst and the patient think they are mainly doing. Whatever the merits of these explanations, it is difficult to answer questions about whether and how a correct interpretation or construction works, if one has no independent handle on the epistemological question, "How do we know that it is correct?" In putting it that way I am of course referring to its content correctness and not to its technical correctness, not to the output aspect of the analyst's interpretation. It would be strange, would it not, if we were able to investigate the technically relevant components of the output side of analytic interpretation without having some independent test of its cognitive validity? That is, how would I research the question whether, for instance, summary interpretations at the end of the session are, on the average, more efficacious than tentative ones dropped along the way, (cf. Glover 1940), if the problem of inexact interpretation or totally erroneous "barking up the wrong tree" were wholly unsettled? I do not advance the silly thesis that one must know *for sure* whether the main content of an interpretation is cognitively valid before investigating these other matters. But without some probabilistic statement as to content correctness, it is hard to imagine an investigation into the comparative therapeutic efficacy of the two interpretative tactics. The usual statement that an interpretation is "psychologically valid" when it results in a detectable dynamic and economic change may be all right as a rule of thumb, but it does not satisfy a Fliessian critic, and I cannot convince myself that it should. Although there occur striking experiences on the couch or behind it in which the quality, quantity, and temporal immediacy of an effect will persuade all but the most anti-Freudian skeptic that something is going on, these are not the mode. Furthermore, "Something important happened here" is hardly the same as "*What* happened here is that a properly timed and phrased interpretation also had substantive validity and hence the impulse-defense equilibrium underwent a marked quantitative change."

There are few phenomena—and I do mean *phenomena*, that is, virtually uninterpreted raw observations of speech and gesture, not even first-level thematic inferences—that are so persuasive to the skeptic when he is himself on the couch, or so convincing (even when related without tape recordings or verbatim protocol) to clinical students, as the *sudden* and *marked* alteration in some clearly manifested mental state or ongoing behavior immediately following an analytic interpretation. For readers without psychoanalytic experience, I present a couple of brief examples.

When I was in analysis, I was walking about a half block from the University Hospitals to keep my analytic appointment and was in a more or less "neutral" mood, neither up nor down and with no particular line of thought occupying me, but rather observing the cars and people as they passed. I perceived approaching me a man and woman in their late thirties, both with distinctly troubled facial expressions and the woman weeping. The man was carrying a brown paper sack and over his arm a large Raggedy Ann doll. It is not, of course, in the least surprising (or requiring any special psychodynamic interpretation) that the thought occurred to me from their behavior, the doll, and the fact that they were leaving the University Hospital, that a child was very ill or possibly had just died. It would not be pathological for a person of ordinary human sympathy, and especially a parent, to feel a twinge of sympathetic grieving at such a sight. That is not what befell me on this occasion, however. I was suddenly flooded with a deep and terrible grieving and began to weep as I walked. I don't mean by that that I was a little teary; I mean that I had difficulty restraining audible sobs as I passed people, and that tears were pouring down my face. I told myself this was absurd, I must be reacting to something else, and so on and so forth, none of which self-talk had the slightest discernible effect. On the elevator to go up to my analyst's office were two of our clinical psychology trainees who looked at me somewhat embarrassedly, saying "Good morning, Dr. Meehl," vainly trying to appear as if they had not noticed the state I was in. Even under those circumstances, in an elevator full of people, I literally could not control the weeping, including muffled sobbing sounds. I did not have to wait more than a minute or two for my analyst to appear. Trying to ignore the puzzled expression of a psychiatric social worker whose hour preceded mine, I went in, lay down, and at that point began to sob so loudly that I was unable to begin speaking. After acquiring enough control to talk, I described briefly the people I had met, whereupon my analyst (who, while he had had analysis with Helene Deutsch and Nathan Ackerman, had been exposed to strong Radovian influences in his training institute) intercepted with the brief question, "Were you harsh with Karen [my five-year-old daughter] this morning?" This question produced an immediate, abrupt, and total cessation of the inner state and its external signs. (I had spoken crossly to Karen at the breakfast table for some minor naughtiness, and remembered leaving the house, feeling bad that I hadn't told her I was sorry before she went off to kindergarten.) I emphasize for the nonclinical reader, what readers who have had some couch time will know, that the important points here are the *immediacy* and the disappearance of any problem of *control*—no need for counterforces, "inhibition" of the state, or its overt expression. That is, the moment the analyst's words were perceived, the affective state immediately vanished. I don't suppose anyone has experienced this kind of phenomenon in his own analysis without finding it one of the most striking direct behavioral and introspective evidences of the concepts of "mental conflict," "opposing psychic forces," and "unconscious influences"—the way in which a properly timed and formulated interpretation (sometimes!) produces an immediate dynamic and economic change, as the jargon has it.

Comparable experiences when one is behind the couch rather than on it, usually carry less punch. The reason is not that analysis is a "religious experience," as my behaviorist friends object when I point it out, but that the analysand is connected with his inner events more closely and in more modalities than the analyst is, which fact confers an evidentiary weight of a different qualitative sort from what is given by the analyst's theoretical knowledge and his relative freedom from the patient's defensive maneuvers. True, it is generally recognized that we see considerably fewer "sudden transformations" today than apparently were found in the early days of the analytic movement. We do not know to what extent this reduced incidence of sudden lifting of repression with immediate effects, especially dramatic and permanent symptomatic relief, is attributable to the cultural influence of psychoanalytic thinking itself (a development Freud predicted in one of his prewar papers). There are doubtless additional cultural reasons for changes in the modal character neurosis. There was perhaps some clinical peculiarity (that still remains to be fathomed) in some of the clientele studied during the early days, such that true "Breuer-Freud repression," the existence of a kind of "cold abscess in the mind" that could be lanced by an analytic interpretation-cum-construction that lifted the repression all at once, was commoner in the 1890s than today. These are deep questions, still poorly understood. But it remains true that from time to time symptomatic phenomena that have been present for months or years, and have shown no appreciable alteration despite the non-interpretative adjuvant and auxiliary influences of the therapeutic process (e.g. reassurance, desensitization, and the mere fact that you are talking to a helper) do occur and help to maintain therapist confidence in the basic Freudian ideas.

I recall a patient who had among her presenting complaints a full-blown physician phobia, which had prevented her from having a physical examination for several years, despite cogent medical reasons why she should have done so. She was a professionally trained person who realized the "silliness" of the phobia and its danger to her physical health, and attributed the phobia—no doubt rightly, but only in part—to the psychic trauma of a hysterectomy. Her efforts to overcome it were unsuccessful. Repeatedly she had, after working herself up to a high state of drive and talking to herself and her husband about the urgency of an examination, started to call one or another physician (one of whom was also a trusted personal friend who knew a lot about her) but found herself literally unable to complete even the dialing of the telephone number. Now, after seventy-five or eighty sessions, during which many kinds of material had been worked through and her overall anxiety level markedly reduced, the doctor phobia itself remained completely untouched. From themes and associations, I had inferred, but not communicated, a specific experience of a physical examination when she was a child in which the physician unearthed the fact of her masturbation, which had unusually strong conflictful elements because of the rigid puritanical religiosity of her childhood home (and of the physician also). During a session in which fragments of visual and auditory memory and a fairly pronounced intense recall of the doctor's examining table and so on came back to her, and in which she had intense anxiety as well as a feeling of nausea (sufficient to lead her to ask me to move a wastebasket over in case she should have to vomit), she recalled, with only minimal assistance on my part, the physician's question and her answer. This occurred about ten minutes before the end of the hour. She spent the last few minutes vacillating between thinking that she had been "docile," that I had implanted this memory, but then saying that she recalled clearly enough, in enough sense modalities, to have a concrete certainty that it was, if imperfectly recalled, essentially accurate. As one would expect in a sophisticated patient of this sort, she saw the experience as the earlier traumatic happening that potentiated the effect of the adult hysterectomy and led to her doctor phobia. She called me up the following morning to report cheerily, although a bit breathlessly, that she had refrained from making a doctor's appointment after the session yesterday, wondering whether her feeling of fear would return. But when, on awakening in the morning, she detected only a faint anxiety, she found it possible without any vacillation to make a phone call, and now reported that she was about to leave for her appointment and was confident that she would be able to keep it. I think most fairminded persons would agree that it takes an unusual skeptical resistance for us to say that this step-function in clinical status was "purely a suggestive effect," or a reassurance effect, or due to some other transference leverage or whatever (75th hour!) rather than that the remote memory was truly repressed and the lifting of repression efficacious.

Some argue simply that "clinical experience will suffice to produce conviction in an open-minded listener." We are entitled to say, with Freud, that if one does not conduct the session in such and such a way, then he will very likely not hear the kind of thing that he might find persuasive. But the skeptic then reminds us of a number of persons of high intelligence and vast clinical experience, who surely cannot be thought unfamiliar with the way to conduct a psychoanalytic session, who subsequently came to reject sizable portions of the received theoretical corpus, and in some instances (e.g., Wilhelm Reich, Albert Ellis, Melitta Schmideberg, and Kenneth Mark Colby) abandoned the psychoanalytic enterprise. Nobody familiar with the history of organic medicine can feel comfortable simply repeating to a skeptic, "Well, all I can say is that my clinical experience shows . . . ."

The methodological danger usually labelled generically "suggestion," that of "imposing theoretical preconceptions" by "mind-reading one's own thoughts into the patient's mind," is itself complex. An experimental or psychometric psychologist (I am or have been both) can distinguish four main sources of theory-determined error in the psychoanalytic process. First, *content implantation*, in which memories, thoughts, impulses, and even defenses are explicitly "taught" to the patient via interpretation, construction, and leading questions. Second, *selective intervention*, in which the analyst's moment-to-moment technical decisions to speak or remain silent, to reflect, to ask for clarifications, to call attention to a repetition, similarity, or allusion, to request further associations, to go back to an earlier item, etc., can operate either as *differential reinforcement* of verbal behavior classes (a more subtle, inexplicit form of implantation!) or as a *biased evidence-sifter*. By this latter I mean that even if the patient's subsequent verbalizations were uninfluenced by such interventions, what the analyst has thus collected as *his* data surely has been. Third, on the "input" side, there is the purely perceptual-cognitive aspect of subjectivity in discerning the "red thread," the thematic allusions running through the material. (As my Skinnerian wife says, we want the analyst to *discern* the "red thread," we don't want him to spin it and weave it in!) Fourth, supposing the theme-tracing to be correct, we make a *causal* inference; and what entitles us to infer the continued existence and operation of an unconscious background mental process *guiding* the associations (Murray's *regnancy*)? Such a construction does not follow immediately from correct detection of a theme *in* the associations. I focus the remainder of my remarks almost wholly on the third of these dangers, the subjective (critics would say "arbitrary") construing of what the verbal material *means*, "alludes to," "is about."

I do not trouble myself to answer superbehaviorist attacks, such as those that say that science can deal only with observables, hence an unconscious fantasy is inherently an illicit construct; since these attacks, besides being dogmatic, are intellectually vulgar, historically inaccurate, and philosophically uninformed. *The crunch is epistemological, not ontological.* The problem with first-level psychoanalytic constructs is not that they are not observable as test-item responses or muscle twitches or brain waves, but that their inferential status, the way in which they are allegedly supported by the data base of the patient's words and gestures, is in doubt.

I also reject, in the most high-handed manner I can achieve, the typical American academic psychologists' objection that psychoanalysis is not "empirical," which is based upon a failure to look up the word "empirical" in the dictionary. There is, of course, no justification for identifying the empirical with the quantitative/experimental other than either behaviorist or psychometric prejudice, nor to identify the quantitative/experimental with the scientific, nor to identify any of these with what is, in some defensible sense, "reasonable to believe." These mistaken synonymies involve such elementary errors in thinking about human knowledge generally, and even scientific knowledge in particular, that I refuse to bother my head with them.

My late colleague Grover Maxwell used to ask me why I think there is a special problem here, once we have shed the simplistic American behaviorist identification: reasonable = empirical = quantitative/experimental = scientific. Do we not recognize the intellectual validity of documentary disciplines like law, history, archaeology, and so on, despite the fact that they (with interesting exceptions, such as the cliometrists) proceed essentially as we do in psychoanalysis? Or, for that matter, what about all of the decisions, judgments, and beliefs we have in common life, such as that we could probably lend money to our friend Smith, or that our wife is faithful to us, or that one Swedish car is better than another?

An analogy between psychoanalytic inference and decision making or beliefs adopted in "ordinary life" is defective for at least three reasons, and probably more.

Most "ordinary life" beliefs do not involve high-order theorizing, but concern fairly simple connections between specific happenings, easily and reliably identified. Herewith a list of ten circumstances that affect the degree of confidence or skepticism with which nonquantified impressions from clinical experience should be assessed:

1. Generalized observations about a variate that is of a "simple, physical, quickly-decidable" nature are more to be trusted on the basis of common experience, clinical impressions, anecdotal evidence, "literary psychology," or the fireside inductions generally (essay 15, this volume) than claims about variates, however familiar to us from common life or sophisticated clinical experience, that are not "observable" in a fairly strong and strict sense of that slippery word. Thus shared clinical experience that persons in a grand mal epileptic seizure fall down is more dependable than the (equally shared) experience that schizotypes readily act rejected by a clumsy therapist's remark in an interview. The fact that an experimental animal stops breathing is more trustworthy protocol, absent solid data recording, than the "fact" that an experimental animal shows "anxious exploring behavior." We would think it odd if somebody published an article proving, with scientific instrumentation and significance tests, that if you hold a bag of kittens under water for an hour, they will be dead!

2. Contrasted with the preceding are three main categories of not simply observable variates that are readily inferred by us, both in common life and in clinical practice: (a) Inferred inner states or events ("anxiety," "dependency," "hostile," "seductive," "manipulative," "passive-aggressive," "anhedonic," "guarded," "paranoid"); (b) clusters, composites, behavior summaries — more generally *traits*, a trait being conceived as an empirically correlated family of content-related dispositions; and (c) inferred external events and conditions, either current but not actually under the clinician's observation (e.g., "patient is under work stress") or historical (e.g., "patient is obviously from a lower-class social background").

3. Even simple physical observables, however, can sometimes be distorted by theory, prejudice, or otherwise developed habits of automatic inference. A classic example is Goring's study of the English convict in which estimated heights of foreheads were positively correlated with intelligence as estimated by prison personnel, although the estimated intelligence (like the estimated forehead height) did not correlate with *measured* forehead heights! The interesting methodological point here is that guards and prison officials could agree quite reliably on how bright a man is, intelligence being a socially relevant property and one that we know (from many data in educational, military, and industrial settings) has an interjudge reliability of .50 or better, so that pooled judgments can have a high reliability; but because these persons shared the folklore belief that high forehead goes with brains, they apparently "perceived" a prisoner's forehead as higher when they thought the prisoner was bright.

4. If the event being correlated is something strikingly unusual, such as an occurrence or trait that deviates five standard deviations from the mean in populations with which the observer is accustomed to dealing, it is obviously going to be easier to spot relationships validly.

5. States, events, or properties that fluctuate spontaneously over time are hard to correlate with causative factors such as intervention, compared to those that do not fluctuate much "spontaneously" (that is, absent intervention) over time.

6. States, properties, or dimensions that normally move monotonically in a certain direction over time (e.g., patients usually get progressively sicker if they have untreated pernicious anemia) are more easily relatable than those that show numerous spontaneous "ups and downs" (e.g., spontaneous remissions and exacerbations in diseases such as schizophrenia or multiple sclerosis). The long list of alleged beneficial treatments for multiple sclerosis that have been pushed enthusiastically by some clinicians and have subsequently been abandoned as enthusiasm dies out or controlled quantitative studies are performed, is due not only to the urgency of trying to help people with this dread illness, but also to the normal occurrence of spontaneous remissions and exacerbations, the considerable variability in interphase times, in their severity, and in the functional scarring following an acute episode of this illness (see Meehl 1954, p. 136).

7. The more causal influences are operative, the harder it will be to unscramble what is operating upon what. In the case of cross-sectional correlation data in the social sciences, the intractability of this methodological problem is so great as to have resulted in a special methodological approach, known as path analysis, disputes about whose conceptual power in unscrambling the causal connections still persist to the extent that some competent scholars doubt that it has any widespread validity.

8. If a causal influence shows a sizable time lag to exert its effect, which is often true in medical and behavioral interventions, it is harder to correlate validly than if its effect, when present, is immediate. The other side of this coin is the tendency of minimal effects in behavior intervention to fade out with time. Differences in the impact of an educational procedure—such as the difference between two methods of teaching fractions to third graders—if it is barely statistically significant but not of appreciable size immediately after learning, the chances are good that the children's ability to do fractions problems two years later (let alone as adults) will not be different under the two teaching methods. Yet in opposition to this admitted tendency of interventions to fade out, we have some tendency—claimed but not well documented, if at all—for long-term influences of successful psychotherapeutic intervention to escape detection in immediate post-treatment assessment. Whatever the influence of these opposed tendencies, the point is that the existence of the first and the probability (at least in some cases) of the second greatly increase the difficulty of ascertaining an effect.

9. If the time lag between an influence and its consequence, whatever its av-

erage size, is highly variable among individuals (or over different occasions for the same individual), a valid covariation is harder to discern.

10. If there are important feedback effects between what we are trying to manipulate and the subsequent course of our manipulation, the relationships are harder to untangle, especially because there are likely to be sizable differences in the parameters of the feedback system.

More generally, a complicated and controversial topic deserving more discussion than the present context permits, we still do not have an adequate methodological formulation as to the evidentiary weight that ought rationally to be accorded the "clinical experience" of seasoned practitioners when it is not as yet corroborated by quantitative or experimental investigation that meets the usual "scientific" criteria for having formal "researched status." This problem is troublesome enough when the situation is that of practitioners asserting something on the basis of their clinical experience, which, when pressed, they can document only by what amount essentially to an educated guesser's anecdotes, whereas the "anecdotal method" is repudiated as an unacceptable method in any sophomore general psychology course! The problem is made worse when purportedly scientific research on the clinician's claims has been conducted and seems to be unfavorable to his generalization.

On the one side, it must be admitted that some laboratory or even field survey studies of clinical hypotheses are clumsy, naive, and unrealistic in one or more ways, so that one cannot fault a good clinician for dismissing them as irrelevant to what he intended to say. I think, for instance, of a silly study by some academic psychologist (whose familiarity with psychoanalysis must have been confined to reading one or two tertiary sources) who published a paper in a psychology journal alleging to refute Freud's idea of the Oedipal situation because a simple questionnaire item administered to college undergraduates asking whether they preferred their father to their mother, showed that both boys and girls preferred their mother but the latter more so. One can hardly blame Freud for not spending much time monitoring the journals of academic psychology in the 1920s if this is the kind of production they were coming up with. I think it appropriate, being myself both an experienced practitioner *and* a psychometric and experimental psychologist, to venture an opinion as to the main sources of this "pseudoscientific unrealism" on the part of some academics attempting to study a clinical conjecture. (I think it also fair to say that it happens less frequently today than it did, say, between World Wars I and II, during which time very few academic social scientists had any real firing-line experience with mental patients or with intensive psychotherapy.) First, the nonclinician literally fails to understand the clinician's theoretical conjecture with sufficient precision and depth to know what would constitute a reasonable statistical or experimental test of it. Of course, sometimes this is partly the fault of the clinician for not troubling to expound the theory with even that minimal degree of scientific rigor that the state of the art permits. Second, one can understand the essential features of the theory but make simplistic auxiliary assumptions, the most tempting of which is the reliance upon instruments that the clinician would probably not trust (the above undergraduate questionnaire being a horrible example). Third is the possibility that, although the instruments employed are adequate for the purpose, the particular psychological state of affairs is not qualitatively of the same nature or quantitatively as intense as that which the clinician had in mind; as, for example, paradigm studies of psychotherapy in which, rather than having a full-blown clinical phobia brought in by a suffering patient, one has a small-scale "artificial phobia" generated in the psychology laboratory. Fourth, clinicians are likely to do an inadequate job of characterizing the clientele, so that a selection of individuals from a population may yield an incidence of something whose base rate in that population is so different from that of the clinic that a statistically significant result is hard to achieve with only moderate statistical power. (How the clinician can have detected something here that the statistician can't is such a complicated question that I must forgo discussion of it here, but it deserves an article in its own right.)

Against all of these proclinical points must be a simple, clear, indisputable historical fact: In the history of the healing arts, whether organic medicine or psychological helping, there have been numerous diagnostic and therapeutic procedures that fully trained M.D.s or Ph.D.s, who were not quacks and who were honorable and dedicated professionals, have passionately defended, that have subsequently been shown to be inefficacious or even counterproductive. No informed scholar disputes this. I cannot see the following as anything but a form of intellectual dishonesty or carelessness: A person with a doctorate in psychology advocates a certain interpretation of neurosis on the basis of his clinical experience. He is challenged by another seasoned practitioner who has, like himself, interviewed, tested, and treated hundreds or maybe thousands of patients, and who is familiar with the conceptual system of the first clinician, but persists in not believing it, and denies the causal relations that the first clinician alleges. The first clinician persists in repeating "Well, of course, I *know* from my clinical experience that . . . ."

I suspect that this kind of cognitive aberration occurs partly because introductory psychology courses no longer emphasize the classic studies on the psychology of testimony, the psychology of superstitions, and the inaccuracy of personnel ratings from interviews and the like, which used to be a staple part of any decent psychology course when I was an undergraduate in the 1930s. It is absurd to pretend that because I received training in clinical psychology, I have thereby become immunized to the errors of observation, selection, recording, retention, and reporting, that are the universal curse on the human mind as a prescientific instrument. Nobody who knows anything about the history of organic medicine (remember venesection!) should find himself in such a ridiculous epistemological position as this. Fortunately, we do find statements about certain classes of patients agreed on by almost all clinicians (it is perfectionistic to require *all*, meaning "absolutely every single one") provided they have adequate clinical exposure and do not belong to some fanatical sect, *their diagnostic impressions being shared despite marked differences in their views on etiology and treatment*. Although consensus of experienced practitioners is strictly speaking neither a necessary nor sufficient condition for the truth—it would be as silly to say that here as to say it about consensus of dentists, attorneys, engineers or economists— presumably something that practitioners trained at different institutions and holding divergent opinions about, say, a certain mental disorder, agree upon is *on the average* likely to be more trustworthy as a clinical impression than something that only a bare majority agrees on, and still less so something that is held by only a minority. One says this despite realizing from history, statistics, or general epistemology that a group that's currently in a small minority may, in the event, turn out to have been right after all.

Suppose, for example, that two psychologists have each spent several thousand hours in long-term intensive psychotherapy of schizophrenics, either psychotic or borderline. They may disagree as to the importance of genetic factors or the potentiating impact of the battle-ax mother. But it would be hard to find *any* experienced clinician, of whatever theoretical persuasion, who would dispute the statement that schizophrenics have a tendency to oddities of thought and associated oddities in verbal expression. Even a clinician who has bought in on the labeling-theory nonsense and who doesn't think there is any such mental disease as schizophrenia (if there are some funny-acting people in the mental hospitals, they surely don't have anything wrong with their brains or genes—a view that it takes superhuman faith or ignorance of the research literature to hold at the present time), will hardly dispute that one of the main things that leads *other* wicked practitioners to attach the label "schizophrenia" is a fact that he himself has observed *in the people so labeled*; to wit, that they have funny ways of talking and thinking, and it's a kind of funniness that is different from what we hear in neurotics or people who are severely depressed or psychopathic or mentally deficient.

But there simply isn't any way of getting around the plain fact that individuals in the healing arts are not immune from overgeneralization and are sometimes recalcitrant in the presence of refuting evidence, even when the statistical or experimental study cannot be faulted on any of the clinical grounds given above. Everyone knows that this is true in the history of organic medicine (where, by and large, we expect the clinical phenomena to be relatively more objective and easier to observe than in a field like psychotherapy), so that for a long time physicians practiced venesection or administered medicinal substances that we now know have no pharmaceutical efficacy. Surely this should lead an honest psychotherapist to face the possibility that he might *think* that he is helping people or—the main question before us in the present paper—that he is making more correct than incorrect inferences from the patient's behavior, even though in reality he is not doing so, and is himself a victim of a large-scale institutionalized self-deception. Even a practitioner like myself who finds it impossible to really believe this about say, a well-interpreted dream, ought nevertheless to be willing to say in the metalanguage that it *could* be so. His inability to believe it belongs in the domain of biography or "impure pragmatics" rather than in science or inductive logic.

Several thousand people are today totally blind because they developed the disease called retrolental fibroplasia as a result of being overoxygenated as premature newborns. For twenty years or so, obstetricians and pediatricians debated hotly the merits of this allegedly "prophylactic" procedure. It was only when an adequate statistical analysis of the material was conducted by disinterested parties that the question was finally resolved. It is incredible to me that psychotherapists familiar with this kind of development in organic medicine nevertheless counter objections to psychotherapeutic interpretations by doggedly reiterating, "My clinical experience proves to my satisfaction that . . . ."

It is not easy to convey to the nonclinician reader how a seasoned experienced practitioner who has had plenty of diagnostic and therapeutic exposure to a certain clientele could come into collision with another one, without giving examples outside psychoanalysis. Consider, for instance, the widely-held view that the battle-ax mother (often called by the theory-laden term "schizophrenogenic mother," despite rather feeble quantitative support for her causal relevance) has a great deal to do with determining the psychopathology of schizophrenia and, perhaps, even its very occurrence. The point is that the clinicians who are convinced of her etiological importance have not made up the raw data, and this explains why other equally experienced clinicians skeptical of the schizophrenogenic mother hypothesis don't find that their (similar) clinical experience convinces them of the same etiological view. I have not talked to any experienced practitioner, whatever his views of schizophrenia or its optimal treatment, who disputes certain "observations" about the way schizophrenics talk when they get on the subject of their mother or subsequent mother figures. But collecting these chunks of verbal behavior about battle-ax mothers is several steps removed inferentially from the common (American) clinicians' conclusion that this patient is psychotic mainly because of the way his battle-ax mother treated him. There are half a dozen plausible factors tending to generate this kind of verbal behavior, and they are not incompatible, so that when taken jointly, it is easy to construct a statistical-causal model that will explain the widespread extent of this clinical experience by practitioners without assuming even the tiniest causal influence of the battle-ax mother syndrome upon the subsequent development of a schizophrenia (see Meehl 1972, pp. 370–71). For a more general discussion of the relationship of clinical or anecdotal generalizations to criticism and the difficulty of assessing the relative weight to be given to it in relation to more scientifically controlled studies, see essay 15, this volume, especially pp. 461–67.

Even those ordinary-life conclusions that are not themselves explicitly statistical nevertheless are often *based upon* experimental or statistical findings by somebody else. Sometimes these findings are known to us, sometimes we rely on reports of them because we have previously calibrated the authorities involved. Thus, for instance, in buying life insurance we rely upon actuarial tables constructed by insurance statisticians, and we also know that the law constrains what an insurance company can charge for a given type of policy on the basis of these statistics. The actuarial table's construction and interpretation is a highly technical business, beyond the insured's competence to evaluate. But he does not *need* to understand these technicalities in order (rationally) to buy life insurance.

In most ordinary-life examples, one is forced to make a decision by virtue of the situation, whereas a psychology professor is not forced to decide about psychoanalytic theory. If somebody replies to this by saying that the *practitioner* is forced to decide, that's not quite true, although it has a valid element. The practitioner is not forced to decide to proceed psychoanalytically in the first place; and pushing the point even farther back, the psychologist was not forced to be a psychotherapist (rather than, say, an industrial psychologist).

For these three reasons, the easy analogy of a psychoanalytic inference about an unconscious theme, or mechanism, or whatever, with those less-than-scientific, action-related inferences or assumptions we require in ordinary life, is weak, although not totally without merit.

Suppose one drops "ordinary life" as the analogy and takes instead some other nonexperimental, nonstatistical but technical scholarly domain, such as law or, usually, history. The evidence in a law court is perhaps the closest analogue to psychoanalytic inference, but inferences in history from fragmentary data and empirical lawlike statements that cannot be experimented on are also a good comparison. The analogy breaks down somewhat in the case of law, however, in that the application of legal concepts is not quite like an empirical theory, although the lawyer's inferences as to the fact situation are epistemologically similar to those of psychoanalytic inference.

A difficulty in relying on Aristotle's dictum about "precision insofar as subject matter permits" is that this rule doesn't tell us whether, or why, we ought to have a high intellectual esteem for a particular subject matter. If the subject matter permits only low-confidence, nonquantitative, impressionistic inferences, operating unavoidably in a framework not subjected to experimental tests in the laboratory, or even file-data statistical analysis, perhaps the proper conclusion is simply that we have a somewhat shoddy and prescientific discipline. Doubtless some physical scientists would say that about disciplines such as history, or the old-fashioned kind of political science, as well as psychoanalysis. In either case one cannot take very much heart from the analogy. It is, I fear, really a rather weak defense of psychoanalytic inference unless we can spell it out more.

However, an interesting point arises here in connection with the flabbiness of statistical significance testing as a research method. I think it can be shown—but I must leave it for another time—that the use of either a Popperian or a Bayesian way of thinking about a criminal case gives stronger probabilities than those yielded by null hypothesis testing. This is an important point: The fact of "explicit quantification," i.e., that we have a procedure for mechanically generating *probability numbers*, won't guarantee strong inference or precision, although it looks as if it does, and most psychologists seem to think it must. I am convinced that they are mistaken. The "precision" of null hypothesis testing is illusionary on several grounds, the following list being probably incomplete:

1. Precision of the tables used hinges upon the mathematical exactness of the formalism in their derivation, and we know that real biological and social measures don't precisely fill the conditions. That a statistical test or estimator is "reasonably robust" is, of course, no answer to this point, when precision is being emphasized.

2. Random-sampling fluctuations are all that these procedures take into account, whereas the most important source of error is systematic error because of the problem of validity generalization. Almost nothing we study in clinical psychology by the use of either significance tests (or estimation procedures with an associated confidence belt) is safely generalizable to even slightly different populations.

3. The biggest point is the logical distance between the statistical hypothesis and the substantive theory. For a discussion of this see Meehl (essay 1, this volume, pp. 27-37; Meehl 1967/1970; Lykken 1968; and Meehl 1954, pp. 11–14, Chapter 6, and passim).

As to the analogy of psychoanalytic inference with highly theoretical interpretive conjectures in history (e.g., hypotheses about the major factors leading to the fall of Rome, of which there are no fewer than seven, including that the elite all got lead poisoning from drinking wine out of those pewter vessels!), I find critics are as skeptical toward these as they are toward psychoanalysis. So that one doesn't get us very far, at most taking us past the first hurdle of a simplistic insistence that nothing can be "reasonable" or "empirical" unless based upon laboratory experiments or statistical correlations. We have to admit to the critic that not all psychoanalytic sessions are understandable, and even a session that is on the whole comprehensible has many individual items that remain mysterious, as Freud pointed out. We must also grant the point that physicians and psychologists who have certainly had the relevant clinical experiences—thousands of hours in some cases—have "fallen away" from the Freudian position, and claim to have rational arguments and evidence *from their clinical experience* for doing so. And finally, as a general epistemological point, we have to confess that human ingenuity is great, so that if you have loose enough criteria you can "explain anything."

It may help to ask, "Just *why* is there a problem here?" Why, in particular, do some of us find ourselves caught in the middle between, on the one hand, people who think there is no problem, that we know how to interpret, and that any seasoned practitioner has his kit of tools for doing so; and on the other, those skeptical people (e.g., Sir Karl Popper) who think our situation is conceptually hopeless because of a grossly uncritical methodology of inference? I can highlight the dilemma by examining Freud's jigsaw-puzzle analogy. The plain fact is that the jigsaw-puzzle analogy is false. It is false in four ways. There are four clearcut tests of whether we have put a jigsaw puzzle together properly. First, there must not be any extra pieces remaining; second, there must not be any holes in the fitted puzzle (Professor Salmon has pointed out to me that although this requirement holds for jigsaw puzzles, *provided all the pieces are present*, it is too strong for such cases as a broken urn reconstructed by an archaeologist, since a few "holes" due to unfound pieces do not appreciably reduce our confidence in the reconstruction); third, each piece has to fit cleanly and easily into a relatively complicated contour provided by the adjacent pieces; finally, when a piece is fitted "physically," that which is painted on it also has to fit into a meaningful gestalt as part of a picture. Now the first two of these do not apply to the great majority of psychoanalytic sessions; and the second two apply only with quantitative weakening. Combining this point with the variation among psychoanalytic sessions (ranging from sessions almost wholly murky, in which neither patient nor analyst can even be confident about a generic theme lurking behind the material, to a minority in which it seems as though "everything fits together beautifully"), we recognize a statistical problem of *selective bias*, emphasizing theoretically those sessions that are, so to say, "cognitively impressive." A good Skinnerian will remind us that the interpreter of psychoanalytic material is on an intermittent reinforcement schedule and that therefore his verbal behavior and his belief system will be maintained, despite numerous extinction trials that constitute potential refuters. The statistical problem presented here is that when, in any subject matter, a large number of arrangements of many entities to be classified or ordered is available, and some loose (although not empty) criterion of "orderliness" has been imposed, then we can expect that even if the whole thing were in reality a big random mess, *some expected subset of sequences will satisfy the loose ordering criteria*. This is one reason why we worry about significance testing in the inexact sciences, since we know that articles with significant *t* tests are more likely to be accepted by editors than articles that achieve a null result, especially with small samples.

If you wonder why this problem of selecting an orderly-looking subset of cases from a larger mass arises especially in psychoanalysis, my answer would be that it does not arise there more than it does in other "documentary" disciplines, in which the interpreter of facts cannot manipulate variables experimentally but must take the productions of individuals or social groups as they come, as "experiments of nature," to use Adolf Meyer's phrase for a mental illness. My conjecture is that this is a far more pervasive and threatening problem than is generally recognized. It appears distressingly frequent, to anyone who has once become alerted to it, in diverse domains other than psychodiagnosis, including the nonsocial life sciences, the earth sciences, and in almost any discipline having an important "historical" dimension. To digress briefly, lest this point be misunderstood for want of nonpsychoanalytical examples, I give two.

Philosophers of science have recognized in recent years that the largely non-historical, nonempirical, "armchair" approach of the Vienna Circle can be misleading. Most of us would hold that a proper philosophy of science must (as Lakatos has emphasized) combine critical rational reconstruction with tracing out the historical sequence of the growth of knowledge as it actually occurred. Hence we find an increasing use of evidence for or against various philosophies of science from historical examples. I find it odd that so few agree with me that this problem involves a constant danger of selecting one's examples tendentiously. Thus, for instance, my friend Paul Feyerabend loves to talk about Galileo and the mountains on the moon in order to make a case against even a sophisticated falsificationism; whereas almost any article by Popper can be predicted to contain a reference to the quick slaying (with Lakatos's "instant rationality") of the Bohr-Kramers-Slater quantum theory by a sledgehammer falsification experiment. I don't think I am merely displaying the usual social scientist's liking for doing chi squares (on tallies of practically anything!) when I say that this seems to me an inherently statistical problem, and that it cannot be settled except by the application of formal statistical methods.

A second example occurs in paleontology. Almost any educated person takes for granted that the horse series, starting out with little old terrier-size, four-toed *Eohippus*, is chosen by paleontologists for effective pedagogy, but that there are countless similar examples of complete, small-step evolutionary series in the fossil record—which in fact there are not. I think the evaluation of the fossil evidence for macroevolution is an inherently statistical problem, and is strictly analogous to such documentary problems in copyright law as whether a few bars of music should be considered plagiarized, or a few words of verbal text lifted. (See Meehl 1983.) In the evolution case, given a very large number (literally hundreds of thousands) of species of animals with hard parts that existed for various periods of time; and given the heavy reliance on index fossils for dating rocks (because in most instances neither the radium/lead clock nor purely chemical and geological criteria suffice); it stands to reason that some subset of kinds of animals should, *even if the historical fact of evolution had never occurred at all*, give an appearance of evolutionary development as found in the famous horse series.

We deal here with what I learned in elementary logic to call "the argument from convergence." In the light of a hypothesis H we can see how certain facts f_1, f_2, f_3 would be expected (ideally, would be deduced—although in the biological and social sciences that strict deducibility is rare). So when we are presented with f_1, f_2, f_3 we say that they "converge upon" the hypothesis H, i.e., they give it empirical support. I believe it is generally held by logicians and historians of science (although the late Rudolf Carnap was a heavyweight exception, and I never managed to convince him in discussions on this point) that the argument from convergence in inductive logic (*pace* Popper!) is inherently weaker than the argument from prediction, given the same fact/theory pattern. That is to say, if the facts that support hypothesis H are f_1, f_2, and f_3, let's contrast the two situations. First we have pure convergence, in which the theorist has concocted hypothesis H in the presence of f_1, f_2, f_3 and now presents us with the pure argument from convergence; second, we have a mixed argument from convergence *and prediction*, in which the theorist has concocted hypothesis H in the presence of facts f_1, f_2 and then predicted the third fact f_3, which was duly found. Every working scientist (in any field!) that I have asked about this says that Carnap was wrong and Popper is right. That is, the second case is a stronger one in favor of the hypothesis, despite the fact that precisely the same data are present in both instances at the time of the assessment, and their "logical" relationship to the theory is the same. If the logicians and philosophers of science cannot provide us with a rational reconstruction of why scientists give greater weight to a mixed argument from convergence and prediction than to a pure argument from convergence (given identical fact/theory content), I think they had better work at it until they can.

The danger of content-implantation and the subtler, more pervasive danger of differential reinforcement of selective intervention, combine here with the epistemological superiority of prediction over (after-the-fact) convergence to urge, "Wait, don't intervene, keep listening, get more uninfluenced evidence." But our recognition of the factor of resistance often argues the other way, as, e.g., to get a few associations to a seemingly unconnected passing association, especially when the patient seems anxious to get past it. We simply won't *get* certain thoughts if we never intervene selectively, and those never-spoken thoughts may be crucial to our theme-tracing. The technical problem posed by these countervailing considerations is unsolved.

In my own practice, I usually follow a crude rule of thumb to avoid an intervention (whether requesting further associations to an item or voicing a conjecture) until I receive at least two fairly strong corroborator associations. If the corroborators are weak or middling, I wait for three. *Clinical example:* The manifest content of a male patient's dream involves reference to a urinal, so one conjecture, doubtless at higher strength in my associations because of his previous material, is that the ambition-achievement-triumph-shame theme is cooking. (Cf. Freud 1974, p. 397, index item "Urethral erotism.") Halfway through the hour he passingly alludes to someone's headgear and suddenly recalls an unreported element of the dream's manifest content, to wit, that hanging on a wall peg in the urinal was a "green hat." This recalls to my mind, although not (unless he is editing) to his mind, a reference several weeks ago to a green hat. The patient had an uncle of whom he was fond and who used to be an avid mountaineer, given to recounting his mountain-climbing exploits to the boy. Sometimes when the uncle was a bit in his cups, he would don a green Tyrolean hat that he had brought back from Austria. The uncle had several times told the boy the story about how Mallory, when asked why he wanted so much to conquer the Matterhorn, responded, "Because it's there." The uncle would then usually go on to say that this answer showed the true spirit of the dedicated mountain climber, and that it should be the attitude of everybody toward life generally. We may choose to classify the passing allusion to a green hat as belonging to the same thematic cluster as this material. Later in the session, if it doesn't emerge spontaneously by a return to that element in the associations, we may decide (how?) to ask the patient to say more about the hat, ascertaining whether he says it was a Tyrolean hat and, even better, a Tyrolean hat "such as my uncle used to wear." I call this a strong corroborator for the obvious reason that the base rate of green-hat associations for patients in general, and even for this patient, is small. That generalization isn't negated by the fact that he *once before* had this thought. Once in scores or hundreds of hours is still a pretty low base rate. But more important is the fact that the sole previous mention is what enables us to link up a green hat with the achievement motive.

On the other hand, the presence of alternative and competing hypotheses tends to lower the corroborative power of our short-term prediction. How much it is lowered depends on how many competitors there are, how good a job they do of subsuming it, and, especially, on the antecedent or prior probability we attach to them. This prior probability is based upon general experience with persons in our clinical clientele but also, of course, upon the base rate for the particular patient. For example, in the present instance the patient, although not an alcoholic, has reported having a minor drinking problem; he has also revealed—although it has not been interpreted—a linkage between alcohol and the homoerotic theme. The uncle's tendency to tell this story when in his cups, and his further tendency to get a little boy to take a sip of beer, produces an unwelcome combination of competing hypotheses.

We have also the possibility, frequently criticized by antipsychoanalytic skeptics as a form of "fudging," that what appear at one level of analysis to be competing hypotheses are, at another level (or one *could* say, "when properly characterized thematically"), not competitors but aspects or facets of a core theme.

In the present instance, at one level one might view the major determiner of manifest content about urinals and a Tyrolean hat as being *either* ambition or homoeroticism, and unfortunately the cluster of memories concerning the uncle can allude to both of these competing thematic hypotheses (and hence be useless for predictive corroboration). But we may without artificiality or double talk point out that achievement, especially that which involves marked features of competition with other males, has a connection with the theme of activity vs. passivity, strength vs. weakness, masculinity vs. femininity, the latent fear in males of being aggressively and/or homosexually overpowered by other males. (One thinks here of the ethologists' observations on our primate relatives, in which a "subordinate" male wards off threatening aggressive behavior from a dominant male by adopting the "sexual presenting" posture of females.) It could easily be that the additional associative material in the session is useful to us primarily as a means of separating these linked themes of homosexuality and achievement but, although we recognize their thematic linkage and overlapping dynamic sources, is primarily useful in differentiating the aspects of that common cluster as to what the "predominant" emphasis is at the moment. We do not need to force an arbitrary and psychologically false *dis*connection between the ambition theme and defense against passive feminine wishes and fears in order to ask and, in probability, answer the question, "Is the regnant [Murray 1938, pp. 45–54] wish-fear aspect of the theme today, and in the creation of the dream, that of homosexual passivity or that of competitive achievement ["male aggressiveness"]?"

The mathematical psychoanalysis of the utopian future would be plugging in values, or at least setting upper and lower bounds on values, of three probability numbers—none of which we know at the present time, but which are in principle knowable. The first probability is the prior probability of a particular theme, whether from patients in general or from the patients in a particular clinic or therapist clientele or, as presumably the most accurate value, this particular patient. The second probability number would be the conditional probability going from each competing theme to the associative or manifest content element taken to corroborate it. (It boggles the mind to reflect on how we would go about ascertaining that one! Yet it has some objective value, and therefore it should be possible to research it.) Third, we want the probability of the associative or manifest content item without reference to a particular dynamic source. The reason we want that is that we need such a number in the denominator of Bayes's Formula, and the only other way to ascertain that number is to know the probability of each of those elements on the whole set of competing dynamic or thematic hypotheses, a quantity that is as hard to get at as the second one, and maybe harder.

But there is worse to come. Even the pure argument from convergence gets its strength when the facts that converge upon the hypothesis are numerical point predictions, i.e., facts having low prior probability, an argument that can be made from either a Popperian standpoint of high risk-taking or from the non-

Popperian standpoint of the Bayesians — in this respect, the two positions come to the same thing. We have to admit that the deductive model in which H strictly entails facts f_1, f_2, f_3 is not satisfied by psychoanalytic inference, although we can take some comfort from the fact that it is not satisfied in other documentary disciplines either. Freud points out, after discussing the dream work, that it would be nice if we had rules for actually constructing the manifest content from the latent dream thoughts arrived at by interpretation, but that we cannot do this. Hundreds, or in fact thousands, of alternative manifest contents could be generated from the list of latent dream thoughts, plus knowledge of the precipitating event of the dream day that mobilized the infantile wish, plus the stochastic nomologicals (if I may use such a strange phrase; or see essay 1, this volume, pp. 11-14, "stochastologicals") that we designate by the terms condensation, displacement, plastic representation, secondary revision, and symbolism. The situation is rather like that of a prosecutor making a case for the hypothesis that the defendant killed the old lady with the ax, when he tries to show that there was a motive, an opportunity, and so forth. That the defendant decides to kill her does not tell us on which night he will do so, which weapon he will use, whether he will walk or drive his automobile or take a taxi, and the like. Whether a Hempel deductive model can be approximated here by designating a suitably broad *class* of facts as what is entailed, and by relying upon probabilistic implication (a notion regrettably unclear), I shall not discuss.

There is the further difficulty that the mind of the interpreter plays a somewhat different role in the argument, either from prediction or convergence, than it does in the physical and biological sciences. In order to "see how" a dream element or an association "alludes to" such and such a theme, one makes use of his own psyche in a way that most of us think is qualitatively different from the way in which we solve a quadratic equation. This is, of course, a deep and controversial topic, and one thinks of the nineteenth-century German philosophers of history who emphasized the qualitative difference between *Naturwissenschaften* and *Geisteswissenschaften*, or the famous thesis of Vico — which sounds so strange to contemporary behaviorist and objectivist ears — that man can understand history in a way he cannot understand inanimate nature, because of the fact that history, being human actions under human intentions, is of his own making, whereas the physical world is not! Whether or not Brentano was correct in saying that intentionality is the distinctive mark of the mental, I think we can properly say that there is a role played in psychological understanding of words and gestures that involves so much greater reliance upon the interpreter's psychological processes and content — the fact of the similarity between his mind and that of the other person — that it would be a case of "quantity being converted into quality." In recent years, the business of intentionality has led some philosophers, especially of the ordinary language movement, to deny that purposes can be causes and especially that reasons can be causes, a view I consider to be a mistake — as I am certain Freud would. (See essays 2 and 3, this volume.)

In this connection, it is strange that one common objection to idiographic psychoanalytic inferences is that they seem too clever, an objection Fliess once made to Freud. I call attention to an unfair tactic of the critic, a "heads I win, tails you lose" approach — unfair in that he relies on the relative weakness of the pure argument from convergence when the facts are limited in number and especially when the facts are qualitatively similar (like replicating the same experiment in chemistry five times, instead of doing five different *kinds* of experiments, which everybody recognizes as more probative); but when presented with a more complicated network in which this epistemological objection is not available, he then objects on the grounds that the reconstruction *is* too complicated! It's a kind of pincers movement between epistemology and ontology such that the psychoanalytic interpreter can't win. If the thing seems fairly simple, it doesn't converge via multiple strands (and hence not strongly), or it can be readily explained in some "nonmotivational" way, as by ordinary verbal habits and the like; if the structure is complex, so that many strands and cross connections exist, tending to make a better argument from convergence than the simple case, he thinks it unparsimonious or unplausible, "too pat," "too cute," "too clever" for the unconscious to have done all this work.

My response to this pincers movement is to blunt the second, that is, the ontological pincer. I do not accept the principle of parsimony, and I am in good company there because neither does Sir Karl Popper, no obscurantist or mystic he! I see no reason to adopt the "postulate of impoverished reality" (as an eminent animal psychologist once called it). I see no reason to think that the human mind must be simpler than the uranium atom or the double helix or the world economy. Furthermore, the critic contradicts himself, because when he says that the interpreter is attributing to the subject's mind something too complicated for the mind to concoct, he is of course attributing that complicated a concoction to the interpreter himself! It doesn't make any sense to say, "Oh, nobody's head works like that," when the subject matter has arisen because Freud's head, for one, obviously *did* work like that. With this rebuttal, the second pincer is blunted and can be resharpened only by saying that the conscious mind does it; but obviously the unconscious couldn't be that complicated. I cannot imagine the faintest ground for such a categorical denial about a matter of theoretical substance; and it seems to me obvious that there are rich and numerous counter-examples to refute it.

In the experimental literature there is a vast body of non-Freudian research dealing with the establishment of mental sets, with the superior strength of thematic similarity over sound similarity in verbal conditioning, and so forth. Or, for that matter, take the righting reflex of the domestic cat. It was not until the advent of modern high speed photography, permitting a slow motion analysis of the movement, that this amazing feline talent was understood from the standpoint of physics. The cat's nervous system, wired in accordance with what must be an awesome complication in DNA coding, embodies, so to speak, certain principles of mechanics concerning the moment of inertia of a flywheel. As the cat begins to fall, he extends his rear limbs and adducts his forelimbs so that his front section has a small radius of gyration and hence a small moment of inertia, whereas his rear is large in these respects. The torque produced by appropriate contractions of the midriff musculature consequently produces a greater rotation of the forebody, so that the rear twists only a little and the front a great deal. When he is nearly "head up" from this first half of the maneuver, he then extends the forelimbs and adducts the rear limbs and again uses his muscles to apply opposed torques, but now his front has a greater moment of inertia and therefore twists less than the rear. This is an extraordinarily complicated behavior sequence, and nobody supposes that the cat is familiar with differential equations for the laws of mechanics. I therefore meet the second prong of the criticism with sublime confidence, because I know the critic cannot possibly demonstrate, as a general thesis of mammalian behavior, either (a) that the nervous system is incapable of complex computings or (b) that all of its complex computings are introspectable and verbally reportable.

As I pointed out in a previous paper on this subject (essay 10, this volume), however, answering a silly objection is merely answering a silly objection, and does not suffice to make an affirmative case. Recognizing the weakness of the jigsaw analogy, and recognizing that complicated inference in the other documentary disciplines, while it might reassure us to know that we are in the same boat with historians and historical geologists and prosecuting attorneys and journalists is not, upon reflection, terribly reassuring in the face of methodological criticism; what are the possibilities for reducing the subjectivity of psychoanalytic inference? I hope it is clear that in putting this question I am not focusing on the possible development of some cookbook mechanical "objective" procedure to be employed in the interview. (See Meehl 1956, 1957.) I still try to distinguish between Hans Reichenbach's two contexts, i.e., the context of discovery ("how one comes to think of something") and the context of justification ("how one rationally supports whatever it is he has come to think of"). A caveat is imperative here, however, if we are to be intellectually honest: Distinguishing between these two contexts, important as it is epistemologically, should not lead to the mistaken idea that there is a clean qualitative distinction between a high probability (and hence, in some sense, "cookbook" process?) relied on, and a low probability in a more idiographically creative one. Freud himself relies upon both; witness his acceptance of Stekel's view that there are more or less standard dream symbols and scattered remarks that claim universality. For example, when the patient says, "I would not have thought of that," the remark can be taken as a quasi-definitive confirmation of the interpretation; or when he says, "My mind is a blank, I am not thinking of anything now," this is almost invariably a violation of the Fundamental Rule with respect to transference thoughts. With this warning, I focus then upon research procedures that aim to reduce the subjectivity, in the special sense that they ought to be rationally persuasive to a fair-minded skeptic who himself has not experienced or conducted analyses, leaving open to what extent such research might add to the list of high-probability "rules of thumb" that already exist in psychoanalytic lore. I list five approaches, without evaluating their merits and without claiming that they are entirely distinct, which they aren't.

First, I am convinced that sheer laziness, aggravated by excessive faith in the received tradition (plus the fact that most practitioners are not research-oriented, plus the lamentable dearth of psychoanalytic protocols), has prevented the application of simple and straightforward nonparametric statistics to test some basic, "first-level" psychoanalytic concepts (not the metapsychology yet). To take my favorite example because of its simplicity, when in 1943 I was seeing a patient (as a graduate student, before my own analysis) and proceeding in a modified Rogersian fashion, the patient reported a dream about firemen squirting water on a burning building. Almost all of the rest of the interview dealt with ambition as a motive and its correlated affects of triumph or shame, which struck me forcibly because it just happened that I had been reading one of Freud's long footnotes on the puzzling "urethral cluster" of urinary function, pyromania, and ambition. Being in those days extremely skeptical of psychoanalytic thinking, I resolved to take note in the future of exceptions to such a crude rule. Now, some forty years later, I can report that I have as yet never found one single exception *among male patients* to the induction that, if the manifest content of a dream deals with fire and water, the dominant theme of the rest of the session will be in the domain of Murray's *n Recognition* (or its aversive correlate *n Infavoidance*) and the associated affects of triumph and elation on the one side or shame and embarrassment on the other. Now such a finding (which I cannot record in the research literature because, stupidly enough, I haven't been keeping affirmative tallies but only waiting vainly to find the first exception) does not exist as a "statistic" because nobody—myself included—has bothered to analyze it systematically. And what I am claiming about this relationship is that it yields a fourfold table with one empty cell—a thing we almost never find in the behavioral sciences. I believe that simple chi squares applied to such intermediate levels of psychoanalytic inference should be computed, and that no new techniques need to be developed for this purpose.

Second, it is possible that the application of existing statistical techniques of various complexity, such as factor analysis and cluster analysis, might be helpful. (Cf. Luborsky's factor analysis of time-series correlations based on Cattell's P-technique, in Luborsky, 1953.) I am inclined to doubt the value of these approaches because I am not persuaded that the factor-analytic model is the appropriate formalism for this subject matter. I think it fair to say that what few studies have been done along these lines have not been illuminating.

A third possibility is the application of new formalisms, kinds of mathematics with which social scientists do not customarily operate, chosen for their greater structural appropriateness to the problems of the psychoanalytic hour. I am particularly open to this one because my own current research is in taxometrics and has convinced me that a psychologist with even my modest mathematical competence can come up with new search techniques in statistics that are superior to those customarily relied on. The taxometric procedures I have developed over the last decade appear, so far, to be more sensitive and powerful than such familiar methods as factor analysis, cluster analysis, hierarchical clustering, and Stephenson's Q-technique. (I do not believe that interdisciplinary exchange between mathematical statisticians and psychoanalytic psychologists is likely to be fruitful unless each party possesses some real understanding of the other one's subject matter, a rare situation.) If someone were to ask me what novel formalisms I have in mind, I don't know enough mathematics to come up with good examples, although graph theory with its nonmetric theorems about paths, nodes, and strands of networks is urged by a colleague of mine. I do not suggest that a really new branch of mathematics needs to be invented, but I would not exclude even that, since I think the social sciences have had an unfortunate tendency to assume that their kind of mathematics has to look like the mathematics that has been so powerful in sciences like chemistry and physics. There have been kinds of mathematics that had no application to empirical scientific questions for long periods, the standard example in the history of science being Galois's invention of group theory in the 1820s, a branch of mathematics that found no application in any empirical science until somebody realized over a century later that it was useful in quantum theory.

A fourth possibility is along the lines of computer programming for complex content analysis that we find in the book by Stone, Dumphy, et al., *The General Inquirer* (1966). In my 1954 monograph on statistical prediction I tried to make a case against T. R. Sarbin and others who imagined that there could be a "mechanical" method for analyzing psychotherapeutic material, at least at any but the most trivial level. I think today we must be extremely careful in setting limits on the computer's powers. Ten years ago computers could play a pretty good game of checkers, and had been programmed to search for more parsimonious proofs of certain theorems in Russell and Whitehead's *Principia Mathematica*; but no computer, although it could obey the *rules* of chess, could play even a passable chess game. Recently in Minneapolis two computers were entered as competitors in our Minnesota Chess Open Tournament, and they did rather well. In 1979 a computer got a draw with an international grand master. On the other hand, machine translation of foreign languages has turned out to be so intractable a "context" problem (so my colleagues in psycholinguistics inform me) that even the Russians have dropped it. I don't really want to push the computer as psychoanalyst. I merely warn you that it would be rash for people like me who do not possess computer expertise to say, "Well, whatever they program the damn things to do, it's obvious they will never be able to interpret dreams." Maybe they will, and maybe they won't.

No doubt one reason for persistence of the Achensee Question is that objectification of psychoanalytic inference, in any form that would be persuasive to psychometricians, behaviorists, and other social science skeptics who have scientific doubts about the validity of the psychoanalytic interview as a data source, would presumably rely on well-corroborated *quantitative* lawlike statements from several disciplines that are themselves in their scientific infancy. Since psychoanalysis deals mainly with words, the most obvious example of such a related discipline would be psycholinguistics, whose conceptual and evidentiary problems (I am reliably informed by its practitioners) are not in much better scientific shape than psychoanalysis itself. But cognitive psychology more broadly — the psychology of imagery, the general psychology of motivation, the social psychology of the psychoanalyst as audience, not to mention the recent non-Freudian experimental work on the mental and cerebral machinery of dreams — would all have to be put together in some utopian integrated whole before it would be possible to write the sort of nomological or stochastological (essay 1, this volume, p. 11–14) relations that would generate any sort of plausible numerical probabilities for the inferences. I am not here lamenting lack of exact numerical values; I am referring rather to the difficulty of expressing crude forms of functional dependencies that would yield any numbers at all. Suppose the "objectifier" requires a kind of evidentiary appeal *more explicit* than, "Well, just look at these clusters and sequences of speech and gesture. Don't you agree that they sort of hang together, if you view them as under the control of a certain (nonreported) guiding theme?" I am not accepting here that it is imperative to meet such a standard of explicitness. I am simply reacting to the social fact that most objectifiers would not be satisfied with less. Now since we don't have a good *general* psychology of language, of imagery, of dreams, of short-term fluctuations in state variables like anxiety or anger or erotic impulse (and obviously we cannot turn to psychoanalysis itself for that when the Achensee Question is before us), then it is almost pointless for anyone in the present state of knowledge to even speculate utopianly about how such a psychology might look. We do not even know whether the kinds of mathematics favored among social scientists would be appropriate. Thus, for instance, it may be that the mathematical formalisms of factor analysis (Harman 1976) or taxometrics (Meehl and Golden 1982) are much less appropriate for tracing themes in the psychoanalytic interview than, say, something like graph theory (Read 1972, 914–58) or finite stochastic processes (Kemeny, Snell, and Thompson 1957). All of this is music of the future, and I shall not discuss it further.

Does that mean that we have to put the whole thing on the shelf for another century, pending satisfactory development and integration of these underpinning disciplines? One hopes not, and let me try to say why that *may* not be required (although it may!). When we think about the relationship of a mathematical psycholinguistics to a mathematical science of short-term motivational state variables, we are fantasizing a rather detailed prediction (or explanation) of the analysand's choice of words and their sequence. Not perhaps the specific word, which is likely to be beyond the power of utopian psycholinguistics, just as the prediction of precisely how a collapsed bridge falls today is beyond our advanced science of physics; but at least a kind of intermediate-level analysis of the verbal material. Suppose we can bypass that by permitting a somewhat more global categorization of the patient's discourse, allowing for a kind of global subsumption under motivational themes by some kind of partly objective, partly subjective procedure of the sort that I discuss in the research proposal below. That is, we aren't (pointlessly?) trying to predict exactly which verb, or even which class of active or passive verbs, will be emitted during a specified small time interval of the session, having been preceded by a narrowly specified number of allusions to the "mother theme," or whatever. What we are saying is that we have a small collection of rather broadly identified remarks (or gestures or parapraxes), and we hope to persuade the skeptic (assuming we have convinced ourselves) that it is more reasonable to construe this small set of happenings as produced by one dynamic state or event—I shall simply refer to *a theme* in what follows—rather than to reject that possibility in favor of multiple separate psychological hypotheses that are unrelated dynamically or thematically, but each of which might easily be capable of explaining the *particular* individual remark, gesture, or parapraxis that is treated as *its* explanandum.

In several places Freud likens the analytic detective work to that of a criminal investigation, and the analogy is a good one on several obvious counts. We do not consider the prosecutor's summation of evidence to the jury, or the judge's standardized instructions on how to assess this evidence, as somehow irrational or mystical or intuitive, merely because it is not possible to express the invoked probabilistic laws *in numerical form*, let alone ascribe a net joint "empirical support" *number* to the total evidence. As I have said elsewhere in this essay, there are other disciplines that we consider intellectually respectable and worth pursuing and, in certain important private and social decision makings, even deserving of our reliance in grave matters, despite the absence of an effective procedure (algorithm) for computing a numerical probability attachable to outcomes, or to alleged explanations of events that have already taken place.

I don't intend to get much mileage out of those nonpsychoanalytic examples. But it is important, before we proceed, to recognize that the domain of the rational and empirical is not identical with the domain of the statistical-numerical, as some overscientized psychologists and sociologists mistakenly believe. What reservations must be put by a rational skeptic on the force of such extrapsycho-analytic analogies I discuss elsewhere herein; and I agree with the skeptics that those reservations are discouragingly strong. But the point is that we can and do talk about evidence converging, of explanations as being parsimonious or need-lessly complicated, and so forth, with an idealized inductive logic (if you don't like that phrase, an idealized empirical methodology), including one that accepts a particular *kind of inferential structure* — say, a Bayesian inference — even though, in the concrete domain of application, we cannot plug in any actual *probability numbers*. If we do hazard mention of numerical values — and this is an important point one should never forget in thinking about psychoanalysis and al-lied subjects — at most we have some upper and lower bounds, acceptable by almost all members of our clinical and scientific community, on the numerical values of expectedness, priors, and conditionals in Bayes's Formula. I think it is generally agreed that we can "think Bayesian" and, thinking Bayesian, can come up with some reasonable numerical bounds on likelihood ratios and poste-rior probabilities, without claiming to have determined relative frequencies empirically as the initial numbers that get plugged into Bayes's Theorem. (See Carnap's discussion of the two kinds of probability, Carnap 1950/1962, passim.) For someone who is uncomfortable even with that weak a use of a widely ac-cepted formalism (which is, after all, a high-school truth of combinatorics and does not require one to be a "strong Bayesian" in the sense of current statistical controversy), at the very least one can point to a list of separate causal hypotheses to explain half a dozen interview phenomena and then to a single causal hypothesis — the psychoanalytic one — as doing the job that it takes half a dozen others to do as its joint competitors.

Example: A patient drops her wedding ring down the toilet. In speaking of her husband, Henry, she mistakenly refers to him as George, the name of an old flame of hers. An evening dining out in celebration of their wedding anniversary was prevented because the patient came down with a severe headache. Without any kinds of challenge to the contrary, she "spontaneously" makes four state-ments at different times in the interview about what a fine man her husband is, how fortunate she is that she married him, and so on. Now you don't have to go through any elaborate psycholinguistics or even any of that "within-safe-bounds" application of Bayes's Theorem, to argue that it may be simpler and more plausible to attribute these four phenomena to the unreported guiding influence of a single psychological entity, namely, some ambivalence about her husband, than to deal with the four of them "separately." In the latter case we would be, say, attributing the wedding ring parapraxis to nondynamic clumsiness (the patient happens to be at the low end of the O'Connor Finger Dexterity Test); the anniversary headache to insufficient sleep and oversmoking; the misnaming George-for-Henry to the fact that old George was in town recently and called her up; and the unprovoked overemphasis on her happy marriage to some recent observations on the unhappy wives that are her neighbors on either side. Setting aside the independent testing of those alternatives, it's basically a simple matter. We have four competing hypotheses whose separate prior probabilities are not much higher than that of the marital ambivalence hypothesis, although some of them might be a little higher and others a little lower. We think that the conditional probabilities are also roughly in the same ball park numerically as the conditional probability of each of the four observations upon the ambivalence hypothesis. The argument that one would make if he knew nothing about statistics, Bayesian inference, or inductive logic but did know legal practice, or common sense, or diagnosing what's the matter with somebody's carburetor, would be: ''We can easily explain these four facts with one simple hypothesis, so why not prefer doing it that way?''

It is not difficult to tighten this example up a bit and make it semi-formal, to such an extent that it is the skeptic who is put on the spot—provided, of course, that he will accept certain reasonable bounds or tolerances on the estimated numbers. Thus, suppose the average value of the four priors is not greater than the prior on the ambivalence hypothesis; and suppose the average value of the four conditionals required to mediate an explanation of each of the four observations is not greater than the average conditional of the four observations on the ambivalence theory. Since the ''expectedness'' in the denominator of Bayes's Theorem is some unknown but determinate true value (however we break it up into the explanatory components associated with the possibilities), and since a dispersion of four probabilities yields a product less than the fourth power of their average, then when we compute a likelihood ratio for the ambivalence hypothesis against the conjunction of the separate four (assuming these can be treated as essentially independent with respect to their priors, quite apart from whether they are explanations of the four explananda), things cancel out, and we have a ratio of the prior on the ambivalence hypothesis to the product of the other four priors. If, as assumed above, the dynamic hypothesis is at least as probable antecedently as the other four average priors, a lower bound on this likelihood ratio is the reciprocal of the prior cubed. So that even if the priors were all given as one-half—an unreasonably large value for this kind of material—we still get a likelihood ratio, on the four facts, of around eight to one in favor of the psychodynamic construction.

Before setting out my fifth (and, as I think, most hopeful) approach to psychoanalytic theme-tracing, it will help clarify a proposed method to say a bit more about theory and observation, at the risk of boringly repetitious overkill. I think our characterization of the theory/observation relation is especially important here because (a) both critics and defenders of psychoanalytic inference have tended to misformulate the issue in such a way as to prevent fruitful conversation, and (b) the pervasive influence of the antipositivist line that all observations are theory-infected (Kuhn, Feyerabend, and Popper) lends itself readily to obscurantist abuse in fields like psychopathology. Having mentioned Popper in this connection, I must make clear that I do not impute to him or his followers any such abuse; and, as is well known, Popper himself is extremely skeptical about the alleged scientific status of psychoanalytic theory.

As a starter, let us be clear that there are two methodological truisms concerning the perceptions and subsumptions (I think here the line between these two need not be nicely drawn) of "experts," in which the expertise is partly "observational" and partly "theoretical." One need not be appreciably pro-Kuhnian, let alone pro-Feyerabendian, as I most certainly am not, to know that technical training, whether in the methods of historiography or electron microscopy or psychodiagnosis or criminal investigation, enables the trained individual to perceive (and I mean literally *perceive*, in a very narrow sense of that term that would have been acceptable even to Vienna positivism) things that the untrained individual does not perceive. Anybody who has taken an undergraduate zoology class knows this; it cannot generate a dispute among informed persons, whatever their views may be on epistemology or history of science. On the other hand, it is equally obvious, whether from scientific examples or everyday life, that people tend to see and hear things they expect to see and hear, and that, given a particular close-to-rock-bottom "perceptual report," the expert's theoretical conceptions will affect under what rubric he subsumes the observation. These truisms are so obvious that my philosophy-trained readers, who comfortably accept both, will be puzzled to learn that the situation is otherwise in psychology; but it is. Psychoanalytic clinicians have become accustomed to relying on analogies of psychoanalytic method to the microscope or telescope or whatever, together with the alleged combination of sensitization to unconscious material and reduced defensive interferences, supposedly producing *some* variant of "objectivity," consequent upon the analyst's personal analysis and the corrective experiences of his control cases. Nonpsychoanalytic clinicians, especially those coming from the behaviorist tradition, fault the analytic theme-detector for failing to provide "objective operational definitions" in terms of the behavior itself, of constantly going behind the data to concoct unparsimonious causal explanations, and the like. The same polarization is true for nonpractitioners, i.e., academic theoreticians with psychoanalytic versus antipsychoanalytic orientations. In these disputes, when the parties are not simply talking past each other (the commonest case), the difficulty is that each thinks that his methodological principle clashes with his opponent's methodological principle, which is almost silly on the face of it. Consider the following two statements:

M_1: "It takes a specially skilled, specially trained, clinically sensitized, and theoretically sophisticated observer to notice certain sorts of behavioral properties and to subsume them under a psychodynamically meaningful rubric."

M_2: "Training in a special kind of observation predicated upon a certain theory of (unobserved) states and events underlying the behavior being observed may sometimes have the result, and presents always the danger, of seeing things that aren't there, or subsuming them in arbitrary ways, or forcing a conceptual meaning upon them that has no correspondence to the actual causal origins of the behavior observed."

These two methodological assertions M_1 and M_2 are perfectly compatible with each other, as is obvious so soon as we state them explicitly. In fact, in large part each of them flows from the *same* imputed characteristics of the "sensitive" and "insensitive" observer! They just aren't in conflict with one another as assertions. Why would anyone have supposed they were, or (better), argued as if he supposed that?

The problem is that they are in a kind of pragmatic conflict, even though they are logically and nomologically compatible, in that there is a tension generated in anyone who accepts both of them, between his aim to discover the nonobvious (an aim pursued by reliance on M_1) and his aim to avoid theoretically generated self-deception or projection (an aim aided by remembering M_2). This epistemic tension between two aims that are both reasonable and legitimate is not, I suggest, any more puzzling than some better-understood cases, such as the fact in statistical inference that one has tension between his desire to avoid Type I errors (falsely inferring parameter difference from the observed statistical trend) and Type II errors (wrongly sticking with the null hypothesis of "no difference" when there is a difference in the state of nature). There isn't any mathematical contradiction, and under stated and rather general conditions, one uses a single coherent mathematical model to compute the trade-off and assign it numerical values. Nor is there any sort of philosophical collision or semantic confusion. It is simply a sad fact about the human epistemic situation, even for a fairly developed and rigorous science like mathematical statistics, that when we wish to apply it to such a simple task as detecting bad batches of shotgun shells, we experience a pragmatic tension, and that tension has, so to speak, a realistic (not a "neurotic") basis.

Similarly, in dealing with material of appreciable complexity such as the stream of speech and gesture produced by an analysand, if the observer (NB: *noticer, attender*), classifer, and interpreter lacks certain kinds of training and expertise, he won't be able to do the job. But if he does have those kinds of training and expertise, he may be seduced to do a job that is too good. So the first thing one has to do in thinking rationally about this problem is to get away from the pseudo-collision of Principles M_1 and M_2, to wholeheartedly and unreservedly accept both of them, recognizing that the two principles are logically consistent and even flow from the same facts about the human observer and interpreter and the effects of his training and experience. They lead to a pragmatic tension generated by our reasonable desire to avoid two kinds of errors which might be described as errors of omission versus commission, errors of "under-discovery" versus "over-belief," or even William James's famous errors of the tenderminded and the toughminded. One thinks of James's comment on William Kingdon Clifford's stringent "ethics of belief," to the effect that Professor Clifford apparently thought that the worst possible fate that could befall a man was to believe something that wasn't so!

Excursus on Observations

Because of some current tendency in psychology to rely on the Kuhn-Feyerabend "theory-laden" doctrine, I shall permit myself here a few general remarks on the controversy about meaning invariance and theory-ladenness, because it seems to me that the situation in psychology is importantly different from the favorite examples employed by philosophers and historians of science in discussing this difficult and important issue. First, the theory-ladenness of observational statements and the associated meaning-variance is most clearly present and most important in what Feyerabend calls "cosmological theories," i.e., theories that say something about everything there is (as he once put it to me in discussion). I believe a psychologist can be seduced into attributing undue importance to the Kuhn-Feyerabend point if he takes it as a matter of course that philosophical arguments concerning meaning variance and theory-ladenness applying to the Copernican hypothesis or relativity theory or (less clearly?) quantum mechanics, apply equally strongly *and equally importantly* to rats running mazes or psychoanalytic patients speaking English on the couch. I recall a Ph.D. oral examination in which the candidate, a passionate and somewhat dogmatic Kuhn-Feyerabend disciple, was asked by one of my philosophy colleagues to explain just how the protocol "Rat number 7 turned right in the maze and locomoted to the right-hand goal box" was theory-laden; in what sense the emperimenter would experience a perceptual gestalt-switch if the experiment converted him from being a Tolmanite to being a Skinnerian; and which of the words in the protocol sentence would undergo a meaning change as a result of his theoretical conversion? It was a good question, and our surprise was not at the candidate's utter inability to deal with it, but the extent to which he was prepared to go in a hopeless cause. What he said was that the very genidentity of rat number 7 from yesterday's trial run to today's test run, and the very fact that we called today's run a "test run," were theory-laden. (I think this is pathetic, but if there are readers who don't, I won't press the point.) Of course the "theory" that today's rat is genidentical with yesterday's rat, is not a psychological theory in any sensible or interesting use of the word "psychological," and even if it were, it is firmly believed (I should say presupposed) by both Tolman and Skinner as well as all of their followers, including those that are in transition to the opposing paradigm. If one wants to say that the ordinary common-sense world view that macro-objects as described in Carnap's "physical thing language" are spatiotemporally continuous constitutes a kind of theory, I have no strong objection to this, although I don't find it an illuminating way to speak. But the point is that if it is a theory, it is a theory that cuts across psychological theories of animal learning. And, of course, it's for that reason that the candidate was unable to point to any of the words in the sentence that would have undergone a meaning change as a result of the experimental psychologist's conversion from one theory of learning to another.

The question whether theory defines the concept "test day" is another piece of obscurantism, since, although the theory is what *leads us to make a certain test* (not in dispute), this fact is quite incapable of showing meaning variance or theory-ladenness of the behavioral terms describing what the rat *does* on the test. Witness the fact that an undergraduate with correct 20/20 vision and normal hearing, who is nonpsychotic and familiar with the macro-object English terms "right" and "left," could be safely trusted to make the relevant observations even if he knew nothing about the latent learning concept or about differences between the rat's condition (hungry? anxious?) this night and on previous nights. In most latent learning experiments, the question about test (or critical pre-test) occasions "How is this night different from all other nights?" has its answer either in the precedent *operations* of feeding (or fasting), or what, if anything, is present in the goalbox that wasn't there on previous occasions.

In psychological research on behavior, whether animal or human, the theory-dependence of observations and the theory-ladenness of operational meanings involve a cluster of questions that are related but clearly distinguishable, as follows:

(1) Instruments of observation are usually theoretically understood, whether in the inorganic or life sciences. (Not quite always, e.g., the Wasserman test!) Such instruments are used (a) to control all causally influential variables, (b) to extend the human sensorium, (c) to dispense with human perception by substituting a physical record for the human sense-report, and (d) to replace human memory by a more reliable record (storage and retrieval). In physics and astronomy (I do not know about chemistry, but I imagine there also) there is sometimes a theoretical question concerning the extent to which the instrument can be relied upon for a certain experimental purpose, because the laws of physics involved as auxiliaries in the test proposed are themselves "connected," via overlapping theoretical terms, with the conjectured laws (including dispositional, causal, and compositional properties attributed to conjectural entities) that the experiment is designed to test. There are problematic entities whose role in the nomological net would be altered importantly (for the experiment) if certain other adjacent re-

gions of the net were altered in such-and-such respects. This may happen in psychology also, but it is not as common in good research as those who emphasize theory-ladenness seem to assume. Whether the observing instrument is the unaided human eye, the kymographic recording of a lever press, or a photo cell showing which alley the rat passed through, these are all instruments that rely on no currently competing theory of animal learning. For that matter, no reasonable person believes their deliverances are dependent upon a theory of how the rat's brain works in choosing which direction to turn in a T-maze.

(2) Auxiliary theories, and hence auxiliary particularistic hypotheses formulated in terms of these theories, may be problematic but essentially independent of the subject matter under study. An example would be an auxiliary theory about the validity of the Rorschach Ink Blot Test as a detector of subtle cognitive slippage in schizoidia. We might wish to rely on this in testing the dominant schizogene theory of that disorder, but it is an auxiliary theory that is highly problematic and, in fact, as problematic as the major substantive hypothesis under test (essay 1, this volume, pp. 19–24). A less problematic auxiliary theory used in listening to psychoanalytic session discourse would be the vague (but not empty) "theory" that speech is determined by interactive causal chains between the current stimulating field (is the analyst moving restlessly in his chair?) and the subject's inner states and dispositions, whether those latter are characterized in brain language (not presently available except for very rough statements of certain systems or regions of the brain that are more relevant to verbal behavior than, say, to keeping one's balance when standing up) or in the molar language (whether behavioristic or phenomenological) again. We tacitly presuppose the "theory" that people cannot speak a language they have not learned. Suppose I know that a patient is a classics professor, and that his wife's name is Irene. Then the possibility that a dream about a "peace conference" conjoined with an association during the session about "knocking off a piece" is connected with his wife, is plausible only because of our tacit auxiliary theories about language. If he didn't know any Greek, he could still link in his unconscious the homophones "peace" and "piece," but he would not link that with the name of his wife because he wouldn't know the etymology of the female name "Irene." (NB: If the therapist doesn't know that amount of Greek, he won't be able to create the thematic conjecture either!)

(3) *Did* this particular investigator design the experiment in the light of the theory he was interested in testing (a biographical question of fact)?

(4) *Could* a seasoned, clever researcher have designed this experiment without the disputed learning theory in mind—perhaps without any learning theory in mind except the minimal nondisputed statement (hardly a technical doctrine of animal psychology) that organisms usually have a knack to "learn things"?

(5) Granted that a purely atheoretical, "blind inductive" ethologist *could* have designed a certain experiment, is it *likely* that he would have designed this particular one and chosen to observe the things he chose to observe, absent this theory? Ditto, absent some other theory about learning?

(6) Whatever has led, or plausibly could lead, to the designing of the experiment and the specification of what was to be observed on the test night, *could* a theoretically naïve person with normal sensory equipment make and record the observations without the theory?

It is a grave source of confusion to lump all these questions together by the single seductive statement, "Observations are theory-laden." One can make entirely too much of the simple fact that people's visual and auditory perceptions, and their imposition of a spatial or other reference frame upon what comes to them through distance receptors, is always influenced by their implicit beliefs about the world (genidentity of macro-objects, etc.), their previous experiences, their verbal habits, and their culture's dominant interests and values. Nobody today holds—what one doubts even our philosophical ancestors held—that the favorite epistemological prescriptions of Vienna positivism can be founded upon theorems in formal logic, as if we were to pretend we did not know that we are organisms, occupying space-time, having distance receptors, wired somewhat similarly to one another, able to remember, to speak, and so forth. The agreement among scientists (or critical, skeptical, tough-minded contemporary nonscientists) observing a witchcraft trial as to which witnesses were believable, which sense modalities were generally reliable, could not be achieved without experience of the human mind and society. Does anybody dispute this? On the other hand, these kinds of minimal "epistemological basics" are part of our general theory of macro-objects, formulable in Carnap's "physical thing language," and our knowledge of human beings as observers, recorders, rememberers, and reporters.

These shared, common-sense, well-tested notions are *not* "theories" in the interesting and complex sense we have in mind when we talk about constructing a satisfactory psychology of perception, or an adequate psychology of cognition, or a sound descriptive (non-normative) theory of rat decision making. It is not perfectionist epistemology or vulgar positivism—nor, I think, even an antipathy to ghosts, leprechauns, and capricious deities (not to mention fortune tellers and other epistemological disreputables)—that we form the societal habit of employing instruments of observation and recording as often as we do in the sciences whether these sciences deal with organic or inorganic subject matter. I must confess I see nothing complicated, philosophically earthshaking, or especially interesting about the fact that since humans are not always accurate in noticing whether a visual or auditory stimulus occurred first, one has a problem in such cases about relying on human observation. For that reason one substitutes non-human instruments whose subsequent deliverances to the human perceiver are of a different form, a form chosen by the instrument maker and the scientist who wanted the instrument built so as to be less ambiguous perceptually. (Incidentally, the notion that we cannot do any basic epistemology or formulate any workable methodology of science prior to having respectably developed sciences of perception, cognition, sociology of knowledge, etc., seems very odd to me when I reflect that astronomy, chemistry, physics, and physiology were well advanced sciences, relying on a developed "method" that made them so superior to pre-Galilean thought, long before psychology or sociology were even conceived as scientific disciplines.)

Do we really have to write a big book about this? Maybe for a critical epistemology of astrophysics, or quark theory; but not, I urge, for animal conditioning, or classical psychometrics, *or even psychoanalysis.* In N. R. Campbell's (today underrated) *Physics: The Elements* (1920/1957) he has a nice section (pp. 29–32) about judgments for which universal assent can be obtained. He is of course exaggerating somewhat when he refers to these judgments as being "universal," and one supposes that even if we eliminate known liars, psychotics, persons with aberrant vision and hearing — things which can be independently tested — we still might have a minuscule fraction of observers who would puzzlingly persist in making judgments out of line with the rest of us. Note that even in such extremely rare cases, it is usually possible without vicious ad hockery to give a satisfactory *causal* explanation of why the incurably deviant response is made. But let's admit that it is not always so. Nothing in the method of science requires that we should come to a quick decision in such cases. What happens is that (a) we get a steady accumulation of protocols from the reliable observers (calibrated in the past in other contexts); (b) we are able to give a satisfactory explanation, again without vicious ad hockery, of the discrepant observer's findings; so (c) we decide to "pull a Neurath" (Neurath 1932/1959) by simply refusing to admit the aberrant protocol into the corpus. We prefer to rest decision (c) on a conjunction of (a) and (b), but if (a) is sufficiently extensive and varied, and the theory forbidding the aberrant protocol is doing well enough, we will dispense with (b) — while keeping our hopes up. Thus, e.g., physicists dealt "Neurath-style" with the irksome Dayton C. Miller ether-drift protocol for some 30 years before Shankland and colleagues provided an acceptable (b). But I think it unfortunate that psychologists do not at least read and reflect upon Campbell's discussion or that of an undervalued contributor — C. R. Kordig (1971a, 1971b, 1971c, 1973) before jumping on the popular Kuhn-Feyerabend bandwagon. Campbell sets up three kinds of perceptual judgments on which universal assent could be attained among normal calibrated observers — to wit, judgments of simultaneity, consecutiveness, and betweenness in time; judgments of coincidence and betweenness in space; and judgments of number. Now this is a pretty good list. Everyone knows that the plausibility of Eddington's famous statement "science consists of pointer readings" (wrong, but not a stupid remark at the time) arises from the very large extent to which pointer readings of instruments substituted for the human eye and ear at the first interface with the phenomenon under study have replaced the human eye and ear as Aristotle and Pliny used them. Again, I don't see anything mysterious about this, and it flows directly from Campbell's principles. That a pointer lies *somewhere between* the line marked "7" and the line marked "8" on a dial is an example of spatial betweenness; that this may be an observation made *during* a few seconds interval during which a single tone was being sounded is an example of (local grammar) temporal coincidence. Now whenever we find that most people's theoretical notions unduly affect consensus in perceiving alleged N-rays (or auras, or levitations) — not to mention "anxiety" in the rat or "latent hostility" in the psychiatric patient — we have recourse to some stratagem in which we try to achieve an equivalent of the physicist's pointer reading *without throwing away perceptual input that is relevant*.

I cannot insist too strongly that the raw data of the psychoanalytic hour are speech, gesture, and posture *and* — unless the analyst claims to have telepathic powers — *nothing else*. If my psychodynamic theory allows me to say that I *"observed the patient's hostility"* when the existence of the patient's (latent, nonreported, denied) hostility is what is under dispute between me and, say, a certain kind of behaviorist, then my observations are here theory-infected to an undesirable extent, and I am scientifically obligated to move down in the epistemic hierarchy closer to the behavior flux itself (MacCorquodale and Meehl 1954, 220 ff). If I refuse to do this, or at least to concede the epistemic necessity to do it (given your denial and request for my evidence), then I may be a perceptive analyst and a skillful healer, but I have opted out of the game "science." We have now reached little-boy impasse, "My Dad can lick your Dad," "Can not!", "Can so!", "Can not", etc., irresolubly ad nauseam.

Now the rock-bottom data in the clinical example below I shall confine to the patient's speech and, in fact, to features of the speech that can be fairly adequately represented in the transcript without a tape, although everyone knows "something is lost" thereby. Thus pauses, gross fluctuations in rate of speech, and volume level can be measured objectively from the tape and indicated by a suitable notation in the transcript. We are, however, going to rely almost wholly upon the content, because that's what my proposed theme-tracing procedure deals with. (One cannot deal with everything at once!) In a way, our problem of tradeoff between errors of omission (insensitive, untrained listener not perceiving) and errors of commission (theoretically biased listener projecting) can be stated quite simply in the light of what was said above. Stating it thus leads fairly directly to my theme-tracing proposal. The problem is this: Restricted segments of the verbal output (blocks, hereafter) can be subsumed under a variety of thematic rubrics, and which rubric it is subsumed under by a psychoanalytically sophisticated listener or protocol reader will, of course, be affected by his tentative subsumption of the other blocks, all guided by his acceptance of the minimal Freudian theory. Now this interblock influence is what we want to get away from if possible, because we are sensitive to the skeptic's objection that "human ingenuity can fit almost anything together if you're not too fussy," based upon the several lines of criticism set out above. We want the clinician to use his psychodynamically sophisticated mind to achieve the subsumption of a verbal block. Yet we would like the conclusion of his subsuming activity to have as a work product something that cannot be easily defeated by the skeptic's "Well, so what? It's all very clever, you do make it sound as if it hangs together; but I am not impressed."

It is not that we think that a proper method of protocol analysis should be *coercive* with respect to a sufficiently determined skeptic, which it is foolish to require. We do not require that "good arguments" for the roundness of the earth be capable of convincing the (still surviving!) Flat Earth Society members. No, the problem is not that we foolishly seek an automated truth-finding machine, some kind of algorithm for particularistic inductive inference in this kind of material, which very likely cannot be come by and is not anticipated even for the utopian phase of psycholinguistics or psychodynamics. Rather the problem is that we ourselves, "pro-Freud leaners" with scientific training and epistemological sophistication, are fully aware of the merits of the skeptic's complaint. That being so, our aim is to use the clinically sensitive mind of the psychoanalytically trained listener or reader to discern the red thread running through the discourse, to carry out the theme-tracing that we are reasonably sure could not be done by a competent clerk or a non-Freudian psycholinguist (Meehl 1954, chapter 6, 7 and passim). But we would like those red thread discernings to be at what might be called an intermediate level of complexity and persuasiveness, so that given the thematic subsumption of blocks of the discourse, the preponderance or strength of allusions to the "segments of red thread" recurring in the various blocks will speak for themselves when we add them up across blocks. That is what the proposed method of theme-tracing tries to do.

So I present this somewhat simple-minded approach, which involves no fancy mathematics but which attempts to do partial justice to Freud's notion of the "red thread of allusions" running through the patient's material. The approach appeals to me because it combines the advantages of the skilled, empathic, thematically perceptive clinical brain with at least partial safeguards against contamination effects. Let's put the question thus: "How can we make use of the classificatory powers of the skilled mind without that mind's classifications being contaminated by theory, hence rendering the whole process especially vulnerable to the Achensee Question?" We want to use the clinician's brain to do something more complicated than associate tables with chairs or plug in *mother figure* for "empress," or, idiographically, to search his memory bank for previous references by this patient to green Tyrolean hats to find that they always relate to the uncle. But if we start using the skilled clinical mind to do something more interesting and complicated than these jobs, then comes the critic with the Achensee objection, telling us that we are brain-washed Freudians and therefore we naturally read our thoughts into the patients and "see" meanings, metaphors, and subtle allusions when they are not there.

To sharpen somewhat the distinction between the first method (doing a simple chi-square on a four-fold table showing the association between an objectively, i.e., clerically scorable, dream content on the one hand and a subjective, impressionistic, skilled clinician's uncontaminated discernment of the theme in the subsequent associations on the other) and the fifth method, which I shall christen "Topic Block Theme Tracing," I choose a short clinical example that is in most respects as straightforward as the fire/ambition example, but *not quite* — and the "not quite" introduces terrible complexities for objective scoring, even by such a clever device as the computerized General Inquirer. A patient begins the session by reporting: *I dreamed there was a peculiar water pipe sticking into my kitchen.* My Radovian training suggests a minor intervention here, for clarification only, so I ask, "Peculiar?", to which the patient responds, "Yes, it was a peculiar water pipe because it seemed to have some kind of a cap on it, I couldn't understand how it could work." The standard symbology here [*waterpipe* = penis, *kitchen* = female genitals] is familiar to undergraduates, but knowing it would only permit the trained clerk or the supertrained clerk (e.g., the General Inquirer) to infer a heterosexual wish. What makes it interesting is the "peculiar cap," juxtaposed with the word "work" [= coitus, at least semi-standard]. Here an idiographic low-frequency consideration enters our minds, mediated by the fact that the patient is Jewish and I am gentile. I conjecture that the capped pipe is an uncircumcised (i.e., gentile) penis, and that the dream expresses an erotic positive transference impulse. I further conjecture (more tentatively) that the current manifestation of these transference feelings involves negative feelings toward her husband, unfavorable fantasied comparisons of me with him, and that the focus of these invidious comparisons will be something in the Jewish/gentile domain. Except for the one word, "Peculiar?", I remain silent until the last five minutes of the session. Everything the patient talked about during that period alluded directly, or almost directly, to the conjectured theme. Space does not permit me to present all of the associations, but to give you an example: She recounted a recent episode in which she and her husband visited a drugstore with whose proprietor the husband had formerly done business, and the patient was irritated with her husband because he slapped the counter and put his hand on the druggist's shoulder and asked in a loud voice how his profits were going. The patient noted the presence in the store of a slightly familiar neighbor woman named Stenquist, who the patient mentions is a Norwegian Lutheran. (She knew from the newspapers and other sources that I was a Lutheran and of Norse origins.) She had the conscious thought in the drugstore that her husband was "carrying on in exactly the way anti-Semites have the stereotype of the way Jewish people talk and act in public.'' She then talked about a non-Jewish boy she had gone with briefly in high school but quit because her parents disapproved, emphasizing that he was ''quiet'' and ''somewhat shy'' and had ''very nice manners.'' She went on to say she liked men who were gentle (note further phonetic link between ''gentle'' and ''gentile''), and after a bit of silence said that she realized it was my business to be gentle in my treatment of her but that she imagined I was the same way in real life. Some more hesitation, then a complaint that sometimes her husband was not gentle in bed; and then finally a reluctant expression of the thought that I would no doubt be gentle in bed.

Now this example presents only minor difficulties for an objective classification of the associative material, since I have picked out material that illustrates the theme. But in the ''figure-ground'' situation they are less clear, and one *could* miss the point without having his switches properly set by the symbolized uncircumcised penis in the manifest content of the dream. And although it is dangerous to impose limits on what the souped-up computer programs of the future will achieve, it will take some doing on the part of the content analyst who writes the General Inquirer's ''dictionary'' to deal with this case. That one (low-frequency) idiographic element, a manifest dream element that I have never heard before or since in thousands of hours of therapeutic listening, and that no one in any psychotherapist audience I have asked has had—that would mean a minimum of 100,000 hours of our collective experience—makes all the difference. It is for this reason that we need the psychoanalytic retrieval machinery of our own minds, i.e., that we are still the superprogrammed General Inquirers.

From this example it is only one step to cases in which the manifest content contains little of the received symbology, but is itself idiographic to such a degree that its meaning becomes evident only as we listen to the associations in the ensuing session. So we have a situation in which one cannot see a particular ''fact'' as bearing upon a particular conjecture except in the light of the conjecture itself. Crudely stated, we don't know that a fact is of a certain kind without knowing what it means, and in the work of the mind we don't know what it means without having purposes and intentions available as potential ''explainers.'' In psychoanalytic listening we impose the relevant dimensions of classification on what, for the behaviorist, are just noises (of course he doesn't really proceed that way, but he pretends to, and tries to impose this impossible methodology upon us!). Our ''imposing of relevant dimensions''—the important truth in the Kuhn-Feyerabend line as it applies to psychoanalysis—is precisely what makes us vulnerable to the Achensee Question.

It is almost impossible, as Freud points out in his introduction to the study of Dora, to illustrate the more complex (and, alas, commoner!) kinds of theme-tracing without making multiple reference to previous sessions and to the whole structure of the patient's life. I shall present you with a short example that involves a specific postdiction, namely, what the patient was reading the night before, and whose photograph looked like the person dreamed of. I use it as a kind of litmus test on my Minnesota colleagues to diagnose who is totally closed-minded against psychoanalytic thinking. If this sort of instance doesn't at least mobilize a rat psychologist's or psychometrician's intellectual curiosity to look into the matter further, he is a case of what the Roman Church would call "Invincible Ignorance."

Businessman, late thirties, wife had been a patient of mine; he refused to pay for her psychotherapy because "didn't believe in it, nothing to it." (She cashed an old insurance policy for payment.) Wife benefited greatly, to the point he became interested. Bright, verbal man of lower-class background (father was a junk-dealer). Patient went to University of Minnesota for almost two years, premedical course. Quit ostensibly because family needed money (in depression years), but he was flunking physics at the time and his overall grades would not get him into Medical School. Older brother Herman used to reprimand him for laziness. Brother got top grades, Ph.D. in chemistry. For a while patient worked in brother's drugstore. Brother was a pharmacist, who finished graduate school while continuing in drugstore business to make a living. I knew (from wife's therapy) that the brother had mysteriously died during surgery in what was thought to be a fairly routine operation for stomach ulcer, the family having been greatly impressed by the fact that on the night before the surgery, Herman expressed with great dread an unshakable conviction that he would die on the operating table. (Some physician colleagues have told me that — whatever the explanation of this phenomenon, which has been reported in medical folklore before — they would have considered it undesirable to operate on the patient under those circumstances.) During the first interview the patient related to me in a mixed fashion, including: a) nonchalance, unconcern, "minor problems"; b) jocularity; c) deference; d) competitiveness. (I won't fully document these impressions as noted after the first hour, but an example: He fluctuates between addressing me as "Dr." and "Mr.," and once corrects himself twice in row — "Dr., — uh, Mr., — uh, Dr. Meehl.")

In the fourth session he had reported a dream that was quite transparent, even prior to associations, about a waiter who provided poor service, making the patient "wait a long time before providing anything. Also, I couldn't say much for the meal [= Meehl; I have learned, as have most analytic therapists whose names readily lend themselves to punning, that dreams about food, meals, dinners, lunches, etc. frequently are dreams of transference nature — as in my own analysis, I learned that, like some of my analyst's previous patients, if I dreamed about "buses," it likely referred to him because 'Bus' was his nickname]; and the bill was exorbitant, so I refused to pay it." He went off on discussion of ways his wife had and had not improved, alluded to the parking inconvenience on campus, time taken coming over here, expressed "hope we can get this thing over

328   SUBJECTIVITY IN PSYCHOANALYTIC INFERENCE

with fairly rapidly.'' At end of hour asked what bill was [$10—my modest fee back in the ancient days before inflation!] and ''tell me something about the waiter'' (blond, blue-eyed, crew-cut, mustached—an exact description of me in those days). I asked directly what thoughts he had about our sessions. He said he had wondered why I wasn't saying anything much. He contrasted our sessions disappointedly with some sessions his wife had told him about, in which she had been fascinated by interpretations of her dream material. I then interpreted the dream and summarized the corroborating associations. He asked ''When did you figure out what I had on my mind?'' I said I guessed it at the beginning, as soon as he reported the dream. (Debated matter of technique: Because of my Radovian analyst and supervisor, I frequently depart from the classical technique, following the practice of Freud himself and some of his early colleagues that part of the ''educative'' phase early on is to gain leverage by establishing a conviction in the patient that the process has a meaning, even if that involves saying something about the therapist's inferential processes and when they occurred. The dangers of this are obvious, but doing it carefully to avoid gross one-upmanship is part of what I believe to be involved in intellectually mobilizing suitable patients by engaging their cognitive needs, their need to understand themselves, and the sheer element of intellectual interest that is part of what aligns the observing ego to enter into the therapeutic alliance. Part of what one does early on is to engage the patient's reality-based, mature cognitive interest in the psyche and its machinery. Persons who cannot think psychologically and cannot distance themselves from their own puzzling experiences are unsuitable for psychoanalytic therapy; even patients who are able to think psychologically about themselves and others usually lack a firm, concrete, gut-level conviction about the unconscious. Any professional in psychiatry or clinical psychology who has had analysis can report his surprise during early sessions at the fact that ''all this stuff is really true, even for me!'') My patient seemed to be very impressed by this, chuckling and repeating, ''By God, that's fascinating,'' and, ''To think I didn't know what I was talking about, and you did!''

In the fifth session, following the session about the waiter dream, patient enters smiling, remarks before reclining, ''Sure was interesting last time, *you knew* [emphasis!] all along what was going on and I didn't.'' First dream: *An Oriental, some kind of big shot, Chinese ambassador or prime minister or something—he's hurt—he has a big bloody gash in his abdomen.* Second dream: *I am measuring out some pills from a bottle.*

His associations continued as follows: Drugstore with brother—patient was partner but not registered pharmacist—at times he put up prescriptions when brother not in—nothing to some of them—silly to take the task so seriously—brother's Ph.D. degree—''he studied—I was lazy—lacked ambition—still do—make more money if I had more ambition—brother also brighter to start with—how bright am I, really?—always caught on to things quickly—poor work habits—wanted to be a physician, but not hard enough—I don't like doctors much—haven't seen one in years—some are pretty dumb"—(long discussion of wife's gynecologist who missed her diagnosis when patient got it right)—in drugstore patient used to advise customers about medication—often felt confident he had diagnosed a condition their doctor wasn't treating them for—(rambles on about various incompetent physicians he has known, detailed anecdotes with use of medical terminology, including narrative of brother Herman's unexplained surgical death, insensitivity of surgeon in pooh-poohing Herman's fear, then back reference to Herman's getting the Ph.D. by his brains and hard work). Comments on "experts who don't necessarily know much more than an intelligent amateur." But doesn't want to "overgeneralize that." (Pause—the first even short pause in the stream of the associations. Here one asks the tactical question whether to wait the silence out, which is sometimes appropriate, but in my experience, frequently not. I believe the tendency to wait it out regularly, as developed in this country during the twenties and thirties, is one reason for interminable analyses of people who are actually good prospects for help. We want to know what the patient is thinking that makes him pause, and I know of no really persuasive technical reason not to ask.) (Q Thinking?) "Still can't get over our last session—that *you knew* what was on my mind when I didn't—not just that I didn't—that's to be expected—but that *you knew*, that really gets me!"

Here, after the third over-stressed phrase "You knew," I had an association. The previous night I had been reading *TIME*, and saw a photo of the Burmese prime minister U Nu. So one hypothesizes a pun, mispronouncing the name, hence there is a linkage to me via this pun: Meehl = "You knew" = U Nu = Oriental in dream.

So I asked him for further thoughts about last session. "Surprised" [Pause] (Q Go on) "Impressed—what else can I say? [Pause] (Q Just keep talking) "Taken aback, sort of—why didn't *I* recognize it, if you did?—pretty obvious— then the $10 bill and all that stuff—shouldn't take an expert to see that!" [Laughs] (Q Any negative feelings at all?) "No—no negative feelings—irked with myself." (No resentment at all, toward me?) [At such moments one must be persistent] "No—or if so, very faint—I'd hardly call it resentment even." (Q But a feeling as if I had sort of won a round, or had one up on you, perhaps?) [Laughs] "A bit of that, sure—it's kind of humiliating to go yackety-yacketing along and then find out *you knew* all along—so I suppose you could say there was a little element of resentment there, yes."

I then asked if he was reading last night ("Yes, *TIME*"). Pressed for recall— "business, foreign affairs" (Q Picture in foreign affairs?) "Hey! By God—that oriental in the dream was a photo in *TIME*." Patient can't recall name—I tell him "U Nu" and point out that again, as last session, a play on words is involved. The dream shows how strong this reluctantly reported and allegedly faint resentment is, in that he has me wounded (killed, castrated, made into a woman?), linked perhaps by the associations to his wife's vaginal problem and the professional's misdiagnosis; then there is the obvious connection with the abdominal wound that surgerically killed his competitor, harder-working Ph.D. brother Herman. The interpretation of this material led to some further fruitful associations regarding his competitive feelings toward his business partner, whom he had originally described to me as "entirely compatible" and "a sympathetic person." I had external evidence, not discussed with him before this session, from his wife that in fact the business partner tended constantly to put down the patient, to underestimate his abilities, to pontificate to him about cultural matters in which the patient was as well informed as he (the business partner, like brother Herman, had completed his college education with high grades). As a result of this interpretation, some of that ambivalence toward the business partner came out, and several subsequent sessions were especially fruitful in this regard.

I should be surprised if any psychoanalytically experienced readers disagreed about the essentials of this dream's meaning. (As stated earlier, I bypass here questions of optimal technique, the "output" side of therapist interpretation, except to remind ourselves how *avoiding* intervention helps avoid theory-contamination of the patient's associations.) I have found in every audience of nonanalysts several listeners whose sudden facial "Aha!"-expressions showed the moment they "got it," sometimes with the irresistible bubbling up of laughter that so often accompanies a good interpretation (thus fitting Freud's theory of wit). It is equally clear that the lay audience (that includes some clinical psychologists in this context) displays wide individual differences in how soon various members begin to "catch on." And, of course, some tough-minded behaviorists or psychometrists (while smiling willy-nilly) shake their heads at the gullibility of Meehl and the other audience members. So Achensee—justifiably—is with us yet! The two diagrams say most of what needs saying by way of reconstruction. In Figure 1, the session's associative material is presented running sequentially (as it occurred) along the left and bottom. My first intervention (neglecting any unintended signals of changed breathing, throat-clearings, or chair squeakings) occurs after the first short pause by the patient ("editing," in violation of the Fundamental Rule), after his mentioning not-so-knowledgeable experts he "wouldn't want to overgeneralize about." The postulated guiding theme ("unconscious wish-fulfilling fantasy," if you will) is shown at center. One sees that associations viewed as "topics" are all loosely connected with the second dream's manifest content, and with each other. In Figure 2, I have avoided the "causal arrow" in favor of nondirectional lines (without arrowheads), as here we merely conjecture associative linkages that perhaps strengthen some of the final verbal operants; but we do not say which way the causal influence runs, nor assign any time-order. The strengthening of associations here is loosely "contextual," and some connections are obviously more speculative than others.

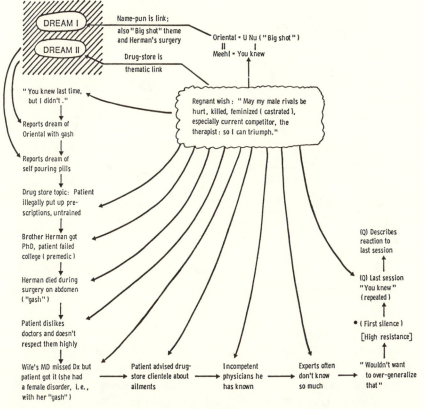

Figure 1.

The first dream finds no plausible place in this network, except via the (hence crucial) "U Nu = You knew" word-play (and, of course, the dream-day event involving *TIME*). We also, bootstrapping (Glymour 1980), invoke Freud's rule of thumb (Freud 1900/1953, 315–16, 333-35, 441-44) that two dreams of the same night deal with the same thing and often express a cause-effect relation, the first dream usually (not always) being the antecedent of the causal "if . . . then." Read here: "*If* Meehl [= U Nu = "you knew"] is killed, like my earlier sibling competitor Herman, *then* I will be the triumphant, learned, be-doctored expert who is perfectly capable of prescribing pills, etc." This inferred latent structure I do not here pretend to "quantify," and I am not convinced it needs to be quantified. All that the theme-tracing method to be proposed would perhaps do for us is to reduce somewhat the "subjective ad hockery" component in the skilled clinician's discerning the "red thread" allegedly woven into the associations. (For a similar approach to a non-psychoanalytic interpretative problem of psychology see Meehl, Lykken, et al., 1971.)

What is nomothetic and, in principle, "computerizable" contributes to our

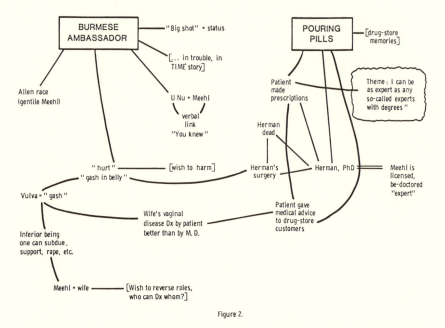

Figure 2.

understanding, but is rather feeble here unless combined with the idiographic components. A male figure with an abdominal wound would presumably occur in a psychoanalytic content analysis dictionary tagged with "castration" and "aggression" themes. But we don't have a place for pouring out pills, we don't have a place for Orientals, and we certainly couldn't get to the postdiction about *TIME* via the pun on U Nu. The pincers that "close together" to make the Achensee Question hurt do so, in this kind of situation, because the complex ontology (one pincher) requires a complex imposition of thematic content by the analytic listener and hence the other pincer (subtle epistemology) closes simultaneously. Detecting the "red thread" of allusions in the associative material, performing our psychoanalytic Vigotsky on blocks varying in many ways other than shape, size, and color, invalidates the jigsaw analogy, at least in the eyes of the skeptic. We have to discern what is common in the blocks of verbal output, but "what is common" resists any simplistic semantic or syntactic categorization. At the risk of overstating my case, I repeat, one must begin to formulate his conjectures before he can discern that a certain speech sequence tends to confirm them. To quote a previous paper of mine on this subject:

> Skinner points out that what makes the science of behavior difficult is not — contrary to the usual view in psychoanalytic writing — problems of observation, because (compared with the phenomena of most other sciences) behavior is relatively macroscopic and slow. The difficult problems arise in slicing the

pie, that is, in classifying intervals of the behavior flux and in subjecting them to powerful conceptual analysis and appropriate statistical treatment. Whatever one may think of Popper's view that theory subtly infects even so-called observation statements in physics, this is pretty obviously true in psychology because of the trivial fact that an interval of the behavior flux can be sliced up or categorized in different ways. Even in the animal case the problems of response class and stimulus equivalence arise, although less acutely. A patient in an analytic session says, "I suppose you are thinking that this is really about my father, but you're mistaken, because it's not." We can readily conceive of a variety of rubrics under which this chunk of verbal behavior could be plausibly subsumed. We might classify it syntactically, as a complex-compound sentence, or as a negative sentence; or as resistance, since it rejects a possible interpretation; or as negative transference, because it is an attribution of error to the analyst; or, in case the analyst hasn't been having any such associations as he listens, we can classify it as an instance of projection; or as an instance of "father theme"; or we might classify it as self-referential, because its subject is the patient's thoughts rather than the thoughts or actions of some third party; and so on and on. The problem here is not mainly one of "reliability" in categorizing, although goodness knows that's a tough one too. Thorough training to achieve perfect interjudge scoring agreement per rubric would still leave us with the problem I am raising. (Essay 10, this volume, p. 274)

I say again, we require the subsuming powers of the clinical brain, but we need a reply to the skeptic who says that there is so much play in the system that we can subsume arbitrarily, any way we want, by some mixture of general theoretical preconceptions and the prematurely frozen conjectures that we arrived at from listening to the dream and first association. My fifth proposal for making a dent in this problem is not very elegant, and I have not worked out any fancy statistics for doing it, partly because I think that they will not be necessary. We first have a clinically naïve but intelligent reader break the patient's discourse into consecutive blocks, which I shall label "topics." This initial crude categorizing is done without reference to inferred motives by someone ignorant of such things as defense mechanisms, symbols, and the like, essentially in the way a highschool English teacher instructs students to paragraph a theme by topics. Passing intrusions from the manifest content of some other block are simply ignored (e.g., a one-sentence allusion "as I said, Jones was the sergeant" does not fractionate a block of discourse dealing with a single "non-Jones" episode of barracks gambling). In Table 2 I have done this by three crude topic designations running along the top of the table. The purpose of this breaking up by crude manifest topics is essentially to provide separable chunks of material sufficiently large for a clinician to discern possible themes, but sufficiently small to prevent

Table 1. Themes Discerned by Five Analysts Independently Reading Discourse Block I (Crude Topic: Brother Herman). Hypothetical Data.

Theme Rubrics

Analyst A: "Competition with males"
           "Sibling rivalry"
           "Object-loss" [Herman's death]

Analyst B: "Object-loss"
           "Competition with another male"
           "Childhood family"

Analyst C: "Sibling rivalry"
           "Educational failure"
           "Intellectual snobbery"

Analyst D: "Competition with males"
           "Object-loss"
           "Self-sabotage" [didn't study]

Analyst E: "Inadequacy-feelings"
           "Childhood family"
           "Sibling rivalry"

his contaminating himself by themes discerned when looking at other blocks. So each crude topic block of discourse is submitted to *different* psychoanalytic therapists with instructions to write down whatever theme occurs to them as "present in it," "underlying it," "alluded to by it." This requires several teams of readers who do not have access to any of the crude topic blocks that the other teams are reading. We then type up (on 3 by 5 cards) the set of conjectured themes that have been generated in our analytic readers by a particular block. These cards are given either to another team (or, in this phase, I see no harm in the same team doing it) and we ask them to rank (or rate, or Q-sort—I think the psychometric format unimportant here) each theme as to its likelihood (or strength?) as a thematic contributor to that block. Writing the instructions for this third phase will be tricky, because there is a certain opposition between base rates on the one side and low probabilities (as being stronger evidence) on the other side, which is one of the reasons we need clinicians as judges. We employ the 2-phase rating scheme because we believe that a clinician especially skilled (or hyper-responsive to a particular theme) may *sometimes* discern something that the other clinicians will quickly see as a good bet even if they didn't come up with it themselves.

When these batches of rated themes are colligated in a single table, one now reads horizontally instead of vertically, to see whether the thematic "red thread" is apparent. In Table 2 I have illustrated this with fictional ratings. The summed (weighted) ratings for "competition with males" being the largest $\Sigma w_i = 17$) the red thread would be crudely quantified by these imaginary results. I do not have an appropriate significance test for evaluating the end result of this process, but I am not much interested in statistical significance testing anyway. A couple of ob-

Table 2. Summed (Weighted) Ratings of Themes Discerned within Blocks by Three Independent Sets of Analysts. Hypothetical Data.

Block I: Brother Herman		Block II: Drug-Store		Block III: Wife's Physician	
Theme	Σw_i	Theme	Σw_i	Theme	Σw_i
Competition with males	8	Self-aggrandizement	7	Intellectual snobbery	6
Sibling rivalry	6	Economic insecurity	5	Self-aggrandizement	6
Object-loss	6	Negative transfer	5	Competition with males	6
Childhood family	3	Hostility to experts	4	Negative transfer	5
Inadequacy feelings	3	Super-ego defiance	3	Dislike of doctors	4
Educational failure	2	Sibling rivalry	3	Object-loss	3
Self-sabotage	1	Competition with males	3		
Intellectual snobbery	1				

vious possibilities are to establish a crude baseline for "chance congruency" by slipping in blocks that belong to a different session or even to a different patient. One interesting question is how often we can "make sense" of the associations given to a dream even if the manifest content was not dreamed by the associater—a claim made against psychoanalysis forty years ago by Rudolf Allers in his book *The Successful Error* (Allers 1940) and never, to my knowledge, answered.

Space does not permit an adequate treatment of such a method's limitations, but there is one major defect that must be mentioned. Sometimes the allusions are few in number, perhaps *only* two or three, buried in high-resistance "sawdust," but are given evidentiary weight because of some delicate mix of very low nomothetic base rate ("expectedness" in the denominator of Bayes's Formula) with very high idiographic linkage ("conditional probability" in the numerator of Bayes's Formula). In such sessions, the Topic Block Theme Tracing method would fail utterly; and, I fear, so would all the others.

Summary

Summarizing this essay is rather like pulling together the material from a murky psychoanalytic hour, which is perhaps diagnostic of my cognitive condition. I *do* have a theme of sorts, but it's hard to verbalize briefly. In a word, I am ambivalently saying that Fliess's Achensee question deserves a better answer than it has yet received. Granted that there are respectable documentary disciplines (like history) that rely mainly upon qualitative evidence, a mind's discernment of intentionality, and the argument from convergence—disciplines that are neither experimental nor statistical in method; and granted that the "experimental/quantitative" (often called the "scientific") is not coextensive with the empirical, nor with the reasonably believable; and granted that the usual behaviorist and psychometric objections to the *concepts* of psychoanalysis (e.g., not "operationally specified") are simplistic and philosophically uninformed; granted all this, it remains problematic just what *is* the state of our evidence from the best source, the analytic session. I have suggested five directions we might take in an effort to ascertain how much of what the "thought reader" reads — admittedly using his own mind — is also objectively there, in the mind of the other.

References

Allers, R. 1940. *The Successful Error*. New York: Sheed & Ward.

Campbell, N. R. 1920. *Physics: The Elements*. Reprinted as *Foundations of Science*. New York: Dover Publications, 1957.

Carnap, R. 1950. 2d ed. 1962. *Logical Foundations of Probability*. Chicago: University of Chicago Press.

Freud, S. 1954. *The Origins of Psychoanalysis*. Ed. Marie Bonaparte, Anna Freud, Ernst Kris. London: Imago Publishing Co., Ltd.

Freud, S. 1900. *The Interpretation of Dreams*. In *Standard Edition of the Complete Psychological Works of Sigmund Freud*, ed. J. Strachey, Vols. 4–5. London: Hogarth Press, 1953.

Freud, S. 1974. *Standard Edition of the Complete Psychological Works of Sigmund Freud*, ed. James Strachey, Vol. 24 (Index). London: Hogarth Press.

Glover, Edward. 1940. *An investigation of the Technique of Psychoanalysis*. Baltimore: Williams & Wilkens.

Glymour, C. 1980. *Theory and Evidence*. Princeton: Princeton University Press.

Harman, H. H. 1976. *Modern Factor Analysis*. (3rd Ed.) Chicago: University of Chicago Press.

Kemeny, J. G., Snell, J. L., and Thompson, G. L. 1957. *Introduction to Finite Mathematics*. Englewood Cliffs, N.J.: Prentice-Hall.

Kordig, C. R. 1971a. The Theory-Ladenness of Observation. *Review of Metaphysics* 24: 448–84.

Kordig, C. R. 1971b. The Comparability of Scientific Theories. *Philosophy of Science* 38:467–85.

Kordig, C. R. 1971c. *The Justification of Scientific Change*. Dordrecht: D. Reidel.

Kordig, C. R. 1973. Discussion: Observational Invariance. *Philosophy of Science* 40:558–69.

Luborsky, L. 1953. "Intraindividual Repetitive Measurements (P technique) in Understanding Psychotherapeutic Change." In *Psychotherapy: Theory and Research*, ed. O. H. Mowrer, chapter 15, pp. 389–413. New York: Ronald Press.

Lykken, D. T. 1968. Statistical Significance in Psychological Research. *Psychological Bulletin* 70:151–59. Reprinted in *The Significance Test Controversy*, ed. D. E. Morrison and R. Henkel. Chicago: Aldine, 1970.

MacCorquodale, K. and Meehl, P. E. 1954., "E. C. Tolman." In *Modern Learning Theory*, ed. W. K. Estes, S. Koch, K. MacCorquodale, P. E. Meehl, C. G. Mueller, W. N. Schoenfeld, and W. S. Verplanck. New York: Appleton-Century-Crofts, pp. 177–266.

Marmor, Judd. 1968. *Modern Psychoanalysis*. New York: Basic Books.

Meehl, P. E. 1954. *Clinical versus Statistical Prediction: A Theoretical Analysis and a Review of the Evidence*. Minneapolis: University of Minnesota Press.

Meehl, P. E. 1956. Wanted — A Good Cookbook. *American Psychologist* 11:263–272.

Meehl, P. E. 1957. When Shall We Use Our Heads Instead of the Formula? *Journal of Counseling Psychology* 4:268–73.

Meehl, P. E. 1967. Theory-Testing in Psychology and Physics: A Methodological Paradox. *Philosophy of Science* 34:103–15. Reprinted in *The Significance Test Controversy*, ed. D. E. Morrison and R. Henkel. Chicago: Aldine, 1970.

Meehl, P. E. 1972. A Critical Afterward. In I. I. Gottesman and J. Shields. *Schizophrenia and Genetics: A Twin Study Vantage Point*. New York: Academic Press, pp. 367–416.

Meehl, P. E. and Golden, R. R. 1982. "Taxometric Methods." In *Handbook of Research Methods in Clinical Psychology*, ed. P. C. Kendall and J. N. Butcher. New York: Wiley, pp. 127–81.

Meehl, P. E., Lykken, D. T., Schofield, W., and Tellegen, A. 1971. Recaptured-Item Technique (RIT): A Method for Reducing Somewhat the Subjective Element in Factor-Naming. *Journal of Experimental Research in Personality* 5:171–90.

Meehl, P. E. 1983. "Consistency Tests in Estimating the Completeness of the Fossil Record: A Neo-Popperian Approach to Statistical Paleontology." *Minnesota Studies in the Philosophy of Science*, vol. x, *Testing Scientific Theories*, ed. J. Earman. Minneapolis: University of Minnesota Press, pp. 413–73.

Murray, H. A. 1938. *Explorations in Personality*. New York: Oxford University Press.

Neurath, O. 1959. Protocol Sentences. In *Logical Postivism*, ed. F. J. Ayer. New York: Free Press, pp. 199–208. (Originally published in German in 1932.)

Read, R. C. 1972. *A Mathematical Background for Economists and Social Scientists*. Englewood Cliffs, N.J.: Prentice-Hall, pp. 914–58.

Reik, T. 1948. *Listening with the Third Ear: The Inner Experience of a Psychoanalyst*. New York: Farrar, Strauss and Co.

Sears, R. R. 1943. Survey of Objective Studies of Psychoanalytic Concepts. New York: *Social Research Council Bulletin* No. 51.

Silverman, L. H. 1976. Psychoanalytic Theory: "The Report of My Death Is Greatly Exaggerated." *American Psychologist* 31:621–37.

Stone, P. J., Dumphy, B., Smith, M., and Ogilvie, B. 1966. *The General Inquirer: A Computer Approach to Content Analysis*. Cambridge, Mass: MIT Press.

12

The Virtues of M'Naghten

with Joseph M. Livermore

Imposing punishment on those who transgress criminal proscriptions has been thought to serve the interests of society in a number of ways. The painfulness of the punishment is designed to deter others from engaging in conduct inimical to these interests. Similarly, to the extent that an offender is likely to offend again, his imprisonment will protect society from further depredations by him. Finally, punishment and other therapeutic means utilized during imprisonment may rehabilitate the offender into a useful and law-abiding citizen.[1]

That individual conduct has adversely affected interests protected by the criminal law, however, has rarely been enough to invoke the sanctions of that law. Before punishing one who has invaded a protected interest, the criminal law has generally required some showing of culpability in the offender.[2] The basic *mens rea* concept, the notion that one has not violated the law unless he knows or in some cases should know the facts making his conduct criminal, is the most notable device to excuse those who are thought not blameworthy.[3] Provision of trial by jury and police and prosecutorial discretion in the invocation of the criminal process are other means used to sift out "innocent" offenders from those to be subjected to punishment.

There is a condition, then, to the general use of the criminal process to effect social ends. Before punishment may be exacted, at least with respect to most major crimes, blameworthiness must be present in the offender. That some deterrent, restraint, or rehabilitative purpose may be served is not in itself enough.

This emphasis on blameworthiness has led some commentators to assert that the criminal law is nothing more than a sophisticated vehicle for exacting retribution.[4] No doubt that purpose also is served. But there is nothing inconsistent in upholding an institution on solid utilitarian grounds that also serves a function many find to be distasteful. And much may be said, if only to still disquietude, for demanding blameworthiness as a pre-condition in those who are used as good soldiers in the fight for a better social order.[5]

338

Moreover, the exaction of retribution is more than the hangover from our barbaric past that most observers choose to characterize it.[6] The utility of the criminal law inheres not only in those simplistic notions of deterrence, restraint, and rehabilitation already described. It is based, too, on the creation of an individual abhorrence of certain conduct that is far more effective in discouraging that conduct than the largely fictional intellectual balancing of relative pain of imprisonment against pleasure of engaging in a forbidden act. That instinctive aversion is created by viewing criminal conviction as a societal judgment of moral condemnation. By allowing the rest of society to view the criminal as wicked and deserving of punishment, emulation of the criminal's conduct is discouraged.[7] Another related function of the criminal law is the promotion of a sense of individual responsibility for the effects of one's conduct on others. By holding to account those who violate the law, all are led to recognize that they too will be held to account for their conduct. This recognition in turn may lead individuals to a higher level of conduct than the minimum demanded by the criminal law.[8]

Obviously, the promotion of responsibility and the creation of abhorrence through moral condemnation are part of a larger goal of minimizing socially harmful acts. The criminal law effects this purpose in three distinguishable ways. First, it deters by creating an inducement — imprisonment — to avoid certain conduct. Second, it implants or reinforces an instinctive abhorrence of certain conduct by labeling that conduct evil and by excising from society those who engage in such conduct. Finally, it creates or bolsters a more thoughtful approach to one's place in society by fostering the recognition that individual responsibility must be taken for the effect of one's conduct on others.

The criminal law, in short, reduces the number of socially dangerous acts in more ways than by inviting a Benthamite intellectual assessment of relative pain and pleasure. To be sure, the reason most of us do not engage in rape is not because imprisonment for life is more painful than forced intercourse is pleasurable. But the criminal sanction against rape has helped create our abhorrence of the act and recognition of our responsibility to society for the damage it would cause our victims.

The imposition of punishment as a means of expressing the moral condemnation of society, barbaric retribution though it may be in the view of some, is justified to the extent that such an expression is related to and promotive of the senses of responsibility and abhorrence that are necessary to the attainment of the goal of minimizing socially harmful conduct. Disapproval of and desire to punish criminals may be necessary concomitants of those senses of abhorrence and responsibility that are themselves highly desirable. To fail to satisfy the desire to punish is to undercut the abhorrence and responsibility that prevent damage to others.[9]

These propositions, of course, are too easily overblown. Much as deterrence through threatened punishment is a matter of faith with respect to many crimes, so is the idea that the senses of abhorrence and responsibility partially bred by punishment will diminish if punishment is ended. It is impossible to know, and difficult even to speculate as to what, over time, the views of society would be toward socially dangerous but unpunished conduct. If, however, the societal need for moral condemnation through retribution, for the feeling that another is not getting away with something not permitted to most, is continually frustrated,[10] it is not unfair to conclude that the utility of the criminal law would be impaired.

Perhaps it suffices to say that attainment of the present goals of the criminal law depends in large part on social acceptance of the methods used and the results achieved in individual cases. Just as the institution of the criminal law may be brought into disrepute by the too easy attribution of criminality in situations where the label criminal is generally thought inappropriate,[11] so also may the institution be undercut if it releases as noncriminal those society believes should be punished. This does not mean that the criminal law may not be a means of educating the public as to the conditions under which moral condemnation and punishment is inappropriate.[12] It does mean that the results may not depart too markedly from society's notions of justice without risking impairment of the acceptability and utility of the institution.[13]

Our purpose is to explore the place of the insanity defense within the framework and purposes of the criminal law. Initially, it is clear that to the extent offenders generally may be thought to need restraint for the protection of society and rehabilitation to function well as members of society, the same may be said of mentally diseased offenders. Indeed, these needs would seem even greater for the diseased person who has committed a criminal act. Similarly, the deterrence of certain behavior in others by the imposition of punishment on some will not be diminished, and may be marginally increased, by imprisoning as criminals those offenders who now elude such punishment by use of the insanity defense.[14] Why, then, should we excuse from criminal responsibility those or some of those suffering from mental illness?

In traditional terms, the insanity defense can be justified only on the supposition that mental illness may negate that normal prerequisite to use of the criminal process, the culpability of the offender.[15] To test the utility of the defense, one must be able to identify the elements distinguishing blameworthy conduct from other conduct. Preliminarily, we reject the notion, frequently advanced, that deterrability is the touchstone of responsibility.[16] It is obvious that all offenders are nondeterrable in the sense that they were not deterred by the existing system of criminal sanctions. It is similarly obvious that all offenders could be deterred by some set of circumstances. And it is far from obvious, although it may be true, that insane offenders can be deterred only by means far more immediate in application than necessary to deter noninsane offenders.[17] We should and do attach moral condemnation to the person engaging in conduct that has not been and probably by any reasonable means could not be prevented.[18] If deterrence, abhorrence, and responsibility are to be promoted, condemnation must follow moral failure.

A more promising place to begin is with the inquiry whether insanity is inconsistent with moral failure. A person may be morally blameless if under the circumstances it would be unreasonable to expect avoidance of the forbidden conduct.[19] The criminal law has long taken account of this notion in many of its defenses. Thus, a man is permitted to kill if he reasonably believes it to be necessary to defend himself from being killed. Similarly, through the *mens rea* concept, a man is excused from criminality if he reasonably did not know the facts making his conduct criminal. And the defense of duress has excused in select cases where the threatened harm to the actor was far more severe than the harm caused to the victim by the criminal conduct.

At least two difficulties arise in equating the reasonableness of expecting compliance with moral blameworthiness. First and most obvious is the absence of any standard by which to judge the reasonableness of expecting compliance. In addition, even in those cases where opinion is nearly unanimous that compliance cannot reasonably be expected, the criminal law has often imposed moral condemnation. Thus, in a nondefensive situation, one may not take another's life to save one's own even though it is known that the actor will almost certainly do so.[20] That one acting reasonably is ignorant of the existence of a particular penal statute is no defense though one cannot reasonably be expected to comply with an unknown rule. One is not excused if an unreasonable mistake of fact causes the actor to believe his conduct is lawful. In all these cases, looking at the actor at the moment he acts, it is unreasonable to expect compliance. Nonetheless, the law condemns because the actor is expected to have the power of compliance.

The presence of moral blameworthiness then is less a quality of the offender, resting on his actual ability or inability to conform, than of the normative judgment of others that he ought to have been able to conform.[21] We have come full circle by saying a man is culpable when we intuitively believe him culpable. Yet this is not simply a begging of the question. It is only a recognition that the aims of the criminal law frequently conflict. Rejection of certain demonstrations that an offender could not reasonably have been expected to do otherwise can be justified on utilitarian grounds. In those cases, the value of demanding blameworthiness before punishment is thought to be overridden by other values. Thus, strict liability is generally justified on the ground that the punishment of those who are blameless tends to increase the level of compliance with the law by others and that to try *mens rea* issues in the wholesale prosecutions of public welfare offenses would unduly burden the court.[22] For our purposes, whether these justifications are persuasive is unimportant. What is important is the recognition that culpability, in the sense that society can reasonably expect the actor to do other than he did, is not an ultimate value but only one of the many values that must at times give way. Our own preferences are for the widest possible recognition of nonblameworthiness as an excuse. But given the utilitarian functions of the criminal law and the difficulty in assessing culpability, we do expect to compromise.

Beginning then with an admission of philosophical inability, we propose to examine the insanity defense, in all its forms, in terms of its effectiveness in isolating those elements which by common consent negate culpability. Our framework will be the notions of culpability inherent in the existing criminal law. We recognize that notions of culpability vary and that no formulation can satisfy all moral sensibilities. Nonetheless, we believe an effort so directed is valuable if only to emphasize the consideration we believe to be fundamental, a consideration always subsumed but rarely alluded to in discussions of this topic.

At the outset we should make it clear that we take the criminal law seriously. We believe that a criminal conviction is a societal condemnation that should not be imposed lightly.[23] Consequently, we believe that it is meaningful to examine the efficacy of the insanity defense as a device to exclude a group not properly subject to this condemnation. We recognize that there are those who view this as a merely semantic quarrel wasteful of societal resources at best and heedless of the crucial issue. To these commentators, insanity is relevant only to disposition and unnecessary to a finding of guilt.[24] We admit that it is appealing to contemplate the demise of the insanity defense with the consequent ending of the agonizing effort that has gone into its administration. And it is also appealing to contemplate a more careful approach in the disposition of offenders. If the purpose of the insanity defense, as suggested by the framers of the Model Penal Code, were solely to distinguish between those cases ''where a punitive-correctional disposition is appropriate and those in which a medical-custodial disposition is the only kind that the law should allow,''[25] then surely it would be more useful to approach the matter administratively at the disposition stage where a more refined determination could be made.

But it is clear that resolution of this treatment question is not the function of any of the present or proposed insanity defenses, and, in our view, it is equally clear that it ought not to be the function. First, the disposition of the offender is irrelevant to the issue of whether one has committed an offense. Yet, the insanity defense is used to negate criminal guilt.[26] Second, no proponent of a test of criminal responsibility seriously contends that his test resolves appropriate disposition. And it would be burdensome to the administration of criminal justice to inject that issue in a meaningful way into a criminal trial.

The major objection to destruction of the insanity defense in favor of confining insanity to resolution of the disposition question is that it would either permit the assessment of moral blame where it is inappropriate[27] or cut loose the criminal law from its moorings of condemnation for moral failure. Once one has started down this road, there is no defensible stopping point short of strict liability with the question of culpability being raised at the stage of disposition.[28]

While it is possible to construct a new system, and perhaps a more rational one, on these lines, we assume that such radical reconstruction is neither imminent nor appropriate so long as present social attitudes toward criminals and toward the utilitarian functions of the criminal law continue.[29]

Some preliminary mention must also be made of the problem of determinism. To the extent that the notion of culpability rests on the judgment that the actor ought to have done otherwise, and to the extent that determinism holds that an actor can never have done otherwise, there is an irreconcilable conflict.[30] Without plumbing these philosophical depths, it is enough for our purpose to say that the utilitarian functions of the criminal law are consistent with, indeed dependent on, the notion of determinism. It is expected that the structure of the criminal law will be a determinant on others. And assessing moral blame, regardless of the impropriety of this in the view of the determinists, will make the criminal law a more effective determinant.[31] The theory that it is unreasonable to expect anyone to do other than he did is speculative at best. This, and the additional fact that to embrace the theory is to destroy the existing postulates of the criminal law, require its rejection as a working principle of nonresponsibility.

Finally, we must briefly examine the notion of economy of punishment. In Bentham's terms this has meant that punishment ought not to be imposed where unnecessary to fulfill the purposes of the criminal law.[32] Thus, it has been argued that insane offenders need not be punished because insane potential offenders cannot be deterred, and the exclusion from punishment of such offenders would not impair the general deterrent function of the criminal law on noninsane potential offenders.[33] In our judgment, this argument has two major defects. First, it again separates blameworthiness from the criminal law. We view it as morally reprehensible to treat equally blameworthy persons differently on the fortuitous basis of the effect of such treatment on others.[34] Second, the economy argument focuses only on the criminal law purpose of deterrence by intellectual balancing of pleasure and pain. The creation of the senses of abhorrence and responsibility might well be impaired by such an approach. And the community's respect for the justness of the criminal law, on which its utility must rest, would almost certainly be reduced. Finally, it is not at all clear that the existence of an insanity loophole would not diminish to some degree the general deterrent effect of the criminal law.[35]

There are two basic and unavoidable problems in framing an insanity defense. First, mental condition cannot be split neatly into disease and health as the criminal law demands because of the need to find a defendant either innocent or guilty. Recognizing that mental health usually involves, among other things, "adjustment to a particular culture or to a particular set of institutions,"[36] mental disease or disorder involves slight incremental gradations of nonadjustment. Wherever on this continuum a line is drawn for any purpose, it is necessarily somewhat arbitrary as between those cases on either side and close to that line.[37]

The second problem is that, assuming the existence of a mental illness, the question of whether the defendant would have acted differently had he been free of mental illness is necessarily one of probability. An expert testifying to this issue can state only his belief and the basis for that belief. Certainty is impossible.

The oldest and most widely used test of criminal responsibility is that enunciated by the House of Lords in *M'Naghten's Case*:[38] The accused is not responsible if, at the time of committing the act, he "was labouring under such a defect of reason, from disease of the mind, as not to know that nature and quality of the act he was doing; or, if he did know it, that he did not know he was doing what was wrong."

Although the admonition has been uttered many times, it is always necessary to start any discussion of *M'Naghten* by stressing that the case does not state a test of psychosis or mental illness. Rather, it lists conditions under which those who are mentally diseased will be relieved from criminal responsibility. Thus, criticism of *M'Naghten* based on the proposition that the case is premised on an outdated view of mental disease is inappropriate. The case can only be criticized justly if it is based on an outdated view of the mental conditions that ought to preclude application of criminal sanctions.[39]

Before it is possible to assess whether *M'Naghten* is a satisfactory test of criminal responsibility, it is necessary to examine the meaning of the *M'Naghten* language. Although it is usually assumed that the meaning is obvious, as with most legal formulae, this is simply not the case. What follows is an attempt to put psychological meat on these legal bones.

From the psychologists' viewpoint, the noun "reason" refers to certain psychological functions, held together by virtue of a conceptual unity.[40] This unity lies in the fact that, in carrying out any of these functions adequately, inference takes place. That is, some sort of mental transition occurs between one mental content and another where there is a rational or logical relation between the contents justifying the inferential step. The existence of this rational relation is a condition to a justifiable making of this transition. The adequacy of these inferential transitions usually tends to be somewhat correlated in spite of differences in the particular subject matter or logical form of the relation. That is, one would expect that a person who reasons more ably than most people in solving riddles will more likely than not reason more ably in other domains. If a person's momentary state (e.g., sickness, fatigue, intoxication, rage) greatly impairs his ability to do arithmetic problems, it will also impair his working of crossword puzzles.

Identity of logical form and similarity of content will not, however, guarantee perfect correlation between reasoning abilities as displayed in two reasoning tasks. If the tasks differ appreciably in context or content (as they must if they are really two tasks), they will involve specific (task-tied) abilities over and above the cognitive abilities they share. Further, especially in mentally abnormal persons, they may arouse markedly different motivational or emotional states. Such noncognitive influences may aid, or may impede, the reasoning process. Fear anger, shame, boredom, competing interests, bias, and all such we shall designate generically, insofar as they exert an adverse influence, as "interfering factors." In ordinary language, we do not usually attribute to defective reason those inferential errors caused by interfering factors. For example, if a man thinks rationally about everything except politics (he is a zealous member of the Prohibition Party), we tend to describe him as "prejudiced" or "buggy about booze," rather than invoking a defect of reason. Ordinarily, we would not postulate a defect of reason unless we had evidence of considerable generality over diverse content domains, and preferably, also lacked good evidence for exaggerated influence of interfering factors. In this respect the psychologist proceeds rather closely in accord with the usages of ordinary speech. A possible difference, however, is that given a sufficiently extreme irrationality in a single domain (e.g., delusion of persecution), the psychologist is likely to invoke the notion of a defective ego, a concept that does imply at least the potential for defective reasoning over many or all domains. Whether ordinary usage resembles "psychologese" here is hard to say, partly because ordinary usage does not attempt these refinements for the extreme case. We rather suspect, however, that the layman would tend to question the financial judgment of a man who thought he was Napoleon. It is probable that common usage actually inflates the generality of reason.

In psychologese, then, a defect in reason would be a defect in the class of mental functions involved in performing psychological transitions between mental contents on the basis of a logical relation between them. In our view this is a sensible construction of these words and one which is wholly consistent with current psychological knowledge and practice. The argument often advanced by *M'Naghten* detractors that this phrase involves an outmoded conception of mental life[41] is simply not so.

In addition to the process of reasoning, the phrase "defect of reason" may also include the ability to perceive. The process of perception and categorization, the subsuming of the perceived item into its logical category, involves to some extent the ability to properly infer. Furthermore, when perceptions are demonstrably false, as when one hallucinates the voice of God speaking to him, the ability to reason is, usually, generally impaired. Accordingly, while a defect in perception does not always involve a defect in inferring, for purposes of *M'Naghten* such defects should be included in the concept defect in reason. This, in turn, changes the psychologese of defect in reason to defect in the cognitive ego functions—perceiving, remembering, inferring, classifying, judging, etc.— the meaning traditionally assigned to *M'Naghten*.

Defect of reason, of course, shares with the concept of mental abnormality the problem of degree. Inferential errors in the process of reasoning vary considerably in magnitude and depend on a variety of factors. It is impossible to say precisely how great a defect in reason is necessary to satisfy the *M'Naghten* rule. Words such as "substantial" or "gross" only mask the user's view. The substantial defects we have in mind, however, correspond roughly to the present distinction between psychosis and other mental abnormalities. In the words of Page:

> [In the neurotic] there is no deterioration of personality, intellect, or social habits, and no significant organic pathology. Rapport with the world of reality and the social group is maintained. Speech and thought processes are logical and coherent. Behavior is in conformity with cultural demands and responsive to social pressures. . . . The psychotic, on the other hand, is sharply differentiated from the normal individual by the bizarreness of his actions, the incoherency of his speech, the absurdity of his hallucinations and delusions, the inappropriateness of his emotional responses, and his general mental confusion. . . . Especially marked is the psychotic's loss of contact with the social group. The psychotic has withdrawn from reality. . . . Consequently his behavior and thoughts are unaffected by rules of logic, cultural mores, or outside happenings.[42]

The second phrase in the *M'Naghten* formulation is "disease of the mind," a term that appears in all the existing or proposed tests of insanity. As several writers have observed, this phrase more than any other poses problems for the administration of the criminal law.[43] Disease of the mind could mean an organic abnormality in brain structure or performance. It could also mean any diagnostic category in general usage in the psychiatric profession. Finally, it could be indicated by any strikingly abnormal conduct. As used, it has meant all these things and more. From the standpoint of the purposes for which the term is used, any of the usages may be entirely proper. From the standpoint of the criminal law, however, more refined usage is essential.

Restricting the meaning of mental disease to organic abnormality of brain structure or performance is too narrow for the purposes of the criminal law. Traditional psychiatric disorders such as schizophrenia may have no organic manifestations. Despite this, those afflicted with such disorders may not be culpable as that term is generally used.

But once the meaning of mental disease is broadened beyond organic disorders, reasoned analysis becomes even more difficult. In the first place the phrase, according to one commentator, means only a "theory by means of which we 'explain' how the events in question might have occurred."[44] If a crime is the event in question which calls forth an explanation of mental disease, and if those mentally diseased are excused, then there is a reasonable likelihood that most of those engaging in criminal conduct would be excused. This is particularly so because much crime is by definition the sort of abnormal conduct likely to call forth an explanation of mental disease.[45] Moreover, while labeling such a theory of human conduct as mental disease may be a proper shorthand designation of the probable utility of psychiatric treatment, it has little to do with whether blame-worthiness is negated.[46]

We shall explore later in this article how results vary from differing usages of the phrase "mental disease." For the present, we simply note that the criminal law has usually used the term in what one writer has called its core concept,

> i.e., with regard to such conditions in which the sense of reality is crudely impaired, and inaccessible to the corrective influence of experience—for example, when people are confused or disoriented or suffer from hallucinations or delusions.[47]

Under *M'Naghten* this usage is achieved by requiring the mental disease to result in a defect of reason.

With rare exceptions, the verb "know" in *M'Naghten* is used as a dispositional concept. Even though it is a verb grammatically, it usually refers to a state of potentiality rather than to an action or event. Dispositional concepts in psychology designate more or less enduring potentialities of the individual to react in a certain way given certain circumstances. If the circumstances rarely or never arise, the disposition remains unactivated, but it still has reality as a disposition. In this respect, dispositional concepts in psychology are not basically different from those attributed to inanimate objects. Thus, soluble is a dispositional concept, and we consider it literally correct to say that a particular sugar lump is soluble even though it happens never to be put into solution. It is obvious that most of the terms used to describe people, whether in psychologese or ordinary speech, are dispositional in nature. Skills, habits, abilities, and character traits are all dispositional; if it were otherwise we could never attribute any such trait to a person unless he was momentarily manifesting it. When we say, "Jones knows the date of the Norman Conquest," we do not require that he be saying or think-ing it. His knowing is his disposition (power, potentiality, ability) to say, or think, or write "1066" under suitable eliciting circumstances. When we say that Jones knows the date of the Norman Conquest, we cannot predict for sure he will be able to come up with the correct response on each and every occasion. He may have a momentary blockage for any of a number of reasons. The only way to cover all such contingencies so as to formulate an accurate dispositional state-ment is to exclude the entire class of interfering factors among the preconditions. But since this list is, strictly speaking, unknown to us, the only way of referring to it is by saying "and other interfering factors being absent," which renders the dispositional statement tautologous and empirically applicable only after the fact.

What does it mean to "know . . . that his act was wrong"? If a psychologist were to employ this language, he would be intending either (or both) of two com-ponents. One of these components is of an ethical-cognition nature; the other is of a guilt-signal nature. For short, let us designate these components by notations "e_c" and "g_s," respectively.

The primarily cognitive component e_c consists of a whole family of dispositions to perceive, classify, expect, think, recognize, infer, and *talk* (especially internally) about actions with respect to their allowed or forbidden character. These dispositions are, of course, the product of life experiences of many kinds, including explicit instruction in moral rules, observation of and identification with significant figures, and the whole reward-punishment regime which the institutions of the family, peer-group, and society have provided. We italicized "talk" because the ability to produce verbal responses in oneself, which in turn act as behavior controllers, is one of the most important dimensions in ethical choice. As we all know, a person can permit himself all sorts of inconsistent ethical behavior as long as he can avoid "talking to himself" about the real ethical nature of his actions. However, because the word talk has a social and out-loud implication, we shall employ the more neutral word "token," used by logicians and psycholinguists, as a generic term for the whole class of psychological events that have a symbolic nature sufficient to justify treating them as essentially propositional.[48] Thus when we say "Jones tokened red," we mean that there occurred within Jones a psychological event of a symbolic, referential, representational character—that in some sense, however attenuated, he said to himself or thought or intended the English sign red. He may have spoken it aloud, or his vocal chords may have formed the word silently, but these are not necessary conditions for a tokening event.

The cognitive component e_c involves a family of dispositions including dispositions to token such statements as "this is forbidden," "I shall deserve punishment," "if I do that I am wicked," "I'll hate myself later," and the like. While philosophers dispute about what is the essential element of ethical tokenings, psychologically we cannot—at least presently—assign clearly privileged status to some of these over others. The main point is that a person's moral training (all kinds, from all sources, and largely inexplicit) results in his having a family of dispositions to token statements containing ethical concepts such as wrong, illicit, forbidden, duty, ought, bad, sinful, unfair, and the like. If we could make an exhaustive survey of these tokening dispositions, and could then sort out the common features of those actions he is disposed to categorize one way or the other, we would have arrived inductively at the content of his particular ethical system.

The noncognitive component g_s is a motivational-affective state or event which is normally elicited by the activation of the dispositions e_c and which in turn functions as a behavior inhibitor. It is called a signal because it warns of future consequences (punishment, disapproval, guilt feeling, loss of self-esteem). As Freud points out, we learn by experience how to turn off this internal anxiety signal aroused by our impulse to forbidden actions. Most of the time our forbidden impulses are suppressed so quickly and automatically that the anxiety signal consists only of the faintest, briefest "blip" of internal warning, and is often not reportable (consciously introspectable) by the individual.

When psychologists say, then, that a person knows something is wrong, they may mean two different things.[49] First, an ethical-cognition signal may be meant. This, as we have indicated, is only the tokening of the phrase "this act is forbidden." A guilt signal, on the other hand, involves some emotional response such as anticipatory anxiety. In ordinary language, the distinction may be illustrated by the speeding driver who knows (i.e., tokens an ethical-cognition signal) that his act is illegal but does not feel that he is acting wrongly (i.e., does not adequately appreciate, in the sense of emotional-motivational overtones, that he may be imperiling the lives of himself and others). For *M'Naghten* purposes, it is obvious that the former meaning of "know" must be meant. That an offender has no conscious appreciation that he is presently acting dangerously, experiences no internalized inhibitory signal, and feels no guilt or remorse is irrelevant.

Returning to the e_c component of knowing that an act is wrong, we have interpreted this expression to mean that the individual, at the time he performed the act, had the disposition to token "this is wrong" or other roughly equivalent ethical statements. What *M'Naghten* says is that if he lacks this disposition, and if the cause of his lacking it is a defect in cognitive ego functions, then he is not criminally responsible. The writers of *M'Naghten* were aiming at a critical psychological distinction. Presumably anyone raised in our society (given at least some exposure, whether in home, church, school, or from peers) will have acquired ethical tokening dispositions. But whether an e_c disposition is activated at a given time depends upon a whole complex of factors, including the interference factors, operative at that moment. It obviously will not do to exculpate the agent solely because something impeded the activation of the e_c disposition,[50] because that impeding something may be any of the motives and emotions which impel a man to commit wrong acts and concurrently impair his momentary ability to token a member of e_c. If nondisposition to token an e_c signal were enough in itself, then the plea "my client didn't think his act was wrong at the time, because he hated the victim and intensely wished him dead" would, if factually established, justify acquittal. To avoid such absurd results, the rule specifies that the cause of the failure to token a member of e_c must be not an emotional or motivational factor, but a defect of reason.

The *M'Naghten* rule can be restated in these terms: The defendant will be excused if at the time of the criminal act he had a mental disease or defect which included among its symptoms or consequences an impairment in one or more of the psychological functions requisite for reasoning (i.e., cognitive ego functions) which, in turn, reduced the strength of his disposition to token "this is wrong" to a negligibly low value and, as a result, he did not in fact token "this is wrong" though, if the impairment of reasoning had not been present, the probability of his so tokening would have been materially greater. We recognize that this formulation can hardly be said to improve on the surface clarity of *M'Naghten*. But, as we have observed, this surface clarity is delusive and, in dealing with the human mind, simple formulae cannot be expected.

The meaning we have given the *M'Naghten* language, while consistent with existing definitions, is not to our knowledge generally recognized.[51] Almost all commentators have agreed that knowledge of wrong means more than the ability to say that murder is wrong.[52] To hold to the contrary would be to destroy the defense, for no one in our society is unaware of the illegality and immorality of murder.[53] Beyond this, there is no agreement. As one court put it, "The usual practice is to just say 'know' to the jury, and let it go at that."[54]

This is not to say that commentators have not attempted, just as we have above, to give rationalizing construction to those words.[55] Perhaps the most sophisticated attempt was by Sir James Fitzjames Stephen in 1883. In his view, a man could not know his act was wrong if he "was deprived by disease affecting the mind of the power of passing a rational judgment on the moral character of the act which he meant to do."[56] In explanation, he stated: "Knowledge has its degrees like everything else and implies something more real and more closely connected with conduct than" the faint "perception of reality" possessed by the insane.[57] By defining self-control as "a power to attend to distant motives and general principles of conduct, and to connect them rationally with the particular act under consideration,"[58] he was then able to conclude "that a man who by reason of mental disease is prevented from controlling his own conduct is not responsible for what he does."[59] Stephen's analysis is remarkably similar to our own. Indeed, if we were to reduce it to psychologese, we would reach the same result.[60]

Other writers have reached similar conclusions by focusing on the words "nature and quality of his act." "Nature" is usually explained by asking whether the actor knew that he was knifing someone. Thus, to use one of Professor Wechsler's examples, "a madman who believes that he is squeezing lemons when he chokes his wife"[61] does not know the nature of his act. "Know" is used in a different sense here than we have used it before. Rather than a disposition to respond, "know" in this usage refers to present awareness of surrounding physical facts.[62] The "nature" portion of *M'Naghten* is unimportant for two reasons. First, it almost never arises in actual practice. Second, most cases excusable under it would also be reached by knowledge of wrongfulness. It does have some theoretical interest in a case where the madman believes he is illegally choking his neighbor's dog when he is actually choking his neighbor. But one with such distorted awareness would almost certainly be suffering from a defect of reason creating a minimal disposition to token the appropriate ethical rule.

The word "quality," on the other hand, has more elastic possibilities. The most mentioned meaning is that it refers to the actor's recognition of the consequences of his act.[63] An example of Stephen's makes the point: "An idiot once cut off the head of a man whom he found asleep, remarking that it would be great fun to see him look for it when he woke."[64] Stephen assumed that the idiot knew his act was wrong in the sense that he knew his elders would reproach him for his mischievousness in forcing the man to look for his head. But it is clear that the idiot did not appreciate the enormity of what he had done. The difficulty with this approach is that very few criminals at the time of the crime have a real recognition of the extent of their wrong. If they did, crime might diminish. If quality is to take on the meaning of appreciation of enormity, its usage must be limited to gross cases such as that posed by Stephen. A test premised on complete understanding of what the consequences to the victim will be would exculpate almost every criminal.[65]

The *M'Naghten* rule has been the subject of much criticism.[66] Consider first the claim that since modern science has shown that the mind is an integrated whole, a rule such as *M'Naghten* which is formulated in terms of the rational or cognitive functions is counterscientific.[67] The first thing to be clear about is what we mean by saying that the mind is an integrated whole. If this rather imprecise expression is taken to mean that modern medical and behavioral science does not recognize the existence and operation of part-functions in mental life and behavior, in the sense that the mind or the person-in-action is conceived of by psychologists and psychiatrists as a kind of undifferentiated blob, the generalization is simply false as a summary statement of the teachings of these sciences. We are unaware of any theoretical formulation, however many or few professional adherents it commands, which treats of mind or behavior as an undifferentiated unity of the sort which this phrase might seem to suggest to an uncritical reader. If we examine the conceptualizations of human behavior and experience arising from such different approaches as clinical psychiatry, the statistical analysis of performance on psychological tests (differential psychology), or the experimental study of human and animal learning, we find, in spite of the vast differences in methodology and in the resulting substantive content of such theories, that they all utilize a model of the mind which postulates the existence of distinguishable processes, state-variables, part-functions, factors, intrapsychic "structures," and the like.[68]

Everyday experience demonstrates the ease with which psychological part-functions can be isolated. Consider, for example, a Siamese cat which, we are informed, has learned to shake hands. Interested in testing the truth of this somewhat unlikely allegation, a psychologically untrained layman offers his hand to the cat and says "shake." The cat fails to lift his paw. What are the possibilities that explain this failure of response? Since the cat, unlike the dog, is relatively weak in its susceptibility to control by purely social reward (such as a pat on the head and verbal approval, "Good cat!"), if he has been taught to shake hands to human command, the teaching very likely proceeded by the use of a more basic biological reward, such as a bit of food. This suggests the possibility that the cat fails to lift his paw because he has recently been fed to satiety and is in a state of minimal hunger drive. The layman knows that in order to test this particular hypothesis, the rational procedure is to prevent the animal from having access to food for a sufficient number of hours to ensure that the hunger drive will again be at high strength. Alternatively, it could be that the cat-trainer was a Frenchman so that the cat does not understand a verbal command uttered in English. Or, it may be that the cat is unusually shy of strangers and his normal response tendencies are being emotionally impaired by the interfering affective state of fear. Even in this simple animal case, we recognize that in order for certain behavior to appear, the organism must *know* something, must *want* something, and must not be too *emotionally disturbed*. That is, we take for granted that a given bit of behavior, or the absence thereof, is susceptible of alternative explanations, in terms of distinguishable psychological variables, processes, or states. The difference between this homespun kind of example and the application of a complex, highly abstract psychological theory, great as it is and differing in important details, is fundamentally a matter of degree.

A second frequently voiced objection to *M'Naghten* is that "reason" is not a psychological concept. With regard to the existence of a general reasoning factor, the statistical evidence is unclear.[69] This may be attributable to the reliance most such studies place upon psychological tests (rather than clinical manifestations) as applied to samples of subjects drawn from the mentally healthy population. When abnormal individuals compose a large part of the sample, and the data subjected to factorization are ratings by skilled clinicians based on extensive diagnostic contact, a strong factor of cognitive slippage (ego weakness, thought disorder) emerges, being reflected in high factor loadings on such phenomena as disturbances of conceptualization, perceptual distortions, illogical or unrealistic thinking, altered states of consciousness, associative dyscontrol—in short, the group of abnormalities traditionally considered evidential of a psychotic process.[70] Such a statistical finding, of course, should not be surprising to those versed in the psychodynamic system which measures ego strength in these terms.

Even assuming that there is no such thing as a general reasoning factor in psychology, it still would not follow that the *M'Naghten* reliance on that concept would be either unreasonable or counterscientific. It is important only that the concepts used in the law be compatible with existing scientific knowledge, not that the law utilizes scientific concepts. Whether an individual starting with certain premises consisting of the information from his sensory input, together with certain general principles of conduct which he may be supposed to have learned, is capable of drawing the correct inference as to the moral and legal characteristics of a contemplated action may very well depend upon the presence and operation of several distinguishable psychological factors or functions. The question, admittedly of great interest to the psychometric theorist in psychology, as to whether these distinguishable part-functions are statistically correlated or completely independent does not prevent the moral philosopher or the legislator from asking the question, for legal purposes, whether the individual's net ability to think reasonably is materially impaired. That is to say, the notion of rationality is properly viewed as what the philosophers call an attainment concept, a concept referring to the efficacy or validity of a certain behavioral outcome quite apart from the detailed causal analysis of the various parts of the mental machinery that must play their proper role in attaining this outcome. Thus if I am an employer hiring a retail clerk, it is important for me to assess the job applicant's ability to make change correctly. For my purposes, this outcome disposition is what is pragmatically important. This trait or disposition of the person can be assessed without carrying on a psychological inquiry into the system of part-functions which must be intact in order for it to exist, and into the question of whether these part-functions are in any way correlated.

To take another example, suppose a law firm is interested in hiring an attorney to handle automobile accident cases and in writing letters of inquiry the firm speaks of "auto accident case winning ability." A vocational psychologist undertakes a job analysis of what a lawyer does in working up such cases, devises a set of tests which he shows empirically to be severally predictive of these various job components, and then performs a factor analysis upon the matrix of intercorrelations among these tests. As a result of this factor analysis, he is able to show that the ability to win automobile accident cases is a complex composite of several distinct psychological dimensions which are completely independent of one another. He might, for instance, discover that lawyers who have a strong medical interest, a special detective talent in collecting bits and pieces of evidence, a knack for spotting potential jurors who will be free with the insurance company's money, and who know how to get under the skin of medical witnesses on cross-examination are the ones who tend to win this type of case. Since these factors are logically distinguishable, and show up in the statistical analysis to be unrelated to one another, the psychologist tells the law firm that they ought to stop talking about "automobile accident case winning ability" because his research has demonstrated that there is no such unitary trait or function in the mind. We doubt that the senior partners of the firm would find this argument persuasive, given their purposes.

Another frequent criticism of *M'Naghten* is that it improperly attempts to define insanity in terms of the single symptom of defective reasoning.[71] But this again confuses the issue of mental disease with that of criminal responsibility. If a symptom is the only relevant one for purposes of blameworthiness, the law has no choice but to define responsibility in terms of it. Moreover, this criticism implies that cognitive functions have been relegated to a minor status in diagnostic psychiatry. The opposite is true. For example, in diagnosing psychosis, the extent to which the patient's cognitive ego functions are intact is the single most important basis for distinguishing the psychotic from the nonpsychotic. The model of the mind which would seem presupposed by *M'Naghten* is a human being subject to various conflicting impulses and forces from within and without, that his behavior is the resultant of these forces, and that the mode of resolution of opposing forces (as, for instance, avarice impelling to larceny countervailed by fear of imprisonment and social shame if detected) is mediated by the operation of certain broadly cognitive processes. This model is, of course, precisely the model of the mind accepted in the psychodynamic picture of the role of the rational ego.[72] Under such a model, there is nothing strange about requiring, as a condition for criminal responsibility, that this rational ego must be capable of carrying out its weighing, judging, and decision-making functions.[73]

While technical philosophical considerations in legal thinking should be kept to a minimum, we are persuaded that part of the confusion and controversy surrounding the rationale and especially the case application of the *M'Naghten* rule arises from a lack of philosophical clarity about such core concepts as "knowing" and "reason." If a tendency (readiness, power, capacity) to respond in a certain way is conceived as a disposition of the first order, then the tendency or capacity or power to acquire or lose a disposition of the first order may properly be looked upon as a disposition of the second order. Thus in the realm of inanimate objects, the term "magnetic" designates a physical disposition of the first order. A magnetic bar is disposed to be attracted to the iron hull of a ship and is disposed to attract iron filings toward itself. These movements of bodies are individual events, located in space-time. By contrast, a disposition is not thought of as a short-term event or episode but as a state or power or potentiality having a more extended duration. (These distinctions are not offered as philosophically precise but as adequate for present purposes.) The property of being magnetic is, therefore, a disposition of the first order. Now a bar of iron may or may not be magnetic depending upon its history, this history having resulted in a certain microstate. By placing an iron bar in a sufficiently powerful electromagnetic field we can confer upon it the first-order disposition magnetic. By heating a magnetized bar, on the other hand, we can disarrange its molecular domains and render it nonmagnetic. A bar of iron has the potentiality of acquiring the first-order disposition designated by the term magnetic and also of losing this first-order disposition. The same is not true of a chunk of glass since glass is not a magnetizable substance. The property of being magnetizable, as distinguished from the property of being magnetic, is therefore a second-order disposition. Theoretically one can conceive of a hierarchy of dispositions of various orders, although in practice we rarely pass beyond the second, and almost never beyond the third.

In the realm of behavior the ability to calculate sums and products is a first-order disposition. That is, while no one is perpetually in a state of doing mental arithmetic, under suitable circumstances such behavior can be elicited. However, one is not born with this first-order disposition; it must be acquired. The capacity to acquire arithmetical dispositions of the first order is, therefore, a disposition of the second order, one which is lacking, for instance, in a congenital idiot. One might view a genetic defect producing an inborn error of metabolism that would lead an untreated individual to become an idiot as a disposition of the third order, because by suitable chemical procedures (e.g., dietary regime in an infant with phenylketonuria) we can induce in him the second-order disposition called the capacity to learn arithmetic. Another type of feeble-minded individual (say, one who has an anatomical absence of a large number of cells in the brain) cannot be brought into a condition of normal arithmetic-acquiring capacity and, therefore, his third-order dispositions are different from those of the first case.

Applying these concepts to the analysis of the notion "defect of reason," an individual piece of invalid inference is an episode or event characterized by certain properties, these properties being partly specified by the science of psychology and partly by the science of logic. The tendency to reason validly or invalidly at a given moment in time is a disposition of the first order. Whether such reasoning is valid depends upon a variety of factors, chief among which are motivational state (wishes, desires, goals, aversions), emotional state (fear, rage, excitement, arousal), and the whole family of cognitive instrumental habits usually subsumed under the broad rubric "cognitive functions of the ego." No psychologist alive can write the mathematical equations which give the probability of a valid inference. One cannot say with precision whether an individual tokened an ethical sentence judging a contemplated action as wrong. Again we remind the reader that for purposes of the criminal law it is not necessary to do this, and even if it could be done it would not be readily possible to translate it into jury instructions. It suffices for our purposes to recognize the three broad classes of determiners which enter into the insanity defense in a quantitatively significant way. A person may have a negligible probability of tokening the relevant ethical sentence because the combination of three classes of factors is sufficient to impair his first-order disposition to think rationally, to token a sentence which is a highly relevant logical inference from the perception or knowledge he currently possesses. The first of these classes of factors is his motivational state. Thus a very strong motive of avarice may impair an intelligent and informed taxpayer's momentary disposition to token the sentence "fudging on my income tax is wrong." Second, emotional state variables such as fear and rage and perhaps general excitement (extremely heightened arousal) may impair one's disposition to token the appropriate ethical sentence. Third, the set of cognitive instrumental habits broadly subsumed under cognitive ego functions (speaking psychoanalytically) or reasoning functions (speaking psychometrically) may be defective. Schizophrenic thought disorder, feeble-mindedness, organic brain damage, or a very extreme psychometric deviation at the low end of one of the several capacity or ability factors involved in a certain type of cognitive performance would all be examples of this third kind of inadequacy. Now it is obvious that a relatively weak ego will be, in general, more susceptible to the influence of the impairing factors of heightened (or grossly reduced) motivation, or of states of emotional excitement, than a relatively strong ego. From this point of view one may look upon ego strength and specifically the rational functions as second-order dispositions in the sense that they affect the potential influence of the two other classes of factors upon the first-order disposition to think rationally or irrationally, as the case may be, at a given moment in time.

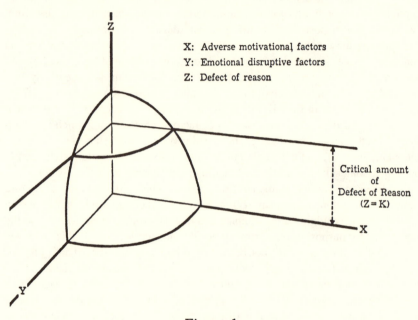

X: Adverse motivational factors
Y: Emotional disruptive factors
Z: Defect of reason

Critical amount of Defect of Reason (Z = K)

Figure 1

Not with the intention of a misleading claim to mathematical precision but for expository purposes, we find it convenient to represent the *M'Naghten* rule criterion geometrically. The x-axis (running from left to right in the plane of the page) corresponds to the influence of the broad class of factors called "motivational," thedirection of increased impairment of the disposition to token rationally increasing as we move toward the right. The point of origin at zero is for present purposes taken as the optimal motivational state for thinking rationally. The y-axis (pointing out toward the reader, perpendicular to the plane of the page) may be taken to represent the composite impairing influence of the broad class of emotional disruptive factors such as fear, rage, and general heightened physiological arousal or excitement. The vertical z-axis (perpendicular to the other two and lying in the plane of the page) represents cognitive ego weakness: Strong ego is at the origin and the readiness of rational function to be impaired increases as we move away from the origin. On any particular occasion, an individual's psychological state for purposes of the *M'Naghten* rule is then representable as a point in this space, the x, y, and z coordinates of this point representing the adverse strength of influence of motivational, emotional, and ego weakness factors respectively. As we move further away from the origin in this geometrical representation of the psychological functions, the disposition to token appropriately, the ability to think rationally, decreases. If we translate such common-sense terms of the law as "unable" or "substantial incapacity to . . . " as meaning a negligible probability or near-zero disposition, say a momentary disposition state such that the probability of tokening the appropriate legal or ethical sentence is less than .01, then we can represent this negligible probability (substantial incapacity) to token appropriately as a surface, such as the sphere shown in the diagram. Momentary states of an individual in which the combination of the strength of factors is such that the values of the relevant variables x, y, and z lie outside this surface are occasions in which we would say, for legal purposes, that the individual cannot think correctly about a situation or a contemplated action. Inside the sphere are coordinates of the points representing momentary values of the motivational, affective, and cognitive variables such that the probability of a correct and relevant ethical or legal tokening exceeds this low value. It may still have a probability considerably less than one-half, so that one would still be entitled to predict that the individual would not token appropriately, but the law does not exculpate anybody merely on the grounds that he had less than a fifty-fifty probability or chance of passing the correct moral judgment on what he is about to do. (Obviously if we proceeded on that basis, it would follow as a mathematical consequence that half of all criminal offenders should be excused, since, on the average, half of them will below that probability level.)

The *M'Naghten* rule for exculpation requires more than that, at the time of the action, the accused's momentary state correspond to a point lying somewhere outside the sphere representing the tokening probability of .01. It adds the further condition that, given a negligible probability of the offender's tokening the correct ethical sentence, the defect in the third component (i.e., the rational second-order disposition) must be above a certain critical value.

The explanation we have given may also be represented arithmetically. If x equals the effect of adverse motivational factors, y the effect of adverse emotional factors, and z the effect of the second-order disposition ego weakness, then there is an unknown function, f, which gives the e_c tokening probability, p, for any combination of these factors. If not knowing an act to be wrong means both a failure to token e_c and a probability of less than .01, then *M'Naghten* first requires that the joint values of x, y, and z were such at a given time that: $p = f(x, y, z) < .01$. Under *M'Naghten*, if $p < .01$, but e_c occurs, then conviction is required. If $p > .01$, whether or not e_c occurs, conviction is required. Only if $p < .01$ and e_c fails is acquittal possible.

It is not sufficient, however, that $p < .01$ and e_c fail. *M'Naghten* also requires that the adverse z component (ego weakness, cognitive slippage, thought disorder) must exceed a certain value in the pathological direction, k. As we have said before, this value cannot be precisely stated. Words such as "marked," "extreme," "pathological" can be used. Alternatively, one could say two standard deviations meaning psychometrically a condition experienced by less than 3% of the population. Either of these explanations, of course, is arbitrary. They are merely illustrative.

The full *M'Naghten* requirement, then, is that defendant fail to token e_c, that $p = f(x, y, z) < .01$, and that $z > k$. If $z < k$, while tokening may still not occur because of the strength of x and y, conviction must follow because the defendant had the second-order disposition, the capability of thinking rationally at the time of the act.

The immediately preceding material deals with the explication of the *M'Naghten* rule with emphasis upon a philosophically and psychologically adequate analysis of the verb "to know." It goes without saying that a similar diagram or equation can then be drawn in which the output variable or event is the overt response which is the subject matter of the offense. Given whether and how clearly a defendant tokens one or more sentences containing a moral or legal judgment upon the act he is about to commit, then whether he will in fact proceed to perform it will again be a function of the three classes of variables. But in this second diagram, the probability surface of interest is the probability of performing the overt act rather than, as in the diagram shown, the probability of a correct ethical-legal tokening event.

But whereas the psychologist is interested in the manner in which this second probability is related to the three major classes of factors, the *M'Naghten* rule is not. It nowhere denies that cognitive, conative, and affective components are inextricably involved jointly in determining the defendant's conduct; it merely disclaims any interest given the prior occurrence of a relevant ethical-legal tokening e_c. It is important to recognize this two-stage situation, because without such recognition one would be led to the erroneous conclusion that a rule which focuses attention upon the impairment of cognitive function is committed to the view that cognitive function is not susceptible of being impaired by motivational and emotional factors.[74] This *M'Naghten* does not deny. What it does deny is that it is legally and morally relevant whether, given an adequate disposition to token an appropriate ethical-legal judgment upon one's contemplated act (i.e., given the person's knowledge of the act's wrongness), the act was performed anyway because of strong feelings or urges. The important point is that from the standpoint of the community's sense of justice, while we are understandably reluctant to exculpate a criminal action on the ground that, although the person performed it knowing it was criminal, he was impelled so to do by strong criminal motives or emotions, we are much more willing to exculpate if his emotions and motives impaired his ability to be capable of thinking rationally.

Our defense of *M'Naghten* is not to be understood as defending all, or even perhaps most, of its application in current administration of the criminal law. It is our view that the inadequate analysis of knowing as a disposition, with the resultant inability or reluctance of expert witnesses to render their expertise into what they take to be the *M'Naghten* concepts, has in part resulted in the unedifying "battle of the experts," all too often present when insanity is at issue, and has contributed to the widespread disaffection among psychiatrists and social scientists with the *M'Naghten* rule itself. It is our position that when a proper analysis of moral and legal knowing is made, it is generally possible for an expert witness to translate the *M'Naghten* language into his own familiar clinical or scientific mode of thought, and that he can be responsive to counsel's questions without doing violence to his professional concepts. But, of course, this presupposes that the expert witness is not himself tendentious with respect to the criminal law, or hostile to its underlying policy of implementing the community's sense of justice.

Because of the widespread criticism of *M'Naghten* based on that test's alleged defects many attempts have been made to formulate better rules of responsibility. These attempts have embraced one or more of four separable approaches to the problem of criminal responsibility.

The most interesting new formulation is that advocated by a majority of the Royal Commission on Capital Punishment. They would "leave the jury to determine whether at the time of the act the accused was suffering from disease of the mind (or mental deficiency) to such a degree that he ought not to be held responsible."[75] In short, the jury is asked as the community in microcosm to apply its sense of justice to determine whether, given his mental condition, the accused ought to have been able to obey the law. If it is important that the criminal law reflect the societal sense of justice, this test meets that challenge on its own terms.[76]

This proposal has been most strongly criticized for its failure to provide any standard by which jury decision is to be guided.[77] For its application to be consistent with the rest of criminal law, the jury would have to be lectured on the purposes of the criminal law and the notions which generally control responsibility there. If this is to be done, it can better be done in the formulation of the test of insanity. On the other hand, if the test is to be applied intuitively, other problems arise. First, since intuitions will vary, similar cases will be treated differently. While that threat is always present, it has been the purpose of all legal systems to minimize rather than accentuate it.[78] More serious in our view is the underlying assumption that mental disease or deficiency is itself a reason to allow open jury nullification when it is forbidden elsewhere.[79] The jury is never asked directly whether this accused should be punished, although we cannot prevent that consideration from affecting their judgment on the issues left to them. Why should the fortuity of mental disease change the nature of the submission?[80] The only justifiable answer to this question is that mental disease inevitably so affects conduct that the accused ought not to be held responsible. But if this is so, then the question left to the jury ought to be whether the accused is suffering from a mental disease. If it is not so, then the question of justice of punishment ought to be left to the jury only in those cases in which the mental disease is of a type having a serious and substantial effect on conduct. Once this point is reached, the formulation that the Royal Commission avoided making must be made.

The besetting sin of the Royal Commission's test, as in all the proposed insanity rules, is the ambiguity of the phrase "mental disease or defect." As we have observed before,[81] the concept is simply not susceptible of any but a normative definition.[82] It means what the user wants it to mean. Even to limit it to the diagnostic categories of the American Psychiatric Association is illusive. It would be an unusual criminal who could not be placed by a friendly expert witness in one of the following categories: inadequate personality,[83] emotionally unstable personality,[84] sociopathic personality disturbance,[85] and transient situational personality disturbance.[86] It is no answer to say that these are not mental diseases unless we can also say what are mental diseases. And, to allow the jury to disregard expert testimony on this issue on the basis that the accused ought to be punished is simply to mask the fact that the announced test is not the test at all.

This is well illustrated by the experience of the District of Columbia under the *Durham* rule. Under that test, "an accused is not criminally responsible if his unlawful act was the product of mental disease or mental defect."[87] In *Blocker v. United States*,[88] the court felt compelled to grant a new trial because the doctors at St. Elizabeth's hospital had relabeled sociopathy a mental disease after having characterized it as merely a personality disturbance at the initial trial. Such a change in nomenclature may be useful, even necessary, for some purposes. But it is extremely unlikely that the psychiatrists considered the purposes of the criminal law in making their decision. Moreover, it is doubly unlikely that a delegation to psychiatrists of power to establish rules of criminal responsibility was the intent of the *Durham* decision.

It has been suggested that this result could be avoided by making mental disease an issue for decision by the jury.[89] But this is to return to the unprincipled decision that has been the basis of criticism of the Royal Commission test. If we have standards of what mental diseases are appropriate bases for excuse, why not state them in the rule? If we do not, how is the jury to decide the issue except on an intuitive judgment of whether the accused ought to be punished?

In *McDonald v. United States*,[90] the court modified the *Durham* rule by limiting the meaning of mental disease or defect to "any abnormal condition of the mind which substantially affects mental or emotional processes and substantially impairs behavior control." Unfortunately, ambiguity remains. It is unlikely that anything will ever be labeled a mental disease which does not have manifestations of abnormal mental or emotional processes. The chameleon "substantial" does not provide an effective limitation; necessarily it must bear the meaning the user wishes. The effect on processes is substantial enough to consider the individual diseased. How can one answer how much more substantial, if at all, the effect must be before it is substantial enough to qualify as a mental disease for *McDonald* purposes? How can the jury decide that issue? If the jury is permitted to say to the experts that what is substantial enough for you is not for us, are we not again simply covertly asking the jury to intuitively apply its own sense of justice?[91] If we want to do this we should do it openly. The second requisite for a *McDonald* mental disease, a substantial impairment of behavior control, can, in our view, only be taken as a restatement of the product rule discussed below. If the crime would not have occurred but for the mental disease, how can it be said that the mental disease has not substantially affected behavior control.[92]

Of course, it is unreasonable to ask that the concept mental disease dichotomize in the same way as guilt and innocence. Given the fact, however, that mental disease will often be used to characterize deviations from normality that have no criminological significance, it is important to recognize that the concept serves a very slight limiting function. If it is important to provide some standard for the jury, then a characteristic of those mental diseases that ought to affect responsibility should be isolated. This in our view is what the defect in reason requirement of *M'Naghten* does.

The most criticized portion of the *Durham* rule is the phrase "product of." As used by the court, it has meant that if the conduct would not have occurred but for the presence of mental disease, then the conduct is a product of that disease.[93] To the extent that mental disease is a hypothesis as to why the accused acted as he did, the product question is already answered. This is a problem of the concept of disease, of course. But given its existence, normal causative principles may serve no limiting function. Observers have also criticized the inherently speculative nature of the question asked. As Judge Brosman put it, "There may be some controversy concerning the scientific validity of the premise that a criminal act may be committed which is *not*, in some sense, a product of whatever mental abnormality may coexist."[94] While the "but for" rule may limit the scope of this dilemma, it does not end it. Indeed, a harder problem is raised, for it is practically impossible to say that a different individual would not have acted differently.[95] This last criticism is partially unsound. The question of the extent to which the mental disease affected the conduct is, though crucial, necessarily speculative. The expert can legitimately provide a conclusion only as to probabilities. This problem exists under any insanity test, but is accentuated in the *Durham* jurisdiction because once mental disease is established, the burden is on the government to prove that the conduct was not a product of that disease.[96] Since the product question is very difficult, perhaps impossible to answer, this burden could very well lead to acquittal of all who are mentally diseased, a result unrelated to common notions of blameworthiness.

Two other approaches have been advanced by those who believe that *M'Naghten* is faulty and that neither *Durham* nor the Royal Commission offer adequate alternatives. Both are present in the Model Penal Code approved by the American Law Institute:

> (1) A person is not responsible for criminal conduct if at the time of such conduct as a result of mental disease or defect he lacks substantial capacity either to appreciate the criminality [wrongfulness] of his conduct or to conform his conduct to the requirements of law.

> (2) As used in this Article, the terms "mental disease or defect" do not include an abnormality manifested only by repeated criminal or otherwise antisocial conduct.[97]

The first part of this formulation is a careful attempt to obviate what some observers believe to be *M'Naghten's* defects. The phrase "substantial capacity" avoids the problem of whether non-disposition to token must be absolute.[98] And the use of the word "appreciate" has been thought to remove any lingering doubt that more than mere knowledge that murder is wrong is required.[99] Also, the Code makes clear that a mental defect is to be treated in the same way as a mental disease, a point not expressly resolved under *M'Naghten*.[100] The issue of moral or legal wrongfulness is left unanswered.

The major defect, in our view, in this reworking of *M'Naghten* is that it excises those portions of the old rule that provide workable standards for judicial administration of the defense. Instead of the limiting device of defect of reason, a standard containing understandable fact issues,[101] the framers have rested on the illusion of mental disease. We can only say again that this leaves responsibility in the hands of labelers. That the framers were neither unaware of nor unbothered by this problem is obvious from their exception in the second clause of sociopathy from the category of mental disease.[102] Unfortunately, more than the exception of one troublesome case is necessary to avoid the ambiguity of mental disease. The excision of the old "nature and quality" clause, while not terribly significant, does remove that hedge against inappropriate attribution of responsibility in those few cases mentioned above in which there is a disposition to token that the act is forbidden but for other reasons there is no real understanding of the conduct engaged in.

The addition to *M'Naghten* contained in the Model Penal Code is the excusing condition of substantial incapacity to conform conduct to the requirements of the law. This raises the most relevant philosophical question. If a man is rendered incapable of obeying the law by mental disease, how can we find him morally blameworthy? The rub is that the question is unanswerable. In terms made familiar by the long debate over irresistible impulse, how do you distinguish an irresistible impulse from an impulse that was not resisted? In the terms of the Model Penal Code, how do you distinguish incapacity from indisposition?[103] There are several ways out of this impasse. One can move intuitively and ask whether the offender ought to have been capable, but this, of course, destroys the test. Alternatively, one can invoke the principle of causality and inquire, as the test seems to suggest, whether the disease was a cause of the conduct. But we know of no way to answer this question except by a *Durham*-like inquiry— whether, but for the disease, that act would have occurred. Finally, it is possible to construe the test as requiring an examination of the strength of the desire. As a theoretical matter, if impaired cognition should excuse, why should not magnified desires that make existing cognition useless for purposes of control? To administer such a rule would be impossible.[104] There is simply no way to measure the strength of desires. One further problem exists if ability to conform is read in this way. Even if related to mental illness, can level of desire be related to culpability? If normal or near normal inhibitory potential exists, can outrageous desires be blameless?[105]

As a means of testing the utility of *M'Naghten* and the newer rules, we have constructed a series of cases in which mental disease or defect is arguably present in one engaging in criminal conduct.[106] We will attempt to demonstrate how results will vary under the different formulations and how expert witnesses could reasonably testify in response to those formulations.

Case 1

Defendant, an adult living at home with his parents, is a mentally deficient individual with an IQ in the imbecile range. He has been watching some neighbor boys play cops and robbers with capguns, and upon finding a loaded revolver in the glove compartment of his father's car, he shoots and kills one of the neighbor boys. The patient's intellect is such that he does not discriminate between a capgun and a revolver, does not understand the meaning of death, does not know the difference between a television actor who falls down upon being shot and one of the neighbor boys who falls down pretending to be killed, and so forth. While in jail he asks whether the slain person will come to visit him. He shows no comprehension of what he has done or why he is involved with the police and is thoroughly baffled by the whole proceeding.

Diagnosis: 000-x903 Mental deficiency (severe).

While it is apparent that defendant is suffering from a defect of reason, his acquittal under *M'Naghten* will depend on whether ''disease of the mind'' includes mental deficiency. If it does, then defendant should fall under either branch of *M'Naghten* for failure to know the nature and quality of his act and to know that the act was wrong. Such a result is clearly dictated by the modified *M'Naghten* rule of the Model Penal Code.[107]

Results under the other tests are not so clear. The Royal Commission's rule precludes predictability and the result in this case would depend on the particular jury's view of the appropriateness of punishment. Under the capability approach of the Model Penal Code, we cannot predict. If capability means that but for the defect the conduct would not have occurred, the *Durham* inquiry, we would assume that an acquittal would follow. Beyond this, we are unable to give meaning to the test.

Case 2

A patient previously diagnosed as epileptic on the basis of typical *grand mal* seizures but hitherto without general disturbances in behavior suffers instead of his usual *grand mal* attack a so-called epileptic equivalent, a clouded state with deep confusion, hallucinations, fears, and violent outbreaks, in the course of which he commits a homicide. Persons in an epileptic equivalent are almost completely uninfluenceable by social stimuli and behave as in an automatic state. They usually have complete amnesia for the episode. Nevertheless, the patient's condition is definitely unlike that of the more usual motor seizure because the motor pattern itself instead of being the purposeless contraction of opposed muscles as in a *grand mal* fit, or a brief loss of consciousness as in the *petit mal* attack, has the usual characteristics of organized motor output with sequential movement patterns quite appropriate to what might be called at least the short-term or subsidiary goals. Thus, for example, a patient sent to the hospital by the court for psychiatric evaluation following an apparent unmotivated assault suffered an epileptic clouded state during his hospitalization in which he systematically dismantled the bed in his room, apparently to use the parts as weapons. The epileptic equivalent, however, is a member of the same disease family if not the same exact disorder as *grand mal* epilepsy.

Diagnosis: 000-550 Acute Brain Syndrome associated with convulsive disorder (epileptic equivalent).

This case is easily handled under each of the insanity formulations.[108] In the "but for" sense, the conduct is the product of the defect. Presumably, the jury under the Royal Commission test would be inclined to acquit. Under *M'Naghten* the disposition to token the e_c signal would be, we assume, wholly absent. The one problem would be whether this nondisposition resulted from a defect in reason. To some extent, the person's ability to carry out purposive conduct demonstrates an ability to reason, but this is true of anyone no matter how impaired he might be. Various tests, such as an EEG, demonstrate a marked organic change during an epileptic equivalent. This plus the amnesia after the event and the inability to influence conduct during the attack by external stimuli lead us to conclude that a defect of reason is present. Under almost any meaning given those tests requiring an inability to conform, the accused would also be acquitted.

Case 3

Patient is an extreme case of paranoid schizophrenia with delusions and hallucinations, who believes that the Masons are plotting to take over the government and that, because of their having learned that he is aware of their intentions, they have decided to do away with him as a potential informer. A salesman with a Masonic button in his lapel comes to the front door. As a result of his delusional misinterpretation of certain things he has heard in listening to a news broadcast, the patient has concluded that today is the day for his execution and is in an acute state of panic. He has armed himself and upon seeing the Masonic button he is sure that the salesman is the triggerman who has been sent to kill him. When the salesman puts a hand in his coat pocket to take out a personal card identifying himself, the patient is convinced that he is reaching for a revolver. The patient draws his own weapon and shoots first in self-defense.

Diagnosis: 000-x24 Schizophrenic reaction, paranoid type.

Under *M'Naghten*, an acquittal would occur. A thought disorder, or defect in reason, is the hallmark of schizophrenia.[109] This in turn, on the facts posited, has created a minimal disposition to token the appropriate signal. An argument could also be made that the disease-induced mistake prevents him from knowing the nature or quality of his act since he believed himself to be acting in justifiable self-defense. This would create a seeming inconsistency with normal rules of mistake of fact. While an unreasonable belief in the need for self-defensive action would inculpate, an outrageous belief would exculpate. But this is not a real problem so long as only those outrageous beliefs caused by defects of reason excuse.[110] Acquittal should also follow under *Durham* and the Model Penal Code.

Case 4

Patient is a professionally trained woman (Ph.D. degree in political science and some interest in the law) who is in psychotherapy with presenting complaints of diffuse anxiety, inability to relate socially and get along with colleagues, some irrational and nongratifying sexual acting out, and a history of a possibly genuine suicide attempt. While the presenting complaints and the superficial clinical picture are those of a neurotic who is chronically unhappy but by no means incapacitated for work and for at least a socially acceptable modicum of interpersonal relations, intensive therapeutic exploration and psychological testing make evident a basically schizoid personality structure with the attendant tendencies to cognitive slippage, extreme ambivalence, defective capacity for pleasure experiences, and a pervasive and recalcitrant interpersonal aversiveness ("distrust," "social fear," "closeness-panic"). The patient does at times think that others are looking at her or paying some special kind of attention to her when they actually are not. Her concern about the reactions of others when this social anxiety is sufficiently intensified and her hypersensitiveness and over-concern, which we normally consider to be neurotic, verges rather markedly into distortions of reality of sufficient deviation, and entertained sufficiently seriously by the patient, to be considered delusional. If these episodes, instead of lasting for hours or at most days, persisted and were unattended by some degree of self-awareness on the patient's part of her tendencies to distort, she would properly be diagnosed as schizophrenic reaction paranoid type instead of pseudoneurotic schizophrenia.

During one of these micropsychotic episodes in which she thought that some of her coworkers were speculating as to whether she was an alcoholic and as to whether she was illegitimately pregnant, she expressed the idea to the therapist that her administrative superior had as part of his supervisory responsibilities the duty to put a stop to this malicious gossip, and that since he did not seem to be doing so, he obviously was hostile to the patient. She was baffled by her supervisor's hostile attitude but was very indignant that he did not carry out his proper moral responsibility in defending her against this vicious character assassination. During this episode of delusional mentation she manifested what was for her a very rare expression of overt anger, clenching her teeth and with glaring eyes saying that she had put up with about as much of this kind of thing as she was going to stand for and that she intended if necessary to take some action to put a stop to it. Asked by the therapist what she had in mind, she said that she had not made up her mind what to do, whether to confront this superior, to go to somebody above his head and complain, to go to the police, or to take legal action. She was reluctant to go to the police since she thought perhaps the police were in some way involved and perhaps had been alerted to put her under surveillance. She then said, with an expression of mixed hatred and fear upon her face, that "after all, even the law recognizes a person's right to kill in self-defense." In describing the attitude and behavior of her fellow workers and the delinquent supervisor she had employed terms like character assassination, annihilation, or—a favorite term of paranoid patients—the verb "destroy." Thus she said, "I don't have to just sit and let these people destroy me."

Now as events turned out, while the therapist went through a period of some professional anxiety, this micropsychotic episode quickly subsided. The patient, while insisting that the people at work had some negative feelings toward her, indicated that she had perhaps slightly overdone things. Let us suppose, however, that instead of this harmless outcome, the patient had taken some form of direct violent action against the allegedly delinquent supervisor.

Diagnosis: 000-x26 Schizophrenic reaction, chronic undifferentiated type.

This case well illustrates the cognitive slippage associated with schizophrenia. By leaping from apparent dislike to desire to destroy, the patient is able to subsume her action under the heading self-defense and to believe that her action is morally and legally right. The ability to engage in reasoning of a sort is demonstrated by the patient's use of the following syllogism:

Major Premise: A homicide in self-defense is justifiable.
Minor Premise: My (contemplated) homicide is in self-defense.
Conclusion: My (contemplated) homicide is justifiable.

While its formal structure is irreproachable, this legal-moral syllogism is based upon a material fallacy of equivocation in the use of the term ''self-defense.'' In the major premise the expression ''self-defense'' has the meaning given it in the law, that defensive force may be used when one has reasonable grounds to believe that he is in immediate danger of death or serious bodily harm by a physical attacker. In the minor premise, however, given the facts which the patient herself has presented (neglecting that these ''facts'' are themselves paranoid distortions), she is not in immediate danger of death or serious bodily harm but only of damage to her reputation. The material fallacy of equivocation which she commits upon the middle term ''homicide in self-defense'' is in turn predicated upon an equivocation in a presupposed underlying syllogism which she does not token overtly in the interview (but which she may well have tokened implicitly prior to the interview) and which involves further equivocations upon words like ''attack,'' ''annihilate,'' and ''destroy.'' Now every clinician is familiar with the tendency of paranoid schizophrenics to utilize the word ''destroy,'' and we know that this word has a meaning for these patients that includes the notion of annihilation and the death of the self. And by ''meaning'' here we do not refer only to the noncognitive elements of meaning such as the motivational and affective features, although they are certainly crucial in the psychopathology of schizophrenia; we are saying that the cognitive meaning, the role in the entire associative network of verbal linkages which are the psychological basis of all logical transitions in symbolic thought, is aberrated in the schizophrene.[111] We emphasize the fact that it is the system of this patient's emotional and motivational forces — of her psychodynamics — that leads her to commit this egregious fallacy, one which a person with many years less education and many points lower IQ than she would hardly be capable of committing. There is no implication here that the rest of the personality, that is, her motives and her emotions, are utterly unrelated to the cognitive functions of this woman. On the contrary, it is precisely those other forces that lead her to commit the fallacy in question. But the point is that normal individuals or neurotics or sociopaths free of schizoid cognitive defect, would not be able to commit such a gross logical mistake. It is her schizoid ego weakness, her second-order disposition to cognitive slippage, that makes it psychologically possible for her to make a mistake of this sort. If she were to undertake the planning of a homicide under these circumstances, her ego is sufficiently intact (at this stage of the disease) so that she would be quite capable of rationally planning it, the reason being that the motivational and emotional system will not, in a patient with this degree of preservation of ego-function, suffice to impair her rationality as regards instrumental (means-to-end) connections.

It might be objected that this woman surely knows that defense against physical attack is *not* conceptually identical with defense against verbal damage to reputation, and, therefore, the *M'Naghten* rule would require that she be found guilty. But this objection overlooks the dispositional character of the word "know." It is true that if she were asked whether there were a difference between these two kinds of attack, she would probably be capable of tokening the appropriate differentiating sentences. But it is part of her semipsychotic ego defect that her disposition to token this self-critical sentence also has a negligible probability, and that is one of the crucial ways in which she differs from a normal or neurotic person. Putting it in another way, having studied a course in undergraduate logic, somewhere in her brain is stored the necessary cognitive material to permit her to form a sentence to the effect that she has just committed a material fallacy of equivocation. But she has a negligible disposition to token any such self-critical sentence, and that is one of the most important respects in which she differs from the rest of mankind.

A useful analogy in thinking about this type of cognitive slippage is to imagine a person intending to play according to the rules of solitaire but who is playing with very badly printed cards, a smudged deck, so that denominations and suits get mixed up. He might be playing by the formal rules of solitaire, but he would be making mistakes. A schizoid person is playing with a partly smudged deck of conceptual cards. Not all suits or denominations are equally smudged. And on some occasions of misplaying a card, he has done so because he very much wants to win the game. When it is psychologically convenient he does not look as carefully at a card that "fits" the rules as he would at another. Admittedly the degrees of cognitive slippage in the major mental disorders may sometimes be very subtle, hard to detect, and difficult to evaluate quantitatively. But in this respect, psychiatric testimony is not essentially different from any other kind of expert testimony where questions of amount and degree may at times be very difficult to answer.

In our opinion a *M'Naghten* defect in reason is present. As a result, the patient has a minimal disposition to token an e_c signal and she must be acquitted.[112] Similar results would occur under the Model Penal Code and *Durham*.

Case 5

The patient has the same degree of psychopathology as in Case 3, with a clinically manifest thought disorder resulting in a breakdown of the reality testing functions of the ego in the form of delusions and hallucinations. The difference between this case and that one lies in the relation between the content of the delusional ideation and the illegal act performed. This patient has the delusion that he is a special agent of God and experiences auditory hallucinations in the form of divine commands (a not uncommon symptom of paranoid schizophrenia). God tells him that the Episcopal bishop is corrupting the diocese into heresy (the patient is a devout Episcopalian) and God's hallucinated voice instructs him that the bishop should be "done away with." In his thought disorder the patient conceives himself as a religious martyr who will perhaps be badly handled by the organized institution of the church as was true of Jesus and of the great reformers. He also recognizes that shooting bishops for heresy is against the criminal law. He nevertheless commits a homicide involving careful planning and lying in wait outside the Episcopal residence for the bishop to appear so he can shoot him. Testimony is presented, and he also admits the fact that he drove away from the vicinity of the bishop's residence upon seeing a squad car come into the block. When interrogated by the police he states that he assumed that the institutions of society would, as usual, line up with the ecclesiastical hierarchy and that he expected to be persecuted for his God-inspired action. The presence of the schizophrenic psychosis is not in question, and no psychiatric testimony is offered to rebut the claim that the patient has paranoid schizophrenia and that his particular reaction was the direct psychological consequence of his psychotic delusion and hallucination.

Diagnosis: 000-x24 Schizophrenic reaction, paranoid type.

This case presents the question of the definition of wrong—does it mean legally or morally wrong? Courts have split on this issue.[113] While no untoward results would occur from allowing a broader definition in the case of commands from God,[114] it is obvious that at some point the accused must not be allowed to impose his own morality on the social system. Consequently, while we prefer the broader definition, we recognize that general acceptability of that morality may be an issue.[115] On the present facts we believe that the hallucination prevented the tokening of an e_c signal and that the defendant ought to be acquitted.

Case 6

The following language is taken from *People v. Wolff*:[116]

[I]n the year preceding the commission of the crime [the fifteen year old] defendant "spent a lot of time thinking about sex." He made a list of the names and addresses of seven girls in his community . . . whom he planned to anesthetize by ether and then either rape or photograph nude. One night about three weeks before the murder he took a container of ether and attempted to enter the home of one of these girls through the chimney, but he became wedged in and had to be rescued. In the ensuing weeks defendant apparently deliberated on ways and means of accomplishing his objective and decided that he would have to bring the girls to his house to achieve his sexual purposes, and that it would therefore be necessary to get his mother (and possibly his brother) out of the way first.

The attack on defendant's mother took place on Monday, May 15, 1961. On the preceding Friday or Saturday defendant obtained an axe handle from the family garage and hid it under the mattress of his bed. At about 10 p.m. on Sunday he took the axe handle from its hiding place and approached his mother from behind, raising the weapon to strike her. She sensed his presence and asked him what he was doing; he answered that it was "nothing," and returned to his room and hid the handle under his mattress again. The following morning defendant arose and put the customary signal (a magazine) in the front window to inform his father that he had not overslept. Defendant ate the breakfast that his mother prepared, then went to his room and obtained the axe handle from under the mattress. He returned to the kitchen, approached his mother from behind and struck her on the back of the head. She turned around screaming and he struck her several more blows. They fell to the floor, fighting. She called out her neighbor's name and defendant began choking her. She bit him on the hand and crawled away. He got up to turn off the water running in the sink, and she fled through the dining room. He gave chase, caught her in the front room and choked her to death with his hands. Defendant then took of his shirt and hung it by the fire, washed the blood off his face and hands, read a few lines from a Bible or prayer book lying upon the dining room table, and walked down to the police station to turn himself in. Defendant told the desk officer, "I have something I wish to report. . . . I just killed my mother with an axe handle." The officer testified that defendant spoke in a quiet voice and that "His conversation was quite coherent in what he was saying and he answered everything I asked him right to a T."[117]

In conversation with police officers, the defendant stated that he knew his act to be wrong.

Diagnosis: The four expert witnesses at trial testified that defendant suffered from schizophrenia, although they disagreed on type, but that he knew his act was wrong.

If the experts were using "knowing the act to be wrong" in the sense that we believe to be proper, then, of course, the defendant must be convicted under

M'Naghten. Whatever meaning they attributed to those words, their testimony effectively insured conviction. Nor could this result be avoided by their further testimony that the defendant's sense of wrong, his careful planning, and his calm were all consistent with the medical diagnosis. As the California court observed, schizophrenia itself is not a defense to crime: If that schizophrenia did not substantially impair the defendant's knowledge of wrongness, his conduct was no less culpable than any other criminal's conduct.

It may well be that the schizophrenia contributed to or was evidenced by the defendant's rather bizarre desires and the failure to satisfy them once having started in that direction. But it is not yet the law that unusual desires are an excuse for crime. *Durham* would lead to an acquittal, for under that test it probably could not be said that, absent the schizophrenia, the conduct would still have occurred. The ability-to-conform test might similarly lead to acquittal. In our view, such results demonstrate the fallibility of those formulations. We are unable to distinguish, in terms of culpability, abnormal desires in mentally diseased persons from abnormal desires in undiseased persons. Sexual fantasies are not exactly rare in teenagers, and, given a relatively equal inhibitory potential, we cannot see why as between two individuals who criminally act to realize those fantasies, only the one who concurrently suffers from mental disease should be acquitted.

All this may be an unnecessary quarrel with the expert evidence in the *Wolff* case. It is possible that the experts could have testified that the defendant was minimally disposed to token the appropriate e_c signal. On the other hand, and perhaps more likely, at least from the facts given by the court, the experts may have been too quick to explain the unusual desires by the label "schizophrenia." While such desires may evidence schizophrenia, considerably more is required before that diagnosis can be made. Assuming, however, the existence of schizophrenia coupled with the unusual desires of defendant and his failure to rationally effectuate his purpose, it may be more probable than not that at the time of the homicidal act his defect in reason prevented the necessary tokening.[118] The strength of this probability rests on the nature and severity of the schizophrenia and on the view taken of the bizarreness of defendant's actions.[119]

Case 7

A 35-year-old woman without previous history of mental illness develops a depressive episode of psychotic proportion with the usual symptoms of extreme sadness of mood, weight loss, sleep disturbances, loss of interest in her usual activities, preoccupation with negative thoughts of guilt and hopelessness of the future, and psychomotor retardation. During the deepest phase of the depression, the psychomotor retardation is such that she is massively inhibited from doing almost anything, including anything dangerous to herself or others. As the depression begins to lift, however, the psychomotor retardation is somewhat reduced, permitting her to make a few decisions and take a few actions, and since her affective state is still one of very black mood and her thinking is still along lines of hopelessness, she kills both of her children and makes an unsuccessful suicide attempt. On that day, she kept the children home from school, called up the cleaning woman and told her not to come as scheduled, and in various other ways showed clear evidence of systematic planning and premeditation of the killings. Emerging from the depression, she is at the time of trial essentially "normal" in all respects, and has a recollection although a somewhat dim one both of the events that transpired and of her mental state at the time. Insofar as she can recall how she felt and what she thought, her recollection is in accordance with the statements she made to police officers at the time, namely that while God did not command her to do anything and no voices were heard, it seemed perfectly clear to her that the situation was hopeless and that the killing was the only right thing to do because of the terrible state of the world and the terrible kind of mother she had been and would no doubt continue to be. The question as to whether she was doing something forbidden by law did not enter her consciousness in any form, although obviously she recognized the necessity of performing the act in some sense surreptitiously, when her husband and the cleaning lady and so on were not around. The evidence indicated, and the psychiatric testimony was to the effect, that the suicide attempt was genuine and miscarried quite inadvertently.

Diagnosis: 000-x12 Manic depressive reaction, depressed type. An alternative possible diagnosis would be 000-x14 psychotic depressive reaction, depending upon the relative emphasis placed by the diagnosing clinician on the absence or presence of previous marked mood swings versus the presence of environmental precipitating factors.

Within the ambit of the depressive attack, the patient suffers from a defect of reason. There is significant impairment of intellectual function and conceptualizing powers.[120] The patient's views of the world, though not necessarily delusional in the sense of objectively false, are not subject to change by rational argument. Thus, no demonstration that this patient was in fact as good or better a mother than most would have any chance of affecting her belief that she was not. In turn, this defect of reason reduced her disposition to token the appropriate e_c signal. This is true despite her efforts to keep others away because of her recognition that they would disapprove of her acts. The absence of the appropriate disposition is evidenced by her feeling that the act was right and it is not negated by her feeling that others would disapprove.

Whether this defendant is acquitted under *M'Naghten* depends on the view taken of the meaning of the word "wrong." If it means illegal, she must be convicted because she was disposed to token that phrase. If it means morally wrong, so long as the morality is consistent with social views generally, conviction might still follow. Only if wrong means morally wrong in the sense that the defendant honestly did not believe in the moral propriety of her action will acquittal occur. We believe this last construction is the proper one and for that reason favor acquittal.[121]

Case 8

Defendant is a psychopath possessing all those characteristics that so exasperate observers. Although showing no psychotic or neurotic traits, he engages in inadequately motivated antisocial behavior without feelings of guilt. He has no real insight into his condition and he is unable to learn by experience.[122] Well known in the town for his past trials with the law on petty charges, he once again passes bad checks in circumstances where it is obvious that he will be apprehended.[123] Indeed, he makes no effort to cover his tracks.

Diagnosis: 000-x61 Sociopathic personality disturbance, antisocial reaction.

M'Naghten would require conviction because psychopathy does not involve a defect of reason. The results under the Model Penal Code are less easy to judge. We believe that the psychopath is minimally disposed to token the relevant e_c signal. Thus, he may be said not to appreciate the criminality of his conduct and not to be able to conform his conduct to the requirements of the law. Undoubtedly, there will be testimony that psychopathy is a mental disease.[124] But the second paragraph of the Model Penal Code expressly excludes from the term mental disease any "abnormality manifested only by repeated criminal or otherwise antisocial conduct."[125] On its face this serves to exclude only those psychopaths whose only manifestation of abnormality is antisocial conduct. While the unusual antisocial conduct is normally what brings the psychopath to the psychiatrist's attention, other manifestations of abnormality are almost always present.[126] Thus, although it is clear that the framers of the Model Penal Code meant to exclude the psychopath, it is not at all clear that they did so.[127] The resolution of that question controls whether this defendant will be acquitted or convicted.

The question yet unanswered is whether the psychopath should be acquitted. There is some evidence that his disorder is neurophysiological, and there is overwhelming evidence that he differs markedly from the normal criminal. The impulsive, rationally purposeless nature of his conduct demonstrates that the law is not and cannot be a significant restraining influence on his actions. Yet on the surface he appears mentally healthy. To acquit him is to create an appearance of arbitrary action.[128] To the public it will seem that the more unrestrained and irresponsible one is, the less likely that one will be held to account.[129] This can only undermine the public's view of the justness of the criminal law. Further, to the extent that punishment of those transgressors who appear to be similar to the class that is to be deterred is essential to general deterrence, acquittal in these circumstances would subvert that function of the law as well. Consequently, while it may be unreasonable to expect the psychopath to comply with the law, there are also considerations requiring the law to insist on compliance.

Case 9

Defendant is an adult male homosexual invert of long standing. While he sometimes has affairs with adult males, his preference is for adolescent boys. The present offense involves a fourteen-year-old boy whom the defendant homosexually seduced. The defendant is free of any signs whatsoever of psychosis or even psychoneurosis, and is essentially "normal" in all respects except for the fact of his homosexuality.

Diagnosis: 000-x63 Sociopathic personality disturbance, sexual deviation, homosexual.

Again, since a defect of reason is not present, conviction under *M'Naghten* is required. The Model Penal Code presents more difficulties. While this homosexual is classified as a sociopath he is entirely different from the sociopath in Case 8. The only similarity in fact is in name. Many experts would, therefore, refuse to testify that homosexuality is a mental disease even though they would say that other sociopaths are mentally diseased. Even if experts did conclude that homosexuality was a disease, the second paragraph of the Model Penal Code formulation might prevent a finding to that effect. Again, however, homosexuals manifest other abnormalities than antisocial behavior. While we would conclude that this homosexual was disposed to token the e_c signal, we are not certain that he was capable of conforming his conduct to the requirements of the law. If that test is a restatement of *Durham*, acquittal should follow. But for his homosexuality, he would not have committed this act. Similarly, if the test refers to the strength of the desire as against normal inhibitory potential, acquittal might be necessary. While such measurements are impossible, we could not negate, and someone would surely testify to, the proposition that homosexual desires are unusually strong.

Since we share the common view that both homosexuals and heterosexuals must keep their criminal desires merely desires, we prefer conviction on these facts.[130] If the law is to promote responsibility, it must impose responsibility. There is nothing to satisfactorily demonstrate that this defendant should be free to pursue his desires while the generality of mankind must exercise restraint. Nothing would more quickly bring the criminal law into disrepute than to admit as a defense what is in effect the plea "I wanted very badly to do the act."

Case 10

Defendant, a hair fetishist, is charged with assault for snipping off a girl's pig-tail while standing on a crowded bus. His description, well supported by corrob-orating psychiatric testimony and by an acquaintance with whom he discussed his problem several days before the event, is one of mounting tension with a feeling tone close to anxiety and with a masked flavor of erotic excitement. Although he made various efforts to distract himself or to systematically place himself in sit-uations where he would be safe from performing such an act, he finally gave in to the impulse and got onto the bus with a pair of scissors in his pocket. Outside the area of the pathological impulse itself he does not show any gross psychiatric abnormality but on more careful study there is considerable evidence of a neu-rotic character structure with predominantly obsessive-compulsive features and also a possibility of a schizoid makeup. No gross thought disorder is present and a diagnosis of schizophrenia would not be warranted on the evidence.

Diagnosis: 000-x63 Sociopathic personality disturbance, sexual deviation, fe-tishism.

Resolution of the insanity defense in this case is almost exactly the same as in Case 9. *M'Naghten* leads to conviction both because there is no defect in reason and because there is a disposition to token the appropriate signal. Assuming that fetishism is a mental disease, *Durham* leads to acquittal.[131] If ability to conform involves an assessment of the strength of the desire, acquittal might follow under that portion of the Model Penal Code test. This is true even though the defen-dant's prior actions demonstrate some ability to control if substantial inability is construed as meaning markedly more difficult to avoid the prohibited conduct.

Case 11

Defendant is a nonpsychotic individual who, exhibiting the paranoid person-ality makeup, has for many years been characterized by a pattern of traits includ-ing over-sensitiveness, especially to affronts to pride or apparent slights, a ten-dency to "take note of" speech or gestures by other people more than most do, a kind of rigid self-righteousness, a heavy emphasis upon rules and principles, a tendency to irritability, an intense resistance to being told what to do, and, smol-dering, often very close to the surface, a great deal of chronic anger which at times is rather frightening because it may take the form of a burst of volcanic rage. In addition, he is suspicious, envious, and stubborn.

Defendant puts up a no-trespassing sign to keep out picnickers. When he finds that does not keep them away, he sets out a lot of bear traps and puts up a sign saying that trespassers enter at their own risk. A picnicker comes onto the property, steps into one of the bear traps, and as a result is so badly injured that he has to have his leg amputated. Defendant is charged with aggravated assault.

Diagnosis: 000-x44 Paranoid personality.

Under *M'Naghten*, a conviction would be obtained. A paranoid personality does not involve a sufficient defect of reason. Second, even though a negligible disposition to token the appropriate phrase exists, this is not caused by defendant's abnormal personality. It results instead from simple ignorance of the law. It is possible to argue that the disorder prevents defendant from appreciating the consequences to others of his conduct and thus prevents him from subsuming his action under the heading assault. But even if this construction is given, the failure to token would not result from the cognitive disorders included in defect of reason.

Under *Durham* and the Model Penal Code, the result would hinge on whether paranoid personality is a mental disease. If it is, then the conduct was a product of it if the argument above is accepted. And, in Model Penal Code terms, the mental disease caused a substantial inability to appreciate the wrongness of his action. If that much is assumed, then defendant also was substantially unable to conform. In order to conform, defendant would have had to be capable of self-criticism about his own self-righteousness concerning his legal rights on his land and capable of at least some empathy and sympathy for the possibly maimed trespasser.

Paranoid personality may be just a technical way of referring to a mean, envious, spiteful, over-sensitive, suspicious, and self-righteous person. If nonresponsibility ever goes this far, it is difficult to imagine who will be responsible. Our efforts to understand why people act as they do should not lead us to a deterministic conclusion that because he did as he did, he could not have done otherwise. At least we should not reach that conclusion unless we are willing to junk the criminal law as it presently exists.[132]

Case 12

The chief manifestation of the defendant's emotional instability is a pronounced tendency to "temper tantrums" or "rage attacks" when his pride is hurt or he feels unfairly treated. Defendant is an unattractive, ugly, undersized little squirt whose chief basis of security is that he is a very adept poker player. He has recently, however, had a run of bad luck and is rather deeply in debt. He is being pursued by several creditors including an underworld character who has lent him money at usurious rates and is known for beating up people who do not pay their debts promptly. He becomes involved in an all-night poker game in which one of the participants is a very famous gambler. Defendant knows his reputation but has not previously played poker with him. The famous gambler has been egged on by some of the others in the group, because of their dislike of the defendant, to needle the defendant. The gambler keeps up a running fire of sarcastic remarks during the course of the game. The defendant loses consistently and in desperation uses the rest of his money in an effort to bluff. The gambler successfully calls and says snearingly, "I'll teach you to try to bluff me, you little pip-squeak!" The defendant is overcome with rage and strikes the famous gambler. The gambler falls over backward, strikes his head, and subsequently dies from a subdural hematoma. Defendant is charged with manslaughter.

Diagnosis: 000-x51 Emotionally unstable personality.

Once again, because defendant's negligible disposition to token the e_c signal does not proceed from a defect of reason, he would be convicted under *M'Naghten*. Under the looser right-wrong test of the Model Penal Code, he might be acquitted. If an emotionally unstable personality is a mental disease,[133] then his nondisposition to token results from that disease. The circularity of the Code is thus highlighted. The diagnostic category is an explanation of the conduct which in turn excuses it. Similarly if capability of conforming is read in terms of *Durham* causality, acquittal must follow. And if that language is meant to refer to relative strength of impulse as against strength of control system, this case might well present a substantial inability to conform.

Case 13

Defendant is an enlisted man who mysteriously disappeared from a military post and turned up three weeks later in a distant city where he walked up to a military policeman standing in a bus depot and turned himself in. Investigation revealed that the defendant had bought a ticket to this city at a small town near the military post, had acted somewhat confused at the time, had upon arrival in the city rented a hotel room and signed a false name, and had laid aside his uniform and purchased a civilian suit. The military policeman testified that the defendant seemed somewhat puzzled and confused when he turned himself in and did not seem to be clear about what city he was in or what the date was. Detailed interviewing led the psychiatrists and the clinical psychologists to testify that in their opinion the defendant had a complete amnesia for the intervening period. The psychiatrists described him from the mental status examination as a classical hysterical personality with dissociative trends, and the psychometric data are strongly supportive of this assessment of the personality structure.[134]

Diagnosis: 000-x02 Dissociative reaction (fugue).

Since defendant literally did not know who he was or what he was doing, it is quite obvious that he did not know the nature or quality of his act (AWOL) or that it was wrong. On the assumption that defect of reason includes impairment of cognition such as this, an acquittal under *M'Naghten* is necessary. Similar results would follow under the other tests.[135]

Case 14

Defendant in an epileptic, his susceptibility to *grand mal* seizures being fairly well controlled by anticonvulsive medication. He also exhibits a not uncommon characteristic of epilepsy, a coexisting tendency to irritability and temper explosions. Defendant commits a serious assault in overreacting to a minor slight by an acquaintance. There is psychiatric testimony that defendant's rage differs from "normal rage" in that it is far more intensive, it is grossly disproportionate to the instigation, and it is attributable to an "epileptic brain."[136]

Diagnosis: Convulsive disorder (epilepsy), a condition not numbered as a psychiatric disorder except when manifested as an epileptic equivalent.[137]

Since defendant did not suffer from a defect of reason at the time of the act, he is not excused by *M'Naghten*. If an epileptic makeup is a disease or defect, as it surely is given a common-sense definition of those terms, then under the Model Penal Code and *Durham*, defendant must be acquitted. Defendant was minimally disposed to token the e_c signal and this indisposition resulted from his makeup. Consequently, he was also substantially unable to conform.

This case again raises a difficult question of culpability—whether we can reasonably expect defendant to do other than he did. Surely he is not to blame for his genetic makeup. But then neither is the homosexual nor, for that matter, the hoodlum who has acquired the criminal values of the environment in which he was blamelessly forced to grow up. It is a pity that we expect as much of these people as of those who by heredity and environment find obedience to the law much less taxing. Nonetheless, we do and it is difficult to see how we can do otherwise consistent with present social values. To isolate the cause of conduct is not yet to excuse it. Consequently, we are inclined to the view that this defendant should be convicted.[138]

Case 15

Defendant is charged with bank robbery. The psychiatric examination shows no evidence of thought disorder, true sociopathic personality, or organic brain damage. Defendant is of average intelligence and not particularly neurotic. His mother was a low-level nightclub entertainer and part-time prostitute, and his father was a bootlegger and thug. Defendant has two older brothers, both of whom became delinquent at an early age and have entered a life of professional crime. He grew up surrounded by persons who were either criminals or very marginal members of society, and from his early teens took it for granted that one did not work for a living but entered some kind of a racket. The problem of vocational choice for him was essentially which racket he should go into. The psychological and psychiatric examination shows an intact ego-function but a severely aberrant superego function, not in the sense that guilt or shame are impossible for this defendant, since he feels guilty if he does not pay a gambling debt, and he felt ashamed to have done such a clumsy job in the bank robbery as to get caught, but the content of his superego is that of a professional criminal. In other words, it is not so much that he lacks a conscience in the functional sense but that he lacks a properly informed conscience, as St. Thomas would say. The causal analysis of this man's criminal makeup is not essentially psychiatric or psychological in the clinical sense but is primarily sociological.

Diagnosis: 000-x62 Sociopathic personality disturbance dyssocial reaction.

Perhaps the best way to begin discussion of this common hoodlum is to quote the American Psychiatric Association's description of his mental disorder:

> Dyssocial reaction applies to individuals who manifest disregard for the usual social codes, and often come in conflict with them, as the result of having lived all their lives in an abnormal moral environment. They may be capable of strong loyalties. These individuals typically do not show significant personality deviations other than those implied by adherence to the values or code of their own predatory, criminal, or other social group.[139]

We do not suppose that most experts would call this condition a mental disease. We are wary, however, of how long this state of affairs will continue. It is now viewed as a mental disorder, presumably in this case a shorthand designation for an aberrancy in adjustment to existing social and cultural values. Since mental disease has no confining definition, we cannot be certain that this disorder will not become a disease, at least in the sense that it will be viewed as something susceptible of psychiatric treatment. Being declarative, surely criminal responsibility cannot be made to rest on medical opinion of appropriateness of treatment.

Conclusion

At this point it should be obvious what we believe the virtues of *M'Naghten* to be. The phrase ''defect of reason'' provides a test that, consistent with the remainder of the criminal law, allows a judgment as to whom we cannot reasonably expect to comply with the law. This test has both legal and psychiatric virtues. In terms of the legal system, it isolates those persons whose sense of reality and ability to think rationally is crudely impaired. This, in turn, is that group that is popularly viewed as insane. Their acquittal will not offend the community sense of justice nor will it impede the other functions of the criminal law.

In psychiatric terms, the phrase "defect of reason," which we have translated in current psychologese as impairment of cognitive ego-functions, including particularly perception of reality and ability to think logically and coherently, addresses itself to the distinction between psychoses and neuroses. Psychoanalytically the degree of ego weakness or strength, the extent to which the ego's cognitive functions are overwhelmed by the combination of pressures from the id and the external world, is the touchstone of psychosis.

While more refined formulations may be possible, it is our contention that the 124-year-old *M'Naghten* rule with its focus on cognitive impairment is sounder from the standpoints of the purposes of the criminal law, of present psychiatric knowledge, and of ease of judicial administration than any of the newer tests. We have noted the difficulty of giving meaning to terms such as "mental disease," "substantial inability to conform," and "product." Whenever the effort is made to make these terms consistent with general social views of responsibility, a retreat to *M'Naghten* is required. If the drafters of rules of criminal responsibility for the deranged are to remain true to general principles of responsibility, they must take account of societal views on the blameworthiness of conduct engaged in by mentally abnormal persons and of the effect of ignoring those views on the utility of the criminal law. It may be that to do this is to embrace consistency at the expense of substance and that the policies thought to support criminal sanctions are merely myths which have held us in thrall too long. But this position is better addressed to the criminal law as such and not to a small, in this respect indistinguishable, portion of it.

Notes

1. We do not mean to imply here, or in the discussion below, that we would agree that the justifications of the criminal process bear all the weight that they are sometimes made to bear. We do, however, suggest that if one wishes to use the existing criminal law in the traditional way, including the guilt-innocence dichotomy, consideration must be given to fulfilling the functions thought to justify the criminal law.

2. See Brett, *An Inquiry into Criminal Guilt* (1963), 37 passim; H. M. Hart, "The Aims of the Criminal Law," *Law and Contemporary Problems*: 23 (1958):401. No matter how high the predictability that a particular individual will commit an offense, most people intuitively abhor the thought that he ought to be imprisoned or treated before he has done so. See generally Meehl, *Clinical Versus Statistical Prediction* (1954).

3. See Packer, "Mens Rea and the Supreme Court," *1962 Supreme Court Review*, 107; Sayre, "Mens Rea," *Harvard Law Review* 45 (1932): 974.

4. E.g. Lukas, "A Criminologist Looks at Criminal Guilt," in 2 *Conference on Social Meaning of Legal Concepts—Criminal Guilt* (ed. Cahn, 1950), pp. 113, 151–52.

5. H. L. A. Hart, *The Morality of the Criminal Law* (1964), 20; H. L. A. Hart, *Punishment and the Elimination of Responsibility* (1962), 27–30.

If I were having a philosophical talk with a man I was going to have hanged (or electrocuted) I should say, I don't doubt that your act was inevitable for you but to make it more avoidable by others we propose to sacrifice you to the common good. You may regard yourself as a soldier dying for your country if you like. But the law must keep its promises.

1 *Holmes-Laski Letters* (ed. Howe, 1953), 806.

6. See Cohen, "Moral Aspects of the Criminal Law," *Yale Law Journal* 49 (1940): 987, 1011.

7. Roche, *The Criminal Mind* (1958), 79; Cardozo, "What Medicine Can Do For Law," in *Law and Literature* (1931), 70, 88–89; Andenaes, "General Prevention—Illusion or Reality?", *Journal of Criminal Law, C. & P.S.* 43 (1952): 176, 180; Cohen, "Moral Aspects of the Criminal Law," *Yale Law Journal* 49 (1940):987, 1017; Michael, "Psychiatry and the Criminal Law," *American Bar Association Journal* 21 (1935):271, 275; Wechsler, "The Issues of the Nuremberg Trial," *Political Science Quarterly* 62 (1947): 11, 16. See Alexander and Staub, *The Criminal; The Judge, and the Public* (rev. ed., 1956), 131; Flugel, *Man, Morals, and Society* (1945), 133–34; West, *Conscience and Society* (2nd ed., 1950), 165–76.

8. Alexander & Staub, *The Criminal, The Judge, and the Public* (rev. ed., 1956), 130; H. M. Hart, "The Aims of the Criminal Law," *Law and Contemporary Problems* 23 (1958): 401, 410; Cf. Moberly, *Responsibility* (1956), 22–23.

9. 2 Stephen, *History of the Criminal Law of England* (1883), 79–80.

10. See Alexander and Staub, *The Criminal, The Judge, and The Public*, (rev. ed. 1956), 211–23; Flugel, *Man, Morals and Society* (1945), 169–74; Ehrenzweig, "A Psychoanalysis of the Insanity Plea—Clues to the Problems of Criminal Responsibility and Insanity in the Death Cell," *Yale Law Journal* 73 (1964): 425.

11. H. M. Hart, "The Aims of the Criminal Law," *Law and Contemporary Problems* 23 (1958): 401, 423.

12. See H. L. A. Hart, *Punishment and the Elimination of Responsibility* (1962), 16–18.

13. "In the determination of guilt age old conceptions of individual moral responsibility cannot be abandoned without creating a laxity of enforcement that undermines the whole administration of criminal law." Fisher v. United States, 149 F. 2d 28, 29 (D. C. Cir. 1945) (Arnold J.), *aff'd*, 328 U.S. 463 (1946). See also *In re* Rosenfield, 157 F. Supp. 18(D.D.C. 1957); Alexander and Staub, *The Criminal, The Judge, and The Public* (rev. ed., 1956), 213–14; Wootton, *Social Science and Social Pathology* (1959), 336; Learned Hand, *A Letter*, University of Chicago Law Review 22 (1955): 319.

14. H. L. A. Hart, "Legal Responsibility and Excuses," in *Determinism and Freedom in the Age of Modern Science* (ed. Hook, 1958), 81, 94–96; Cohen, "Moral Aspects of the Criminal Law," *Yale Law Journal* 49 (1940): 987, 1008; Silving, "Mental Incapacity in Criminal Law," *Current Law and Social Problems* 2 (1961): 3, 25.

15. Brett, *An Inquiry Into Criminal Guilt* (1963), 172; H. M. Hart, "The Aims of the Criminal Law," *Law and Contemporary Problems* 23 (1958): 401, 414 n.31; Silving, "Mental Incapacity in Criminal Law," *Current Law and Social Problems* 2 (1961): 3.

16. Guttmacher and Weihofen, *Psychiatry and the Law* (1952), 412, 420; *Model Penal Code* § 4.01, comment (Tent. Draft No. 4, 1955); Davis, "Some Aspects of the Currens Decision," *Temple Law Quarterly* 35 (1961): 45, 46; Kuh, "The Insanity Defense—An Effort to Combine Law and Reason," *University of Pennsylvania Law Review* 110 (1962): 771, 782. See generally Schlick, *Problems of Ethics* (1939), 143–58; Wechsler, "The Criteria of Criminal Responsibility," *University of Chicago Law Review* 22 (1955): 367, 374. Discussions of deterrability in this context may not be directed to the culpability of the offender. Thus, the assumption is often made that punishment of the insane will add no particular force to the deterrent efficacy of the law toward other insane potential offenders. This proposition, of course, ignores the fact that punishment of insane offenders may have a deterrent effect on potential noninsane offenders. Hill, "The Psychological Realism of Thurman Arnold," *University of Chicago Law Review* 22 (1955): 377, 392; see text accompanying note 14 *supra*. Those who stress deterrability may also be proceeding, *sub silentio*, on an economy of punishment theory. See text accompanying notes 31–35 *infra*.

17. See Wechsler and Michael, "A Rationale of the Law of Homicide: I," *Columbia Law Review* 37 (1937): 701, 753 n.179.

18. See text accompanying note 20 *infra*.

19. H. L. A. Hart, *Punishment and the Elimination of Responsibility* (1962), 20; Raab, "A Moralist Looks at the Durham and M'Naghten Rules," *Minnesota Law Review* 46 (1961): 327, 329.

20. E.g., Regina v. Dudley & Stephens, 14 Q.B.D. 273 (1884).

21. Mercier, *Criminal Responsibility* (1935), 40–41; Roche, *The Criminal Mind* (1958), 86, 249; Davidson, "Criminal Responsibility: The Quest for a Formula," in *Psychiatry and the Law* (ed. Hoch and Zubin, 1955) 61, 67; Silving, "Mental Incapacity and Criminal Law," *Current Law and Social Problems* 2 (1961): 3, 13. Many commentators on the insanity defense assume there is some underlying notion of culpability that will easily resolve cases appropriately. Thus, it is said that the insanity defense negates *mens rea*. E.g., United States v. Currens, 290 F. 2d 751, 761 (3d Cir. 1961); Biggs, *The Guilty Mind* (1955) 82–84; Davis, "Some Aspects of the Currens Decision," *Temp. Law Quarterly* 35 (1961): 45, 46; Goldstein and Katz, "Abolish the 'Insanity Defense' — Why Not?'', *Yale Law Journal* 72 (1963): 853. But absence of *mens rea* is just a shorthand designation for "a series of situations in which a man will be held by the criminal law to be without guilt, unified by a very broad and vague statement of principle." Brett, *An Inquiry into Criminal Guilt* (1963), 40. See also H. L. A. Hart, *The Morality of the Criminal Law* (1964), 6. To say that insanity negates *mens rea* is to imply falsely that an insane offender is never responsible. Such an assertion says nothing about the actual or appropriate content of the defense.

22. See Wasserstrom, "Strict Liability in the Criminal Law," *Stanford Law Review* 12 (1960): 731, 737–39.

23. On the morality of punishing where one cannot blame, see H. L. A. Hart, *The Morality of the Criminal Law* (1964), 28; 2 Stephen, *History of the Criminal Law of England* (1883), 172; De Grazia, "The Distinction of Being Mad," *University of Chicago Law Review* 22 (1955): 339, 348; Michael, "Psychiatry and the Criminal Law," *American Bar Association Journal* 21 (1935): 271, 275; Wechsler, "Panel Discussion: Insanity as a Defense," *F.R.D.* 37 (1964): 365, 381–82.

24. Wootton, *Social Science and Social Pathology* (1959), 245–54; Diamond, "From M'Naghten to Currens, and Beyond," *California Law Review* 50 (1962): 189, 204–05; Guttmacher, "The Psychiatrist as an Expert Witness," *University of Chicago Law Review* 22 (1955): 325, 327; Weintraub, "Criminal Responsibility: Psychiatry Alone Cannot Determine It," *American Bar Association Journal* 49 (1963): 1075; see Newsome v. Commonwealth, 366 S.W.2d 174, 180 (Ky. 1962) (dissenting opinion), *cert. denied*, 375 U.S. 887 (1963).

25. *Model Penal Code* § 4.01, comment (Tent. Draft No. 4, 1955).

26. See Acheson, "McDonald v. United States: The Durham Rule Redefined," *Georgetown Law Journal* 51 (1963): 580, 581.

27. See note 23 *supra*. It can be argued that as much social opprobrium attaches to being labeled insane as to being labeled criminal. See De Grazia, "The Distinction of Being Mad," *University of Chicago Law Review* 22 (1955): 339, 350, 355. While this may be so practically, the purpose of the insanity label in a criminal trial is to extract the opprobrious connotations from having committed a criminal act. Wechsler, *supra* note 23, at 398. So long as we maintain the present structure of the law, we must take this distinction seriously. Compare Pigg v. Patterson, 370 F.2d 101 (10th Cir. 1966), *with* Rouse v. Cameron, 373 F.2d 451 (D.C. Cir. 1967).

28. Wootton, *Crime and the Criminal Law* (1963), 32–57.

29. H. L. A. Hart, *The Morality of the Criminal Law* (1964), 27–29.

30. That there are causes for a person's act is not inconsistent with his having the power to do other than he did. Edwards, "Hard and Soft Determinism," in *Determinism and Freedom in the Age of Modern Science* (ed. Hook, 1958), 104, 106; Sellars, "Fatalism and Determinism," in *Freedom and Determinism* (ed. Lehrer, 1966), 141; University of California Associates, "The Freedom of the Will," in *Readings in Philosophical Analysis* (eds. Feigl and Sellars, 1949), 594; Hobart, "Free Will

as Involving Determinism and Inconceivable Without It, *Mind* 43 (1934): 1; Raab, "Free Will and the Ambiguity of 'Could'," *Philosophical Review* 64 (1955): 60. Some determinists go further than this and assert that causes exist which preclude choice. It has been argued that determinism precludes moral blameworthiness to the extent that the determining psychological forces operative are unconscious. Hospers, "Free-will and Psychoanalysis," in *Readings in Ethical Theory* (eds. Sellars and Hospers, 1952), 571. See generally McConnell, *Criminal Responsibility and Social Constraint* (1912); Whitlock, *Criminal Responsibility and Mental Illness* (1963), 54–71; Louisell and Diamond, "Law and Psychiatry: Détente, Entente, or Concomitance," *Cornell Law Quarterly* 50 (1965): 217. *But see* Fingarette, "Psychoanalytic Perspectives on Moral Guilt and Responsibility: A Reevaluation," *Philosophy and Phenomenological Research* 16 (1955): 18. For a prosecutor's forceful presentation of the collision between legal concepts of blameworthiness, responsibility, free choice, and the typical psychiatric emphasis upon viewing antisocial conduct nonmorally, as a kind of sickness which is strictly determined by the offender's past and in a sense beyond his voluntary control, see Goulett, *The Insanity Defense in Criminal Trials* (1965), 21–25.

31. Brandt, "Determinism and the Justifiability of Moral Blame," in *Determinism and Freedom in the Age of Modern Science* (ed. Hook, 1958), 137, 138–39.

32. Bentham, *An Introduction to the Principles of Morals and Legislation* (ed. Dolphin, 1961), 164, 184.

33. The underlying assumptions of this argument are that insane offenders as a class are non-deterrable, that normal people will not identify with such offenders, and that, consequently, exculpation of these offenders "bespeaks no weakness in the law." *Model Penal Code* § 4.01, comment (Tent. Draft No. 4, 1955). See Board, "Operational Criteria for Determining Criminal Responsibility," *Columbia Law Review* 61 (1961): 221; Waelder, "Psychiatry and the Problem of Criminal Responsibility," *University of Pennsylvania Law Review* 101 (1952): 378, 379. *But see* Silving, "Mental Incapacity in Criminal Law," *Current Law and Social Problems* 2 (1961): 3, 25–26. All these assumptions are open to serious question.

34. An argument could be made for the Benthamite view if insane offenders were necessarily blameless and others were being punished, though blameless, solely for utilitarian reasons. But one need not accept the notion that since punishment is evil, everyone, regardless of blame, should escape it when such escape has no anti-utilitarian consequences.

35. See text accompanying note 14 *supra*.

36. Wootton, *Social Science and Social Pathology* (1959), 218.

37. This arbitrariness remains even if the concept of mental disease is further subdivided. For an attempt to distinguish mental disease, mental illness, and mental disorder, see Naples v. United States, 307 F.2d 618, 629 n.34 (D.C. Cir. 1962).

38. 10 Cl. & F. 200, 210, 8 Eng. Rep. 718, 722 (1843). See Diamond, "On the Spelling of Daniel M'Naghten's Name," *Ohio State Law Journal* 25 (1964): 84. On the history of the insanity defense, prior to *M'Naghten*, see Biggs, *The Guilty Mind* (1955); Platt and Diamond, "The Origins of the 'Right and Wrong' Test of Criminal Responsibility and its Subsequent Development in the United States: An Historical Survey," *California Law Review* 54 (1966): 1227; Platt and Diamond, "The Origins and Development of the 'Wild Beast' Concept of Mental Illness and Its Relation to Theories of Criminal Responsibility," *Journal of the History of the Behavioral Sciences* 1 (1965): 355.

39. E.g., Wechsler, "The Criteria of Criminal Responsibility," *University of Chicago Law Review* 22 (1955): 367, 373.

40. For a discussion of whether "reason" is a unitary concept from a psychologist's viewpoint, see text accompanying notes 69–70 *infra*.

41. E.g. Biggs, *The Guilty Mind* (1955), 132–33; Weihofen, *The Urge to Punish (1957), 11;* Zilboorg, "A Step Toward Enlightened Justice," *University of Chicago Law Review* 22 (1955): 331; see Pierce v. Turner, 87 Sup. Ct. 978 (1967) (Douglas, J., separate opinion).

42. Page, *Abnormal Psychology* (1947), 100. See also *American Psychiatric Association, Diagnostic and Statistical Manual* (1965), 12; Henderson and Gillespie, *Textbook of Psychiatry* (9th ed., 1962), 133; Hinsie and Campbell, *Psychiatric Dictionary* (3rd. ed., 1960), 488, 602; Maslow and Mittelman, *Principles of Abnormal Psychology* (rev. ed., 1951), 305; Masserman, *Principles of Dynamic Psychiatry* (2nd ed., 1961), 61, 305; Noyes and Kolb, *Modern Clinical Psychiatry* (6th ed., 1963), 421; Rosen and Gregory, *Abnormal Psychology* (1965), 7; Strecker, Ebaugh, and Ewalt, *Practical Clinical Psychiatry* (7th ed., 1951), 371–72; White, *The Abnormal Personality* (3rd ed., 1964), 51; Freud, "Neurosis and Psychosis," in *Collected Papers* 2 (1924), 250–51.

43. E.g. Roche, *The Criminal Mind* (1958), 15, 253; Wootton, *Social Science and Social Pathology* (1959), 205–25; Diamond, "From M'Naghten to Currens, and Beyond," *California Law Review* 50 (1962): 189, 192–93; Hakeem, "A Critique of the Psychiatric Approach to Crime and Correction," *Law and Contemporary Problems* 23 (1958): 650; Swartz, " 'Mental Disease': The Groundwork for Legal Analysis and Legislative Action," *University of Pennsylvania Law Review* 111 (1963): 389, 390; see Goulett, *The Insanity Defense in Criminal Trials* (1965), 7.

44. Szasz, "Psychiatry, Ethics, and the Criminal Law," *Columbia Law Review* 58 (1958): 183, 190; see also Szasz, *The Myth of Mental Illness* (1961), at ix.

45. "The occurrence of any crime creates a powerful impetus to construct a theory to explain it." Szasz, *Law, Liberty and Psychiatry* (1963), 134. See also Davidson, "Criminal Responsibility: The Quest for a Formula," in *Psychiatry and the Law* (eds. Hoch and Zubin, 1955) 61, 63; De Grazia, "The Distinction of Being Mad," *University of Chicago Law Review* 22 (1955): 339, 343.

46. "Discussion of addiction as a mental illness in a broad social context or for treatment purposes is quite a different matter from labeling addiction 'mental disease' in the context of determining criminal responsibility." Heard v. United States, 348 F.2d 43, 46 (D.C. Cir. 1964); see Campbell v. United States, 307 F.2d 597, 608–10 (D.C. Cir. 1962) (dissenting opinion); Blocker v. United States, 288 F.2d 853, 859–62 (D.C. Cir. 1961) (concurring opinion).

47. Waelder, "Psychiatry and the Problem of Criminal Responsibility," *University of Pennsylvania Law Review* 101 (1952): 378, 384.

48. A propositional mental event is one capable of being either true or false.

49. It is frequently said that whether a person knew his act was wrong is an unanswerable question. Cassity, *The Quality of Murder* (1958), 6; Guttmacher and Weihofen, *Psychiatry and the Law* (1952), 408; Diamond, "Criminal Responsibility of the Mentally Ill," *Stanford Law Review* 14 (1961): 59, 60–61; Roche, "Criminality and Mental Illness—Two Faces of the Same Coin," *University of Chicago Law Review* 22 (1955): 320, 321. For the reasons discussed, we believe this assertion is false.

50.

A person of sound mind and discretion will not be exempted from punishment because he might have been a person of weak intellect or one whose moral perceptions were blunted or ill developed or because his mind may have been depressed or distracted from brooding over misfortunes or disappointments, or because he may have been wrought up to the greatest and most intense mental excitement from sentiments of disappointment, rage, revenge or anger.

State v. Andrews, 187 Kan. 458, 465, 357 P.2d 739, 744 (1960), *cert denied*, 368 U.S. 868 (1961).

51. But see Davidson, "Criminal Responsibility: The Quest for a Formula," in *Psychiatry and the Law* (eds. Hoch and Zubin, 1955), 61, 68.

52. E.g., Hall, *General Principles of Criminal Law* (2nd ed., 1960), 481; Williams, *Criminal Law* (2nd ed., 1961), 495–97.

53. E.g., Weihofen, *Mental Disorder as a Criminal Defense* (1954), 76; Diamond, "Criminal Responsibility of the Mentally Ill," *Stanford Law Review* 14 (1961): 59, 61; Guttmacher, "The Psychiatrist as an Expert Witness," *University of Chicago Law Review* 22 (1955): 325, 328.

54. Sauer v. United States, 241 F.2d 640, 649 (9th Cir.), *cert. denied*, 354 U.S. 940 (1957).

55. E.g., Maudsley, *Responsibility in Mental Disease* (1897), 103; Rubin, *Psychiatry and Criminal Law* (1965), 20. See also United States v. Westerhausen, 283 F.2d 844 (7th Cir. 1960); Chase v. State, 369 F.2d 997 (Alaska 1962); People v. Wolff, 61 Cal. 2d 795, 799–803, 40 Cal. Rptr. 271, 273–79, 394 P.2d 959, 961–67 (1964); State v. Iverson, 77 Idaho 103, 111, 289 P.2d 603, 607 (1955). It has been suggested that it would be improper to give "know" a meaning unfamiliar to the jury. Kuh, "The Insanity Defense—An Effort to Combine Law and Reason," *University of Pennsylvania Law Review* 110 (1962): 771, 783. While more elaborate, the meaning we have given that word is the common meaning.

56. 2 Stephen, *History of the Criminal Law of England* (1883), 163.

57. Ibid., 166.

58. Ibid., 170.

59. Ibid., 167.

60. But see Mercier, *Criminal Responsibility* (1935), 218.

61. *Model Penal Code* § 4.01, comment at 156 (Tent. Draft No. 4 1955); Wechsler, "Panel Discussion: Insanity as a Defense," *F.R.D.* 37 (1964): 365, 382.

62. Biggs, *The Guilty Mind* (1955), 110; Weihofen, *The Urge To Punish* (1957), 35; Whitlock, *Criminal Responsibility and Mental Illness* (1963), 32.

63. Davidson, *Forensic Psychiatry* (2nd ed., 1965), 5. Courts have generally equated quality with physical nature. Weihofen, *Mental Disorder as a Criminal Defense* (1954), 73; Williams, *Criminal Law* (2nd ed., 1961), 495.

64. 2 Stephen, *History of the Criminal Law of England* (1883), 166.

65. There is a serious danger, we believe, in emphasizing affect, the emotional appreciation of the consequences of an act, as part of true knowledge as some courts and writers would do. See People v. Wolff, 61 Cal. 2d 795, 40 Cal. Rptr. 271, 394 P.2d 959 (1964); Weihofen, *Mental Disorder as a Criminal Defense* (1954), 76–77; Hall, "Psychiatry and Criminal Responsibility," *Yale Law Journal* 65 (1956): 761, 781. "Nothing suggests a doubt of his sanity, unless it is the enormity of his crime; and it would be unsafe to indulge a presumption of a want of sanity from that alone . . . ." Burr v. State, 237 Miss. 338, 342–43, 114 So. 2d 764, 766 (1959), quoting Singleton v. State, 71 Miss. 782, 789, 16 So. 295, 296 (1894).

66. The objection is sometimes made that the *M'Naghten* rule inappropriately requires the psychiatrist to give an either-or judgment and that this ignores the fact that mental disorder is a matter of degree. E.g., Diamond, "Criminal Responsibility of the Mentally Ill," *Stanford Law Review* 14 (1961): 59, 62. Of course, this is so. As put by Stephen, "[I]f criminal law does not determine who are to be punished under given circumstances, it determines nothing." 2 Stephen, *History of the Criminal Law of England*, (1883), 183. But this does not mean that the psychiatric state of a responsible individual is irrelevant for other legal purposes. Thus, the degree of the crime has been reduced when the accused's mental state is such that he could not "*maturely and meaningfully* reflect upon the gravity of his contemplated act." People v. Wolff, 61 Cal. 2d 795, 821, 40 Cal. Rptr. 271, 287, 394 P.2d 959, 975 (1964). See also People v. Goedecke, 56 Cal. Rptr. 625, 423 P.2d 777 (1967); People v. Conley, 64 Cal. 2d 310, 49 Cal. Rptr. 815, 411 P.2d 911 (1966); Early v. People, 142 Colo. 462, 352 P.2d 112, *cert. denied*, 364 U.S. 847 (1960); State v. Gramenz, 256 Iowa 134, 126 N.W.2d 285 (1964); State v. Sikora, 44 N.J. 453, 210 A.2d 193 (1965); State v. Padilla, 66 N.M. 289, 347 P.2d 312 (1959); State v. White, 60 Wash. 2d. 551, 374 P.2d 942 (1962), *cert. denied*, 375 U.S. 883 (1963). But see State v. Rideau, 193 So. 2d 264 (La. 1966); Fox v. State, 73 Nev. 241, 316 P.2d 924 (1957). On other uses of mental condition in criminal law, see Louisell and Diamond, "Law and Psychiatry: Détente, Entente, or Concomitance," *Cornell Law Quarterly* 50 (1965): 217. It is sometimes argued that *M'Naghten* is faulty because it prevents the expert from introducing true understanding of the psychology of the criminal act. See, e.g., Zilboorg, *The Psychology of the Criminal Act and Punishment* (1954), 10. But when this is so it is a function only of the evidential rule of

relevance. Unless such true understanding would lead to a change in assessment of blameworthiness, there is no reason to hear it on the issue of guilt.

> We psychiatrists have not made it sufficiently clear that attempting to understand an individual whom we treat is not necessarily to condone all the behavior of such an individual, or even to expect inevitable penalties for such behavior to be waived merely because he is in treatment.

Menninger, Book Review, *Iowa Law Review* 38 (1953): 697, 703.

67. See, e.g., Biggs, *The Guilty Mind* (1955), 133; Bromberg, *Crime and the Mind* (1965), 51; Weihofen, *The Urge To Punish* (1957), 31.

68. With the single exception of "information theory," which does not purport to be a theory of the mind at all, and which does not have any known relevance to the insanity defense, there is no such holistic presentation. Consider, for example, the broadly psychoanalytic tradition as exemplified in Freudian theory and its derivatives. This theoretical formulation utilizes such part-functions or structures as superego, ego, libido, anxiety signal, the whole family of a dozen or more defense mechanisms, the several instincts and their components, and the like. Again, the psychometric tradition as represented by factor analysis enables us to identify and measure a very large number of components (e.g., at least 120 intellectual factors; see generally Guilford, *Nature of Human Intelligence* [1967]) by means of standard situations or tests, ranging from perceptual capacities or mechanical abilities to personality traits such as social introversion, anxiety-tolerance or emotional reactivity. The general intelligence and reasoning factors emerging from such statistical analysis of differential psychometric data are, presumably, of some relevance to the proper psychological construability of common language terms like "reason" which figure importantly in legal discourse. The third tradition is exemplified by learning theoretical formulations which utilize such concepts as drive, reinforcement, conditioned reinforcement, response chain, discrimination, habit strength, fractional anticipatory goal response, stimulus sample, expectancy, cognitive map, cathexis, conditioned inhibition, or the like. See generally Bush and Estes, *Studies in Mathematical Learning Theory* (1959); Estes, Koch, MacCorquodale, Meehl, Mueller, Schoenfeld and Verplanck, *Modern Learning Theory* (1954); Hilgard and Bower, *Theories of Learning* (3rd ed., 1966); Hull, *Principles of Behavior* (1943); Tolman, *Purposive Behavior in Animals and Men* (1932); Kimble, Hilgard and Marquis, *Conditioning and Learning* (2nd ed., 1961); 2 *Psychology: A Study of a Science* (ed. Koch, 1959); Skinner, *The Behavior of Organisms* (1938). A good test case for our overall thesis regarding the ubiquity of part-functions in psychological theories is provided by the "orthodox Skinnerian line," inasmuch as this form of psychological theory, perhaps the most powerful technologically of any in existence, officially eschews the invocation of multiple hypothetical constructs, and aims to operate as closely as possible to a purely dispositional analysis of behavior itself. Nevertheless a reading of its major sources, e.g., Holland and Skinner, *The Analysis of Behavior* (1961); *Operant Behavior: Areas of Research and Application* (ed. Honig, 1966); Skinner, *Science and Human Behavior* (1953); Skinner, *Verbal Behavior* (1957); Ulrich, Stachnik and Mabry, *The Control of Human Behavior* (1966), makes it obvious that even this chaste, superpositivistic, behavior engineering approach takes it for granted that one must distinguish among several classes of variables of which behavior is a function. Thus, it makes a crucial difference whether an organism's nonresponding on a particular occasion is due to his satiated hunger drive, or an emotional state elicited by an aversive stimulus, or a recent reinforcement following a certain type of reinforcement schedule, or several hours of experimental extinction. While it is true that this relatively atheoretical kind of formulation avoids the postulation of such hypothetical entities as ego, fractional goal response, or perceptual speed factor, the behavior analysis nevertheless proceeds on the underlying assumption that there are experimentally distinguishable classes of operation, e.g., feeding-fasting as contrasted with reward-punishment, which differ importantly in their effects as mediated by different intraorganismic state variables. Thus, for example, food deprivation (a "drive" manipulation) produces changes in the whole family of instrumental acts which have been reinforced with food, apart from their resemblance in response topography; by contrast, the

giving or withholding of reinforcement affects the strength of a class of responses defined by their having similar topography, and emitted on the occasion of physically similar discriminative stimuli. To the extent that the mind-is-a-whole dogma does come from psychological or medical sources, it relies upon quotes from professionals who for some reason are speaking inaccurately about how their own profession really thinks and acts. Somewhat analogous to a minimally theoretical formulation such as Skinner's, consider the so-called "Mental Status Examination" of (descriptive) clinical psychiatry. In assessing the patient's current clinical status, the psychiatrist or psychologist finds it necessary to distinguish such functional rubrics as sensorium and intellect, emotional tone, or mental content. If "the mind is an integrated whole" meant that no distinction between part-functions were possible, the whole Mental Status Examination would have to be junked, since it requires of the clinical examiner that he attempt—difficult though it may be at times—to distinguish between different kinds, and psychological sources, of impairment. Suppose, for example, that a patient seems, superficially, to be disoriented. Is he exhibiting a true disorientation of the organic type, or is he kidding the examiner (manic jocularity), or is he malingering to escape criminal responsibility, or do we have to deal with the pseudodisorientation that may arise in schizophrenia on a delusional or hallucinatory basis? No competent psychiatrist or psychologist will ignore such everyday distinctions as these. Similarly, the intelligence test was originally invented to help make the distinction between genuine intellectual incapacity and other sources of poor school performance (e.g., laziness, perceptual defect, emotional upset).

69. See Adkins and Lyerly, *Factor Analysis of Reasoning Tests* (1952); Ahmavaara, "On the Unified Factor Theory of Mind," *Annales Academiae Scientiarum Fennicae* 106 (1957): Ser. B 1; Botzum, "A Factorial Study of the Reasoning and Closure Factors," *Psychometrika* 16 (1951): 361; Carter, "Factor Analysis of Some Reasoning Tests," *Psychological Monographs* 66 (1952): No. 8, at 66; Guilford, "Basic Conceptual Problems in the Psychology of Thinking," *Annals of New York Academy of Sciences* 91 (1960): 6; Guilford, Kettner, and Christensen, "The Nature of the General Reasoning Factor," *Psychological Review* 63 (1956): 169; Guilford, "The Structure of Intellect," *Psychological Bulletin* 53 (1956): 267; Guilford, "The Structure of Intellect Model: Its Uses and Implications," *University of California Psychological Laboratory, Report* No. 24 (1960); Matin and Adkins, "A Second-Order Factor Analysis of Reasoning Abilities," *Psychometrika* 19 (1954): 71. See also Guttman, "A Faceted Definition of Intelligence," *Scripta Hierosolymitana* 14 (1965): 166; Guttman, "The Structure of Interrelations among Intelligence Tests," *Proceedings of the 1964 Invitational Conference on Testing Problems of the Educational Testing Service*.

70. See Glueck, Meehl, Schofield, and Clyde, "The Quantitative Assessment of Personality," *Comprehensive Psychiatry* 5 (1964): 15; Schofield, Meehl, Glueck, and Clyde, "A Comprehensive Phenotypic Personality Description—Sources and Content," (unpublished paper read at the convention of the American Psychological Association) (New York City, September 4, 1966). As is to be expected in research of this sort, variations in patient population studied, quality and duration of clinical contact, construction of the item pool, and choice of alternative mathematical solutions to the factor problem will all influence the results. And similar or identical factors may be differently named by the investigators, since name choice is somewhat arbitrary. (Thus cognitive slippage, ego weakness, thought disorder, and conceptual disorganization may all refer to the same kind of psychological defect as it emerges under slightly different guises in several research studies.) It may be that ego weakness in the form of perceptual distortion is sufficiently different from conceptual disorganization to warrant speaking of two factors, although in the work of Glueck, et al., one powerful cognitive slippage factor appeared saturating both symptomatic forms. For an excellent summary of the methodological problems and the present state of the evidence, including cross-matching of factors from different studies, see Lorr, Klett, and McNair, *Syndromes of Psychosis* (1963).

71. E.g., Durham v. United States, 214 F.2d 862, 872 (D.C. Cir. 1954); Guttmacher and Weihofen, *Psychiatry and the Law* (1952), 417; Sobeloff, "From McNaghten to Durham and Beyond," in *Crime and Insanity* (ed. Nice, 1958), 136, 138.

72. "The ego represents what we call reason and sanity, in contrast to the id which contains the passions." Freud, *The Ego and the Id* (1927), 30.

73. "The conscious ego utilizes the information imparted by the senses, subjects such data to the discerning and integrative processes of the intellect and so evaluates the milieu in terms of available sources and means of gratification as opposed to possible dangers of frustration or injury." Masserman, *Principles of Dynamic Psychiatry* (2nd ed., 1961), 29.

Thus the most important part of the ego is its intellectual process.

> This intellectual activity, "after considering the present state of things and weighing up earlier experiences, endeavors . . . to calculate the consequences of the proposed line of conduct." Thus by means of its faculties of judgment and intelligence, by the application of logic and reality-testing, the ego blocks the tendency of the instincts toward immediate discharge.

Hinsie and Campbell, *Psychiatric Dictionary* (3rd ed., 1960), 578. See also Freud, "Formulations Regarding the Two Principles in Mental Functioning," in *Collected Papers* 4 (1911), 13; Freud, *Inhibitions, Symptoms, and Anxiety* (1926); Freud, *New Introductory Lectures on Psychoanalysis*, (1933), ch. 3; Freud, *The Ego and the Id* (1927); Hartmann, *Ego Psychology and the Problem of Adaptation* (1958), 60, 65; *Organization and Pathology of Thought* (ed. Rapaport, 1951).

74. See Weihofen, *Mental Disorder as A Criminal Defense* (1954), 4, 66–67; Weihofen, *The Urge to Punish* (1957), 12, 34; Glueck, *Law and Psychiatry* (1962), 48; Whitlock, *Criminal Responsibility* (1963), 35; Davis, "Some Aspects of the Currens Decision," *Temple Law Quarterly* 35 (1961); 45, 46.

75. Royal Commission on Capital Punishment, "1949–53 Report," *Cmd. No. 8932* (1953), at 116.

76. This approach is often associated with the opinion of Judge Thurman Arnold in Holloway v. United States, 148 F.2d 665 (D.C. Cir. 1945), *cert. denied*, 334 U.S. 852 (1948). He there wrote:

> But the issue of the criminal responsibility of a defendant suffering from mental disease is not an issue of fact in the same sense as the commission of the offense. The ordinary test of criminal responsibility is whether defendant could tell right from wrong. A slightly broader test is whether his reason had ceased to have dominion of his mind to such an extent that his will was controlled, not by rational thought, but by mental disease. The application of these tests, however they are phrased, to a borderline case can be nothing more than a moral judgment that it is just or unjust to blame the defendant for what he did. Legal tests of criminal insanity are not and cannot be the result of scientific analysis or objective judgment. There is no objective standard by which such a judgment of an admittedly abnormal offender can be measured. They must be based on the instinctive sense of justice of ordinary men. This sense of justice assumes that there is a faculty called reason which is separate and apart from instinct, emotion, and impulse, that enables an individual to distinguish between right and wrong and endows him with moral responsibility for his acts. This ordinary sense of justice still operates in terms of punishment. To punish a man who lacks the power to reason is as undignified and unworthy as punishing an inanimate object or an animal. A man who cannot reason cannot be subject to blame. Our collective conscience does not allow punishment where it cannot impose blame.
>
> * * *
>
> Psychiatry offers us no standard for measuring the validity of the jury's moral judgment as to culpability. To justify a reversal circumstances must be such that the verdict shocks the conscience of the courts.

Ibid. at 666–67. See generally Hill, "The Psychological Realism of Thurman Arnold," *University of Chicago Law Review* 22 (1955): 377. Hints that legal rules are a fantastic semantic charade," People v. Johnson, 13 Misc. 2d 376, 169 N.Y.S.2d 217, 218 (Sup. Ct. 1957), masking a nonrational submission to the jury of the question whether the accused ought to be punished recur in the cases. E.g., Durham v. United States, 214 F.2d 862, 876 (D.C. Cir. 1954); People v. Nash, 52 Cal. 2d 36, 49–50, 338 P.2d 416, 423–24 (1959); Sellars v. State, 73 Nev. 248, 252–53, 316 P.2d 917, 919 (1957); Brook v. State, 21 Wis. 2d 32, 47, 123 N.W.2d 535, 542–43 (1963).

77. *Model Penal Code* § 4.01, comment 5 (Tent. Draft No. 4, 1955); Royal Commission on Capital Punishment, "1949–1953 Report," *Cmd. No. 8932*, (1953) at 286–87.

78. Davidson, "Criminal Responsibility: The Quest for a Formula," in *Psychiatry and the Law* (eds. Hoch and Zubin, 1955), 61, 65; Silving, "Mental Incapacity in Criminal Law," *Current Law and Social Problems* 2 (1961): 3, 29.

79. Silving, "Mental Incapacity in Criminal Law," *Current Law and Social Problems* 2 (1961): 3, 21.

80. Hill, "The Psychological Realism of Thurman Arnold," *University of Chicago Law Review* 22 (1955): 377, 382–83.

81. See text accompanying notes 43–47 *supra*.

82. Weihofen, *The Urge To Punish* (1957), 75–76; Whitlock, *Criminal Responsibility and Mental Illness* (1963), 74; Guttmacher, "The Psychiatrist as an Expert Witness," *University of Chicago Law Review* 2 (1955): 325, 327. The Group for the Advancement of Psychiatry defined mental illness for this purpose as "an illness which so lessens the capacity of a person to use (maintain) his judgment, discretion and control in the conduct of his affairs and social relations as to warrant his commitment to a mental institution." GAP Report No. 26, *Criminal Responsibility and Psychiatric Expert Testimony* (1954) 8. This creates the need for a definition of when capacity is sufficiently lessened to warrant commitment. Additionally, of course, it ignores the different purposes of the law of commitment and the law of criminal responsibility.

83. 000-x41 Inadequate personality

Such individuals are characterized by inadequate response to intellectual, emotional, social, and physical demands. They are neither physically nor mentally grossly deficient on examination, but they do show inadaptability, ineptness, poor judgment, lack of physical and emotional stamina, and social incompatibility.

American Psychiatric Association, *Diagnostic and Statistical Manual* (1952), 35.

One expert labeled inadequate personality a mental disease in United States v. Naples, 192 F. Supp. 23, 43 (D.D.C. 1961), *rev'd*, 307 F.2d 618 (D.C. Cir. 1962).

84. 000-x51 Emotionally unstable personality

In such cases the individual reacts with excitability and ineffectiveness when confronted by minor stress. His judgment may be undependable under stress, and his relationship to other people is continuously fraught with fluctuating emotional attitudes, because of strong and poorly controlled hostility, guilt, and anxiety.

This term is synonymous with the former term "psychopathic personality with emotional instability."

American Psychiatric Association, *Diagnostic and Statistical Manual* (1952), 36.

Emotionally unstable personality was characterized as a mental disease by the experts in Campbell v. United States, 307 F.2d 597, 608 (D.C. Cir. 1962), as was passive-aggressive personality disorder in King v. United States, 372 F.2d 383, 387 (D.C. Cir. 1967).

85. 000-x60 Sociopathic Personality Disturbance

Individuals to be placed in this category are ill primarily in terms of society and of conformity with the prevailing cultural milieu, and not only in terms of personal discomfort and relations with other individuals. However, sociopathic reactions are very often symptomatic of severe underlying personality disorder, neurosis, or psychosis, or occur as the result of organic brain injury or disease. Before a definitive diagnosis in this group is employed, strict attention must be paid to the possibility of the presence of a more primary personality disturbance; such underlying disturbance will be diagnosed when recognized. Reactions will be differentiated as defined below.

000-x61 Antisocial reaction

This term refers to chronically antisocial individuals who are always in trouble, profiting neither from experience nor punishment, and maintaining no real loyalties to any person, group, or code. They are frequently callous and hedonistic, showing marked emotional immaturity, with lack of sense of responsibility, lack of judgment, and an ability to rationalize their behavior so that it appears warranted, reasonable, and justified.

The term includes cases previously classified as "constitutional psychopathic state" and "psychopathic personality." As defined here the term is more limited, as well as more specific in its application.

000-x62 Dyssocial reaction

This term applies to individuals who manifest disregard for the usual social codes, and often come in conflict with them, as the result of having lived all their lives in an abnormal moral environment. They may be capable of strong loyalties. These individuals typically do not show significant personality deviations other than those implied by adherence to the values or code of their own predatory, criminal, or other social group. The term includes such diagnoses as "pseudosocial personality" and "psychopathic personality with asocial and amoral trends."

American Psychiatric Association, *Diagnostic and Statistical Manual* (1952), 38.

Sociopathic personality disturbances have been recognized as mental disease under both the *Durham* and Model Penal Code formulations. See e.g., United States v. Freeman, 357 F.2d 606, 612 (2d Cir. 1966); United States v. Currens, 290 F.2d 751, 755 (3d Cir. 1961); Blocker v. United States, 288 F.2d 853, 874 (D.C. Cir. 1961) (Miller, J., dissenting), 274 F.2d 572 (1959).

86. Transient Situational Personality Disorders

This general classification should be restricted to reactions which are more or less transient in character and which appear to be an acute symptom response to a situation without apparent underlying personality disturbance.

The symptoms are the immediate means used by the individual in his struggle to adjust to an overwhelming situation. In the presence of good adaptive capacity, recession of symptoms generally occurs when the situational stress diminishes. Persistent failure to resolve will indicate a more severe underlying disturbance and will be classified elsewhere.

American Psychiatric Association, *Diagnostic and Statistical Manual* (1952), 40.

A situational depression was part of the expert diagnosis in State v. Trantino, 44 N.J. 358, 365, 209 A.2d 117, 120 (1965), *cert. denied*, 382 U.S. 993 (1966), but the court held that, standing alone, it did not establish a *M'Naghten* mental disease.

87. Durham v. United States, 214 F.2d 862, 874–75 (D.C. Cir. 1954). Disease and defect were defined in that case as follows:

We use "disease" in the sense of a condition which is considered capable of either improving or deteriorating. We use "defect" in the sense of a condition which is not considered capable of either improving or deteriorating and which may be either congenital, or the result of injury, or the residual effect of a physical or mental disease.

Ibid. at 875.

88. 274 F.2d 572, 572–73 (D.C. Cir. 1959). See generally Blocker v. United States, 288 F.2d 853, 857 (D.C. Cir. 1961) (Burger, J., concurring).

89. King v. United States, 372 F. 2d 383, 387–88 (D.C. Cir. 1967); McDonald v. United States, 312 F.2d 847, 851 (D.C. Cir. 1962); Stewart v. United States, 214 F.2d 879, 882 (D.C. Cir. 1954). See Krash, "The Durham Rule and Judicial Administration of the Insanity Defense in the District of Columbia," *Yale Law Journal* 70 (1961): 905, 932–33.

90. 312 F.2d 847, 851 (D.C. Cir. 1962).

91. Such an approach is suggested in King v. United States, 372 F.2d 383, 388 (D.C. Cir. 1967): "The [mental disease] question for the jury requires the application to medical knowledge, and the lay evidence as well, of the understanding and judgment of the community as reflected in the jury."

92. Acheson, "McDonald v. United States: The Durham Rule Redefined," *Georgetown Law Journal* 51 (1963): 580, 587.

93. E.g., Carter v. United States, 252 F.2d 608, 617 (D.C. Cir. 1957); Wright v. United States, 250 F.2d 4, 12–13 (D.C. Cir. 1957).

94. United States v. Smith, 5 U.S.C.M.A. 314, 322, 17 C.M.R. 314, 322 (1954). "If the disease produces a mental derangement of such character as necessarily to influence the accused's every action, there is no further problem." Carter v. United States, 252 F.2d 608, 616 (D.C. Cir. 1957). See also Roche, *The Criminal Mind* (1958), 267 ("the product question is answerable by psychiatry only in the affirmative"); Davidson, "The Psychiatrist's Role in the Administration of Criminal Justice," in *Criminal Psychology* (ed. Nice, 1962), 13, 20.

95. "[O]nly Omniscience can say whether the act would have been committed had the taint not existed." People v. Hubert, 119 Cal. 216, 223, 51 Pac. 329, 331 (1897). See also King v. United States, 372 F.2d 383, 386–87 (D.C. Cir. 1967); Acheson, "McDonald v. United States: The Durham Rule Redefined," *Georgetown Law Journal* 51 (1963): 580, 583. Some commentators have suggested that the product question is just another way of leaving the issue to the jury's instinctive sense of justice without standards to control the exercise of that judgment. Roche, *The Criminal Mind* (1958), 268; Wechsler, "The Criteria of Criminal Responsibility," *University of Chicago Law Review* 22 (1955): 367, 372.

96. E.g., Frigillana v. United States, 307 F.2d 665 (D.C. Cir. 1962); Satterwhite v. United States, 267 F.2d 675 (D.C. Cir. 1959).

97. *Model Penal Code* § 4.01 (Proposed Official Draft, 1962). In varying forms it has been adopted by statute in four states and by judicial decision in two circuits and states. See 38 Ill. Rev. Stat. ch. 38, § 6–2 (1965); N.Y. Penal Law § 1120 (1965) (omitting substantial capacity to conform); Vernon's Ann. Mo. Stat. §§ 552.010, .030 (Supp. 1966); 13 Vt. Stat. Ann. § 4801 (1959); United States v. Freeman, 357 F.2d 606 (2d Cir. 1966); Wion v. United States, 325 F.2d 420 (10th Cir. 1963), *cert. denied*, 377 U.S. 946 (1964); Commonwealth v. McHoul, 226 N.E.2d 556 (Mass. 1967); State v. Shoffner, 31 Wis. 2d 412, 143 N.W.2d 458 (1966) (burden of proof on accused). It is also the basis for the test in another circuit. United States v. Currens, 290 F.2d 751, 774 (3d Cir. 1961). The court stated:

> The jury must be satisfied that at the time of committing the prohibited act the defendant, as a result of mental disease or defect, lacked substantial capacity to conform his conduct to the requirements of the law which he is alleged to have violated.

Ibid. Presumably an approach similar to the Model Penal Code is intended by those jurisdictions which frame insanity defenses in terms of impairment of cognition or volition. See Davis v. United States, 165 U.S. 373 (1897); Pope v. United States, 372 F.2d 710 (8th Cir. 1967); United States v. Williams, 372 F.2d 76 (7th Cir. 1967); Dusky v. United States, 295 F.2d 743 (8th Cir. 1961), *cert. denied*, 368 U.S. 998 (1962); Hall v. United States, 295 F.2d 26 (4th Cir. 1961); Howard v. United States, 232 F.2d 274 (5th Cir. 1956); Terry v. Commonwealth, 371 S.W. 2d 862 (Ky. 1963); State v. White, 58 N.M. 324, 270 P.2d 727 (1954). Of course, these jurisdictions vary as to how great the impairment of either faculty must be.

98. E.g., Allen, *The Borderland of Criminal Justice* (1964), 116; Weihofen, *The Urge To Punish* (1957), 63.

99. E.g., Glueck, *Law and Psychiatry* (1962), 69.

100. Compare Williams, *Criminal Law* (2nd ed., 1961), § 147 with Wootton, *Social Science and Social Pathology* (1959), 230. See also State v. Fuller, 229 S.C. 439, 93 S.E.2d 463 (1956); State v. Deyo, 358 S.W.2d 816 (Mo. 1962).

101.

> Most important of all the merits of the M'Naghten formula, however, is the fact that a defence of intellectual insufficiency can be tested by criteria external to the actions which it is invoked to excuse. The proof that a man is deluded or lacks understanding lies, not in the fact that he commits a crime, so much as in his behaviour before and afterwards, or even in his capacity to understand things that have nothing to do with his offence.

Wootton, *Social Science and Social Pathology* (1959), 231.

102. *Model Penal Code* § 4.01, comment (Tent. Draft No. 4, 1955).

103. Weihofen, *The Urge To Punish* (1957), 70.

104.

So it may be that the act of the sexual pervert or the kleptomaniac is due, not to the weakening of moral restraint, but to the overpowering strength of the prompting desire. It may be that this is so, but we do not know that it is so; and, if it were determined affirmatively, I am not sure that it would influence our view of the responsibility of the actor, though perhaps it ought to do so.

Mercier, *Criminal Responsibility* (1935), 172.

105. Davidson, *Forensic Psychiatry* (2nd ed., 1965), 20.

The medical evidence most favorable to him was that he possessed a personality which made it a little more difficult to adhere to the right. A mental capacity to adhere to the right may vary in individuals but so long as a person is able to do so he is not legally insane. To overcome that deficiency, which may arise out of moral and not mental deterioration, a person might be required to exercise more self-discipline, but that alone does not legally excuse the commission of a crime.

United States v. Edwards, 4 U.S.C.M.A. 299, 303–04, 15 C.M.R. 299, 303–04 (1954).

106. In our discussion of these cases we have assumed away all evidential problems. We, of course, recognize that there will often be conflicting expert opinion, that much expert opinion may be inherently improbable, and that in many jurisdictions even uncontradicted expert testimony may be disregarded. We have, however, deliberately chosen to ignore these problems of the administration of the defense in order to better focus on its substantive content. For an excellent detailed treatment of practical problems in qualifying and examining expert psychiatric and psychological witnesses, see Goulett, *The Insanity Defense in Criminal Trials* (1965).

107. See note 100 *supra*.

108. See generally Barrow and Fabing, *Epilepsy and the Law* (2nd ed., 1966), 124–33; Glueck, *Mental Disorder and the Criminal Law* (1927), 338–42.

109. See generally Arieti, *Interpretation of Schizophrenia* (1955); Bellak, *Schizophrenia: A Review of the Syndrome* (1958), 18; Bleuler, *Dementia Praecox; or, The Group of Schizophrenias* (1950); Fenichel, *The Psychoanalytic Theory of Neurosis* (1945), 416, 421; Jung, *Psychology of Dementia Praecox* (1909); Kraepelin, *Textbook of Psychiatry* (8th ed., 1913); *Language and Thought in Schizophrenia* (ed. Kasanin, 1944); Maslow and Mittelman, *Principles of Abnormal Psychology* (rev. ed., 1951), 523–24; Payne, "Cognitive Abnormalities," in *Handbook of Abnormal Psychology* (ed. Eysenck, 1961), 248–50; Payne and Hewlett, "Thought Disorder in Psychotic Patients," in *Experiments in Personality* 2 (ed. Eysenck, 1960), 3; Piotrowski and Lewis, "Clinical Diagnosis of Manic-Depressive Psychosis," *Proceedings of American Psychopathological Association* 42 (1952): 25; Rabin and King, "Psychological Studies," in *Schizophrenia: A Review of the Syndrome* (ed. Bellak, 1958), 216; Strecker, Ebaugh, and Ewalt, *Practicalial Clinical Psychiatry* (7th ed., 1951), 275–79; Winder, "Some Psychological Studies of Schizophrenia," in *The Etiology of Schizophrenia* (ed. Jackson, 1960), 191. Eisenstein, "Differential Psychotherapy of Borderline States," *Psychiatric Quarterly* 25 (1951): 379; Hoch and Polatin, "Pseudoneurotic Forms of Schizophrenia," *Psychiatric Quarterly* 23 (1949): 248; Lewis, "Criteria for Early Differential Diagnosis of Psychoneurosis and Schizophrenia," *American Journal of Psychotherapy* 3 (1949): 4; Meehl, "Schizotaxia, Schizotypy, Schizophrenia," *American Psychologist* 17 (1962): 827; Zilboorg, "The Problem of Ambulatory Schizophrenias," *American Journal of Psychiatry* 113 (1956): 519.

110. For an interesting analysis of the insanity defense with reference to its similarities to the defense of mistake, see Silving, "Mental Incapacity in Criminal Law," *Current Law and Social Problems* 2 (1961): 3, 35.

111. Fenichel, *Psychoanalytic Theory of Neurosis* (1945), 49, 421; Hinsie and Campbell, *Psychiatric Dictionary* (3rd ed., 1960), 247, 658. See also authorities cited note 109 *supra*.

112. That the ability to subsume a concrete act under its proper legal category is part of the *M'Naghten* test is argued in Oppenheimer, *Criminal Responsibility of Lunatics* (1909), 141, and ap-

proved by Glueck, *Mental Disorder and the Criminal Law* (1927), 219 and Weihofen, *Mental Disorder as a Criminal Defense* (1954), 80.

113. Compare United States v. Freeman, 357 F.2d 606 (2d Cir. 1966), State v. Kirkham, 7 Utah 2d 108, 319 P.2d 859 (1958), and State v. Allen, 231 S.C. 391, 98 S.E.2d 826 (1957), with Terry v. Commonwealth, 371 S.W.2d 862 (Ky. 1963). See generally Guttmacher and Weihofen, *Psychiatry and the Law* (1952), 405; Hall, *General Principles of Criminal Law* (2nd ed., 1960), 479–80; Williams, *Criminal Law* (2nd ed., 1961) § 159; Annot., 45 A.L.R.2d (1956) 1447, 1454–55.

114. At least two reported cases, however, involve an attempt to fake an insanity defense on the basis of hallucinatory commands from God. United States v. Mathis, 15 U.S.C.M.A. 130, 35 C.M.R. 102 (1964); People v. Schmidt, 216 N.Y. 324, 110 N.E. 945 (1915). We cannot resist quoting Stephen on this problem:

> My own opinion, however, is that, if a special Divine order were given to a man to commit murder, I should certainly hang him for it unless I got a special Divine order not to hang him. What the effect of getting such an order would be is a question difficult for anyone to answer till he gets it.

Stephen, *History of the Criminal Law of England* 2 (1883), 160 n.1.

115. See People v. Wood, 12 N.Y.2d 69, 187 N.E.2d 116 (1962); Devlin, "Mental Abnormality and the Criminal Law," in *Changing Legal Objectives* (ed. Macdonald, 1963), 71, 84.

It may be that so long as the sense of moral propriety is honestly held by the defendant and sufficiently connected with the defect in reason, acquittal should follow. Although the cases have talked about the requirement of consistence with general moral views, this has usually been in connection with a scarcely believable defendant. Thus, in the Wood case, the court's opinion seemed to rest on a general disbelief that the defendant believed it morally right to kill degenerates. Similarly, there may be a causal question. One may view euthanasia as morally right without that view being connected with the concurring defect in reason. Cf. Regina v. Windle, [1952] 2 All. E.R. 1.

116. 61 Cal. 2d 795, 40 Cal. Rptr. 271, 394 P.2d 959 (1964).

117. 61 Cal. 2d at 806-07, 40 Cal. Rptr. at 277–78, 394 P.2d at 965–66.

> Defendant lived with his mother and older brother since his parents were divorced some 13 years previously. However, his father remained on good terms with the family; he drove by their house each morning to ascertain that they had not overslept, and he often ate with them in the evening.

61 Cal. 2d at 806 n.6, 40 Cal. Rptr. at 277 n. 6, 394 P.2d at 965 n.6.

118. See Frigillana v. United States, 307 F.2d 665 (D.C. Cir. 1962); Satterwhite v. United States, 267 F.2d 675 (D.C. Cir. 1959); Weihofen, "The Flowering of New Hampshire," *University of Chicago Law Review* 22 (1955): 356, 361.

119. A jury question would be presented on the "craziness" of the accused's actions. The expert witness has no particular expertise on the rationality of the defendant's conduct; this is almost exclusively a matter of social judgment. Consequently, the jury should be instructed that if irrational behavior is found, the expert's opinion should be considered on the issue of insanity, otherwise not. For such conditional use of expert testimony, see United States v. Hopkins, 169 F. Supp. 187 (D.C. Md. 1958); State v. Bertone, 39 N.J. 356, 188 A.2d 599, *cert. denied*, 375 U.S. 853 (1963). On motiveless behavior, see Wootton, *Social Science and Social Pathology* (1959), 233–35. For a case where a rational motive did not overcome other proof of insanity, see Wright v. United States, 250 F.2d 4 (D.C. Cir. 1957).

120. See Kraines, *Mental Depressions and Their Treatment* (1957), 257–81; Beck, "Thinking and Depression: Idiosyncratic Content and Cognitive Distortions," *Archives of General Psychiatry* 9 (1963): 324; Beck, "Thinking and Depression: Theory and Therapy," *Archives of General Psychiatry* 10 (1964): 561.

121. For a somewhat similar case, see Commonwealth v. Woodhouse, 401 Pa. 242, 164 A.2d 98 (1960).

122. See generally Cleckley, *The Mask of Sanity* (4th ed., 1964); McCord and McCord, *Psychopathy and Delinquency* (1956); *Psychopathic Disorders and Their Assessment* (ed. Craft, 1966); Guttmacher, "The Psychiatric Approach to Crime and Correction," *Law and Contemporary Problems* 23 (1958): 633, 638.

123. For a similar case under the *Durham* rule, see United States v. Amburgey, 189 F. Supp. 687 (D.D.C. 1960).

124. E.g., Diamond "From M'Naghten to Currens, and Beyond," *California Law Review* 50 (1962): 189, 192.

125. *Model Penal Code* § 4.01 (Proposed Official Draft, 1962).

126. E.g., Rubin, *Psychiatry and Criminal Law* (1965), 68; Overholser, "Criminal Responsibility: A Psychiatrist's Viewpoint," *American Bar Association Journal* 48 (1962): 527, 530.

127. Compare Allen, *The Borderland of Criminal Justice* (1964), 122, and Kuh, "A Prosecutor Considers the Model Penal Code," *Columbia Law Review* 63 (1964): 608, 626, with People v. DeSimone, 67 Ill. App. 2d 249, 260, 214 N.E.2d 305, 311 (1966).

128. In one psychiatrist's view, to convict him is to create the reality of arbitrary action. Diamond, "From M'Naghten to Currens, and Beyond," *California Law Review* 50 (1962): 189, 194.

129. The courts have reflected this lay concern. E.g., Williams v. United States, 312 F.2d 862, 864 (D.C. Cir. 1962) ("A long criminal record does not excuse crime."), *cert. denied*, 374 U.S. 841 (1963); Snider v. Smyth, 187 F. Supp. 299, 302 (E.D. Va. 1960) ("That he has a strong anti-social personality and is blunted morally and ethically affords no legal defense for his atrocious crime."), *aff'd*. 292 F.2d 683 (4th Cir. 1961).

130. See Menninger, Book Review, *Iowa Law Review* 38 (1953): 697, 703. "If you cannot resist an impulse in any other way, we will hang a rope in front of your eyes and perhaps that will help." King v. Creighton, 14 Can. Crim. Cas. 349, 350 (1908). Of course, we pass by the question whether certain consensual homosexual activity ought to be proscribed.

131. See Briscoe v. United States, 248 F.2d 640 (D.C. Cir. 1957), change of plea allowed, 251 F.2d 386 (D.C. Cir. 1958) (setting fires to gratify sexual urges). See also Krash, "The Durham Rule and Judicial Administration of the Insanity Defense in the District of Columbia," *Yale Law Journal* 70 (1961): 905, 927–28.

132. Consider also the person suffering from an "aggressive reaction" indicating "that the accused would be more likely than a completely normal individual to 'respond explosively in the face of what would be a mild provocation.' " United States v. Dunnahoe, 6 U.S.C.M.A. 745, 750, 21 C.M.R. 67, 72 (1956) ("Savagery alone does not show a lack of mental responsibility.").

133. It has been so characterized. Campbell v. United States, 307 F.2d 597 (D.C. Cir. 1962).

134. This case was suggested by United States v. Carey, 11 U.S.C.M.A. 443, 29 C.M.R. 259 (1960).

135. We included this case of typical dissociative reaction in part to distinguish it from what typically passes as a dissociative reaction in the cases. Courts should be wary of the claim that everything went black. Dissociative reactions are rare and are almost never attended by violent actions. It is extremely unlikely that armed robbers or murderers are correctly diagnosed as having a dissociative reaction. See Isaac v. United States, 284 F.2d 168 (D.C. Cir. 1960); Pollard v. United States, 282 F.2d 450 (6th Cir. 1960).

136. See Glueck, *Mental Disorder and the Criminal Law* (1927), 341.

137. See Case 2 *supra*. "930-x01 Grand Mal" is the standard medical designation for *grand mal* epilepsy.

138. It is far easier to feel that an individual afflicted with neurophysiological aberrations is not blameworthy than it is to reach a similar conclusion about another individual who is genetically endowed with or has otherwise acquired a particularly explosive temper. There is little logic in this, and it is difficult to establish a defensible category of excusable bad temper.

139. American Psychiatric Association, *Diagnostic and Statistical Manual* (1952), 38.

13

On the Justifications for Civil Commitment

with Joseph M. Livermore and Carl P. Malmquist

Involuntary confinement is the most serious deprivation of individual liberty that a society may impose. The philosophical justifications for such a deprivation by means of the criminal process have been thoroughly explored. No such intellectual effort has been directed at providing justifications for societal use of civil commitment procedures.[1]

When certain acts are forbidden by the criminal law, we are relatively comfortable in imprisoning those who have engaged in such acts. We say that the imprisonment of the offender will serve as an example to others and thus deter them from violating the law. If we even stop to consider the morality of depriving one man of his liberty in order to serve other social ends, we usually are able to allay anxiety by referring to the need to incarcerate to protect society from further criminal acts or the need to reform the criminal. When driven to it, at last, we admit that our willingness to permit such confinement rests on the notion that the criminal has justified it by his crime. Eligibility for social tinkering based on guilt, retributive though it may be, has so far satisfied our moral sensibilities.[2]

It is, we believe, reasonably clear that the system could not be justified were the concept of guilt not part of our moral equipment. Would we be comfortable with a system in which any man could go to jail if by so doing he would serve an overriding social purpose? The normal aversion to punishment by example, with its affront to the principle of equality, suggests that we would not. Conversely, could we abide a rule that only those men would be punished whose imprisonment would further important social ends? Again, the thought of vastly different treatment for those equally culpable would make us uneasy.[3]

Our reflections on the justifications for civil commitment were greatly aided and in part actuated by the excellent collection of material in J. Katz, J. Goldstein & A. Dershowitz, *Psychoanalysis, Psychiatry and Law* (1967). See also T. Szasz, *Law, Liberty and Psychiatry* (1963); Dershowitz, "Psychiatry in the Legal Process: A Knife That Cuts Both Ways," *Trial* 4 (Feb./Mar. 1968), at 29. The latter article is particularly perceptive.

Similarly, if we chose to justify incarceration as a means of isolating a group quite likely to engage in acts dangerous to others, we would, without the justification of guilt, have difficulty explaining why other groups, equally or more dangerous in terms of actuarial data, are left free. By combining background environmental data, we can identify categories of persons in which we can say that 50 to 80% will engage in criminal activity within a short period of time.[4] If social protection is a sufficient justification for incarceration, this group should be confined as are those criminals who are likely to sin again.[5]

The same argument applies when rehabilitative considerations are taken into account. Most, if not all, of us could probably benefit from some understanding psychological rewiring. Even on the assumption that confinement should be required only in those cases where antisocial acts may thereby be averted, it is not at all clear that criminals are the most eligible for such treatment. In addition, most people would bridle at the proposition that the state could tamper with their minds whenever it seemed actuarially sound to do so.

Fortunately, we can by reason of his guilt distinguish the criminal from others whom we are loathe to confine. He voluntarily flouted society's commands with an awareness of the consequences. Consequently, he may serve utilitarian purposes without causing his imprisoners any moral twinge.

This same sort of analysis is not available once we move beyond the arena of the criminal law. When people are confined by civil process, we cannot point to their guilt as a basis for differentiating them from others. What can we point to?

The common distinguishing factor in civil commitment is aberrance. Before we commit a person we demand that he either act or think differently from the way we believe he should. Whether our label be inebriate,[6] addict,[7] psychopath,[8] delinquent,[9] or mentally diseased,[10] the core concept is deviation from norms.[11] Our frequently expressed value of individual autonomy, however, renders us unable to express those norms, however deeply they may be felt, in criminal proscriptions. We could not bring ourselves to outlaw senility, or manic behavior, or strange desires. Not only would this violate the common feeling that one is not a criminal if he is powerless to avoid the crime, but it might also reach conduct that most of us feel we have a right to engage in. When a man squanders his savings in a hypomanic episode, we may say, because of our own beliefs, that he is "crazy," but we will not say that only reasonable purchases are allowed on pain of criminal punishment. We are not yet willing to legislate directly the Calvinist ideal.

What we are not willing to legislate, however, we have been willing to practice through the commitment process. That process has been used to reach two classes of persons, those who are mentally ill and dangerous to themselves or others[12] and those who are mentally ill and in need of care, custody, or treatment.[13] While those terms seem reasonably clear, on analysis that clarity evaporates.

Mental Illness

One need only glance at the diagnostic manual of the American Psychiatric Association[14] to learn what an elastic concept mental illness is. It ranges from the massive functional inhibition characteristic of one form of catatonic schizophrenia[15] to those seemingly slight aberrancies associated with an emotionally unstable personality,[16] but which are so close to conduct in which we all engage as to define the entire continuum involved. Obviously, the definition of mental illness is left largely to the user and is dependent upon the norms of adjustment that he employs. Usually the use of the phrase "mental illness" effectively masks the actual norms being applied.[17] And, because of the unavoidably ambiguous generalities in which the American Psychiatric Association describes its diagnostic categories, the diagnostician has the ability to shoehorn into the mentally diseased class almost any person he wishes, for whatever reason,[18] to put there.

All this suggests that the concept of mental illness must be limited in the field of civil commitment to a necessary rather than a sufficient condition for commitment. While the term has its uses, it is devoid of that purposive content that a touchstone in the law ought to have. Its breadth of meaning makes for such difficulty of analysis that it answers no question that the law might wish to ask.[19]

Dangerousness to Others

The element of dangerousness to others has, at least in practice, been similarly illusive. As Professors Goldstein and Katz have observed, such a test, at a minimum, calls for a determination both of what acts are dangerous and how probable it is that such acts will occur.[20] The first question suggests to a criminal lawyer the answer: crimes involving a serious risk of physical or psychical harm to another. Murder, arson, and rape are the obvious examples. Even in criminal law, however, the notion of dangerousness can be much broader. If one believes that acts that have adverse effects on social interests are dangerous, and if one accepts as a generality that the criminal law is devoted to such acts, any crime can be considered dangerous. For example, speeding in a motor vehicle, although traditionally regarded as a minor crime, bears great risk to life and property, and thus may be viewed as a dangerous act. Dangerousness can bear an even more extensive definition as well. An act may be considered dangerous if it is offensive or disquieting to others. Thus, the man who walks the street repeating, in a loud monotone, "fuck, fuck, fuck," is going to wound many sensibilities even if he does not violate the criminal law. Other examples would be the man, found in most cities, striding about town lecturing at the top of his lungs, or the similar character in San Francisco who spends his time shadow boxing in public. If such people are dangerous, it is not because they threaten physical harm but because we are made uncomfortable when we see aberrancies. And, of course, if danger-ousness is so defined, it is at least as broad a concept as mental illness. The cases are unfortunately silent about what meaning the concept of danger bears in the commitment process.[21]

Assuming that dangerousness can be defined, the problem of predictability still remains. For the man who can find sexual release only in setting fires, one may confidently predict that dangerous acts will occur. For the typical mentally aberrant individual, though, the matter of prediction is not susceptible of answer. However nervous a full-blown paranoiac may make us, there are no actuarial data indicating that he is more likely to commit a crime than any normal person. Should he engage in criminal activity, his paranoia would almost certainly be part of the etiology. But on a predictive basis we have, as yet, nothing substantial to rely on.[22]

Even if such information were available, it is improbable that it would indicate that the likelihood of crime within a group of individuals with any particular psy-chosis would be any greater than that to be expected in a normal community cross-section.[23] Surely the degree of probability would not be as high as that in certain classes of convicted criminals after their release from prison or that in certain classes of persons having particular sociological or psychological charac-teristics.

Dangerousness to Self

The concept of "dangerousness to self" raises similar problems. The initial thought suggested by the phrase is the risk of suicide. But again it can be broad-ened to include physical or mental harm from an inability to take care of one's self, loss of assets from foolish expenditures, or even loss of social standing or reputation from behaving peculiarly in the presence of others.[24] Again, if read very broadly this concept becomes synonymous with that of mental illness. And, of course, reliable prediction is equally impossible.

In Need of Care, Custody, or Treatment

The notion of necessity of care or treatment provides no additional limitation beyond those imposed by the concepts already discussed. One who is diagnos-ably mentally ill is, almost by definition, in need of care or treatment.[25] Surely the diagnostician reaching the first conclusion would reach the second as well. And, if a man is dangerous, then presumably he is in need of custody. The problem, of course, lies with the word "need." If it is defined strictly as, for example, "cannot live without," then a real limitation on involuntary commitment is created. In normal usage, however, it is usually equated with "desirable," and the only boundary on loss of freedom is the value structure of the expert witness.

It is difficult to identify the reasons that lie behind incarceration of the mentally ill. Three seem to be paramount:

(1) It is thought desirable to restrain those people who may be dangerous;
(2) It is thought desirable to banish those who are a nuisance to others;
(3) It is thought humanitarian to attempt to restore to normality and productivity those who are not now normal and productive.

Each of these goals has social appeal, but each also creates analytic difficulty.

As already mentioned, in order to understand the concept of danger one must determine what acts are dangerous and how likely it is that they will occur. There is a ready inclination to believe that experts in the behavioral sciences will be able to identify those members of society who will kill, rape, or burn. The fact is, however, that such identification cannot presently be accomplished. First, our growing insistence on privacy will, in all but a few cases, deny the expert access to the data necessary to the task of finding potential killers. Second, and of much greater importance, even if the data were available it is unlikely that a test could be devised that would be precise enough to identify only those individuals who are dangerous. Since serious criminal conduct has a low incidence in society, and since any test must be applied to a very large group of people, the necessary result is that in order to isolate those who will kill it is also necessary to incarcerate many who will not. Assume that one person out of a thousand will kill. Assume also that an exceptionally accurate test is created which differentiates with 95 percent effectiveness those who will kill from those who will not. If 100,000 people were tested, out of the 100 who would kill 95 would be isolated. Unfortunately, out of the 99,900 who would not kill, 4,995 people would also be isolated as potential killers.[26] In these circumstances, it is clear that we could not justify incarcerating all 5,090 people. If, in the criminal law, it is better that 10 guilty men go free than that one innocent man suffer, how can we say in the civil commitment area that it is better that 54 harmless people be incarcerated lest one dangerous man be free?

The fact is that without any attempt at justification we have been willing to do just this to one disadvantaged class, the mentally ill. This practice must rest on the common supposition that mental illness makes a man more likely to commit a crime. While there may be some truth in this, there is much more error. Any phrase that encompasses as many diverse concepts as does the term "mental illness" is necessarily imprecise. While the fact of paranoid personality might be of significance in determining a heightened probability of killing, the fact of hebephrenic schizophrenia probably would not. Yet both fit under the umbrella of mental illness.

Even worse, we have been making assessments of potential danger on the basis of nothing as precise as the psychometric test hypothesized. Were we to ignore the fact that no definition of dangerous acts has been agreed upon, our standards of prediction have still been horribly imprecise. On the armchair assumption that paranoids are dangerous, we have tended to play safe and incarcerate them all. Assume that the incidence of killing among paranoids is five times as great as among the normal population. If we use paranoia as a basis for incarceration we would commit 199 non-killers in order to protect ourselves from one killer.[27] It is simply impossible to justify any commitment scheme so premised. And the fact that assessments of dangerousness are often made clinically by a psychiatrist, rather than psychometrically and statistically, adds little if anything to their accuracy.[28]

We do not mean to suggest that dangerousness is not a proper matter of legal concern. We do suggest, however, that limiting its application to the mentally ill is both factually and philosophically unjustifiable. As we have tried to demonstrate, the presence of mental illness is of limited use in determining potentially dangerous individuals. Even when it is of evidentiary value, it serves to isolate too many harmless people.[29] What is of greatest concern, however, is that the tools of prediction are used with only an isolated class of people. We have alluded before to the fact that it is possible to identify, on the basis of sociological data, groups of people wherein it is possible to predict that 50 to 80% will engage in criminal or delinquent conduct. And, it is probable that more such classes could be identified if we were willing to subject the whole population to the various tests and clinical examinations that we now impose only on those asserted to be mentally ill. Since it is perfectly obvious that society would not consent to a wholesale invasion of privacy of this sort and would not act on the data if they were available, we can conceive of no satisfactory justification for this treatment of the mentally ill.

One possible argument for different treatment can be made in terms of the concept of responsibility.[30] We demonstrate our belief in individual responsibility by refusing to incarcerate save for failure to make a responsible decision. Thus, we do not incarcerate a group, 80% of whom will engage in criminal conduct, until those 80% have demonstrated their lack of responsibility—and even then, the rest of the group remains free. The mentally diseased, so the argument would run, may be viewed prospectively rather than retrospectively because for them responsibility is an illusory concept. We do not promote responsibility by allowing the dangerous act to occur since, when it does, we will not treat the actor as responsible. One way of responding to this is to observe that criminal responsibility and mental illness are not synonymous, and that if incarceration is to be justified on the basis of irresponsibility, only those mentally ill who will probably, as a matter of prediction, commit a crime for which they will not be held responsible should be committed.[31] A more fundamental response is to inquire whether susceptibility to criminal punishment is reasonably related to any social purpose. Granted that there is a gain in social awareness of individual responsibility by not incarcerating the responsible in advance of their crime, it does not necessarily follow that it is sufficiently great to warrant the markedly different treatment of the responsible and the irresponsible.

The other possible justification for the existing differential is that the mentally diseased are amenable to treatment. We shall explore the ramifications of this at a later point. It is sufficient now to observe that there is no reason to believe that the mentally well, but statistically dangerous, individual is any less amenable to treatment, though that treatment would undoubtedly take a different form.

Another basis probably underlying our commitment laws is the notion that it is necessary to segregate the unduly burdensome and the social nuisance. Two cases typify this situation. The first is the senile patient whose family asserts inability to provide suitable care. At this juncture, assuming that the family could put the person on the street where he would be unable to fend for himself, society must act to avoid the unpleasantness associated with public disregard of helplessness. This caretaking function cannot be avoided. Its performance, however, is a demonstration of the psychological truth that we can bear that which is kept from our attention. Most of us profess to believe that there is an individual moral duty to take care of a senile parent, a paranoid wife, or a disturbed child. Most of us also resent the bother such care creates. By allowing society to perform this duty, masked in medical terminology, but frequently amounting in fact to what one court has described as "warehousing,"[32] we can avoid facing painful issues.

The second case is the one in which the mentally ill individual is simply a nuisance, as when he insists on sharing his paranoid delusions or hallucinations with us. For reasons that are unclear, most of us are extremely uncomfortable in the presence of an aberrant individual, whether or not we owe him any duty, and whether or not he is in fact a danger to us in any defensible use of that concept. Our comfort, in short, depends on his banishment, and yet that comfort is equally dependent on a repression of any consciousness of the reason for his banishment. It is possible, of course, to put this in utilitarian terms. Given our disquietude, is not the utility of confinement greater than the utility of liberty? Perhaps so, but the assertions either that we will act most reasonably if we repress thinking about why we are acting or, worse yet, that our legislators will bear this knowledge for us in order to preserve our psychic ease make us even more uncomfortable than the thought that we may have to look mental aberrance in the eye.

Again, we do not wish to suggest that either burden or bother is an inappropriate consideration in the commitment process. What we do want to make clear is that when it is a consideration it ought to be advertently so. Only in that way can intelligent decisions about care, custody, and treatment be made.

The final probable basis for civil commitment has both humanitarian and utilitarian overtones. When faced with an obviously aberrant person, we know, or we think we know, that he would be "happier" if he were as we are. We believe that no one would want to be a misfit in society. From the very best of motives, then, we wish to fix him. It is difficult to deal with this feeling since it rests on the unverifiable assumption that the aberrant person, if he saw himself as we see him, would choose to be different than he is. But since he cannot be as we, and we cannot be as he, there is simply no way to judge the predicate for the assertion.

Our libertarian views usually lead us to assert that treatment cannot be forced on anyone unless the alternative is very great social harm. Thus while we will require smallpox vaccinations[33] and the segregation of contagious tuberculars, we will not ordinarily require bed rest for the common cold, or a coronary, or even require a pregnant woman to eat in accordance with a medically approved diet. Requiring treatment whenever it seemed medically sound to do so would have utilitarian virtues. Presumably, if death or serious incapacitation could thereby be avoided, society would have less worry about unsupported families, motherless children, or individuals no longer able to support themselves. Similarly, if the reasoning were pursued, we could insure that the exceptionally able, such as concert violinists, distinguished scholars, and inspiring leaders, would continue to benefit society. Nonetheless, only rarely does society require such treatment.[34] Not only does it offend common notions of bodily integrity and individual autonomy, but it also raises those issues of value judgment which, if not insoluble, are at least discomforting. For example, is the treatment and cure of the mentally ill individual of more benefit to society than the liberty of which he is deprived and the principle (lost, or tarnished) that no one should assert the right to control another's beliefs and responses absent compelling social danger?

The reason traditionally assigned for forcing treatment on the mentally ill while making it voluntary for other afflicted persons is that the mentally ill are incapable of making a rational judgment whether they need or desire such help.[35] As with every similar statement, this depends on what kind of mental illness is present. It is likely that a pederast understands that society views him as sick, that certain kinds of psychiatric treatment may "cure" him, and that such treatment is available in certain mental institutions. It is also not unlikely that he will, in these circumstances, decide to forgo treatment, at least if such treatment requires incarceration. To say that the pederast lacks insight into his condition and therefore is unable to intelligently decide whether or not to seek treatment is to hide our real judgment that he ought to be fixed, like it or not.[36] It is true that some mentally ill people may be unable to comprehend a diagnosis and, in these instances, forced treatment may be more appropriate. But this group is a small proportion of the total committable population. Most understand what the clinician is saying though they often disagree[37] with his view.

We have tried to show that the common justifications for the commitment process rest on premises that are either false or too broad to support present practices. This obviously raises the question of alternatives. Professor Ehrenzweig has suggested in another context that the definition of mental illness ought to be tailored to the specific social purpose to be furthered in the context in question.[38] That is what we propose here.

Returning to the first of our considerations supporting commitment, we suggest that before a man can be committed as dangerous it must be shown that the probabilities are very great that he will commit a dangerous act. Just how great the probabilities need be will depend on two things: how serious the probable dangerous act is and how likely it is that the mental condition can be changed by treatment. A series of hypotheticals will indicate how we believe this calculus ought to be applied.

Case 1: A man with classic paranoia exhibits in clinical interview a fixed belief that his wife is attempting to poison him. He calmly states that on release he will be forced to kill her in self-defense. The experts agree that his condition is untreatable. Assume that statistical data indicate an 80% probability that homicide will occur. If society will accept as a general rule of commitment, whether or not mental illness is present, that an 80% probability of homicide is sufficient to incarcerate, then this man may be incarcerated. In order to do this, of course, we must be willing to lock up 20 people out of 100 who will not commit homicide.

Case 2: Assume the same condition with only a 40% probability of homicide.[39] We do not know whether, if the condition is untreatable, commitment is justified in these circumstances. If lifetime commitment is required because the probabilities are constant, we doubt that the justification would exist. Our own value structure would not allow us to permanently incarcerate 60 harmless individuals in order to prevent 40 homicides. On the other hand, if incarceration for a year would reduce the probability to 10%, then perhaps it is justified. Similarly, if treatment over the course of two or three years would substantially reduce the probability, then commitment might be thought proper.

Case 3: A man who compulsively engages in acts of indecent exposure has been diagnosed as having a sociopathic personality disturbance. The probability is 80% that he will again expose himself. Even if this condition is untreatable, we would be disinclined to commit.[40] In our view, this conduct is not sufficiently serious to warrant extended confinement. For that reason, we would allow confinement only if "cure" were relatively quick and certain.

The last case probably is more properly one of nuisance than of danger. The effects of such conduct are offensive and irritating but it is unlikely that they include long-term physical or psychical harm. That does not mean, however, that society has no interest in protecting its members from such upset. Again, the question is one of alternatives. Much nuisance behavior is subject to the control of the criminal law or of less formal social restraints. In mental institutions patients learn that certain behavior or the recounting of delusions or hallucinations will be met with disapproval.[41] Accordingly, they refrain from such behavior or conversation. There is no reason to believe that societal disapproval in the form of criminal proscriptions or of less formal sanctions will be less effective as a deterrent.[42] And, from our standpoint, the liberty of many mentally ill individuals is worth far more than the avoidance of minor nuisances in society.

> *Case 4*: A person afflicted with schizophrenia walks about town making wild gestures and talking incessantly. Those who view him are uncomfortable but not endangered. We doubt that commitment is appropriate even though it would promote the psychic ease of many people. Arguably we would all be happier if our favorite bogey man, whether James Hoffa, Rap Brown, Mario Savio, or some other, were incarcerated. Most of us would be outraged if any of these men were committed on such a theory. If we cannot justify such a commitment in these cases, we doubt that it is any more justifiable when social anxiety is a consequence of seeing mentally ill individuals. While it might be proper to commit if speedy cure were possible, such cures are, as a matter of fact, unavailable. Moreover, we have some difficulty distinguishing the prevention of psychic upset based on cure of the mentally ill and prevention based on neutralizing other upsetting behavior.[43]

The next justification of commitment is more solid, though it too presents the question of the necessity of utilizing less burdensome alternatives. This is the rationale of care for the person who is unable to care for himself and who has no one else to provide care for him. As we suggested earlier, such care must be provided if we are unwilling to allow people to die in the streets.

> *Case 5*: An elderly woman with cerebro-vascular disease and accompanying cerebral impairment has the tendency to leave her home, to become lost, and then to wander helplessly about until someone aids her.[44] At other times she is perfectly able to go shopping or visit friends. She has no relatives who will care for her in the sense that they will prevent her from wandering or will find her when she has become lost. In some ways, this is another case of a public nuisance and it may well be that it is impossible to find a justification for incarcerating this woman. On the other hand, to allow this woman to die from exposure on one of her forays is as disquieting as the loss of her freedom. Since her condition is untreatable, provision of treatment offers no justifica-

tion for confinement. It might be justifiable to exercise some supervision over her, but surely that justification will not support total incarceration. In these circumstances, we believe that if the state wishes to intervene it must do so in some way that does not result in a total loss of freedom.[45] The desire to help ought not to take the form of simple jailing.

Case 6: A schizophrenic woman is causing such an upset in her family that her husband petitions for commitment. It is clear that the presence of this woman in the family is having an adverse effect on the children. Her husband is simply unwilling to allow the situation to continue. All the alternatives here are unpleasant to contemplate. If the husband gets a divorce and custody, he may accomplish his end. But the social opprobrium attaching to that solution makes it unlikely. The question, then, is whether the state should provide a socially acceptable alternative. If that alternative is her loss of freedom, we find it hard to justify. Assuming that the condition is untreatable, that the woman is not dangerous, and that her real sin is her capacity to disrupt, it is almost incomprehensible that she should be subject to a substantial period of incarceration. Yet that is what it has meant. Presumably, in order to isolate the woman from her family, it is necessary to transport her to a location where she will no longer bother her family. Then, if she is able to support herself she could have complete freedom. If she is not able, the state will have to provide care. That care, of course, need not involve a total deprivation of freedom.[46]

The final justification for commitment—the need to treat—is in many ways the most difficult to deal with. As we have said before, society has not traditionally required treatment of treatable diseases even though most people would agree that it was "crazy" for the diseased person not to seek treatment.[47] The problem has been complicated by the fact that religious beliefs against certain forms of treatment often are present[48] and by the fact that most cases of stubborn refusal to accept treatment never come into public view.[49] There is, however, a competing analogy that suggests that mandatory treatment may sometimes be appropriate.

Without going into unnecessary detail, we think it can be said that one of the reasons society requires compulsory education is that it believes a certain minimum amount of socialization is necessary for everyone lest they be an economic burden or a personal nuisance.[50] That principle can also be used to support mandatory psychiatric rewiring if the individual to be refurbished is in fact a burden or nuisance and can be fixed. The difficulty, of course, lies in the extent to which the principle can be carried. To take a mild example outside the field of mental disease, assume an unemployable individual who is unable to support his large and growing family. Could society incarcerate him until he had satisfactorily acquired an employable skill?[51] In the context of mental disease, then, can society demand that an individual obtain an employable psyche?

Case 7: An individual has been suffering from paranoid schizophrenia for several years without remission and has lost his job because of his behavior. He is divorced, but he is able to support himself from prior savings. He is not dangerous, and if he is committed it is unlikely that he will be cured since the recovery rates from such long-term schizophrenia are very low.[52] In addition, the availability of treatment in a state mental institution is problematic.[53] We doubt that he can justifiably be committed. If treatment is an adequate basis for confinement, it surely ceases to be so either when the illness is untreatable or when treatment is in fact not given or given in grossly insufficient amounts. No other basis for commitment being present, it is unjustifiable.

Case 8: A distinguished law school professor, known for a series of brilliant articles, is suffering from an involutional depression. His scholarship has dried up, and, while he is still able to teach, the spark is gone and his classes have become extremely depressing. There is a chance, though probably not more than 25%,[54] that he will commit suicide. He has been told that he would recover his old élan if he were subjected to a series of electroshock treatments but this he has refused to do. In fact, in years past when he was teaching a course in law and psychology, he stated that if he ever became depressed he wanted it known that before the onset of depression he explicitly rejected such treatment. Should he be compelled to undergo treatment? The arguments of social utility would suggest that he should. Yet we are unable to dislodge the notion that potential added productivity is not a license for tampering.

Case 9: A woman suffers from a severe psychotic depression resulting in an ability to do little more than weep. Again shock treatment is recommended with a reasonable prospect of a rapid recovery. The woman rejects the suggestion saying that nothing can make her a worthy member of society. She is, she claims, beyond help or salvation. It is possible to distinguish this from the preceding case on the ground that her delusional thought processes prevent her from recognizing the desirability of treatment. But any distinction based on a proposed patient's insight into her condition will probably be administered on the assumption that any time desirable treatment is refused, insight is necessarily lacking. And that, of course, would destroy the distinction.

These cases suggest that the power to compel treatment is one that rarely ought to be exercised. We are unable to construct a rationale that will not as well justify remolding too many people to match predominant ideas of the shape of the ideal psyche. We recognize, of course, that we are exhibiting a parade of horrors. In this instance, however, we believe such reference justified. The ease with which one can be classified as less than mentally healthy, and the difficulty in distinguishing degrees of sickness, make us doubt the ability of anyone to judge when the line between minimum socialization and aesthetically pleasing acculturation has been passed. Regardless of our views, however, it seems clear that if society chooses to continue to exercise the power to compel treatment, it ought to do so with constant awareness of the threat to autonomy thus posed.

Different considerations are present when commitment is not based on the need to treat. If one is committed as dangerous, or as a nuisance, or as unable to care for oneself, and treatment can cure this condition, then it is easier to strike the balance between deprivation of liberty and the right to refuse treatment in favor of compulsory treatment. If told that this is the price of freedom, the patient may accede; if he prefers confinement to treatment, perhaps the state ought not to override his wishes. But at least in this situation the question is ethically a close one.

The difficulty with present commitment procedures is that they tend to justify all commitments in terms that are appropriate only to some, and to prescribe forms of treatment that are necessary in only some cases. Thus, while danger stemming from mental illness may be a proper basis for commitment, it does not follow that all mentally ill are dangerous, or that the standards of danger should be markedly less rigid in cases of mental illness. Similarly, because mentally ill people may be a nuisance and some means of preventing such nuisance must be found, it does not follow that nuisance commitments ought to involve the same restraints as commitments based upon potential danger. Finally, because treatment is humanitarian when applied to those confined for danger, nuisance, or care, does not in itself suggest that treatment can be applied whenever administrators believe it proper or humane to do so.

We recognize that many people will not agree with the manner in which we have drawn the balance in individual cases. We hope that few will disagree that the balance must be drawn. We suggest, therefore, that in each case of proposed commitment, the following questions be asked:

I.   What social purpose will be served by commitment?
   A. If protection from potential danger, what dangerous acts are threatened? How likely are they to occur? How long will the individual have to be confined before time or treatment will eliminate or reduce the danger so that he may be released?[55]
   B. If protection from nuisance, how onerous is the nuisance in fact? Ought that to justify loss of freedom? If it should, how long will confinement last before time or treatment will eliminate or reduce the risk of nuisance so that release may occur?
   C. If the need for care, is care in fact necessary? If so, how long will confinement last before time or treatment will eliminate the need for care so that release may occur?
II. Can the social interest be served by means less restrictive than total confinement?

III. Whatever standard is applied, is it one that can comfortably be applied to all members of society, mentally ill or healthy?[56]

IV. If confinement is justified only because it is believed that it will be of short term for treatment, is the illness in fact treatable? If it is, will appropriate treatment in fact be given?

If these questions are asked—and we view it as the duty of the attorney for the potential patient to insure that they are—then more intelligent commitment practices may follow.[57]

Notes

1. But see Ross, "Commitment of the Mentally Ill: Problems of Law and Policy," *Michigan Law Review* 57 (1959): 945, 954–64. It will become obvious that we share the point of view of C. S. Lewis and Francis Allen that confinement is confinement regardless of the name under which it parades.

> To be taken without consent from my home and friends; to lose my liberty; to undergo all those assaults on my personality which modern psychotherapy knows how to deliver; to be re-made after some pattern of "normality" hatched in a Viennese laboratory to which I never professed allegiance; to know that this process will never end until either my captors have succeeded or I have grown wise enough to cheat them with apparent success—who cares whether this is called Punishment or not?

Lewis, "The Humanitarian Theory of Punishments," *Res Judicatae* 6 (1953): 224, 227.

> Measures which subject individuals to the substantial and involuntary deprivation of their liberty contain an inescapable punitive element, and this reality is not altered by the fact that the motivations that prompt incarceration are to provide therapy or otherwise contribute to the person's well-being or reform. As such, these measures must be closely scrutinized to insure that power is being applied consistently with those values of the community that justify interference with liberty for only the most clear and compelling reasons.

F. Allen, *The Borderland of Criminal Justice* (1964), 37.

2. See generally H. L. A. Hart, *Punishment and Responsibility* (1968); H. M. Hart, "The Aims of the Criminal Law," *Law and Contemporary Problems* 23 (1958): 401.

3. Of course, arbitrary punishment would lose its utility if its nature were widely known, but even if it were useful it would generally be viewed as morally wrong. See H. L. A. Hart, *Punishment and Responsibility* (1968), 77–80. Perhaps the reason that inequality in application can exist in the civil commitment area is that it, like secret, arbitrary punishment, does not make us conscious of any threat to our own liberty.

4. See Briggs, Wirt, and Johnson, "An Application of Prediction Tables to the Study of Delinquency," *Journal of Consulting Psychology* 25 (1961): 46; Craig and Glick, "A Manual of Procedure for Application of the Glueck Prediction Table," in *Psychoanalysis, Psychiatry, and Law* (ed. J. Katz, J. Goldstein, and A. Dershowitz, 1967), 394–99; Thompson, "A Validation of the Glueck Social Prediction Scale for Proneness to Delinquency," *Journal of Criminal Law C. and P. S.* 43 (1952): 451. But see S. Hathaway and E. Monachesi, *Adolescent Personality and Behavior: MMPI Patterns of Normal, Delinquent, Dropout, and Other Outcomes* (1963); S. Hathaway and E. Monachesi, *An Atlas of Juvenile MMPI Profiles* (1961); S. Hathaway and E. Monachesi, *Analyzing and Predicting Juvenile Delinquency with the MMPI* (1951); Wirt and Briggs, "The Efficacy of Ten of the Glueck's Predictors," *Journal of Criminal Law C. and P. S.* 50 (1960): 478. See generally Briggs and Wirt, "Prediction," in *Juvenile Delinquency, Research and Theory* (ed. H. Quay, 1965), 170.

In addition to the legal, ethical, and social policy issues upon which we focus in this paper, there is a difficult problem concerning the application of actuarial results to the disposition of the individual case. In the text we have simply referred to the betting odds, the "chances per hundred" that behavior of a stated kind will subsequently occur, without examining such questions as how such numerical estimates are best arrived at, or what should be their precise interpretation when applied to an individual. To go into the logical, epistemological and mathematical issues involved therein (e.g., the very technical controversy over the several alleged meanings of the word "probability") is beyond the scope of this paper. The leading treatment of the so-called "clinical-statistical" issue in the behavioral sciences is P. Meehl, *Clinical Versus Statistical Prediction* (1954). See also G. Kimble and N. Garmezy, *Principles of General Psychology* (3rd ed., 1968), 589; B. Kleinmuntz, *Personality Measurement* (1967), 344; P. Marks and W. Seeman, *The Actuarial Description of Abnormal Personality* (1963); *Research in Clinical Assessment* (ed. E. Megargee, 1966); W. Mischel, *Personality and Assessment* (1968), 128; N. Sundberg and L. Tyler, *Clinical Psychology: An Introduction to Research and Practice* (1962), 197–224; Gough, "Clinical Versus Statistical Prediction in Psychology," in *Psychology in the Making* (ed. L. Postman, 1962), 526; B. Kleinmuntz, "The Processing of Clinical Information by Man and Machine," in *Formal Representation of Human Judgment* (ed. B. Kleinmuntz, 1968), 149; Meehl, "What Can the Clinician Do Well?" in *Problems in Human Assessment* (ed. D. Jackson and S. Messick, 1967), 594; Meehl, "When Shall We Use Our Heads Instead of the Formula?", *Journal of Counseling Psychology* 4 (1957): 268. Without digressing into the merits of that controversy, we cannot avoid at least entering two caveats for the benefit of our law-trained readers who will, in general, be unfamiliar with the relevant research literature, by now very considerable in scope. First, one should not simply assume as somehow obvious that "individual prediction" is fundamentally different from "actuarial prediction," a quick-and-easy distinction very commonly presupposed in many quarters. Second, one should not simply assume that "intensive, clinical, psychological understanding of the individual" leads generally to more trustworthy forecast of behavior than a more behavioristic-actuarial approach to the predictive task. This second assumption seems still to be taken blithely for granted by almost all psychiatrists and — surprisingly, given the research evidence — by many clinical psychologists. The comparative efficacy of different methods of predicting behavior is, of course, a factual question; and in spite of the armchair plausibility of the above mentioned assumptions (to be skeptical of "understanding the individual" is rather like being against motherhood), there exists a very sizable body of empirical evidence to the contrary. The latest published summary of factual evidence is Sawyer, "Measurement and Prediction, Clinical and Statistical," *Psychological Bulletin* 66 (1966): 178, which also presents a very sophisticated and fair-minded methodological reformulation. Of some five dozen published and unpublished research studies known to us, there is only a single study showing, given an acceptable research design, a clearcut superiority of clinical judgment over actuarial prediction. See Lindzey, "Seer Versus Sign," *Journal of Experimental Research in Personality* 1 (1965): 17; Meehl, "Seer Over Sign: The First Good Example," *Journal of Experimental Research in Personality* 1 (1965): 27. But see Goldberg, "Seer Over Sign: The First 'Good' Example?", *Journal of Experimental Research in Personality* 3 (1968): 168. It would be difficult to mention any other domain of social science research in which the trend of the data is so uniformly in the same direction, so that any psychiatrist or psychologist who disfavors the objective, actuarial approach in a practical, decision-making context should be challenged to show his familiarity with this research literature and invited to rebut the theoretical argument and empirical evidence found therein.

5. The habitual criminal statutes may be thought of as one instance where incarceration is based on a judgment that the person incarcerated is dangerous. But such statutes also serve a deterrent function by a Benthamite increase in punishment for those who are viewed as especially likely to commit a crime.

6. See, e.g., Conn Gen. Stat. Rev. § 17–155e (Supp. 1965).

7. E.g., Ala. Code tit. 22, §§ 249–50 (1958); see In re Spadafora, 54 Misc. 2d 123, 281 N.Y.S.2d 923 (Sup. Ct. 1967).

8. E.g., Boutilier v. Immigration and Naturalization Service, 387 U.S. 118 (1967); Minn. Stat. Ann. § 526.09 (1947). See Minnesota *ex rel.* Pearson v. Probate Court, 309 U.S. 270 (1940).

9. E.g., Md. Code Ann. art. 31B, § 5 (1967); see Sas v. Maryland, 334 F.2d 506 (4th Cir. 1963); Director of Patuxent Institution v. Daniels, 243 Md. 16, 221 A.2d 397 (1966), *cert. denied*, 385 U.S. 940 (1966).

10. E.g., Mass. Ann. Laws ch. 123, § 1 (1965):

"Mentally ill" person, for the purpose of involuntary commitment to a mental hospital or school under the provisions of this chapter, shall mean a person subject to a disease, psychosis, psychoneurosis or character disorder which renders him so deficient in judgment or emotional control that he is in danger of causing physical harm to himself or to others, or the wanton destruction of valuable property, or is likely to conduct himself in a manner which clearly violates the established laws, or ordinances, conventions or morals of the community.

11. The concept "abnormal" or "aberrant" is sorely in need of more thorough logical analysis than it has, to our knowledge, as yet received. It seems fairly clear that several components—perhaps even utterly distinct kinds of meaning—can be discerned in the current usage of medicine and social science. The most objective meaning is the purely statistical one, in which "abnormal" designates deviation from the (statistical) "norm" of a specified biological or social population of organisms. Whether an individual specimen, or bit of behavior, is abnormal in this sense is readily ascertained by adequate sampling methods plus a more or less arbitrary choice of cutting score (e.g., found in fewer than 1 in 100 cases). But for legal purposes this purely statistical criterion does not suffice, because the *kind* and *direction* of statistical deviation from population norms, as well as the *amount* of deviation which threatens a protected social interest sufficiently to justify legal coercion, are questions not answerable by statistics alone. Thus, anyone who has an IQ of 180, or possesses absolute pitch, or is color-blind, is statistically abnormal but hardly rendered thereby a candidate for incarceration, mandatory treatment, or deprivation of the usual rights and powers of a "normal" individual. A second component in the concept of normality relies upon our (usually inchoate or implicit) notions of biological health, of a kind of proper functioning of the organism conceived as a teleological system of organs and capacities. From a biological viewpoint, it is not inconsistent to assert that a sizable proportion—conceivably a majority—of persons in a given population are abnormal or aberrant. Thus, if an epidemiologist found that 60% of the persons in a society were afflicted with plague or avitaminosis, he would (quite correctly) reject an argument that "Since most of them have it, they are okay, i.e. not pathological and not in need of treatment." It is admittedly easier to defend this non-statistical, biological-fitness approach in the domain of physical disease, but its application in the domain of behavior is fraught with difficulties. See W. Schofield, *Psychotherapy: The Purchase of Friendship* (1964), 12. Yet even here there is surely something to be said for it in extreme cases, as, for example, the statistically "normal" frigidity of middle-class Victorian women, which any modern sexologist would confidently consider a biological maladaptation in need of repair, induced by "unhealthy" social learnings. A third component invokes some sort of subjective norm, such as an aesthetic, religious, ethical, or political ideal or rule. Finally, whether an a priori concept of "optimal psychological adjustment" should be considered as yet a fourth meaning of normality, or instead subsumed under one or more of the preceding, is a difficult question. In any event, it is important to keep alert to hidden fallacies in legal and policy arguments that rely upon the notion of abnormality or aberration, such as subtle transitions from one of these criteria to another. It is especially tempting to the psychiatrist or clinical psychologist, given his usual clinical orientation, to slip unconsciously from the idea of "sickness," where treatment of a so-called patient is the model, to an application that justifies at most a statistical or ideological or psychological-adjustment usage of the word "norm." Probably the most pernicious error is committed by those who classify as "sick" behavior that is aberrant in *neither* a statistical sense *nor* in terms of any defensible biological or medical criterion, but solely on the basis of the clinician's personal ideology of mental health and interpersonal relationships. Examples might be the current psychiatric stereotype of what a good mother or a

healthy family must be like, or the rejection as "perverse" of forms of sexual behavior that are not biologically harmful, are found in many infrahuman mammals and in diverse human cultures, and have a high statistical frequency in our own society. See generally F. Beach, *Sexual Behavior in Animals and Men* (1950); H. Ellis, *Studies in the Psychology of Sex* (1936); C. Ford and F. Beach, *Patterns of Sexual Behavior* (1951); A. Kinsey, W. Pomeroy, and C. Martin, *Sexual Behavior in the Human Male* (1948); A. Kinsey, W. Pomeroy, C. Martin, and P. Gebhard, *Sexual Behavior in the Human Female* (1953); W. Masters and V. Johnson, *Human Sexual Response* (1966); Ellis, "What is 'Normal' Sexual Behavior," *Sexology* 28 (1962): 364; S. Freud, "Three Essays on the Theory of Sexuality," in *Complete Psychological Works* 7 (ed. J. Strachey, 1962), 123.

12. E.g., Tenn. Code Ann. § 33–604(d) (1967).

13. Ibid. For a discussion of standards applied in the various states, see American Bar Foundation, *The Mentally Disabled and the Law* (1961), 17, 44–51.

14. Diagnostic & Statistical Manual of Mental Disorders (2nd ed., 1968) [hereinafter cited as DSM-II]. The first edition of this manual, published in 1952, will be referred to as DSM-I.

15. DSM-II, 295.24, at 33.

16.

> In such cases the individual reacts with excitability and ineffectiveness when confronted by minor stress. His judgment may be undependable under stress, and his relationship to other people is continuously fraught with fluctuating emotional attitudes, because of strong and poorly controlled hostility, guilt, and anxiety.

DSM-I, 000-x51, at 36. In DSM-II, this disorder is characterized as hysterical personality. DSM-II, 301.5, at 43.

17. "Normal and abnormal, one sometimes suspects, are terms which a particular author employs with reference to his own position on that curve." A. Kinsey, W. Pomeroy, and C. Martin, *Sexual Behavior in the Human Male* (1948), 199. See also Boutilier v. Immigration and Naturalization Service, 387 U.S. 118, 125 (1967) (Douglas, J., dissenting); W. Schofield, *Psychotherapy: The Purchase of Friendship* (1964), 12–13; Weihofen, "The Definition of Mental Illness," *Ohio State Law Journal* 21 (1960): 1.

18. The usual reason for variance in diagnosis is a variance in the theoretical orientation of the diagnosticians.

19. We are not saying that mental illness does not exist or that the disease concept should not be used in the field of "functional" behavior disorders. Compare T. Szasz, *The Myth of Mental Illness* (1961); Albee, "Models, Myths, and Manpower," *Mental Hygiene* 52 (1968): 168; Szasz, "The Myth of Mental Illness," *American Psychologist* 15 (1960): 113; Szasz and Ausubel, "Personality Disorder is Disease," *American Psychologist* 16 (1961): 69; Meehl, "Schizotaxia, Schizotypy, Schizophrenia," *American Psychologist* 17 (1962): 827; Meehl, "Some Ruminations on the Validation of Clinical Procedures," *Canadian Journal of Psychology* 13 (1959): 102. The most objective and sophisticated methodological analysis known to us of the general problem of taxonomy, types, and disease entities in the domain of "non-organic" behavior disorders is Dahlstrom, *Personality Systematics and the Problem of Types* (1972). See also R. Cattell, *Personality and Motivation, Structure and Measurement* (1957), 382; M. Lorr, C. Klett, and D. McNair, *Syndromes of Psychosis* (1963); W. Mayer-Gross, E. Slater, and M. Roth, *Clinical Psychiatry* (2nd ed., 1960), 6; W. Sargant and E. Slater, *An Introduction to Physical Methods of Treatment in Psychiatry* (4th ed., 1963), 4, 14, 305; Cattell, "Taxonomic Principles for Locating and Using Types," in *Formal Representation of Human Judgment* (ed. B. Kleinmuntz, 1968), 99; Foulds, "Psychotic Depression and Age," *Journal of Mental Science* 106 (1960): 1394; Kiloh and Garside, "The Independence of Neurotic Depression and Endogenous Depression," *British Journal of Psychiatry* 109 (1963): 451; McQuitty, "Pattern Analysis Illustrated in Classifying Patients and Normals," *Educational and Psychological Measurement* 14 (1954): 598; McQuitty, "Typal Analysis," *Educational and Psychological Measurement* 21 (1961): 677; Meehl, "Detecting Latent Clinical Taxa by Fallible Quantitative Indicators Lacking an

Accepted Criterion," Research Laboratories, Department of Psychiatry, University of Minnesota (1965), Rep. PR-65-2; Meehl, "Detecting Latent Clinical Taxa II: A Simplified Procedure, Some Additional Hitmax Cut Locators, a Single-Indicator Method, and Miscellaneous Theorems," Research Laboratories, Department of Psychiatry, University of Minnesota (1968), Rep. PR-68-4; Rao and Slater, "Multivariate Analysis Applied to Differences Between Neurotic Groups," *British Journal of Psychology (Statistical Section)* 2 (1949): 17; Wender, "On Necessary and Sufficient Conditions in Psychiatric Explanation," *Archives of General Psychiatry* 16 (1967): 41; Wittenborn, "Symptom Patterns in a Group of Mental Hospital Patients," *Journal of Consulting Psychology* 15. (1951): 290. See generally *Explorations in Typing Psychotics* (ed. M. Lorr, 1966) with its extensive bibliography. For a beautiful methodological analysis of the relation between specific etiology and other quantitative contributors—still very much worth reading in spite of the author's later repudiation of his substantive thesis—see S. Freud, "On the Grounds for Detaching a Particular Syndrome from Neurasthenia Under the Description 'Anxiety Neurosis,' " and "A Reply to Criticisms of My Paper on Anxiety Neurosis," in *Complete Psychological Works* 3 (ed. J. Strachey, 1962), 90, 123.

Even a nodding acquaintance with these works should suffice to convince any scholar that the complexities are enormous, and that writers who find easy solutions to the disease-entity problem (e.g., with a few cliches about "pigeonholing" and "the unique individual") are not even beginning to grapple with it. A fair statement of the present situation in psychiatry and clinical psychology with regard to "disease entities" would be that nobody knows whether or not such entities exist outside the domain of the "organic" psychoses associated with demonstrable damage to the brain by trauma, toxins, infections, vascular disorder, senile changes, etc. The conceptual and statistical problems involved are difficult, recondite, and highly technical. We can only caution our law-trained readers against being "taken in" by plausible, quick and easy verbal resolutions of the issue, which are all too common among psychologists and psychiatrists. The most difficult class is the major functional disorders (e.g., schizophrenia, manic-depression) where hereditary factors appear to play an important causal role, but where the concept "disease" does not have quite its usual medical meaning. We do not think that the moral, policy and legal questions before us hinge upon the resolution of these empirical issues. The clinical status of a psychologically aberrated individual (e.g., "Can he think rationally about his condition?"), his prognosis (with and without hospitalization and treatment), and his probability of socially dangerous or intolerable conduct if left in the community are the relevant considerations. Given a particular quantitative balance among these three behavioral factors, what does it matter whether the behavior-syndrome is truly "taxonomic," and whether the aberration, taxonomic or not, is mainly attributable to germs, genes, toxins, or social learning experiences? It is, we submit, a mistake to rest the cases for and against civil commitment upon the slippery semantics of the term "disease," or upon the unsettled empirical questions concerning the etiology of mental disorder, as does Szasz.

20. Goldstein & Katz, *Dangerousness and Mental Illness: Some Observations on the Decision to Release Persons Acquitted By Reason of Insanity, Yale Law Journal* 70 (1960): 225, 235. *See* Note, *The Nascent Right to Treatment, University of Virginia Law Review* 53 (1967): 1134, 1141-43.

21. But see United States v. Charnizon, 232 A.2d 586 (D.C. Ct. App. 1967), where the probability of the issuance of checks drawn on insufficient funds was found to render the defendant "dangerous."

22. While there is an inclination to equate mental illness and dangerousness, "the fact is that the great majority of hospitalized mental patients are too passive, too silent, too fearful, too withdrawn" to be dangerous. Statement of Albert Deutsch, *Hearings on Constitutional Rights of the Mentally Ill before the Subcommittee on Constitutional Rights of the Senate Comm. on the Judiciary*, 87th Cong., 1st Sess. 43 (1961) [hereinafter cited as *1961 Hearings*]. See also *The Clinical Evaluation of the Dangerousness of the Mentally Ill* (ed. J. Rappeport, 1967); Statement of Thomas Szasz, *1961 Hearings* 270; Dershowitz, "Psychiatry in the Legal Process: A Knife That Cuts Both Ways," *Trial* 4 (Feb./Mar. 1968): at 29; Giovannoni & Gurel, "Socially Disruptive Behavior of Ex-Mental Pa-

tients," *Archives of General Psychiatry* 17 (1967): 146; Rappeport and Lassen, "The Dangerousness of Female Patients: A Comparison of the Arrest Rate of Discharged Psychiatric Patients and the General Population," *American Journal of Psychiatry* 123 (1966): 413; Weihofen, "Institutional Treatment of Persons Acquitted by Reason of Insanity," *Texas Law Review* 38 (1960): 849, 855–57.

23. Of course, the probability of dangerous conduct would increase if the computation was made on the basis of a subclass composed only of mentally ill individuals who had engaged in dangerous behavior before. Even here, though, we have no solid data upon which to rely.

24. E.g., Statement of Hugh J. McGee, *1961 Hearings* 56. Another example of danger to self can be found in a woman enmeshed in a masochistic marriage. Not only may she suffer physical harm at the hands of her sadistic husband but her need for such sadism and her consequent willingness to endure it may lead to more serious psychical deterioration. See Snell, Rosenwald, and Robey, "The Wife Beater's Wife—A Study of Family Interaction," *Archives of General Psychiatry* 11 (1964): 107.

25. That one needs treatment does not answer two other crucial questions: whether there is any known effective treatment for the affliction and whether treatment will be made available.

26. See Meehl and Rosen, "Antecedent Probability and the Efficiency of Psychometric Signs, Patterns, or Cutting Scores," *Psychological Bulletin* 52 (1955): 194; Rosen, "Detection of Suicidal Patients: An Example of Some Limitations in the Prediction of Infrequent Events," *Journal of Consulting Psychology* 18 (1954): 397.

27. Even if we applied the psychometric test earlier hypothesized to a group of paranoids, we would still isolate 10 harmless individuals for every dangerous one.

28. See note 4 *supra*.

29. This is compounded by the natural inclination of institutional psychiatrists and committing courts to protect themselves against possible censure by retaining patients until any possibility of danger has passed. See e.g., Ragsdale v. Overholser, 281 F.2d 943 (D.C. Cir. 1960). This conclusion is reinforced by a study to which Dr. Guttmacher alluded, *1961 Hearings* 152, when he said that "people who were released against hospital advice made about as good an adjustment rate as the people who were released by the hospital." See also Lewin, "Disposition of the Irresponsible: Protection Following Commitment," *Michigan Law Review* 66 (1968): 721.

30. See Note, "Civil Commitment of the Mentally Ill: Theories and Procedures," *Harvard Law Review* 79 (1966): 1288, 1290; Project, "Civil Commitment of the Mentally Ill," *U.C.L.A. Law Review* 14 (1967): 822, 827.

31. It would be even more difficult to predict irresponsibility than it is to predict dangerous conduct. In addition, it is unlikely that the irresponsible will represent a high percentage of the mentally ill. See essay 12, this volume.

32. Sas v. Maryland, 334 F.2d 506, 516 (4th Cir. 1963).

33. Jacobson v. Massachusetts, 197 U.S. 11, 27 (1905): "Upon the principle of self-defense, of paramount necessity, a community has the right to protect itself against an epidemic of disease which threatens the safety of its members."

34. See generally Note, "Compulsory Medical Treatment," *Minnesota Law Review* 51 (1966): 293.

35. See generally Slovenko, "The Psychiatric Patient, Liberty and the Law," *Kansas Law Review* 13 (1964): 59; Note, "Civil Commitment of Narcotics Addicts," *Yale Law Journal* 76 (1967): 1160, 1168–1174; Note, "Civil Commitment of the Mentally Ill: Theories and Procedures," *Harvard Law Review* 79 (1966): 1288, 1295–1298.

36. The circularity of argument is obvious when the refusal to accept treatment is used as evidence of incompetence to decide, which in turn justifies compulsion. It is also present, however, in more refined formulations suggesting that mental illness diminishes liberty and that "mental health treatment should be required when the increase in liberty resulting from treatment outweighs the limitations necessary for the therapeutic process." Comment, "Liberty and Required Mental Health

Treatment.'' *University of Pennsylvania Law Review* 114 (1966): 1067. The circularity is buried even deeper when incompetence to decide is premised on a psychiatric judgment that while the proposed patient cognitively appreciates the nature of the decision, his emotional response or affect is inappropriate.

37. See, e.g., M. Twain, *The Mysterious Stranger* (1916) passim.

38. Ehrenzweig, "A Psychoanalysis of the Insanity Plea—Clues to the Problems of Criminal Responsibility and Insanity in the Death Cell,'' *Yale Law Journal* 73 (1964): 425.

39. The case becomes even more interesting when the condition is usually compensated, thus making the individual a functioning member of society, but can on rare occasions become briefly decompensated with possibly disastrous results. Consider the case of the man who over a period of 15 years had two episodes of catatonic excitement is which he became violently assaultive. Each occurrence came without warning.

40. It should be pointed out, however, that such conduct would most probably violate the criminal law, so that criminal prosecution and incarceration might be in order, even though civil commitment would be improper.

41. See E. Goffman, *Asylums* (1961).

42. For example, a bus driver in Minneapolis began to annoy passengers by inflicting his paranoid ideas on them in conversation. He was advised by his employer that if he continued to do this, he would lose his employment. The offensive conduct stopped and the driver continued to work for many more years.

43. The most famous case of incarceration to relieve psychic anxiety is the segregation of the Japanese in World War II. See Ex parte Endo, 323 U.S. 283 (1944); Korematsu v. United States, 323 U.S. 214 (1944). This episode, however, has never been cited as one that had favorable precedential value. See Rostow, "The Japanese American Cases—A Disaster,'' *Yale Law Journal* 54 (1945): 489.

A statute in the District of Columbia, D.C. Code § 24–301 (d) (1961), providing for mandatory commitment after acquittal by reason of insanity was passed in part to add to "the public's peace of mind." Lynch v. Overholser, 369 U.S. 705, 717 (1962), quoting S. Rep. No. 1170, 84th Cong., 1st Sess. 13 (1955); H. R. Rep. No 892, 84th Cong., 1st Sess. 13 (1955). In the case of Bolton v. Harris, 395 F.2d 642 (D.C. Cir. 1968), the mandatory commitment provision was attacked as failing to provide equal protection of the laws. Judge Bazelon agreed, but instead of holding the entire provision invalid, the court merely read the procedural safeguards of the civil commitment statute into subsection (d). See Comment, "Commitment Following Acquittal by Reason of Insanity and the Equal Protection of the Laws,'' *University of Pennsylvania Law Review* 116 (1968): 924. See also *Model Penal Code* § 4.08, Comment (Tent Draft No. 4, 1955).

44. See Lake v. Cameron, 364 F.2d 657 (D.C. Cir. 1966).

45. Ibid. See also Association of the Bar of the City of New York, *Mental Illness and Due Process* (1962), 43.

46. If nothing short of total confinement can keep the woman away from her family, we may have to temporarily deprive her of all freedom. If this occurs frequently enough, deterrence may be effected. If that, too, fails, then long-term confinement may be necessary, barbaric as that may seem. Obviously, the disruption ought to be very great before this last alternative is embraced.

47. See note 34 *supra* and accompanying text.

48. E.g., Jehovah's Witnesses v. King County Hosp., 278 F. Supp. 488 (W.D. Wash. 1967).

49. See "In Memory of Mr. Justice Jackson," 349 U.S. (1955), xxvii, xxix.

50. A primary purpose of the educational system is to train school children in good citizenship, patriotism and loyalty to the state and the nation as a means of protecting the public welfare." *In re* Shinn, 195 Cal. App. 2d 683, 686, 16 Cal. Rptr. 165, 168 (Dist. Ct. App. 1961). See also State v. Superior Court, 55 Wash. 2d 177, 346 P.2d 999 (1959), *cert. denied*, 363 U.S. 814 (1960).

51. Consider the comment of the Minnesota court in Leavitt v. City of Morris, 105 Minn. 170, 175, 117 N.W. 393, 395 (1908): "The state has the power to reclaim submerged lands, which are a

menace to the public health, and make them fruitful. Has it not, also, the power to reclaim submerged men, overthrown by strong drink, and help them to regain self-control?" But see Golding, "Ethical Issues in Biological Engineering," *U.C.L.A. Law Review* 15 (1968): 443.

52. See, eg., Drasgow, "A Criterian for Chronicity in Schizophrenia," *Psychiatric Quarterly* 31 (1957): 454.

53. That a certain form of treatment is useful in one type of case, of course, does not mean it is uniformly efficacious or even helpful with respect to all mental illnesses. Thus, while milieu therapy, the provision of a structured environment, may be a positive benefit to a psyche that must be removed from existing pressures or stresses, it may be useless or even harmful in other cases requiring other forms of treatment. We applaud the humanitarian concern of the Court of Appeals for the District of Columbia in recognizing a right to treatment in Rouse v. Cameron, 373 F.2d 451 (D.C. Cir. 1966), but we view that effort as misconceived. It suggests that if a patient is receiving any treatment, the state may continue his commitment. This can only be so if the provision of treatment is itself a basis of commitment, a proposition that we find horrifying in its implications. It also tends to direct attention to the limited question of provision of treatment rather than to the more fundamental question whether the state may incarcerate. Finally, by necessity it requires assessment of adequacy of treatment, an issue that because the treating professionals are in disagreement, the courts are ill-equipped to judge. See generally Commonwealth v. Page, 339 Mass. 313, 159 N.E.2d 82 (1959); "Position Statement on the Adequacy of Treatment," *American Journal of Psychiatry* 123 (1967): 1458; Note, "Civil Restraint, Mental Illness, and the Right to Treatment," *Yale Law Journal* 77 (1967): 87; Note, "Due Process for All—Constitutional Standards for Involuntary Civil Commitment and Release," *University of Chicago Law Review* 34 (1967): 633; Note, "The Nascent Right to Treatment," *University of Virginia Law Review* 53 (1967): 1134.

54. *American Handbook of Psychiatry* 1 (ed. S. Arieti, 1959), 543.

55. See generally Dession, "Deviation and Community Sanctions." in *Psychiatry and the Law* (eds. P. Hoch and J. Zubin, 1955), 1, 11.

56. See Morris, "Impediments to Penal Reform," *University of Chicago Law Review* 33 (1966): 627, 640.

57. The proposed statutory formulation that most nearly approaches ours is contained in Royal Commission on the Law Relating to Mental Illness and Mental Deficiency, 1954–1957 Report, Cmd. No. 169, at 111 (1957):

> We consider that the use of special compulsory powers on grounds of the patient's mental disorder is justifiable when:—
>
> (a) there is reasonable certainty that the patient is suffering from a pathological mental disorder and requires hospital or community care; and
>
> (b) suitable care cannot be provided without the use of compulsory powers; and
>
> (c) if the patient himself is unwilling to receive the form of care which is considered necessary, there is at least a strong likelihood that his unwillingness is due to a lack of appreciation of his own condition deriving from the mental disorder itself; and
>
> (d) there is also either
>
>   (i) good prospect of benefit to the patient from the treatment proposed—an expectation that it will either cure or alleviate his mental disorder or strengthen his ability to regulate his social behaviour in spite of the underlying disorder, or bring him substantial benefit in the form of protection from neglect or exploitation by others; or
>
>   (ii) a strong need to protect others from anti-social behaviour by the patient.

14

Psychology and the Criminal Law

The two opposite errors a lawyer may make in evaluating the social scientist's contribution to law are to be overly critical and hostile, or to be unduly impressed and uncritically receptive. I have seen examples of both mistakes. The extreme form of the first attitude is shown by the lawyer who frankly believes that psychology, psychiatry, and sociology are mostly "baloney," pretentious disciplines which have abandoned common-sense knowledge of human life[1] but whose claim to have substituted scientific knowledge is spurious. I would like to believe that this hostile attitude is always based upon misinformation or ignorance; but unfortunately, if I am honest with myself, I must admit that *sometimes* lawyers feel this way in spite of their being knowledgeable. Thus, for example, the late Harlan Goulett, by whom I had the dubious pleasure of being cross-examined in a murder case when he was assistant county attorney, took a dim view of the scientific status of psychiatry in his excellent book *The Insanity Defense in Criminal Trials*; and he was able to document his cynicism by quoting cloudy, tendentious, and incompetent remarks from textbooks, articles, and trial transcripts. I should like to say explicitly, as a social scientist, that there are some pretty bad examples of pseudoscience in my field. It is not easy for a lawyer, no matter how fair-minded and intelligent he may be, to separate the gold from the garbage in fields like psychology, psychiatry, and sociology. Nevertheless, I must insist that we do have something to offer you, and that there are lawyers who dismiss our contribution without bothering to look into it fairly.

The opposite error, of being overly impressed and insufficiently critical, is perhaps less common; but it is on the increase and in some respects may be even more dangerous. This error was brought dramatically to my attention when I gave

Public lecture delivered at the University of Richmond, February 3, 1970, celebrating the one hundredth anniversary of the founding of the T. C. Williams School of Law. Preparation of this lecture for publication was aided by the Carnegie Corporation which supported the author's summer appointment as Professor in the Minnesota Center for Philosophy of Science.

expert testimony in a child-custody case some years ago before an extremely able and psychologically oriented judge who, I believe, was somewhat surprised when I, having been qualified as a recognized authority on a certain personality test, criticized the report of the court psychologist by pointing out that it was impossible for her (or anybody else!) to infer from the test findings many of the statements she had made. It is important that lawyers, judges, and legislators be fully aware that while some branches of the social sciences are in fairly good shape, the area of personality assessment is still extremely primitive. Psychological tests are particularly seductive to a favorably disposed judge because they are expressed in numbers and can be plotted on a graph, which tends to give them a kind of "scientific" or "objective" aura which they may or may not deserve. It is unwise for those concerned with the conduct of human affairs to treat psychology and sociology as if they were scientifically on a par with internal medicine or mechanical engineering. I do not think that it is my trade-union bias that leads me to add that this caveat holds even more strongly for psychiatry, which can hardly lay any claim to being a scientific discipline at the present time.

With respect to the psychologist's attitudes toward the law, it has been my impression that many of my brethren are characterized by a combination of ignorance and mild hostility. It distresses me that psychologists, who would not permit themselves a dogmatic opinion concerning some area of psychology outside of their competence, are often willing to make very strong evaluative statements—usually negative—about the law, even though they have had neither academic nor practical contact with it and probably could not give you an adequate definition of "tort" or "contract" or even list the four traditional functions of the criminal law. One area of conflict which is particularly cliché-ridden is in the relation between normative and factual concepts. Unfortunately, many psychologists are philosophically uneducated, which makes it possible for them to say some pretty dumb things about norms and rules if they happen to have hostile attitudes toward the legal system. Example: "Social science teaches us not to pass judgment but to understand behavior," a cliché which I have heard or read perhaps a hundred times and am beginning to find rather tiresome. It is hardly necessary to expose the fatuous character of this remark, so I will content myself with saying two things. First, the value neutrality of a descriptive science obviously gives it *no* competence to pass an "empirical" judgment on the statements of a normative discipline such as ethics, law, or political theory; second, I have yet to find a social scientist who makes this remark and is internally consistent on this issue. For example, the same person who makes a remark like the one quoted may, in the next breath, pronounce an adverse moral judgment on prosecutors, or policemen, or members of the community who wish to see criminals severely punished. That both of these obvious undergraduate bloopers are widespread among psychologists, psychiatrists, and sociologists can be ex-

plained only by some combination of emotional attitudes with inadequate philosophical education.[2]

I think there may be a danger of "overselling" the behavioral sciences to the
legal profession, and I would hate to see us make the mistake that some psychologists made in the 1920s when they oversold the IQ to schools and to industry,
making claims which could not be substantiated and which resulted in intelligence testing — a perfectly good thing in itself — getting somewhat of a black eye
among many educators and businessmen. I think it fair to say that the alleged
power of psychology and psychiatry to alter the behavior of criminal offenders is
an example of such overselling. Among well-educated and humanitarian citizens, there is a widespread belief that we could get rid of crime if we would hire
more psychiatrists, psychologists, and social workers to work in our correctional
system. I am always fascinated when, on the occasion of a particularly news-
worthy crime, letters to the editor fall into two distinct categories. The first kind
of letter, from what might be called the "horsewhip school," takes the view that
if policemen would shoot a few more people and if capital punishment and long
mandatory nonparoleable prison sentences were to be imposed, these terrible
things wouldn't happen. Opposed to this punitive group there are letters from
what might be called the "bleeding heart school," who state confidently that if
the taxpayer would only shell out more money for social workers and "head-
shrinkers" we could put a stop to crime. These writers are opposite in attitude;
neither of them can make a rational empirical case. Naturally, as a psychologist
and a humanitarian, I find myself more in sympathy with the "bleeding hearts"
than with the "horsewhippers." But as a social scientist I have to admit that, so
far as the evidence goes, there is no reason to believe that hiring a thousand clinical psychologists in the state correctional system would have appreciably more
effect than introducing severe penalties or improving the odds of detection and
conviction. The painful fact of the matter is that *we do not know how to treat, or
"cure," or rehabilitate, or reform* criminal offenders. What scientific research
there is — and there is not nearly as much as there should be — on the efficacy of
either psychological or social treatment does not indicate that we have a technology of criminal prevention or reform available at the present time.[3] Please understand that I am *not* saying that no criminal offenders refrain from further
crime, or that all recidivism figures are pessimistic. That is, as you know, untrue.
What I am saying is that we do not possess a powerful behavior technology for
influencing these probabilities, except perhaps for a new approach, as yet unresearched, which I shall mention below.

Correctional practitioners, and even social scientists, sometimes apply a
double standard in evaluating evidence, emphasizing the methodological inade-
quacies of statistical studies as to the deterrent effect of the criminal law, but not
applying the same rigorous standards of scientific criticism to the evidence for
social and psycho-therapeutic rehabilitative techniques. As I read the record, I

am forced to agree with Professor Andenaes[4] that, on presently available evidence, there is at least as much support for the idea that the threat of the criminal sanction deters certain classes of offenses (e.g., the dramatic rise in crimes attendant upon a police strike or breakdown of law enforcement in periods of political disruptions)[5] as there is for the prevention or cure of an individual's delinquent tendencies by social work or psychotherapy. In fact about the only evidence that has come to my attention that suggests any real efficacy of behavior-engineering is an unpublished research study by a Minnesota psychologist who has been applying the powerful behavior modification techniques relying on the work of Professor Skinner, and I am willing to go out on a limb and prophesy that effective rehabilitation lies in this direction.

One fact about psychology and psychiatry which makes the hard-headed lawyer suspicious as to their scientific claims is the existence of diverse ''schools'' such as Freudian, Rogerian, Sullivanian, Adlerian, and the like. I freely admit that the existence of such dogmatic schools, which often seem more like religious sects or political parties than they do like scientific investigations, is properly taken as suspicious. The lawyer approaching psychology should realize that the disagreements among these schools of thought are frequently at a deep theoretical level, so that there may be much less disagreement at the ''factual'' or ''descriptive'' level, and therefore less disagreement on practical questions involving a minimum of theory. For example, in the field of psychology known as ''learning theory,'' there are persisting disagreements as to the basic nature of the process called ''reinforcement'' [= reward, roughly] and its precise role in how organisms learn. An outsider approaching this controversial literature de novo might throw up his hands in disgust and say, ''These psychologists can't agree among themselves, so why should I bother with them?'' But this would be a mistake. There is a sizable body of knowledge concerning the descriptive, factual aspects of the learning process which no informed person, whatever his theoretical biases, would dispute. I, for example, am not an orthodox Skinnerian by a long shot, although I had the great privilege to study under Professor Skinner when he was at Minnesota. But I can say without fear of successful contradiction that Skinner's approach has developed a technology of behavior-control compared to which all other schools are hardly in the running. There are well-established *factual* generalizations about such matters as the effect of various kinds of time relationships in administering rewards—known in our jargon as ''reinforcement-schedules''—that hold over a variety of drives, rewards, situations, and species, and which have a demonstrated practical value in such areas as the technology of teaching. These generalizations do not hinge upon one's ''whole hog'' acceptance of the Skinnerian *theoretical* framework as being adequate to explain everything about the human mind.[6] Psychologists can provide useful information to college students on how to study more efficiently, we can advise the military on the selection and training of radar operators, we can design programmed textbooks and teaching machines, we can help a drug company check out new psychotropic drugs on rats and chimpanzees—all of this without having resolved some basic theoretical controversies as to the fundamental nature of learning.

Similarly, nobody knows at the present time what is the precise psychological nature or the exact causation of the mental disorder schizophrenia. There are several theories and one cannot choose among them on present evidence.[7] But it is an established fact, not disputed by any informed person, that there is a pronounced tendency for schizophrenia to run in families. It is an established fact that patients diagnosed schizophrenic by a competent psychiatric staff will, over the long pull, have an unfavorable prognosis, with or without treatment. To take a different illness, whatever may be one's theoretical views as to the nature of a psychotic depression, it is an established fact that patients with this kind of disorder represent a major suicide risk, and that they show a favorable response to electroshock therapy, so much so that this is close to being the only "specific therapy" in the whole field of psychiatry.

One way I have tried to satisfy lawyers who are puzzled by the various competing schools of thought in psychology is to make an anology to their own field of jurisprudence. There are "schools of thought" in jurisprudence, and the controversies among them have persisted for a very long time, as articles in contemporary law reviews attest. But these disagreements on rock-bottom questions, such as the nature of a right, or the philosophical theory of judicial decision making, are not taken by lawyers to prove that lawyers have no genuine expertise in how to write a will, or how to set up a corporation for achieving certain purposes, or how to advise a client as to whether a contemplated tort action has a good chance of collecting damages. The fact is that some areas of psychology are highly scientific and others are much less so. Those which are less so happen to be those which are more directly relevant to problems of the law. Since the expert opinion rule is practically forced upon courts as a matter of necessity (even though it is a sort of *ad verecundiam* fallacy), there is a great difficulty for the lawyer and judge, because an expert witness may act just as confident of the scientific status of his field of expertise when it is not scientifically advanced as when it actually is.

As regards collisions of experts that are based not mainly on disagreement concerning the *facts* but upon interpretative differences arising from fundamental theoretical divergencies, I can offer one piece of advice to counsel which I have rarely seen followed in a courtroom or read about in trial reports where psychiatric testimony was involved, although it is fairly common in general medicine or other expertise. As a way of reducing the weight of an expert's opinion that is more or less independent of theoretical biases, there is nothing in the law of evidence to prevent this line of questioning, if done properly. In cross-examining an opposing witness, one can at least bring out the fact that he is literally *uninformed* about the available scientific studies supporting a theoretical position different from his. If one's own witness shows that he is informed about the controversy and has drawn one conclusion, whereas the opposing witness, while drawing the opposite conclusion, turns out to be ignorant of the names, treatises, issues, arguments, and evidence, I should think this would have a considerable impact upon a fair-minded jury. For example, there is a controversy in social science concerning the relative accuracy of two methods of predicting behavior, namely, the actuarial or statistical method—which proceeds more like an insurance company does in setting life-tables—and the clinical judgment method relied upon by most psychiatrists.[8] Now it is not evidence of incompetence in a psychiatrist to disagree with my views on this subject, since there are well-informed psychologists who do so.[9] But suppose your psychiatrist witness expresses the confident opinion that his clinical judgment—or the judgment of any qualified expert— would be more accurate than a computerized prediction based upon a mathematical combination of relevant data. When pressed on cross-examination, he says (as most psychiatrists and many clinical psychologists persist in saying) that "the superiority of clinical judgment to any mechanical rule or mathematical formula is well recognized in my profession," or words to that effect. It is surely damaging—and given the rationale for departing from the rule against opinions, it *ought* to be damaging—for opposing counsel to elicit the fact that this witness is literally unfamiliar with the very *existence* of a scholarly controversy, arising from a sizable body of empirical literature (amounting now to over 60 studies) which overwhelmingly indicate that he is mistaken in this generalization. *It is difficult to come up with so much as one single well-designed research study in which the clinician's predictions are better than the statistical table or formula; in most studies the clinician is significantly worse.* There are very few domains of social science in which so sizable a body of evidence is so consistently in the same direction. If a medical or social science witness is not even broadly familiar with this literature and the generalization it supports, he is a poorly qualified witness in the area of personality assessment and behavior forecasting, no matter how many degrees he holds or how many hundreds or thousands of patients he has examined. Every experienced judge and trial lawyer knows that it is easy to get psychiatric testimony on either side of a case, and that the courtroom "battle of the experts" is rarely edifying. One of the obvious advantages of actuarial or statistical methods over the clinical approach is that they are more objective and depend less on sheer authority. As plaintiff's counsel in a wrongful death action, which would you prefer to rely on: life-expectancy tables, or the opinion of a physician that "the deceased impressed me as healthy, I opine he would have lived quite a while"? Similarly, it is permissible for an expert to disagree about the causation of schizophrenia, but if the possibility of its being inherited were a material question in the litigation, a psychiatrist who is not informed about the schizophrenia research on twins—a little sticky to bring out, but it should be possible by laying the right foundation—can hardly command the respect of the trier-of-fact that he would if he at least knew about this evidence but merely chose to interpret it differently.

It would be desirable for law schools to offer courses in the forensic aspects of the behavior sciences, provided that somebody on the law faculty is sufficiently well informed to make a reasonable judgment as to who should teach what. Whether it is better to hire a psychologist who is scientifically oriented (and therefore rather eclectic in his theoretical position) or instead to present a smorgasbord of experts who disagree and allow the law student to arrive at his own conclusions, I am not prepared to say. But if I were a law school dean, let me say frankly that I would temper my enthusiasm for interdisciplinary teaching involving the social sciences with a good deal of hard-nosed skepticism, because it is probably just as bad for law students to be brainwashed into a doctrinaire position about mind and society as it is for them to come out largely ignorant in these matters. "A little knowledge is a dangerous thing" is at least as true in the field of social science as it is anywhere.

That proverb is illustrated by the prediction problem alluded to above. It is generally supposed that one legal context in which medical and social science should play an important role is in the pre-sentence investigation of a convicted offender. While there is a great deal of variation in this matter, it is safe to say that judges today are relying more heavily upon social science practitioners than in the past. And I suppose the same can be said of parole boards, youth conservation commissions, and the like. At the risk of making my colleagues mad at me, I must mention the possibility that the average level of scientific competence of the professionals available to judges for this purpose, taken together with the present unsatisfactory state of the art, may sometimes mean that society would be better off if the judge had relied upon his own common sense and experience rather than alleged expertise. For example, it is a rather strong generalization in social science that *the best way to predict somebody's behavior in the future is his behavior in the past*. There are numerous individual exceptions to this, and a hard-nosed, rigid application of the principle would be both inhumane and inefficient. But as a general statement, it has been repeatedly supported in a variety of domains. Now this statement is one which I suspect the average judge or attorney would believe, even if he were totally uninformed about social science research on the question. Most of us know that it is not a prudent move to lend money to a long-time deadbeat, or have your client tried before a "hanging judge." Whereas a *little* knowledge of social science or psychiatry, without a sophisticated study of the present state of predictive techniques, might lead a judge to play down his own experience and common-sense knowledge in favor of the opinion of a psychologist or psychiatrist who is supposedly an expert. Suppose that the professional is relying upon psychological tests and psychiatric interviews of moderate or low predictive power, which will usually be the case.

Reliance upon his professional judgment in deciding upon the disposition of the offender may actually represent a lowering of accurate decision-making from what would have been achieved had the judge looked only at the "record." I do not say that this is in fact the case; I merely emphasize that it is a live possibility.

A flagrant example, which gave rise to a great deal of critical comment in the Minneapolis newspapers recently, was a brutal slaying in connection with an armed robbery by a young man in his twenties who had recently been let loose on society by the responsible correctional board in spite of a history of 14 previous convictions for crimes of violence against the person! The public—and I find myself as a psychologist in agreement with them—were understandably horrified and puzzled as to why the responsible agency had seen fit to let this person out. A spokesman for the board, feeling it necessary to reply to the mass of adverse criticism, admitted that an error had been made but said that the reason they decided to return him to society was that "he appeared very cooperative" in his interview with them. Now as a psychologist having some expertise in the prediction problem, I have to point out that to permit one's impressionistic judgment as to an offender's "cooperative attitude" to countervail a behavioral history by age 24 of 14 aggravated assaults, armed robberies, and attempted homicides can only be described as preposterous. It indicates that the board does not know how to think straight about these questions, and is not even decently informed as to the available scientific evidence. Even at the level of clinical judgment, any adequately trained psychologist would know that the combination of making a favorable interview impression with an objective history this malignant *is in itself a diagnostic sign of a well-known entity known as the sociopathic personality type*.[10] So that the "favorable impression" is actually evidence for a diagnosis that should rationally lead to the opposite disposition instead of the one made. Unfortunately, I am not satisfied that putting a psychiatrist or psychologist or social worker in the role of decision-maker in this kind of case would be much better. Because the fact of the matter is that such a professional might also be naïve in this area, and if he belonged to the "bleeding heart" rather than the "horsewhip school" (as social scientists tend to if they are doctrinaire), he might take the position that this friendly tousle-headed 24-year-old lad may have shown poor judgment in sticking a switchblade into somebody, but his favorable attitude in the interview entitles us to be optimistic. This is just dumb, but it requires advanced education (M.D., Ph.D., or M.S.W.) to do it with flair. My point here is that unless one had some administratively workable means of assuring that the medical or social science practitioner is himself well-informed and a clear critical thinker, it is possible that his role in the total decision-making process may be, over the long run, adverse to the interests of both society and the offender.

Let me now turn to something that is music of the future but by no means in the class of science fiction, arising from what Professor Schwitzgebel, a psychologist associated with the Harvard Law School, calls "behavior electronics."[11]

His work has dealt thus far mainly with the possibility of keeping tabs on the location of a paroled offender by picking up radio signals from a transmitter worn by the individual, which already raises some ethical and legal questions, to which Dr. Schwitzgebel addresses himself in his publications. More difficult questions will arise from probable technological developments (based upon improved electronic gadgetry and advances in our knowledge of brain physiology) that will take place within the next decade. Research on animals and humans has shown the existence of specific regions in the brain whose activity is the basis of different emotions and drives, and it is known that direct intracranial stimulation via permanently implanted electrodes can exert a more powerful control over an organism's behavior than that usually attainable by the delivery of ordinary positive and negative reinforcements, such as a pellet of food or a punishing electric shock to the feet.[12] There is some clinical research showing that unpleasant psychological conditions of anxiety or depression in psychiatric patients can be "turned off" by the patient at will, simply by pressing a button on an electronic gadget in his pocket.[13] Given only a little advancement in our knowledge of the brain and our electronic instrumentation, it will be feasible to have implanted electrodes appropriately placed in the brain of a chronic recidivist that will reveal the fact that he is approaching a potentially dangerous state of rage readiness, or sexual arousal, or anxiety level nearing panic, or other states which in his case are a major factor in producing episodes of antisocial conduct. This cerebral "danger signal" could either be monitored by a central receiving station — sort of a computerized parole officer! — or the patient trained to respond as his own electro-therapist by pushing the right button on his equipment to "turn off the undesirable state." He might even be wired directly so that such a dangerous brain-signal would give rise, in the apparatus worn, to an appropriate "turn-off" electronic input, thus bypassing the patient's own volition as well as any decision by the central monitoring agency. Query whether a constitutional issue, not to say a basic ethical issue, would arise if the offender's submission to such "brave-new-world" wiring of his brain were made a legal condition for his being returned to society? An analogy has been made between this situation and the one in which society can isolate a patient with active pulmonary tuberculosis if he refuses chemotherapy; but for most of us, such analogies are imperfect in an important respect, to wit, that we do not readily view what is called "voluntary conduct" as quite comparable with the presence of infectious disease.

Apart from the immediate legal questions that will have to be faced when such feats of electronic behavior engineering become technologically practicable, one suspects that their indirect influence on our *attitudes* toward antisocial conduct may be even more significant in the long run. I have in mind the traditional conflict between psychological determinists and believers in free will, and the bearing of this ancient controversy upon how society conceives the functions of the criminal law. I think it is true, whether it is rational or not, that the concrete showing of a pronounced control of behavior via the physical influencing of brain-processes has considerably more impact upon our ethical stance than does a mere abstract philosophical argument in favor of psychological determinism. For example, I think most persons are not willing to exculpate, either ethically or legally, an offender on the grounds that he probably inherited a "bad temper" or an "impetuous disposition." But if, as some fairly persuasive evidence now suggests, it should turn out that some individuals are overly prone to aggressive behavior because the cells of their bodies contain an extra Y-chromosome, this kind of biological causation influences us to view the antisocial propensities as similar to a true *disease*, comparable to color blindness or diabetes, for which we want strongly to say that "such a thing is surely not the individual's own fault." Future developments in psychophysiology of the brain and electronic control of behavior via direct brain-stimulation will probably have an impact upon the thinking of educated persons concerning the concept of criminal responsibility, and the functions of the criminal law, that will be far greater than the hackneyed arguments employed by Clarence Darrow in his famous "deterministic defense" of Loeb and Leopold.

By referring to Darrow's famous speech as hackneyed, I do not mean to dismiss the problem of psychological determinism and moral responsibility, which I view—unlike some contemporary philosophers of the "ordinary language school"—as a real one of terrifying complexity. You will recall that Loeb and Leopold, two bright and sophisticated youths from wealthy families, carried out a carefully planned murder of a neighbor boy just for "kicks," and to prove that they were clever enough to plan and perform the perfect crime. The prosecution had the goods on them, including their confessions; so Darrow's approach to avoid the death penalty was, pyrotechnics aside, essentially a rejection of the criminal sanction itself as presently understood. Darrow argued that while these defendants were not legally insane, their behavior was a product of their heredity and environment. Absent any showing of mental illness (or even anything special about their heredity or their environment that could be plausibly linked to the crime) what this argument really amounts to is that since human behavior is determined, the sanctions of the criminal law ought not to be imposed. Let me say parenthetically that I myself am strongly opposed to capital punishment and am not arguing that Loeb and Leopold should have been executed; my point is that the rationale of Darrow's summing-up, if extrapolated, would presumably mean nobody should be punished (whether fined, incarcerated, or executed) for anything. Now it just will not do to pitch it at that level if we are interested in policy questions instead of merely persuading a jury. Much as I hesitate to enter into the complexities of the determinism issue, I do not suppose anybody here would feel he "got his money's worth" if a psychologist talking about the criminal law failed to say something about this old question. Perhaps the commonest stereotype that lawyers and judges have of psychologists and psychiatrists is that our belief in psychological determinism leads us to "side with the criminal against society." There are psychiatrists and psychologists who exhibit this prejudice, and who even write articles and books to this effect; but I myself am not in sympathy with them. Some of the statements that I have seen by psychiatrists on the subject of crime are not scientifically supportable, and are so muddleheaded philosophically that they are embarrassing to read. I will ask you to set aside any anti-psychological prejudices you may have and listen open-mindedly to what I have to say, because I assure you that I do not say it tendentiously with any kind of softheaded animosity toward the criminal law. I repeat, I do not belong to either the "horsewhip school" or the "bleeding heart school" of criminology.

What is psychological determinism? Certain ways of stating it are inaccurate and morally misleading, such as, "Psychological determinism means that you have to do certain things whether you want to or not." What a person *wants* to do is part of his psychological state, and human voluntary behavior is controlled by our motives in a way that involuntary responses (such as the knee-jerk reflex or, in my view, even an attack of psychosomatic asthma) are not. Simply put, psychological determinism is the doctrine that all human behavior is strictly caused by the antecedent conditions, both within the individual and external to him; or, to avoid the troublesome word "cause," that all human behavior instantializes or satisfies laws of nature. It is most unfortunate that the same term "law" is used for such natural regularities as for human statutes, but there is no other term. So the determinist believes that, theoretically, somebody who knew that exact physical state of my brain and Dean Gray's brain when we first met [this morning] would have been able to predict exactly how the course of our conversation proceeded. I am not concerned here to argue the merits of this position, with which I daresay you are all familiar. It is an extrapolation of something everybody knows from common life, i.e., that a large part of human conduct can be predicted with high confidence. We do not expect children born and raised in Spain to grow up as hard-shell Baptists; we often explain somebody's conduct by pointing out that his parents didn't discipline him properly as a child, or that he inherited his bad temper from his grandfather, and the like. Even in matters of ethical decision, where traditionally the emphasis upon the individual's "freedom to choose" has been the greatest, we rely on the stability of long-term character when we say confidently, "He would never do such a thing, that's not the sort of person he is." Note that I have not made any reference to coercion, or compulsion, or any term that suggests a person has to do something against his will. That is not the point of determinism at all. The point is that the motivational state of his will is also determined by his genes and his life history and the fried eggs he had for breakfast. I think the main difference between psychologists and others in this respect is not that nonpsychologists reject psychological determinism; the common-life examples I just cited show that everybody implicitly relies on the orderliness of behavior as a general rule. The point is that most of us are not always consistent about it. The psychologist, since his subject matter is the prediction and control of behavior (whether of pigeons, rats, or people) assumes that everything is strictly determined and could be predicted if we only knew enough about it. Whatever the merits of that extreme position, I readily admit it is partly an article of faith by the psychologist. But it is based upon extrapolation from both ordinary life and the psychological laboratory, where the more we control the variables, the more predictable the behavior becomes. You can predict the rat's behavior to some extent just watching him run around in a free field situation and knowing nothing about his past. You can predict his behavior better if he has been raised in the laboratory and you know his previous history of experiences and you have him running around in a maze under standard conditions. If you put him in a soundproof, lightproof box with practically perfect control of the stimulus conditions, and study some objectively countable kind of behavior like pressing a lever, the degree of regularity exhibited by this behavior, while still not perfect, is very impressive. When we combine the experimental psychology of learning with Freud's clinical material indicating that even the most trivial "accidental" occurrences of common life (such as slips of the tongue or mislaying objects) are explainable in terms of unconscious motives; and then remind ourselves that, after all, behavior is the movement of muscles under the control of impulses from the brain; and the brain is, however complicated, still a system of physico-chemical processes, and it is not so *very* far-fetched for the psychologist to hazard the opinion that the behavior of human beings is, in the eyes of "Omniscient Jones," just as orderly and strictly deterministic as the behavior of other physical systems about which we happen to possess more detailed information.

Now my point about Clarence Darrow is that his speech to the jury relied on general philosophical arguments. When we find out that the murderer Speck had inherited an extra Y-chromosome, this somehow impresses us more than saying that a criminal offender inherited a bad temper. But it is hard to think of any good philosophical reason why an extra Y-chromosome should somehow reduce Speck's moral or legal responsibility, whereas inheriting 15 genes that would add up to a bad temper should not do so. The difference between one chromosome and 15 genes is not a philosophically relevant one, but I suppose that a single causative factor, one which is visible under the microscope, somehow carries more weight with us than 15 genes which we have to refer to vaguely as a "polygenic system" and cannot even locate at the present time. My point in this example is that how strongly the idea of psychological and biological determinism "grabs us" depends partly on how concrete and simple the causative factor happens to be. Most of us would be distressed to find a man convicted of manslaughter if he struck a nurse while flinging his arms about during a delirium induced by typhoid fever. However, when the causal chain becomes more complicated, subtle, and more difficult to discern (even though we may suppose that it is clear in the eyes of God), the determinist thesis does not pack its usual wal-lop for us.

What, if anything, is the relevance of psychological determinism to our think-ing about crime? The most general statement is an encouraging one, in spite of our limited knowledge at the present time. The general statement would be that *if* all behavior is strictly determined by biological, psychological, and social factors in the person's life history, then since criminality is a form of behavior and there-fore is strictly determined, like any other kind of behavior it should presumably be controllable in principle. If we know what causes something in sufficient de-tail, we should be able to put a stop to it, provided, of course, that we are both willing and able to do something about the causes. That preliminary general comment should keep us from feeling pessimistic about the long run; but I hasten to add that it is not a very helpful remark, given the present state of our psycho-logical knowledge and the attitudes of our society.

We must ask ourselves a question which is outside the psychologist's baili-wick, namely, what are we trying to do by means of the criminal law? A psy-chologist or sociologist relates to you, as citizens and taxpayers, as does an en-gineer or bacteriologist, in that he can tell you something about the causal relation of ends and means (including sometimes telling you things you do not want to hear, to the effect that certain means will not in fact achieve the ends you are assuming they do). Equally important is that we can tell you something about *methods of investigating* whether certain means work or do not work. But you have to tell the social scientist what your goals are. Now the first difficulty is that the criminal law does not have one single defining aim on which everyone in our society agrees. Traditionally, it has had at least four purposes. These are: (1) Physical isolation of the individual offender, to prevent his committing fur-ther antisocial acts by removing him from the social group; (2) Reform, rehabil-itation or treatment of the offender so as to lower the probability of his commit-ting further offenses upon release; (3) General deterrence, lowering the probability of offenses by persons, who might be disposed to such, by the threat of the criminal sanction; and (4) Retributive justice, in the sense that society should exact suffering from an individual to make him "pay for what he did." Whatever may be the moral and political justifications for these four functions of the criminal law, and whatever may be the adequacy of our available techniques for achieving them, there is no assurance that the same techniques will maximize all four. Hence, you have to decide which of them you consider more important, and then combine that choice of aims with the best available scientific informa-tion as to the efficacy of procedures for achieving each, yielding a conclusion as to what we should be doing until further notice.

At present, the four traditional functions do not have an equal status in the judgment of informed persons. It is depressing to say it, but I cannot emphasize too strongly that the only one of these four functions that we can be confident about our ability to perform is the first one — social isolation of the offender. One does not need any scientific research to be confident that if somebody is securely locked in the state prison, he cannot steal my car or rape my wife or burn my house. If there were no other considerations (salvaging a human personality, saving taxpayer money, avoiding needless suffering), the obvious easy solution would be life imprisonment for all criminal offenses, non-paroleable, in a maximum security prison. Although I should point out to you that if that were the approach, ignoring all aims except the first, there would be no good reason for making it into a prison. What we would want is a beautiful, comfortable, southsea island with a pleasant climate and plenty of free coconuts and bananas. We should probably import some dancing girls (although, of course, we could have criminals of both sexes on the same island). It would be humanitarian to provide medical care, but it would be easy to find dedicated missionary doctors to go there. We either have the place surrounded by sharks, or periodically we dump some radioactive salt in the ocean surrounding it, so that we need not even bother with guards. The offenders can enjoy themselves, and meanwhile sociologists and anthropologists could study the kind of legal system they would develop (there is no question at all that they would develop one). Everybody there would be "living it up and happy as a clam," and meanwhile we would not have to worry about them. The attitude that would inspire this solution — and for four-time losers, given to crimes of violence against the person, I might be prepared to defend this proposal with complete seriousness — would be: "I have no desire to make criminals suffer for their crimes, I experience no impulse for vengeance, and I have no need to extract a pound of flesh. I do not even understand the concept of an 'injury to society' as involving some kind of hedonic bookkeeping that must be balanced. I don't want to make the man unhappy, or to deprive him of food or sex or poker games — all I want is to keep him away from me." It seems to me that this would be an eminently humanitarian and rational approach, given the assumption (which none of us *really* makes) that the sole function of the criminal law is to reduce as much as possible the probability that the individual will do further social harm to the larger community. The point of my example is partly to highlight the fact of disparate aims that must be reconciled, but also that this is one function we do know how to perform if we could honorably set ourselves single-mindedly to it.

As to the laudable aim of rehabilitating or reforming the offender, I have already said that there is no persuasive evidence that we know how to do so by any of the available methods. While criminology is not my area of professional expertise, I am somewhat familiar with the research literature; and I have it on the authority of a first-class sociologist colleague that there is at present no good research evidence to show that harsh punishment, psychotherapy, group counseling, reducing the case load of probation officers, neighborhood programs, or anything else significantly reduces the probability of delinquency in predelinquent individuals, the probability of parole violation, or the probability of criminal recidivism. An exhaustive survey of the research literature led one scholar to conclude bluntly that the amount of outcome optimism in various studies was inversely proportional to the scientific rigor of the investigation! The better the study was conducted according to the methodological canons of social science, the more discouraging were the research findings.[14] This trend is now becoming so clear that one threat to further research is the "correctional establishment" itself, which in some instances has gone to considerable lengths to suppress the results of scientific research, even to the point of trying to prevent a state legislature from having access to the research outcomes.

The approach to delinquent and criminal behavior which makes the most theoretical sense to me as a psychologist, and which I urge you to encourage and foster by dollars and influence, is the behavior modification approach stemming from the work of B. F. Skinner.[15] If you hear that an enterprising psychologist wants to introduce it experimentally into your correctional system, do not allow yourself to be brainwashed by some psychiatrist, clinical psychologist, or social worker with a bunch of clichés implying that psychotherapists and social workers know how to rehabilitate criminals, because such is simply not the case. Nobody knows how. So you might as well let a zealous Skinnerian try *his* hand at it, because the available evidence shows that we are not accomplishing much of anything with the present conventional methods.

The case for general deterrence (i.e., a deterrent effect not upon the offender himself after release, but upon the rest of us who experience varying opportunities and temptations to commit crime) is not much better than that for reform but—this may surprise you coming from a psychologist—as I read the record it is *slightly* better. There is evidence to support the idea that at least *some* kinds of potential offenders are deterred to *some* appreciable extent from committing *some* classes of crimes. It appears plausible, for instance, that crimes against the person are not as much influenced by the threat of apprehension as are crimes against property. This makes good psychological sense, because crimes against the person (such as rape, murder, and aggravated assault) are almost certainly indicative of a greater degree of psychological and social pathology, and are less likely to be "decided on" in the way that the traditional Benthamite theory of punishment as a general deterrent would suppose. How many of you, for instance, think that the chances of your committing rape or murder would be materially increased if you discovered that there was no law against it in the state of Virginia? The point is that one who is at all likely to commit this kind of crime has usually got something very much wrong with him (I do not mean that he is insane in the legal sense) and most such crimes are probably committed under somewhat abnormal conditions of passion, or by persons who lack the very kind of deliberation, rational foresight, and impulse control that the criminal law presupposes when it tries to deter such conduct by the threat of punishment. But there are crimes against property and white-collar crimes which are fairly tempting to persons within the relatively normal range of socialization and mental health. Some kinds of white-collar crimes, such as fudging on one's income tax, are widespread among persons who are otherwise law-abiding. It is not surprising that statistical studies of crime-rate fluctuations under special circumstances (such as Nazi inactivation of the Danish police) show a considerably greater increment in crimes against property than crimes against the person. You sometimes hear members of the "bleeding heart school" argue that we know the criminal sanction does not deter because capital punishment does not seem to decrease the murder rate, but this is a psychologically fallacious argument. The "horsewhip school" is probably wrong about capital punishment, but murder is such a low incidence crime, is so suggestive of severe personal and social pathology, and the threat of being imprisoned for life is such a severe threat already, that extrapolating to other crimes and other classes of offenders from the rather well-established finding that the death penalty does not *further* deter is illegitimate.

Finally, with regard to retributive justice, two things must be said. Granted that some able minds (such as Immanuel Kant) have considered this a legitimate function—he said that even if civil society were to be dissolved tomorrow, we should have to hang the last murderer before disbanding, so that justice could be done—and while some first-class contemporary thinkers (such as Professor Herbert Morris) write persuasively about the moral bookkeeping, the retributive justice function is pretty hard to defend. Even if, as a general principle, I were contented with it (which I am not), I would have to say that as a psychologist it seems to me extremely rash for us to try to "make the punishment fit the crime," as the saying goes, in light of present psychological, sociological, and genetic knowledge. I simply do not see how I, or anyone else, or any group of persons, lay or professional, can be in a sufficiently God-like position of knowledge to decide, as between two persons who committed antisocial acts, which one "deserves" to suffer the greater penalty. Short of gross mental disorder (which I think should exculpate an offender from being officially labeled "criminal"),[16] I believe strongly that this kind of moral balancing is at present, and for the foreseeable future, beyond our powers. Therefore I am not inclined even to argue the retributive justice aim on the philosophical merits, since I do not believe our methods of unraveling the individual case are accurate enough to enable us to perform the Solomonic task required if we are to do it justly.

Where does that leave me? Pending good research on innovative approaches to rehabilitation; recognizing that if some potential offenders can be deterred, they will be deterred even though general deterrence is not our main aim (absent more convincing demonstration of its efficacy); and rejecting retributive justice as an aim, both for philosophical and empirical reasons—I conclude that by far the heaviest weight in writing and applying the criminal law should be given to the only one of the four traditional functions that is clearly defensible philosophically and that we know we can perform, to wit, isolate the offender from the rest of us so long as he has appreciable probability of committing further serious depredations.[17] Most of you will not agree with me when I add that I would try to make his period of isolation a relatively pleasant one. I strongly suspect that imprisonment per se plus, for those of us who are not professional criminals or sociopathic personality types (and they will not be deterred anyway!), the social opprobrium of being sent to prison and labeled "convicted criminal" are the chief deterrents, rather than our expectations as to whether we will have beer and skittles once we are there. I cannot believe, for instance, that it improves the general psychological state of anybody to be deprived for 10 years of a normal sexual outlet and to engage in homosexual relations in prisons as a substitute, which is what we know happens. I, therefore, strongly favor the Latin American custom of letting prisoners be visited by their wives or, if they don't have wives, by their girl friends. In fact I would include such visits, along with many other rewards, ranging from whether you can have cigarettes or watch the color TV instead of the plain one, to weekend passes, or money to hire an expensive call girl, as among the reinforcements for shaping up behavior in a variety of ways. I suppose these suggestions will offend many of you. I frankly choose them for that purpose. I am not a parson. I am a psychologist and my concern with crime is that of a behavioral engineer. In my professional capacity, I am not in the least interested in making people good or getting them into heaven. I am interested in lowering the probability that they will subsequently commit antisocial acts that I as a citizen find frightening.

To a psychologist it is not really surprising that the conventional methods of preventing delinquency or reducing recidivism are relatively feeble in their impact. Whatever may be the best taxonomy of criminal personalities (and a nonarbitrary classification of offenders is one of the most important research problems),[18] there are two categories that will surely be included in any such classification system. There is the deeply pathological specimen who suffers from diagnosable mental disorder, manifesting itself in other ways besides his legal delinquency; and there is the psychiatrically normal "professional criminal" type, the causation of whose antisocial conduct lies in genetic and social factors of a kind not essentially different from the explanation of why someone is an extravert or a Republican or a skilled mechanic or an Episcopalian or a good poker player. The usual correctional methods do not provide the duration or depth of therapeutic interaction appropriate for the pathological type. Furthermore, the effectiveness of conventional psychotherapy and casework is itself limited, and in fact not strongly supported by evidence of efficacy even for non-criminals.[19] As for the professional criminal, consider the psychological forces operative on such a person, especially the reward system for his style of life. His associates, his self-concept, his feelings of personal worth, his pride in his professional skill

in picking pockets or "cracking" safes, his social and sexual life, the very vocabulary in which he talks and thinks, his long habituation to a life of autonomy
to do as he pleases (e.g., to sleep late mornings) so long as he pulls a successful
"job" now and then, his low tolerance for boredom, and (especially if he has
undergone considerable imprisonment) a diffuse hatred and contempt for what he
perceives as the hypocritically so-called law-abiding society and its law enforcement agencies—all of these militate against shifting to a law-abiding career. It
may be that special methods of rewarding even moderate amounts of productive
economic work should be applied to such individuals, in which the best available
know-how about the psychology of learning is brought to bear. Thus, for example, it might be necessary to deliver economic rewards to such individuals on a
different schedule and in greater amounts, because we have a very strong collection of habit systems working against us when we try to change such a person.
Instead of the usual procedure of revoking parole for any technical violation,
learning principles would suggest such control techniques as rewarding violation-
free intervals that are then made progressively longer, grading the rewards and
punishments in proportion to the kind of violation, and so forth. The point is that
psychology today has a pretty powerful tool-kit for behavior modification which
is not being used—in fact is almost unknown—in the correctional system. But
such special approaches would require firm, informed, clearheaded adoption of a
consistent behavior-engineering viewpoint. The first reaction one has to such
ideas is likely to be, "Why should this crook get paid more or more frequently or
on a different basis from Honest John citizen?" To which my reply is, "Make up
your mind what you are trying to do. If you have to treat some people in a rather
special way for a while in order to get their behavior running along the lines you
want, you cannot afford as a taxpayer (and potential victim) to be preoccupied
with giving everyone his due. You have to decide firmly whether you want to
reduce the crime rate more than you want to maintain some kind of cosmic ethical bookkeeping" The answer to the question why should somebody be treated
specially is the counterquestion, what are you trying to accomplish?

   The same is true with respect to ameliorating the background conditions
which raise the probability of delinquent behavior, such as slum environment,
unemployment, racial discrimination, and the like. If one is primarily oriented
toward ethical or political categories, he is likely to say, "Well, I know a fellow
who was raised in a slum dwelling and whose father was a drunkard and his mother
was a prostitute and his older brother was a pickpocket; but that fellow grew up
to be a successful law-abiding citizen." So what? Fine for him! But where is one
supposed to go with this argument? The anecdote shows that criminal behavior is
predictable only in statistical probability from certain kinds of background factors but not with certainty. Personally, I cannot as a citizen and taxpayer take any
satisfaction, in case a more typical product of a bad neighborhood and family
environment commits a crime against me, in knowing that some *other* persons

from similar backgrounds turn out better. What good does it do me to know this? I repeat, you have to make up your mind what you are trying to do. The difficult thing in this area is to "keep your eye on the ball." I am not trying to eliminate all application of the categories of justice, but I would confine emphasis on them to the specific question involved when a trial court concludes as to a defendant's guilt or innocence as charged. Outside of that issue, I would minimize reference to ethical and equitable notions in the same spirit that I think it more important to reduce the incidence of venereal disease among our soldiers than to see that individuals pay for their sexual sins by becoming infected because catching syphilis or gonorrhea is "their own fault."

Let me give you a noncriminal example of this tension between concern with ethical and political categories and concern with efficient behavioral engineering. I recently heard a Ph.D. oral in which the candidate was a psychologist who reported on the application of Skinner's method of behavior control to a variety of problems, including that of a man who had been chronically unemployable for many years because he got into the habit of utilizing the most minor physical or mental discomforts as an excuse to stay home in bed, as a result of which his irregular work attendance led to his discharge from any job. His wife was working full-time to support them. Conventional psychotherapy had been almost without effect, except perhaps to make the man feel a little more comfortable in his parasitic role! The student psychologist worked out a detailed plan of rewards and deprivations — which included persuading the patient to make an attorney the receiver of his salary checks — and by a slow, careful, scientifically-graded process lasting over several months, worked the man out of his long-time habits and by the time of the thesis writing the patient had been steadily employed at the same job for over a year, the first time in his life he had ever held any position more than a few weeks. But many special provisons had to be made, including rather inconvenient arrangements with his employer and supervisor, in order to bring about this result. Now suppose we are tempted to say, "Why should we go to so much trouble about this fellow? Why should he have such special privileges when he is just a lazy goldbrick good-for-nothing? If he doesn't show up for work, he deserves to be fired. Other people do their jobs without such special psychological handling. Shame on him!" Without entering into the merits of these evaluative judgments, which I confess I share (since I agree with my sainted namesake that "he who does not work should not eat"), such responses on our part are socially inefficient, because while they give us the satisfaction of looking down our noses at an apparently inferior being, the fact is that they do not shape him up. It is far more socially desirable to take the trouble over a period of months to change his behavior so that he becomes, and hopefully will remain, a functioning economic unit. I repeat: We have to make up our minds what we want to do. For my part, I am much less interested in speculating about people's fundamental moral responsibility for being the way they are, than I am in trying to change them in a socially desirable direction.

I should like to close with a political observation and a political plea. The high visibility in American society of the crime problem imposes a terrible burden upon law enforcement agencies, correctional personnel, and political officeholders. I agree with psychologist Donald T. Campbell[20] that there is need for a change in the political atmosphere as regards crime and similar social problems, toward a more open recognition that we do not know exactly how to proceed, that no man or group of men or political party knows how to proceed, so that persons running for elected office, or holding appointive office in correctional and law enforcement systems, would feel a freedom that they do not currently feel in our political atmosphere to say that for the next few years such-and-such a social experiment is going to be tried. The mandate should not be to stamp out crime (or poverty, or discrimination, or inflation) but the mandate should be to embark, whole-heartedly but skeptically, upon the social experiment to see whether or not it works. Society is continually experimenting on its problems whether we label it by that name or not. It should not be a disgrace for a politician to say that Method Number One was given a good try during his term in office, and it appears not to be successful. It is no disgrace for a scientist to report the negative results of an experiment. The point is that the experiment had to be done before one could find out that the results were negative. Only in such a political atmosphere can the psychologist reach the full potential of his contribution to the amelioration of social problems.

Notes

1. See essay 15, this volume.

2. Karl Menninger objects to the lawyer's concern for "justice," on the ground that this concept is not considered relevant in bacteriology! I am at a loss even how to formulate such an argument for criticism. See K. Menninger, *The Crime of Punishment* (1966), 17. May one suppose that Dr. Menninger would accept an argument that the concept "unconscious wish" is illegitimate because it is not used in metallurgy? When such egregious non sequiturs are found in psychiatric writing, it is surely no wonder that many scholars trained in the logical habits of legal thought look upon psychiatric thinking with contempt.

3. Ward and Kassebaum, "Evaluations of Correctional Treatments: Some Implications of Negative Findings," in *Law Enforcement Science and Technology* (ed. S. Yefsky, 1967); Christie, "Research into Methods of Crime Prevention," *Collected Studies in Criminological Research* 1 (1967): 55; Hood, "Research on the Effectiveness of Punishments and Treatments," *Collected Studies in Criminological Research* 1 (1967): 73; Lerman, "Evaluating the Outcomes of Institutions for Delinquents: Implications for Research and Social Policy," *Social Work* 13 (1968): 40.

For an excellent introduction to the evaluation problem by one of the most sophisticated, hardheaded, fair-minded social scientists working in the area, see L. Wilkins, *Evaluation of Penal Measures* (1969), written so as to presuppose no expertise in social science methods or data. For examples of the kind of controlled research study that regularly tends to yield substantially negative results, the reader might have a look at Miller, "The Impact of a 'Total-Community' Delinquency Control Project," *Social Problems* 10 (1962): 168; and—the *locus classicus* of a large-scale study whose discouraging findings are still being explained away twenty years later by social workers and psychotherapists—E. Powers and H. Witmer, *An Experiment in the Prevention of Delinquency* (1951). But see Witmer, "Prevention of Juvenile Delinquency,"*Annals of the American Academy of Political and Social Science* 322 (1959), a collection which, *caveat lector*, illustrates the tendency mentioned in note 14 *infra*.

4. Andenaes, "General Prevention—Illusion or Reality?" *Journal of Criminal Law, Criminology and Police Science* 43 (1952): 176; Andenaes, "The General Preventive Effects of Punishment," *University of Pennsylvania Law Review* 114 (1966): 949. These should be "must" readings for clinicians and social scientists approaching the study of criminal law. They could, having had their social science prejudices shaken up a bit by Andenaes, profitably follow with the carefully reasoned H. Hart, *Punishment and Responsibility* (1968), and H. Packer, *The Limits of the Criminal Sanction* (1968), the latter providing a very helpful bibliographic note along with its informed, wise, and fair-minded analysis of this difficult problem.

5. See, e.g., Newman, "Punishment and the Breakdown of the Legal Order: The Experience of East Pakistan," in *Responsibility: Nomos III* (ed. C. Friedrich, 1960). Indirectly relevant is the interesting "vigilante" phenomenon, the organizing of citizens' (procedurally) illegal self-help groups to enforce (substantive) law when adequate political institutions do not exist or their officials are excessively inefficient, distant, nonfeasant, or corrupt. See H. Bancroft, *Popular Tribunals* (1887); R. Brown, *The South Carolina Regulators* (1963); A. Valentine, *Vigilante Justice* (1956).

6. Lawyers seeking a non-technical introduction to the "Skinnerian line" should read B. Skinner, *Science and Human Behavior* (1953). For additional references requiring varying amounts of psychological sophistication see J. Holland and B. Skinner, *The Analysis of Behavior* (1961) (a programmed text which I recommend to busy lawyer readers seriously approaching this subject-matter for the first time). See also T. Ayllon and N. Azrin, *The Token Economy: A Motivational System for Therapy and Rehabilitation* (1968); L. Krasner and L. Ullmann, *Research in Behavior Modification* (1965); L. Ullmann and L. Krasner, *Case Studies in Behavior Modification* (1965). My own grave doubts as to the "long-run, total, theoretical adequacy" of Skinner's program arise from my conviction that he and his followers underestimate (a) The verisimilitude in Freud's constructions, (b) The importance of genetic factors—and resulting taxonomic entities—in behavior disorder, and (c) The complexity of language behavior. See Chomsky, Book Review, *Language* 35 (1959): 26, and the reply of MacCorquodale, Book Review, *Journal of Experimental Analysis of Behavior* 13 (1970): 83 (reviewing B. Skinner, *Veral Behavior*). See also W. Honig, *Operant Behavior: Areas of Research and Application* (1966); B. Skinner, *Contingencies of Reinforcement, A Theoretical Analysis* (1969); B. Skinner, *The Technology of Teaching* (1968); R. Ulrich, T. Stachnik and J. Mabry, *Control of Human Behavior* (1966).

7. A. Buss and E. Buss, *Theories of Schizophrenia* (1969); I. Gottesman and J. Shields, *Schizophrenia and Genetics* (1972); I. Gottesman and J. Shields, "In Pursuit of the Schizophrenic Genotype," in *Progress in Human Behavior Genetics* (ed. S. Vandenberg, 1968); D. Jackson, *The Etiology of Schizophrenia* (1960); S. Kety and D. Rosenthal, *The Transmission of Schizophrenia* (1968); T. Millon, *Theories of Psychopathology* (1967); E. Slater and M. Roth, *Mayer-Gross, Slater and Roth: Clinical Psychiatry* (3rd ed., 1960), at 237.

8. See essay 13, this volume, especially note 4 and the references thereat, to which should now be added B. Kleinmuntz, *Clinical Information Processing by Computer* (1969), and, for further development of the counter-actuarial view, Holt, "Yet Another Look at Clinical and Statistical Prediction: Or, is Clinical Psychology Worthwhile?", *American Psychologist* 25 (1970): 337. See also Marks and Sines, "Methodological Problems of Cookbook Construction," in *MMPI: Research Developments and Clinical Applications* (ed. J. Butcher, 1969); Einhorn, "The Use of Nonlinear, Noncompensatory Models in Decision Making," *Psychological Bulletin* 73 (1970): 221; Pankoff and Roberts, "Bayesian Synthesis of Clinical and Statistical Prediction," *Psychological Bulletin* 70 (1968): 762; Peterson and Lynch, "Man as an Intuitive Statistician," *Psychological Bulletin* 68

(1967): 29; Sines, "Actuarial Versus Clinical Prediction in Psychopathology," *British Journal of Psychiatry* 116 (1970): 129.

9. See, e.g., Holt, "Clinical and Statistical Prediction: A Reformulation and Some New Data," *Journal of Abnormal and Social Psychology* 56 (1958): 1; Holt, "Clinical Judgment as a Disciplined Inquiry," *Journal of Nervous and Mental Disease* 133 (1961): 369; Holt, *supra* note 8.

10. H. Cleckley, *The Mask of Sanity* (4th ed., 1964), whose beautiful delineation of the type makes it worth more than all other books and articles combined. Any of my law readers who have docilely accepted the widespread psychiatric cliche that "There is no such entity as the psychopath [= sociopath], it's just a wastebasket term for patients we don't like" should *study* Cleckley's brilliant portrayal of the syndrome and evaluate his thesis in the light of their experience. See also W. McCord and J. McCord, *The Psychopath* (1964). The unfortunately common carelessness in diagnosis (worsened by incoherencies in the received nomenclature), which gives rise to the "waste-basket" cliche, cannot tell us whether there nevertheless exists a core group of true-blue psychopaths, who make up perhaps 30 or 40 percent of all patients "officially" labelled as sociopathic. The great merit of Cleckley's book is to teach us how to spot the real ones and what to look for. Formal delinquency arising from antisocial conduct is *not* the clinical touchstone. I am myself convinced that Cleckley's type exists, and is a very special breed of cat, at least as homogeneous as other recognized diagnostic entities. For some fascinating psychometric and psychophysiologic data bearing on the taxonomic issue, see Lykken, "A Study of Anxiety in the Sociopathic Personality," *Journal of Abnormal and Social Psychology* 55 (1957): 6; *replicated by* Schachter and Latané, "Crime, Cognition, and the Autonomic Nervous System," *Nebraska Symposium on Motivation* 12 (1964): 221. See also Hare, "Psychopathy and Choice of Immediate Versus Delayed Punishment," *Journal of Abnormal Psychology* 71 (1966): 25; Hare, "Acquisition and Generalization of a Conditioned Fear Response in Psychopathic and Nonpsychopathic Criminals," *Journal of Psychology* 59 (1965): 367; Hare, "Temporal Gradient of Fear Arousal in Psychopaths," *Journal of Abnormal Psychology* 70 (1965): 442. I think that the "essential psychopath" develops on the basis of some sort of (genetic) malfunction of the anxiety-signal systems of the brain, and we do have considerable (albeit conflicting) evidence that these persons manifest an aberrant brain-wave pattern. The electroencephalographic research is difficult to interpret, mainly because the *behavioral* side of the brain-wave-to-behavioral correlation is not studied in a way that is both (a) objective and (b) sophisticated [= theoretically informed]. It is pointless—worse, downright counterproductive because it misleads us—to study the EEG patterns of so-called "sociopaths" without measuring, rating, classifying the behavior deviations with a theory like Cleckley's in mind, since without such the investigator is really dealing with a "waste-basket" bunch of psychologically heterogenous "antisocials." For a nice example of how misleading it would have been to report brain-wave data on the crude category, see the careful but little-known study by Simmons and Diethelm, "Electroencephalographic Studies of Psychopathic Personalities," *Archives of Neurology and Psychiatry* 55 (1946): 619. About the vexed issue of diagnostic rubrics in behavior disorders generally (commonly "settled" these days in a remarkably shoddy, dilettante fashion) see essay 13, this volume. See also Meehl, "Specific Genetic Etiology, Psychodynamics, and Therapeutic Nihilism," *International Journal of Mental Health* 1 (1970); Murphy, "One Cause? Many Causes? The Argument from a Bimodal Distribution," *Journal of Chronic Diseases* 17 (1964): 301; Wender, "On Necessary and Sufficient Conditions in Psychiatric Explanation," *Archives of General Psychiatry* 16 (1967): 41.

11. Schwitzgebel, "Issues in the Use of an Electronic Rehabilitation System with Chronic Recidivists," *Law and Society Review* 3 (1969): 597. See also "Development of an Electronic Rehabilitation System for Parolees," *Law and Computer Technology* 2 (1969): 9; "Electronic Innovation in the Behavioral Sciences: A Call to Responsibility," *American Psychologist* 22 (1967): 364; Note, "Anthropotelemetry: Dr. Schwitzgebel's Machine," *Harvard Law Review* 80 (1966): 418.

12. The great initial discoveries here were Olds and Milner, "Positive Reinforcement Produced by Electrical Stimulation of Septal Area and Other Regions of Rat Brain," *Journal of Comparative*

and Physiological Psychology 47 (1954): 419; and the same year, independently, Delgado, Roberts, and Miller, "Learning Motivated by Electrical Stimulation of the Brain," *American Journal of Physiology*, 179 (1954): 587. Reviews of subsequent developments may be found in Olds and Olds, "Drives, Rewards, and the Brain," in *New Directions in Psychology* 2 (ed. T. Newcomb, 1965), 327; Olds, "Hypothalamic Substrates of Rewards," *Physiological Review* 42 (1962): 554; Trowill, Panskepp, and Gandelman, "An Incentive Model of Rewarding Brain Stimulation," *Psychological Review* 76 (1969): 264. See also Roberts, "Hypothalamic Mechanisms for Motivational and Species-typical Behavior," in *The Neural Control of Behavior* (eds. R. Whalen, R. Thompson, M. Verzeano, and N. Weinberger, 1970).

13. Heath and Mickel, "Evaluation of Seven Years' Experience with Depth Electrode Studies in Human Patients," in *Electrical Studies on the Unanesthetized Brain* (eds. E. Ramey and D. O'Doherty, 1960). But no dry, scientific verbal reports or graphs can convey the sense of powerful control over behavior and subjective experience that one gets from viewing Dr. Heath's sound movies of his wired-up patients!

14. Bailey, "Correctional Treatment: An Analysis of One Hundred Correctional Outcome Studies, *Journal of Criminal L.C. and P.S.* 57 (1966): 153.

15. See authorities cited note 6 *supra*.

16. Livermore and Meehl, essay 12, this volume. Objections of my brethren in psychology have persuaded me that the application of our M'Naghten-Rule exegesis to Case 14 (at 378) yields an untoward result. At this writing my law colleague Livermore is inaccessible so I cannot speak for him.

17. Reactions of hearers of this lecture and readers of the manuscript indicate that "serious depredations" needs underscoring and expansion, especially in relation to the penal South Sea Island fantasy *supra* where my specific restriction to "four-time losers, given to crimes of violence against the person" seems readily missed by those whose reflex identification is with the criminal offender rather than with his actual *and potential* victims. The point deserves, of course, much more than a footnote. I am assuming that most of my fellow-citizens are like me in fearing crimes involving violence to the person (or threat thereof) more than crimes against property. Furthermore, one can protect himself against property crimes in ways that do not make much psychological sense when applied to personal-violence crimes. No amount of life or disability insurance will recompense me if a hoodlum or psychopath kills me or gouges my eye out; nor would the fact of being "adequately" insured prevent my living in fear if the Hobbesian war of every man against every man prevailed. Whereas it seems fair to say that the various buffers against property crimes, ranging from a fidelity bond to vandalism coverage on one's automobile, serve adequately to relieve most of us from catastrophic consequences and the chronic fear of such. For my part, therefore, I want the muggers, knifers, armed robbers, rapists, kidnappers (and night-time burglars?) put away safely, more than I do the shoplifters, car-thieves, embezzlers, forgers, and con men.

The reference to "four-time losers" was an arbitrary choice of cutting score, recognizing that a number of previous offenses has a high prognostic power. (See e.g., the impressive curves in Figure 1 of Wilkins, *supra* note 3, at 55. I am confident that no psychological test scores and no psychiatric clinical ratings, singly or jointly, could come even close to competing with these actuarial recidivism functions in steepness.)

In considering the merits of imprisonment for property offenses, someone should cost-account our correctional system with an eye to the disturbing question, "Does it cost the average taxpayer more to incarcerate felon Jones [larceny of $150 TV set] for five years than it would cost to let Jones go free but group-insure adequately against Jones's statistically expectable larcenies during the ensuing 5-year interval?" I have no idea what such a cost accounting would show, but I would be most curious to see it done. It is not inconceivable that 50 years hence the several-year imprisonment of a TV-set thief will seem as strange to educated persons as the fellow-servant rule for industrial accidents seems to us today, accustomed as we are to the universal enactment of workmen's compensation statutes. Setting aside *both* employer's fault and contributory negligence by the injured workman—

surely "unfair" to one thinking in terms of ordinary tort concepts—we have come to consider it rational to collectivize this risk by law, making the consumer pay for it as part of production costs.

A recent Finnish study (personal communication, abstract only available, from my sociologist colleague Dr. David Ward) showed that recidivism-rates for offenders convicted of property crimes or drunken driving did not differ as between those incarcerated in closed prisons and those placed in "open institutions" (labor colonies). The abstract concludes that "It seems to be possible to achieve remarkable savings in cost of prison systems and at the same time avoid needless human suffering to prisoners and their families by decreasing use of closed prisons and replacing with labor colony type institutions." Of course this study cannot answer the question whether closed imprisonment would, in the *very* long run, exceed labor-colony service in its *general* deterrent effect (on potential but non-actualizing offenders). Suppose that statutory probation for the first *n* property offenses were yet a third form of "social treatment." I find it pretty hard to believe that *zero* change in commission-rate of these crimes would occur as a result. But would the increase be large enough to render such a rule diseconomic? I submit that we really do not know; and we surely ought to be doing research to find out! See also "Preliminary Report on the Costs and Effects of the California Criminal Justice System and Recommendation for Legislature to Increase Support of Local Police and Correction Programs," (Research Office of California Assembly, 1969).

18. T. Ferdinand, *Typologies of Delinquency: A Critical Analysis* (1966).

19. The younger generation of law professors has to some extent been brainwashed by psychiatrists and social scientists into implicit acceptance of the efficacy of conventional psychotherapy, including psychoanalysis. While I myself have experienced it, urge it upon my clinical students, and have for some twenty years been earning a sizeable fraction of my income as a psychotherapeutic practitioner, I cannot emphasize sufficiently to my law-trained readers that psychotherapy is today a problematic and marginal operation, such that sane and intelligent minds can—and do—seriously raise the question whether it has any efficacy whatever. I personally "believe it works" for *some* patients if they are lucky enough to have the right psychotherapist. See Meehl, "Discussion of Eysenck's "The Effects of Psychotherapy," *International Journal of Psychiatry* 1 (1965): 156. But I cannot really prove this scientifically. If there are readers to whom this revelation (of a truism among scientifically competent psychologists) comes as a shocking novelty, I recommend perusal of the entire journal issue cited. See also Bergin and Strupp, *Changing Frontiers in the Science of Psychotherapy* (1972); A. Ellis, *Reason and Emotion in Psychotherapy* (1962) (especially his superb Chapter 20, "The limitations of psychotherapy" at 375); A. Goldstein and S. Dean, *The Investigation of Psychotherapy* (1966); A. Herzberg, *Active Psychotherapy* (1945); *Research in Psychotherapy* 1 (eds. F. Rubinstein and M. Parloff, 1959); *Research in Psychotherapy*, 2 (eds. H. Strupp and L. Luborsky, 1962); D. Wiener, *A Practical Guide to Psychotherapy* (1968); "Symposium: The Hospital Treatment of the Schizophrenic Patient," *International Journal of Psychiatry* 8 (1969); 699; and the periodic reviews of research in *Annual Review of Psychology* under headings "Psychotherapy" or "Psychotherapeutic Processes" by Snyder, 1 (1950): 221; Hathaway, 2 (1951): 259; Raimy, 3 (1952): 321; Sanford, 4 (1953): 317; Saslow, 5 (1954): 311; Meehl, 6 (1955): 357; Harris, 7 (1956): 121; Winder, 8 (1957): 309; Snyder, 9 (1958): 353; Luborsky, 10 (1959): 317; Rotter, 11 (1960): 381; Seeman, 12 (1961): 157; Strupp, 13 (1962): 445; Wirt and Wirt, 14 (1963): 365; Colby, 15 (1964): 347; Matarozzo, 16 (1965): 181; Dittmann, 17 (1966): 51; Ford and Urban, 18 (1967): 333; Cartwright, 19 (1968): 387; Gendlin and Rychlak, 21 (1970): 155. I must confess as a practitioner that most of the psychotherapy research strikes me as curiously unilluminating.

20. Campbell, "Reforms as Experiments," *American Psychologist* 24 (1969): 409.

15

Law and the Fireside Inductions: Some Reflections of a Clinical Psychologist

The Psychology of the Fireside

Lawmen will immediately see the point of my title, but for social science readers I should explain. The phrase "fireside equities" is legalese for what the legal layman feels intuitively or common-sensically would be a fair or just result (see, e.g., Llewellyn, 1960). Sometimes the law accords with the fireside equities, sometimes not; and lawyers use the phrase with derisive connotation. Analogously, by the language "fireside inductions" I mean those common-sense empirical generalizations about human behavior which we accept on the culture's authority plus introspection plus anecdotal evidence from ordinary life. Roughly, the phrase "fireside inductions" designates here what everybody (except perhaps the skeptical social scientist) believes about human conduct, about how it is to be described, explained, predicted, and controlled.

One source of conflict between the social scientist and practitioner of law — especially the legislator — is the former's distrust of common knowledge concerning human conduct and the latter's reliance upon this common knowledge. Such reliance is often associated among lawyers with doubts about the value of generalizations arising from systematic behavioral science research involving quantification and experimental manipulation in artificial situations. Reliance upon "what everyone knows" (simply by virtue of being himself a human being) was hardly critically scrutinized prior to the development of the experimental and statistical methods of contemporary social science. This historical fact provides a built-in preference for the common-sense knowledge of human behavior embod-

I am indebted to the Carnegie Corporation for support of a summer appointment as Professor in the Minnesota Center for Philosophy of Science, and to my Law School colleagues Carl A. Auerbach, John J. Cound, and Joseph M. Livermore for their critical readings of the manuscript.

This article is part of the discussion, "Socialization, the Law, and Society," edited by June L. Tapp, which was published as Number 2, Vol. 27 (1971) of the *Journal of Social Issues*.

ied in positive law. But psychologists mistakenly suppose that the lawyers' continued reliance upon the psychology of the fireside is wholly attributable to inertia, and these misunderstandings warrant consideration. Without being honorific or pejorative, I shall use "fireside inductions" to refer broadly to those expectations and principles, largely inchoate although partially embodied in proverbs and maxims (e.g., "The burnt child dreads the fire," "Blood is thicker than water," "Every man has larceny in his heart," "Power always corrupts") arising from some mixture of (a) personal anecdotal observations, (b) armchair speculation, (c) introspection, and (d) education in the received tradition of Western culture prior to the development of technical social science method. It is not clear where nonquantitative, nonexperimental but psychologically sophisticated ideas, such as those of contemporary psychoanalytic theory and therapy, should be classified, but for the moment I will set this aside.

With my fellow psychologists I share a considerable skepticism concerning the fireside inductions. Even universally held generalizations about the origins and control of human conduct should be subjected to (at least) *quantitative documentary* research and, where feasible, to systematic *experimental* testing. Obviously the degree of skepticism toward a dictum of common-sense psychology should increase as we move into those areas of social control where our efforts are hardly crowned with spectacular success. For example, there is no known system for the prevention or cure of crime and delinquency that is so strikingly successful that anyone can suggest we are doing so well at this social task that it is hardly necessary to call our techniques into question, absent specific research that casts doubt upon them (essay 14, this volume). That the psychological presuppositions underlying the criminal law should be subjected to merciless armchair scrutiny and quantitative research is not said *pro forma*, but expresses a sincere conviction.

Unfair Controversial Tactics Sometimes Used by Lawyers and Psychologists

Nor is this merely a platitude—"we need research"—that everyone accepts. One does come across rational, educated persons who disagree, at least when presented with concrete instances. I know, for instance, a very able law professor (formerly a practicing attorney) whose ignorance of the behavioral sciences was systematic and deliberate and who, although he regarded me highly as an individual intellect, made no secret that he thought most scientific research on law, such as quantitative studies of jury behavior, had little point. Over several months, I realized that he had a foolproof heads-I-win-tails-you-lose technique dealing with intellectual threats from the social sciences, to wit: If I introduced a quantitative-documentary or experimental study of some behavioral generalization having relevance to the law, the findings either accorded with his fireside inductions, or they did not. If they did, he typically responded, "Well, I suppose it's all right to spend the taxpayer's money researching that, although anybody could have told you so beforehand." If the results were *not* in harmony with the fireside mind-model, he refused to believe them! When I called this kind of dirty pool to his attention, he cheerfully admitted this truth about his debating tactics.

Without defending such illegitimate, systematic resistance to the inroads of behavior science data upon legal thinking, I direct my behavior sciences' brethren to some considerations that may render my law colleague's tactics less unreasonable than they seem at first glance. Some behavior scientists, particularly those ideologically tendentious and often completely uninformed with respect to the law, reveal a double standard of methodological morals that is the mirror image of my legal colleague's. They are extremely critical and skeptical about accepting, and applying in practical circumstances, fireside inductions but are willing to rely somewhat uncritically upon equally shaky generalizations purporting to be rigorous deliverances of modern behavior science. A shrewd lawyer, even though he might not know enough philosophy, logic of science, experimental method, or technical statistics to recognize just *what* is wrong with a particular scientific refutation of the fireside inductions, may nevertheless be right in holding to what he learned at his grandmother's knee or through practical experience, rather than abandoning it because, say, "Fisbee's definitive experiment on social conformity" allegedly shows the contrary.

Example: Punishment as a General Deterrent

Consider the threat of punishment as a deterrent, one of the most socially important and widely disputed issues relating behavior science to law. While I have not kept systematic records of my anecdotal material (fireside induction!), the commonest reaction of psychologists upon hearing of my interest in studying law and teaching in the Law School, is a surprised, "Well, Meehl, I have always thought of you as a hard-headed, dustbowl-empiricist, quantitatively-oriented psychologist—how can you be interested in that medieval subject matter?" When pressed for an explanation of why they consider law medieval, my behavior science colleagues generally mention the outmoded and primitive (sometimes they say "moralistic") reliance of the criminal law upon punishment, which "is out of harmony with the knowledge of modern social (or medical) science." This kind of rapid-fire sinking of the lawyer's ship quite understandably tends to irritate the legal mind. However, the same psychologist who says punishment doesn't deter relies on its deterrent effect in posting a sign in the departmental library stating that if a student removes a journal without permission, his privilege to use the room will be suspended but his use fee not returned. This same psychologist suspends his children's TV privileges when they fight over which channel to watch; tells the truth on his income tax form (despite feeling that the government uses most of the money immorally and illegally) for fear of the legal consequences of lying; and drives his car well within the speed limit on a certain street, having been informed that the police have been conducting speed traps there. It will not do for this psychologist to say that as a citizen, parent, professor, taxpayer, automobile driver, etc., he must make such judgments upon inadequate evidence, but when contemplating the legal order he must rely only on scientific information.

Psychologists and psychiatrists (especially the latter) say strange things when pressed to document their statement, often made with dogmatic assurance and an attitude of scientific superiority to the benighted legal profession, that the criminal law cannot deter. They say, for example, that the only way to control behavior is to get at its source or origin, rather than penalizing it; that capital punishment has been shown not to deter murderers; that experimental research on the behavior of infra-human animals has demonstrated that punishment is an ineffective mode of behavior control. These are the three commonest responses, along with a general overall flavor to think about crime "scientifically" instead of "in moralistic categories (e.g., *justice*)." I set aside this last as outside my province *qua* behavior scientist, although in my experience those who object to the introduction of ethical, theological, or juridical concepts in dealing with the problem of criminal conduct usually include some moral judgment upon present practices or upon society, frequently in a self-righteous manner. They seem blissfully unaware of the elementary philosophical point that you either allow ethical categories into your discourse or not, and you cannot forbid them to your opponent and then use them polemically yourself. Karl Menninger's *The Crime of Punishment* (1969) contains a dreadful example, although it's a powerful and perceptive book in many respects. The book is full of moralizing and judgmental language about society, never the criminal offender. Why do the terms of ethical theory apply to social groups but not to individuals? Why is society blameworthy although (presumably) causally determined, and the individual not? Whether psychological determinism precludes all application of ethical terms is beyond the scope of this article, and Menninger does not appear to appreciate its philosophical difficulty. As a psychologist-citizen, I incline to agree with Spinoza (and our contemporary social critic Albert Ellis) that "blaming" behavior is one of the more useless human responses. Antisocial conduct should be approached as a problem of genetics, economics, and behavior engineering, because that orientation tends to minimize the intrusion of emotions into our problem solving, thereby fostering rationality. "Blame" words are emotion elicitors; their use tends to impair the cognitive functions of blamer, blamee, and interested third parties. Regrettably, practically all the words available to designate infractions of moral or legal rules, or persons disposed thereto, are blame laden; since society cannot articulate its legal processes without using the concept of a rule, of its violation, and of a rule violator. We could profitably dispense with words like heinous, dastardly, brutal, bloodthirsty, or wicked. But few would want a society whose legal system had no use for the words justice, fair, equal treatment, malicious intent, offender, obliged, or responsible. Avoiding affect-arousing "blame" words while retaining an axiological vocabulary adequate for the purposes of law is a terribly difficult task. But we can strive for consistency, and it is both inconsistent and unfair to forbid application of ethical descriptors to a burglar while freely applying condemnatory labels to society (= the rest of us) for our less-than optimal treatment of his problem. Nor is such selective moralizing likely to induce the objective attitude that Menninger believes—I think rightly—would facilitate rationality and flexibility in our approach to crime control. If a psychiatrist tells a frightened shopkeeper, whose friend has recently been murdered by an armed bandit, that he, the shopkeeper, is wicked because he wrongly thinks of the bandit as wicked, his most probable reaction is to conclude that psychiatrists must be wicked, rather than to examine critically whether wickedness is a useful conceptual tool in thinking about law as a mode of social control. In addition to the mentioned inconsistency, Menninger advances the strange argument that lawyers should not invoke the concept "justice" in dealing with crime, because this concept is not used in surgery or bacteriology (1969, p. 17). Presumably this reasoning would preclude using concepts like unconscious wish or reaction formation, inasmuch as these notions are superfluous in metallurgy. When such fuzzy-headedness is retailed by a distinguished psychiatrist, can we wonder that lawyers, whose stock in trade is largely clarification of verbal inference, often view "mind experts" with contempt?

A well-known sociologist actually objected to the criminal law's reliance on (threatened) punishment as a deterrent on the ground that it does not work, since we find persons in jail who knew they would go there if convicted of crime! One can hardly understand the commitment of this low-level methodological mistake (pointed out repeatedly by criminologists and jurists, e.g., Andenaes, 1952, 1966) by a social scientist other than from ideological motives. That some persons commit crimes despite the criminal law, and that incarcerated burglars report verbally that they knew burglary was illegal, is as helpful in evaluating the deterrent effect of the criminal sanction as it would be to study the prophylactic effect of a drug by conversing with a sample of patients who had fallen ill despite its administration! When a law professor hears a psychologist, sociologist, or psychiatrist argue this way, it is hardly surprising that his regard for the logical incisiveness of social science thinking is not increased. The amazing thing is that there are actually scholarly monographs written, lectures delivered, and press releases made by university professors in the social or medical sciences, which rely upon an argument whose structure is identical with the following: Medicine has always tried to prevent disease and death; but since people still get sick, and everybody finally dies, we can safely conclude that the medical sciences are a waste of time. Would anybody be impressed with this argument unless he had some sort of ideological ax to grind?

A more subtle mistake is inferring nondeterrency from the inefficacy of the threat of capital punishment (when compared with the threat of noncapital punishment) for murder. This is an instructive example of a little learning being a dangerous thing. One may know barely enough methodology to recognize the desirability of statistical study and experimental control, the necessity to make statistical significance tests between homicide rates in two jurisdictions, or in one jurisdiction before and after a change in the penalty for murder; but this minimal amount of social science sophistication is not always sufficient to recognize the limitations of such findings for generalizing about the effectiveness of the criminal sanction as a general deterrent. It is somewhat embarrassing to find that trained social scientists can make this higher-level mistake, so that a law professor (Andenaes, 1952, 1966) has to make—in ordinary language and without reliance upon technical psychometric concepts—a few elementary points which anyone familiar with learning theory, behavior genetics, and psychometric theory ought to arrive at with a little thought.

Levels of Sophistication in Social Science Method

This levels-of-sophistication question is of great importance in interdisciplinary work and in legal education. Any lawyer knows that having the more meritorious case does not guarantee winning it, a main interfering factor being skill of counsel. Differing levels of sophistication in any technical domain, even possession of a special vocabulary, often lead to misleading impressions as to who has the better of a theoretical or practical dispute. The parish priest can refute the theological objections of an unlettered Hausfrau parishioner. The priest, in turn, will lose a debate with the intellectual village atheist. C. S. Lewis will come out ahead of the village atheist. But when C. S. Lewis tangles with Bertrand Russell, it gets pretty difficult to award the prizes. This dialectical-upmanship phenomenon has been responsible for some of the friction between lawyers and social scientists, especially when the social scientist tendentiously presents what purport to be the findings of modern social science but is expressing the particular psychologist's, psychiatrist's, or sociologist's ethos or theoretical (ideological) prejudices. Undergraduate sophistication sufficiently questions the efficacy of criminal law sanctions as a deterrent (although some college-educated legislators appear to be naïve about this!), and recognizes the desirability of adequate statistics on comparable jurisdictions or within the same jurisdiction before and after a change in severity (or certainty) of penalty. However, to understand threshold effects, asymptotes, second-order interactions, nonlinear dependencies, rate changes at different points on a growth function—considerations hardly profound or esoteric—already takes us beyond the level of sophistication of many social and medical writers who have addressed themselves to legal problems.

Example: Ineffectivness of Capital Punishment

Consider the rapid-fire dismissal of the general idea that increasing a penalty will be effective, on the ground that capital punishment is not effective (i.e., more effective than life imprisonment) as a general deterrent to murder. To draw such a general conclusion from this instance is illegitimate, but the levels-of-expertise problem requires a certain amount of social science know-how even to talk about difficulties in choosing a murder-rate index and calculating a significance test. (It takes more technical know-how to handle the data when time changes in the same jurisdiction are relied on. See, e.g., Campbell, 1969; Campbell & Ross, 1968; Glass, 1968; Ross, Campbell, & Glass, 1969.) Just a bit more sophistication takes into account problems of extreme values, curvilinearity, and the like involved in such a far-out deviation from social norms as murder. You do not need a Ph.D. in Axiology or Social Psychology to know that murder is a crime *malum in se* rather than *malum prohibitum*; that (allowing for varying definitions) it is forbidden in all known societies, literate and preliterate; that it is regularly attended by strong moral disapprobation and severe legal penalities; that it is explicitly forbidden by all known recorded moral codes; that it is a crime of high deviation threshold, having a very low incidence compared with crimes against property, sexual offenses, and so forth. Given these facts, it may be safely assumed that we deal largely with individuals who are aberrated socially or psychiatrically (I do not mean insane or even formally diagnosable, see essays 12 and 13, this volume) or who were responding to extreme and unusual stresses in low-probability contexts. Furthermore, the alternative to capital punishment is life imprisonment, a sufficiently extreme penalty that, assuming a Benthamite rational calculation model, a person would not take a chance on this consequence appreciably more than on the death penalty if the probabilities of detection and conviction were other than small. We are comparing the deterrent effects of two penalties, both of which are sufficiently far out on the hedonic continuum that their difference is probably not very great at the Benthamite calculational stage, *even when* such calculation occurs—presumably rarely in this crime. Evidently we cannot extrapolate, with any confidence at all, from "Capital punishment does not reduce murder rates" to "The notion of general deterrence in criminal law is empirically unsound."

Now the special-case question: Is capital punishment an efficacious general deterrent when operating (a) with less extreme personality deviates, and in a social context which (b) makes apprehension quasi-certain and (c) the penalty well publicized? That is, we inquire whether the threat of death as a sanction can be effective under conditions that come closer to the idealized Benthamite-calculus-user situation than is probably the case for most murderers or rapists. It is not easy to find examples, but the military setting is a pretty good one, and we have a fairly clear case in connection with the mass insubordination, defection, and mutiny of the French army during World War I. In 1917, following the collapse of the Nivelle offensive, morale in the French army was desperately low. The constant danger of death or horrible wounds, the obvious pointlessness of the attacks, and the overall conditions of daily existence must have provided a set of psychological instigations whose pervasiveness, intensity, and duration were beyond anything found in civilian life. In some units, refusals to obey orders had the full character of a mass mutiny and over half of the French army's divisions experienced such mutinies. In the Ninth Division, all three regiments formed a protest march in which they sang the *Internationale* and shouted, "We won't go up the line!"

> Not even units with the finest war records were immune from the profound discontent. . . . In one such army corps there was a large number of mutineers, who shut themselves in their huts or threatened to open fire on anyone who came near them. . . . Half of Petain's army therefore was mutinous. (Barnett, 1965, p. 220)

Petain, who had replaced Nivelle, understood the instigations to mutiny and took appropriate steps to see that some (e.g., insufficient rest between attacks) did not occur. But he also recognized that the current emergency situation, in which half the army was mutinous, required drastic summary treatment. "I set about suppressing serious cases of indiscipline with utmost urgency" (Barnett, 1965, p. 237). Verdicts of guilty were passed on over 23,000 men, i.e., one in every 100 men in the field army on the Western front. Only 432 were sentenced to death and only 55 of these were actually shot, the remainder being sent to penal settlements in the colony. But, of course, every soldier and officer knew that the new commander was determined to punish mutineers, and the tiny number of executions were carefully dispersed and widely publicized. The general deterrence notion in criminal law presupposes knowledge (or, more precisely, belief) as to sanctions, and in civilian life such expectations doubtless vary a good deal. Petain saw the importance of making examples, writing:

> It is essential that the High Command impresses on all ranks that it is resolved on the strictest discipline and obedience, from top to bottom of the military structure. It must ruthlessly make examples where necessary and bring them to the knowledge of the army. (Barnett, 1965, p. 226)

As the fireside inductions would predict, the mutinies ceased entirely and immediately. Presumably, the efficacy of Petain's approach lay in some near-optimal combination of (a) reduced instigations to mutiny, or the hope thereof, under new command, (b) severity of the penalty, and (c) near certainty of detection. As for (c), in 1764 the great Italian criminologist Beccaria (1963) noted that the certainty of punishment is more important than its severity. Severity and certainty combined would predict a high efficacy of general deterrence. Persuasive anecdotal support comes from the area of narcotics law enforcement. Law-enforcement officers cannot get into the high echelons of the drug traffic because the small-fry peddlers toward the terminal end of the chain cannot be effectively pressured by a prosecutor, under the usual threats and promises, to tell anything about the next level of the higher-ups. Peddlers have a solid conviction, amounting to a subjective certainty, that if they are known or strongly suspected to have turned stool pigeon, they will be killed by the organized international narcotics underworld (Lindesmith, 1965, p. 39). An Illinois state's attorney describes a defendant (from whom he was trying to get information about the pushers, sellers, and the higher-ups) as saying, "Well, what can you do? You can give me a couple of years. I have been there before. You can give me time. If I tell you and it gets out, I would be dead before the week is over." Here we have an example of what the underworld sees as a very serious offense, being a stool pigeon, punished with great severity (death) and with near certainty. Why as a psychologist should I dismiss this kind of evidence as worthless because it is not "scientific" but merely anecdotal?

Indirect Evidence as to General Deterrence

Indirect evidence that some of us not now engaged in criminal conduct might commit crimes if the general deterrent pressure of the criminal law were removed is the statistical finding that local crime rates rise dramatically when apprehension probabilities are greatly reduced by suspension of law-enforcement functions (e.g., police strikes, Nazi arrest of the entire Danish police force; see Andenaes, 1952, 1966), and the rates fall quickly when normal police functions are reinstated. Looting associated with natural catastrophes is expected; hence National Guard troops are regularly called out in such emergencies. Conversations with ex-soldiers about the looting and raping that often occurs when a town is occupied—its citizenry may belong to an allied nation—supports the fireside induction, "Many people will do illegal things if they know they can get away with it." I have a close friend, very law-abiding and moral in civilian life, who has recounted to me (with retrospective amazement) his stealing armfuls of books from a bombed French bookshop during World War II, thinking "Everyone was doing it and nobody could stop us, so what the hell?" When law enforcement is ineffective, (e.g., Wild West days), the crime rate often becomes intolerably high, approximating Hobbes's "war of every man against every man," so that all live in constant fear. Contrary to the connotation of "vigilante" as a riotous lynching mob, vigilante organizations were formed by reputable, law-abiding citizens, with their own courts and procedural rules, set up in desperation to enforce substantive law because the legitimate political authority could not or would not protect the community from predators (Bancroft, 1887; Brown, 1963; Newman, 1960; Valentine, 1956). They seem to have been fairly effective in deterrence.

The reactions of some social scientists to the problem of reducing campus violence is predicated on behavioral assumptions that there is no good reason to prefer over the fireside inductions. I have heard it argued that punitive measures cannot have any effect because they do not get at the source of the unrest. Nobody has ever proved this generalization. No scientific proof exists as to what the *source* is for most of the rioters. Neither psychological theory nor the fireside inductions suggest that the source of a student's seizing a building or manhandling a dean is the same from one participant to another. Suppose that photographs of law violators involved in campus disturbances were taken in order to clinch identification; suppose that severe academic penalties and the legal penalties for the felonies involved were imposed; suppose that these consequences were widely publicized; and suppose that these practices were uniform over all campuses. My prediction is that campus disturbances involving violence would shortly be reduced to negligible incidence. A (nonpsychotic) college student who knows that he will be apprehended, thrown permanently out of school, and convicted of a felony carrying a three-year prison term is not appreciably more prone to commit a crime of violence than a looter is likely to steal the silverware from a wrecked house while a National Guardsman with an automatic rifle is observing him. Some of my fellow social scientists, actuated by their own identification with the offenders' cause (a different question, arguable on the moral merits*) attempt to countervail the fireside inductions in a matter of grave importance by invoking "modern behavioral science" as if they were talking about the well-established and highly generalizable principles of mechanics. I would not presume, *qua* psychologist, to instruct a government adviser with a Ph.D. in economics on the adequacy of Keynesian theory in forestalling a major depression should a recession commence, relying upon Ayllon's beautiful studies of the "token economy" in a state hospital (Ayllon & Azrin, 1968) or Cowles's classic ex-

---

*It is irrelevant but in these troubled times perhaps desirable to state for the record that I am myself so strongly opposed to the Indochina War that if I were draftable and not classifiable as a conscientious objector I would emigrate rather than enter the armed services. It should not be necessary to point out (but wide current use of *ad hominem* arguments suggests it is) that one's agreement with student protesters on substantive issues has nothing to do with the empirical means-end question: Can criminal sanctions and optimally deployed counterforce reduce illegal campus violence? That rule-regulated force (or the threat thereof) is intrinsic to law is, I take it, recognized by all informed persons, being the main difference between law and ethics or etiquette.

periments (Cowles, 1937) on the efficacy of differently colored poker chips as token rewards for the chimpanzee. But some social scientists dare extrapolations equally dangerous as these.

When we generalize from laboratory research on punishment in infra-human animals, the situation is extraordinarily complex, and few statements can be made unqualifiedly. It was already known before the advent of Skinnerian learning theory that, by and large, punishment (negative reinforcement, aversive control) is a relatively nonpreferable form of behavior engineering as contrasted with well-designed regimes of differential positive reinforcement when the latter are situationally feasible. That generalization seems overall a safe one on the evidence we have, and it is probably broadly applicable at the level of the human child or adult. Overreliance upon aversive control can confidently be counted as one respect in which the old fireside mind model was badly in error, and I wish to state clearly, before continuing with my modulated pro-deterrence argument, that the average citizen's faith in more and tougher laws as the main way to reduce crime is unsound. The punitive technique combined inefficient behavior engineering with much needless human suffering (Skinner, 1948, 1953, 1961 especially Part I, 1968, 1969 especially Part I). But when we go on to quantitative details, necessary qualifications, and practical applications to influencing the adult human criminal offender (or deterring the rest of us potential offenders) matters become pretty complicated.

Consider the merits of severely punitive legislation against drunken driving, setting aside the recent statistical time series data (Ross, Campbell, & Glass, 1969). Advocates of a stiffer law may rely upon the fireside inductions. Psychologists or sociologists may rely upon the allegedly scientific generalization that "punishment doesn't prevent crime." What is the part of rationality? Who makes the riskier extrapolation: The lawmaker, contrasting his own behavior and introspections about driving his car to a cocktail party in the United States and in Copenhagen, or the psychologist, extrapolating from Estes's experiments on the white rat (Estes, 1944) and generalizing from what a severely disturbed juvenile delinquent told him in a therapeutic interview? Without denigrating these latter kinds of data, I cannot say that they are clearly more persuasive than introspection and the (remarkably uniform) anecdotes about the Scandinavian drunk-driving sanctions. (That it is often considered methodologically unsound to ask persons why they do things is one of the strange developments from behaviorism — here allied for a change with psycho-analysis.)

The Concepts Empirical, Experimental, Quantitative

Rational discussion of the law's reliance on the fireside inductions may be rendered needlessly difficult by an unfortunate semantic habit as to the honorific word "empirical." Since I have myself been fighting a running battle with my psychological associates for some years against this bad semantic habit, I would dislike to see it accepted by legal scholars. The following methodological equation, often implicit and unquestioned, is being taken over by lawyers from behavior science:

$$Empirical = Experimental\text{-}and\text{-}Quantitative = Scientific$$

This equivalence is objectionable on several grounds. It is epistemologically inaccurate since there is a great deal of the empirical (i.e., arising in or supported by observations or experiences, including introspective experiences) that is neither experimental nor quantitative. Furthermore, the middle term assumes a false linkage because (a) not all experimental research is quantitative and (b) not all quantitative research is experimental. Third, several disciplines (to which hardly anybody would refuse the term scientific) exhibit varying amounts of experimental manipulation conjoined with varying amounts of the qualitative/quantitative dimension, e.g., astronomy, ecology, comparative anatomy, botany, human genetics, paleontology, economics, meteorology, geography, historical geology, epidemiology, clinical medicine.

What is an experiment? I am not prepared to give an exactly demarcated definition of the term. Roughly, an experiment is a systematic, preplanned sequence of operations-cum-observations, the system of entities under study being relatively isolated from the influence of certain classes of causal factors; other causal factors being held quasi-constant by the experimenter; and still others manipulated by him, their values either being set for different individuals in the system or changed over time at the experimenter's will; and output is recorded at the time. Some (under Sir R. A. Fisher's influence) would add, but I would not, that remaining causally efficacious factors (known, guessed, or completely unidentified but assumed to exist) must be rendered noncorrelates of the manipulated variables by a randomizing procedure permitting their net influence to be estimated (statistical significance test).

This definition says nothing about apparatus, instruments, measurement, or even being in the laboratory. I disapprove of stretching the word "experiment" to include clinical or sociological research based upon ex post facto assessment processes, entering files of old data, naturalistic observations in the field or in public places, and so forth. But Campbell's "quasi-experiment" is useful to denote a subset of these possessing certain methodological features that render them relatively more interpretable (see Campbell, 1969). The word "experiment" has become invidious because biological and social scientists tend to denigrate nonexperimental sources of knowledge (such as clinical experience, analysis of documents, file data, or the fireside inductions). Then, by equating "experimental" with "empirical" with "scientific," they often imply that any knowledge source other than experimental is methodologically worthless (armchair speculation, appeal to authority, metaphysics, folklore, and the like). But the fireside inductions *are empirical*. No logician would hesitate to say this. Their subject matter is the domain of empirical phenomena, and one who invokes a fireside induction will, when pressed to defend it, appeal to some kind of experience which he expects the critic will share with him, whether personally or vicariously.

Even the traditional law review article which traces, say, the development of a juridical concept like "state action" or "substantive due process" through a historical sequence of appellate court opinions is empirical, since its subject matter is the verbal behavior, recorded in documents, of a class of organisms, and the researcher studies the changes in this verbal behavior over time. The presence of analytical discourse in such a traditional law review paper does not render it non-empirical, but to argue this is beyond the scope of the present paper (see Feigl & Meehl, essay 3, this volume; essay 2, this volume; Skinner, 1969, ch. 6).

There are important differences between the traditional law review article and the kind of article we expect to find in *Law and Society Review*. But we have some perfectly good words, more precise and less invidious, to characterize the difference. For a study of files or documents utilizing the statistical techniques of behavior science we can say simply "statistical," a straightforward word that means pretty much the same thing to most people and that is not loaded emotionally. If structural statistics (such as factor analysis or multidimensional scaling, see Meehl, 1954, pp. 11–14) are employed, we have the word "psychometric." Distinguishing the quantitative or statistical from the experimental dimension is particularly important in discussing methodology of research on law because—as in clinical psychology and personology—one research method in these fields is the application of statistical and psychometric techniques of analysis to documents (e.g., diaries, interview transcripts, jury protocols, Supreme Court opinions). It would be misleading to say that one "performs an experiment" if he plots a curve showing the incidence of concurring opinions over time in the behavior output of an appellate court, but it is equally misleading to say that a traditional law review article which draws no graphs and fits no mathematical functions but traces through a set of opinions over time with reference to the incidence of split votes and dissents, presented in ordinary text, is not empirical. Research does not cease to be empirical, or even behavioral, when it analyzes behavior products instead of the ongoing behavior flux itself.

Since the control of variables influencing a dependent variable is a matter of degree, situations arise in which one is in doubt as to whether the word "experiment" is applicable. But this is merely the familiar problem of drawing an arbitrary cut whose location matters little. For research designs methodologically more powerful than studying a slice of cross-sectional file data because we have changes over time in relation to a societal manipulation (e.g., amendment of a penal statute), we have the expression "quasi-experiment" (Campbell, 1969).

Mental Tests and Social Class:
The Levels-of-Sophistication Point Exemplified

The sophistication-level effect is beautifully illustrated by the vexatious problem of interpreting socioeconomic differences on mental tests. I suppose the minimum sophistication level necessary in order even to put the interesting questions is that of understanding why and how intelligence tests were built and validated, including basic concepts of correlation, content-domain sampling, reliability, validity, developmental growth curves, etc., that one learns about in an elementary psychology class. Exposure to basic psychometric theory and multiple strands of validation data (Campbell & Fiske, 1959; Cronbach & Meehl, 1955; Jackson, 1969; Loevinger, 1957) should eliminate some common anti-test prejudices and excessive reliance upon anecdotal refutations. (*Example*: "I knew a kid with an IQ of 196 who became a bum.") I find it odd, by the way, that some lawyers will pronounce confidently to me about what intelligence tests do and do not measure, when the pronouncer could not so much as define IQ, factor loading, or reliability coefficient. I cannot conceive myself asserting to a lawyer that "the Hearsay Rule is silly" without having at least taken a course or read a treatise on the law of evidence, where the rationale of the Rule and its exceptions was discussed. But I am uncomfortably aware that some psychologists permit themselves strong—usually negative—views about the law without knowing anything about it.

This bottom level of psychometric sophistication would suffice for an employer to consider using psychological tests in screening job applicants. At a higher level, one thinks about the social-class bias in tests. If he stops there, relying upon the class-score correlations as definitive proof of test bias, he will perhaps avoid using tests, either because he may "miss" some good candidates (a poor reason, statistically) or from considerations of fairness, justice, equal opportunity (a good reason, provided his psychometric premise concerning bias is substantially correct). Moving one step higher in sophistication, we realize that the SES-IQ correlation is causally ambiguous, and that the limitations of statistical method for resolving this causal ambiguity are such that no analysis of file data can tell us what causes what. No one knows and, worse, no one knows how to find out to what extent the SES-IQ correlation is attributable to environmental impact and to what extent it is attributable to genetic influence. This causal ambiguity, while rather obvious (and clearly pointed out over 40 years ago in Burks & Kelley, 1928) is, as I read the record, somewhat above the sophistication level of many sociologists and psychologists, who talk, write, and design experiments on the (implicit) assumption that social class is entirely on the causal input side of the equation.

The terrible complexity of this problem cannot be discussed here, but I have treated it elsewhere (Meehl 1969, 1970a, 1971). I can briefly concretize it by reference to the Coleman Report (Coleman, Campbell, & Hobson, 1966) on equality of educational opportunity. In the course of an interdisciplinary discussion at the University of Minnesota branch of the Law and Society Association one law professor argued: Since the Coleman Report showed that the psychological characteristics of a student's peer group were more closely correlated with his measured ability and achievement than either the school's physical plant or the characteristics of the teaching staff, these "empirical data of behavior science" would indicate that the way to achieve equal educational opportunity should be mandatory busing to provide disadvantaged pupils with the presumably better stimulation from abler peers. Whatever the legal merits of mandatory busing in relation to de facto segregation, the methodological point is important and requires a level of psychometric sophistication a notch above my law colleague's. It is possible that the higher statistical correlation between peer-group attributes and student's academic level is attributable mainly to geographic selective factors mediated by the family's social class, rather than causal influence of peer-group stimulation. Parental intelligence, personality, and temperament factors are transmitted to the child in part genetically (no informed and unbiased person today could dispute this, but many social scientists are both uninformed and prejudiced against behavior genetics) and partly through social learning. If physical-plant characteristics and teacher characteristics are correlated with the biological and social inputs of the child's family only via the (indirect) economic-neighborhood-location and political (tax-use) factors, they will have a lower statistical relationship with the child's cognitive level than is shown by indicators of the cognitive level of other children attending the same neighborhood school. Roughly, peer-group attributes happen to be a better (indirect) measure of average family and neighborhood causal factors—genetic and environmental—than teacher or physical-plant attributes. The differential correlation would reflect more a psychometric fact (about the factor loadings and reliabilities of certain measures) than a causal fact (about peer-group influence).

Whether one analyzes these data by inspecting a correlation table or by more complex statistical devices such as regression equations or analysis of covariance, neither the crude zero-order relationships, beta-weights, nor sums of squares tell us much about the direction of causal influence. We cannot infer whether social stimulation from other students is causally more efficacious than having better qualified teachers or a newer, better lighted, cleaner school building. The correlations with peer-group attributes cannot even tell us whether the impact upon a lower-IQ child of being in a classroom with more bright, dominant, articulate, and intellectually self-confident children does more harm than good.

In the opinion of Judge Skelley Wright in Hobson v. Hansen (1967) one cannot find a single sentence indicating recognition of this methodological problem. I do not suggest that awareness of it would have led to a different result. But a single sentence obiter would surely occur somewhere in his careful, scholarly opinion of 109 pages had the judge thought of it or counsel argued it in connection with the Coleman Report's significance. One may feel, as I do, that the problems of racial discrimination and educational disadvantagement are so grave that the society should lean over backwards — within limits set by principles of distributive justice to individuals — to change things, since we are confronted with a frightful combination of gross inequities and a major social emergency. Under such pressing circumstances the adoption and implementation of policy cannot await definitive solution of difficult scientific questions, especially when the kind of controlled experiment or even semi-controlled quasi-experiment (Campbell, 1969) capable of yielding clear answers cannot be performed and statistical techniques presently available are not adequate for the purpose of unscrambling causal influence. The Coleman Report shows that minority-group children receive substandard educational treatment, and I for one am willing to call that discriminatory, ipso facto. What concerns me here is the legal generalizability of a causal inference methodology. The kind of reliance upon social science data found in Hobson v. Hansen, lacking adequate clarification of the concept "unfair discrimination" in relation to correlational findings, might produce some untoward results in other contexts where the interpretative principles would be difficult to distinguish. And if judges should become cynical about the trustworthiness of what psychologists and sociologists assert, we might be faced with a judicial backlash against the social sciences. One can hardly blame Judge Wright for making a flat statement that intelligence tests do *not* measure innate intelligence, or for repeating the old chestnut that intelligence is "whatever the test measures" [Hobson v. Hansen, 1967, p. 478]. The Coleman Report states flatly, with no hint that disagreement exists among psychologists on the highly technical and obscure issues involved, "recent research does not support [the] view" that intelligence tests measure more fundamental and stable mental abilities than achievement tests (Coleman et al., 1966, p. 292). "Ability tests are simply [*sic*] broader and more general measures of education" follows at the same locus, again without the faintest whiff of doubt or qualification to warn the legal reader that this is a complex and controversial issue. We read further, "The findings of this survey provide additional evidence that the 'ability' tests are at least as much affected by school differences as are the 'achievement' tests," the causal language "affected by" being again unqualified, with no mention made that some psychologists would interpret the parallelism of ability-score differences and achievement-score differences as suggesting that the achievement differences are not primarily due to school differences but to intelligence differences (an interpretation that would fit well with the report's other findings). It is well recognized among psychologists concerned with the ex post facto design's deficiencies that the report is dangerous reading for the nontechnically trained, because of its pervasive use of causal-sounding terms: influence, affect, depend upon, account for, independent effect (*sic*). This causal atmosphere cannot be counteracted by the brief methodological sections, which contain the usual caveats. One wonders whether the report's authors were really clear about what regression analysis can and cannot do (Guttman, 1941, pp. 286–92). I am not arguing the merits, except to show that an unresolved scientific controversy exists which we psychologists have no right to sweep under the rug when we talk or write for lawyers and judges. If we present a distorted picture even in a good cause, implying that certain technical matters are settled when in fact they are obscure and controversial, the powerful forces of the lawyers' adversary system will, sooner or later, ferret out the secret. Could we then complain if the findings of social science were treated with less respect than those of chemistry, geology, or medicine by less tractable, more wised-up judges?

Consider a nonracial example that I predict will arise in the near future. There is some correlation between the vocational interests of fathers and sons (Forster, 1931; Strong, 1943, 1957) and part of this correlation has a genetic basis (Carter, 1932; Vandenberg & Kelly, 1964; Vandenberg & Stafford, 1967). Nichols (1966, Table 2) also presents persuasive data which he under-interprets through neglect of the statistical power function (Cohen, 1962). This neglect, combined with his disappointment in the heritability coefficient as a precise, stable, clearly interpretable measure (see Elston & Gottesman, 1968; Fuller & Thompson, 1960, pp. 62–68; Hirsch, 1967, p. 423; Roberts, 1967, pp. 233–42) and his following the traditional practice of simply sorting results into "significant" and "nonsignificant," leads him to be baffled by sex patterns that should not baffle him and that are probably theoretically uninterpretable because they have no systematic meaning (except to a statistician interested in power functions). The "biggest" fact in Nichols's Table 2 is that 23 out of 24 (MZ-DZ) correlation differences are in the expected direction and respectable in size. Even with his large samples, an (MZ-DZ) difference less than around .14 Pearson r units will have less than 50% power $(1 - \beta)$. We ought not be surprised by sex differences in the pattern of significant variables under such circumstances. A sophisticated consideration of the question would involve a currently unstable area of social science method, where matters are murky and the social science establishment is maintaining a conspiracy of silence (see Bakan, 1966; Hogben, 1958; Lykken, 1968; Meehl, 1967; Rozeboom, 1960; and references cited therein). Whatever the merits, the point is that there exists a technical controversy which an appellate court justice with an M.A. in psychology would have difficulty following, let alone adjudicating. If the judge relies on expert testimony as to current accepted practice, he stands a good chance of being taken in by sincere diploma'd experts who will themselves be unaware how big a methodological storm is brewing. The discrepancy between Nichols's findings and the other twin studies provides a beautiful illustration of the levels-of-sophistication problem. Most law professors are just now learning about the significance test. It will be 20 years or more before they learn what is wrong with it (Badia, Haber, & Runyon, 1970; Morrison & Henkel, 1970).

There is a sizable correlation between fathers' and sons' intelligence, the larger part of which is probably of biological origin (Burt, 1958, 1966, 1967; Erlenmeyer-Kimling & Jarvik, 1963—a short paper which alone almost suffices to prove the point; Fuller & Thompson, 1960, ch. 7; Gottesman, 1963, 1968a; Honzik, 1957; Jenkins & Paterson, 1961; Manosevitz, Lindzey, & Thiessen, 1969, sections 5–6; Robinson, 1970; Shields, 1962; Thompson, 1967; Vandenberg, 1968; Waller, 1971; Whipple, 1940—thirty years old but still very much worth reading on this issue). Given these interest and ability correlations and other factors, the sons of physicians are more frequently admitted to medical schools than the sons of nonphysicans, and much more frequently than the sons of, say, unskilled laborers. Medical school selection committees allegedly have shown a preference for physicians' sons. To avoid this bias, some schools exclude father's occupation from the application blank, but a statistical association persists.

Suppose a WASP premedical student of proletarian origins brings an action against a state-supported medical school alleging occupational discrimination, offering in evidence the somewhat higher incidence of admission among physicians' sons. The school defends by showing that father's occupation does not appear on the application blank, and argues that selection is based upon a combination of premedical grades, scores on the Strong Vocational Interest Blank, and the Medical Aptitude Test. The student replies that the SVIB and Medical Aptitude Test are biased in favor of physicians' sons and, further, that both are generically biased against proletarians. If psychometric bias is defined ipso facto by tests yielding differences between groups identified socio-demographically (e.g., by parental occupation, father's income, neighborhood, race, religion) all such tests are biased. Pushed to the limit, the position is that, whatever may be the social or biological origins of individual differences in intellectual capacity, vocational interest, study habits, temperament, etc., any selection variable reflecting these differences and shown to be a correlate of parental occupation is discriminatory (in the sense of unfair).

Nor could this consequence be avoided by eliminating all use of psychological tests and relying solely upon undergraduate grades, inasmuch as the latter also correlate with father's occupation, education, and income. Point: The problem of interpreting correlations and the influence of "nuisance variables" is not a hair-splitting academic exercise, it is a major methodological stomach ache, arising in many legal contexts where social science findings are relevant to fair treatment or equal protection.

Away from the Fireside and Back Again

The levels-of-sophistication problem has a time component reflecting the stage of scientific knowledge. We psychologists should be cautious when an alleged principle of modern behavioral science appears to conflict with the fireside inductions. There are some embarrassing instances of overconfident generalization and unjustified extrapolation which were subsequently corrected by movement back toward the fireside inductions. It would be worth knowing how often such back-to-the-fireside reversals have taken place, and whether there are features of subject matter or methodology that render the counter-fireside pronouncements of social science prone to reversal or modification. Sometimes psychologists seem to prefer negating the fireside inductions, especially those embedded in the received scholarly tradition (e.g., Aristotle should be beaten up wherever possible). For example, the experimental psychologists' revival of the constructs "curiosity" and "exploratory drive" seems strange to a nonpsychologist who has observed children or pets—or who remembers the opening sentence of Aristotle's *Metaphysics*, "All men by nature desire to know."

Consider three examples relevant to law as a means of social control. Traditional reliance upon punishment (aversive control) in socialization, both in suppressing antisocial conduct and in education, is horrifying to the contemporary mind. One reads about the execution of a 14-year-old for larceny in the 1700s, or Luther's description of his schooling, in which corporal punishment was not even confined to infractions of discipline, but was the standard procedure of instruction. If a child didn't give the right answer, he would be rapped on the knuckles with a rod. Research on white rats and, to a lesser extent, on human subjects led to the generalization that, by and large, punishment is a mode of behavior control inferior to reward (positive reinforcement). Thirty years ago, I was taught that the useful role of punishment was to suppress undesirable responses sufficiently (in the short run) so that alternative competing behaviors could occur, and the latter could then be positively reinforced. This is still a fair statement of the practical situation.

Following the publication of Skinner's epoch-making *The Behavior of Organisms* (1938), his student Estes's doctoral dissertation (1944), and especially Skinner's *Science and Human Behavior* (1953) and his Utopian novel *Walden Two* (1948), aversive control fell into extreme disfavor. These writings combined with the gruesome stories told to us clinical psychologists by adult neurotics about their aversively-controlled childhoods to produce a rejection of both the general deterrent and rehabilitative functions of the criminal law. But this could be an illicit extrapolation, conflating the rehabilitative and general deterrent functions of the criminal law under the generic rubric "punishment." Supporters of general deterrence need not assume the same psychological process operates

on deterrable persons as that involved when punishment is unsuccessful in reforming convicts. Only punishment as a reformer even approximates the laboratory model of an aversive consequence following emission of the undesired response. Furthermore, the criminal sanction is rather more like withholding
positive reinforcement (given elimination of flogging and similar practices from
the penal system), both fines and imprisonment being deprivations. The distinction is becoming fuzzed up by experimental work with animals because manipulations such as "time out" (during which the instrumental act cannot be performed because the manipulandum is unavailable, or a stimulus signals that
reinforcement will now be withheld) has aversive (punishing) properties. Having
neither expertise nor space for the details, I refer the reader to Honig (1966),
especially the chapter by Azrin and Holtz, which should be read asking, "To
what extent do the current experimental findings refute, confirm, or modify the
fireside inductions concerning punishment?" How would the psychologist classify a statutory provision that threatens to deprive the citizen of, say, money that
the citizen had never learned to expect, e.g., the Agricultural Adjustment Act
(see U.S. v. Butler, 1936, p. 81), where Mr. Justice Stone's dissent hinges partly
on the semantics of coercion, which he argues must involve "threat of loss, not
hope of gain." Can the experimental psychologist speak to this issue? I doubt it.

A second example concerns imitation. The folklore is that both humans and
infrahumans learn by imitation. (The criminal law, as lawyers and psychologists
agree, is invoked to handle trouble cases, where the normal processes of socialization have not been applied or have failed to work. I trust my selecting the notion of general deterrence as a fireside induction will not be misconstrued as a
belief in its major socializing role, which I daresay no psychologist would care to
defend.) Our policy concerning TV and movie presentation of social models of
aggression or forbidden sexual behavior is influenced by our beliefs about imitation. Despite the related Freudian emphasis upon identification as a mechanism
of character formation, when I was a student the tendency in academic psychology was to minimize the concept of imitation to the point of skepticism as to
whether there was any such process at all. I was taught that the classic experiments of E. L. Thorndike on the cat (*circa* 1900) had demonstrated that, for
infrahuman organisims at least, there was no learning by imitation. This alleged
laboratory refutation was presented as an example of how scientific research had
overthrown part of the folklore. The failure of Thorndike's cats to learn one particular problem-box task, under his special conditions of drive and so forth, was
overgeneralized to the broad statement, "Infrahuman animals cannot learn by
imitation." The received doctrine of scientific psychology became so well en-
trenched that a well-designed experiment by Herbert and Harsh (1944) was
largely ignored by the profession (see Barber, 1961). But beginning slightly earlier with Miller and Dollard's *Social Learning and Imitation* (1941), a book that
cautiously reintroduced the concept and made important conceptual distinctions

as to kinds of imitation, the subject came to be restudied, especially by developmental psychologists in relation to aggressive behavior (see, e.g., Bandura & Walters, 1963; Megargee & Hokanson, 1970). A recent article by John, Chesler, Bartlett, and Victor (1969) makes it probable that Thorndike's negative dictum at the turn of the century was just plain wrong, even for *Felis catus*. *Point*: A lawyer in 1930 might have lost a cocktail party debate with an animal psychologist, but the lawyer would have been closer to the truth.

A third area important in such legal contexts as presentence investigation is that of forcasting behavior probabilistically. The fireside inductions say that you should rely heavily upon the record of an individual's past conduct. As I have argued elsewhere (essay 14, this volume), it may be that a naïve judge will (over the long run) make better decisions than one who knows just enough psychology or psychiatry to rely on medical or social science experts' making an intensive study of the offender. The efficiency of actuarial prediction is almost always at least equal to, and usually better than, prediction based upon (purported) clinical understanding of the individual subject's personality (see references in footnote 4 in essay 13 and footnote 8 in essay 14). Second, behavior science research itself shows that, by and large, the best way to predict anybody's behavior is his behavior in the past (known among my colleagues as Meehl's Malignant Maxim). Hence the naïve judge's reliance on the fireside inductions may yield better results than the intermediate-level sophistication which knows enough to ask a psychologist's or psychiatrist's opinion, but does not know enough to take what he says *cum grano salis*, especially when clinical opinion conflicts with extrapolation from the offender's record.

The subtle interaction between levels of sophistication and the developing state of scientific knowledge is nicely illustrated by the Supreme Court's attitude toward statutes postulating inherited tendencies to mental deficiency and criminalism. In Buck v. Bell (1927) the court upheld the constitutionality of an involuntary sterilization statute for mental defectives, in an opinion famous for Mr. Justice Holmes's "Three generations of imbeciles is enough." The opinion naturally does not display sophistication about the varieties of mental deficiency, such as the distinction between high-grade familial deficiency (usually nonpathological, being merely the low end of the normal polygenic distribution) and the Mendelizing or developmental anomaly varieties, characteristically yielding a lower IQ, relatively independent of social class, and presenting differing eugenic aspects since some of them have no discernible hereditary loading and others a clearcut one. Without entering into such technical issues in genetics, the court came to what I would regard as the right result (see Reed & Reed, 1965). In Skinner v. Oklahoma (1942) involuntary sterilization of a habitual criminal was disallowed, again a right result in my view. The fireside inductions that underlay Oklahoma's statute are perhaps as strong and widespread for criminal or "immoral" tendencies as for mental deficiency. But the scientific data on inherited dispositions are much stronger in the one case than in the other, and *that* much social science knowledge the Court did possess. Suppose that a more refined taxonomy of delinquents and criminals should enable us to discover that some persons disposed to antisocial behavior get that way in part on a genetic basis (see footnote 10 in essay 14), although in most delinquents the etiology is social. A modified form of the fireside inductions underlying Oklahoma's unconstitutional statute would then be defensible, and a properly redrafted statute combining habitual criminality as a legal category with psychogenetic categories or dimensions could be upheld on the same grounds as Virginia's sterilization statute. But the court's new task would demand far more technical sophistication, especially given the ideological components that would saturate social scientists' opinions in the briefs, than was required for handling Buck v. Bell and Skinner v. Oklahoma.

Direct Application of Experimental Results to Legal Problems: Some Rational Grounds for Caution

As a clinical practitioner who was trained at a hard-nosed, quantitatively-oriented, behavioristic psychology department (Minnesota has been called the "hotbed of dustbowl empiricism" by some of its critics), I sense a deep analogy between the problem faced by judge or legislator in balancing the fireside inductions against purportedly scientific psychological or sociological findings, and the perennial problem of how far we clinicians are entitled to rely upon our clinical experience, lacking (or apparently contradicting) experimental or quantitative research. For myself as clinician, I have not been able to resolve this dilemma in an intellectually responsible way, although I have been steadily conscious of it and engaged in theoretical and empirical research on it for over a quarter-century. So I am hardly prepared to clean up the analogous dilemma for lawyers. However, dwelling on this analogy may enable me to offer some tentative suggestions. There is a similarity in the pragmatic contexts of law and clinical practice, in that something will be decided, with or without adequate evidence, good or bad, scientific or anecdotal. A judge cannot leave a case undecided — although a logician could point out that law, being an incomplete postulate set, renders some well-formed formulas undecidable.

Let us strip the concept "scientific experiment" to its essentials, as I have tried to do in a rough meaning stipulation *supra*. Forget the usual images of glass tubing and electronic equipment operated by bearded gents wearing white coats in a laboratory. What, for instance, is the purpose of gadgetry? Scientific apparatus performs one of two functions. Either it plays a role on the input side, contributing to the physical isolation of the system under study and to the control or manipulation of the variables, or it facilitates the recording of observations (output side). We conceive a situation space whose dimensions are all physical and social dimensions having behavioral relevance. In research on human subjects, this set of dimensions will include such minor variables as the material of the experimenter's desk, since in our society the social stimulus value of an oak desk differs from that of pine.

If we are studying the impact of a psychoanalytic interpretation and design an experiment to smuggle this real-life phenomenon into the laboratory, what happens? We move in the situation space from the ordinary-life context of psychotherapy to the experimental context. This movement is in the interest of locating the system studied more precisely, because in the ordinary-life, nonlaboratory situation, the values of certain variables known (or feared) to have an influence are neither assigned by the investigator nor measured by him (with the idea of their influence being removed statistically).

There is no mystery about this, no conflict between a scientific and nonscientific view of the subject matter. The problem presented is quite simple—it is the solution that presents complexities. In order either to eliminate certain causal variables, hold them constant, or manipulate them, or to measure them, we move to a different region of the situation space. By (a) eliminating, (b) fixing, (c) manipulating, or (d) measuring (and "correcting for") the input variables, we intend to test generalizations as to what influences what, generalizations we could not reach in the natural, field, nonexperimental situation. The price we pay is that these generalizations are only known to hold for the new region of the situation space; their application in the ordinary-life context is an extrapolation.

This untoward consequence of the experimental method does not flow from tendentious, polemic formulations polarizing a scientific against a nonscientific frame of reference (empirical versus armchair psychology). Such locutions are misleading, as they locate our methodological stomach ache in the wrong place. The problem can be stated in general terms within the scientific frame of reference. To concretize it: Suppose I am interested in the behavior of tigers. If I rely uncritically on anecdotes told by missionaries, hunters, native guides, etc., my evidence will suffer both on the input and output sides, i.e., from indeterminacy of the input and inaccuracy of the output. If I have accurate output data (e.g., carefully screened independent, convergent testimony by skeptical, reliable, scientifically-trained observers, use of telescopic camera recording, high-fidelity tapes of the tiger's vocalizations), I may be able by such means to take care of the recording-accuracy problem (although hardly the recording-completeness problem). But I will still be troubled by indeterminacy on the input side. I don't know all of the inputs to this tiger when I am photographing him at a distance. I do not know his inputs an hour earlier when he was invisible to me, and I have reason to believe that those previous inputs alter his momentary state and change his behavioral dispositions.

Suppose, to get rid of this uncertainty on the stimulus side, I capture my tiger and put him in a zoo or bring him to my animal laboratory. I eliminate the influence of variations in the chirping of a certain bird as part of the tiger's surround. There is a sense in which I now don't have to be concerned about birds chirping, the only birds that chirp in a proper psychological laboratory being those that the experimenter himself introduces. But there is another sense in which I should be worried about the influence of bird chirping. An average level and fluctuation of bird chirps is part of the normal ecology of tigers in the wild. If I want to extrapolate my laboratory findings to the behavior of wild tigers, this extrapolation is problematic. The background of bird chirps may have a quantitative impact upon the tiger's behavioral dispositions, and perhaps upon his second-order dispositions to acquire first-order dispositions (Broad, 1933; Meehl, 1972).

In research on human subjects, it is frequently found that the influence of variable x upon variable y is dependent upon values of variable z, called by statisticians an "interaction effect." Interaction effects regularly occur whenever the sensitivity of the experimental design suffices to detect them. It is not absurd to suppose that, in human social behavior, almost all interactions of all orders (for instance, the influence of variable v on the interaction effect of the variable z on the first-order influence of variable x on variable y) would be detected if our experiments were sufficiently sensitive. When we liquidate the influence of a variable, either by eliminating it through physical isolation or holding it fixed, we are in danger of wrongly generalizing from our experimental results to the natural, real-life setting.

Law-trained readers unfamiliar with social science statistical methods may have found the preceding rather abstract. Suppose I am a developmental psychologist interested in the deterrent effects of punishment and I argue that the sanctions of the criminal law are inefficacious, relying on "Fisbee's classic experiments on punishment in nursery-school children." In Table 1 I list differences that might be relevant in extrapolating from the laboratory study to the legal context.

One need hardly be obscurantist or anti-scientific in his sympathies in order to be nervous about extrapolation in the joint organism-situational space from the region of the left-hand column to that of the right as ground for repealing a statute penalizing larceny. In the foreseeable future, lawmakers will unavoidably rely upon a judicious mixture of experimental research, quasi-experiments, informal field observation, statistical analysis of file data, *and* the fireside inductions. The legislator, prosecutor, judge, and public administrator—like the clinical psychologist—cannot adopt a scientistic purist posture, "I will not decide or act until fully adequate standards of scientific proof are met by the evidence before me." The pragmatic context forces him to act. In these matters, not doing anything or not changing anything we now do is itself a powerful form of action. When the fireside inductions are almost all we have to go on, or when the fireside

Table 1. Extrapolating from Fisbee to Real-Life

Experiment	Criminal Sanction Against Larceny
Four-year-olds	Adults
Mostly upper middle class	Mostly lower and lower middle class
Mostly biologically normal	Numerous genetic deviates in group
Time-span minutes or hours	Time-span months or years
Social context: Subject alone	Social context: Criminal peer-group inputs
Reward: Candy	Rewards: Money, prestige, women, autonomy, leisure, excitement
Punishment: Mild electric shock	Punishment: Deprivations of above rewards [Punishment more like non-reward or time-out than strictly aversive stimulus onset]
Punished response emitted; experimenter aims at reform	Punished response not emitted by most; law aims at general deterrence
Subject's perception of situation: Who knows?	Subject's perception of situation: Who knows?

inductions appear to conflict with the practical consequences of extrapolated experimental research or psychological theory, it would be nice to have some sort of touchstone as to pragmatic validity, some quick and easy objective basis for deciding where to place our bets. Unfortunately there is none.

Are Some Classes of Fireside Inductions More Trustworthy than Others?

This problem is so important in a society which has become sophisticated and self-conscious as to its own modes of social control that one might reasonably argue in favor of support for second-level empirical research aimed at developing a taxonomy of fireside inductions, enabling us to sort them into categories having different average levels of accuracy. We do not even possess a corpus of the explicit fireside inductions upon which our law relies. To ferret these out from statutes, appellate court opinions, the Restatements, and so forth would be a monstrous and thankless task, although I suggest that a random sampling of the documents might be worth doing. One might inquire, apart from whether the fireside inductions are corroborated by social science research, how many legal rules, principles, and practices accord even with the fireside inductions of contemporary men. Most law professors will readily agree, I find, that much of our law is predicated on notions about human conduct that hardly anybody would care to defend. *Example*: A lawyer will advise a testator to leave a dollar to one of his children whom he wishes to disinherit, because courts have held that, since a parent naturally tends to bequeath property to his child, failure to do so creates a legal presumption that the testator omitted him by inadvertence. I doubt that this presumption accords with the fireside inductions. Laymen agree with me that if a father is sufficiently *compos mentis* to write a valid will at all, his failure to mention a son is not attributable to forgetfulness. *Example*: One class of exceptions to the Hearsay Rule is "declarations against interest," when the declarant is unavailable as a witness. The unavailability creates a special need for hearsay, and the fireside induction is that the declaration's having been made against interest renders it more trustworthy. But the interest is required to be pecuniary, not penal (Livermore, 1968, pp. 76–78; McCormick 1954, pp. 546–51). Surely our fireside inductions do not suppose that a man is more likely to be careless or mendacious in admitting rape than that he borrowed money! Similar oddities have been noted in the Hearsay exception for "Admissions of a party-opponent," where a litigant's predecessor or joint tenant falls under the exception, but not a tenant in common or a co-legatee (McCormick, 1954, pp. 523–25). I cannot imagine that the fireside inductions concerning motivations for accuracy would support these distinctions, which arose not from empirical considerations in the psychology of testimony but through formalistic intrusion of property-law metaphysics into the law of evidence.

A taxonomy of fireside inductions based upon their substantive, methodological, and psychological properties might permit a rough ordering of inductive types as to accuracy, comparing the fireside inductions in each category with social science generalizations available in the literature. If strong taxonomic trends existed among researched cases, we would have some basis for judging the probable trustworthiness of those unresearched. We could inquire whether the following methodological features of a fireside induction are associated with a higher probability of its being scientifically corroborated:

Hardly anyone entertains serious doubts about the induction. Persons of different theoretical persuasions agree about the fireside induction almost as well as persons holding the same theoretical position. There is a consensus of the fireside that cuts across demographic variables such as education, occupation, social class, religious belief, ethnic background, and the like. Within the legal profession prosecutors, defense lawyers, law professors, and judges are in substantial agreement. Personality traits (e.g., dominance, social introversion, hostility, rigidity) are not appreciably correlated with adherence to the induction. The particular fireside induction involves an observation of actions, persons, or effects that occur with sufficient frequency so that most qualified and competent observers will have had an extensive experience as a generalization basis. The fireside induction deals with relatively objective physical or behavioral facts rather than with complicated causal inferences. The policy implications of the induction are such that nobody's political, ethnic, religious, moral, or economic ideology or class interest would be appreciably threatened or mobilized by its general acceptance in the society or by lawmakers' or administrators' reliance upon it in decision-making. Sophisticated armchair considerations do not reveal a built-in observational or sampling bias that would operate in the collection of anecdotal support or refutation of the induction. The induction is qualitative rather than one that claims to make quantitative comparisons despite the lack of a reliable measuring device.

I do not profess to know the relative importance of items in this list, and I can think of exceptions to any of them as a touchstone. Thus, for example, the height of a person's forehead is a relatively simple physical fact. But judgments of forehead heights of prison inmates by their guards were shown* to be correlated with guards' estimates of their intelligence, whereas objectively measured forehead heights were not. (*Explanation*: The erroneous fireside induction that a low forehead—low-brow—indicates stupidity led guards' perceptions and/or memories of this simple physical feature to be infected with their behavior-based estimates of a prisoner's intellect.)

And Are Some Experimental Findings Safer to Extrapolate?

One asks here about the comparability of two groups of organisms as to species, developmental period, and status. What motives, what rewards and punishments, what time relationships are shared between the experimental context and the natural setting? An indirect lead as to extrapolability can sometimes be picked up from the experimental literature itself, asking, "To what extent do the experimental findings replicate over a variety of species, drives, instrumental responses, rewards, and punishments?" If we cannot generalize within the laboratory, moving to the field is presumably risky. How sizable are the relationships? A social scientist who countervails a lawyer's fireside induction by extrapolating from psychological research yielding two correlation coefficients $r = .25$ with $r = .40$ is just plain silly; but an unsuspecting law-man, overly impressed with social science statistical methods, might be taken in. *Point*: Random sampling errors aside, this correlational difference represents an increment of less than 10% in variance accounted for, and could easily be liquidated by moving to a not very distant region of the situation space.

To have the best of both worlds, one would want accurate recording on the output side and proper statistical treatment, but with the situation being very similar to the one to which we wish to extrapolate. Accurate observations, accurate records (instead of memory and impressions), appropriate statistical analysis are all attainable in the field or natural life setting, lacking experimenter manipulation of the input. I am therefore inclined to view Campbell's "Reforms as Ex-

---

*I cannot trace the reference, which is from the late Professor Donald G. Paterson's lectures.

periments'' (1969) not as a second-best substitute for laboratory investigation, but as often intrinsically preferable, because the situational-extrapolation problem is so grave that the scientific precision of laboratory experiments with college students or school children is largely illusory.

The Lawmaker's Dilemma

The legislator's, judge's, or administrator's situation is most comfortable when there is a sizable and consistent body of research, experimental and non-experimental (file data and field observation data), yielding approximately the same results as the fireside inductions. While one may be scientifically skeptical even in this delightfully harmonious situation, in the pragmatic context of decision-making, rule-writing, policy-adopting, etc., such rigorous skepticism can hardly lead to pragmatic vacillation. Some sort of action is required, and all we have goes in the same direction. The methodologically unsatisfactory situations can be divided into three groups, differing in degree rather than kind: (a) No quantitative or experimental evidence is available or readily collectable before action must be taken. Here we rely upon the fireside inductions, these being all we have. A healthy skepticism concerning the fireside inductions, engendered by the study of social science, makes us nonetheless uncomfortable. (b) We have a large-scale, adequately conducted study in the field situation, supplemented by file data from different jurisdictions varying in relevant parameters (e.g., offense rate, community socioeconomic indices); these field-observation and file-data results accord with theoretical concepts developed experimentally on humans and infrahumans; but the conclusion conflicts with the fireside. Such a massive and coherent body of information should countervail the fireside inductions, even those with the admirable properties listed above. It seems difficult to dispute this, since by including file data from the nonlaboratory setting to which we wish to extrapolate, we are in effect comparing two sets of anecdotal data, one of which has the methodological advantage of being based upon records instead of relying upon our fallible and possibly biased memories of observations gathered nonsystematically as regards representativeness of persons and situations. *Example*: If statistics show that accuseds released without bail pending trial have such a low incidence of pretrial criminal offenses or failure to appear for trial that the bail system has negligible social utility (combined with its obvious inequity to the poor), our fireside inductions to the contrary should not countervail. But a nagging doubt persists, since other relevant statistics (e.g., ratio of reported felonies to arrests) tend to support the fireside induction that some fraction of these defendants have committed further crimes during their pretrial freedom, and we cannot accurately estimate this fraction (see the excellent paper by Tribe, 1970). A lively sense of the lawmaker's dilemma can be had by reading the Senate debate on the District of Columbia crime bill (*Congressional Record*, 1970). (c) The most difficult situation is that in which there is a collision between a fireside induction having several of the good properties listed above, and a smattering of social science research that is strong enough to give us pause about the fireside inductions, but not strong enough to convince us. Thus, the research may not be entirely consistent from one investigator to another; or it comes only from the experimental laboratory and consequently involves considerable extrapolation in the situation-space; or, if a large-scale quantitative nonexperimental survey, it has the causal-ambiguity and variable-unscrambling difficulties intrinsic to such studies (Meehl, 1969, 1971a). One hardly knows what to suggest in such collision situations except the social scientist's usual "more research is needed."

Conclusion

Unavoidably the law will continue to rely upon the fireside inductions. They should be viewed with that skepticism toward anecdotal evidence and the received belief system that training in the behavioral sciences fosters, but without intellectual arrogance or an animus against fireside inductions in favor of overvalued or overinterpreted scientific research. I can summarize my position in one not very helpful sentence since nothing stronger or more specific can be said shortly: In thinking about law as a mode of social control, adopt a healthy skepticism toward the fireside inductions, subjecting them to test by statistical methods applied to data collected in the field situation; but when a fireside induction is held nearly *semper, ubique, et ab omnibus* a similar skepticism should be maintained toward experimental research purporting, as generalized, to overthrow it.

Postscript

I find, on reading what I wrote almost 20 years ago, that there is little to change on the basis of theoretical arguments or empirical evidence that have appeared since that time. There are, however, a few matters that fall under the general umbrella of social science research in relation to the "common sense" or "general knowledge" that lawyers, lawmakers, and judges must unavoidably rely on, that I did not discuss and that are at least as important as those that I did. Space limitations prohibit consideration of all the pros and cons; so my presentation may sound dogmatic. Perhaps the best way to view the text that follows is as raising questions, which, whether my answers to them turn out to be right or wrong, I think no informed person could deny are of legal importance.

Abuse of Significance Tests in Appraising Theories

It seems to be the fate of social scientists, in their impact on other professions, to begin by converting them to a procedure or substantive view that is slowly assimilated by the other group; and then the task of the social scientist is to emphasize the dangers of overdoing the lesson learned! I believe we have oversold statistical significance tests to law professors. Not that one should abandon them. When a newspaper account of the short-term change in number of homicides fails to ask whether it is merely a "chance upward fluctuation," the psychologist must criticize it and hope that lawmakers and criminal justice system personnel do not overreact to something analogous to flipping pennies. My local newspaper publishes annually the achievement test scores of students in different schools, mislabeling the results as "grading the schools," without warning that some of the differences between schools, and between two testings in the same school, are probably chance variations. So it is appropriate to ask whether a difference between groups, or a trend line over time, is a genuine phenomenon, which we answer by doing a statistical significance test. For many questions in the social sciences, the first thing to ask about a set of data is whether their orderliness (trend, correlation, difference, change) is only apparent, i.e., could plausibly be due to random or chance factors. One sometimes says "tests of statistical significance are *necessary but not sufficient*," especially when the aim is to corroborate a causal theory for purposes of social action. In recent years there has been increasing criticism, both by statisticians and social science theorists, of the excessive reliance on statistical significance testing (proving that an observed sample difference could not plausibly be attributed to chance, so that the real difference, if we could observe the whole population, would be nonzero) as a way of proving that a substantive causal theory has verisimilitude (Bakan, 1966; Carver, 1978; Chow, 1988; Lykken, 1968; Meehl, 1967, essay 1, this volume, 1990a, 1990b; Morrison & Henkel, 1970; Rozeboom, 1960). Wherever possible, significance tests should be replaced by a statement of confidence intervals, that is, the numerical range within which one can have a stated assurance (*p* value) that the true population value lies. Preferable to that, when statistics are used to assess the verisimilitude of a substantive theory, efforts should be made to strengthen the theory sufficiently to permit prediction not merely of a nonzero difference but of the shape of a mathematical function, or the rank order of a set of groups, and—ideally—the numerical point value, as is done in the more advanced sciences such as physics, chemistry, and genetics (essay 1, in this volume).

Failure to Report Overlap

When statistics are employed not primarily for evaluating a causal theory but for some technological purpose, such as justifying the use of a test in a military selection situation, or arguing for one remedial procedure over another in dealing with handicapped pupils, it is bad reporting to state the statistical significance level and not provide the reader with numbers indicating the overlap. I take a strong stand on this. I believe that it is unscholarly to submit such a paper, and that it is equally unscholarly that editors continue to accept such. There are legitimate disagreements as to the optimal way to express this matter of overlap, and which one is preferable depends on the pragmatic context. An obvious answer when there is doubt about how to express the overlap between two groups (say, one group treated with psychotherapy and the other with drugs, or one group of offenders paroled and the other incarcerated) is to report several of the generally accepted overlap measures and let readers take their pick. Whenever two groups are contrasted with respect to the impact of a procedure (therapeutic, education, reforming), the investigator should state what percentage of the one group reached or exceeded standard reference percentiles of the other group. Thus, we might read, "Seventy percent of those treated with Elavil exceeded the 50th percentile (median) of the control group." My own preference is to use standard reference points at the 10th, 25th, 50th, 75th, and 90th percentiles of the other group. Another measure increasingly accepted is the *Effect Size* advocated by Glass, McGaw, and Smith (1981) and Hunter (1982), in which the mean difference of the two groups is divided by the standard deviation of the control group, or sometimes by the composite of the two standard deviations. In case the two distributions are each close to normal, there is a well-known statistic devised by Tilton (1937) called the *Tilton Overlap*. I repeat that I do not urge this as merely a kind of frosting on the scholarly cake, but as a *minimum necessity for adequate scientific reporting*. The sad fact that journal editors are sloppy about requiring it does not justify the common practice of merely reporting "the two groups differed significantly at the .05 level of probability." A law reader who knows some elementary statistics will find it instructive to draw a couple of normal curves which, with sample size 100, show a statistically significant difference at the .05 level. The reader will find that relying upon such a procedure of change, or such an instrument of selection, will do only a few percentage points better than one could do by flipping pennies. Many devices employed in clinical psychology are not cost effective for this reason, although in an industrial or military setting when N is large, and depending upon the *selection ratio* (= applicants/jobs), even a test of rather poor validity may pay off.

Causal Inference from Correlation

Doubtless every introductory course in social science, and every beginning statistics lecturer or text, informs the student that "correlation doesn't prove causality.'' This is a loose way of saying it, since if a correlation between two variables is not due to chance and can be replicated in subsequent samples, it does prove *some kind of causality* at work; what it does not prove, taken as it stands, is a direct causal connection between the two variables measured. Thus if IQ is negatively correlated with dental caries (which it is, or at least used to be in the old data), there must be something causing this relationship if it is statistically stable. But we do not know whether bad teeth lowers the IQ, as some dental hygienists argued in the 1920s from these correlations, or whether people with lower IQs don't take proper care of their teeth, or whether some third unmeasured factor affects both of these and they have no direct causal connection with each other. The last is the current interpretation, because when we partial out the influence of social class the correlation vanishes.

The ideal way to ascertain direct causal influence is to manipulate variables, which is why the experimental method is preferred over collecting statistics when it is applicable. Sometimes a social change, such as enactment of a criminal statute, comes sufficiently close to an experiment to be illuminating as to causality (Campbell, 1969). Sometimes "experiments of nature" can play this role. We have several examples of police strikes, or absent or distant law enforcers, or the Nazi inactivation of the Danish police, which were followed immediately by a significant rise in crime. Lacking experiments and quasi-experiments, untangling the causal paths in a system of correlated variables is a complicated problem, about which there continues to be dispute among social scientists and statisticians. Lawyers should be familiar with the concept of *path analysis* which, while it is not usually capable of providing a solid gold affirmative argument for a certain causal understanding of a many variable system, is usually capable of *refuting* a particular causal interpretation (Duncan, 1966; Werts & Linn, 1970; but see Li, 1975; Loehlin, 1987; Meehl, 1989; Shaffer, 1987). Sometimes it can at least provide plausibility considerations, as, for example, the IQ/tooth decay relationship described above. If that correlation goes away when you hold social class constant, it remains conceivable, but not plausible, to say that bad teeth lower the IQ. If only three causal models are viable, and two of the three path diagrams can be clearly refuted, it is often reasonable for the policymaker to act in reliance on the sole unrefuted one, absent competitors.

Immediate Transition from Statistical Discrimination to "Unfairness"

One cannot conclude that a psychological test is "unfair" to a particular group (ethnic, geographic, religious, social class, age, sex) merely from the fact that the test shows significant group differences. This should be obvious, but for some reason the media, and some politicians and judges, seem unable to grasp it.

If two groups do differ with respect to a social or psychological trait, then a valid test *should* show a difference between them. It is an empirical fact that many human traits, both of body and mind, exhibit small, medium, and even large differences between groups of individuals demographically specified. There are racial, national, social class, geographical, and sex differences in various abilities, interests, temperamental traits, susceptibility to diseases (physical and mental), and socially "neutral" traits such as the strange difference in the ability to taste the bitter synthetic chemical phenylthiocarbamide (PTC). The incidence of PTC "tasters" varies over the earth's surface from a low of 10% in some ethnic populations to a high of 80% in others, even though this trait has no biologically adaptive significance, as the substance involved does not exist in nature but was created by the chemist. One must distinguish the question whether a test as such is "unfair" (that it invalidly attributes differences between groups) from the question whether it is "valid and fair" for a trait that differs between groups because of a history of social discrimination. In the latter case the *test* is not "unfair," but social practices have been. The prevalence of medically diagnosable chronic alcoholism among Irish is nearly 20 times greater than among Jews. In fact, the only two variables that have been shown statistically predictive of alcoholism are (1) alcoholism in a first-degree relative and (2) being of Irish extraction (Goodwin, 1981; Vaillant, 1983). Evidence from twin and adoption studies proves that alcoholism involves a strong hereditary predisposition, contrary to what most of us were taught in undergraduate sociology classes. Psychometric or biochemical tests for alcoholism, or predisposition to it, would show a large "discrimination" between Irish and Jews, as would the statistics of D.W.I. convictions. Does this prove, or even tend to prove, that such tests are "biased against the Irish," or that the criminal justice system and highway department must have a pro-Jewish prejudice? Of course not. What to do about real differences arising from societal unfairness is a deep and complex problem at the interface between political and ethical theory; e.g., is it morally proper to perpetrate distributive injustice to present *individuals* as means of achieving a kind of "statistical" justice to *groups* composed of *other individuals*? This is obviously not a question on which psychologists possess any special expertise, but discussion of it is not helped by confusions about psychometric validity.

Double Standard of Proof of Generalizability

In the original article I pointed out the extent to which lawyers, lawmakers, and judges rely upon the "fireside inductions," common knowledge available to people just because they have lived in the world, observed human behavior, and perhaps thought about their own behavior. I tried to emphasize evenhandedly that sometimes the fireside inductions are pretty good and should not be lightly discarded on the basis of an alleged scientific proof from the social scientist; but, on the other hand, it is important that lawyers be aware of the extent to which social science research that is not flimsy and tendentious does refute common-sense views our grandmothers cherished. The plain fact is that some fireside inductions are sound, others are unsound, and most are a mixture. I know of no way to find out which, when a dispute arises, except to collect facts in the systematic manner of the social scientist. But I sense that *sometimes* (I do not say usually) the legal profession imposes a double standard in this manner. I give only a single example that relates to the previous mentioned problem of psychometric validity. As I understand it, the courts have held that it is improper for a business concern to use an intelligence test for selection purposes absent clear proof that in that particular setting it has validity for the specific job involved. Now this sounds reasonable, but I submit that it isn't. The law relies on hundreds of "generalizations" about human conduct, about the generality of traits, about the trustworthiness of eye witnesses, about how ordinary people "reasonably" conduct their everyday affairs, that have not been subjected to any kind of objective validation. Many of these generalizations would, if critically studied, turn out to be either false, or at least not highly generalizable from one situation to another. For example, we routinely admit character testimony, presumed probative with respect to whether a party (or witness) would be likely to do so-and-so. But the research on trait generality (starting with the classic study by Hartshorne & May, 1928) shows such high behavioral specificity that some social psychologists can even assert (I think wrongly, but never mind) "there are no traits, there are only situations." By contrast, there are hundreds of research studies, in a variety of settings, involving many thousands of civilians and military personnel, in a variety of kinds of jobs, which show that *proficiency at almost any kind of task will be correlated with the general intelligence factor*. If you don't like the "intelligence" label for the statistical factor, you can simply label it g, as is increasingly the practice among psychologists (Betz, 1986). Hawk (1986) estimates, on the basis of his review of these studies and a consideration of the effect sizes, that the saving in the U.S. economy achievable by using tests of g as a selective factor amounts to around $80 billion a year (but cf. Linn, 1986, who considers that inflated). It may be argued that the existence of ethnic and class differences in measures of g, when combined with the previous history of social unfairness, requires that some sort of commutative justice be done at the expense of distributive justice and economic inefficiency, hence measures of g are bad even when valid for the job. The point I wish to make is that the empirical grounds for believing in the cross-situational validity of measures of g is far greater in amount, quality, and diversity than the grounds we have for believing probably 90% of the unresearched fireside inductions that a judge and jury rely on in the legal process. This is what I mean by saying that a kind of double standard of evidence is being applied.

Social Science in Legal Education

I think it is both difficult and socially unnecessary to instruct law students in the details of social science research method, particularly the technical machinery of mathematical analysis whose interpretation is sometimes disputed among experts. Hardly any lawyers, even those who become professors, will be doing such research solo, without a co-worker who is a social scientist; and the important distinction between being a *critical research consumer* and a *new knowledge producer* should never be forgotten. I hold the same view with regard to the education of clinical psychologists who are vocationally oriented to becoming practitioners rather than university teachers and research investigators (Meehl, 1971b). It is not necessary to put law students through the algebra of Sewall Wright's equations for path analysis. Most of them wouldn't remember how to do it a couple of years later, unless they had continued to do research using it in the meantime. What is important is that they should know that there is such a technique as path analysis, and have acquired a strong readiness to ask the critical questions appropriate as a litigator, judge, or legislative committee member where a psychologist or sociologist is testifying about a matter of social causation. One can learn enough path analysis conceptually, without details of the mathematics, to think rationally about the matter — something that even a bright, reasonable person will have trouble doing if he or she is totally ignorant of the conceptual issues and metatheory involved. Grave mistakes in reasoning are made by U.S. senators who are not stupid or uneducated but who are sadly uninformed about matters of this particular kind. *Example*: Recently a senator arguing against federal financial aid to secondary schools (a subject on which I have no opinion) pointed to the fact that the average SAT score of high school seniors in Mississippi, which has a low per capita support for education, exceeded that of high school seniors in Michigan, which has a high per capita support for education. In making this argument, he ignored the fact that a much smaller percentage of Mississippi students intend to go on to college, and they are the ones who take the test, which is not required of all high school seniors. All he was proving was a difference in the percentage of cases above a certain region on the normal distribution curve, self-selected for their educational plans. I am confident that a properly designed course in law school would sophisticate law students so that they would routinely think of asking this kind of critical question in the presence of such an argument, and that would be far more useful to them and to society than to teach them how to perform a Kolmogorov-Smirnov significance test or an analysis of covariance. "How to parse complex social causality" can be explained with numerical *illustrations* from the path-analysis literature, without trying to teach lawyers the computational procedures for *doing* one, or the underlying mathematical theorems.

Incompetent Testimony by Psychologists

Psychologists, like other professional experts, have benefitted in prestige and income from the current litigation explosion. Only 20 years ago, after two days on the witness stand in a murder case, I was asked the "M'Naghten hypothetical," and the prosecutor objected on the grounds that I was not a physican. Today, so far as I know, every jurisdiction admits testimony by psychologists as to mental illness, competence to make a will, suitability as a parent in child custody cases, impairment of function due to brain injury, etc. As one who enjoys the courtroom scene and is pretty good at it, I can hardly find these social changes objectionable. Scientific integrity, however, compels me to comment on some unwholesome features of the testimony situation.

It is well known by members of my profession that psychology is a heterogeneous subject matter, probably more so than any other allegedly "scientific" discipline (Meehl, 1987). I have academic colleagues, both psychologists, who can hardly converse with each other about their work, because one studies the electrochemistry of the walleyed pike retina and the other writes about Jung's theory of dreams! It is not invidious or turf-protective to recognize a plain fact, that these qualitative differences in subject matter (and, correspondingly, research method) are associated with differences in scientific status. How firmly corroborated are the facts, generalizations, and explanatory theories of a psychologist's subdomain? How clearly and objectively defined are its leading concepts? How much consensus exists among "accredited" persons working in a domain? In my own specialty areas (clinical psychology, psychometrics, behavior genetics) I know that the validity of diagnostic instruments, the factual support of theories, and the efficacy of therapeutic interventions varies from *high* and *clear* to *low* and *doubtful*. Unfortunately there are practitioners who either do not know these facts or choose to ignore them in practice, including forensic contexts. I have observed psychologists on the witness stand, and read trial transcripts and depositions that led me to wonder how such a person could get through an accredited doctoral program without learning the rudiments of critical, scientific, quantitative thinking in which I was trained at Minnesota. I have concluded that there are numerous licensed practitioners who are, literally, *not competent* to evaluate data in a scientific fashion. Law readers can easily convince themselves of this by reading the excellent treatise by Ziskin and Faust (1988), "must" reading for any lawyer or judge who has to deal with expert testimony by psychologists. (If one lawyer has studied it and his opponent has not, the latter will probably be totally *crushed*, if the former puts on seasoned experts of the scientific kind.) A frightening eye-opener in the special area of child sexual abuse is Wakefield and Underwager (1988).

This sorry situation of "incompetent expertise," which I could explain sociologically if space permitted, presents a grave problem to the courts. Reliance on the opinions of experts, permitting questions and answers that our Anglo-American rules of evidence disallow for lay witnesses, presupposes that the expert *is* objectively "expert," that he or she knows more facts and thinks more incisively about them than a nonexpert could or would. The trial scenario is not a good forum for the resolution of complex technical issues involving scholarly disagreement. (Hence the usual emphasis on the expert's "qualifications," typically piled on to dazzle the jury far in excess of what is necessary to establish expertise.) A judge, in admitting expert testimony and instructing the trier of fact about it, naturally assumes that while experts may disagree, any expert knows the basic facts and tools of the trade, and knows how to reason about them properly. A plumber can be safely presumed to know what the most competent plumbers know about plumbing; ditto an orthopedic surgeon, accountant, or electrical engineer. *In the "soft" areas of psychology (clinical, counseling, community, social, personality, developmental) this cannot be safely presumed.*

I do not conclude from this that expert psychological testimony should be disallowed, although I admit that a case can be made for that conclusion. I do believe that trial judges should feel free to exclude some of it, when it would not be reversible error to do so. An important kind of expert testimony should consist of a scholarly showing that no trustworthy expertise exists (either side!) in certain areas. But because of widespread scientific incompetence among practitioners, such critical testimony will collide with the customary legal standard expressed by, "Doctor, is it generally held by your profession that. . . . " The correct answer to this question is often, "*Yes, it is generally held, but erroneously.*" If our evidentiary rules do not permit this critical, consensus-challenging role for the expert, then the idea of greatly restricting areas of psychological expertise (e.g., to straight actuarial generalizations, analogous to an insurance actuary's testimony concerning the empirical numbers appearing in life tables, in a wrongful death action) becomes, regrettably, more appealing. I find myself ambivalent on this score, partly because I cannot persuade myself that the insanity defense to a criminal charge should be liquidated, although my views as to its needed reform are extremely radical and arguably open to constitutional objections (essays 12 and 16, this volume; but compare Lykken, 1982).

References

Andenaes, J. 1952. General Prevention: Illusion or Reality? *Journal of Criminal Law, Criminology, and Police Science* 43: 176–98.
Andenaes, J. 1966. The General Preventive Effects of Punishment. *University of Pennsylvania Law Review* 114: 949–83.
Ayllon, T., and Azrin, N. 1968. *The Token Economy*. New York: Appleton-Century-Crofts.
Azrin, N., and Holtz, W. 1966. In *Operant Behavior: Areas of Research and Application* (ed. W. K. Honig). New York: Appleton-Century-Crofts.
Badia, P., Haber, A., and Runyon, R. P. (eds.). 1970. *Research Problems in Psychology*. Reading, Mass.: Addison-Wesley.

Bakan, D. 1966. The Test of Significance in Psychological Research. *Psychological Bulletin* 66: 423–37.

Bancroft, H. H. 1887. *Popular Tribunals*. San Francisco: History Company.

Bandura, A., and Walters, R. H. 1963. *Social Learning and Personality Development*. New York: Holt, Rinehart & Winston.

Barber, B. 1961. Resistance by Scientists to Scientific Discovery. *Science* 134: 596–602.

Barnett, C. 1965. *The Swordbearers: Supreme Command in the First World War*. New York: Signet.

Beccaria, C. B. 1963. *On Crimes and Punishments*. New York: Bobbs-Merrill. (Originally published in 1764.)

Betz, N. E. (ed.). 1986. The *g* Factor in Employment (Special Issue). *Journal of Vocational Behavior* 29: (3).

Broad, C. D. 1933. *Examination of McTaggart's Philosophy*. Cambridge: Cambridge University Press.

Brown, R. M. 1963. *The South Carolina Regulators*. Cambridge, Mass.: Harvard University Press.

Buck v Bell. 1927. *United States Reports*, 274: 200–208.

Burks, B., and Kelly, T. L. 1928. Statistical Hazards in Nature-Nurture Investigation. *Twenty-Seventh Yearbook of the National Society for the Study of Education, Nature and Nurture, Part I: Their Influence upon Intelligence*. Bloomington: Public School Publishing.

Burt, C. 1958. The Inheritance of Mental Ability. *American Psychologist* 13: 1958.

Burt, C. 1966. The Genetic Determination of Differences in Intelligence: A Study of Monozygotic Twins Reared Together and Apart. *British Journal of Psychology* 57: 137–53.

Burt, C. 1967. The Genetic Determination of Intelligence: A Reply. *British Journal of Psychology* 58: 153–62.

Campbell, D. T. 1969. Reforms as Experiments. *American Psychologist* 24: 409–29.

Campbell, D. T., and Fiske, D. W. 1959. Convergent and Discriminant Validation by the Multitrait-Multimethod Matrix. *Psychological Bulletin* 56: 81–105.

Campbell, D. T., and Ross, H. L. 1968. The Connecticut Crackdown on Speeding: Time Series Data in Quasi-Experimental Analysis. *Law and Society Review* 3: 33–53.

Carter, H. D. 1932. Twin Similarities in Occupational Interests. *Journal of Educational Psychology* 23: 641–55.

Carver, R. P. 1978. The Case against Statistical Significance Testing. *Harvard Educational Review* 48: 378–99.

Chow, S. L. 1988. Significance Test or Effect Size? *Psychological Bulletin* 103: 105–10.

Cohen, J. 1962. The Statistical Power of Abnormal-Social Psychological Research: A Review. *Journal of Abnormal and Social Psychology* 65: 145–53.

Coleman, J. S., Campbell, E. Q., and Hobson, C. 1966. *Equality of Educational Opportunity*. Washington: U.S. Government Printing Office.

Congressional Record, 1970, 116 (121), July 17, 1970.

Cowles, J. T. 1937. Food-Tokens as Incentives for Learning by Chimpanzees. *Comparative Psychology Monographs* 14: 1–96.

Cronbach, L. J., and Meehl, P. E. 1955. Construct Validity in Psychological Tests. *Psychological Bulletin* 52: 281–302.

Duncan, O. D. 1966. Path Analysis: Sociological Examples. *American Journal of Sociology* 72: 1–16.

Elston, R. C., and Gottesman, I. I. 1968. The Analysis of Quantitative Inheritance Simultaneously from Twin and Family Data. *American Journal of Human Genetics* 20: 512–21.

Erlenmeyer-Kimling, L., and Jarvik, L. F. 1963. Genetics and Intelligence: A Review. *Science* 142: 1477–79.

Estes, W. K. 1944. An Experimental Study of Punishment. *Psychological Monographs* 57 (Whole No. 263).

Forster, M. C. 1931. A Study of Father-Son Resemblance in Vocational Interests and Personality Traits. Doctoral dissertation, University of Minnesota.

Fuller, J. L., and Thompson, W. R. 1960. *Behavior Genetics*. New York: John Wiley & Sons.

Glass, G. V. 1968. Analysis of Data on the Connecticut Speeding Crackdown as a Time-Series Quasi-Experiment. *Law and Society Review* 3: 55–76.

Glass, G. V., McGaw, B., and Smith, M. L. 1981. *Meta-Analysis in Social Research*. Beverly Hills: Sage.

Goodwin, D. W. 1981. *Alcoholism: The Facts*. New York: Oxford University Press.

Gottesman, I. I. 1963. Genetic Aspects of Intelligent Behavior. In *Handbook of Mental Deficiency* (ed. N. Ellis). New York: McGraw-Hill.

Gottesman, I. I. 1968a. A Sampler of Human Behavior Genetics. In *Evolutionary Biology*, vol. 2 (ed. T. Dobzhansky, M. K. Hecht, and W. C. Steere). New York: Appleton-Century-Crofts.

Gottesman, I. I. 1968b. Biogenetics of Race and Class. In *Social Class, Race, and Psychological Development*, (ed. M. Deutsch, I. Katz, and A. R. Jensen). New York: Holt, Rinehart, & Winston.

Guttman, L. 1941. An Outline of the Statistical Theory of Prediction. In *The Prediction of Personal Adjustment, SSRC Bulletin, No. 48* (ed. P. Horst). New York: Social Science Research Council.

Hartshorne, H., and May, M. A. 1928. *Studies in Deceit*. New York: Macmillan.

Hawk, J. 1986. Real World Implications of *g*. *Journal of Vocational Behavior* 29: 411–14.

Herbert, M. J., and Harsh, C. M. 1944. Observational Learning by Cats. *Journal of Comparative Psychology* 37: 81–95.

Hirsch, J. (ed.). 1967. *Behavior-Genetic Analysis*. New York: McGraw-Hill.

Hobson v Hansen. 1967. *Federal Supplement* 269: 401–519.

Hogben, L. 1958. *The Relationship of Probability, Credibility, and Error: An Examination of the Contemporary Crisis in Statistical Theory from a Behaviorist Viewpoint*. New York: W. W. Norton.

Honig, W. K. (ed.). 1966. *Operant Behavior: Areas of Research and Application*. New York: Appleton-Century-Crofts.

Honzik, M. P. 1957. Developmental Studies of Parent-Child Resemblance in Intelligence. *Child Development* 28: 215–28.

Hunter, J. E., Schmidt, F. L., and Jackson, G. B. 1982. *Meta-Analysis: Cumulating Research Findings across Studies* vol. 4, *Studying Organizations: Innovations in Methodology*. Beverly Hills: Sage.

Jackson, D. N. 1969. Multimethod Factor Analysis in the Evaluation of Convergent and Discriminant Validity. *Psychological Bulletin* 72: 30–49.

Jenkins, J. J., and Paterson, D. G. (eds.). 1961. *Studies in Individual Differences: The Search for Intelligence*. New York: Appleton-Century-Crofts.

John, E. R., Chesler, P., Bartlett, F., and Victor, I. 1969. Observational Learning in Cats. *Science* 159: 1489–91.

Li, C. C. 1975. *Path Analysis: A Primer*. Pacific Grove, Calif.: Boxwood Press.

Lindesmith, A. R. 1965. *The Addict and the Law*. Bloomington: Indiana University Press.

Linn, R. L. 1986. Comments on the *g* Factor in Employment Testing. *Journal of Vocational Behavior* 29: 438–44.

Livermore, J. 1968. *Minnesota Evidence: Minnesota Practice Manual 22*. Minneapolis: University of Minnesota General Extension Division.

Llewellyn, K. N. 1960. *The Common Law Tradition: Deciding Appeals*. Boston: Little, Brown.

Loehlin, J. C. 1987. *Latent Variable Models*. Hillsdale, N. J.: Lawrence Erlbaum Associates.

Loevinger, J. 1957. Objective Tests as Instruments of Psychological Theory. *Psychological Reports* (Whole Monograph Supplement 9).

Lykken, D. T. 1968. Statistical Significance in Psychological Research. *Psychological Bulletin* 70: 151–59.

Lykken, D. T. 1982. If a Man be Mad. *The Sciences* (Journal of the New York Academy of Sciences) 22: 11–13.

McCormick, C. T. 1954. *Handbook of the Law of Evidence*. St. Paul: West Publishing Company.

Manosevitz, M., Lindzey, G., and Thiessen, D. 1969. *Behavioral Genetics: Methods and Research*. New York: Appleton-Century-Crofts.

Meehl, P. E. 1954. *Clinical versus Statistical Prediction: A Theoretical Analysis and a Review of the Evidence*. Minneapolis: University of Minnesota Press.

Meehl, P. E. 1967. Theory-Testing in Psychology and Physics: A Methodological Paradox. *Philosophy of Science* 34: 103–15.

Meehl, P. E. 1969. Letter in "Input." *Psychology Today* 3 (6): 4.

Meehl, P. E. 1970. Nuisance Variables and the ex post facto Design. In *Minnesota Studies in the Philosophy of Science*, vol. 4, *Analyses of Theories and Methods of Physics and Psychology* (eds. M. Radner and S. Winokur). Minneapolis: University of Minnesota Press.

Meehl, P. E. 1971a. High School Yearbooks: A Reply to Schwarz. *Journal of Abnormal Psychology* 77: 143–48.

Meehl, P.E. 1971b. A Scientific, Scholarly, Nonresearch Doctorate for Clinical Practitioners: Arguments Pro and Con. In R. R. Holt (ed.), *New Horizon for Psychotherapy: Autonomy as a Profession* (pp. 37-81). New York: International Universities Press.

Meehl, P. E. 1972. Specific Genetic Etiology, Psychodynamics, and Therapeutic Nihilism. *International Journal of Mental Health* 1: 10–27.

Meehl, P. E. 1987. Theory and Practice: Reflections of an Academic Clinician. In *Standards and Evaluation in the Education and Training of Professional Psychologists* (eds. E. F. Bourg, R. J. Bent, J. E. Callan, N. F. Jones, J. McHolland, and G. Stricker), 7–23. Norman, Okla.: Transcript Press.

Meehl, P. E. 1990a. Appraising and Amending Theories: The Strategy of Lakatosian Defense and Two Principles That Warrant It. *Psychological Inquiry* 1:108-41. Reply to the Commentators, 1:173-80.

Meehl, P. E. 1990b. Why Summaries of Research on Psychological Theories Are Often Uninterpretable. *Psychological Reports* 66: 195-244. In *Improving Inquiry in Social Science: A Volume in Honor of Lee J. Cronbach* (eds. R. E. Snow and D. Wiley). Hillsdale, N.J.: Lawrence Erlbaum Associates, 1991.

Megargee, E. I., and Hokanson, J. E. (eds.). 1970. *The Dynamics of Aggression*. New York: Harper & Row.

Menninger, K. A. 1969. *The Crime of Punishment*. New York: Viking Press.

Miller, N. E., and Dollard, J. 1941. *Social Learning and Imitation*. New Haven: Yale University Press.

Morrison, D. E., and Henkel, R. E. (eds.) 1970. *The Significance Test Controversy*. Chicago: Aldine.

Newman, K. J. 1960. Punishment and the Breakdown of the Legal Order: The Experience in East Pakistan. In *Responsibility: Nomos III* (ed. C. J. Friedrich). New York: Liberal Arts.

Nichols, R. C. 1966. The Resemblance of Twins in Personality and Interests. *National Merit Scholarship Reports* 2 (Whole No. 8).

Reed, E. W., and Reed, S. C. 1965. *Mental Retardation: A Family Study*. Philadelphia: Saunders.

Roberts, R. C. 1967. Some Concepts and Methods in Quantitative Genetics. In *Behavior-Genetic Analysis* (ed. J. Hirsch). New York: McGraw-Hill.

Robinson, D. N. (ed.). 1970. *Heredity and Achievement*. New York: Oxford University Press.

Ross, H. L., Campbell, D. T., and Glass, G. V. 1969. The British Crackdown on Drinking and Driving: A Successful Legal Reform. Laboratory of Educational Research Paper No. 29, University of Colorado, May 1969.

Rozeboom, W. W. 1960. The Fallacy of the Null-Hypothesis Significance Test. *Psychological Bulletin* 57: 416–28.

Shaffer, J. P. (ed.). 1987. *Journal of Educational Statistics* (Special Issue). 12 (2).

Shields, J. 1962. *Monozygotic Twins Brought Up Apart and Brought Up Together*. London: Oxford University Press.

Skinner, B. F. 1938. *The Behavior of Organisms*. New York: Appleton-Century-Crofts.

Skinner, B. F. 1948. *Walden Two*. New York: Macmillan.

Skinner, B. F. 1953. *Science and Human Behavior*. New York: Macmillan.

Skinner, B. F. 1961. *Cumulative Record*. New York: Appleton-Century-Crofts.

Skinner, B. F. 1968. *The Technology of Teaching*. New York: Appleton-Century-Crofts.

Skinner, B. F. 1969. *Contingencies of Reinforcement: A Theoretical Analysis*. New York: Appleton-Century-Crofts.

Skinner v Oklahoma. 1942. *United States Reports* 316: 535–47.

Strong, E. K., Jr. 1943. *Vocational Interests of Men and Women*. Stanford: Stanford University Press.

Strong, E. K., Jr. 1957. Interests of Fathers and Sons. *Journal of Applied Psychology* 41: 284–92.

Thompson, W. R. 1967. Some Problems in the Genetic Study of Personality and Intelligence. In *Behavior-Genetic Analysis* (ed. J. Hirsch). New York: McGraw-Hill.

Tilton, J. W. 1937. The Measurement of Overlapping. *Journal of Educational Psychology* 28: 656–62.

Tribe, L. H. 1970. An Ounce of Detention: Preventive Justice in the World of John Mitchell. *Virginia Law Review* 56: 371–407.

U.S. v Butler. 1936. *United States Reports* 297: 1–88.

Vaillant, G. E. 1983. *The Natural History of Alcoholism*. Cambridge, Mass.: Harvard University Press.

Valentine, A. 1956. *Vigilante Justice*. New York: Reynal.

Vandenberg, S. G. 1968. The Nature and Nurture of Intelligence. In *Genetics* (ed. D. C. Glass). New York: Rockefeller University Press.

Vandenberg, S. G., and Kelly, L. 1964. Hereditary Components in Vocational Preferences. *Acta Geneticae Medicae et Gemellologiae* 13: 266–74.

Vandenberg, S. G., and Stafford, R. E. 1967. Hereditary Influences on Vocational Preferences as Shown by Scores of Twins on the Minnesota Vocational Interest Inventory. *Journal of Applied Psychology 51: 17–19.*

Wakefield, H., and Underwager, R. 1988. *Accusations of Child Sexual Abuse*. Springfield, Ill.: Charles C. Thomas.

Waller, J. H. 1971. Social Mobility: Father-Son Difference in Social Position Related to Difference in IQ Score. *Social Biology* 18: 252–59.

Werts, C. E., and Linn, R. R. 1970. Path Analysis: Psychological Examples. *Psychological Bulletin* 74: 193–212.

Whipple, G. M. (ed.). 1940. Intelligence: Its Nature and Nurture. *39th Yearbook of the National Society for the Study of Education*. Bloomington: Public School Publishing, 2 vols.

Ziskin, J., and Faust, D. 1988. *Coping with Psychiatric and Psychological Testimony* (Vols. 1–3). Marina del Rey, Calif.: Law and Psychology Press.

16

The Insanity Defense

The proximate cause of my being invited to present this lecture was concern among Minnesota psychologists about what the legislature might do, perhaps with insufficient reflection on the complexities, by way of amending the Minnesota statute covering the insanity defense to a criminal charge. In a previous session, a bill was introduced that excluded the insanity defense except insofar as the patient's mental condition went to the possibility of intent as a material element of the crime. Within a larger social context, we know that there is widespread concern about the insanity defense, leading to what some consider ill-advised legislation in several states. This was largely attributable to public dissatisfaction with the outcome of the Hinckley case, about which I have no informed opinion since I do not read the newspapers or watch the television news. It is my understanding, from what informed persons have told me, that the outcome was arguably erroneous, and it seems to have violated the community sense of justice. Current social pressures aside, the whole problem of the insanity defense to a criminal charge is a topic on which psychologists should reflect. As in most such matters of professional expertise (real or alleged!) it is desirable for practitioners and scholars to examine the situation and contemplate possibilities for improvement at leisure, rather than as a reaction to urgent social pressures such as can arise in a state legislature.

I do not propose to discuss here the various rules for the insanity defense, partly because the empirical data on jury behavior suggests that while there are some statistically significant differences, they are numerically smaller than one might have supposed. Although it is true that the proportion of cases in the Washington, D.C. circuit where insanity was pleaded did show a marked increase in the 1950s following the famous Durham opinion. If you are familiar with these competing rules, such as M'Naghten and ALI, there's no need for me to remind you; and if you aren't familiar with them, telling about them briefly won't help much. In any case, I felt it would be more interesting for all of us if I address myself to some more fundamental issues rather than to the specific language of the various rules.

I'm not prepared to say that, as presently formulated and administered in Minnesota, the insanity defense results in any appreciable amount of injustice, granted the inevitable percentage of incorrect results that the criminal justice system has to put up with whether madness is at issue or not. On the basis of some unpublished MMPI research that my psychiatrist colleague Carl Malmquist did on statistics in Hennepin County, I'm inclined to think that to the extent that injustice is done, it is more commonly in conviction of persons who ought to have been acquitted than the other way around; but I cannot assert this confidently. This is, of course, opposite to the lay opinion that all sorts of bad characters get off the hook by successfully pretending to be crazy. One reason for concern among psychologists—which I do not think should be lightly dismissed as mere trade unionism—is that the public image of the psychologist (and psychiatrist) is one of a ''muddleheaded, bleeding heart shrink'' going into court and getting some murderous switchblade artist out of his just dues by selling the jury a bill of goods that the accused didn't get enough breastfeeding or was born on the wrong side of the tracks. I'm going to presume in what follows that if either the philosophical justification, or the statutory formulation, or the administration of the insanity defense is gravely disharmonious with the community sense of justice, it is bad for our profession, it is bad for the public attitude toward the criminal justice system, and, more to the point, it won't be carried out. There is ample evidence that neither police nor juries will consistently do things that violate the community's sense of justice. If a psychologist believes that the community sense of justice is ill informed, it may be his or her responsibility to contribute, by writing and popular lecturing and by the way he or she conducts a professional practice, to improving the community sense of justice. But it is not one's professional prerogative to slant testimony or otherwise accept a professional role that essentially consists of subverting the community sense of justice when he or she has not succeeded in persuading the citizenry that their moral and political views are mistaken.

I doubt that anyone who has functioned as a witness, or as a courtroom observer of psychological testimony, or has read transcripts of trials, would claim that as presently conducted the spectacle of the ''battle of the shrinks'' in the courtroom arena is edifying. In my opinion, there are mainly four reasons for its scientifically frustrating and clinically disedifying character. First, we have to face the fact that quite a few people in the mind business are not very smart, not very logical, not very well informed about relevant disciplines (e.g., ethics, political theory, jurisprudence, and alas, even statistics and probability theory) or are, even when cognitively competent, effective on the witness stand. Second, some lawyers are not very good courtroom lawyers, and are particularly inept about the insanity issue if they have not made it their specialty. We have here also the problem of inadequate preparation of counsel. For example, an expert witness should prepare the lawyer as to what sorts of questions will bring out the relevant points, especially how counsel can protect on redirect examination from effective cross-examination of the expert that, if unrebutted, leaves a misleading appearance of refutation. Third, while I myself am fond of the courtroom scene, admire lawyers, and find the legal process fascinating, I think it fair to say that there are some built-in defects of the criminal court as a forum for exploring the insanity defense. It is, of course, stupid for psychologists or other social scientists to say that the courtroom situation is not a disinterested pursuit of the truth, which obviously it cannot be because people's lives and liberty are at stake. It is irrational to expect a conflict of factual interpretations, backed up by the terrible power of the state, to be conducted like a philosophy of science seminar or a psychotherapy session. But the Anglo-American rules of evidence and the whole procedure of the adversary system (I include here the important factor of the enforced passivity of the trial judge) are not always conducive to bringing out the psychological truth. I must add, however, that if the first two defects (that is, of incompetent experts and poorly prepared or incompetent counsel) were removed, I believe that the leeway given to expert witnesses in the format of their testimony, even in our adversary system, would usually permit adequate exploration of all the issues and bringing out the relevant material. Fourth, despite my view that the presently formulated insanity defense is better than some critics think, if I were dictator of the universe trying to construct the best of all possible legal worlds in this respect, I would make some radical changes in the statutory definition and the associated judge's charge to the jury.

How does the problem arise in the first place? Consider a patient suffering from typhoid fever delirium (which is technically a psychosis). He misperceives the nurse, who comes to give him an injection, as a Klu Kluxer planning to kill him. Under this misapprehension, he knocks her down and she suffers a fatal brain concussion. Even disciples of Thomas Szasz would agree that it is inappropriate to convict this individual of murder. To do so would be neither just nor socially efficient. I find that lay persons who are completely innocent of psychology, even those who have a suspicion of shrink testimony in murder cases, will readily agree that it would be both stupid and unfair to punish this individual as a murderer by locking him in a cage for many years. Why? Because, as the layman would say, he was out of his head, he was not himself, he was nuts, he didn't know what he was doing. Correlated with that assessment, and of great importance to lay thinking in the matter, when he gets over his typhoid fever, he will also be free of his delirium, and consequently he will not be a menace to the rest of us any more than a randomly chosen person would be. Laymen, I find, do not like predators loose who will rape them or stick them with switch blades or take their property by violence, and I confess that, unlike some people, I have not reacted to my many years' training in social science by developing a fondness for predators. In this respect my views are closer to the layman's than to some social scientists'.

A slightly harder case, but one which I find is also persuasive to the lay mind (although it may take a little more doing) is that of a pious, conventional home-maker with no criminal history who becomes severely depressed. (It helps here to point out to the layman that psychotic depression is a biochemical disease of the brain produced by abnormal genes.) Evidencing the classical textbook signs of a psychotic depression (e.g., marked weight loss, severe intractable insomnia, delusions of guilt, complete loss of hope) she follows the hallucinatory instructions of the devil by putting her baby in the oven and turning on the gas, and then makes an unsuccessful suicide attempt. When further informed that this woman's depression will probably lift spontaneously in a matter of months (unless she's one of the unlucky ones), and in two or three weeks in most cases with anti-depressant medication, after which time she will be her former, noncriminal self again and no more risk to society than you or I, I find the layman says, as in the typhoid fever case, that it would be both unfair and inefficient to send her to prison as a murderer. The point I want to make here is that there is no appreciable disparity between the professional view of a major mental illness leading to what would otherwise be a criminal act, and the way the ordinary psychologically naïve layman thinks of the matter. Historically, the idea that a person is not crim-inally responsible if he is "out of his mind" goes back to the 13th century in our Anglo-Saxon legal tradition.

Now, in explicating this lay intuition one must ask what are the functions of the criminal law? One cannot address the question under what circumstances of mental condition an individual ought not be held responsible for a rape or a mur-der without a background understanding of why we do hold people responsible otherwise. As you know, there are a half dozen commonly recognized functions of the criminal sanction—four big ones and two minor ones. First, *incapacita-tion*: He can't kill me or steal my car while he is locked up, or on Devil's Island or in Siberia, or has been executed. Second, *reform*: He will learn his lesson, or he will learn something else while locked up which will lower the odds of his being criminal on being released. A subheading of reform is like "punishment" in the animal psychology sense, learning a lesson via unpleasant consequences so you won't do it again, and is generally called "special deterrence" by criminologists. Third, *general deterrence*: By locking criminals up, we give public notice to oth-ers who might be tempted that it's not a smart move to commit a crime. Fourth, *retributive justice*: We keep the society's moral bookkeeping straight, we give predators their just deserts. I note that even those who don't officially believe in this one affirmatively, are likely to become upset if you violate it negatively, that is, if you punish people who didn't do anything wrong for the purpose of deter-ring others, or propose to incarcerate a non-offender because his pattern of per-sonal and social attributes shows him statistically to be at high risk for criminal conduct. So the idea that it is unjust to punish the nonguilty is present even among those social scientists who reject any notion of retributive justice to the guilty as an affirmative obligation of the state.

These four biggies are supplemented by two that are emphasized mainly by Scandinavian jurisprudes, namely, the siphoning off of society's counteraggression (which is not the same as retributive justice, because we might consider it necessary as a matter of social engineering, even if we reject retribution as a moral or political concept); and moral education, not as dumb as it sounds. It's one of a half dozen ways society inculcates people with a sense of what is and is not a baddie, and how bad a baddie is by the knowledge that some baddies are penalized far more severely than others. While family training and peer group models are doubtless more important in this respect, I do not believe we should hastily dismiss the idea that the background awareness of the criminal penalty does have some effect in moral education.

Now given these six distinct functions of the criminal law, we have what any economist will tell us is an intractable mathematical problem. Whatever "input" variables are involved in the criminal justice system—taxes spent on cops versus social workers, or surveillance versus group therapy, severity of sentencing, the kind of milieu provided in the prison, and the like—the six output variables are obviously not going to be the same mathematical function of the several inputs that the society can manipulate, even if society proceeded totally "rationally" in an effort to optimize results. This mathematical problem would be present even if there were social agreement on still disputed empirical questions, such as the efficacy of special deterrence. Hence, absent some assignment of different utilities to the six functions, there is simply no way of deciding what to do. As we all know, there is far from universal consensus on the relative importance of these six aims. While this presents problems for selecting a good insanity rule and implementing it procedurally, I don't think it makes as much difference here as in non-insanity cases, because I think that in the clear-cut insanity cases, where the layman and the professional would easily come to close agreement (as in my typhoid fever or depressed homemaker examples), it is plausible to argue that *none* of the six functions of the criminal law is appreciably advanced by a conventional criminal penalty to the psychotic person.

Without deciding what is the incidence of injustice under the present rules of our system, or whether it errs more often by false positives than false negatives, I don't have much to suggest "institutionally" regarding poor preparation of counsel or inadequate competence of experts, since these are primarily matters of the internal policing of the professions involved. Statutorily we might require that an expert witness be more than any generally qualified psychologist or physician, whereas in the present system special competence in the forensic area or in psychopathology is not required. Whether one is a psychiatrist or a GP, or whether one is a clinical psychologist or some other kind, only goes, in the lawyer's jar-

gon, to the weight and not the admissibility of the testimony. It would probably
be unconstitutional to exclude less qualified testimony than real experts, but one
could require that they testify simply as laymen and not with technical expertise.
I myself would advocate that an expert witness must be a boarded clinical psychologist or psychiatrist; but I realize that I wouldn't get very many takers on
such a stringent proposal.

As to the character of the forum, I advocate a bifurcated trial (despite some
allegedly unsatisfactory experiences with that in a couple of states) in which psychological evidence in the first trial at most bears upon the question of *mens rea*,
and then the second "trial" would deal with the defendant's exculpability under
whatever insanity rule was in effect. The second trial would be conducted more
like a hearing by an administrative tribunal. It would not use a jury, but instead a
three- or four-person panel consisting of a lawyer (the chairman, for well-known
reasons), a psychiatrist, and a clinical psychologist, plus a lay member. (Because
of the Asch Phenomenon, one might want to have two lay persons.) There would
be a rebuttable presumption of sanity, and I would put the burden on the defendant, provided the Nine Holy Persons in Washington will hold still for that,
which I guess they won't. I would define that burden as a preponderance of the
evidence, although perhaps we could squeak through easier with the Supreme
Court by making it something closer to "probable cause" or "any warrant in the
record" — some lower degree of evidentiary support as occurs in administrative
law. I would require that the professional panel members, in addition to their general qualifications and experience, pass a written and oral examination in the specific area of forensic psychology and psychiatry, assuring that the lawyer is
knowledgeable in these areas, and the psychologist and the psychiatrist are
knowledgeable about criminal law, jurisprudence, political theory, and ethics. I
realize this is radical because in the United States, people are sometimes appointed to judgeships on the basis of minimal scholarly qualifications (plus being
an old poker-playing crony of the executive). In European countries candidates
embark on formal curricula with the specific vocational goal of becoming a
judge, and must pass rigorous examinations in "judgin'." The only "political"
or "ideological" considerations that would come up for examination before appointment to such panels would be ascertainment that the candidate is not some
sort of ax-grinder out to impose his own set of ideas in defiance of the community
sense of justice, or who has resistance to applying such technical knowledge as
psychology, psychiatry, statistics, and genetics genuinely possess.

The rules would be like those of an administrative tribunal, and the panel
members would play an active role as interrogators. I do not mean that all elements of an adversary proceeding would be eliminated, which would be inappropriate. Counsel would be present, but the various reasons that have been accepted
for the development of administrative tribunals instead of the ordinary courtroom
battle would seem to apply here. I give you two brief examples. I don't think I've

ever participated in, observed, or read an insanity defense where the prosecutor failed to bring out the fact that the defendant was oriented for time and place, that he remembered somebody's name, or even knew the telephone number of the Yellow Cab Company (a point made much of in the Eubanks murder case where I was an expert witness). Suppose the defendant is pleading paranoid schizophrenia. Then whether he is oriented, and whether he remembers a telephone number, is not only not dispositive, it is not even *relevant*. An objection of the traditional kind ought to be sustained, although I've never seen a lawyer try it. Such facts are completely irrelevant to the probandum. To a lay jury, it sounds important. To such a sophisticated panel of experts, its irrelevance would be apparent. They would, without waiting for objection by opposing counsel, simply stop the line of questioning and say, "Counsel, the defendant is pleading paranoid schizophrenia as a form of mental illness. Are you unaware that the retention of orientation and ordinary memory is one of the accepted medical criteria for diagnosis of paranoid schizophrenia? Defendant is not claiming organic brain syndrome or delirious hypermania, so why are you bringing up the irrelevant fact that he was oriented and remembered a phone number?" Similarly, on the other side, if counsel for the defendant tries to bring in the fact that he had an older brother who was a pickpocket, his father was a mean bastard, and his mother was a drunk, none of this bears upon exculpability under the sort of insanity rule that I'm going to propose below. So again, without requiring objection by the prosecutor, the panel would simply put a stop to it on the grounds it has nothing to do with what is being pleaded in exculpation. As you can see, my proposal for a bifurcated trial is not simply a matter of "loosening things up." It's loosening them in some directions while tightening them in others, bringing them closer to rational criteria of psychotic exculpability.

There is a constitutional problem here because of the right to trial by jury. I can think of two ways of handling this, and there are probably others a lawyer could cook up. One is to make the expert panel optional, hoping that defense counsel would gradually learn that they stood a better chance with such a panel of experts than with the usual lay jury and courtroom rules, which I assume the empirical statistics would bear out after a while. Second, we could allow a plea in the *first* trial of "guilty but mentally ill," as is done in Michigan, and then we don't consider this second hearing as a "trial" in the strict sense at all, but rather as administrative handling of a *convicted* (but specially labeled) person from the standpoints of forecasting and treatment. This requires suitable machinery of interlocking between the criminal justice system and the mental health system. Whether there would be some constitutional objections even to this, I am not enough of a lawyer to say. One can imagine a class action in which it was argued that offenders who go through this second process are being treated in a special way that is subtly unfair to other convicted persons, because it amounts to kind of an "exculpatory second trial" whether we call it a trial or not. Again, we have to be careful not to violate the community sense of justice, complaining that a panel of so-called experts rather than a lay jury gets to decide whether somebody "pays for his crimes" as he justly should. This brings me to the radical substantive proposal I have about the statute.

To capture the essence of the community's sense of justice—that a person should be exculpated from criminal responsibility only if he was "crazy," "nutty," "out of his mind," "didn't really know what he was doing," "totally out of control for a medical reason"—it might be desirable to write the statute so that pleading not guilty by reason of insanity (or guilty while mentally ill) amounts to pleading psychosis. I say this despite current emphasis by the psychiatric profession that 'psychosis' is a medical term and 'insanity' a legal one, a true but trivial observation that doesn't tell us anything useful about the extent to which they denote the same class of individuals. I think that they usually do, with exceptions so few that it would be unwise to attempt covering the exceptions by special statutory language. It is therefore my proposal that a list of exculpable psychotic diagnoses, *nosological rubrics*, be put into the statute. I'm not certain of that list's composition, but it would be quite short. My own candidates would include: manic depressive disease, unipolar psychotic depression, paranoid schizophrenia, catatonic schizophrenia (I have here in mind the rare cases of Bleuler's "catatonic raptus"), coarse brain syndrome (with definite clouding, memory loss, and disorientation) and the psychomotor epileptic equivalent. Nothing else goes. So you can't plead not guilty by reason of mental illness on the grounds that you had a battle-ax mother, or a pickpocket uncle, or a poverty-stricken childhood, or whatever. It is true that if a person is psychologically or socially disadvantaged by aberrant parents or racial prejudice or going to a crummy school, the community sense of "fairness" increasingly recognizes that he or she is entitled to some sort of special aids and reparative benefits. But the community sense of justice as regards criminal conduct does not hold that because I had a battle-ax mother or an alcoholic father or a poverty-stricken slum background that I am somehow entitled to stick knives into people or rape them or rob a bank. I might be open to a suggestion that irresistible impulse (which I am rather inclined to doubt really exists) could be included. But in that case I would specify proof of a classic textbook severe compulsion neurosis. The point is that mere intensity of motivation, of whatever character and origin, is not an excuse for predatory conduct.

Putting aside the Szaszian claim that there is no mental illness (I'm really not interested in discussing things with people who are 30 years behind in their reading of the literature on genes and biochemistry, not to mention taxometrics and the reliability of improved psychiatric mental examination methods), I'm aware that the suggestion to include a list of nosological labels right in the statute itself bothers most lawyers. It seems to bother lawyers and law professors a great deal. What they usually tell me is that "we don't write statutes in specific terms but in general language.'' My response to this is two-fold. First, there may be times when we *ought* to write statutes in quite specific terms, and we do, as in speed limits, or the percentage of alcohol in beer, or permissible interest rates, or the properties of a negotiable instrument. More important, this "general language" principle is no longer an accurate description of American Law, which today has all sorts of very detailed language about chemical substances and landlord tenant relationships and corporate management and child care and medical procedures and the environment and so on and on. It is simply not true that all statutory language is in highly general terms, so I do not find myself much influenced by this argument.

I wish time permitted me to expand on the formal nosology problem, both as to its intrinsic validity (i.e., construct meaning) and its interjudge reliability aspects. We may confidently assume that counsel will become more sophisticated and critical about psychodiagnostic labels, as a result of law school exposure and especially the rapidly growing number of faculty with double degrees. These Ph.D.–J.D. amphibians (e.g., Jay Ziskin, Stephen Morse) write articles and books that are read by lawyers and judges. The "critique of nosology" in social science will affect trial tactics under prevailing rules, and, of course, would have major importance in considering statutory change along the radical lines I have suggested. Unfortunately, the conceptual level of much social science criticism is sophomoric, being "sophisticated" more than the ordinary M.D. practitioner, but pitiable when judged by a scholarly clinician knowledgeable in genetics, taxometrics, philosophy of science, and history of medicine. I find—even in the academy, where intellectual responsibility is supposedly a top virtue—a depressing reliance on anti-nosologic clichés, such as "everyone knows that psychiatric diagnoses are completely unreliable."

This was not an empirically validated statement even before the reliability oriented interview developments of recent years, and I am amazed at psychologists who cite, say, Schmidt and Fonda's classic study as anti-nosological evidence, when the interjudge reliability of the "schizophrenia/nonschizophrenia" dichotomy was tetrachoric .95. The careful recent studies show that diagnostic reliability in psychiatry is at least as good as that of organic medicine. In a murder case, we want as high a reliability as we can get, and we as psychologists should be imaginative in applying our psychometric and decision-theoretic know-how to improving it. *Example*: The Spearman Brown Prophecy Formula has been in our psychometric tool kit for over 70 years. Why don't we use it? The fact that human ratings behave like test items in closely following this old equation has been known since the 1920s. So if clinicians' ratings on "paranoid delusion" had a pairwise interjudge reliability of only .70 (we can do better than that) the old Formula tells us that we need four clinicians to get a pooled rating reliability of .90 and six raters would yield .933 (permitting, if content-valid, a net attenuated construct validity of .97, which should satisfy anybody!).

This sounds like a lot of clinical raters, but two to four clinicians independently viewing say, two videotaped standardized mental status interviews conducted by two others would cost less than the usual four "experts" (two on each side) being put through their courtroom paces as we now do it. I admit that persuading lawyers to accept the fact that statistically combined numerical ratings are superior to unformalized talk would be a difficult educational task, especially since I have thus far had negligible success in educating supposedly scientific psychologists in such matters. *Another example*: One merit of taxonic models is that when the inferred entity is a taxon (e.g., manic depressive disease) rather than a dimension (e.g., general intelligence, social introversion) the distribution of the diagnostic probabilities yielded by Bayes's Formula is deeply U-shaped, with clear cusps at the ends, and the lowest sign-pattern frequencies occur in the mid-region of doubtful diagnoses. Thus, for a taxon base rate $P = \frac{1}{2}$ and only three diagnostic signs, each no better than an MMPI scale (and quasi-independent within taxa), 62% of cases are classifiable with 99% confidence, and the other 38% with 85% confidence. This is, of course, due to the multiplicative structure of Bayes's Theorem whose applicability depends on the difference between a taxometric and ordinary dimensional situation. How many forensic psychologists use this in their work—or, for that matter, how many know about it?

So one must counter the clichéd objection that psychiatric diagnosis is completely unreliable, but that's a question of informing people who have been falsely brainwashed in some social science course as to the present state of the evidence. I find that some lawyers and law professors have a double standard of epistemological morals in this regard, because they seem to require that psychiatric diagnosis show reliability vastly superior to what is found in studies of the reliability (and validity against pathologist's findings) of diagnoses in organic medicine. Equally double-minded are those psychologists who derogate formal nosology on unreliability grounds and then proceed to predict (or explain) from complicated psychodynamics as inferred from the Rorschach! Furthermore, if we insisted on reliability coefficients of .95 for any procedure that is used to make important judgments about human beings—their health or income or freedom—most of the legal system would have to be junked as judged by its present functioning.

I have given less thought than I should to the question of subsequent handling of a person found not guilty by reason of insanity or guilty while mentally ill, but certain things seem fairly obvious, given the initial assumption that a defense of this sort is rational at all. Commitment to a mental hospital of good security should be automatic upon either of these verdicts, despite the fact that the verdict itself hinges upon mental state at the time of the offense rather than the trial. This is because the behavioral engineering element now predominates over (I would say to the exclusion of) concepts of general or special deterrence or of retributive justice, so that the only thing that's relevant here is the protection of society and the individual from future predatory behavior on his part. I can see no good reason to keep such a person in custody once the empirical probabilities of his dangerous behavior are ascertained to be quite low, although it is not obvious without further discussion that they should be lowered to the level of a "randomly chosen member of the population." The terrible problems of forecasting dangerousness are known to all of you, and that controversy on present evidence deserves a lecture longer than this one, so I can say little about it. If my proposed list of nosological categories were in effect, the ascertainment that somebody has made a clinical recovery from a major affective disorder is fairly easy, but probability of subsequent recurrence is around .80. However, search of the literature by Malmquist and me failed to reveal one single instance of a psychotically depressed patient who, after an altruistic homicide of a family member (unlike paranoid schizophrenics, depressed patients don't kill strangers or neighbors) was a repeater. When it comes to schizophrenia, the problem is stickier. As Rado says, "A schizotype is one from vume to tume," and there is fairly high probability of future attacks, which in their early stages, and in some clinical forms, are probably harder to detect than a depressive episode, at least on an outpatient, rare-contact basis. Presumably lesser degrees of confinement where the psychiatric offender is dealt with like the paroled criminal offender, with careful monitoring of status, is the best we can do. One of the main reasons for maintaining some carefully defined insanity defense as fully exculpatory is that consideration of "just deserts" and of general deterrence having been eliminated from consideration by that kind of verdict, what remains is purely social engineering, that is, clinical and statistical forecasting problems. Of course, if psychologists persist in employing irrational and low-validity means of prediction, it won't help much.

The community sense of justice applies also to the moral or policy issue before a legislator in assigning utilities to the two kinds of errors. If, for instance, the taxpayer is most concerned about his own and his family's safety from predators—the inactivation function of the criminal law (the only one of the six that we know, without any systematic research, is achievable!)—it is reasonable to require that some defensible assignment of weights to the false positive and false negative errors exist both in the criminal justice system and the mental health system for persons who have in fact performed a dangerous social act like raping or killing a human being, whether the verdict was one of criminal responsibility or insanity acquittal. There is a widespread cliché among social scientists, based upon uncritical interpretation of some well-known studies of criminal recidivism, that the false positive rate in recidivism prediction is so high that there is something inherently "unfair" about incarcerating even offenders who have committed dangerous acts. To think clearly about this, one must remember that the crime reporting rate, as shown by victimization studies for the seven index felonies of the Unified Crime Reports (homicide, rape, robbery, aggravated assault, burglary, grand larceny, and car theft) is less than 50%, for a variety of complicated social and psychological reasons. The clearance rate, that is, percentage of reported cases which police consider effectively solved and hence close investigation, is very much less than 50%, as for example in the case of burglary and aggravated assault, less than 10% in most studies. And then finally, of cases reported and cleared, less than 50% result in conviction for an index crime, the rest being cases of prosecutorial discretion as to insufficient evidence, or police carelessness about Miranda, or derailment from the criminal justice system to some other such as chemical dependency or mental health, or simply being asked to leave the jurisdiction, and then, finally, the two biggest factors, plea bargaining and cases tried but acquitted. Multiplying these probabilities we see that the upper bound for tallying a recidivating offense is 12%, that is, for every tallied recidivating event there are seven that do not appear in the statistics. Of course, I've used upper limits on all three probabilities, so a more realistic ratio would be two or three times larger than that! That means that a recidivism study reporting a valid positive rate of only 10% means that, in reality, the valid positive rate is at least 80%. I don't know why it is necessary to explain such elementary arithmetic to social scientists, except that so many of them have a greater emotional identification with predators than with their victims. If it is objected that we only have an 80% *group* figure, and we don't know about the individual, I would reply that we don't need to at the level of legislative policy. One of the main reasons for having an insanity defense that declares some people ''innocent of crime'' is that such cases are now candidates for purely behavioral engineering disposition, whereas the criminal offender can have a penalty attached related to the social severity (and, in the community's sense of justice, the moral turpitude) of the offense. Within that permissible sentence I cannot see why a reduction of the degree of security (such as represented by an electronically monitored parole) offends either the community sense of justice or a rational intellect's ethical principles.

If a homicide is acquitted as insane, his disposition presents moral, political, and statistical problems essentially the same as those we face in ordinary civil commitment. The main difference is that our acquitted killer is *known* to be ''dangerous'' in the strong sense that he actually *has done* a fearful antisocial act, rather than only being inferentially ''disposed to'' such. Unfortunately, stating this difference rigorously is a surprisingly difficult task. As to the arguments on civil commitment generally, while I am a card-carrying member of the Libertarian Party and my fear of the State is probably as great as anyone's in this room, I am unpersuaded by Szasz and Co. that it is always wrong, although it is unquestionably subject to abuse (as I saw concretely during my three years on the Hastings State Hospital Review Board). The core issue is not psychology; it is an issue at the moral/political philosophy interface: Under what conditions, if any, should the community be permitted to use force in restraining someone, to prevent probable self-injury or harm to others? The first element presents the problem of paternalism, the second that of preventive detention; both are issues of formidable complexity, currently *sub judice* among moral philosophers, political theorists, and jurisprudes. A psychologist who settles them offhandedly or dogmatically shows a lack of scholarship.

As regards the paternalistic issue in civil commitment or upon successful insanity defense, I find it surprising how many of my colleagues (and educated persons generally) are very uptight about interfering with a paranoid schizophrenic's behavior against his will for his own benefit no matter how crazy he is, but these same people think it's all right to have mandatory investment in a poor investment program (to wit, social security), to compel people to go to school when they don't want to, to pay extra for air bags in automobiles, not to mention a large number of things which we do by way of protecting the consumer. I don't mind if the law requires honest packaging in my soda pop. But if Regents' Professor Meehl, with a respectable IQ and not insane, has to be protected against his own folly, should he ingest saccharin in his Diet Coke, I think it odd that someone who is clearly psychotic and wants to assassinate the governor should not be entitled to protection by the community.

Operating on the general principle that we wish to implement the community sense of justice in formulating statutory language, it might be further specified that exculpation for a criminal act (as found in the first trial) should depend upon there being some sort of "intimate content relationship" between the psychotic delusional or hallucinatory material and the criminal act performed. In the case of Mr. Hinckley—and I repeat I'm not familiar with the details of this, except second hand—it is admittedly a peculiar way of thinking for him to believe that he could get this actress to love him by shooting the president. If pressed, I might be willing as a clinician to say that this is goofy enough mentation that probably he was schizophrenic as alleged. But I gather it was not alleged that he actually had paranoid delusions as part of his schizophrenia. While in terms of social engineering I *might* be willing to concede that he should be treated as a nonresponsible person, it's a debatable point. I fear that here my clinical instincts may not be harmonious with the community sense of justice, because I think that the reflective layman would argue that even if one has a strange notion of how you make somebody fall in love with you this does not, so to speak, entitle you to shoot the president. For that reason it might be cleaner to add to the list of nosological rubrics a specific requirement that for the defense to be successfully maintained, it must be shown, at least by reasonable inference, that the action was performed in close connection with the delusional ideas. I don't think that this will get us into the sort of difficulty that the Durham rule did by its merely referring to "a product of . . . " which is more difficult to ascertain. Going back to my case of the depressed woman who puts the baby in the oven and then unsuccessfully attempts to suicide, we know that the content of psychotic depression includes delusions of guiltiness and hopelessness. In the case of parents, these delusional ideas often involve not meeting their responsibilities toward their children. This is something we know clinically about such patients generally, most of whom do not perform any acting out behavior that results in a criminal charge. She sincerely believes the devil told her that the kids would be better off dead because she was such an awful mother, that she would be doing them a favor, and that seemed quite reasonable to her at the time. I repeat that I'm not quite satisfied with this "content-connected" criterion clinically. But I'm trying to arrive at some reasonable compromise between the community sense of justice (as imperfectly informed) and what *we* might look upon as optimal from the standpoint of psychopathology.

These radical suggestions are predicated upon the assumption that the thing cannot be made to work satisfactorily if one of the currently available rules, such as ALI or M'Naghten, are retained in the statute. As I said at the beginning, I am not myself persuaded that they cannot be made to work better than they currently do. I am not even convinced that there is an inordinately high percentage of injustice being done as they are presently defined and implemented. It was argued in your *ad hoc* committee (that Dr. Long chaired) that sometimes it's better for a professional group to "let well enough alone." The committee was impressed by our inability to come up with good examples when one of the lawyers in the legislature asked whether there were any clear cases where we were satisfied as clinical psychologists that a serious injustice had definitely been done, particularly an injustice of the kind where an individual has been wrongly acquitted when he was guilty. I do know of several instances of the opposite result, and Malmquist's unpublished study on MMPIs of unsuccessful insanity defense pleaders leads me to think that there are some people in Stillwater Prison who really ought to be in a mental hospital or long since released. But I wasn't able, nor was anybody else on the committee, to come up with any clear examples of the other sort. The proposed statutory changes, both in the Minnesota legislature and the ones that have been enacted in other jurisdictions, are uniformly in the direction of tightening up the grounds of exculpability rather than loosening them. It isn't obvious that it's advantageous for these defendants, or for society's protection, or for our professional image, to take a strong stand in advocating such radical changes as the ones I have been here discussing.

There is a mixed metaphysical/moral/political bugbear which, while not directly related to the insanity defense, lurks in the shadows of discussion about it, and I believe contributes to the layman's suspiciousness about psychologists. It is the idea that if we exculpate some persons for psychological reasons, philosophical consistency will push us to exculpate everybody, since everybody's behavior is determined by his genes, his upbringing, his race, his peer group, his economic status, etc. You know the line — we all had bull sessions about free will, determinism, and accountability as sophomores — so I needn't elaborate it. It would be absurd for me to try resolving this old controversy in a few minutes, but let me list briefly, without argument, the main components as I see them. First, "moral blameworthiness" in the sense of some omniscient cosmic evaluation of a human act (or life!), is not the same as "accountability" in the legal or political sense, although these concepts are related. Second, whether strict psychological determinism entails nonresponsibility is a dreadfully complex question, about which the ablest intellects in moral philosophy continue to disagree. The majority of contemporary philosophers are so-called compatibilitists, holding that determinism and free choice (in whatever sense of 'free' is required for accountability) are not inconsistent. Third, while strict psychological determinism is a plausible extrapolation from empirical evidence to date, it *is* an extrapolation, and we do not know it to be true. Some eminent philosophers of science (e.g., Sir Karl Popper) don't believe it, and claim to have strong arguments against it. Fourth, even if determinism holds and precludes blameworthiness, it does not follow that society should give equal weight to the predator's interest and the victim's. (If I see a big angry dog about to slay a kitten, I try to protect the kitten, although I don't regard dogs as rational moral agents, capable of deserving blame in the sense that persons can.) Fifth, one must be careful about this word 'society' in excusing those who commit antisocial acts. Even if I believed that "society" forces people to be criminal (which I don't), that claim doesn't translate into, "The widow washerwoman, whom Jones mugs and robs, deserves no protection because — being part of 'society' — *she* is responsible for Jones's becoming a thief." That is, because Smith didn't give Jones a good job, the washerwoman deserves to suffer, and the rest of *us* are estopped from protecting her, whether *we* in turn ever treated Smith unfairly or not. The absurdity of such an inference, when stated thus explicitly, is so obvious as to require no comment.

In summary, I have tried to make several points, doubtless somewhat dogmatically under the constraints of time and format. The insanity defense should be retained, on grounds of both fairness and social efficiency. The disharmony between a sophisticated professional view and the community sense of justice has been exaggerated. Whether the insanity defense errs excessively as currently defined and administered, I do not know; but I opine that errors of false conviction preponderate. Its main defect is perhaps the public image of us and of the criminal justice system, where a few atypical cases filtered through the media's muddy lenses can arouse widespread fear and anger in the public mind. As a blueprint for the utopian future, I advocate a bifurcated trial with the second trier being a specially qualified and carefully screened panel of lawyer, psychologist, and psychiatrist, plus a layman. The statutory criterion of exculpability would be narrowed to psychosis and mental deficiency, and I even advocate listing formal nosological rubrics in the statute. It is urged that psychologists show more imagination and resourcefulness in applying their technical knowledge of human ratings, taxometrics, and decision theory to improve accuracy and to save taxpayer money. Finally, unless we think there's a decent chance of accomplishing such perfectionistic refurbishments, one strategy our profession should consider is letting well enough alone.

17

Compatibility of Science and ESP

with Michael Scriven

As two of the people whose comments on an early draft of George Price's article on "Science and the Supernatural" he acknowledged in a footnote, we should like to clarify our position by presenting the following remarks.

Price's argument stands or falls on two hypotheses, only the first of which he appears to defend. They are (1) that extrasensory perception (ESP) is incompatible with modern science and (2) that modern science is complete and correct.

If ESP is *not* incompatible with modern science, then the Humean skeptic has no opportunity to insist on believing modern science rather than the reports about ESP. If modern science is *not* believed to be complete or correct, then the skeptic is hardly justified in issuing a priori allegations of fraud about experimenters even when they claim that they have discovered a new phenomenon that requires reconsideration of the accepted theories.

In our view, both of Price's hypotheses are untenable. Whatever one may think about the comprehensiveness and finality of modern physics, it would surely be rash to insist that we can reject out of hand any claims of revolutionary discoveries in the field of psychology. Price is in exactly the position of a man who might have insisted that Michelson and Morley were liars because the evidence for the physical theory of that time was stronger than that for the veracity of these experimenters. The list of those who have insisted on the impossibility of fundamental changes in the current physical theory of their time is a rather sorry one. Moreover, unhappy though Price's position would be if this were his only commitment, he cannot even claim that specifiable laws of physics are violated; it is only certain philosophical characteristics of such laws that are said to be absent from those governing the new phenomena.

It is true that Price attempted to give a specific account of the incompatibilities between ESP and modern science, rather than relying on Broad's philosophical analysis, but here the somewhat superficial nature of Price's considerations becomes clear. Of his eight charges, seven are unjustified.

497

1. He claims that ESP is "unattenuated by distance" and hence is incompatible with modern science. But, as is pointed out in several of the books he refers to, since we have no knowledge of the minimum effective signal strength for extrasensory perception, the original signal may well be enormously attenuated by distance and still function at long range.

2. He says that ESP is "apparently unaffected by shielding." But shielding may well have an effect: the evidence shows only that the kind of shielding appropriate to electromagnetic radiation is ineffectual; since detectors indicate that no such radiation reaches the percipient from the agent, this is scarcely surprising.

3. He says "Dye patterns . . . are read in the dark; how does one detect a trace of dye without shining a light on it?" The two most obvious answers would be by chemical analysis and physical study of the impression (which is usually different for different colors).

4. "Patterns on cards in the center of a pack are read without interference from other cards." The word *read* is hardly justified in view of the statistical nature of the results; however, this phenomenon is always used by parapsychologists as evidence against a simple radiation theory, which it is. But no simple radiation theory can explain the Pauli principle and one can no more refute it by saying "How could one electron possibly know what the others are doing?" than one can refute the ESP experiments by saying "How could one possibly read a card from the middle of the pack without interference from those next to it?" These questions are couched in prejudicial terms.

5. "We have found in the body no structure to associate with the alleged functions." Even if true, this hardly differentiates it from a good many other *known* functions; and among eminent neurophysiologists, J. C. Eccles is one who has denied Price's premise [originally in *Nature* 168 (1951)].

6. "There is no learning but, instead, a tendency toward complete loss of ability," a characteristic which Price believes has "no parallel among established mental functions." Now it would be reasonable to expect, in a series of experiments intended to show that learning does not occur, some *trial-by-trial* differential reinforcement procedure. Mere continuation, with encouragement or condemnation after *runs of many trials* can hardly provide a conclusive proof of the absence of learning in a complex situation. We ourselves know of *no* experiments in which this condition has been met and which show *absence* of learning; certainly one could not claim that this absence was established. Furthermore, *even if it had been established*, it would be very dangerous to assert that there is "no parallel among established mental functions." In the psychophysiological field particularly, there are several candidates. Finally, *even if it had been established and there were no parallel among mental functions*, there would be no essential difficulty in comparing it with one of the many familiar performances that exhibit no learning in adults—for example, reflex behavior.

7. "Different investigators obtain highly different results." This is the most distressingly irresponsible comment of all. ESP is a capacity like any other human capacity such as memory, in that it varies in strength and characteristics from individual to individual and in the one individual from one set of circumstances to another. The sense in which Rhine and Soal (Price's example of "different investigators") have obtained "highly different results" is when they have been dealing with different subjects or markedly different circumstances—for example, different agents; and exactly the same would be true of an investigation of, for example, stenographers' speed in taking dictation or extreme color blindness.

There remains only statistical precognition, which is certainly not susceptible to the types of explanation currently appropriate in physics: but then it is not a phenomenon in physics. Even if it were, it is difficult to see why Price thinks that we properly accommodated our thought to the distressing and counterintuitive idea that the earth is rotating whereas we should not accept precognition. His test for distinguishing new phenomena from magic is hopeless from the start ("The test is to attempt to imagine a detailed mechanistic explanation") because (1) it is of the essence of the scientific method that one should have means for establishing the facts *whether or not* one has already conceived an explanation and (2) it would have thrown out the Heisenberg uncertainty principle and action across a vacuum—that is, nuclear physics and the whole of electricity and magnetism—along with ESP.

Finally, Price's "ideal experiments" are only Rube Goldberg versions of the standard tests plus a skeptical jury. The mechanical contrivances would be welcome if only parapsychologists could afford them, and the jury is obviously superfluous because, according to Price's own test, we should rather believe that they lie than that the experiments succeed. However, in our experience, skeptics who are prepared to devote some time and hard work to the necessary preliminary study and experimenting are welcome in the laboratories at Duke and London. Without the training, one might as well have (as Price would say) 12 clergymen as judges at a cardsharps' convention.

The allegations of fraud are as helpful or as pointless here as they were when they were made of Freud and Galileo by the academics and others who honestly believed that they *must* be mistaken. They are irresponsible because Price has not made any attempt to verify them (as he admits), despite the unpleasantness they will cause, and because it has been obvious since the origin of science that any experimental results, witnessed by no matter how many people, *may* be fraudulent.

18

Precognitive Telepathy I:
On the Possibility of Distinguishing It
Experimentally from Psychokinesis

It has sometimes been argued that we cannot, in principle, design an experiment which would permit us to distinguish between precognitive telepathy and psychokinesis as alternative theoretical explanations of those extra-chance parapsychological effects usually taken to indicate "backward (telepathic) causality." (See, e.g., discussion in Mackie, 1974, pp. 160–92 and references therein; see also Soal and Bateman, 1954, pp. 80–82, 89; Mundle, 1950, 1952; Wheatley and Edge, 1976, especially Section III.) The reasoning is simple and straightforward, and on first hearing appears compelling; but I shall attempt to show that it is nevertheless unsound, by describing an experimental arrangement, easily realizable with presently available technology, that would enable a decision to be made with as much confidence as we customarily settle for in scientific research. I do not, of course, wish to maintain that I have devised an *experimentum crucis* in any "absolute" sense of that phrase, since without prejudging the outcome of the continuing Duhemian Thesis debate (Grünbaum, 1960, 1962, 1969, 1976; Lakatos, 1970, 1974) I doubt the possibility of solid-gold *modus tollens* crucial experiments in psychology. I do, however, urge that my experiment is about as close to being potentially decisive as we can get in the inexact sciences. Reflection upon the design and interpretation of this quasi-crucial experiment serves to illuminate some general issues of psychophysical theory, especially the notions of choice, cause, determinism, predictability, chance, and freedom that are of philosophical interest, as to both their ontology and epistemology.

It may be objected that, in evaluating such "preposterous" effects as those alleged by parapsychologists, the usual evidential standards (e.g., levels set for statistical significance tests, confidence intervals, likelihood ratios, information theoretic approximations) are inappropriate because of low prior probability on the theoretical postulates invoked in parapsychological explanation. However, I deal here with a comparison between two alleged parapsychological processes either of which would be assigned, on the received doctrines of human cognition and action, a minuscule prior probability. ("Why?" is an intriguing question I do not here consider.) I presuppose throughout that we set some limit upon the "Humean strategy" of rejecting evidence as fraudulent (or merely inexplicable) whenever it tends to prove the occurrence of an event which the received theoretical framework nomologically forbids (Price, 1955; Meehl and Scriven, essay 17, this volume). Thus, I shall assume that we are willing to entertain the possibility that genuine experimental findings exist which are *prima facie* of the precognitive kind, so that the theoretical decision-problem consists of choosing *between* precognition and psychokinesis. The theoretical difficulties of either interpretation are so horrendous that one can hardly employ differential prior probability as a criterion of choice between them.

The oft-claimed impossibility of an experimental test arises from an apparent arbitrary option between two directions of the hypothetical causal arrow, given the fact of extrachance correlation between the percipient's call series and the target series. Suppose, for example, the target series consists of a sequence of distinguishable physical states, such as brief illuminations of one or the other of two milk-glass plates on which are painted symbols 'L' and 'R'. These target plates are in the visual field of an agent (= "sender") who, therefore, perceives (via "normal" sensory channels) the target as input. A *prima facie* case for precognitive telepathy is then made by showing that if the percipient's successive calls "Left," "Right," etc., are displaced in time by some fixed amount, say, two seconds, as in the case of Basil Shackleton (Soal and Bateman, 1954), then the correspondence of this percipient-call series lrr . . . with the target series LRR . . . of plate-illuminations is significantly greater than chance expectancy allows. Roughly speaking, the experimental result suggests that the percipient "knows what is going to happen (in the agent's mind) two seconds in the future."

The trouble is, of course, that an alternative hypothesis exists, namely, the percipient's call "left" at a time t exerts a psychokinetic effect upon whatever physical process is being used to determine the target event L occurring at time $(t + 2)$. And however complicated this latter target-determining process is made, it seems that we could not rule out the psychokinetic possibility as an explanation. (If the target series is determined by a pre-existent random number list, *non*-precognitive telepathy or psychokinesis are both possibilities, as they are when the target series is determined by the experimenter's concurrent physical drawing of counters from a bag as the experiment proceeds.)

The experimental design I propose derives its theoretical power from three mutually reinforcing considerations. First, we determine the target series by means of events (occurring post-call) which are presumably random, according to theoretical physics. Second, we apply statistical significance tests to decide whether the target series is *in fact* random (i.e., whether physical theory is falsified by the precognitive telepathy experiment). Third, we utilize the fact that human guessing-behavior is never completely random, a generalization itself subjected here to further empirical test by statistical methods. While the randomness of our target-determining physical process is taken to have a high prior probability on grounds of theoretical physics, this is to be regarded mainly as a technological device for generating a random target sequence—an intended result which is itself to be subjected to experimental test within our data. Thus the target series' physical randomness is, while theoretically anticipated, a *hypothesis* rather than an *assumption*, as these terms are employed by statisticians.

The experimental arrangement is as follows: Having by preliminary exploration ("pre-test" pilot study) located a *sensitive*, defined as a percipient capable of psi-hitting, and an *agent* ("sender") to whom he is precognitively "attuned," we experimentally determine the optimal precognitive lead time between the percipient's call and the presentation of the physical target stimulus to the agent. This lead time, say two seconds, is a resultant of psychologically distinguishable components, such as the percipient's verbal or manual reaction-time to his own inner percept, the neurological transmission time between plate-illumination and the perceptual events in the agent's visual cortex, and a (negligibly small) time occupied by electrical transmission within the apparatus—*plus* the optimizing increment Δt that the experimenter introduces by use of a time delay relay. There is no methodological necessity to assess the values of these time-components with high accuracy. The true "precognitive lead time" is that between the agent's visual perception of the target and the percipient's cognitive event, consciously reportable or not. Neither Basil Shackleton nor Gloria Stewart experienced visual imagery of the target (Soal and Bateman, 1954), but presumably there occurs some sort of "cerebral representative event" that is the causal ancestor of the "call" response as a motor event, laryngeal or manual. Our preliminary experimental exploration aims to optimize the sum of all these time components in an average sense, such that the best mean value of the true precognitive lead time is achieved.

Having determined (in preliminary trials) the optimal call/target-presentation interval, we set up our apparatus so as to yield that average value as an experimentally imposed condition. The milk-glass targets are illuminated by independent circuits each of which is independently activated by the discharge of a Geiger counter, the wiring being such that as soon as either counter discharges, it (a) illuminates its stimulus plate and (b) prevents subsequent discharge in the other counter from illuminating the other plate. The whole system is rendered operative by an electrical impulse from the percipient's call-response (e.g., a voice-key, or one of two manual keys which he depresses to indicate his call "left" or "right" as the case may be). The Geiger counters are randomly discharged by a suitably chosen radioactive salt, such that the time-distribution of discharge latencies is negligibly small in mean and variance relative to the two-second precognitive lead time. Thus from the moment a two-second interval timer activates the Geiger counters to the moment of one counter's discharge there is a time-lapse of a few micro-seconds at most. The variance of these times can, of course, be made negligibly small in relation to that produced by the quasi-random events in the nervous systems of agent and percipient which generate variable reaction-times in all such organic performances.

According to physical theory, the radioactive decay processes utilized to generate the target sequence are completely random, both "internally" and "externally." That is, the target series LRRLR . . . is presumably random, both in its internal structure *and* in relation to all other physical events preceding it (except, of course, for the percipient's brain-state if he is genuinely precognitive).

On the other hand, we know that human guessing behavior (Wagenaar, 1972) or, for that matter, animal choice-behavior, as in a rat's successive turns to right and left in a T-maze when food-reward is available in both arms (Dennis 1939; Hilgard, 1951, p. 533) is never completely random. Even a mathematically sophisticated human subject, endeavoring to generate a random series of calls of "heads" and "tails," is not quite able to manage it, and his departures from randomness will, however slight, be statistically detectable in a sufficiently long series.

We do not, however, need to rely upon this well-known psychologist's generalization in performing the present experiment—any more than we intend to rely fully upon the theoretical randomness of radioactive decay processes. We merely utilize this prior knowledge about both series' properties in setting up our experimental situation. Then we *test* the two series (target and call) for their departures from randomness. The procedure is simple. We run the following statistical tests:

1. Is there an extra-chance correspondence between the call series and the target series under the experimental condition? (The basic phenomenon of interest—something parapsychological is going on.)

2. Does this correspondence disappear under "control" conditions? We should get "chance" results under such circumstances as these (used in the Shackleton and Stewart series by Soal and his collaborators):

   a. Clairvoyant trial, where agent does not look at the target panel, or where Geiger counters fire but plates are unilluminated.

   b. Stretching delay time, e.g., to five seconds, beyond precognitive span of percipient.

   c. Use of an agent to whom the percipient is regularly insensitive.

   d. Use of two agents, one of whom is higher in the percipient's preference hierarchy (as in Stewart series).

   e. Cross-check: Use of a target series taken from a different day's run.

These and other special comparisons are employed as corroborative evidence for the phenomenon's reality, and are (I think appropriately) rather more persuasive to most scholars than the mere "statistical significance" of call-target matching taken by itself (see Lykken, 1968; Meehl, 1967; Morrison and Henkel, 1970; Badia, Haber, and Runyon, 1970).

But now we make some further statistical tests, which, I believe, have not been suggested hitherto, and which permit a reasonable decision as between precognition and psychokinesis. We reason as follows: The ordinary tendency of the percipient is to generate a call series which departs from internal (sequential) randomness. If left to his own "normal" devices (i.e., with no telepathic influence on his guessing behavior) he will, willy-nilly, display dispositions to alternation, avoidance of very long runs, unconscious attempts to "balance things out," and similar (poorly understood) sequential constraints in calling. Some of these sequential effects have already been studied by Pratt and Soal in their re-analysis of the internal structure of Mrs. Stewart's guesses (Soal and Pratt, 1951; Pratt and Soal, 1952). Fortunately, we need not possess a complete *positive* mathematical model of the latent structure underlying these "distortions" away from sequential randomness. It suffices that we can strongly corroborate a *negative* thesis, namely, that the internal structure of the call series departs from randomness. Thus, if the radioactive decay processes are physically random, the probability of target L occurring at any given position in the target sequence remains at $p(L) = \frac{1}{2}$ regardless of whether the just-preceding target value was L or R. Whereas even if the human subject's call were at most affected by the just-preceding call but not by any calls farther back (Markoff process), his transitional probabilities would differ from those generated by radioactive decay. In actuality, of course, the Markoff model is inadequate for human guessing, which characteristically manifests transitional probabilities that are dependent upon states more than one step backward in the series.

Now if the percipient's internal tendencies are away from randomness, while the radioactively-generated target series remains wholly random, *the statistical effect of precognition will be to shift the call-series in the direction of greater (internal) randomness*. That is, to the extent that a nonrandom association exists *between* call-series and target-series, and the latter is wholly random but the former is not, the random character of the latter influences the former to be more random than it would otherwise be. The "normal" psychological factors operative in human guessing will still tend to interfere, as Soal showed in the case of Mrs. Stewart. Thus, for example, her hit-rate is significantly lowered on the subset of targets that are identical with just-preceding calls (or, therefore, just-preceding targets). Hence, the randomness of the call series should be intermediate between the (purely random) target series and a call-series not constrained toward randomness by telepathic influence. This reasoning leads to further statistical tests:

3. Does the target series deviate significantly from internal randomness on control trials? (If physics is true, it had better not!)

4. Does the target series deviate significantly from randomness on the experimental runs? (If psychokinesis is the explanation of extra-chance hit-rates, this should occur; and theoretical physics may have to be modified by pressure from a strange evidentiary source, i.e., psychological research.)

5. Does the call-series shift significantly away from internal randomness on the control trials? (It should, if percipient is precognitive on the effective trials.)

If these statistical tests come out as expected, we should, I think, reject psychokinesis and opt instead for precognition as the theoretical interpretation. Consider the argument in its full force: We have a target series which should be internally random according to physical theory, and which should not be influenced by anything the percipient does, says, or thinks two seconds prior to the target-determining event (radioactive decay). As expected, the mathematical structure of this sequence is unaffected by whether the agent is in the system, what the percipient calls, etc. On the other hand, the mathematical properties of the percipient's calls *are* influenced by the target series, but only on "experimental" runs. It would seem to be a rather straightforward decision as to "what is influencing what," since the target-series' statistical properties are invariant with respect to both the call-series and our experimental manipulations, whereas the call-series' properties *are* dependent upon these arrangements, and the mode of their dependence is to shift toward conformity with the (always-random) target series. There are few more clearcut bases for decisions concerning "direction of causality" than this.

In information-theory terms, we argue from an increase in call-series entropy to the conclusion that the call-series is the dependent variable, since the target series possesses maximum entropy, the nontelepathic (control) series has the lowest entropy of the three, and the target-series' maximum entropy remains uninfluenced by experimental manipulation.

Fortunately, it is not relevant here to expound the statistical details of entropy measurement in guessing sequences, let alone to adjudicate persisting disagreements about the best way of doing it, a task for which I am not fully competent. For nonpsychologist readers acquainted with thermodynamics, it should be noted that most information theorists from Shannon (1948; Shannon and Weaver, 1949) on have (perhaps unfortunately) used the term 'entropy' to designate a quantity that is analogous to, and in some circumstances formally and contentually identical with, the mathematical expression called 'entropy' in thermodynamics, except, alas, for a minus sign. Let p_i be the probability of an event of kind i in an event sequence, such as the probability of a coin toss showing H, conditional on the preceding toss having shown H. The reference class ("collective") is all tosses that are preceded by a toss H, and p_i is the relative frequency of H in that collective. Then the first order "entropy," or "uncertainty" of such a sequence is measured by the general information theory formula $H = \Sigma p_i \log_2 p_i$. The conventional base 2 for the logarithm arises from a stipulation that a single "bit" of information is transmitted when we resolve an uncertainty as to the occurrence of one or the other of two equally probable outcomes. The ratio of the observed uncertainty to the maximum possible uncertainty H_{max} (given the number of alternatives) is the *relative uncertainty*, and its complement $1 - H/H_{max}$ is called the *redundancy*. In analyzing the entropy statistics for a sequence of calls, departures from complete "disorder" may be detected at different levels of complexity, such as a p_j of event H in the collective defined as "coin falls immediately following a triadic pattern of events *HTH*." So the general entropy and redundancy formulas can be re-applied at each possibly significant order. For a large number of alternatives and strong intrasequence dependencies this will lead to the number of required computations increasing at an exponential rate. However, the research on human guessing of alternatives in general, and psi-guessing in particular, indicates that intrasequence call dependencies ("constraints") do not extend forward by more than four or five calls, so that the transitional probabilities of a particular call conditioned upon the preceding sequence can be adequately handled by studying pre-call blocks of one, two, three, and four precedent calls. When we go backward beyond five previous calls the earlier history of the call sequence becomes irrelevant in computing the probability associated with a particular call. The information measure for a sequence of four calls can be written recursively as $H_4 =$ H(tetragram) $-$ H(trigram), the H(trigram) similarly in terms of H(digram) and so on. (See Attneave, 1959, p. 23, Table 1 and adjacent text.)

To explain this somewhat by example, suppose a human guesser were capable of generating a completely random series and one which was unbiased with respect to the two alternatives. Then Formula 1 above will have the value $H = -pi$ $\log_2 p_i = 2$, which is also the value of H_{max} for the limiting case of two equiprobable alternatives, and the redundancy is zero. If, instead, a human caller generated a Markov process, such that while the overall probability of calling R or L was unbiased (so that the first order redundancy remains zero), he tended to avoid repetitions so the probability of calling R drops from .5 to, say, .4 when he has just called 'R,' then the redundancy computed for a one call precedent block as the basis for a conditional probability of inferring the next call would yield an entropy value $H = -\Sigma p_i \log_2 p_i = -(.4 \log .4 + .6 \log .6) = .97$, which, given the maximum entropy $H_{max} = 1$ for the dichotomous case, yields a redundancy R = .03.

Considering all possible "types" of 4-call blocks as immediate predecessors from which the conditional probability of the instant call is to be estimated, we have $2^4 = 16$ distinguishable kinds of blocks, and the intrasequence constraints involved in the psychology of human guessing behavior are considerable. Thus, for instance, in a completely random series the redundancy is zero and the probability of calling 'R' remains one-half regardless of whatever has preceded it in the sequence (as is presumably true of the radioactive decay generated target sequence in our experiment). Whereas the human guesser, in addition to generating a somewhat reduced incidence of homogeneous blocks of 4 (i.e., he avoids tetragrams of type RRRR), will also have an excessively shy avoidance of following whatever small number of such (RRRR) blocks he does generate by still a fifth call 'R.' So that if we identify, in a long series of thousands of guesses, all of the (RRRR) precedent blocks and then examine the relative frequency with which the successor call for these (RRRR) blocks is another R, we will find it is markedly less than one-half. Despite existence of recursion formulas for deriving uncertainties of various orders, there are some irksome statistical problems in information theory, such as the unpleasant fact that the maximum likelihood estimate of uncertainty is not unbiased in Fisher's sense (see, e.g., Frick, 1959; Luce, 1960, p. 46). Monte Carlo approaches to these problems would surely suffice, but the important point for purposes of the present discussion is that the good sensitives like Stewart and Shackleton were able to maintain fairly stable rates of psi-hitting for months at a time running hundreds of calls per night to generate many thousands of calls. We are not dealing, as in much of the information-theory research on language with paragraphs or words in which our numbers are in the scores or hundreds; we are dealing instead with many thousands of events. For that reason the analytical deriviation of "precise" statistical significance tests, which has been overdone in social science anyway (see cites of Lykken, Meehl, *et al.*, *supra*) is not important. A simple unsmoothed graph showing the redundancies for preceding blocks of 1, 2, 3, and 4 calls plus application of ordinary chi-square statistics (despite the relatively low power of chi-square) would, with this kind and mass of research materials, be pretty sure to yield dramatic "statistical significance" if anything worthwhile were taking place along the lines herein theorized.

If, in a sequence of events, the character of event E_{i+n} at position $(i + n)$ is influenced by the character of event E_i at position i, that is, there is an effect carrying over n steps, we may wish to measure the average *amount* of such influences for that displacement over a long sequence. A convenient rough statistic for that purpose is the "coefficient of constraint" (Newman and Gerstman, 1952; Attneave, 1959, pp. 35–37; Luce, 1960, pp. 58–59) which takes the value zero when the events are independent and goes to unity as the $(i + n)$th event is uniquely determined by its predecessor event i at n steps removed. An increase in the internal disorder of a percipient's call sequence could be easily detected simply by calculating the Newman-Gerstman coefficients for, say, all five displacements from $n = 1$ to $n = 5$, comparing the values for experimental and control (non-psi-hitting) runs.

My former colleague, Dr. Harold L. Williams, points out that the information-theory formalism may not, despite its obviousness when the internal entropy of a sequence is the object of study, be the best method for approaching this problem, and suggests the use of autocorrelation and cross-lag correlation methods instead. My competence to exposit these briefly is even less than I have with respect to information-theory formulas, so I hope it suffices to say that one can compute the correlation coefficient (of which the so-called phi-coefficient for a four-fold table of dichotomous values is a special case algebraically) between the attribute of a binary event and the corresponding attribute in the event preceding it. Over a sequence of such events this correlation coefficient answers the question, "To what extent does a call tend to match or not match its content with the immediately preceding call?" If we are comparing call events with call events rather than call events with target events, we are correlating a variable with itself, hence the term 'autocorrelation.' When the event being autocorrelated with event e_i in the sequence is an event at position $(i - 1)$ we have an autocorrelation of "lag one" or "displacement one." If we were to set up a four-fold table and compute a phi-coefficient in which the horizontal axis is the call in question and the vertical axis represents the content of a call two steps back, we have an autocorrelation $\varphi_{i(i - 2)}$ of displacement 2, and so on. If one plots the autocorrelations as a function of the displacements, the various statistics of this graph, called the *autocorrelogram*, provide another way of representing the internal relationships of a sequence. For example, the autocorrelogram of the radioactive target sequence is flat at $r = 0$ for all displacements, since none of the radioactive decay events has theoretically (again assuming physics is correct) any influence upon any other Geiger counter-determined event in the target series. While the various distribution properties of the autocorrelogram are sensitive to certain changes (and, according to some, involve less dubious assumptions than information-theory statistics), it is my understanding that call dependencies upon various kinds of immediately preceding N-grams involving dependency structures of higher orders would not be reflected adequately in the autocorrelogram. It may be that some combination of information-theory formalism with autocorrelograms extracts the necessary information, but I do not attempt to discuss those questions here.

It is clear that whether these statistical relationships exist or not is a contingent matter, that the experiment could have the outcome described above. Such a result would support the precognitive as against the psychokinetic interpretation. It is hard to imagine anyone's admitting such empirical data, and agreeing that they were paranormal, but insisting upon the psychokinetic view of them. There are, however, some knotty problems about the quantitative aspects of merely stochastic constraints, which do permit the concoction of ingenious *ad hoc* hypotheses to preserve a psychokinetic interpretation. These will be discussed below.

What then are we to make of the philosophical objection to the idea of pre-cognition, namely, that it is analytically excludable on the basis of the semantics of the term 'causation'? I conceive three broadly "philosophical" objections that might be voiced against employing the notion of backward causality. The first is the familiar Oxbridge complaint that what we *mean* "ordinarily" when we say that an event E_1 causes an event E_2 (I grossly simplify the terrible complexities of causal talk for the present purpose) includes, as a matter of common usage, the idea that the alleged cause E_1 precedes in time the alleged effect E_2. As to this objection, I confine myself to saying that the question of what most people would ordinarily mean by a quasi-technical term if they were to analyze their usage (which they don't and usually can't) is to me a matter of thundering uninterest. I have no objections to somebody who has that interest pursuing it, although I agree with Sir Karl Popper that the surest path to intellectual perdition is worry-ing or quarreling about words and their meanings. In any case, when we deal with such scientifically abhorrent and philosophically obscure matters as telepa-thy and psychokinesis, reliance upon what somebody supposes to be "ordinary usage" as a means of adopting an optimal technical vocabulary for scientific and philosophic analysis seems to me preposterous.

A complaint deserving of more respect is that if we allow the verb 'to cause' in sentences of the form "E_2 causes E_1," where E_2 occurs at t_2 and E_1 occurs at t_1 ($t_2 > t_1$), we permit assertions that, while admissible standing alone despite their oddity in vulgar speech, turn out to involve us in contradictions and para-doxes when taken together with the total body of systematic received usage among scientists and philosophers.

A third objection, perhaps subsumable under the second, takes the form of specific thought experiments propounded by objectors to the idea of precognitive telepathy and therefore can be conveniently treated separately as a technical *sci-entific* problem. This is the objection that "empirical contradictions" will de-velop, in the sense that if one permits himself to speak of the kind of backward causality implied by the notion of precognitive telepathy, experimental designs are easily conceivable which lead to apparent absurdities in the predicted results.

As to the second objection, my philosophical colleagues in astronomy and physics inform me—and I do not have the competence to do other than accept what they say on authority—that in most of physical theory the noun "cause" and the verb "causes" are not commonly employed in a technical sense anyway, and that most (not all) equations of theoretical physics do not indicate the "causal arrow's direction." In any case, it would seem reasonable to suggest that anybody discussing *scientific* interpretations of causality in the special domain of telepathy research would have made it sufficiently clear what subject matter do-main he was operating in, and a couple of sentences of explanation and warning would be sufficient to alert us that we ought to be prepared for some odd (= unfamiliar) usages given the special nature of the empirical subject matter under consideration.

The only interesting objection of these three is the third one, which alleges the possibility of "experimental contradictions" (to speak loosely). But in order to discuss it, we must further explore the question: "Just what is it about the experimental setup in the Shackleton research that would lead one to postulate the kind of backward causality implied by the phrase 'precognitive telepathy' in the first place?" I shall first discuss this from a standpoint of the concrete experimental situation, relying on a more or less common-sense, garden variety scientific understanding of the so-called causal handle function; and then I shall reexamine it ontologically rather than epistemologically, i.e., from the standpoint of Omniscient Jones. I believe that an adequate analysis of the situation requires adopting O. J.'s perspective, but I shall not press that point, which I think will be evident to the reader at the end of our discussion.

What led investigators Soal, Goldney, Bateman et al. to invoke the notion of precognitive telepathy on the basis of their experimental results? Despite the philosophical complexities that appear upon reflection, at first blush the argument is simple and straightforward. What we find is a nonchance correlation between Shackleton's recorded guesses and the objective target series, whether that latter is defined by a page from a random number table (selected by Professor C. D. Broad the afternoon preceding the particular evening's experiment) or determined by a physical randomizing process carried out during the course of the experimental run, to wit, one of the experimenters' drawing a counter from a bag of counters on which are stamped appropriate symbols designating the five target cards to be telepathized. What do we find on analysis of the experimental results? We find that Shackleton's extra-chance matching of the target series ("hits") consistently occurs when the target series is defined as the symbol that will be perceived by the agent ("sender," human subject from whose brain/mind system Shackleton is picking up the telepathic impulses postulated) two seconds subsequent to Shackleton's recording his guess. Now the role of this event, the agent's perception (by "normal" visual means) of the target image, in the experimental arrangement is not arbitrarily chosen by the investigator's whim, but flows from the statistical findings. That is, we discover that Shackleton can consistently "receive" from some agents, and consistently cannot receive from others. Further, suppose that, unknown to Shackleton (and, apparently, not subconsciously telepathizable by him!) we insert a "pure clairvoyant" trial in the course of an evening (that is, a trial in which the counters are drawn, or the second experimenter in the other room takes note of the random number table before him and touches the appropriate target card, but the target cards are laid face down, or are covered up, or the agent keeps his eyes shut and does not look at them when touched); so that if Shackleton were to score a (non-lucky) hit he would have to be scoring it either (a) via telepathy involving the experimenter (who, as it happens, is not a successful agent for Shackleton) or, alternatively, (b) without the intermediation of another living brain but directly apprehending the target object or the random number series (i.e., pure clairvoyance rather than telepathy). Under these pure clairvoyance conditions, Shackleton consistently drops to chance level in his hit rate. Third, if we stretch out the time lag between Shackleton's guess and the agent's perception event from the quasi-optimal two-second time lag to, say, a time lag of five seconds, Shackleton also drops to chance level. What do experimental findings of these kinds add up to? They indicate that the event E_2, which is the "adequate agent's" normal visual perception of the target card, plays a crucial role in the total experimental situation; and if that agent event E_2 does not occur, or occurs too far forward in time, Shackleton's telepathic powers cannot function successfully. If we omit the oddity of the time relationships and the inherent strangeness of telepathic influence of any kind, and simply substitute neutral letters for the events involved, we would have a fairly simple and ordinary kind of scientific inference from experimental data, namely: It turns out that a certain event E_2 has to take place in order for another event E_1 to occur; hence, the necessary event E_2 is assigned a crucial causal role in the system.

The experimental inconsistency objection, which I believe was first propounded to me by Professor Gilbert Ryle during a session of the Minnesota Center for Philosophy of Science in the 1950s (but I am not sure of this so do not wish definitely to attribute it) runs as follows: Suppose we assume that the percipient does precognitively telepathize the two-seconds-in-the-future psychophysical state of the agent's brain/mind. Then we develop a kind of experimental paradox by devising simple physical arrangements that will falsify all such precognitions. The possibility of such an experimental arrangement guaranteeing the falsification of the percipient's purported precognitive knowledge is then taken as a *reductio ad absurdum* of the precognitive concept, somewhat in the same way that God's foreknowledge of human free action has been held by some to involve a self-contradictory notion, inasmuch as by not doing act A which God purportedly foreknew, I could falsify his foreknowledge and hence genuine human freedom is held to be incompatible with divine omniscience. One could easily devise a simple experimental arrangement that would falsify Shackleton's precognitive guesses. For instance, instead of permitting Shackleton to write or vocalize his calls, we require him to depress an appropriately marked key. In the two-target case I am here considering for simplicity, he depresses a right telegraph key with his right hand for the call r (corresponding to target R, the right-hand glass plate illuminated in visual field of agent) or a left telegraph key with his left hand if he precognizes that the left plate target L is about to be illuminated. Then we wire up the apparatus at "cross purposes," so that whenever Shackleton precognizes r, the plate that will be illuminated two seconds in the future before the agent's eyes is instead target plate L, and conversely for the precognitive call L. Of course such an arrangement "fixes things" not merely so that Shackleton will perform at a chance level, but so that he will perform with perfect error. (We could presumably modify the setup carefully so as to bring him down to a chance hit-rate—although if this experimental effort at a fixed quantitative *reduction* failed, that would be a most interesting finding.) While the cross-rigging possibility of falsifying precognitions is initially distressing to one who accepts the genuineness of precognitive telepathy, I do not think it ought to be so. My simple answer is that what this thought experiment (one which we hardly need to perform because we know what will happen!) proves is that it is possible to set up an experimental situation in which the phenomenon of precognitive telepathy will not (i.e., cannot) be manifested, even by a usually sensitive percipient. But such an experimental possibility does not contravene the genuineness of precognition in the normal experimental situation. In order to get any phenomenon in the scientific laboratory you have to arrange the apparatus and the subjects in such and such ways, ways that do not require violation of *any* natural laws in order for the desired effects to occur. The precognitive-falsification experiment shows that it is possible to prevent Shackleton from being precognitive by *yet* another means besides the familiar devices of inserting too long a delay, using an agent to whom he is not sensitive, and requiring him to perform clairvoyantly. Other interferences no doubt exist but have not been tried because they are not interesting (e.g., injecting him with a massive dose of sodium pentothal, or occupying his brain with the simultaneous carrying out of competing complex mental operations). If we assume that the ordinary laws of physics are not violated psychokinetically under the conditions of the thought experiment, what it amounts to is merely that no experiment can produce an effect which is counternomological, i.e., that all effects in the laboratory must instantiate the nomologicals, whether on dualistic or monistic premises about the ontology of things. If the only way a "normally precognitive sensitive" could successfully achieve a precognitive hit would be by psychokinetically violating the laws of physics that are relevant to the functioning of the apparatus being used, then, of course, it follows that either he will not be able to perform precognitively, or that the laws of physics require modification. (I set aside here the important question of whether physics as it stands asserts, or implies, or presupposes, that its present list of kinds of forces is complete; and, if not, whether adding a new psychoidal force, capable of countervailing other familiar forces, as electrostatic and magnetic forces were found to countervail mechanical or gravitational ones, should be viewed as modifying the *old* laws, or merely augmenting them). This turns out, unless I am mistaken, to be a rather unexciting thought experiment, because it really derives its paradoxical punch from the initial oddity of precognition; whereas the essential substantive point shown by the thought experiment is that a phenomenon which violates laws of nature will not occur. There are a number of ways to prevent somebody from being telepathic, and cross-wiring happens to be one of them. So much for the alleged experimental paradox.

Assuming that I have made a *prima facie* case in favor of the introduction of precognitive telepathy and hence the postulation of an instance of backward causality, I turn now to the theoretical ontology of this situation as seen by Omniscient Jones rather than by the incompletely informed human investigator. Without prejudging any substantive issues as to the metaphysics of mind, upon which I myself have no settled opinion (and intend, so far as possible, not to introduce into the present discussion) it will be notationally convenient to settle on an expression for designating the "normal, nontelepathic physiological laws of brainfunction" which are operative in the precognitive telepathy experiments both in the cerebral processes of the agent and in those of the percipient. For example, the agent's image of an elephant in the Shackleton series has as its immediate causal ancestor the "normal" visual input received by his retinal receptors when he looks at the elephant target card designated by the experimenter, whose designation of that card is in turn determined "normally" by the experimenter's inspection of the random number table (or the counter drawn from the bag). Similarly, on the percipient's side we may assume the operation of the "ordinary, nontelepathic" influences that jointly determine verbal guessing behavior in such situations, the most important of which is probably the pattern of the immediately preceding guesses. The total configuration of causal chains whose confluence eventuates in a particular percipient's guess without the alleged precognitive telepathic influence would be taken, on deterministic assumptions, to instantiate the set of psychophysiological laws traditionally listed under such familiar rubrics as "sensation," perception," "association," "short-term memory," "alternation effects," "perseverative tendencies," and the like. In the agent's case, his perceptual event E_2, barring low-probability pathological aberrations which we shall exclude here (e.g., hallucination, schizophrenic drift out, *petit mal* attack) is determined completely by his visual input from the momentarily presented target card. The nontelepathic psychophysiological laws involved in either the agent's perceptions of the target or the percipient's call (when not telepathically controlled) I shall for brevity lump together by the one covering expression 'phi-nomologicals' and an event that instantiates them (and requires no confluent contribution from psi-influences) I shall call 'phi-determinate.' It will be convenient for present purposes to adopt the Feigl (1967) identity-thesis concerning the mind body problem and shorten "psychophysiological" to "physiological," although again I do not believe that this simplification, here adopted for expository purposes, prejudges the philosophical issues I wish to discuss. Radical metaphysical dualism will be mentioned as a counterhypothesis later in the paper, but we cannot discuss everything at once.

There is a problem about the "normal" and "para-normal" (= telepathic) calls, especially because nontelepathic calls may also be "hits" (correspond to the target card) despite the absence of any telepathic causal influence. The frequency of such nontelepathic hits is given by the "chance" probability calculations, the refutation of which constitutes the positive result in such experiments. We, therefore, focus upon the telepathic hits, which we cannot do presently as human investigators but which we can do in the role of Omniscient Jones. The causal situation can be seen most clearly for this purpose by imagining perfect performance on the part of the percipient, and asking how this flawless matching of the call series with the target series could be brought about by the instantiation of the phi-nomologicals in both events E_1 and E_2.

If no para-normal effects occur, so that there are neither psychokinetic influences running from E_1 to E_2 nor precognitive telepathic influences "running backward" from E_2 to E_1, what is the nomological situation in the eyes of Omniscient Jones? Well, it is not physically contradictory, but it is, to say the least, strange. We have a guessing event E_1 instantiating the normal phi-nomologicals of human quasi-random choice in which everything from the fried eggs percipient Shackleton had for breakfast to a momentary itching of scalp dandruff or a passing thought concerning an overdue debt owed him by one of his photographic studio customers and, most important, *the state of his cerebral cell assemblies consequent upon the short-term effects of his immediately preceding calls*, phi-determines the instant call as, say, '1.' Two seconds hence, the left-hand target plate is illuminated in the visual field of the agent, and the determination of this target element as being L is a nomological consequence of the experimenter's visual perception of an odd number rather than an even number at position i, j, k in the random number table that Professor Broad brought to the experiment that evening, having selected it randomly in the course of the afternoon.

That the two causal series terminating in events E_1 and E_2 have certain recent and remote overlappings in the sense of shared links in their causal chains (e.g., both Broad and Shackleton were acquainted with Professor Soal because the latter had the intention to get in touch with them; or, more remotely, suppose both Broad's and Shackleton's ancestors arrived in Britain during the Norman Conquest) is useless for explanatory purposes, because these kinds of causal overlaps are not of such a character as to account for the matching between the percipient's call at time t_1, and the agent's normally produced perception at time t_2. Essentially we are in the same situation as a biologist investigating the influence of vitamin deficiency on a sample of guinea pigs. The biologist would hardly consider it an adequate causal explanation of a correlation between vitamin deficiency and weight loss if someone were to remind him of the existence of just *any* sort of "causal overlap" between the chains of causality terminating in his selective administration of vitamins on the one hand and the weight loss on the other. That both sets of animals were purchased from the same supplier, that the purchases were made by one and the same investigator with a particular experiment in mind, that the vitamin supplements and the lab cages were delivered on the same day by the same campus delivery employee, and the like, are all examples of causal chain overlap useless for explanatory purposes, because they do not explain the specific covariations which the experiment brought to light. So that if, in the Shackleton series, we were in a position to say that both events E_1 and E_2 are perfect instantiations of normal nontelepathic nomologicals, and that the relevant properties of the events correlate in an extra-chance way, we would confront a frightening scientific mystery. It looks like what we would in ordinary language refer to as a 'coincidence,' but the statistics show it can't be a coincidence in the sense of a chance-based, "nonlawful" set of occurrences. The only hypothesis that occurs to one is some sort of Leibnizian pre-established harmony, in which the two chains of causes eventuating in C. D. Broad's choice of a random number page and leading to Shackleton's guess are so constituted as to generate hits, the basis being The Great Jokester's suitable assignment of initial conditions of the cosmos before the Lemaîtrean "Big Bang."

An objection which I hear repeatedly from critics, but which I must have some sort of blind spot in understanding (and hence difficulty in responding to) is, "Well, it appears that certain events are mysteriously correlated with other events; but why would you want to postulate backward causality? That is, how do you *know* that the causality doesn't go in the usual (= forward) direction?" I will meet this objection as clearly as I can, despite my awareness that I don't fully understand what motivates it. The events in the agent's brain are, by hypothesis, taken to be explained without residue by the "ordinary" (nontelepathic) phi-nomologicals of physics, physiology, and psychology. That is, in order to understand why the agent's brain is in the "L-perceiving state" at time t_1, given our utopian psychophysiology, we need only invoke (a) the laws of physics as regards the transmission of light through the illuminated target screen in the agent's experimental cubicle, (b) the laws of geometrical optics regarding the transmission of this light to the agent's eyes, (c) the laws of optics and sensory physiology concerning the events transpiring within the agent's eyeball (including the activation of a certain geometrical pattern of rods and cones on the agent's retina), (d) the configuration of neural impulses through the second cranial nerve and the topological mapping of the retinal form within the lateral geniculate bodies, and so on back to Brodmann's Area 17 in the agent's visual cortex. *Nothing that happens in the brain of the agent requires any reference to events in the brain of the percipient, or in anybody else's brain, in order to be explained.* The agent's perceptual brain-event is adequately explained by reference to the visual inputs he is momentarily receiving from the illuminated target plate L. If I can explain this event without residue, meanwhile avoiding any mention of any other organism's cerebral occurrences, and, in particular, avoiding any mention of the percipient's psychophysiological state or his calls, there is no affirmative reason why I ought to invoke the events in the percipient's brain as causal contributors to the events in the agent's brain. Isn't this how we generally "do science"? On the present hypothesis (and this conjecture is one we make in the light of our finding that the agent's brain event is a necessary part of the experimental setup if the percipient's brain is to map the target series to an extra-chance extent) it turns out we cannot explain (= quasi-derive, "make understandable," give a causal account of) the cerebral events going on in the percipient's brain without making a reference to the agent's brain event with which it is correlated.

Consider this *experimentum crucis*: Our utopian psychophysiologist might be able to manipulate directly the agent's brain events so that despite the agent's receptors being currently exposed to the illuminated target plate L, his brain event was sometimes an R-event instead, that is, the kind of brain event normally associated with a retinal input from the right-hand target plate (see essay 7, this volume). What would happen? We today are not utopian psychophysiologists, but even our currently available molar behavior data from Shackleton's series tell us what we can confidently anticipate would happen under those circumstances. We expect that the percipient would show an extra-chance "hit" rate when the target series is redefined as *cerebral events of the agent*, rather than being defined by the sequence of target plate illuminations. Reason? Since Shackleton is telepathic rather than clairvoyant, we know that his brain events do not follow the target but instead they follow the agent's brain-events. The point is that unless we have done something special to interfere with the normal perceptual-cognitive machinery of the agent's brain, the agent's brain states are isomorphic with the objective target series. So what we have is an extra-chance correlation of two series of events, where one series of events can be "explained without residue" ignoring the other series, *but not conversely*. This is our reason for postulating backward causality.

Despite the intuitive plausibility of the above argument about "constraints" imposed upon the target or call series by the fact of psi-hitting, it is, unfortunately, impossible to develop strictly algebraic constraints without additional theoretical assumptions, except for some interesting (and perhaps critical) extreme cases to be discussed below. One must be careful in formulating these intuitions because of the merely stochastic character of the relations obtaining between the molar events of a target illumination and a percipient's call. From the qualitative statements that A is correlated with B and that B is correlated with C, one cannot infer directly that A is correlated with C. We know that ordinary correlation coefficients (such as the Pearson r) permit a surprising "play" in such a system, so that variables x and y can each be correlated to a considerable degree with variable z and yet be zero or negatively correlated with one another. There are quantitative restrictions at the extremes, however, which are easily derived from the partial correlation formula and the fact that $r_{xy.z}$, like any other Pearson r, lies between -1 and $+1$. Thus, for example, if $r_{xz} > .7$ and $r_{yz} > .7$ we know that $r_{xy} > 0$—a rather weak restriction. In considering what further causal and statistical assumptions are required in explicating one's intuitions about mutual "constraint'' between the call and target series, we need some simple notation. Suppose the target events are coin flips, hence either a *head* or a *tail*. We designate the target events by capital letters and the call events by corresponding lower case letters, and indicate serial position in the two series by subscripts. Since our percipient is either precognitive or psychokinetic, we set the call subscripted 'i' into scoring correspondence with the target subscripted 'i,' although experimentally the event designated by the target subscripted 'i' occurs two seconds later in time than the call event subscripted 'i.' So the symbols 'H_i,' 'T_i,' 'h_i,' and 't_i' designate target events (heads and tails respectively) in general position 'i' and the call events of heads and tails corresponding to those target events, that is, precognitive of them by two seconds or so in Shackleton's case. A target "block" of, say, 4 target events preceding the target event subscripted 'i' will be represented by a capital letter 'B_i,' so that 'B_i' means the set of 4 target events preceding the target event with subscript 'i' in the target sequence; and, similarly, a lower case letter 'b' subscripted as 'b_i' refers to the call block preceding the call at position 'i' in the call sequence. Assuming the intraserial "influence" on transitional probabilities does not extend back beyond 4 preceding calls (or targets, as the case may be), the $2^4 = 16$ possible precedent call patterns define 16 call-*types*. One of these is a call sequence of four heads preceding the 'i' call, so then $b_i = h_{i-4}, h_{i-3}, h_{i-2}, h_{i-1}$. Correspondingly there are 16 possible block-types for B_i in the target series. Conditional probabilities within or across series will be represented by the small letter 'p' followed by the usual parenthesis and slash notation. Thus, for example, the notation '$p(h_i/b_i)$' means the probability of calling a head at position i given that the percipient has just called a block of 4 calls of type j. Suppose, for instance, that in accordance with the usual bias of human guessers to avoid long runs and (unconsciously or consciously) to commit the "gambler's fallacy" of assuming that if one has just called 4 heads in what is supposed to be random sequence he ought not to call another head—a phenomenon clearly exhibited in the internal call relationships of the Shackleton and Stewart series—a call block of the type $_1b_i = (h_{i-4}, h_{i-3}, h_{i-2}, h_{i-1})$, which from here on we will designate without the subscript detail simply as "of type *hhhh*," yields a transitional probability of only $p = .1$ to call a head at position i. Suppose further that the target event probabilities are required to remain internally random and random with respect to previous call blocks, although of course if psi-hitting is to take place successfully, one cannot consistently add the further requirement that a target H_i must have a probability unaffected by the *call i*, since that would amount to saying no extra-chance success in psi-hitting is occurring.

Representing the four call × target cells of our fourfold table by the conventional a, b, c, d (these being relative frequencies so that $a + b + c + d = 1$) it is easily seen that the excess concordance owing to psi-hitting cannot exceed the smaller of the two call-rates, if the target sequence is to maintain $H = T = \frac{1}{2}$ as randomness requires. Suppose the smaller call-rate is for heads, as would be

Table 1

Targets

		H$_i$	T$_i$	
	h$_i$	a	b	a + b
Calls	t$_i$	c	d	c + d
		a + c	b + d	1

found among the subcollective of calls that are preceded by a strongly "biasing" call-block such as (hhhh). Say this conditional head-call rate is $p(h/hhhh) = .1$ and no psi-hitting occurs. This situation is represented by the proportions in Table 2. The bottom marginals are the fixed target rates $H = T = \frac{1}{2}$ required by our random-target condition, and on the precognitive hypothesis must not be influenced by shifts in the table entries to reflect psi-hitting. Now suppose that

Table 2

Targets

		H$_i$	T$_i$	
	h$_i$	5	5	10
Calls	t$_i$	45	45	90
		50	50	100

some psi-hitting occurs, as shown in Table 3. The hit-rate is now .6 rather than the chance value .5, and has been achieved by shifting 10% of the cases from cell b → a and, necessarily (to preserve the bottom marginals of the target rates), by shifting an equal 10% from cell c → d. But we see from these tables that the hit excess cannot exceed the smaller call marginal. Put generally, the target marginal constraints require that a psi-hitting increment in the smaller concordant cell must be "balanced" by an exactly equal increment in the larger concordant cell,

Table 3

Targets

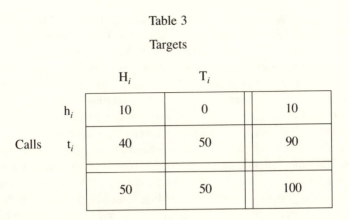

	H_i	T_i	
h_i	10	0	10
t_i	40	50	90
	50	50	100

Calls

each in turn being balanced by equal decrements in the two discordant cells. Thus we know that:

$$a + c = b + d = \tfrac{1}{2}$$
$$\Delta a = \Delta d$$
$$-\Delta a = \Delta b = \Delta c = -\Delta d$$

So $\Delta(a + d) = 2\Delta a$. Therefore maximizing $\Delta(a + d)$ is maximizing Δa. But the greatest Δa occurs when $a = a + b$ and $b = 0$. Hence, the hit-excess cannot exceed the smaller call marginal. Therefore, if some call blocks yield low transitional probabilities for a head or a tail on the next call, the overall hit rate achieved by the percipient may be higher than is reachable in the subset of calls following such "strong biasing" call blocks. This would be a situation in which the internal patterning of the call series was sufficiently great (i.e., some blocks sufficiently strong in influencing call probabilities of heads and tails) *and* the basic overall hit rates sufficiently above chance summed over all kinds of calls and call blocks, so that there was a numerical limit imposed upon the hit rates of some subsets of calls. If the high hit rate were to be maintained over all kinds of place selections, it would then have the effect intuitively inferred above of (strictly) constraining the call series in the direction of greater entropy, i.e., decreased patterning, weakened internal constraining effects.

Reflection on Tables 2–3 makes us careful lest we formulate our cross-series constraint intuitions too strongly, since it is evident that some freedom or "play" exists within the overall constraints imposed by the fixed marginals in redistributing call-target combination frequencies over the four cells of such a table. That this redistribution possibility within the constraints imposed by the marginals does not deprive the intuitive argument of all theoretical force, even if we could not find any such extreme blocks as in the tables, will be argued further below.

The simplest form of a psychokinetic interpretation would be to conjecture that the percipient exerts a fixed psychokinetic "influence" upon the target, thus deflecting its probability somewhat away from $p(H_i) = \frac{1}{2} = p(T_i)$; and that this causal influence is exerted by the instant call i upon the associated target event i and does not extend farther backward in the call or target series. If desired this hypothesis can be investigated directly (and presumably can also be experimentally realized) by increasing the time lag between successive calls. One next wonders whether the notion of a fixed psychokinetic "influence" is better captured by some linear increment or multiplicative function on the target base rate probabilities. In some situations this guess would be an important choice, but it does not matter here because the theoretical target base is $p(H_i) = \frac{1}{2}$ and multiplying this base probability by a constant and adding something is equivalent to adding something. Of course, the molar probability event may not be a linear measure of psi-influence strength and a theoretical statement about this relation could take any of many possible forms relating a molar probability to a latent variable, such as an ogive, log function, or whatever. Suppose we assume that the average psi-influence is fixed, which is not to say it is equally strong on every call (that we presumably already know is false?) but that it does not vary with place selection or with the character of the call. Thus, for instance, whatever it is that determines Shackleton to call heads at position i, the conditional probability of the target being heads, given the call h_i exerting a psychokinetic effect on the target, is not itself a function of the prior causal events that influence the *call* to be what it is. This means that we can apply the multiplication rule in computing the relevant probability, that is, the conditional probability of a target H_i given a call h_i can be multiplied by the conditional probability of a call h_i given the immediately precedent call block b_i, and these can be multiplied to get the conditional probability of a target head on the precedent call block i on this simple psychokinetic hypothesis. From this it is apparent that the character of the target at position i will not be independent of the preceding *target* block B_i, because on these assumptions the conditional probability of a call block b_i of a given type is not invariant with respect to the target block, since if it were (for all 16 types of blocks) no psi-hitting would have occurred, *either* precognitive or psychokinetic. So we see that on these assumptions the nonrandom character of the call block internal transitional probabilities, taken together with the requirement of psi-hitting which yields a correlation between target blocks and call blocks preceding call i, leads us to expect differences in target probabilities of heads and tails over the 16 types of precedent target blocks. So that the constraint upon the internal disorder of the target series intuited above follows as a consequence of the psychokinetic hypothesis, provided that this hypothesis postulates a psychokinetic influence dependent solely upon the resultant call at position i. One way of saying this is that the "influence" (in the statistical sense) of the preceding call block b_i and its associated (and correlated!) target block B_i is "mediated solely *via* the causally efficacious call event at position *i.*"

For purposes of exposition here I much oversimplify the empirical facts of psi-hitting, which appear to result from several converging kinds of influence, both intraserial (call → call) and cross-series (target ↔ call) in nature. For example, the percipient's overall bias against calling doublets (which in Mrs. Stewart's data amount to a reduction from the "chance"-theoretical doublet frequency of .2 to an observed value of only .14, see Soal and Bateman, 1954, p. 320) must interact in a complex way with "reinforcement" influences from other targets displaced -1, $+1$, $+2$, etc. Furthermore, the Stewart series reveals a significant tendency to "miss" on the *first* target of a target doublet, even though she was not significantly precognitive when the target displaced $+1$ is itself used in scoring hits. Analysis of both Stewart and Shackleton data does show that in order to score a hit on the second member of a target doublet, the percipient must deviate from his usual guessing pattern, which is the main feature I want to rely on here. Despite the complexities revealed when differently defined subcollectives of calls or targets are statistically examined, they are all, of course, findings as to *some kind of internal order*, and will, therefore, be reflected in the appropriate redundancy measures. The interested reader may consult Soal and Bateman, especially their Chapter XIX devoted to "position effects with Mrs. Stewart," for details that would needlessly complicate the argument of this paper. For our purposes here, it is sufficient to consider all (feasibly calculable) kinds of intrasequence redundancy as contrasted with the zero redundancy (all orders) expected within the radioactively generated target series. We exemplify this contrast by examining a simplified influence model where only one target event has causal efficacy (no "reinforcement" effects) and the negentropy of the call series is attributable to nontelepathic mental habits.

Suppose that the experimental outcome is that which we have intuitively considered to be *prima facie* precognitive, but that in reality the effects are causally generated by psychokinesis; what manner of psychokinetic functioning by Shackleton's brain would this supposition require? The call outcomes are extra-chance conditionally probable on the targets, this is, $p(h_i/H_i) > \frac{1}{2}$ and $p(t_i/T_i) > \frac{1}{2}$, and ditto, of course, for the inverses of these probabilities. The call transitional probabilities are highly variable over the 16 precedent call block types. The latter are correlated, although not as greatly, with their associated target block types, otherwise there would be no significant psi-hitting. But, within the algebraic constraints imposed by the numerical values of these several probabilities, the target probability does not depend upon the immediately precedent call block or target block type. Thus any association between target and immediately preceding call block is "mediated by" their mutual associations with the target block's associated call. Finally, we assume that the imagined experiment with the Geiger counters continues to show the same sort of "weak (stochastic) constraints" (i.e., a statistical relationship but not an algebraic necessity) that was observed in the actual Shackleton and Stewart series, namely, that when the immediately precedent call block is such as to lead to a strong statistical bias against a specified successor call, and that specified successor call would in its content correspond to the object target against which it is scored, the psi-hitting not only drops but, in fact, becomes significantly worse than chance. This reasoning fits our original intuitions about precognition rather than psychokinesis, because it suggests that the precognitive telepathic force is able to operate best when the recipient's brain is in a delicately balanced, marginal, "knife edge" call situation, and cannot usually countervail the very strong biasing effect against calling a "head" that is brought about by an immediately preceding call block of type (hhhh).

Despite this straightforward common-sense indication favoring telepathy as the explanation of such a statistical pattern, it is not always possible strictly to *exclude* a sufficiently tailored psychokinetic interpretation, as witness the following theoretical concoction: We imagine that Shackleton unconsciously weakens his psychokinetic force, or that he simply fails to exercise it, in the great majority of cases in which he calls t_i following a strongly biasing call block of type (hhhh), since if he exerted his usual psychokinetic force to its full effect, the target i would be strongly constrained away from randomness in the subset of target events defined by their following a "strong" call block of type (hhhh); and this would in turn generate some internal structure in the target series, since there will be an extra-chance correlation between call blocks of type (hhhh) and the associated target block type (HHHH). Furthermore, this subtle "rigging" of the effective magnitude (or perhaps a dichotomous "on or off" exercising at various rates?) of the psychokinetic force must be delicately adjusted with extreme precision in order to prevent the appearance of a statistically significant negentropy in the target series when it is analyzed over many thousands of calls. While such a state of affairs is logically possible, I invite the reader to contemplate what a jerry-built *ad hoc* theory we have here concocted. Consider: Like other human or animal subjects, Shackleton does not spontaneously generate a random series of his own calls; and we will further presume—although this ought to be systematically investigated in such an experiment as herein envisaged—that he *cannot* do so, as has been shown to be true of other human subjects, who cannot generate a random series even when they are alerted to the characteristic sources of negentropy in human guessing. Despite these disabilities, the hypothesis requires that he is nevertheless able (unconsciously) to adjust his psychokinetic force magnitudes (or proportions of dichotomous exercising and not exercising) so as to redistribute the tallies in the kind of fourfold table we have seen above with an exact preservation of the target marginals and complete sequential randomness within the target series. Why would we opt for this super *ad hoc* theoretical explanation? I do not believe one must be a strict Popperian or Lakatosian (as I am not) in order to view such a theory as content-decreasing, viciously *ad hoc*, and "degenerating."

Those who hold some variant of the received inductionist (pre-Popperian) view that recommends theoretical simplicity *per se* would presumably opt for the precognitive telepathy theory rather than the rigged force psychokinetic theory, given the complexities elaborated above. And it appears not to be merely a question of how many *ad hoc*, "artificial" nomologicals are required. There is also something counterpersuasive, although admittedly hard to spell out, about a requirement in the modulated psychokinetic interpretation that the percipient's brain must be capable of generating internal randomness via delicate adjustment of PK forces, despite the same brain's inability, in common with other mammalian species brains that have been studied in alternation contexts, to do so "directly" in the sense of randomizing the pattern of molar calls generated. We would consider it especially unparsimonious or artificial to postulate that although Shackleton cannot psychokinese without the agent's brain in the system, despite the fact that on this hypothesis the agent's brain is an irrelevancy both causally and in the scoring—nor can he generate a random series in his calls— yet he can effectively psychokinese with the agent's brain in the system and he can assure stability of the base rates and internal randomness in the target series. For those of us who are dubious about simplicity as such, for instance Popperians or Bayesians who would view simplicity as an index of theoretical desirability only by virtue of its being correlated with falsifiability or with "reasonable priors"—assuming there are any reasonable priors when psi-phenomena are the subject matter—I think the argument is fairly easy to make, although it is easier from the neo-Popperian point of view than from the Bayesian, as is usual when the priors are not quantified but somewhat vague and tacit expectations of the way the world will turn out to be. Speaking neo-Popperian, specifically Lakatosian, the argument would run thus: He who postulates precognitive telepathy is already aware, psi-phenomena aside, that call series generated by human and animal subjects display internal constraints which, in the case of "strong" pre-call blocks such as (hhhh), are quantitatively severe. Such a theoretical conjecture would lead him, if he were totally ignorant of Soal's internal analyses of the Stewart and Shackleton data, to expect that the backward psi-influence would be hard put to generate hits when the subset of calls considered was those in which the target required a call of heads and the precedent call block was of strongly pro-tail type, such as b_i = (hhhh). Without claiming this inference would be deductively tight, it would *ceteris paribus* be the expected consequence of such a precognitive telepathy theory. And a finding of lowered hit rates—in the Shackleton and Stewart analyses, actually subchance hitting for the case of five possible targets—is not only compatible with this theory but constitutes a nice further corroborator of it. *Per contra*, one who interprets psi-hitting in the (apparently) precognitive case as psychokinetic would have, so to speak, no prior affirmative reason in such a theory to expect a modulation of the psychokinetic force one way or the other; in fact, if one were asked, given such a theory initially silent with respect to variations in the psychokinetic force, how he would expect it to vary as a function of the immediately preceding call block, he might well think this would be especially strong under such circumstances. If anything, the psychokinetic force might be expected to be somewhat enhanced in favor of a target event H following a call block (hhhh), as the intra-call series then has a strong tendency for the succeeding call to be a tail. The discovery of a declining hit rate under constraint of fixed vertical margins for target base rates requires an *ad hoc* adjustment that does not increase the content and would, therefore, unless I am mistaken, be a Lakatosian degeneration.

References

Attneave, F. 1959. *Applications of Information Theory to Psychology.* New York: Holt, Rinehart and Winston.

Badia, P., Haber, A. and Runyon, R. P. 1970. *Research Problems in Psychology.* Reading, Mass.: Addison-Wesley.

Dennis, W. 1939. Spontaneous Alternation in Rats as an Indicator of the Persistence of Stimulus Effects. *Journal of Comparative Psychology* 28: 305–12.

Feigl, H. 1967. *The "Mental" and the "Physical": The Essay and a Postscript.* Minneapolis: University of Minnesota Press.

Frick, F. C. 1959. "Information Theory." in *Psychology: A Study of a Science*, vol. 2, *General Systematic Formulations, Learning and Special Process*, ed. S. Koch 611–36. New York: McGraw-Hill.

Grünbaum, A. 1960. The Duhemian Argument. *Philosophy of Science* 11:75–87.

Grünbaum, A. 1962. Falsifiability of Theories: Total or Partial? *Synthese* 14: 17–34.

Grünbaum, A. 1969. Can We Ascertain the Falsity of a Scientific Hypothesis? *Studium Generale* 22: 1061–1093.

Grünbaum, A. 1976. *Ad Hoc* Auxiliary Hypotheses and Falsificationism. *The British Journal for the Philosophy of Science* 27:329–62.

Hilgard, E. R. 1951. "Methods and Procedures in the Study of Learning." In *Handbook of Experimental Psychology*, ed. S. S. Stevens. New York: Wiley.

Lakatos, I. 1970. "Falsification and the Methodology of Scientific Research Programmes." In *Criticism and the Growth of Knowledge*, eds. I. Lakatos and A. Musgrave. Cambridge: Cambridge University Press.

Lakatos, I. 1974. The Role of Crucial Experiments in Science. *Studies in History and Philosophy of Science* 4: 309–25.

Luce, R. D. 1960. "The Theory of Selective Information and Some of its Behavioral Applications." In *Developments in Mathematical Psychology*, ed. R. D. Luce. Glencoe, Ill.: The Free Press.

Lykken, D. T. 1968. Statistical Significance in Psychological Research. *Psychological Bulletin* 70: 151–59.

Mackie, J. L. 1974. *The Cement of the Universe: A Study of Causation.* Oxford: Oxford University Press.

Meehl, P. E. 1967. Theory Testing in Psychology and Physics: A Methodological Paradox. *Philosophy of Science* 34: 103–15.

Morrison, D. E., and Henkel, R. (eds.). 1970. *The Significance Test Controversy.* Chicago: Aldine.

Mundle, C. W. K. 1950. The Experimental Evidence for PK and Precognition. *Proceedings of the Society for Psychical Research*. 49: 61–78.

Mundle, C. W. K. 1952. Some Philosophical Perspectives for Parapsychology. *The Journal of Parapsychology* 16: 257–72.

Newman, E. B. and Gerstman, L. J. 1952. A New Method for Analyzing Printed English. *Journal of Experimental Psychology* 44: 114–25.

Pratt, J. G. and Soal, S. G. 1952. Some Relations between Call Sequence and ESP Performance. *Journal of Parapsychology* 16: 165–86.

Price, G. R. 1955. Science and the Supernatural. *Science* 122: 359–67.

Shannon, C. E. 1948. A Mathematical Theory of Communication. *Bell Systems Technical Journal*. 27: 379–423, 623–56.

Shannon, C. E. and Weaver, W. 1949. *The Mathematical Theory of Communication*. Urbana, Ill.: University of Illinois Press.

Soal, S. G. and Bateman, F. 1954. *Modern Experiments in Telepathy*. New Haven, Conn: Yale University Press.

Soal, S. G. and Pratt, J. G. 1951. ESP Performance and Target Sequence. *Journal of Parapsychology* 15: 192–215.

Wagenaar, W. A. 1972. Generation of Random Sequences by Human Subjects: A Critical Survey of Literature, *Psychological Bulletin*: 77: 65–72.

Wheatley, J. M. O. and Edge, H. L. (eds.). 1976. *Philosophical Dimensions of Parapsychology*, Springfield, Ill.: Charles C. Thomas.

19

Precognitive Telepathy II: Some Neurophysiological Conjectures and Metaphysical Speculations

For expository simplicity in a paper that is philosophical rather than scientifically substantive (in the sense of seriously defending a specific neurophysiological theory about how the brain works in ESP experiments), I shall permit myself some framework assumptions about the functioning of CNS subsystems and single neurons. This will make it easier to discuss the methodological issues than if I were to invent a new "general substantive vocabulary" or—so clumsy as to be unfeasible—to set up a disjunction of alternative conjectures about brain function which would, even if wearisomely long and conceptually difficult, obviously have to be incomplete. Thus: I shall speak of 'cell-assemblies' without implying thereby everything that went into Hebb's exposition as to their structure, function, and development, but only the weaker and vaguer idea that neurons are synaptically linked together in functional systems in the general way that he sets forth in his classic work (Hebb, 1949). I shall refer throughout to neurons as the functional elements in experience and behavior control, despite currently open questions about whether what were formerly thought of as purely sustentacular or otherwise ancillary cells (e.g., glia) participate in processing information. Despite the large and complicated mass of evidence that has accumulated over the last decades indicating that information is "coded" in the CNS in other ways besides transmission of the classical spike potential along the fiber, I shall set aside such other forms as graded potentials, electrotonic coupling, amplitude changes in the spike, etc.

I think it obvious that none of these simplifications affects the methodological argument, so long as we may consistently (and, on the basis of what evidence we presently have, without flying in the face of well-corroborated experimental facts) conjecture that (a) the molar call depends upon the occurrence of classical spikes and that (b) in the causal chain leading finally to the integrated firing of motoneurons directly controlling the call, nonspike informational states and events in a final neuron C which is anatomically linked to an earlier A only via internuncial neuron B, are normally (always?) dependent upon the production of a spike in B. Finally, in order to present some speculative "micro-statistics" in relating the idea of quantum uncertain local outcomes to the molar call, we will use the idea that a relatively small number of neurons in one cell assembly, or in a functionally connected system of cell assemblies, can be "critical" or "determinative." Given suitable momentary states of the other elements in the assembly, if such and such a pattern or number of a selected group of such critical neurons fires within a specified interval, the assembly will be activated, or its activity level will exceed a threshold level of intra-assembly pulse frequencies sufficient to discharge another final common pathway neuron, or whatever the critical event farther along in the chain may be for determining the content of molar call.

The existence of what have been variously called "critical," "command," or "pontifical" neurons has been well corroborated in several species, including primates; and command neurons are believed to exist in both perceptual and motor systems of man, although in humans the evidence is as yet only suggestive (Perkel and Bullock, 1969, pp. 468–70; Rosenbaum, 1977; Rosenbaum and Radford, 1977). A "determining influence" by a relatively small number of critical neurons (e.g., 10 of them, as hypothesized in examples *infra*) is not as unplausible as it may seem to readers accustomed to emphasizing the mass action and stochastic character of CNS processes, being actually less dramatic an example of privileged element causality in neuronal chains than some that have been empirically found by neurophysiologists. For example, the complex serial integrated movements constituting the defense reaction in crayfish can be set off by stimulating a single "command neuron" fiber with a simple train of evenly spaced electrical shocks lacking phasic or patterning relationship to the output pattern (Wilson, 1970, p. 402), which pattern involves more than half the musculature of the entire crayfish body. This phenomenon was first reported as far back as 1952 (Wiersma, 1952). A single Mauthner axon in aquarium fishes commands the sudden "jump" elicited by the stimulus of tapping the glass. In the mollusk *Tritonia* there exists a command neuron in which a *single spike impulse* suffices to elicit a long sequence of swimming movements involving much of the animal's musculature. The command fibers controlling crayfish abdominal posture affect large sets of muscles, in some cases requiring the mediating action of 300 motor neurons. Grillner and Shik (1975) have found command neurons in the cat. Schiller and Koerner (1971) found evidence that single neurons in the superior colliculus of monkey are responsible for triggering different eye movement saccades. (A corresponding many-one situation on the "input" side is also known to exist, e.g., in the visual system of the cat, see Hubel and Wiesel, 1962.) We may perhaps consider the existence of command neurons as merely the "logical" extreme case of that hierarchial organization that is ubiquitous in the CNS of complex organisms. So there is nothing antecedently improbable, and surely nothing outlandish or counternomological, in the imagined circumstance that 10 critical neurons "determine the call." All these neural elements need not, of course, be found in the same cell assembly. Each of them might play its "pontifical" role in each of 10 non-overlapping cell assemblies, or cell assembly systems, which nevertheless converge upon another "pontifical" internuncial neuron which in turn "commands" the molar call subsystem of the brain.

Taking the "total cerebral event" as a reductive complex (Reichenbach, 1938, pp. 105–11; Meehl, essay 2, this volume, p. 71) of its part events, and taking the unit of analysis as the synapse (although it might very well be more "micro" than this, such as the quantity of disturbance at a specific locus on the synaptic scale induced by the arrival of a presynaptic spike potential at that terminal knob, with its resultant release of transmitter substance), it seems clear that the configuration of local outcomes, and, I repeat, the cerebral event that is explicitly definable as a reducible complex of these, can, on the occasion of any given cerebral event generating a molar "call," *whether a hit or a miss*, be one of three kinds:

1. *Phi-determinate*. This means that each of the local events instantiates the "ordinary neurophysiological laws," no psi-influence by the agent's brain-event being required.

2. *Phi-violative*. This means that one or more of the local events fails to instantiate the ordinary neurophysiological laws. There is an ambiguity, as always, about when a "law of nature is transgressed," because one must explain whether he is treating the received system of nomologicals as causally complete. Thus, the laws of mechanics, if taken to be a complete empirical system for inanimate bodies in motion, seem to be "violated" or "transgressed" when a magnet deflects a steel ball rolling on a table; but when electromagnetic forces are added to the explanatory system, then the Newtonian laws relating acceleration to imposed forces are preserved, because the nomological network of mechanics is now supplemented by the nomological network of electromagnetic theory. For the telepathic situation we could find that our physico-chemical laws concerning the activity of neurons do not suffice to subsume (explain, derive) some of the local events, and for present purposes it does not matter whether we choose to view that as a case of "transgression" or as a case of "incompleteness." Either way, something is happening at the synapse which finds no place in the received law network of neurophysiology, the singular synaptic event is not an instantiation of the received phi-nomologicals, but instead constitutes an "exception" to them.

3. *Phi-indeterminate*. This means that some (conceivably all) of the local events are known to be quantum-uncertain, *again without reference to any telepathic influence*, and the configuration of those which are quantum-uncertain is such that for some proper subset of calls we may speak of the total cerebral event, which determines the cognitive character of the molar call, as quantum-uncertain.

It must be stressed that the identification of these three subsets of the entire set of calls can be made without reference to the psychokinetic or precognitive telepathic relation. To identify these distinguishable subsets of calls it suffices to examine the configuration of Shackleton's brain at the moment in terms of the received "non-psi" laws of optics, visual perception, physiology of the speech [= "tokening"] mechanism, etc.

There is an irksome problem of distinguishing between a quasi-determinate state and a significantly quantum uncertain state, analogous to the Second Law of Thermodynamics' being, strictly speaking, inconsistent with the statistical mechanics of the kinetic theory of heat. It can be shown in pre-quantum physics that "once in a while" dropping an ice cube into a boiling cup of tea should result in further heating up the tea. And physicists do not worry about the influence of quantum uncertainty upon, say, Hooke's Law applied to a bathroom scale. Some outcomes in the apparatus a physicist uses to study processes that are "small enough" so that the size of the quantum of action becomes relevant could, nevertheless, not occur with theoretical probability sufficient to require even *pro forma* mention when the physicist reports his experiment. For example, when I use macro-apparatus to study beams of electrons or patterns of photons, I do not for that purpose concern myself with the question whether closing a switch might, for quantum uncertain reasons, fail to activate the apparatus. The quantum theory does not impel us to worry much about the accuracy of a scintillation counter.

The clean, simple case would be such that when the cerebral system is phi-determinate, the hit rate for a standard 5-symbol ESP deck is exactly 1/5 but that when the system is phi-indeterminate, a target "hit" is scored. This would fit our expectations that the received physical nomologicals are all right, and that the physical$_2$ (Meehl and Sellars, essay 6, this volume) isolation of the percipient's brain from the receiver's brain by experimental means has been successful. The target series is internally random, and is also random (on any sensible theory) with respect to the call series. So we have two presumably independent causal chains that happen to have been brought together in this laboratory by some experimenter but the *content patterns* of the two sequences have no rational connection with one another.

We then conjecture that in the subset of cases which independent examination of the percipient's momentary brain state shows to be quantum uncertain—so that there exists a subset of possible configurations of local quantum uncertain synaptic events for which the resultant molar consequence *would* be a hit—then the realized outcome on all such occasions *will* be a hit. On this theory, there is a simple numerical relationship between the observed hit rate and the proportion of phi-determinate calls as follows:

Let p_d = Proportion of calls phi-determinate. Then the hit-rate is

$$p_h = p_d(_dp_h) + (1 - p_d)(_ip_h) \text{ where } _ip_h = 1 \text{ as hypothesized,}$$

$$= (1/5)(p_d) + (1 - p_d)$$
$$= 1 - (4/5)(p_d)$$

Thus, if Shackleton ran about 30% hits (i.e., 10% extra-chance) we could infer that .875 of his calls were phi-determinate. If our utopian neurophysiologist had a sufficiently accurate micro-method of estimating the proportion of phi-indeterminate calls, and combined this value of $_{\text{d}}p_h$ with the theoretical postulate of "perfect psi-hitting when possible" to yield a predicted molar hit-rate, corroboration of that predicted hit-rate would strongly corroborate the postulate.

While for expository purposes I have spoken of a quasi-perfected "utopian psychophysiology," it should not be supposed that this requires direct micro-level ascertainment of each of the large (but finite) set of local synaptic states immediately preceding a specific call. The notion of an advanced physiology of perception and psycholinguistics does not imply that by a combination of theory and super instrumentation we could answer all possible "local" questions about an actual ongoing cerebral state (without dismantling the recipient's brain or interfering with his cerebral processes), any more than an advanced theory of thermodynamics demands that in order to apply the mathematics of Maxwell, Boltzman & Co. the theoretical physicist claims to be able, *or needs to be able*, to say what each individual molecule has as its instantaneous components of momentum. The rate at which psychophysiology and neurology are developing today, especially since the introduction of microelectrodes permitting both local stimulation and local unit response readings, makes it thinkable that within a generation and probably less, it will be possible to combine our molar behavior statistics on simple guessing tasks with detailed knowledge of the neuroanatomy and neurophysiology of the cerebral subsystems concerned—not, be it noted, ascertained upon the subject currently under molar experimental study—such that upper and lower bounds on the theoretical incidence of phi-indeterminate calls could be calculated by putting together this general knowledge with the molar statistics of the particular percipient's calls. Thus we would not require that thousands of microelectrodes be stuck into various of Shackleton's individual neurons by opening his skull in order to infer important neurophysiological statements from his molar guessing behavior during non-psi-effective calls (e.g., when the agent is one from whom he is routinely unable to receive, or when the lead time for the target event is pushed beyond four or five seconds into the future, or when a pure clairvoyant run is inserted during the course of the evening). We could, in utopian psychophysiology, put together what we know of cerebral physiology and psycholinguistics and information theory plus the internal sequential properties of his molar-level calls so as to infer, say, that approximately 87% of his calls are phi-determinate. This inference makes no reference to his telepathic powers, nor to any properties, either on specific call occasions or in the long run, of the target series. This number, in quasi-utopian psychophysiology, would be computable solely by reliance on Shackleton's nontelepathic call series' properties and our general knowledge of how the visual perception and verbal systems work. The latter theory will be very complicated and based mainly upon micro-level data collected on brains other than Shackleton's. Given the estimate of around 13% phi-indeterminate calls, we extrapolate that value to the phi-effective condition for Shackleton—a conjecture, but a testable one. We then conjoin a further bold conjecture, to wit, that the psi-influence is infallible, i.e., that whenever the psi-influence *can* act on a phi-indeterminate brain state, it *does* so in such a manner as to produce a precognitive hit. Substituting these values in the above formula, we conclude that the expected hit rate should be about 30%. Corroboration of this numerical prediction corroborates our conjunction of conjectures.

Returning to the three possibilities listed above (phi-determinate, phi-violative, phi-indeterminate) how would we view each of them if a clear psi-hitting trend were in evidence? I shall say something about each but focus mainly on the third. I daresay most of us would find the first one stupefying in its spooky implications. It would mean that despite psi-hitting, the percipient's brain events run off in accordance with the ordinary micro-laws of physiology and chemistry when the agent is effectively in the system just as they do when the agent is not effectively in the system. The paradoxicality of this language does not reflect a real inconsistency, since "effective agency" means a conjunction of two things,

a. Extra-chance call/target correlation (= psi-hitting); and

b. Correlation of (a) with selected agent's presence, eyes open, target illuminated, time lag short enough, etc.,

neither of which contains any reference or implication as to percipient's local synaptic events. The circularity here is only apparent, since we are able to ascertain fairly stable properties of agents and of the precognitive lead time which we can then subsequently manipulate in the course of the experiment to eliminate successful precognition of the target series. So, Case 1 means that Shackleton's local brain events are determined in the usual neurophysiological way, by such things as the fluctuation in his blood sugar or a mosquito biting him or the movement of a curtain in his peripheral vision or—most important—persistence, alternation, and other more complex intraserial effects belonging to the field of psycholinguistics. When we employ an agent to whom he is consistently insensitive, or extend the precognitive lag to five seconds or more, or insert a pure clairvoyant call (in which the Geiger counters discharge but either the stimulus plates do not light up or the agent keeps his eyes shut), the same closed system of neurophysiological laws explains the pattern of Shackleton's local micro-events, and hence the molar call outcome, as when the agent is "effectively in" the causal system so that the call series tends statistically to match the target series.

One hardly knows what to say about such a state of affairs, unless theological explanations are permitted. This would be pre-established harmony with a vengeance. The Great Jokester has so arranged the cosmos that the ordinary (non-psi) physico-chemical nomologicals, together with the initial conditions of the Big Bang, entail that Shackleton's brain-states are correlated with the agent's brain states (provided that certain time relations are satisfied) but that not all human beings can appear in the role of pseudo-agents for this purpose. It boggles the mind, and I shall not discuss it further here. I realize that the causal, statistical, and metaphysical issues involved in a depth-analysis of this "crazy coincidence" argument are from some viewpoints still controversial, and must content myself here with referring the reader to Grünbaum (1974), Popper's reply (1974b), his section 30 on debates with Schroedinger (1974a, pp. 108–109), and the references cited in those sources. Popper's (1956a) example, reversing a movie film depicting the disturbance of a pond's surface owing to dropping a stone, makes the "coincidence" point well. "It would," as he says, "demand a vast number of distant coherent generators of waves the coordination of which, to be explicable, would have to be shown, in the film, as originating from one centre. This, however, raises precisely the same difficulty again, if we try to reverse the amended film" (Popper, 1956a). Again, in replying to a criticism of the first paper, he says that to explain the reversed film sequence "we do not wish to accept the coherence of the generators as *an ultimate and inexplicable conspiracy of causally unrelated conspirators*" [my italics] (Popper, 1956b, p. 384). Despite its metaphorical character, the "ultimate and inexplicable conspiracy of causally unrelated conspirators" expresses the point beautifully. Popper attributes the same argument to Einstein in a 1909 paper, not read by me.

(Would it support Malebranche in a way he could not easily have imagined? A nontheological occasionalism that rejects the telepathic influence explanation has been held by some scientific contemporaries, as, e.g., Paul Kammerer, the unfortunate Lamarckian who postulated a kind of law of [noncausal but extrachance] coincidences. See Appendix 1, "The law of seriality," in Koestler [1971, pp. 135–43], and Chapter 3 "Seriality and synchronicity" in Koestler [1972, pp. 82–104].)

In this connection, it is perhaps worth noting that the usual contemporary view of miracles as genuinely counternomological differs importantly from that held by (some) ancient theologians of the three Semitic religions, in that extraordinary occurrences working "in behalf of" God's people or prophets, and revelatory because of their aberrant causal structure when viewed at one level of analysis, were considered to be nevertheless "lawful" in some deeper sense. See e.g., Goldman (1975, p. 122). I have heard a conservative Christian physicist, relying on modern knowledge of the *koine* Greek phrase for heliacal rising (mistranslated in Matthew 2:2 KJV "in the East") argue from astronomical calculations that the Star of Bethlehem was a conjunction in 7 B.C. of Jupiter and Saturn in the constellation Pisces which would have been easily visible to the naked eye and in a direct line from, say Sippur through Bethlehem. Such a dramatic celestial display would have symbolic significance to Babylonian astronomers (and to Jews residing in Babylon) because Saturn was the "Jewish planet," Jupiter the "royal planet," while Pisces was the zodiacal sign of the West (to Chaldeans) and of Messiah (to Jews). Hence this "miraculous sign" was not "miraculous [= counternomological]" in post-Newtonian Faustian man's usual sense. Such a view, of course, fuzzes up our theological distinctions between God's modes of agency in general providence, special providence, and miracles. It involves a physical occurrence entailed by nomologicals + initial cosmic conditions which event, given human cultural beliefs, has a "special meaning"—a kind of astronomical/sociological preestablished harmony (see Keller, 1956, pp. 345–55). I am not suggesting a theological explanation for precognitive telepathy of Case 1 kind, but I think it interesting to note that what I called *supra* "mind-boggling" and "pre-established harmony with a vengeance" is not without historical and contemporary examples outside the parapsychology domain.

The second possibility becomes extraordinarily difficult to explicate in any rigorous way, and I have found myself unable to do so with sufficient precision to make it worthwhile, so I content myself with an analogy. The ordinary phi-nomologicals of (utopian) received neurophysiology suffice to account for Shackleton's cerebral events when he is not functioning as a telepathic sensitive. When he is functioning as a sensitive, with an agent effectively in the system, it is as if the required "new telepathic nomologicals" exert a molar-discernible effect on 13% of the calls. This could be rather like the conjunction of electromagnetism to Newtonian mechanics, where theoretically a child's magnet retards the downhill progress of a big steel truck (as, in gravitation theory, we must hold that by crooking my finger I slightly deflect the course of the planet Jupiter) but in order to lift the truck one needs a gigantic electromagnet. In Case 2 the cerebral system is not quantum-indeterminate, nor does it display any "miracles" (in the sense that nomologicals are "violated"), but the situation is one requiring inclusion of a *new kind of force* (or influence, or field, or whatever) which operates concurrently with the ordinary phi-nomologicals of brain function and which, under some circumstances, cannot suffice to influence the molar outcome. Part of the reason for this "insignificant influence" is that the molar outcome is not finely graded. In fact, any ordinary variations in response topography such as faint differences in the loudness or assurance with which Shackleton makes a precognitive guess, are not recorded; so that every call is either a hit or a miss, no matter how "weak" or "strong" it might be if studied in more detail. And, of course, there could be variations in the cerebral event that are not reflected in measurable features on the molar outcome, a possibility which can easily arise in a variety of ways.

The third possibility is the more interesting and the one I would like to develop at somewhat greater length. It does not matter for our purposes here whether whatever genuinely quantum uncertain event-types exist in the functioning of the human cerebral system are at the "whole synapse" (i.e., involving the "optional transmission" postulated by Lorente de Nó, where 'input' refers to all of the incoming events over the post-synaptic cell's synaptic scale), or whether what is genuinely a quantum uncertain event, considered singly, is whatever happens in the post-synaptic cell membrane directly under a particular synaptic knob when the latter emits a transmitter substance, generates an electrostatic field, or whatever. It will be convenient expositorily to refer simply to a "synaptic locus," keeping in mind that the post-synaptic neuron's optional transmission, while it might itself be "determined" by the configuration of all micro-events at the various loci on its surface, could nevertheless be quantum uncertain as a consequence of the quantum uncertainty of the several more localized synaptic scale micro-events.

I assume that physics can attach a reasonably clear meaning to quantum uncertainty of a local event (such as a discharge or not, or a spread of cell membrane disturbance timed and patterned sufficiently to get the cell over a spike threshold) and I shall speak of this condition ontologically in most of what follows. However, one may ask preliminarily how utopian psychophysiology could conclude that there was quantum uncertain optional transmission? It seems that three lines of evidence, converging on the conclusion of local quantum uncertainty, would be corroborative. First, as is already to some degree the case in the present state of neurophysiology, knowledge of the local micro-processes would suggest this conclusion on theoretical grounds, inasmuch as the distances, times, and energies involved in the transaction are sufficiently minute so that the quantum of action has relevant order of magnitude. Already in the 1930s a theoretical argument of this form was advanced persuasively by Hecht together with experimental findings that a half dozen photons suffice to produce a detectable retinal response. Second, experimental study of the convergence of local influences, whether measured or experimentally produced by us, could show that these synaptic input manipulations, while (like changing slit size in the diffraction experiments) altering the statistical parameters, cannot bring the post-synaptic consequence under strict nomological control, i.e., they can raise or lower the transmission probability but a basic "optional transmission" persists. Third, despite some bias away from a strict 50:50 "chance" of spiking once having assigned the parameter, we might discover that the internal sequential pattern of the cell's firing or not firing was random.

It seems necessary to differentiate between the (theoretically uninteresting) situation where the total cerebral event resulting in a behaviorally identifiable molar outcome ("call") is a random micro-consequence of the configuration of local quantum uncertain synaptic states, in the same sense that the distribution of steel balls at the end of a finite trial on a Galton Board is the outcome of accumulated and dependent random results when each marble strikes various nails on the way down; and the theoretically interesting case in which the molar cerebral event, while still a "resultant" or "configural consequence" of the local synaptic event, including some that are quantum uncertain (while others may not be on a given call), is not such a random result but shows a "configural selection" with respect to the precognitive target. We must also forestall any important element of stochastic slippage between those local synaptic events that are, so to speak, "decider" events and the subsequent events in the chain of cerebral occurrences that direct the controllee tokening machinery. That is, we avoid concern about phenomena like aphasia, Freudian mis-speaking, non-Freudian slips of the tongue, and the like which are not of interest for the present purpose. It is not necessary to assume that no such phi-determined aberrations in the subsequent causal sequence ever take place, but presumably they are relatively rare in this situation; and in any case their influence should be to reduce psi-hitting to the extent that they have a statistically discernible effect in the molar call series. Hence, it seems a harmless simplification for present purposes to assume that there is quasi-complete determinism obtaining between the "deciding" mechanisms of the brain and the tokening mechanism that produces the vocal or written molar call. If the molar call is a quasi-nomological consequence of the configuration of local synaptic events on those occasions in which Shackleton's brain is on the knife-edge, that is, when the call is phi-indeterminate, and, further, if the distribution of local synaptic events, no matter how considered with respect to one another or with respect to the previous sequence of events of the same loci, satisfy a random statistical model by all of the usual tests of randomness, sequential and configural, then I shall refer to the molar cerebral event as determined by a *quantum uncertain cascade*. Roughly, this phrase means that "everything is random with respect to everything," including all configural features, in the sequence of patterns of local events. However, we note that three kinds of uncertainties may jointly obtain, *and strictly so*, despite what might be a good — even a perfect — rate of psi-hitting:

1. Each local synaptic event is quantum uncertain, as explained above.

2. Each local synaptic event is completely random with respect to the remaining synaptic events, taken singly and collectively.

3. Each local synaptic event is random with respect to the target.

Nevertheless, each single synaptic event may have a stochastic inferability (and some of them, under some occasions of the total cerebral state, may have perfect inferability) *when we consider jointly the pattern of other local events and the target*. If Shackleton's brain scores a hit whenever a hit is scorable, configural laws would obtain such that a disjunction of conjunctions of locally uncertain synaptic events can be necessitated by a requirement that the target must be successfully "hit" by the molar call.

A more interesting conceivable case, which is also somehow more plausible, perhaps because the molar guessing behavior has the properties of a constrained stochastic process, is one in which the configuration of quasi-nomological phi-determinate cerebral systems active at the moment of the percipient's call renders the brain rather like a "biased coin," that is, where the cerebral system is quantum uncertain but the distribution of probabilities is not symmetrical with respect to the molar character of the call h or t. It seems antecedently an improbable hypothesis that all cerebral situations that could *possibly* (i.e., by at least one configuration of quantum uncertain local synaptic outcomes) yield a specified molar call, say, "heads," would be so constituted as to the locus and potential causal influence of each of the quantum uncertain synaptic events that these events, when considered collectively, would make either molar outcome equally probable. The molar guessing behavior suggests the contrary, to wit, that whether there are no radically indeterminate cerebral events in the eyes of Omniscient Jones, or whether, as we are currently conjecturing, there are *some* radically quantum uncertain cerebral events, the probabilities in either case are not routinely symmetrical for all molar call outcomes but tend instead to have varying degrees of statistical bias. How would this "biased brain state" be constituted at the utopian neurophysiologist's micro-level?

Consider the hypothetical case of 10 "critical neurons" each of which is in a quantum uncertain state (to fire or not to fire) during the causally effective time interval just preceding a molar call. For simplicity we will assume that each *individual* quantum uncertain synaptic event has $p = \frac{1}{2}$ (hardly the way it would work, but that refinement makes no difference in the present argument). Suppose further that the condition for a molar call of character h is that any 9 of the 10 quantum uncertain critical neurons should fire. So if two or more fail to fire, the call will be t. If this configural event is internally random and the psi-hitting phenomenon is of psychokinetic origin, what do we expect? The probability of a molar call h is the sum of the last two terms in the binomial expansion $(\frac{1}{2} + \frac{1}{2})^{10}$, that is, the molar probability of a hit in such a situation is $p < .011$, so that considering the subcollective of such calls, almost 99% of them should be "tail" calls. On a straightforward application of the psychokinetic theory of psi-hitting, if we define the subset of targets that follow two seconds after calls arising on this type of cerebral configuration, we should expect to see a distinct, and possibly quite pronounced, psychokinetic "influence" shifting the target distribution away from H:T symmetry toward $p(H) << p(T)$. If, on the other hand, the target marinals of our psi-hitting table remain fixed at approximately $\frac{1}{2}$ for this subset of targets defined by the cerebral constellation of the associated calls, it means either that the hit rate must decline or, at least, that the hits which occur must be heavily concentrated on successful calls of tails. On the precognitive telepathy interpretation, we expect that there will be a nonrandom configural selection under such cerebral circumstances, so that the relative frequency of 9:10 *h*-favorable quantum uncertain firings will *not* be correctly estimated by summing the last two terms of the appropriate binomial, that is, the character of the target as a head or a tail influences the selection of the configuration of local synaptic outcomes so as to produce the usual high hit rate. It would of course be especially interesting if, as postulated *supra*, the configuration of local outcomes should *always* be such as to generate a hit whenever the immediately preceding phi-determination of the total cerebral system gave rise to a momentary pattern of quantum uncertain synaptic states such that at least one selection of the possible configurations of local outcomes would generate a molar call to match the target. But such an extreme case as this is not required to make the argument. It suffices to show a departure from the pure chance expectancy over the 1,024 possible patterns of local outcomes at 10 quantum uncertain synaptic loci. The combination of a stable symmetry of target marginals with systematic distortions from a random distribution of the configuration of quantum uncertain local outcomes argues strongly against psychokinesis in favor of precognitive telepathy. Here again, the defender of the counterhypothesis is in the position of saying that when the agent is in the system, etc., the percipient's brain delicately adjusts the psychokinetic force so as to maintain the hit frequency while also maintaining symmetrical target marginals in the fourfold table. Such an interpretation does not flow naturally from the simple psychokinetic conjecture but is content-decreasing and *ad hoc*, in addition to the oddity mentioned earlier that the percipient's brain "knows how" to generate psychokinetically a random sequence in the target but not in its own guessing pattern. I have described the situation ontologically and without reference to what kind of utopian neurophysiological micro-techniques would be needed. But I take it as obvious that there is a molar counterpart to these micro-cerebral circumstances, consisting of what has already been observed in the actual analysis of the Shackleton and Stewart series about the difficulties of psi-hitting following certain strongly biased pre-call blocks.

There is a philosophically fascinating "configural selection" possibility that I plan to develop elsewhere but will briefly adumbrate here by way of conclusion. We need a bit more terminological stipulation to consider it, which I hope extends, without confusing, the brain-event semantics proposed *supra*. If the momentary stimulus situation conjoined with the cerebral state consequent upon the immediately preceding events (especially the preceding call sequence as far back as it is influential) nomologically entail a particular call, the system may be described as *micro-determined*. Suppose that this condition does not strictly obtain, but that the joint firing probabilities for all the elements in the relevant cell assemblies are such that the molar character of the instant call is nearly certain (in the same sense that the experimental physicist considers it "certain" that an ice cube will be melted when dropped into a cup of hot tea, despite kinetic theory's showing that there is a non-zero probability that the ice cube will get colder and heat up the tea). Then the instant call will be said to be *quasi-micro-determined*. If neither of these conditions obtains, then the system at the moment of the instant call will be said to be *micro-uncertain*. If the cerebral system is quasi-micro-determined, and the nomologically necessary (or overwhelmingly probable) molar outcome matches the target, the system will be said to be *hit-determinate*. If the system is micro-uncertain and there exist one or more possible quantum uncertain patterns at the indeterminate synaptic loci such that, if any one of these outcome patterns were to occur, the outcome would constitute a target hit, the system is described as in a *hit-possible* state. Then there could be evidence for a "systematic molar outcome-selected cerebral process." Such evidence would consist in showing, over a series of hit-possible occasions, that the configural selection of positive and negative fire/not fire outcomes at the relevant quantum uncertain synaptic loci is *not random with respect to the distribution of possible molar call outcomes*, despite the two statistical facts that:

a. Local quantum uncertainty obtains at each synaptic locus w.r.t. its electrochemical input and surround; and

b. The internal sequence of outcomes ("fire/not fire") at each single synaptic locus is random.

Such a state of affairs, in which a nonchance predictability of a local quantum uncertain outcome is possible only by reference to the rest of the configuration when the latter is related to the molar outcome as being a "hit" or a "miss" with respect to the target, would be a rational basis for saying, roughly, "The entire cerebral system 'chooses' freely so as to effect a certain result." If this reasoning is essentially sound, I shall further argue that the usual positivist dichotomy which says, by assuming reducibility of the system function to the component functions, that a person's mind-brain must either be *determined* or *act randomly* ("capriciously," "by chance") is a false dichotomy. It is a natural conclusion for a materialist-reductionist to make, and for most of us reared in the Western scientific tradition it seems "obvious." But it is a mistaken dichotomy when dealing with a system whose parts are quantum uncertain but whose configural events lead nomologically to a molar outcome that can be mapped onto a molar target. The development of this argument, of great interest to moral and juridical philosophy, I must leave to a separate paper (essay 4, this volume).

My colleague Professor Emeritus Herbert Feigl urged upon me (some 20 years ago, in the early days of the Minnesota Center for the Philosophy of Science) a criticism which he does not currently make, but which is plausible enough to be a likely thought of numerous readers, so I shall attempt to deal with it. The criticism is that one ought not to refer to an event as being "indeterminate," whether the indeterminacy is of a quantum-mechanical kind or has the sort of (debatable) indeterminacy that Sir Karl Popper and others allege to hold even in classical physics (Popper, 1950, 1966) if it is theoretically predictable given sufficient knowledge of the conditions. That the configural cerebral event can be correlated with an external event (e.g., psi-target) despite complete randomness both within the local part-event sequences and zero correlation between each local sequence and the target, while surprising to many on first hearing, is easily shown (Meehl, et al., 1958, Appendix E, "Indeterminacy and Teleological Constraints," pp. 328–38, whose line of reasoning I still consider sound after 20 years, although I no longer hold to the Lutheran theology there providing context; essay 7, this volume, pp. 200-201; essay 2, this volume, fn 27, pp. 95-96). In psychometrics the formal situation has been called 'configural scoring' (Meehl, 1950, 1954, pp. 132–33; Horst, 1954). The general principle is that of asymmetry in the relationship between "pairwise independence" and "total mutual independence" among a set of event-variables, the former being a necessary but not sufficient condition for the latter (Cramér, 1946, p. 162; Feller, 1957, pp. 114–17, the theorem being due to S. Bernstein). If we have m synaptic loci and associate them with the (molar) target event, these $(m + 1)$ event variables are not mutually independent if psi-hitting occurs, but they may nevertheless be pairwise independent; so each synaptic variable may be independent of the target variable.

But Feigl's revised objection is not aimed at Bernstein's paradox. Feigl objects to calling the local events "indeterminate" if they are in any way lawful, and surely if they are, in principle, predictable. In the Geiger counter experiment as I have imagined it the event is not predictable, if we believe the received physics, because the configuration of local synaptic events that generates a molar call is, according to the analysis supra, a function of the quantum-uncertain and hence radically unpredictable radioactive decay process two seconds in the future. So 'predictable' is not the right word, if we have in mind forecasting in time by a quasi-Omniscient Jones, who (unlike God) is "inside time" but who (unlike us) has a precise and complete knowledge of the nomologicals and the momentary conditions of the system. If physics is true, quasi-Omniscient Jones cannot predict Shackleton's micro-cerebral events because those events are chosen on the basis of their being a member of the proper subset of configurations of local synaptic outcomes that would generate a molar "hit," and a molar "hit" is not defined the moment before these events occur because the determinative event in the backward causal chain has not taken place yet and is itself, according to physics, radically indeterminate.

The notion of configural selection, where the cerebral subsystem seems "as a whole" to determine one or more quantum-uncertain local events teleologically, could theoretically be made testable in the strong sense by technological advances in single-unit micro-electrode procedures (currently available) that are not so far out as to be science fiction. Suppose the neurophysiologist of A.D. 2000 could identify and analyze pontifical cell-assemblies in telepathic subjects. He could then, at will, micro-stimulate specified subsets of neural elements in such assemblies. Hence he could select varying firing patterns on different trials, such that only certain (pre-calculable) outcomes at the "free" loci would produce a molar "hit." If the transmission probabilities remained stable at each "free" locus, but the patterns of free locus events were strongly influenced by the joint (target + micro-stimulated neural) events—in the extreme case, completely determined by them—such experimental manipulability would strongly support the configural selection hypothesis. Thus, the experimenter selects a pattern F_k of local firings to be brought about by microelectrode single unit stimulation, such that the assembly can "work" to yield a molar call 'l' iff free elements (a, b, c) all fire. It turns out that they *do* so iff target turns out to be L, not if target is R. The experimenter has, so to speak, "manipulated the *abc* events conditionally"—he has employed his microelectrodes to produce F_k which assures that "if L, then l" will be true. Since the long run statistics show that F_k does not influence L, we infer that it operates by influencing l.

But someone may say that an event, though unpredictable, should not be characterized as "indeterminate' if it fits into a nomological system—never mind whether some of the independent variables' values that must be plugged into the laws relied upon happen, in strange cases like precognitive telepathy, to occur at a subsequent time. I do not believe any substantive issue hinges upon the semantics of this objection. If somebody wants to say that the macro-cerebral event is unpredictable but determinate, being a disjunction of a large number of quantum-uncertain micro-events which configurally suffice to generate a molar call that *will* constitute a hit against the target *when the target appears* (so that after the target has appeared we can retrospectively assert that the local outcomes were determined by the character of the target), I have no objection. It remains interesting and important that the individual local outcomes are quantum-uncertain, and that there is no logical or mathematical inconsistency in saying that they are individually quantum-uncertain from the standpoint of their immediate physical surroundings even if we could say (given "idealized psi-hitting") that *one* among the proper subset of local configurations which would suffice to generate a molar hit, whenever a molar hit is possible, will be "chosen." I remind the reader again that the target sequence is internally random, so that even if there were no way in which the many-one correlation of quantum-uncertain local synaptic events with molar call outcomes could permit the sequence of single call events to be wholly random with respect to the properties of all target events and their patterns, they could still be perfectly random, call by call, as a sequence, since they are only required to "match" the target sequence which is itself internally random. It is important to get a clear picture of the nonrandom, systematic relationship involved here, otherwise one fails to see the almost unique character of the kind of causal relation being discussed. What a utopian physiologist knows is that the supernormal hit rate comes about because, on all occasions when the phi-initial conditions of Shackleton's brain are such that given the phi-nomologicals, there exists at least one configuration of locally quantum-uncertain synaptic outcomes that would generate, as a molar consequence, a call that matches the target two seconds in the future, such a call will be made, i.e., such a configuration of local outcomes will "occur." What would we have to know in order to derive this configuration? We would have to know the target, and the quasi-determinate cerebral constraints, in order to ascertain which configurations of locally quantum-uncertain outcomes would generate a molar hit; but we would still not be able to infer which of these hit-effective configurations will be (*or was*) realized. With knowledge of the micro-details (such as even utopian psychophysiology might lack as regards the single occurrence) the evidence for this "choice" would be statistical in nature, and would presumably have to refer jointly to the molar outcome and the target, because from the standpoint of probability theory, any one configuration is as likely as any other.

I speak of this above as being "almost unique," because such configural principles as the Pauli Exclusion Principle (which, as I understand it, is not derivable from more fundamental physical postulates), or the famous two slit experiment, seem similar to our setup, in that a sort of "gestalted" characteristic of a system is referred to in excluding or predicting something about one of its components. That reference must be made to the agent's brain and not to somebody else's brain in Calcutta 20 years ago is comparable to the fact that the Pauli Principle refers to elementary particles belonging to the same system, so that an electron on the earth can have the same four quantum numbers as an electron in Alpha Centauri belonging to a different system, or to another cadmium atom adjacent to it.

It is worth noting that Hume, in setting out the conditions for something being a cause, thought it necessary to mention a conjunction of three things: (a) contiguity, (b) succession, and (c) constant conjunction, without, so far as I can discern, raising the question how one could even begin looking for (b) and (c) without (a). That is to say, in canvassing the possible candidates for "causes" of a certain event or events of a certain kind, the very meaning of 'invariable sequence' involves the other two notions, since we do not search for possible causal ancestors among *all* events however remote in space-time, and we would have no rational basis for including or excluding such if we did fecklessly begin with a blind search throughout the whole space-time continuum. (I once heard a physicist confronted with an anti-Copenhagen query "You don't assume that the elementary particle recorded by your scintillation counter is in a physicist's lab setup in Berlin, do you?" reply "Well, *some* of it is." Does he really mean it?)

It is interesting to consider the analogy between the two slit experiment and the telepathic experiment as here analyzed, because physicists generally assume that there is nothing about that slit through which the photon passes (especially during those low intensity variants in which no two photons are likely to be in the apparatus at the same time) that can be influenced by the presence of the other slit or by other photons passing through it on other occasions. There is nothing "local'' about the condition of slit 1 traversed by Photon Abner that is changed by what Photon Beulah did a micro-second ago in passing through slit 2. And the post-slit momenta of Abner and Beulah are each quantum-uncertain. But the statistical distribution of post-slit momenta as revealed by the photographic scatter pattern is inferrable from knowledge of the total experimental arrangement. The physicist does not feel obliged to ascertain what other macro-apparatus arrangements exist in another building across the campus, let alone one at Cal. Tech. while he is experimenting at MIT! In the precognitive telepathy set up, what I am sketching out is a theoretical interpretation in which there is a rock bottom configural postulate that refers (somewhat vaguely) to an individual human brain in a precognitive telepathy experiment, and then, having made that preliminary molar identification, goes on to say that if there exist possible configurations of local synaptic quantum-uncertain outcomes such that the macro-consequence of those outcomes will be a call that constitutes a hit, one of such will be "selected." I do not know how I would go about discussing attenuated forms of this that would arise if we start moving into the brains of chimpanzees or excised subregions of Shackleton's brain and the like, but colleagues who are informed about the current state of physics assure me that in that respect the relation between micro-events analyzed quantum-theoretically and the experimental situation described classically still remains somewhat puzzling. As I am given to understand, the sometime allegation that the classical laws are *derivable* from the quantum-principles is not based upon valid proofs except for very special cases. Let me hasten to say that I do not intend in the least to invoke the less than satisfactory state of quantum mechanics as an *argumentum per obscurium*. But since I have invoked the conjecture by Schroedinger, Jordan, Eccles, Hecht, and others as to genuine quantum-uncertainty at some micro-level of neural function, it seems appropriate to point out that an inherently and irreducibly *configural* statement of the kind I use: "If a hit is possible . . . ,'' does have analogies in quantum-theory outside the human telepathic domain.

Summary

There appears initially to be a kind of "explanatory symmetry" between precognitive telepathy and psychokinesis, such that a statistical correlation observed between cognizing events in a percipient's cerebral system and the target events cognized could, in principle, be explained either by forward causality (call → target: psychokinetic influence) or by backward causality (call ← target: precognitive telepathy). In this paper I have argued that it is nevertheless possible to design an experiment which would tend strongly to discorroborate one in favor of the other. The experiment relies conjointly upon the randomness of radioactive decay processes and the nonrandomness of human guessing behavior. A target series generated by radioactive decay processes should according to theoretical physics display no internal organization (departure from randomness, negentropy, sequential dependencies) and the information theoretical formulas for various orders of redundancy should over the long run yield maximum entropy on a target series so generated. By contrast, the calling behavior of the human percipient will display significant redundancy, with or without the occurrence of significant psi-hitting. Significant psi-hitting should be reflected, on the psychokinetic hypothesis, in a distortion away from maximum entropy within the target series. Whereas if the causal system is one of precognitive telepathy the target series entropy should be unaffected by the presence/absence of the percipient, operation of an effective/ineffective agent in the system, or by the occurrence/nonoccurrence of significant psi-hitting. It is predicted on the precognitive telepathic theory that the entropy of the call sequence during successful psi-hitting should be increased. These predictions can be made with considerable confidence on the basis of present available molar behavior data, without further refinement in our detailed knowledge of the micro-functioning of the cerebral system. Taking that presently feasible experiment as a jumping-off place, further conjectures are elaborated on three possible ways in which precognitive telepathy might take place in the cerebral system, and the notion of a *gestalted selection of patterns of quantum uncertain synaptic events* is delineated. One consequence of this analysis is rejection of the customary positivist dichotomy between psychological determinism and completely random (capricious, ''chance'') behavior in favor of a conception that involves genuine choice or selection by the total cerebral system, a selection teleologically defined by reference to target matching. On this conjecture, the local synaptic events are individually quantum uncertain, but the statistical properties of selection among possible configurations of such events are incompatible with an interpretation that makes the molar outcome simply a result of independent and random synaptic events (''quantum-uncertain cascade''). While sufficiently complicated *ad hoc* theories might still preserve a psychokinetic interpretation, it is suggested that such interpretations would constitute a content-decreasing, degenerating research program. For some quantitative experimental values of psi-hitting it is shown that a psychokinetic theory would be numerically incompatible with preservation of entropy in the radioactive decay sequence by constraining the target marginals.

References

Cramér, H. 1946. *Mathematical Methods of Statistics*. Princeton: Princeton University Press.

Feller, W. 1957. *An Introduction to Probability Theory and Its Applications* (2nd ed.) New York: Wiley.

Goldman, S. L. 1975. Alexander Kojeve on the Origin of Modern Science: Sociological Modelling Gone Awry. *Studies in the History and Philosophy of Science* 6: 113–24.

Grillner, S. and Shik, M. L. 1975. "Command Neurons in the Cat." Paper presented at the International Conference on Neural Control of Locomotion, September 29–October 2, Valley Forge, Pa.

Grünbaum, A. 1974. "Popper's Views on the Arrow of Time." In *The Philosophy of Karl Popper*, ed. P.A. Schilpp, chapter 25, 775–97. La Salle, Ill.: Open Court.

Hebb, D. O. 1949. *The Organization of Behavior*. New York: Wiley.

Horst, P. 1954. Pattern Analysis and Configural Scoring. *Journal of Clinical Psychology* 10: 3–11.

Hubel, D. H. and Wiesel, T. 1962. Receptive Fields, Binocular Interaction, and Functional Architecture in the Cat's Visual Cortex. *Journal of Physiology London* 160: 106–54.

Keller, W. 1956. *The Bible as History* (trans. W. Neil). New York: William Morrow.

Koestler, A. 1971. *The Case of the Midwife Toad*. London: Hutchinson and Co.

Koestler, A. 1972. *The Roots of Coincidence*. New York: Vintage Books.

Meehl, P. E. 1950. Configural Scoring. *Journal of Consulting* Psychology 14: 165–71.

Meehl, P. E. 1954. *Clinical versus Statistical Prediction: A Theoretical Analysis and a Review of the Evidence*. Minneapolis: University of Minnesota Press.

Meehl, P.E., Klann, H. R., Schmieding, A., Breimeier, K. and Schroeder-Slomann, S. 1958. *What, Then is Man?* St. Louis: Concordia Publishing House.

Perkel, D. H., and Bullock, T. H. 1969. "Neural Coding." In *Neurosciences Research Symposium Summaries*, eds. F. O. Schmitt, T. Melnechuk, G. C. Quarton, and G. Adelman, 405–527. Cambridge, Mass.: MIT Press.

Popper, K. R. 1950. Indeterminism in Quantum Physics and in Classical Physics. *British Journal for the Philosophy of Science* 1: 117–33, 173–95.

Popper, K. R. 1956a. The Arrow of Time. *Nature* 177: 538.

Popper, K. R. 1956b. Irreversibility and Mechanics: A Reply of Richard Schlegel. *Nature* 178: 382–84.

Popper, K. R. 1966. *Of Clouds and Clocks. Arthur Hally Compton Memorial Lecture*. St. Louis: Washington University.

Popper, K. R. 1974a. "Debates with Schroedinger." In *The Philosophy of Karl Popper*, ed. P. A. Schilpp, vol. 1, sec. 30. La Salle, Ill: Open Court.

Popper, K. R. 1974b. "Grünbaum on Time and Entropy." In *The Philosophy of Karl Popper*, ed. P. A. Schilpp, sec. 38, 1140–1144 and "Replies to my Critics." La Salle, Ill: Open Court.

Reichenbach, H. 1938. *Experience and Prediction*. Chicago: University of Chicago Press.

Rosenbaum, D. A. 1977. Selective Adaptation of "Command Neurons" in the Human Motor System. *Neuropsychologia* 15: 81–90.

Rosenbaum, D. A., and Radford, M. 1977. Sensory Feedback Does Not Cause Selective Adaptation of Human "Command Neurons." *Perceptual and Motor Skills* 41: 497–551.

Schiller, P. H., and Koerner, F. 1971. Discharge Characteristics of Single Units in Superior Colliculus of the Alert Rhesus Monkey. *Journal of Neurophysiology* 34: 920–36.

Wiersma, C. 1952. Neurons of Arthropods. *Cold Spring Harbor Symposium in Quantitative Biology* 17: 155–63.

Wilson, D. M. 1970. "Neural Operations in Arthropod Ganglia." In *The Neurosciences: Second Study Program*, ed. F. O. Schmitt, chap. 38, 397–409. New York: Rockefeller University Press.

Acknowledgments

"Theoretical risks and tabular asterisks: Sir Karl, Sir Ronald, and the slow progress of soft psychology" was originally published in *Journal of Consulting and Clinical Psychology* 46 (1978), 806-34, copyright © 1978 by the American Psychological Association, reprinted with permission;

"Psychological determinism and human rationality: A psychologist's reactions to Professor Karl Popper's 'Of clouds and clocks' " (310-72) and "Some methodological reflections on the difficulties of psychoanalytic research" (403-16) were originally published in *Minnesota Studies in the Philosophy of Science*, vol. IV, *Analyses of Theories and Methods of Physics and Psychology*, editedby M. Radner and S. Winokur, (Minneapolis: University of Minnesota Press, 1970);

"The determinism-freedom and mind-body problems" was originally published in *The Philosophy of Karl Popper*, edited by P. A. Schilpp, 520-59, copyright © 1974 by The Library of Living Philosophers, reprinted by permission of Open Court Publishing Company, La Salle, Illinois;

"Psychological determinism or chance: Configural cerebral autoselection as a tertium quid" was originally published in *Science, Mind, and Psychology: Essays in honor of Grover Maxwell*, edited by M. L. Maxwell and C. W. Savage (Lanham, Md.: University Press of America, 1989), reprinted with permission;

"A most peculiar paradox" was originally published in *Philosophical Studies* 1 (1950), 47-48, copyright © 1950 by Kluwer Academic Publishers, reprinted with permission;

545

"The concept of emergence" was originally published in *Minnesota Studies in the Philosophy of Science*, vol. I, *The Foundations of Science and the Concepts of Psychology and Psychoanalysis*, edited by H. Feigl and M. Scriven, 239-52 (Minneapolis: University of Minnesota Press, 1956);

"The compleat autocerebroscopist: A thought-experiment on Professor Feigl's identity thesis" was originally published in *Mind, Matter, and Method: Essays in Philosophy and Science in Honor of Herbert Feigl*, edited by P. K. Feyerabend and G. Maxwell, 103-80 (Minneapolis: University of Minnesota Press, 1966);

"Psychopathology and purpose" was originally published in *The Future of Psychiatry*, edited by Paul Hoch and Joseph Zubin, 61-69 (New York: Grune & Stratton, 1962), reprinted with permission;

"Subjectivity in psychoanalytic inference: The nagging persistence of Wilhelm Fliess's Achensee question" was originally published in *Minnesota Studies in the Philosophy of Science*, Vol. X, *Testing Scientific Theories*, edited by J. Earman, 349-411 (Minneapolis: University of Minnesota Press, 1983);

"The virtues of M'Naghten" (written with J. M. Livermore) was originally published in *Minnesota Law Review* 51 (1967), 789-856, reprinted with permission;

"On the justifications for civil commitment" (written with J. M. Livermore and C. P. Malmquist) was originally published in *University of Pennsylvania Law Review* 117 (1968), 75-96, reprinted with permission;

"Psychology and the criminal law" was originally published in *University of Richmond Law Review* 5 (1970), 1-30, reprinted with permission;

"Law and the fireside inductions: Some reflections of a clinical psychologist" was originally published in *Journal of Social Issues* 27 (1971), 65-100, reprinted with permission; "Postscript: Law and the fireside inductions (with postscript): Some reflections of a clinical psychologist" was originally published in *Behavioral Science & the Law* 7, no. 4 (1989), 540-47, copyright © 1989 John Wiley, reprinted with permission;

"The insanity defense" was originally published in *Minnesota Psychologist* 32 (Summer 1983), 11-17, reprinted with permission; "Compatibility of science and ESP" (written with M. J. Scriven) was originally published in *Science* 123 (1956), 14-15, copyright © 1956 by the AAAS, reprinted with permission;

"Precognitive telepathy I: On the possibility of distinguishing it from psychokinesis" is reprinted with permission of the author and of the editor of *NOÛS* 12 (1978), 235-66;

"Precognitive telepathy II: Some neurophysiological conjectures and metaphysical speculations" is reprinted by permission of the author and of the editor of *NOÛS* 12 (1978), 317-95.

Publications of P. E. Meehl

1. Meehl, P. E. (1945). The dynamics of "structured" personality tests. *Journal of Clinical Psychology, 1*, 296–303. Reprinted with Prefatory Comment in L. D. Goodstein & R. I. Lanyon (eds.), *Readings in personality assessment* (pp. 245–253). New York: Wiley, 1971.

2. Meehl, P. E. (1945). A simple algebraic development of Horst's suppressor variables. *American Journal of Psychology, 58*, 550–554.

3. Meehl, P. E. (1945). An examination of the treatment of stimulus patterning in Professor Hull's *Principles of Behavior. Psychological Review, 52*, 324–332.

4. Meehl, P. E. (1945). An investigation of a general normality or control factor in personality testing. *Psychological Monographs, 59* (4, Whole No. 274).

5. Meehl, P. E., & Jeffrey, M. (1946). The Hunt-Minnesota Test for Organic Brain Damage in cases of functional depression. *Journal of Applied Psychology, 30*, 276-287.

6. Meehl, P. E. (1946). Profile analysis of the Minnesota Multiphasic Personality Inventory in differential diagnosis. *Journal of Applied Psychology, 30*, 517–524.

7. Meehl, P. E., & Hathaway, S. R. (1946). The K factor as a suppressor variable in the Minnesota Multiphasic Personality Inventory. *Journal of Applied Psychology, 30*, 525–564.

8. Meehl, P. E., & McClosky, H. (1947). Ethical and political aspects of applied psychology. *Journal of Abnormal and Social Psychology, 42*, 91–98.

9. Bird, C., Heron, W. T., Meehl, P. E., & Paterson, D. G. (1947). The foreign language requirement for the Ph.D. *American Psychologist, 2*, 136–138.

10. Meehl, P. E. (1947). Minnesota Multiphasic Inventory. In *Fifth Annual Industrial Relations Conference Report*. Minneapolis: University of Minnesota, Center for Continuation Study.

11. Meehl, P. E. (1947). Schizophrenia, catatonic form. In A. H. Burton &

R. E. Harris (Eds.), *Case histories in clinical and abnormal psychology*. New York: Harper.

12. McKinley, J. C., Hathaway, S. R., & Meehl, P. E. (1948). The Minnesota Multiphasic Personality Inventory: VI. The K scale. *Journal of Consulting Psychology, 12*, 20–31.

13. MacCorquodale, K., & Meehl, P. E. (1948). On a distinction between hypothetical constructs and intervening variables. *Psychological Review, 55*, 95–107.

14. Meehl, P. E., & MacCorquodale, K. (1948). A further study of latent learning in the T-maze. *Journal of Comparative and Physiological Psychology, 41*, 372–396.

15. MacCorquodale, K., & Meehl, P. E. (1949). "Cognitive" learning in the absence of competition of incentives. *Journal of Comparative and Physiological Psychology, 42*, 383–390.

16. Meehl, P. E. (1950). On the circularity of the Law of Effect. *Psychological Bulletin, 47*, 52–75.

17. Meehl, P. E. (1950). A most peculiar paradox. *Philosophical Studies, 1*, 47–48.

18. Meehl, P. E. (1950). Configural scoring. *Journal of Consulting Psychology, 14*, 165–171.

19. Meehl, P. E. (1950). *Using the Minnesota Multiphasic Personality Inventory in counseling*. St. Paul: Advisement and Guidance Section, Vocational Rehabilitation and Education Division, Veterans Administration.

20. Hathaway, S. R., & Meehl, P. E. (1951). *An atlas for the clinical use of the MMPI*. Minneapolis: University of Minnesota Press.

21. Meehl, P. E., & MacCorquodale, K. (1951). A failure to find the Blodgett effect, and some secondary observations on drive conditioning. *Journal of Comparative and Physiological Psychology, 44*, 178–183.

22. Meehl, P. E., & MacCorquodale, K. (1951). Some methodological comments concerning expectancy theory. *Psychological Review, 58*, 230–233.

23. Gough, H. G., McClosky, H., & Meehl, P. E. (1951). A personality scale for dominance. *Journal of Abnormal and Social Psychology, 46*, 360–366.

24. Hathaway, S. R., & Meehl, P. E. (1951, July). The Minnesota Multiphasic Personality Inventory. In *Military Clinical Psychology*, Section IX (pp. 71–111). Department of the Army, Technical Manual, TM8–242.

25. MacCorquodale, K., & Meehl, P. E. (1951). On the elimination of cul entries without obvious reinforcement. *Journal of Comparative and Physiological Psychology, 44*, 367–371.

26. Gough, H. G., McClosky, H., & Meehl, P. E. (1952). A personality scale for social responsibility. *Journal of Abnormal and Social Psychology, 47*, 73–80.

27. APA Committee on Test Standards. (1952). Technical recommendations for psychological tests and diagnostic techniques: Preliminary proposal. *American Psychologist*, *7*, 461–475.

28. Meehl, P. E., & MacCorquodale, K. (1953). Drive conditioning as a factor in latent learning. *Journal of Experimental Psychology*, *45*, 20–24.

29. MacCorquodale, K., & Meehl, P. E. (1953). Preliminary suggestions as to a formalization of expectancy theory. *Psychological Review*, *60*, 55–63.

30. Bird, C., Clark, K. E., & Meehl, P. E. (1954). Relationships between objective and oral examinations in psychology. In R. E. Eckert & R. J. Keller (Eds.), *A university looks at its program*. Minneapolis: University of Minnesota Press.

31. MacCorquodale, K., & Meehl, P. E. (1954). E. C. Tolman. In W. K. Estes, S. Koch, K. MacCorquodale, P. E. Meehl, C. G. Mueller, W. N. Schoenfeld, & W. S. Verplanck, *Modern learning theory* (pp. 177–266). New York: Appleton-Century-Crofts.

32. Meehl, P. E. (1954). *Clinical versus statistical prediction: A theoretical analysis and a review of the evidence*. Minneapolis: University of Minnesota Press.

33. Meehl, P. E. (1954). Comment on "Analyzing the clinical process." *Journal of Counseling Psychology*, *1*, 207–208.

34. Meehl, P. E. (1955). Psychotherapy. *Annual Review of Psychology*, *6*, 357–378.

35. Meehl, P. E., & Rosen, A. (1955). Antecedent probability and the efficiency of psychometric signs, patterns, or cutting scores. *Psychological Bulletin*, *52*, 194–216. Reprinted in P. E. Meehl, *Psychodiagnosis: Selected papers* (pp. 32–62). Minneapolis: University of Minnesota Press, 1973.

36. Cronbach, L. J., & Meehl, P. E. (1955). Construct validity in psychological tests. *Psychological Bulletin*, *52*, 281–302. Reprinted in P. E. Meehl, *Psychodiagnosis: Selected papers* (pp. 3–31). Minneapolis: University of Minnesota Press, 1973.

37. Meehl, P. E., & Scriven, M. J. (1956). Compatibility of science and ESP. *Science*, *123*, 14–15.

38. Meehl, P. E. (1956). Clinical versus actuarial prediction. In *Proceedings of the 1955 Invitational Conference on Testing Problems* (pp. 136–141). Princeton: Educational Testing Service.

39. Meehl, P. E. (1956). Wanted—a good cookbook. *American Psychologist*, *11*, 263–272. Reprinted in P. E. Meehl, *Psychodiagnosis: Selected papers* (pp. 63–80). Minneapolis: University of Minnesota Press, 1973.

40. Meehl, P. E., & Sellars, W. (1956). The concept of emergence. In H. Feigl & M. Scriven (Eds.), *Minnesota studies in the philosophy of science: Vol. I. The foundations of science and the concepts of psychology and psychoanalysis* (pp. 239–252). Minneapolis: University of Minnesota Press.

41. Meehl, P. E. (1956). Symposium on clinical and statistical prediction (with C. C. McArthur & D. V. Tiedeman). *Journal of Counseling Psychology*, *3*, 163–173.

42. Meehl, P. E. (1957). Religion and the maintenance of mental health. In *Society's stake in mental health* (pp. 52–61). Minneapolis: University of Minnesota, Social Science Research Center.

43. Meehl, P. E. (1957). When shall we use our heads instead of the formula? *Journal of Counseling Psychology*, *4*, 268–273. Reprinted in P. E. Meehl, *Psychodiagnosis: Selected papers* (pp. 81–89). Minneapolis: University of Minnesota Press, 1973.

44. Fleeson, W., Glueck, B. C., Heistad, G., King, J. E., Lykken, D. T., Meehl, P. E., & Mena, A. (1958). The ataraxic effect of two phenothiazine drugs on an outpatient population. *University of Minnesota Medical Bulletin*, *29*, 274–286.

45. Meehl, P. E., Klann, R., Schmieding, A., Breimeier, K., & Schroeder-Slomann, S. (1958). *What, then, is Man?* St. Louis: Concordia Publishing House.

46. Meehl, P. E. (1959). Some technical and axiological problems in the therapeutic handling of religious and valuational material. *Journal of Counseling Psychology*, *6*, 255–259.

47. Meehl, P. E. (1959). Some ruminations on the validation of clinical procedures. *Canadian Journal of Psychology*, *13*, 102–128. Reprinted in P. E. Meehl, *Psychodiagnosis: Selected papers* (pp. 90–116). Minneapolis: University of Minnesota Press, 1973.

48. Meehl, P. E. (1959). A comparison of clinicians with five statistical methods of identifying MMPI profiles. *Journal of Counseling Psychology*, *6*, 102–109.

49. Meehl, P. E. (1959). Structured and projective tests: Some common problems in validation. *Journal of Projective Techniques*, *23*, 268–272.

50. Meehl, P. E. (1959). Q-technique, pros and cons. In B. C. Glueck (Ed.), Report on *Conference on Social Adjustment Rating Scales* (pp. 11–18). University of Minnesota Center for Continuation Study.

51. Meehl, P. E. (1960). The cognitive activity of the clinician. *American Psychologist*, *15*, 19–27. Reprinted in P. E. Meehl, *Psychodiagnosis: Selected papers* (pp. 117–134). Minneapolis: University of Minnesota Press, 1973.

52. Glueck, B. C., Heistad, G. T., & Meehl, P. E. (1960). Approaches to the quantitative analysis of clinical assessment. *American Psychiatric Association District Branches Publication No. 1* (pp. 202–212). Washington, DC: American Psychiatric Association.

53. Meehl, P.E., & Dahlstrom, W. G. (1960). Objective configural rules for discriminating psychotic from neurotic MMPI profiles. *Journal of Consulting Psychology*, *24*, 375–387.

54. Meehl, P. E. (1960). Treatment of guilt-feelings. In *1957 Symposium of the American Catholic Psychological Association* (pp. 34–41). New York: Fordham University.

55. Meehl, P. E. (1961). Logic for the clinician. *Contemporary Psychology, 6*, 389–391.

56. Meehl, P. E. (1962). Parapsychology. *Encyclopedia Britannica, 17*, 267–269.

57. Meehl, P. E. (1962). Psychopathology and purpose. In P. Hoch & J. Zubin (Eds.), *The future of psychiatry* (pp. 61–69). New York: Grune and Stratton.

58. Meehl, P. E., Schofield, W., Glueck, B. C., Studdiford, W. B., Hastings, D. W., Hathaway, S. R., & Clyde, D. J. (1962). *Minnesota-Ford Pool of Phenotypic Personality Items, August 1962 Edition*. Minneapolis: University of Minnesota.

59. Meehl, P. E. (1962). Schizotaxia, schizotypy, schizophrenia. *American Psychologist, 17*, 827–838. Reprinted in P. E. Meehl, *Psychodiagnosis: Selected papers* (pp. 135–155). Minneapolis: University of Minnesota Press, 1973.

60. Glueck, B. C., Meehl, P. E., Schofield, W., & Clyde, D. J. (1964). The quantitative assessment of personality. *Comprehensive Psychiatry, 5*, 15–23.

61. Meehl, P. E. (1964). *Manual for use with checklist of schizotypic signs* (Report No. PR-73-5). Minneapolis: University of Minnesota, Research Laboratories of the Department of Psychiatry.

62. Meehl, P. E. (1965). Let's quit kidding ourselves about the training of clinical psychologists. In R. D. Wirt (Ed.), *Professional education in clinical psychology* (Mimeo). Minneapolis: University of Minnesota. [Reprint revised as #87]

63. Meehl, P. E. (1965). Discussion of Eysenck's "The effects of psychotherapy." *International Journal of Psychiatry, 1*, 156–157.

64. Meehl, P. E. (1965). Seer over sign: The first good example. *Journal of Experimental Research in Personality, 1*, 27–32.

65. Meehl, P. E. (1965). *Detecting latent clinical taxa by fallible quantitative indicators lacking an accepted criterion* (Report No. PR-65-2). Minneapolis: University of Minnesota, Research Laboratories of the Department of Psychiatry.

66. Meehl, P. E. (1965). The creative individual: Why it is hard to identify him. In G. A. Steiner (Ed.), *The creative organization* (pp. 25–32). Chicago: University of Chicago Press.

67. Meehl, P. E. (1965). Philosophy of science and Christian theology. In J. Bodensieck (Ed.), *Encyclopedia of the Lutheran Church* (Vol. 3, pp. 1894–1896). Minneapolis: Augsburg Publishing House.

68. Lykken, D. T., & Meehl, P. E. (1966). *Contributions to the problem of evaluating autonomic response data: I* (Report No. PR-66-2). Minneapolis: University of Minnesota, Research Laboratories of the Department of Psychiatry.

69. Meehl, P. E. (1966). The compleat autocerebroscopist: A thought-experiment on Professor Feigl's mind-body identity thesis. In P. K. Feyerabend & G. Maxwell (Eds.), *Mind, matter, and method: Essays in philosophy and science in honor of Herbert Feigl* (pp. 103–180). Minneapolis: University of Minnesota Press.

70. Dawes, R. M., & Meehl, P. E. (1966). Mixed group validation: A method for determining the validity of diagnostic signs without using criterion groups. *Psychological Bulletin, 66*, 63–67. Reprinted in P. E. Meehl, *Psychodiagnosis: Selected papers* (pp. 156–164). Minneapolis: University of Minnesota Press, 1973.

71. Meehl, P. E. (1966). *Psychologists' opinions as to the effects of holding five of Ellis's "Irrational Ideas"* (Report No. PR-66-7). Minneapolis: University of Minnesota, Research Laboratories of the Department of Psychiatry.

72. Committee on Scientific and Professional Aims of Psychology. (1967). The scientific and professional aims of psychology. *American Psychologist, 22*, 49–76.

73. Livermore, J. M., & Meehl, P. E. (1967). The virtues of M'Naghten. *Minnesota Law Review, 51*, 789–856.

74. Meehl, P. E. (1967). Theory-testing in psychology and physics: A methodological paradox. *Philosophy of Science, 34*, 103–115. Reprinted in D. E. Morrison & R. E. Henkel (Eds.), *The significance test controversy* (pp. 252–266). Chicago: Aldine, 1970.

75. Meehl, P. E. (1967). What can the clinician do well? In D. N. Jackson & S. Messick (Eds.), *Problems in human assessment* (pp. 594–599). New York: McGraw-Hill. Reprinted in P. E. Meehl, *Psychodiagnosis: Selected papers* (pp. 165–173). Minneapolis: University of Minnesota Press, 1973.

76. Meehl, P. E. (1968). *Detecting latent clinical taxa, II: A simplified procedure, some additional hitmax cut locators, a single-indicator method, and miscellaneous theorems* (Report No. PR-68-2). Minneapolis: University of Minnesota, Research Laboratories of the Department of Psychiatry.

77. Livermore, J. M., Malmquist, C. P., & Meehl, P. E. (1968). On the justifications for civil commitment. *University of Pennsylvania Law Review, 117*, 75–96.

78. Meehl, P. E. (1969). Comments on the invasion of privacy issue. In J. N. Butcher (Ed.), *MMPI: Research developments and clinical applications* (pp. 273–278). New York: McGraw-Hill.

79. Meehl, P. E., Lykken, D. T., Burdick, M. R., & Schoener, G. R. (1969). *Identifying latent clinical taxa, III. An empirical trial of the normal single-indicator method, using MMPI Scale 5 to identify the sexes* (Report No. PR-69-1). Minneapolis: University of Minnesota, Research Laboratories of the Department of Psychiatry.

80. Meehl, P. E. (1969). *Nuisance variables and the ex post facto design* (Report No. PR-69-4). Minneapolis: University of Minnesota, Research Laboratories of the Department of Psychiatry.

81. Gazzaniga, M. S. (1969, June). Violent man—A seven-way conversation (with D. Premack, L. Festinger, S. Schachter, R. L. Sinsheimer, P. E. Meehl, and K. M. Colby). *Psychology Today*, pp. 52–54, 59–60, 62–63.

82. Meehl, P. E. (1970). Psychology and the criminal law. *University of Richmond Law Review*, *5*, 1–30.

83. Meehl, P. E. (1970). Psychological determinism and human rationality: A psychologist's reactions to Professor Karl Popper's 'Of clouds and clocks.' In M. Radner & S. Winokur (Eds.), *Minnesota studies in the philosophy of science: Vol. IV. Analyses of theories and methods of physics and psychology* (pp. 310–372). Minneapolis: University of Minnesota Press.

84. Meehl, P. E. (1970). Nuisance variables and the ex post facto design. In M. Radner & S. Winokur (Eds.), *Minnesota studies in the philosophy of science: Vol. IV. Analyses of theories and methods of physics and psychology* (pp. 373–402). Minneapolis: University of Minnesota Press.

85. Meehl, P. E. (1970). Some methodological reflections on the difficulties of psychoanalytic research. In M. Radner & S. Winokur (Eds.), *Minnesota studies in the philosophy of science: Vol. IV. Analyses of theories and methods of physics and psychology* (pp. 403–416). Minneapolis: University of Minnesota Press. Reprinted *Psychological Issues*, 1973, *8*, 104–115.

86. Meehl, P. E. (1971). High school yearbooks: A reply to Schwarz. *Journal of Abnormal Psychology*, *77*, 143–148. Reprinted in P. E. Meehl, *Psychodiagnosis: Selected papers* (pp. 174–181). Minneapolis: University of Minnesota Press, 1973.

87. Meehl, P. E. (1971). A scientific, scholarly, nonresearch doctorate for clinical practitioners: Arguments pro and con. In R. R. Holt (Ed.), *New horizon for psychotherapy: Autonomy as a profession* (pp. 37–81). New York: International Universities Press.

88. Meehl, P. E., Lykken, D. T., Schofield, W., & Tellegen, A. (1971). Recaptured-item technique (RIT): A method for reducing somewhat the subjective element in factor-naming. *Journal of Experimental Research in Personality*, *5*, 171–190.

89. Meehl, P. E. (1971). Law and the fireside inductions: Some reflections of a clinical psychologist. *Journal of Social Issues*, *27*, 65–100.

90. Meehl, P. E. (1972). Specific genetic etiology, psychodynamics and therapeutic nihilism. *International Journal of Mental Health*, *1*, 10–27. Reprinted in P. E. Meehl, *Psychodiagnosis: Selected papers* (pp. 182–199). Minneapolis: University of Minnesota Press, 1973.

91. Meehl, P. E. (1972). Reactions, reflections, projections. In J. N.

Butcher (Ed.), *Objective personality assessment: Changing perspectives* (pp. 131–189). New York: Academic Press.

92. Meehl, P. E. (1972). Second-order relevance. *American Psychologist, 27*, 932–940.

93. Meehl, P. E. (1972). A critical afterword. In I. I. Gottesman & J. Shields, *Schizophrenia and genetics: A twin study vantage point* (pp. 367–416). New York: Academic Press.

94. Meehl, P. E. (1972). Clinical issues. In S. S. Kety & S. Matthysse (Eds.), *Prospects for research on schizophrenia. M.I.T. Neurosciences Research Program Bulletin, 10* (No. 4), 377–380.

95. Golden, R., & Meehl, P. E. (1973). *Detecting latent clinical taxa, IV: Empirical study of the maximum covariance method and the normal minimum chi-square method, using three MMPI keys to identify the sexes* (Report No. PR-73-2). Minneapolis: University of Minnesota, Research Laboratories of the Department of Psychiatry.

96. Golden, R., & Meehl, P. E. (1973). *Detecting latent clinical taxa, V: A Monte Carlo study of the maximum covariance method and associated consistency tests* (Report No. PR-73-3). Minneapolis: University of Minnesota, Research Laboratories of the Department of Psychiatry.

97. Meehl, P. E. (1973). *Psychodiagnosis: Selected papers*. Minneapolis: University of Minnesota Press.

98. Meehl, P. E. (1973). MAXCOV-HITMAX: A taxonomic search method for loose genetic syndromes. In P. E. Meehl, *Psychodiagnosis: Selected papers* (pp. 200–224). Minneapolis: University of Minnesota Press.

99. Meehl, P. E. (1973). Why I do not attend case conferences. In P. E. Meehl, *Psychodiagnosis: Selected papers* (pp. 225–302). Minneapolis: University of Minnesota Press.

100. Feigl, H. & Meehl, P. E. (1974). The determinism-freedom and mind-body problems. In P. A. Schilpp (Ed.), *The philosophy of Karl Popper* (pp. 520–559). LaSalle, Ill.: Open Court.

101. Golden, R., Tyan, S., & Meehl, P. E. (1974). *Detecting latent clinical taxa, VI: Analytical development and empirical trials of the consistency hurdles theory* (Report No. PR-74-4). Minneapolis: University of Minnesota, Research Laboratories of the Department of Psychiatry.

102. Golden, R., Tyan, S., & Meehl, P. E. (1974). *Detecting latent clinical taxa, VII: Maximum likelihood solution and empirical and artificial data trials of the multi-indicator multi-taxonomic class normal theory* (Report No. PR-74-5). Minneapolis: University of Minnesota, Research Laboratories of the Department of Psychiatry.

103. Golden, R., & Meehl, P. E. (1974). *Detecting latent clinical taxa, VIII: A preliminary study in the detection of the schizoid taxon using MMPI items as*

indicators (Report No. PR-74-6). Minneapolis: University of Minnesota, Research Laboratories of the Department of Psychiatry.

104. Golden, R., Tyan, S., & Meehl, P. E. (1974). *Detecting latent clinical taxa, IX: A Monte Carlo method for testing taxometric theories* (Report No. PR-74-7). Minneapolis: University of Minnesota, Research Laboratories of the Department of Psychiatry.

105. Meehl, P. E. (1974/75). Genes and the unchangeable core. *VOICES: The art and science of psychotherapy*, *10*, 25–35.

106. Meehl, P. E. (1975). Hedonic capacity: Some conjectures. *Bulletin of the Menninger Clinic*, *39*, 295–307.

107. Meehl, P. E. (1975). Control and countercontrol: A panel discussion. In T. Thompson & W. S. Dockens (Eds.), *Applications of behavior modification* (pp. 509–521). New York: Academic Press.

108. Meehl, P. E. (1976). *Difficulties with economic models of voter behavior* (Report No. PR-76-1). Minneapolis: University of Minnesota, Research Laboratories of the Department of Psychiatry.

109. Meehl, P. E. (1977). Specific etiology and other forms of strong influence: Some quantitative meanings. *Journal of Medicine and Philosophy*, *2*, 33–53.

110. Meehl, P. E. (1977). The selfish voter paradox and the thrown-away vote argument. *American Political Science Review*, *71*, 11–30.

111. Hanson, D. R., Gottesman, I. I., & Meehl, P. E. (1977). Genetic theories and the validation of psychiatric diagnoses: Implications for the study of children of schizophrenics. *Journal of Abnormal Psychology*, *86*, 575–588.

112. Golden, R., & Meehl, P. E. (1978). Testing a single dominant gene theory without an accepted criterion variable. *Annals of Human Genetics London*, *41*, 507–514.

113. Meehl, P. E. (1978). Theoretical risks and tabular asterisks: Sir Karl, Sir Ronald, and the slow progress of soft psychology. *Journal of Consulting and Clinical Psychology*, *46*, 806–834.

114. Malmquist, C. P., & Meehl, P. E. (1978). Barabbas: A study in guilt-ridden homicide. *The International Review of Psycho-Analysis*, *5*, 149–174.

115. Meehl, P. E. (1978). Precognitive telepathy I: On the possibility of distinguishing it experimentally from psychokinesis. *NOÛS*, *12*, 235–266.

116. Meehl, P. E. (1978). Precognitive telepathy II: Some neurophysiological conjectures and metaphysical speculations. *NOÛS*, *12*, 371–395.

117. Golden, R., & Meehl, P. E. (1979). Detection of the schizoid taxon with MMPI indicators. *Journal of Abnormal Psychology*, *88*, 217–233.

118. Meehl, P. E. (1979). A funny thing happened to us on the way to the latent entities. *Journal of Personality Assessment*, *43*, 563–581.

119. Golden, R., & Meehl, P. E. (1980). Detection of biological sex: An empirical test of cluster methods. *Multivariate Behavioral Research*, *15*, 475–496.

120. Meehl, P. E. (1981). Ethical criticism in value clarification: Correcting cognitive errors within the client's—not the therapist's—framework. *Rational Living, 16*, 3–9.

121. Meehl, P. E. (1981). Comment on Ellis's reply. *Rational Living, 16*, 41–42.

122. Meehl, P. E., & Golden, R. (1982). Taxometric methods. In P. Kendall & J. Butcher (Eds.), *Handbook of research methods in clinical psychology* (pp. 127–181). New York: Wiley.

123. Meehl, P. E. (1983). The insanity defense. *Minnesota Psychologist, 32* (Summer), 11–17.

124. Meehl, P. E. (1983). Subjectivity in psychoanalytic inference: The nagging persistence of Wilhelm Fliess's Achensee question. In J. Earman (Ed.), *Minnesota studies in the philosophy of science: Vol. X, Testing scientific theories* (pp. 349–411). Minneapolis: University of Minnesota Press.

125. Meehl, P. E. (1983). Consistency tests in estimating the completeness of the fossil record: A neo-Popperian approach to statistical paleontology. In J. Earman (Ed.), *Minnesota studies in the philosophy of science: Vol. X, Testing scientific theories* (pp. 413–473). Minneapolis: University of Minnesota Press.

126. Meehl, P. E. (1984). Foreword. In D. Faust, *The limits of scientific reasoning*. Minneapolis: University of Minnesota Press.

127. Meehl, P. E. (1984). Radical behaviorism and mental events: Four methodological queries. *The Behavioral and Brain Sciences, 7*, 563–564.

128. Meehl, P. E. (1986). What social scientists don't understand. In D. W. Fiske & R. A. Shweder (Eds.), *Metatheory in social science: Pluralisms and subjectivities* (pp. 315–338). Chicago: University of Chicago Press.

129. Meehl, P. E. (1986). Trait language and behaviorese. In T. Thompson & M. D. Zeiler (Eds.), *Analysis and integration of behavioral units* (pp. 315–334). Hillsdale, N.J.: Lawrence Erlbaum Associates.

130. Meehl, P. E. (1986). Diagnostic taxa as open concepts: Metatheoretical and statistical questions about reliability and construct validity in the grand strategy of nosological revision. In T. Millon & G. L. Klerman (Eds.), *Contemporary directions in psychopathology* (pp. 215–231). New York: Guilford Press.

131. Meehl, P. E. (1986). Psychology: Does our heterogeneous subject matter have any unity? *Minnesota Psychologist, 35*(Summer), 3–9.

132. Meehl, P. E. (1986). Causes and effects of my disturbing little book. *Journal of Personality Assessment, 50*, 370–375.

133. Dahlstrom, W. G., Meehl, P. E., & Schofield, W. (1986). Starke Rosecrans Hathaway. *American Psychologist, 41*, 834–835.

134. Meehl, P. E. (1987). Foreword. In J. N. Butcher (Ed.), *Computerized psychological assessment*. New York: Basic Books, Inc.

135. Meehl, P. E. (1987). Theory and practice: Reflections of an academic clinician. In E. F. Bourg, R. J. Bent, J. E. Callan, N. F. Jones, J. McHolland &

G. Stricker (Eds.), *Standards and evaluation in the education and training of professional psychologists* (pp. 7–23). Norman, Okla.: Transcript Press.

136. Meehl, P. E. (1987). 'Hedonic capacity' ten years later: Some clarifications. In D. C. Clark & J. Fawcett (Eds.), *Anhedonia and affective deficit states.* New York: PMA Publishing.

137. Meehl, P. E. (1988). Foreword. In D. N. Wiener, *Albert Ellis, passionate skeptic.* New York: Praeger.

138. Dawes, R. M., Faust, D., & Meehl, P. E. (1989). Clinical versus actuarial judgment. *Science, 243,* 1668–1674.

139. Meehl, P. E. (1989). Autobiography. In G. Lindzey (Ed.), *History of psychology in autobiography, Vol. VIII* (pp. 337–389). Stanford: Stanford University Press.

140. Meehl, P. E. (1989). Schizotaxia revisited. *Archives of General Psychiatry, 46,* 935–944.

141. Meehl, P. E. (1989). Law and the fireside inductions (with Postscript): Some reflections of a clinical psychologist. *Behavioral Sciences and the Law, 7,* 521–550.

142. Meehl, P. E. (1989). Psychological determinism or chance: Configural cerebral autoselection as a tertium quid. In M. L. Maxwell & C. W. Savage (Eds.), *Science, mind, and psychology: Essays in honor of Grover Maxwell* (pp. 211–255). Lanham, Md.: University Press of America.

143. Meehl, P. E. (1990). Schizotaxia as an open concept. In A. I. Rabin, R. Zucker, R. Emmons, & S. Frank (Eds.), *Studying persons and lives* (pp. 248–303). New York: Springer.

144. Meehl, P. E. (1990). Why summaries of research on psychological theories are often uninterpretable. *Psychological Reports, 66,* 195–244. In R. E. Snow & D. Wiley (Eds.), *Improving Inquiry in social science: A volume in honor of Lee J. Cronbach* (pp. 13-59). Hillsdale, N.J.: Lawrence Erlbaum Associates, 1991.

145. Meehl, P. E. (1990). Toward an integrated theory of schizotaxia, schizotypy and schizophrenia. *Journal of Personality Disorders, 4,* 1–99.

146. Meehl, P. E. (1990). *Corroboration and verisimilitude: Against Lakatos's "sheer leap of faith"* (Working Paper, MCPS-90-01). Minneapolis: University of Minnesota, Center for Philosophy of Science.

147. Meehl, P. E. (1990). Appraising and amending theories: The strategy of Lakatosian defense and two principles that warrant using it. *Psychological Inquiry, 1,* 108–141. Meehl's Reply to the commentators. *Psychological Inquiry, 1,* 173–180.

000. Meehl, P. E. (in press). Extension of the MAXCOV-HITMAX taxometric procedure to situations of sizeable nuisance covariance. In D. Lubinski and R. V. Dawis (Eds.), *Assessing individual differences in human behavior: New concepts, methods, and findings.* Minneapolis: University of Minnesota Press.

000. Meehl, P. E. (in preparation). Path analysis: Metatheory matters.

000. Meehl, P. E. (in preparation). Cliometric metatheory: A modest proposal.

000. Meehl, P. E. (in preparation). If Freud could define psychoanalysis, why can't ABPP? APA speech, Boston, 1990.

000. Meehl, P. E. (in preparation). Factors and taxa, traits and types, differences of degree and differences in kind.

000. Meehl, P. E. (in preparation). *The Seven Sacred Cows of Academia.*

000. McClosky, H. & Meehl, P. E. (in preparation) *Ideologies in Conflict.*

Index

impedance to healthy responses in maladaptive behavior, 268

impoverished reality, postulate of, 308

impulse-defense model of psychotherapy, 271

incapacitation:
as aim of criminal law, 428, 484;
only achievable aim of criminal law, 431

incapacity to conform, 362

incompetent testimony by psychologists, 475

incorrigibility of raw-feel statements, 207

indecent exposure, civil commitment case, 403

independence:
pairwise, 146;
total configural, 146

indeterminacy, quantum: of brain events, 142; at synapse, 195

individual differences, 5

indubitability of raw-feel statements, 209

induction:
fireside, 440;
Hume's problem of, xxi

ineffability of raw-feel statements, 221

inerrancy of raw-feel statements, 208

inference: as fact, 67; probable, precise theory of, 15

innocent:
confinement of, on actuarial grounds, 396;
incarceration of, social nuisance, 401

insanity:
clear cases of exculpability, 483;
nosological rubrics in statute, 488

insanity defense, case illustrations, 363;
cognitive slippage in schizophrenia, 367;
dissociative reaction (fugue), 377;
dyssocial, 378;
emotionally unstable personality, 376;
epilepsy, 364, 378;
fetishism, 375;
mental deficiency, 363;
micropsychotic episode, 366;
paranoid personality, 375;
paranoid schizophrenia, 365, 369;
paternalistic issue in, 493;
pseudoneurotic schizophrenia, 365;
psychopathic, 373;
psychotic depression 371;
schizophrenia, 367, 369;
sexual deviation, 374;
sociopathic, 373

insanity defense, reasons why often unsatisfactory, 482

insanity rule: Durham, 360, 493; M'Naghten, 344; Model Penal Code, 362; Royal Commission, 359

instrumental response chains, weak, in psychotherapy patient, 269

instruments, accuracy of, 29

intelligence:
biological influence on, 457;
general, xxiii;
general factor, and task proficiency, 473;
IQ-SES correlation, causal direction problem, 453

intentional characterization of action outcome, 144

intentional words, 137

intentionality, xx, 16; component, of mind-body problem, 204

intentions: and determinism, 46; as effectual, 111

interaction effects in neuron dependencies, 146

interactionism, 155, 192

intersubjective world picture, raw feels in, 235

intervals, narrow, 19

intervening variable:
alternative sets, by decomposing laws, 253;
anchoring by input and output, 256;
characteristics of, 262;
examples of, 258;
proposed convention, 258;
'pure,' 258;
as summarizing only, 255;
Tolman's view of, 255

introspections, kinds of choice, 163

inverted-spectrum problem not formulable in identity theory, 215

invisible hand theories, 28

involutional depression, civil commitment case, 406

IQ-SES correlation, causal direction problem, 453

irrational determiners:
Freud, 115;
Marx, 115;
Pavlov, 115

island for criminals, 429

isolation: only achievable aim of criminal law, 431; physical, as aim of criminal law, 428, 484

miss, due to bias against doublet cells,
521;
objections to backward causality, 509;
preceding calls, effect of, 514;
pre-established harmony as explanation for,
515;
vs. psychokinesis, list of tests for, 505;
shifts call-series toward randomness, 504;
three causal possibilities, 528
predictability, strict, and determinism, 97
prediction:
of behavior from past behavior, 422, 460;
of dangerous acts, 399, 491;
of delinquency as basis for confinement,
396;
and full understanding, 226;
short-term, in psychoanalysis, 305
primary processes, 116
prime numbers: distribution of, 70; largest,
Euclid's proof, 58
Principia Mathematica, xix
prior probability in parapsychology, 500
privacy ("privileged access") of raw-feel
statements, 209
privileged access:
nomological, 195;
and privacy, 209;
of raw-feel statements, 209;
to raw-feels, 194
probabilities: conditional, in telepathy call
sequence, 515; transitional, in telepathic
call series, 506
probability: logical, 19; not always numerically
computable, 37, 275, 313; prior, 19; of
responding, 44; two kinds (Carnap), 314
probable inference, precise theory of, 15
problem: Compton's, 97; Descartes's, 97, 109
projection (Reichenbach), 71
proof, potential, unactualized, 78
propositions, tokening, 190
proprioceptive impulses as hypothetical
construct, 255
protocols: incorrigible, xxvi; reliable, 11–12
proxy variable, 26–27
prudential memory banks, suppressed, 159
pseudoneurotic schizophrenia, insanity defense
case, 365
pseudoscience in social science, 416
psychoanalysis, xxv;
changes in technique of, 285;

classifying statements during, 274;
clumsy studies of, 296;
concepts of, mapping on learning theory
and neurophysiology, 273;
defectors from, 292;
experience of, 274, 439;
Fundamental Rule of, 286;
inexact interpretation in, 289;
jigsaw puzzle analogy, 275, 302;
mathematical, 306;
new formalisms for, 311;
not monolithic, 272;
and psycholinguistics, 35, 312;
protocols, statistics on, 36;
red thread, discerning, 324;
session of, 35;
short-term prediction in, 305;
skilled observer required, 316;
sudden and marked changes during, 289;
too many variables, 275;
topic block theme tracing, 325;
what is observed in, 281
psychoanalyst:
computer as, 312;
as thought reader, 284
psychodynamic, rational ego as, 354
psychodynamics, noble tradition of, 17
psychoid, 156, 198, 200;
continuant as, 201;
location of, 198;
selects configuration, 156;
states of, 199;
throws switches, 156
psychokinetic explanation, of extreme ad hoc
kind, 522
psycholinguistics, and psychoanalysis, 35, 312
psychological causation, irrational, 56
psychological determinism, meaning of, 426
psychological truth, getting at with adversary
system, 483
psychologism:
inescapable element of, 207;
and pure pragmatics, 66
psychologists:
controversial tactics of, 441;
erroneous beliefs widely held by, 476;
incompetent testimony by, 475;
public image of, and insanity defense, 482
psychology: clinical, noble traditions of, 17;
"schools" of, 419

Paul E. Meehl is regents' professor of psychology, professor of psychiatry and philosophy at the University of Minnesota, and past chairman of the psychology department (1951-57). He is also engaged in the part-time practice of psychotherapy in Minneapolis, and his current research is on developing new taxometric methods for classification and genetics of psychopathology. Very active professionally, Meehl is a Diplomate of the American Board of Professional Psychology, Fellow of the Institute for Rational-Emotive Therapy, Fellow of the American Academy of Arts and Sciences, a member of the National Academy of Sciences, and in 1962 served as president of the American Psychological Association. He has received numerous awards including the American Psychological Association Distinguished Scientific Contributor Award, the Bruno Klopfer Distinguished Contribution Award, and the American Psychological Foundation's Gold Medal Award for Life Achievement in the Application of Psychology.

Widely published in such areas as animal behavior, learning theory, psychometric theory, MMPI scale development and validation, methods of actuarial interpretation, forensic psychology, and interview assessment, Meehl has also formulated an integrated biosocial theory of schizophrenia and developed a checklist for the diagnosis of nonpsychotic schizotypy. He cofounded and is a staff member of the Minnesota Center for Philosophy of Science and has published with the Center. Meehl is author of *Psychodiagnosis* (Minnesota, 1973) and coauthored *Modern Learning Theory* (1954), with Estes et al., and *An Atlas for the Clinical Use of the MMPI* (Minnesota, 1951), with Starke R. Hathaway.

C. Anthony Anderson is associate professor of philosophy at the University of Minnesota. He has been an assistant professor of philosophy at the University of Texas at Austin. Anderson has published articles on intensional logic and philosophy of religion and coedited, with C. Wade Savage, *Rereading Russell,* volume XII in the Minnesota Studies in the Philosophy of Science series (Minnesota, 1989).

Keith Gunderson is professor of philosophy at the University of Minnesota and has been a member of the Minnesota Center for Philosophy of Science since 1967. He has taught philosophy at Princeton and UCLA. Gunderson is author of *Mentality and Machines,* second edition (Minnesota, 1985), and edited *Language, Mind, and Knowledge,* volume VII in the Minnesota Studies in the Philosophy of Science series (Minnesota, 1975). He has published four books of poetry, and some of his poems have been set to music by the composers Sydney Hodkinson, Libby Larsen, and Eric Stokes. Parts of Gunderson's poem sequence *Tripping Over the Cat* appeared in *Cat Catalog—The Ultimate Cat Book* and have been choreographed by Linda Shapiro of the New Dance Ensemble.